ELEANOR MARX

ELEANOR MARX

A Life

RACHEL HOLMES

BLOOMSBURY PRESS

NEW YORK · LONDON · NEW DELHI · SYDNEY

Published by Bloomsbury Press, New York
Bloomsbury is a trademark of Bloomsbury Publishing Plc

All papers used by Bloomsbury Press are natural, recyclable products made
from wood grown in well-managed forests. The manufacturing processes
conform to the environmental regulations of the country of origin.

LIBRARY OF CONGRESS CATALOGING-IN-PUBLICATION DATA
HAS BEEN APPLIED FOR.

ISBN: 978-1-62040-970-1

First published in Great Britain in 2014
First U.S. Edition 2015

1 3 5 7 9 10 8 6 4 2

Typeset by Hewer Text UK Ltd, Edinburgh
Printed and bound in the U.S.A. by Thomson-Shore Inc., Dexter, Michigan

Bloomsbury books may be purchased for business or promotional use.
For information on bulk purchases please contact Macmillan Corporate and
Premium Sales Department at specialmarkets@macmillan.com.

For my mother, Karin Anne Pibernik, born Silén

And first, a general idea that has to do with all women. The life of woman does not coincide with that of man. Their lives do not intersect; in many cases do not even touch. Hence the life of the race is stunted.

Eleanor Marx and Edward Aveling, 'The Woman Question', 1886

Is it not wonderful when you come to look at things squarely in the face, how rarely we seem to practise all the fine things we preach to others?

Eleanor Marx to her sister Laura Lafargue, 26 November 1892

'Go ahead!'

Eleanor's favourite motto

CONTENTS

PREFACE

Eleanor Marx changed the world. In the process she revolutionised herself. This is the story of how she did it.

She seems an unfashionable subject. And then there's her father. Yet the public Eleanor Marx is one of British history's great heroes.

The private Eleanor Marx was the favourite daughter of an unusual family. She was nicknamed Tussy, to rhyme, her parents said, with pussy not fussy. Cats she adored; fussy she wasn't. She loved Shakespeare, Ibsen, both the Shelleys, good poetry and bad puns. White was her favourite colour, and champagne her idea of happiness.

The life of Eleanor Marx was one of the most significant and interesting events in the evolution of social democracy in Victorian Britain. Not since Mary Wollstonecraft had any woman made such a profound, progressive contribution to English political thought – and action. She left a colossal, although unacknowledged, legacy for future generations.

Eleanor Marx was a revolutionary woman writer; a revolutionary woman, and a revolutionary. She was a person of words and action.

Social democracy and radical thought were the family trade. Not for profit, but for the progressive transformation of people's lives for the better. Eleanor's parents, and the man she called her 'second father', Friedrich Engels, were children of industrial capitalism. They grew into political adulthood in the revolutionary Europe of the 1840s but their mature ideas were forged from the ashes of that early utopian and idealist socialism. The global triumph of capitalism was declared in the decades after 1848. Their child Eleanor, born in 1855, was heir to their ideas in a different, modern age.

Eleanor went out into the world to put into practice and to test what she'd learned from Marx and Engels at the family hearth. Her quest to 'go ahead', to live it, soon took her into new worlds. The Shakespeare revival, the cultural realms of radical modern theatre, the contemporary novel and the artistic circles of early bohemian

Bloomsbury. She loved steam trains and was an early and enthusiastic adopter of new technology, most notably the typewriter. Eleanor
Marx was a pioneer of Ibsenism in Britain. She translated Flaubert's
Madame Bovary into English for the first time. She took to the stage
herself – with sometimes hilariously misdirected results. She never
noticed any boundaries between the personal and political, even
when she tripped over them and they sent her flying.

Tussy had an extraordinary gift for friendship. Unconventional,
she nevertheless effortlessly attracted and compelled others. People
felt good around her. Her lifelong, loving relationship with Friedrich
Engels and longterm companionships with George Bernard Shaw,
Will Thorne, Wilhelm Liebknecht and Henry Havelock Ellis are just
a few examples of her easy rapports with men. The close and loving
relationship between Eleanor Marx and Olive Schreiner is one of the
great female friendships, not only of literary and political history, but
of life and the heart.

'What is it that we as Socialists desire?' asked Eleanor Marx, and
spent her life searching for answers to this question.

From the time of Eleanor's childhood – the 1860s – socialism was the
ideology primarily associated with the new democratic struggle against
capitalism. There is no neat story of the origins and rise of socialism qua
socialism in Britain because it was by character and intent a broad-based,
diverse alliance of widespread radical thought and action. Tussy's life is
one of the significant primary elements in the composition of the story
of British socialism.

As the late, great Eric Hobsbawm observed, in the 1860s and 1870s
native socialists in Britain might have comfortably fitted into one small-
ish hall. Eleanor, the only Marx who was a native English socialist, and
her friends, might have filled more than half that hall.[1] 'Certainly,'
Eleanor said, 'socialism is at present in this country little more than a
literary movement.'[2] She took this literary movement from its visionary
pages on to the streets and on to the political stage. She lived it, and she
tested it.

Eleanor Marx became an adult in the age of collectivism. Collectivism,
most recognisable in the trade union movement, was an organised
response to unfettered capitalism and the grossly uneven distribution of
the prosperity it generated. The labouring poor produced surplus value,
for the benefit of the happy few who exploited them. Britain was not yet

an electoral democracy. The right to vote was based on property ownership and religion. Working-class men were prohibited from voting.
Women of all classes were prohibited from voting. The poor were
prohibited from voting.

British government, political representation and Parliament were a
closed shop: entrance was restricted to property-owning men of particular religious sects. Trade unions were therefore the first people's
parliaments. Britain had one of the strongest traditions of working-class
organisation in the world, despite the collapse of Chartism and, in the
1850s, the Communist League.

In the 1860s the organised proletariat regrouped, renewing the
attempt to deal with the consequences of capitalism. A new trade unionism emerged in the 1870s, out of which grew Britain's first democratic
political parties: most significantly, the Independent Labour Party and
the Scottish Labour Party. Eleanor Marx was one of the first and most
prominent leaders of the new trade unionism. And she brought feminism to the heart of the trade union movement, both in Britain and in
Europe.

Eleanor often said, 'I inherited my father's nose (I used to tell him I
could sue him for damages as his nose had distinctly entailed a loss on
me) – and not his genius.'[3] Friedrich Engels, George Bernard Shaw,
Olive Schreiner, Henry Havelock Ellis, William Morris and his daughter May, Elizabeth Garrett Anderson, Sylvia Pankhurst, Amy Levy,
Israel Zangwill – amongst many others – would have corrected the error
of this self-assessment. Eleanor did inherit her father's genius. The loss
entailed on her was not her nose, but her sex.

Eleanor Marx was born into a Victorian Britain where she had no
right to education, was barred from university, from voting for the
national government, from standing for parliamentary representation,
from most of the professions and from control of her reproductive and
psychological rights. The historical conditions into which she was born
made her understand from first-hand experience what it meant, and felt
like, to be the member of an oppressed class.

She spent her life fighting for the principle of equality. To a cynical
generation, this might make her sound tiresome. To the people around
the world who are discovering themselves in the new social revolutions
today, her fight may seem more familiar.

Eleanor Marx was the foremother of socialist feminism. Contrary to
current popular misconceptions, feminism began in the 1870s, not the

1970s. Like all ideas that turn into movements, feminism has an empirical history and detectible conception. It did not arrive in Britain delivered by a stork, or left under a gooseberry bush.

In Victorian Britain and its expanding colonies, the problem of sexual oppression was generally described as 'the woman question'. To Eleanor Marx, this question was imprecise. So she moved it on, to 'the working woman debate'.[4] She supported and admired the call for women's suffrage. Some of her best friends were suffragettes. But suffrage reform for middle-class women within existing capitalist society failed to address 'the debate on the attitude of social democracy towards working women.'[5] Eleanor lucidly summarised her position in an open letter to the English socialist leader Ernest Belfort Bax in November 1895:

> I am, of course, as a Socialist, not a representative of 'Woman's Rights'. It is the Sex Question and its economic base that I proposed to discuss with you. The so-called 'Woman's Rights' question (which appears to be the only one you understand) is a bourgeois idea. I proposed to deal with the Sex Question from the point of view of the working class and the class struggle.[6]

Women's suffrage lacked a sufficient analysis of the economic base of the division of labour, production and reproduction. Understanding the role of economics in human society was essential to human happiness, and therefore to the emancipation of women, and men – equally oppressed by patriarchy. Happiness – what, Eleanor wondered, constituted happiness? She found the most important element was work.

Eleanor Marx radicalised 'the woman question' by bringing modern feminism to Britain in 1886.

She created the political philosophy of socialist-feminism, summarised in her treatise 'The Woman Question: From a Socialist Point of View', co-written with Edward Aveling, her spouse. In the same year, Eleanor Marx and the German socialist politician Clara Zetkin together brought feminism to the top of the agenda of the international socialist movement at the first congress of the Second International, held in London. Later, inspired by this intervention, Zetkin co-founded International Women's Day, with Luise Zietz.

'The Woman Question: From a Socialist Point of View' stands alongside Wollstonecraft's *Vindication of the Rights of Women*, Engels's

Origin of Private Property, Family and the State and Virginia Woolf's *A Room of One's Own* in its importance as a revolutionary text.

Eleanor Marx was her father's first biographer. All subsequent biographies of Karl Marx, and most of Engels, draw on her work as their primary sources for the family history, often without knowing it.

In this sense, this book is a biography of a biographer.

Tussy's first childhood memory was of riding on her father's shoulders and being suddenly struck by the different view. I've been able to see much further by standing on the shoulders of the two groundbreaking twentieth-century biographers of Eleanor Marx. Chushichi Tsuzuki published the first full-length biographical evaluation of her life in 1967. Yvonne Kapp followed soon after with her mighty two-volume study published in 1972 and 1976. Both stand their ground as fine accounts and invaluable guides.

Eleanor started writing the first full-length biography of her father in the 1880s. She wrote to Karl Kautsky, reflecting on the project: 'His work must stand as it is, and we must all try to learn from it. And we can all "walk under his huge legs" – and find ourselves not dishonourable but honourable graves.'[7]

Daughters are well positioned to walk under their father's legs, and, if they can, through them and out the other side. And daughters are from their mother's wombs born. 'Cherchez la femme,' Eleanor often said when people sought explanations for the behaviour of others. This is good advice to follow on the quest to understand her life and psychology.

Eleanor Marx was the physical and spiritual daughter of a group of women who defined her as powerfully as her father: most significantly, her mother Jenny Marx, 'second mother' Helen Demuth, and Engels's partner, Auntie Lizzy Burns. In adulthood, her friendships with women sustained and developed her. This sisterhood is as important to understanding the forces that made Eleanor as her family and male lovers.

Eleanor Marx never finished her biography of her father. During the process of writing it she discovered a shocking, unspeakable secret at the heart of her family. She agonised over the consequences of its disclosure. And she thought deeply about the divided duty of daughters. On the one hand, the duty of daughters towards the patriarchs and matriarchs that made them; on the other, the duty of truth to history. Before she had time to reach a conclusion, Eleanor Marx succumbed to a painful and violent death. Some say it was murder, others that she was over-whelmed by the family secret.

Towards the end of her life, Eleanor wrote to her sister Laura about the struggle she was having writing the biography of their father: 'After all, Marx the "Poliker" and "Denker" can take his chance, while Marx the man is less likely to fare as well.'[8] Eleanor was confronted by the challenge of all biography: the story of the individual life taking its chance in the grander scheme of history. Individuals, and our lives, are full of contradictions. We don't conform to abstract ideology or deterministic theories. This is what makes us human, man and woman alike.

The life of Eleanor Marx is as varied and full of contradictions as the materialist dialectic in which she was, quite literally, conceived. Her father, the most famous philosopher in the world, wrote:

> The modern family contains in embryo not only slavery (*servitus*) but serfdom also... It contains within itself in miniature all the antagonisms which later develop on a wide scale within society and its state.[9]

Eleanor's life was a dramatisation of these antagonisms. If Karl Marx was the theory, Eleanor Marx was the practice. This is the story of both the public and the private lives of Eleanor Marx. She wrote, in 'The Woman Question', that for the feminist, the public and the private were indivisible realms.

Her peers – allies and adversaries – regarded her as one of the greatest radical reformers and leaders of their age. Will Thorne, first Secretary of the Trades Union Congress (TUC), said at her funeral that Britain had lost its foremost political economist. The praise, admiration and unqualified esteem in which she was held would fill reams. In fact, the volume of Eleanor-adulation is enough to make a biographer's heart sink. 'It seems impossible to find any unfavourable references to her,'[10] wrote her friend Henry Havelock Ellis.

Fortunately, this is untrue. Eleanor Marx was all too human.

She had many shortcomings, frustrations and spectacular failures. Her life was a mass of contradictions. She is irreducible to either her public or private life. And so we need to know the story of both.

After all, Marx the politician and thinker can take her chance. Whether Marx the woman is likely to fare as well, only her story can tell.

I

Global Citizen

Eleanor Marx tumbles prematurely into the world in London at the moment before dawn on Tuesday 16 January 1855. Puffing anxiously on a cigar in the corner of the overcrowded room at 28 Dean Street, Soho, is Europe's greatest political scientist. Karl and Jenny Marx have another child.

They'd hoped for a boy. It's a girl.

Exhausted, Jenny sips crimson laudanum held to her lips by the attentive Helen Demuth. Lenchen, as she's known to all the family, has been present at the births of all the Marx children. This is Jenny's sixth home delivery. Just one year after her birth her last baby, Franziska, died in this same room from bronchial pneumonia. Jenny is now forty-one, in medical terms an *older gravida* according to the family physician Dr Allen, who has been urgently sent for from nearby Soho Square.

Sweetened with honey, liquorice and anise, the laudanum adds spice and caramel scents to the overheated atmosphere. The reassuring aroma of strong German coffee mingles with the tang of blood, camphor, tobacco smoke and coal dust. Elegant and solidly expensive, the *Kaffeekanne*, a wedding gift from Jenny's mother, looks out of place amongst cracked crockery, shabby, cramped surroundings and dilapidated furniture.

Lenchen snips the umbilical cord, slaps and wipes down the baby girl. Handing her into her father's outspread arms, she pronounces her puny but intact, with a fair fighting chance. Teeny as she is, the Marxes' newborn baby daughter declares her arrival with hearty, indignant yelling, joining her first protest at the shock of existence with the street-life dawn chorus of Soho beneath the second-floor window.

Boots of working Londoners, horseshoes and cartwheels crunch through the fresh morning snow. Superbly drunk revellers weave amongst them three sheets to the wind, tacking vaguely homewards or on to the next tavern, bawling heartily and insensible to the cold and their frost-nipped noses. Glum prostitutes sheltering in the portal to Miss Kelly's Royalty Theatre diagonally opposite 28 Dean Street eye up the soakers and calculate their possible worth.

From the tiny adjoining back room Marx hears, painfully, six-year-old Edgar's monotonous cough. His sole surviving son is battling tuberculosis.

Dr Allen arrives with the daylight for a 'grand consultation'.[1] Marx hasn't paid his last overdue account but Dr Allen, a socialist, admiring of Karl Marx in particular and sympathetic to impoverished activist immigrants in general, comes anyway. Jenny is in no fit state to breastfeed, the doctor warns, and instructs that a local wet-nurse be found immediately for the purpose.

Dr Allen apologises that nothing more can be done for Edgar's infected lungs. Flush-cheeked, bright-eyed, feverish, Marx's once ebullient, vital male heir seems already otherworldly, clinging to a thin precipice of life as his newborn baby sister seizes on to it with clamorous vigour.

Karl and Jenny's old friends Wilhelm and Ernestine Liebknecht, who live around the corner in Old Compton Street, call in to congratulate them. The friends toast the baby girl's arrival. 'A global citizen – *Weltbürgerin* – is born,'[2] pronounces her father with suitable Teutonic emphasis for the occasion.

To match him, Wilhelm Liebknecht, nicknamed 'Library' by the Marxes, plucks a reference from Proverbs, welcoming the baby girl as 'a merry little thing, as round as a ball and like milk and blood'.[3] Library's sanguine 'Milch' and 'Blut' bring an elemental tone to the toast.

This child is to the struggle born.

The following evening Marx writes a reflective note to his best friend Friedrich Engels in Manchester to tell him about the new arrival. The baby is the reason he's slipped his copy deadline for a leader on British military errors in the Crimean War for the *New York Daily Tribune*:[4]

> I could not of course write to the *Tribune* yesterday and could not either today and for some time in the future, for yesterday my wife was delivered of a bona fide traveller – unfortunately of the sex par excellence . . . Had it been a male the matter would have been more acceptable.[5]

More acceptable to whom?

Marx's emphasis on legitimacy and the arrival of the baby as an act of conjugal good faith in this note to his best friend is very odd. Once again a father, Marx doesn't say *to whom* it would have been more acceptable if the new child had been a boy. But he knows Engels will understand *who* would have preferred a son.

Parents already to two daughters – Jenny, eleven, and Laura, ten – Karl and Möhme, as Mrs Jenny Marx is called by her family, are now burdened with another girl. Edgar is not recovering and Dr Allen has told them to expect the worst. They have already lost a son, Little Fawkes – Heinrich Guido – born on 5 November 1849 and dead from meningitis within a fortnight of his first birthday.

Now thirty-seven, Marx is conflicted over the bearing of girls. It's a truism of the age that daughters are all round more economic, social and sexual trouble than sons. The hard-nosed historical materialist can hardly delude himself with the hope that his daughters might transcend entirely their circumstances of being a universal underclass in the nineteenth-century moment into which they are born. Yet, since he was a youngster, Marx has recognised and loved women as equals – at times he even suspects them of being more evolved than men. In their early agitprop *The Communist Manifesto* of 1848 Marx and Engels emphasised the essential need 'to do away with the status of women as mere instruments of production', and argued that 'bourgeois marriage is in reality a system of wives in common . . . i.e. of prostitution both public and private.'[6] Marx still hopes that education and equal treatment might strengthen women's place and possibilities in the world. But like every Victorian patriarch, he wants a son, and this is not one.

The bona fide traveller is named Jenny Julia Eleanor after her mother – like all the Marx daughters. Jenny got her name from her great-grandmother Jeanie Wishart, daughter of an Edinburgh minister, who learned and spoke fluent German with a 'delightful'[7] Scots accent after she married Rhinelander Philipp von Westphalen in 1765 and who lived in Germany for the rest of her life. Eleanor's mother, Jenny von Westphalen, inherited the clear, delicate complexion, dark auburn hair with lustrous blonde tints and bright emerald eyes of her grandmother's Highland ancestry – but not her accent.

The origin of Eleanor's given name is obscure. The claim that it hails from her Scots forebears seems like common sense, but is unsubstantiated. There are several Helens in the genealogical history of the Wisharts of Pittarow, from whom Jeanie descended, but by the time of Eleanor's birth these are vague shades three centuries distant. There are no Ellens or Elaines or Helens or Eleanors in any of the spliced branches of Jenny and Karl's family tree, nor any close friends or inspirational colleagues. The only person with a similar name anywhere near to the family is their lifelong housekeeper Helen Demuth – Lenchen.

For whatever reason it becomes hers, Eleanor is a promising name. In Arabic, Hebrew, Greek and Latin it carries the common root meaning of ray of light and bright illumination. 'Eleanor' holds out the promise of a radiant child with a sunny disposition.

Twelve weeks after Eleanor's birth Edgar dies in Marx's arms. 'I've already had my share of bad luck,' he laments to Engels, 'but only now do I know what real unhappiness is.'[8] Disconsolate, he turns to his newborn daughter and to her he transfers all his love and hopes for his lost son.

By the time she was nine months old, the unbaptised Jenny Julia Eleanor Marx was known by all as Tussy.[9] T-oo-ssy to rhyme, as her parents explained, with pussy and not fussy. Her parents' explanation of the correct pronunciation turned out to be prescient: fussy Tussy was not, but kittens and cats she adored from infancy. Tussy, and its variant endearment Tusschen, was a soubriquet of several possible origins. Perhaps baby Tussy sneezed a lot as her lungs acclimatised to the London fug – coal dust and her father's cigar smoke within, a harsh frozen winter without. *Tousser* is the verb for cough in French, the primary language her sisters spoke with their parents at home. In Dutch, Tusschen is an archaic form of *tussen*, the word for between. Hence the old Dutch saying 'tusschen en tussen' – betwixt and between. Tussy's immediate paternal family were mostly Dutch and living in Holland, where Marx visited them frequently. *Tuzzy* is the Old English word for a garland or knot of flowers. By the 1850s, tussie-mussies were a craze amongst Victorians: nosegays or bouquets of flowers carefully selected and arranged to convey secret messages between lovers and intimacies between friends – love poetry in flowers. Tussy was also street vernacular for vagina.[10]

The numerous likely sources for Tussy's nickname tell us something about the multilingual nature of the Marx ménage. Tussy's sisters, born in Paris and Brussels, spoke French with each other, French and German interchangeably with their mother, and mainly German with their father, Lenchen and Engels. French, German and English were spoken with family and friends.

Of all the family, Möhme was the most fluently multilingual. Her liberal and progressive father Ludwig von Westphalen had seen to it that she began to learn French and English when she was a child. Marx started on his great work on political economy and the workings of capital shortly before Tussy was born and Jenny was his tireless scribe. Jenny copied and edited all her husband's writing, not only because she was one of the few apart from Engels who could decipher his appalling scrawl, but also because her German was, next to his, the best in the family.

From the womb, Tussy swam in a fluid polyphony of German, French and English, with Dutch phrases and Yiddish tags thrown into the rich mix.

An intriguing influence on baby Eleanor's moniker came from China. The Marx household were Sino-obsessed, and avidly followed the politicking of the Dowager Empress of China, Tzu Hi (also TsuTsi or Cixi). Tussy's sister Jenny had been nicknamed Empress of China, but Tussy supplanted her regency and became Successor to the Empress of China. The advice on how to pronounce Tzu-Hi was 'Sue Z' – or Tussy as in pussy, not fussy.

The three sisters all had many topical, amusing or endearing nick-names during their childhoods. For a while Laura was Kakadou, and then became the equally exoticised Hottentot,[11] on account of her black looks – a reference both to her grumpy scowls, famous in the family, and to the dusky African good looks she shared with her father. Hottentot was the nickname that followed Laura into adult-hood and Jennychen the moniker that stuck for Jenny.

Infant Tussy was looked after chiefly by Lenchen, assisted by a wet nurse, her older sisters, her parents and the Liebknechts. 'The soul of the house',[12] Helen Demuth, born of a Rhineland peasant family, had known Jenny since entering service in the von Westphalen home in 1835 when she was just fifteen.

Since then Jenny and Helen had not been separated for more than a few weeks at a time, apart from the single exception of Jenny's extended visit to her mother in 1850 when Lenchen stayed behind to take care of the family. The Marx daughters all described Lenchen as their second mother. Like Gandhi, Churchill and many other great historical figures, Eleanor's relationship with her nanny Lenchen, who performed the role of substitute mother-figure and provider, was a profound influence on her childhood. Lenchen had accompa-nied Jenny and Karl throughout their travels around Europe almost from the beginning of their marriage and had shared their many exiles. One of Marx's sons-in-law described Lenchen as:

> housekeeper and *major domo* at the same time. She ran the whole house. The children loved her like a mother and her maternal feel-ing towards them gave her a mother's authority. Mrs Marx considered her as her bosom friend and Marx fostered a particular friendship towards her; he played chess with her and often enough lost to her.[13]

As her games of chess with Marx attest, Lenchen was also at leisure within the family. Library defined the relationship as follows: 'Lenchen had the dictatorship in the house, Mrs Marx the supremacy.'[14] No man, Library observed, is great in the eyes of his servant, 'and Marx was certainly not in Lenchen's eyes'.[15] She would give her life a hundred times for him and the family, 'but Marx could not impose on her'. She knew all his whims and weaknesses and 'she could twist him around her little finger.' When Marx was irritated and stormed and thundered, she was the only person who would brave the lion's den. 'If he growled at her, Lenchen would give him such a piece of her mind that the lion became as mild as a lamb.'[16]

Grief at Edgar's death was intensified by privation. There was, as ever, a domestic cash crisis. Möhme visited the 'pop-house', as she called the pawnbrokers, so often that she called the amiable local Soho pawnbroker Uncle. 'Pop Goes the Weasel', the nursery rhyme about a shoemaker pawning his tools, was an early favourite of Tussy's. Not that she had a nursery: her bedroom and playroom were the multifunctional twin boxes of the little Soho flat squeezed into by the three grown-ups and her rapidly growing elder sisters. Borrowing against her better linens, wedding silver and the family's clothes, Möhme kept the domestic economy circulating whilst her husband busied himself with the inaugural meetings of the International Working Men's Association and burned the midnight oil to catch up on his overdue articles. Möhme and Lenchen were perennially short on crockery, glasses and sufficient food for the flow of friends and guests to their home, constant as the tide.

Recollected by the rest of her family as the most miserable time of their lives, Tussy never really remembered the pinched Soho years. Twenty-eight Dean Street, without plumbing, gaslight or privacy, was sub-let to the Marxes by a grouchy Irish linguist for £22 per year. The family moved into these lodgings in 1851, shortly after the death of their second son, Little Fawkes. Though Tussy didn't know it, the comprehensive intelligence of a Prussian secret agent sent directly by the Minister of the Interior provides a memorable illustration of Marx family life in the Soho flatlet where she was born.

Tussy arrived into a family of political radicals under constant state surveillance. In 1850 a German newspaper editor calling himself Schmidt arrived in London, purportedly to visit the Great Exhibition. In fact, Schmidt was Agent Wilhelm Stieber, briefed by the Prussian Minister of the Interior to spy on Marx and his associates. Stieber infiltrated German communist meetings and the homes of people connected with the worker and democratic movements, observing in detail the dwelling of its most prominent leader:

> Marx lives in one of the worst and hence cheapest quarters of London. He has two rooms, the one with the view of the street being the drawing-room, behind it the bedroom. There is not one piece of good, solid furniture in the entire flat. Everything is broken, tattered and torn, finger-thick dust everywhere, and everything in the greatest disorder. A large, old-fashioned table, covered with waxcloth, stands in the middle of the drawing-room, on it lie manuscripts, books, newspapers, then the children's toys, bits and pieces from his wife's sewing basket, next to it a few teacups with broken rims, dirty spoons, knives, forks, candlesticks, inkpot, glasses, Dutch clay pipes, tobacco-ash; in a word all kinds of trash, and everything on one table; a junk dealer would be ashamed of it. When you enter the Marx flat your sight is dimmed by coal and tobacco smoke so that you grope around at first as if you were in a cave, until your eyes get used to these fumes . . . Everything is dirty, everything covered with dust. It is dangerous to sit down. Here is a chair with only three legs, there the children play kitchen on another chair that happens to be whole; true – it is offered to the visitor, but the children's kitchen is not removed; if you sit on it you risk a pair of trousers. But nothing of this embarrasses Marx or his wife in the least; you are received in the friendliest manner, are cordially offered a pipe, tobacco and whatever else there is; a spirited conversation makes up for the domestic defects and in the end you become reconciled because of the company, find it interesting, even original. This is the faithful portrait of the family life of the Communist leader Marx.[17]

German Agent Stieber clearly judged Frau Marx and Lenchen utter failures as hausfraus, in his book a shortcoming probably worse than being a communist. Stieber's intelligence led to the arrest of a number of Marx Party members in Germany and ultimately to the infamous Cologne Communist Trial of October 1852. The Prussian government charged eleven members of the Communist League for alleged conspiracy in the 1848 revolution. The prosecution consisted of false testimony and forged evidence. Seven of the eleven were given six-year prison sentences. Furious, Engels later denounced Stieber as one of 'the most contemptible police scoundrels of our century'.[18] Yet even this inveigling snoop who became chief of Bismarck's secret service felt the allure of the friendly welcome and hospitality of the ramshackle Marx home.

The Prussian Minister of the Interior was satisfied with Agent Stieber's report when it landed on his desk, because it confirmed his long-held suspicions of the degeneracy of his brother-in-law Karl Marx. Prussian Minister of the Interior Ferdinand von Westphalen was Jenny's half-brother. He was furious from the instant he heard the rumour in 1836 that his half-sister was secretly engaged to the revolutionary firebrand. Ferdinand spied on Tussy's family throughout her childhood.

Tussy thrived on Dr Allen's milk regime and was no longer 'expected to die every day'.[19] Her first summer was spent in what her family called 'the country', the pastoral suburb of Camberwell, in a cottage loaned to them by their close friend, the socialist Peter Imandt. By September she was attempting to crawl and jump, as her elder sister wrote in a letter to their father who was visiting Engels in Manchester. It seemed she was also an early starter in romance. Jenny reported Tussy 'quite in raptures when the little crucked [sic] greengrocer calls . . . I think, this man is her first amour.'[20] Marx might have hoped the greengrocer wasn't calling by for the settlement of his accounts.

Möhme and Lenchen bought on tick against future income promised from two windfall legacies due to Möhme from the death of both her Uncle George and one of her Scottish relatives. The Marxes spent the money several times over before it finally arrived. Marx urged Jenny to think about finding a new home. Eleanor's ebullience was making the Soho garret feel even more cramped. 'The elder girls', as their mother wrote to a friend, 'foster and fondle her with almost motherly care. It is true that there can hardly be a more lovable child, so pretty, simple and good-natured.'[21]

Eleanor's gregarious disposition buffered the cold front of Möhme's anguish at the loss of 'that truest and best of mothers',[22]

Caroline von Westphalen, in July 1856. Tussy's first journey out of England was at the age of seventeen months, when Möhme took the three girls to Trier in the Rhineland. Eighty-one-year-old Caroline gave her blessing to Jenny and the grandchildren and closed her eyes for the last time. Her modest legacy of a few hundred thalers was divided between Jenny and her brother Edgar.

Shortly after their return from Trier in September, Möhme found a small house in Kentish Town. Tussy's family moved into 9 Grafton Terrace[23] at the end of September when she was twenty-one months old. 'It is a truly princely dwelling compared with the holes we used to live in,' Möhme wrote contentedly to a friend, 'and although it did not cost us more than £40 to furnish it from top to bottom (second hand junk helped a lot) I really felt magnificent at first in our snug parlour.'[24] There were other forms of snugness: Tussy's parents put their new separate bedroom to good use and her mother immediately became pregnant. She miscarried.

The 'princely dwelling' that housed Tussy's emergence into self-consciousness was a small suburban brick home of eight modest-sized rooms spread over a basement, ground floor and two upper storeys. Inside were the new luxuries of gaslight and a kitchen with cold running water. The small garden backed on to open fields and, at the Haverstock Hill end of the terrace, a municipal dump for industrial rubbish from new building development, railway cutting and sewer works. For the first time in London, the family had its own front door on to the street, set into an ornamented façade. Grafton Terrace was a short row of new-build homes classified as '3rd class houses', in the middle of an incomplete housing development contracted in the 1840s when the introduction of overground commuter trains made Kentish Town accessible to central London.

The street was unpaved and unlit when the Marxes arrived, and the house was a bargain due to its unfinished surroundings. Marx grumbled about his exile from his Soho social life, socialist clubs and favourite pubs, but despite the removal of these agreeable distractions from working on his book about the scientific laws of political economy, there were many benefits to this newfound suburban seclusion. Tussy's father now had his own study and separate hearth. All the family was delighted by its new proximity to Hampstead

Heath, its fresh air, wildness and elevated vistas an almost magical escape from a decade in the denlands of Soho.

Möhme was depressed by the twin sorrows of the death of her mother and miscarriage. Marx confided to Engels, 'I do not blame her, under her present auspices, although it annoys me.'[25] When the British Museum opened its new rotunda Reading Room in 1857 Marx was able to escape, commuting from Kentish Town directly into Bloomsbury, where he had his lunch at the Museum Tavern on Great Russell Street, frequented also by Conan Doyle and other popular new writers. The linens, old Scottish damask napkins 'and other small remains of past grandeur'[26] all went back to Uncle's pop-house when their credit ran dry, and this caused Möhme further anxiety.

Laura and Jenny had just started their first schooling at South Hampstead College for Ladies. Run by Misses Boynell and Rentsch, the school was as well-meaning and mediocre as all the other establishments offering unregulated private tuition in a country where there was no formal provision for the education of girls. Prior to this, Jenny and Laura had attended a few terms at a school in Soho and received indifferent coaching from William Pieper, Marx's hopeless so-called 'secretary', who the family nicknamed 'Fridolin'. Fridolin's handwriting was as poor as Marx's and he was a useless administrator. He achieved very little apart from nursing regular hangovers and distracting Marx from his work to discuss literature and philosophy. Möhme used the opportunity of the global recession to dismiss Fridolin. To the background noise of Jenny and Laura thumping out their scales on the very poor piano their father had hired for them, Möhme tidied up her husband's administration and happily resumed her former role of 'copying his scrawly articles'.[27]

Whilst Jenny and Laura learned musical notation, Tussy started to formulate speech. Her father was absorbed by the development of his emerging prodigy. 'The baby,' he marvelled, 'is a remarkably witty fellow and insists that she has got two brains.'[28] The witty fellow took to scribbling on the edge of Marx's letters whilst sitting in his lap at his study desk. Like all of the family and friends, Tussy knew her father by his soubriquet, Mohr – German for 'Moor' – the nickname he earned at university on account of his swarthiness and

plentiful coal-black beard and moustache. Tussy's announcement
that she was double-brained was coincident with the time of her first
conscious memory:

> My earliest recollection ... is when I was about three years old
> and Mohr ... was carrying me on his shoulders round our small
> garden in Grafton Terrace, and putting convolvulus flowers in my
> brown curls. Mohr was admittedly a splendid horse.[29]

Putting Marx in harness was a family tradition. Tussy 'heard tell' that
at Dean Street, Jenny, Laura and her dead brother Edgar would yoke
Mohr to chairs which the three of them mounted as their carriage,
and make him pull. As the youngest and a later arrival, Tussy got her
own mount and his dedicated attention:

> Personally – perhaps because I had no sisters of my own age – I
> preferred Mohr as a riding-horse. Seated on his shoulder hold-
> ing tight by his great mane of hair, then black, but with a hint of
> grey, I have had magnificent rides round our little garden and
> over the fields ... that surrounded our house at Grafton
> Terrace.[30]

Severe whooping cough in the winter of 1858 gave Tussy opportunity to assume dominion of the household: 'The whole family became
my bond slaves and I have heard that as usual in slavery there was
general demoralisation.'[31] The year started badly, without coal or
cash to pay the rental arrears. Whilst Tussy took advantage of being
ill to insist on open house for every street child in the neighbourhood
to keep her company, her father sent to Engels an itemised account
of his debts, lamenting his inability to pay them, 'even if I were to
reduce my expenses to the utmost by, for example, removing the
children from school, going to live in a strictly working-class dwelling, dismissing the servants and living on potatoes'.[32]

The Marxes' immediate neighbours, a respectably petit-bourgeois
master-baker and a builder, were more financially stable than the
notorious local philosopher whose finances were so bad that by 1859
he was served with a county court summons at his front door and

was trying to stop the gas and water companies cutting off their supply due to unpaid bills.

Oblivious to all these adult adversities spirited Tussy, the suburban barbarian, played on increasingly sturdy and sure legs in the muck, rubble and building refuse of the unfinished housing development. Initially, she played tomboyish games with neighbourhood children, barefoot in the red clay of the unpaved street. By the time she was four, the fields around Grafton Terrace were completely built over and the streets she romped around with the seven children of the master-baker and the builder were paved. Naturally gregarious, Tussy formed a circle of friendship with her little peers, introducing her family to their neighbours – skilled tradesmen, shopkeepers, artisans: working people.

Tussy was ringleader of her playmates, trailing her child troupe through the house and hosting impromptu tea parties of milk, bread and biscuits provided by the indulgent Lenchen. Other children accepted Tussy's bossiness and tendency to take the lead in all things because she was friendly and unselfconscious. Fun, bold, laughing continuously, she didn't exclude anyone from the playgroup. Due to her popularity, the Marx family became known to the whole neighbourhood simply as 'the Tussies'.

But Tussy's first friend and primary playmate was Marx. If he was an excellent horse, her adult self recalled, her father 'had a still higher qualification. He was a unique, an unrivalled storyteller.'[33] Laura and Jenny told Tussy about how Mohr told them endless tales as they rambled on their long afternoon walks. 'Tell us another mile,'[34] was the cry of the two girls. Previously too small, the witty little fellow with two brains now had legs strong enough to join in the walks. It was Eleanor's turn to embark on new travels in the imagination with her beloved Dada.

Youngest in the family by a decade and home-schooled by her father, Tussy was as much in the company of grown-ups as her peers. During her fourth and fifth year stories and books became her closest companions and friends. As real as 'kissing the new carpets'[35] and playing with the puppy on the felt hearthrug, the enchanting worlds magically compressed into the books on the second-hand shelves propped in every room in Grafton Terrace flowed into the reality of everyday life. The bookcases could be measured in feet, but the stories within them, as Tussy memorably put it, could be 'measured by miles'.[36]

In the company of her father, the tales left the house and took to the hills of nearby Hampstead Heath on their family walks. Carried on Mohr's shoulders, or her hand nestled safely in his, Tussy absorbed new worlds in words; characters and their adventures taking shape out of the leafy woods and wilderness. After the fecal-stinking midden, slop and smut of their former Soho lodgings, the Hampstead hills were breezy Elysium. It was perfectly sensible to imagine such a verdant fairyland to be the happy hunting ground of supernatural inhabitants and parallel realms.

The tales of the Brothers Grimm, the collected works of Shakespeare and Aristotle, *Robinson Crusoe*, *The Song of the Nibelungs* (*Das Nibelungenlied*) and the recently republished *Arabian Nights* numbered amongst the classics in the Marx family library. There were stacked serialisations of popular fiction and novels by Balzac, Dickens, Gaskell and Wilkie Collins in the house, and volumes of poetry by Goethe, Shelley, Blake and family friend Uncle Heine. Deep collections of history, science and philosophy – including the works of Hegel, Rousseau, Fourier and Darwin's recently published *On the Origin of Species* – held out the promise of mysterious undiscovered terrain for future exploration. The Talmud in Hebrew and Dutch, the Lutheran Bible in German and the King James Version in English sat alongside works on economics and natural sciences.

Everyone in the household was literate. Everything encouraging to the development of Tussy's mind was placed within reach. No stories, books, ideas or questions were out of bounds. Magazines, periodicals, journals, papers, playbills, handbills, flybills, meeting notices, leaflets, letters, free concert programmes, parliamentary reports, legal tracts, postcards, calling cards, birthday cards, Christmas cards, scrapbooks, notes, notebooks, music sheets, exercise books bound in Italian marbled boards, blotting paper, reams of writing paper: these were permanent residents of Tussy's family home. The Marx children were allowed to pick up, read and touch any and all printed words.

In her infant years, the household was short of most things, but books and paper and pencils and ink and nibs and needles, brushes, glue, sewing thread and stubs of charcoal were in plentiful supply. Whatever the other household debts, deficits and scarcity, books, paper and writing materials were as plentiful as the rich deposits in Britain's great industrial coal pits and the newly discovered gold seams of California.

Möhme noticed immediately her baby daughter's love of words and tales. 'The most striking thing about her,' Jenny wrote to a friend in Germany, 'is her love for talking and telling stories.'

> This she got from the Grimm Brothers, with whom she does not part night or day. We all read her those tales till we are weary, but woe betide us if we leave out a single syllable about the Noisy Goblin, King Brosselbart or Snow White. It is through these tales that the child has learned German, besides English which she breathes here with the air.[37]

British children usually encountered the amusing and instructive tales of terror by the Brothers Grimm in the English edition published in 1823, translated by London lawyer Edgar Taylor and illustrated wittily by George Cruikshank. Eleanor, the child of parents steeped in central European romanticism, entered the world of Grimm in the original sonorous German.

In these, her first and favourite stories, native imps, pixies, dwarfs, giants, kobolds and brownies returned from the ancient past to enthral her. Supernatural changelings switched places with healthy human babies to boost their puny physique; animals of all sorts talked, sang and went on fur-raising adventures; elves and fairies skipped on sunbeams. Repulsive frogs, wily foxes and beggars turned out to be virtuous, handsome and eligible young princes or marriageable older King Grisly-Beards in disguise.[38] Tussy revelled in the account of the princess-sisters who slipped out secretly to dance holes in their slippers every night. There were stories of maidens frozen in eternities of time, betrayed to wicked stepmothers by talking mirrors, who ate poisoned apples, were spied on, tricked, entranced and fell into deep comas, only to be awakened by the reviving kiss of handsome total strangers. Whether princess or peasant, girls were liable to be transformed by fairies into caged nightingales or offered up to a lion for his dinner in exchange for a garden rose.

Grimm tales are often gratifyingly violent and sexual: doves peck out the eyes of wicked stepsisters, first cousins are marriageable, unwanted stepsons are decapitated, witches murder their own daughters, dance to death in red-hot iron slippers, or end up baked alive in the oven. Tussy was absorbed by worlds that sprang such marvels.

As her mother notes, it was from the Brothers Grimm that Tussy got her earliest vernacular German. In the same way, it was from the household bible that she first encountered English poetry. That bible was the complete works of Shakespeare, from which her immigrant father studied and improved his knowledge of the national language of the land that hosted him in his exile. When he arrived in England, Marx had a very limited grasp of English. During the early years of their London life he systematically sought out and classified all Shakespeare's original expressions in longhand and then memorised them in order to improve his knowledge of the language. Little Laura and Jenny, whose first languages were French and German, bettered their English by reading aloud and performing Shakespeare. Tussy arrived in a family who knew most of Shakespeare's works by heart. Shakespeare was recited, acted, quoted and debated at the hearth and in the little garden. Tussy's sister Jenny was particularly smitten by the bard and made a shrine to him in her bedroom, described by her mother as 'a sort of Shakespeare museum'.[39] Avid theatregoers, the Marxes followed all aspects of London theatre life, spending money on cheap tickets instead of food and fuel, arguing over the relative merits of actors Sarah Siddons, Ellen Terry and John Kemble, and reading over Möhme's drama reviews for the press.

Aeschylus and Shakespeare, Marx explained to tiny Tussy, were 'the greatest dramatic geniuses humanity ever gave birth to'.[40] A quick student with a sharp ear and retentive memory, Tussy learned fast: 'By the time I was six I knew scene upon scene of Shakespeare by heart.'[41] She recalled that her favourite scenes 'were the soliloquy of Richard III ("I can smile and smile and be a villain," which I KNOW I loved because I had to have a knife in my hand to say it!) and the scene between Hamlet and his mother!' Möhme played the queen, and Tussy would declaim, 'Mother you have my father much offended,' looking at her father 'very pointedly'[42] when she said it, and then collapsing with laughter.

Tussy inherited Marx's unconditional love of Shakespeare. The source of the Marx family passion for Shakespeare was Tussy's maternal grandfather. She would later discover that it was Ludwig von Westphalen who introduced her own father to Homer, Dante and Shakespeare when he was a young Rhineland schoolboy.

As to that other Bible, Christianity, Marx explained to Tussy, figured as an important part of history and a great story cycle alongside all the other great classic texts. Tussy vividly recalled her father telling her the story of Christ: 'the carpenter whom the rich men killed'.[43] Marx christened his baby daughter's imagination with words that glowed and burned long after the telling: 'I do not think it could ever have been told so before or since.'[44] She remembered too his commentary, recalling his observation that, 'After all we can forgive Christianity much, because it taught us the worship of the child.'[45] Her Protestant mother was baptised at birth and her Jewish-born father was baptised a Lutheran Protestant aged six, but Tussy – like her atheist-born sisters and brothers before her – was never baptised.

Respect for children and their rights was one thing, religious adherence to a monotheistic Abrahamic faith quite another. Tussy could recite tragic Shakespearean soliloquies on state power and regicide long before she first set foot in a church. A family trip to a Catholic church to listen to a free concert of 'beautiful' music when she was six brought on unprecedented 'religious qualms'. Confiding these instantly to her father when they got home, she sat upon his knee as he patiently explained that it was the beautiful music that she could hear calling and not the voice of God; 'he quietly made everything clear and straight, so that from that hour to this no doubt could ever cross my mind again.'[46] Tussy was interested in the action-packed, exemplary stories of Jesus and the prophets, but demonstrated no further childhood curiosity about the questions of the Christian

Trinity or existence of this particular God. Her ideal Father was already in the house. She had no need of reference to another.

It is easy to underestimate how unusual and radical it was to bring up such an unreligious child in the middle of the nineteenth century. Tussy was never required to pray, sing to God or go to church.

Marx read aloud to his children: 'Thus to me, as to my sisters before me, he read the whole of Homer, the whole of *Das Nibelungenlied*, *Gudrun*, *Don Quixote*, the *Arabian Nights*, etc.'[47] For a long time Getwerg Albericht, heroic superdwarf of *Das Nibelungenlied* (*Song of the Nibelungs*), gave Tussy her nickname at home.[48] The fearsome Albericht, 'trusty treasurer' to the German folk hero Siegfried, guards the Nibelung treasure locked deep in the heart of the mountain. 'Dwarf Albericht' was an entertaining soubriquet for Tussy, poking fun at her questioning, combative and contrarian spirit, and acknowledging her trusted status in the Marx household as her father's most devoted lieutenant, despite being its most diminutive member. Loyal Albericht is Siegfried's little man: 'Whatever Siegfried wanted the dwarf was ready to do.'[49] But Albericht the bold is no slavish follower – he tests his master and his loyalty has to be earned.

We know from her partiality to *Richard III* that Tussy liked swaggering with swords and daggers, and like the Getwerg Albericht she kept the whole castle awake with her forcefield of energy – chattering, gymnastic tumbling, pranks and uproarious laughter.

It's pleasing to think of the Nibelung treasure buried deep inside the mountain as a metaphor for Marx scribbling away in his upstairs study on what Engels called his 'fat book' – his historical and scientific exploration of political economy and the workings of capital. Tussy had dolls, kittens and puppies, but her father's study was her playroom. Later, she marvelled at her father's tolerance for her constant disruption of his work and thinking, remembering 'the infinite patience and sweetness with which . . . he would answer every question, and never complain of an interruption. Yet it must have been no small nuisance to have a small child chattering while he was working at his great book. But the child was never allowed to think she was in the way.'[50]

Whilst her father worked on the masterwork that became *Capital:*

Critique of Political Economy he created a story saga for Tussy whose antihero Hans Röckle became her great favourite. A swarthy, black-eyed, bearded magician who spends most of his time conjuring wonders at the workbench in his cluttered, fabulous toyshop, Hans Röckle bore a striking resemblance to his creator. 'Of the many wonderful tales Mohr told me, the most wonderful, the most delight-ful one was Hans, Röckle.' It was magical, lively, funny, scary, mysterious, thrilling, by turns tragic and moving, and Tussy eagerly anticipated each instalment. 'It went on for months and months, it was a whole series of stories . . . so full of poetry, wit, of humour!' Hans Röckle, as Tussy describes, was Mohr's own dark materials, his *Karl Marx and the Philosopher's Stone*:

> Hans Röckle himself was a Hoffmann-like magician, who kept a toyshop, and who was always 'hard up'. His shop was full of the most wonderful things – of wooden men and women, giants and dwarfs, kings and queens, workmen and masters, animals and birds as numerous as Noah got into the Ark, tables and chairs, carriages, boxes of all sorts and sizes. And though he was a magician, Hans could never meet his obligations either to the devil or the butcher, and was therefore – much against the grain – constantly obliged to sell his toys to the devil. These then went through wonderful adventures – always ending in a return to Hans Röckle's shop. Some of these adventures were as grim, as terrible, as any of Hoffmann's, some were comic; all were told with inexhaustible verve, wit and humour.[51]

In Hans Röckle Marx pokes fun at himself and the absurdities of the bohemian life to which he subjects his family. In this Faustian pact Marx is Hans, and Uncle at the pawnshop in Soho the affable devil. At another level of abstraction, the Hans Röckle cycle offers a neat allegory of surplus value, alienation and the workings of capital, governed by the diabolical debt cycle and the stygian circulation of commodities. Narrating these adventures to Tussy, Marx constructed a transposed child-friendly version of the subject of his great-book-in-progress: his epic critique of the economic system that would come to be known as capitalism.

The enthralling stories interwove the problems of the different classes of magical and non-magical people attempting to co-exist. The toys, material objects invested with the aura of living things by means of Hans's compact with the devil, went on all manner of exciting and perilous adventures. Overhearing this tale-telling, his wife, Lenchen and Engels recognised the images of the subjugation of poorer people by the rich, and the elective burden of creative labour that creates the freedom and sustenance of pursuing life-changing ideas and adventures of the mind, but not profit and bread that can be put on the table to eat.

Underpinned by reality and drawing on familiar images, through the tales of Hans Röckle Marx introduced Tussy in fable form to the lives and many adventures of her family that preceded her birth – illustrating, through entertaining archetypes and fairy stories, the prequel to her own life story. By this means, Tussy learned the romantic story of how her parents met and married, how Lenchen came to be a member of the family, the adventures of the Marxes' odyssey of European revolutions of the 1840s, of the births of her siblings, of their successive exiles, and how they came to be in England.

In an as yet unimaginable future when she was an extremely old grown-up in her thirties, Tussy would regret that her father's Hans Röckle story cycle was not written down. Combining her recollection of the stories Marx recounted her with a series of autobiographical notes penned by her mother, Tussy did write them down, transferring the archetypes and tales of childhood into their adult form. It is in this way that she became the writer and memorialist who documented the history of her family for posterity; and it is, without exception, from her work, but usually without attribution, that all accounts of her famous father and his family have been drawn. Tussy did not transmit a pre-existing family history, she created it: researched, interviewed, wrote it down, edited and published it before she died. Without Eleanor Marx, the life of one of the greatest men of the nineteenth century and his close family would remain a closed door, and we would know less about Karl Marx than we do about Shakespeare. To understand Eleanor it's necessary to know something of the history of her family. Throughout her life she researched her heritage in preparation for a biography of her father. Tussy never completed this book, but her labour of love left us an atlas of her own origins.

The Tussies

The germ of Eleanor's existence lies in the friendship between two lawyers, one a Royal Prussian Legal Councillor and the other First Councillor of Trier. Eleanor's maternal grandfather, Ludwig, Baron von Westphalen, was a distinguished lawyer who inherited his title from his father Philipp, ennobled as thanks for his service as chief of staff to the Duke of Brunswick during the Seven Years War. The title came at a useful time for Philipp, the son of a postmaster from Hanover, as it helped him win the hand of a spirited Scottish girl half his age, Jeanie Wishart.

Jeanie, Tussy's maternal great-grandmother, was sister-in-law to General Beckwith, commander of the British forces. Aged twenty, she visited her sister in Germany during the war, where she met the forty-year-old chief of staff to the German forces at a dinner party. Philipp went to Edinburgh to ask for Jeanie's hand. Jeanie's father asserted descent from the Earls of Argyll and Angus. There was little substance to this claim to old Scottish nobility, but Philipp's baronetcy appealed to the snobbish Wisharts, for all that he was the son of a petit-bourgeois German postmaster.

Jeanie and Philipp produced four sons, of whom Johann Ludwig, Tussy's maternal grandfather, was the youngest. Sent to study law at the University of Göttingen, Ludwig was more interested in reading Shakespeare, Dante and French philosophers than studying case law. The death of his father whilst he was still a student forced him into a job in the civil service, and his marriage in 1797 to Lisette Veltheim, the aristocratic daughter of a big landowner, into a failed stint as a gentleman farmer.

Ludwig and his first wife Lisette also had four children – two sons, two daughters. Their firstborn was the solemn Ferdinand. Lisette died in 1807 and in 1810 Ludwig married again. His new wife Caroline Heubel, a thirty-five-year-old common-sense woman of the German middle classes, was energetic, conscientious and a good stepmother to his four children. The newly married couple were living in the small north German town of Salzwedel when their first child, Johanna Bertha Julie Jenny von Westphalen, was born on 14 February 1814.

In 1816 Ludwig was appointed First Councillor in the govern-ment of Trier in the Rhineland, close to the French border, under Prussian jurisdiction. Protestant in a dominantly Catholic town and an official in the pay of the reactionary and unpopular Prussian government, von Westphalen and his family were initially outsiders. But they soon found that, beneath the superficial lip-service Trier society paid to French rule and the Catholic church, the citizens were as conflicted as they were about absolute monarchy and lack of democracy. 'We live,' Eleanor's grandfather wrote to a friend whilst her mother Jenny was still an infant, 'in fateful times, a time in which two contradictory principles are at war: that of the divine right of kings and the new one which proclaims that all power belongs to the people.'[1] Von Westphalen struggled all his life to resolve these competing value systems. As a Prussian bureaucrat, Ludwig's profes-sional and family survival depended on upholding the divine right of his king, but his true sympathies were with the new ideas of the French Revolution, free thought, and his love of art, music, literature and – especially – theatre.

Though only a small city of some 12,000 people, Trier had a vibrant cultural life. The von Westphalens had easy access to the local opera house specialising in Mozart, and to the first-rate city theatre with its regular programme of drama by Lessing, Goethe, Racine, Corneille, Marlowe and Shakespeare. Ludwig and his wife were active participants in the Casino Society, a free-thinking liter-ary and social club.

Ludwig's own ambivalence made him sympathetic to the difficulties of other men subject to the conflict between principles and survival. It was in this context that he met and quickly became firm friends with Eleanor's paternal grandfather, Heinrich Marx, one of the town's most successful and sought-after lawyers. In 1817, the same year Ludwig moved his family to Trier, the hitherto named Hirschel ha-Levi Marx became a Lutheran Protestant in order to conform to a declaration by the Supreme Court of the Rhineland declaring that Jews were no longer permitted to hold public office or practise in the professions. Heinrich Marx, as he renamed himself, nominally converted to protect his career, business and family.

Hirschel ha-Levi Marx was born in 1782 in the town of Saarlouis in Saarland, Germany. His family moved to Trier when his father, Meier ha-Levi Marx, became chief rabbi of the city. Meier ha-Levi Marx's gravestone in the Jewish cemetery in Trier records his place of origin as Postoloprty in Bohemia – now the Czech Republic. Heinrich's mother, Eva Lwow, was the daughter of Moses Lwow – also a rabbi in Trier – and like her husband, Eva was descended from generations of rabbinical Rhineland Ashkenazis. Heinrich's brother Samuel, the favoured, wise son, succeeded their father as chief rabbi of Trier. Heinrich excelled at law but had no interest in his faith beyond ritual observance.

Heinrich married Tussy's paternal grandmother Henriette Pressburg, born in 1780 in Nijmegen in the Netherlands. Pressburg was the German name for Bratislava, where Henriette's father, Rabbi Isaak Heyman Pressburg, was born in 1747. His family came from Cracow, and the family line included scholars and a chief rabbi of Padua. A merchant, Isaak Pressburg moved from Bratislava to the Netherlands, where he met and married Nanette Cohen. Nanette's family was long established in the Netherlands, and Henriette grew up in a family where German, Dutch and Hebrew were spoken interchangeably.

Tussy's grandmother Henriette was semi-literate when she married Heinrich. Brought up in the constraint of a customary household, she was uneducated and her only training was in how to be a good wife and cook. She was the more religiously observant and traditionally conservative of the couple. The improvement in her reading and writing was due to the encouragement of her husband. Heinrich, aware of the limitations of her upbringing and informed by his reading of Rousseau, understood that his wife's educational disadvantages resulted from being born a woman in a sexist religion and society. Though not bookish, Henriette was numerate and had a clear grasp of domestic economy and the need for a balance of payments between income and outgoings. Her eldest son Karl might have taken closer note of her domestic economy. Heinrich and Henriette Marx had nine children, of whom four survived beyond the age of twenty-three. The children who survived infancy died of tuberculosis. Their firstborn son died; their second child, Sophie, born in 1816, was followed at 1.30 a.m. on the morning of 5 May 1818 by another son, Heinrich Karl. In August 1824 all Heinrich Marx's children, including Karl, were received into the national evangelical church. Henriette was desperately sad that her only son was baptised and not bar mitzvahed. To a superstitious mind this boded ill for the future.

Like many men and women of his epoch, Heinrich became more progressive as he got older. Heinrich's engagement in moderate nationalist politics brought disillusion. He became critical of the incompetence and prejudice of the absolutist Prussian regime and its resort to repression.[2] A homebody disengaged from her husband's political work, Henriette lacked the opportunity to keep step with the changes in her husband's life.

Looking for answers and new ideas, Heinrich became an enthusiastic member of the Casino Society. He read widely and learned about free-French thought and Enlightenment philosophy. He sang along to the Marseillaise and other revolutionary choruses at club gatherings. When the Prussians promulgated the ban on Jews holding public office or working in the professions, Heinrich formally appealed to the government to lift the anti-Semitic discrimination on behalf of the whole Trier community of his 'fellow believers'.[3] When they refused, Heinrich had to make a strategic conversion of the family to Protestantism. Henriette felt the impact of the conversion more keenly as an attack on her cultural values.

Soon after his conversion Tussy's grandfather Justizrat Heinrich Marx was given the venerable title of Royal Prussian Legal

Councillor, earning the amused remark from Uncle Heinrich Heine that by his conversion he had neatly purchased his 'entrance ticket to European culture'.[4] Heine was Henriette's third cousin and a close friend and frequent visitor to the Marx home in Trier. It was now that Tussy's grandfathers, the new Royal Prussian Legal Councillor and the First Councillor of Trier, met and became firm friends.

Thrown together by the friendship between their fathers, the von Westphalen and Marx children were friends almost from infancy. Jenny von Westphalen was an inquisitive, lively and strikingly pretty child of four when she first encountered Karl Marx, and he still a breastfeeding baby. The future great revolutionary lovers met and knew each other before they knew themselves.

Karl's older sister Sophie, to whom he was closest in his family, was of similar age to Jenny and the little girls became playmates and later confidantes. Karl was home-educated until 1830, then went to the liberal Trier High School, also attended by Jenny's younger brother Edgar, where the two boys became close friends. Karl confided to Edgar that his parents expected him to become a lawyer like his father, but he had every intention of following his own desire, to become a poet.

Meanwhile in Barmen, 250 miles north of Trier, another young man, like Marx, also dreamed of becoming a poet.

The handsome and athletic first son of a wealthy Rhineland entrepreneur, Friedrich Engels was growing up in great material comfort but spiritual discontent. Named after his father, Friedrich was born on Tuesday 28 November 1820, heir to a textile dynasty who made their fortune first from linen yarn bleaching and later from mechanised lace-making and the manufacture of silk ribbons. Friedrich's mother Elise von Haar came from a family of intellectuals and teachers. Hers was a slightly risqué background for a woman married into the merchant elite and living in the extremely Puritan climate of the Wupper Valley.

Friedrich's father diversified into cotton spinning and set up a new company with two Dutch brothers, Gottfried and Peter Ermen. Ermen & Engels established a string of sewing thread factories in Barmen, Engelskirchen and Manchester, England. This was the business into which young Friedrich, eldest son, was expected to follow his father, without question.

Confirmed in the Elberfeld Reformed Evangelical Church in 1837, the child Engels was hand-reared on evangelical fire and brimstone. He was browbeaten into theories of Calvinist predestination in which God's very precise criteria for the pre-selection of the saved and the damned favoured the wealthy, successful and socially elevated. But his mother and her culture-loving father, Gerhard von Haar, an affable unreformed priest, tempered his severe upbringing by introducing him to classical mythology, poetry and novels. When he started school at the Gymnasium in Barmen he showed early flair for languages, history and the classics.

Fascinated by German romanticism, he was drawn into the literary revival of German nationalism. Nationalist romantic legends were the theme of his schoolboy verse, including a piece entitled 'Siegfried', after the swashbuckling hero of the *Song of the Nibelungs*, lord and master to the trusty and valiant Dwarf Albericht. To Eleanor, the little girl who was to become his surrogate daughter, Engels would carefully pass on the poetic charms of legend and classical literature that made up the imaginative realms of his own youth.

Approaching manhood, Engels yearned for a life as a poet-journalist who would support his writing by becoming a lawyer or civil servant. His father was having none of this unprofitable, idle dreaming from his eldest son and heir. Friedrich senior plucked Friedrich junior from school and deposited him into mercantile apprenticeship at the age of seventeen. University was out of the question; he would learn the family business.

The following year, 1837, Engels had to accompany his father to England for the first time, where he learned how to trade in the purchase and sale of silk and encountered the great British cities of Manchester and London. The next stage of the young romantic's very unsentimental education organised by his resolute father was an apprenticeship to a linen exporter in the seaside city of Bremen, where Engels worked as a clerk. The job was dull, but he enjoyed life in a hustling and bustling port and the liberal freedoms of the household with whom he lodged.

In *The German Ideology* (written in 1845–6 and first published in 1932) Marx and Engels poke fun at anarchist philosopher Max Stirner, characterising him as Sancho Panza pontificating to the Duke on the question of the production and supply of bread whilst seated on his high horse of political economy. In one of his own early works on the economic and social conditions of the working classes of Britain, Engels commented on the essential role of bakers in servicing and satisfying the needs of the people. Later, in his study of the role of the sexual division of labour in what he described with masterful clarity as the reproduction of the forces of production, Engels got down to the hard tack of the question of women's domestic labour in holding up not only entire national economies, but the history of the world.

In the history of Tussy's childhood world, Helen Demuth, who came from a family of bakers, was an enormously important member of the family, present at the moment of her birth in Soho. Her role in Tussy's life was as significant as that of Engels. Bread – its price, the lack of it – had often fomented popular revolt. In the person of Helen Demuth, bread, revolution and the universal politics of housework converge in an extraordinary life and personality. Born in the Rhineland village of St Wendel on New Year's Eve 1820, the same year as Engels, Helen Demuth's family background was as humble as Engels's was privileged. Her father was the village baker; little is known of her childhood except that it was short-lived, as she was sent into service as a maidservant in Trier at around the age of eight. Her first employers were brutal, subjugating her as an instrument of child labour within the household. Helen remembered the harshness of the physical work and her mistress for the rest of her life, and always recalled the exact weight of the first, huge baby she was tasked to care for in this job when still just a child herself.

Homesick, longing for her mother, frightened by the formal household regime, sexual prey above and below stairs and bereft of any access to education, little Helen experienced the typical adversity and frustrated childhood of a young European working-class maidservant. Her luck changed at the age of fifteen when she escaped her draconian employers and entered service with the elite, patrician but philanthropic and liberal family of Baron Ludwig von Westphalen, Eleanor's grandfather. Mistress of the lively, fashionable household, the easy-going Caroline von Westphalen took a shine to Helen. She saw to it that the bright, attractive maidservant was provided with a new set of clothes and taught to read, write and account, at which Helen proved an adept and quick student.

Helen's surname is derived from the word *Demut*, German for humility. Like nanny Mary Poppins and canine Nana in *Peter Pan*, it is true that Helen was good-natured and reliable, but these clichéd virtues are not what make her interesting. Helen's expertise at child-care and reliability as a highly skilled servant were consequences of her class and early training. She was gentled by Caroline's decent treatment and encouraged by the improvement in her circumstances. Caroline von Westphalen valued Helen's logical intelligence, insight and good humour. She became a favourite and Caroline gave her discreet but pretty accessories that complemented her fine features, including crimped ribbons and delicate enamelled flower earrings. She also gave her a nickname, Lenchen, and it stuck for the rest of her life.

Jenny was twenty-two years old when Lenchen joined the family. Like her mother, she treated Lenchen respectfully and without affectation. 'Nobody ever had a greater sense of equality than she,' a relative remarked; 'no social differences or classifications existed for her.'[5] Jenny's impartiality to rank defined her character from an early age. Amiable and interested in each other, a friendship developed between Jenny and Lenchen.

Whilst Jenny and Lenchen got to know each other, Jenny's father Ludwig began to take a particular interest in his friend Heinrich's glaringly bright son. Karl was inquisitive, argumentative, attentive and scholarly, and he was physically strong and sporty; more the son Ludwig had hoped for than his own charming but indolent boy Edgar. Ludwig invited Karl to join their long family hikes in the parks and woodlands around Trier.

On these walks, Ludwig introduced the rapt youngsters to the worlds of Aristotle, Aeschylus, Homer, Dante, Shakespeare, Goethe, Rousseau and Shelley. Jenny followed closely, asking questions and arguing with her father. Karl joined in and Ludwig discussed points of aesthetics, ethics and morals.

Between them, the Marx and von Westphalen families spoke five primary languages. In Karl's home, German, Dutch and Yiddish were spoken; in Jenny's, German, French and English. By his maternal Scots heritage, English was Ludwig's second language. This enabled Jenny to pick it up as a mother tongue. On their open-air walks, Jenny quoted Shakespeare and Voltaire in the original, enchanting the youngster Karl, who did not understand English or French. As a little boy, Karl had known Jenny as his big sister Sophie's friend; now he saw her from a new perspective. He was just a diligent and disputatious schoolboy but Jenny was the talk of Trier: an enthralling, desirable and, even to the pugnacious Karl, slightly intimidating young woman of glittering intellect and wit as bright as her beauty.[6]

By all accounts, Jenny was strikingly lovely. Few, it seems, were immune to her beauty, but if it was her bloom that captured Karl's adolescent attentions, it was her intellect that held them and made his heart follow. He loved to hear her speak. It was from Jenny's lips that he first heard the words of Shakespeare and Shelley, and followed, absorbed, the movements of her enquiring mind as she questioned, challenged and debated with all around her.

Ludwig discussed politics with the youngsters, explaining the causes and failures of the French Revolution. The French people rightly revolted against the divine right of monarchy, aristocracy and plutocracy, Ludwig explained, but the Terror and Napoleon's military dictatorship failed to achieve its intentions. He urged them to read the ideas of Saint-Simon, primogenitor of French socialism, who looked for structural economic solutions to the causes of inequality, extreme wealth and inescapable poverty.

The walks gave young Karl cherished opportunities to be with the older Jenny, whom he idolised. But she was inaccessible: a grown-up seventeen-year-old popular at parties, picnics, balls, the theatre, and radical youth league meetings and rallies. Wooed by well-heeled professional men twice her age, Jenny was already a debutante, likely to be spoken for and married before Karl had finished school.

Jenny enjoyed socialising but was at heart an activist and intellectual. Whilst other girls of her age and class practised their coming-out curtsey and vacillated over ribbon shades and glove-lengths, Jenny pinned the tricolour in her hair and got on with reading the work of Genoese Giuseppe Mazzini and her campaigning in the Young Germany youth movement for which she was an elected representative for Trier.[7]

Part of the Young Europe international federation founded in London by Mazzini, Young Germany was led primarily by writers, poets, journalists and theorists opposed to Christian fundamentalism and the apolitical aesthetics of German romanticism. It advocated the separation of church and state, emancipation of Jewry, and the education and equality of women. The Prussian state regarded its democratic, socialist, rationalist principles as seditious and encouraging social instability; it censored many of the publications and authors associated with the movement, including work by Heinrich Heine.

Jenny von Westphalen's leadership role in Young Germany was controversial. No wonder her conservative older half-brother Ferdinand felt dismay. By the measure of Trier society, Jenny was a borderline libertine with breathtakingly progressive views. Ludwig, a follower of Rousseau, strong believer in the education of women and purblind with adoration for his favourite daughter, gave her full rein and shielded her from the criticism. For her numerous suitors, Jenny's loveliness and influential, rich father offset her alarming political and intellectual tendencies that, they no doubt believed, would be subdued by the harness of marriage and baby-making.

However, for one ineligible younger man in Trier, it was precisely that which alarmed other admirers about Jenny's firebrand nature that enticed him. For Karl Marx her analytical mind, passionate politics and disregard for social propriety made her a woman in a million.

Young Karl had no means by which to draw her attention. His very familiarity in her extended family life made him invisible. In October 1835, when he was seventeen, he left Trier to study at the University of Bonn, taking with him unspoken feelings and a good deal of bad love poetry dedicated to the object of his secret desire. Karl worked hard and played hard. Reports of young Marx's 'excellent' academic 'diligence and attention' as a scholar were accompanied by his robust freshman schedule of extra-curricular activities, especially in the Poets' Club, and as co-President of the Men of Trier

Society (the euphemistic title for a drinking club). His antic mishaps resulting from his purchase of a duelling pistol prompted his exasperated father to inquire, 'Is duelling then so closely interwoven with philosophy?'[8]

With the willing collusion of his overanxious mother, Karl dodged the draft at eighteen on the tenuous excuse of a weak chest. Henriette wrote him many letters at university imploring him to 'not get overheated, not drink a lot of wine or coffee, and not eat anything pungent, a lot of pepper or other spices. You must not smoke any tobacco, not stay up too long in the evening, and rise early. Be careful also not to catch cold and, dear Carl, do not dance until you are quite well again.'[9] These maternal admonitions were of course a comprehensive list of his regular activities.

And still he dreamed of unattainable Jenny. Whatever else might be said of Marx's impetuosity, arrogance and obstinacy, he knew his own heart when it came to Jenny von Westphalen. This was no *amour fou*. Twenty-seven years later he would still describe her as the 'most beautiful girl in Trier' and 'queen of the ball'.[10]

Conscription avoided, Marx transferred to study law at the University of Berlin, described by alumnus Ludwig Feuerbach as 'a temple of work'. He persuaded his father that Berlin was the best place for legal studies, but in truth it was a ruse for him to follow his desire to be taught by one of Germany's most contentious philosophers, Georg Hegel, who earned his living as a professor at the university to support his philosophising. From Berlin, Karl was heartbroken to hear from his sister Sophie that Jenny's engagement to Lieutenant Karl von Pannewitz had been announced.

It was an accidental engagement. Jenny accepted Pannewitz's proposal after dancing all night and drinking too much champagne. He had an elite pedigree, but Jenny's father Ludwig was sceptical. His first mother-in-law was from the Pannewitz family and he had no good memories of the experience. He needn't have worried. The effect of the young officer's elegant uniform wore off as fast as the Wachau Valley champagne hangover when Jenny discovered his conversation to be dull, politics neo-conservative and sense of humour banal. The episode was over in a few months. Jenny broke the engagement and Karl, prompted by the close shave, seized his moment and declared himself to her when he went home to Trier from Bonn for his vacation before leaving for Berlin.

After a year away he was newly confident, fashionably hirsute and burnished by scholarship and young man's adventures. He had many new stories to entertain his sisters and friends. Karl's charisma and newly broad shoulders brought him into focus for Jenny in an arresting new way. Stirred by his maturing manly persona, Jenny found herself blushing over the boy she'd known from babyhood.

Jenny probed Sophie for information about Karl. Already alert to her brother's passion for her best friend, Sophie assumed the role of go-between. Lenchen, witness to the exchange of private letters and the arrangement of trysts, was soon taken into Jenny's confidence. Jenny opted for her dark anti-hero, 'my darling little wild boar' – 'Schwarzwildchen' as she called him in her love letters.[11] Karl and Jenny were betrothed, clandestinely, in 1836. Sophie, Edgar and Lenchen were their first confidants. Missives flew thick and fast between them and Karl filled three volumes with love verses all dedicated to Jenny:

> Truly, I would write it down as one refrain,
> For the coming centuries to see –
> LOVE IS JENNY, JENNY IS LOVE'S NAME.[12]

The fact that Jenny was four years older than her fiancé made the match unconventional by the standards of their society; Karl's Jewishness, even more so. Despite their conversion, to all intents and social purposes the Marxes were still culturally Jewish and regarded by Trier society, of which Jenny was a part, as socially and ethnically other.

Jenny's mother Caroline adored Karl and wanted her daughter to follow her heart; but though loyal and supportive, she worried about Jenny's financial security. Karl's mother Henriette was desperately sad and anxious that Jenny was not Jewish. Ferdinand, Jenny's patrician half-brother, was infuriated that she intended to marry a trouble-making Jewish intellectual. He did everything possible to thwart the relationship and tried to bully his father into forbidding it. After several years of civil war more within than between the families, the friendship between the fathers carried the day and the betrothal was formally announced. Ferdinand never forgave either of them.

Jenny's fiancé had to finish his studies. Eleanor summarised the many trials and tribulations of her parents' long engagement with biblical allusion: 'they were betrothed, and as Jacob for Rachel he served her for seven years before they were wed'.[13] Whilst Jacob was working to earn a cash dowry for Rachel, Marx spent seven eventful years in Berlin accumulating intellectual capital and expending his father's money, rather than earning his own.

Regretful but sympathetic, Heinrich conceded to his son giving up law in favour of the study of philosophy whilst at the University of Berlin. Henriette berated Karl. He was abnegating the requirement to be a good husband and father, and avoiding his future responsibilities as head of the family when his father died.

As Jacob for Rachel, Marx's seven years waiting for Jenny 'seemed unto him but a few days, for the love he had for her',[14] nourished by zealous love letters, ardent literary and political debate, and occasional precious periods of time together during his university vacations. In 1841, on an unchaperoned visit to him in Bonn, Jenny cheerfully lost her virginity to Karl, an event that prompted a sparkling and frank letter on the guiltless joys of premarital sex. 'I cannot feel any repentance . . . I know very well what I have done and how the world would dishonour me, I know it, I know it – and yet I am blissfully happy and would not surrender the remembrance of those hours for any treasure in the whole world.'[15]

For Jenny, the seven-year separation caused a great deal of misery and stress. Karl was a young man at large, far busier and more mentally stimulated, his world expanding exponentially faster than hers. She craved further education and occupation. Approaching thirty, she waited faithfully for her absent fiancé, wearying of attending the weddings of her girlfriends and congratulating them on their firstborn babies.

It was during this period, in November 1842, that Karl Marx and Friedrich Engels met for the first time. Their first encounter took place in the offices of the *Rheinische Zeitung* in Brussels. In defiance of his father, Engels had quit his job in Barmen and was trying to make a living as a journalist. Neither made much impression on the other at this initial meeting, but over subsequent months Karl became increasingly interested and impressed by Friedrich's journalism on social history and economics. Neither could have guessed that the intense friendship imminent between them would become a formative factor in the future life of Marx's youngest daughter.

3

Hans Röckle's Toyshop

On a summer morning, 19 June 1843, Jenny and Karl were finally married in the plain Protestant church of the spa town of Bad Kreuznach. Jenny glowed in folds of pale green silk. Her hair was interwoven with pink roses given to her by Karl. In the absence of her father, Edgar gave his sister away to Herr Doktor Karl Marx.

Caroline von Westphalen, the only one of their parents present, wistfully observed how much her husband would have been satisfied to see this day. Ludwig had died the year before, in March 1842. Acknowledging the role of his 'dear fatherly friend' and mentor in 1841, Karl dedicated his PhD dissertation to Ludwig, 'as a token of filial love'. His own father had died in May 1838 whilst Karl was at university.

Karl's mother did not come to his wedding. How could her eldest son get married to a Christian in a *church*? Why could he not have married a nice Jewish girl? She did, however, witness on Karl's behalf the prenuptial contract that gave the pair common ownership of property, each partner promising to pay those debts that the other had 'made, contracted, inherited or otherwise incurred before the marriage',[1] so excluding these debts from community of property. All the debts were on Karl's side, racked up at university and now compounding due to Henriette's refusal to hand over his paternal inheritance.

These debts were far from their minds on their brief but halcyon honeymoon along the Rhine. Caroline gave them a handsome coffer of cash as a wedding present that they spent freely.

Jenny's new husband was between jobs when they got married. Karl's first professional role as editor of the radical *Rheinische Zeitung*, to which he'd been appointed in October 1842, ended in January 1843 when the exasperated government censor shut the paper down. Arnold Ruge responded by inviting Karl to join him in setting up a new publication in liberty-loving Paris, hopefully beyond the iron reach of Prussian censorship. So began the new Herr and Frau Marx's family migration around Europe, an odyssey that lasted seven years.

The newlyweds set up home in Paris in October. The new journal, *Deutsche-Französische Jahrbücher*, was short-lived, running to just one edition, but this first year of their marriage in the centre of the revolutionary world was nevertheless productive. Karl wrote some important developmental work, including his essay 'On the Jewish Question' and the introduction to 'Towards a Critique of Hegel's Philosophy of Right'. On 1 May 1844 their first child was born, a girl named for her mother and known ever after by her parents and family as Jennychen.

Karl started writing for *Vorwärts* whilst Jenny returned to Trier to nurse their newborn with her mother's support. Paris remained the centre of progressive politics and art, but France laboured under the bourgeois monarchy of the pear-shaped Citizen King Louis Philippe with his fat-cat motto, *'enrichissez vous'*. In August 1844 Marx and Engels met again in Paris. After their initial encounter in 1842, Marx continued to follow Engels's journalism. Marx was particularly impressed by a series of essays and reviews Engels submitted to the *Deutsche-Französische Jahrbücher*. He was also curious about Engels's first-hand experience of English industrialisation in the cotton mills of Lancashire. When he heard that Engels was passing through Paris on his way home to Germany, Marx suggested that they meet at a café for aperitifs. That night Marx and Engels started a conversation casually over drinks at the Café de la Régence that lasted ten days and nights, and went on for the remainder of their forever-after combined lifetimes.

During that summer of 1844, Karl poked fun at King Friedrich Wilhelm IV of Prussia in a playful piece for *Vorwärts*. Friedrich complained to Louis Philippe by personal royal dispatch, demanding redress for the insults and libels. A knock on the door in the middle of the night heralded the arrival of a superintendent of the Paris police with an expulsion order for Karl, effective immediately. Brussels provided a safe haven but, in order to stay in Belgium, Karl had to make a statutory declaration that he would abstain from all political activity. This forced him to stop working as a journalist, and he lost his chief source of income.

In September 1845 their second child Laura was born. The new friends Marx and Engels worked together on *The German Ideology* over the hard winter of 1845–6. The Marxes were so overstretched that Jenny dubbed their home 'the pauper colony'. Distressed by her daughter's struggles, Caroline von Westphalen dispatched Helen Demuth to Brussels as 'the best that I can send you, my dear faithful Lenchen'.[2] Dear faithful Lenchen was now a slim, blonde and blue-eyed twenty-five-year-old, six years Jenny's junior but sufficiently similar-looking to her mistress to be mistaken for Mrs Marx, if you didn't see them together. Lenchen took over the running of the household whilst Jenny transcribed her husband's articles and manuscripts, wrote letters and articles of her own, joined in the politicking and activism, and brokered her first deals pawning the silver and fine linen her mother had given her as wedding presents. Effectively, Jenny became first lady and Lenchen mistress of the household. Little Jenny and Laura soon came to regard her as their second mother.

Now in Brussels, unable to earn an income from journalism, Marx accepted his first loan from Engels, who raised it from his father. Engels also raised a collection amongst communists in the Rhineland to support the family and generously promised Marx the proceeds from the royalties of his newly published book on the condition of the working classes in England. They had been unable to find a publisher for *The German Ideology*, and it was put aside – not to be published for another ninety years.

Shortly after his arrival Friedrich invited his lover Mary Burns to join him in Belgium. He paid her passage from England and the two set up home together in Brussels. Mary was a nineteen-year-old Irish textile-worker and political activist, daughter of factory workers Michael and Mary Burns. Friedrich met her when he was in Manchester working for his father's firm. It was Mary who had awakened his real awareness of working-class industrial life and prompted him to the research and journalism that so impressed Karl subsequent to their first meeting. As with Lenchen and the Marxes, Mary was a catalytic force in the life of Engels.

In Brussels, the young allies founded the Communist Correspondence Committee, better known as 'the Marx Party', the cultivar from which all subsequent communist parties grew. Of the eighteen founding signatories, Jenny Marx was the only woman. In 1845 Karl and Friedrich visited England together and met with leaders of English trade unions, Chartists and German communists. Unbeknown to both, this trip presaged the future orientation of the rest of their lives by taking them to the place of their final exile – England.

Back in Brussels, a modest legacy from an uncle of Karl's made life easier. The Marxes moved for the first time into a small house – delightful for being all their own, for all that it was overcrowded for four adults and three children. Their first son, Edgar, was born in December 1846, shortly before the uncle for whom he was named left for America to try his luck in Texas, taking some of his sister's much-needed cash, but freeing up space in the little house. Edgar had been a drain on their resources and Karl and Jenny were quite relieved to see him go, unlike his devastated fiancée Lina Schöler, who he abandoned.

During their peripatetic political adventures around Europe between 1843 and 1848, Karl, Friedrich and Jenny famously explored their thinking on communism. They dispensed with the immaturity of conspiratorial secret societies. Anarchosyndicalism, though an attractive and occasionally useful strategic tool, was idealistic and unprogrammatic. Christian charity was well intended, but sentimental rather than transformative. All these principles had merits in their interpretation of inequality and injustice in the world but none reached the active point of how to change it.

In the course of these five years the Marxes and Engels thought about the nature of power and how to seize it. They argued about the roles of both the bourgeoisie – the middle classes – and the proletariat in real structural transformation. They examined the ways in which it was possible to interpret and understand economic laws. These were early days. Their thinking was often naive and exploratory, but it was an active and formative period, culminating in the profound lessons they learned from the nationalist European revolutions of 1848. The impact of 1848 spread throughout all forms of culture and thought – as could be heard in the new works of composers such as Wagner and Liszt.

Marx and Engels jointly worked out the ideas for what Engels jokingly referred to as the 'Confession of Faith', a statement of principles commissioned by the German Communist League. They missed successive deadlines and, in the end, the single most influential text of the nineteenth century[3] was a rushed job written up by Marx, who holed up for a fortnight with his cigars in January 1848 at 42 Rue d'Orléans in Brussels, whilst his family lodged nearby at the Manchester Hotel.

The German Workers' Educational Society in London published the first edition of *The Communist Manifesto* anonymously in German in the last week of February, to resounding silence. The ink was barely dry on their presses in Liverpool Street when mainland Europe detonated into revolution.

All over the continent, the labouring poor rose up in social revolutions against monarchies and undemocratic states. The immediate prompt for this uprising lay in a trans-European grain famine that took hold in 1846. More generally, 1848 saw the expression of a long-gathering radical movement in Europe of people who wanted more democratic governments, human rights and German unification. Due to the food crisis, prices rose, wages didn't. Profits nosedived, causing a European-wide recession. Mass unemployment and starvation stimulated resentment against undemocratic, unresponsive regimes. Hungry and resentful at the inaction of their rulers, Europe's poor – the majority – were receptive to the idea of revolt.

The 1848 revolutions began in France. In support of the labouring poor who made the revolution, middle-class, liberal lawyers, doctors, traders, retailers and academics – in a word, the bourgeoisie – mobilised for the expansion of suffrage. To raise money for the movement, they launched a 'banquet campaign' to fundraise from subscribed dinners in French cities. On 22 February 1848 Paris bureaucrats ordered the shutting down of a planned banquet on the grounds that it would spark civil unrest. Parisian citizens of all classes, from factory workers to teachers and lawyers, angry at this repression, took to the streets to demonstrate. The National Guard deserted King Louis Philippe and joined the protest, followed by the army garrison stationed in Paris. The king took flight and the people's protest proclaimed the Second Republic on 24 February.

As the age of democracy appeared to be breaking out all around Europe, Belgium became uncomfortable about harbouring the revolution's most loudly crowing cock. Under pressure from the Prussian government, Marx was given his marching orders from Belgium by royal decree in March. King Leopold I was, however, too late. The Marxes were already packing their boxes to head to Paris at the warm invitation of the new provisional French government, who welcomed the return of the 'brave et loyal Marx' to the country whence 'tyranny had banished him, and where he, like all fighting in the sacred cause, the cause of the fraternity of all peoples', would be welcome.[4]

The overthrow of the French monarchy sparked uprising throughout eastern and central Europe. Radical liberals and workers demanded constitutional reform or complete government change. Kaiser Wilhelm IV of Prussia conceded to revolts in Berlin and agreed to create a Prussian assembly. The end of Prussian autocracy encouraged liberals in the divided German provinces to convene at the Frankfurt Assembly to draw up a constitution to unite the German nation. They drew the boundaries for a German state and offered the crown to the Kaiser, who refused it. Minor reforms emerged in the German provinces and in Prussia, but it was the end of hope for a united, liberal Germany.

In Austria, Hungary, Czechoslovakia and Italy movements of national autonomy revolted to set up self-government, democratic assemblies and new constitutions. But from August 1848 the Austrian army crushed every uprising in its empire. In Vienna, Budapest and Prague the Austrian military machine flattened the liberal-democratic impetus and restored the empire to the traditional conservative regime that ruled at the beginning of 1848. Tens of thousands of protesters, hunted down for execution and imprisonment, had to flee the lands of their birth. Karl Marx, his family and most of his friends were amongst them. Known as the Forty-Eighters, these refugees migrated to Britain, America and Australia.

The revolutions of 1848 weakened the image of autocracy, but failed utterly to achieve any substantive change. The December 1848 presidential election in France brought the dictatorial Louis Napoleon, nephew of the former emperor, into office. In Austria the new emperor, Franz Josef I, consolidated Austrian repression over all the minorities of Eastern Europe. In Prussia, the new assembly had no power and was stuffed with the aristocratic elite.

The bourgeois revolutions of 1848 failed because they were badly organised and dominated by an essentially middle-class leadership dedicated to liberal reform, but ultimately fearful of the radicalism of mass, grass-roots, working-class movements. When radicals tried to take control of the revolutions in France and eastern Europe, middle-class liberals ran scared, back into the arms of reaction; they were more comfortable with the familiarity of absolute rule and law and order than the uncertainty of radical revolution.

As Marx and Engels recognised, the uprisings were premature; it was going to take more time and democratic political organisation to achieve the formation of the proletariat into a transnational class that could overthrow bourgeois supremacy and take responsibility for political power. To their disappointment, and contrary to the predictions of their so recently published *Communist Manifesto*, the bourgeoisie in whom Marx and Engels had placed their hope had failed as a revolutionary class.

These were the chief lessons learned from 1848. The happy accident of timing that made this early work of two optimistic radicals coincident with the great, failed European revolutions pushed them to grow up very quickly. The events of 1848 demonstrated, for all time, that textbook bourgeois-democratic revolution was doomed to failure without the development of an independent, democratically organised proletarian movement. The 1848 failure of the bourgeois republican revolutions in Europe turned these young radical hopefuls into pragmatic revolutionaries. The age of utopian socialism was over. Exile and enforced isolation from politics after the upheavals of 1848 enabled Marx and Engels to mature their theories.

The year 1848 was one of hectic transmigration for the Marxes, in the flux of the European revolutions. They lived briefly in Paris, then moved to Cologne to start the *New Rhenish Gazette*, then back to

Paris when the Prussian government banned and closed the paper. France was soon no longer safe. After a month the now-familiar figure of the sergeant of police appeared with the instruction that Karl *et sa dame* must leave Paris within twenty-four hours, otherwise they would be interned at Vannes in marshy Brittany.[5]

The Marxes gathered their possessions and joined the other refugees seeking a safe haven in England, the only country left in Europe that would have them. They arrived in London the year that the Corn Laws were repealed, Disraeli became the first leader of Jewish birth of the Conservative Party, Britain annexed the Punjab, the grand hall of Euston station was opened, and patent was granted for a machine to make envelopes. In literature, it was the period of publication of Charlotte Brontë's *Jane Eyre*, Dickens's *David Copperfield* and Macaulay's *History of England*. Darwin was writing *On the Origin of Species*, and Annie Besant and Charles Bradlaugh were challenging British censorship of sex education. In theatre, the legendary Fanny Kemble, abolitionist and Shakespearean actress, finally divorced Pierce Butler, her wealthy slave-owning husband.

Marx and his family arrived in Britain unnoticed. They would change it for ever.

The British population was about twenty million, over 10 per cent of whom lived in London and its suburbs. During the 1840s more than a quarter of a million people from Britain emigrated to America and three-quarters of a million left Ireland. In the wake of the 1848 revolutions thousands of Forty-Eighters emigrated to Britain. For those who made it to exile rather than jail[6] – many of them radical thinkers, middle-class, or both – London was a key focal point of this diaspora.

By autumn 1849 the family was renting temporary lodgings at 4 Anderson Street, Chelsea. Möhme was pregnant again. Hans Röckle was setting up his toyshop in Europe's biggest metropolis. The 'small belongings' that they brought with them included more books, papers and pamphlets than tables, chairs or cradles, but they had some boxes containing silver and linen from Jenny's mother. When Marx took some of these to a London pawnshop sometime later to raise cash the pawnbroker called police constables. He claims they belong to his wife, explained the pawnbroker, but he's an immigrant beggar tramp and I think he stole them.[7] It's a sharp insight into how some Londoners regarded the newly displaced European immigrants.

London was a safe haven for her family, but it was storm-tossed, to borrow one of the Shakespearean metaphors hovering behind Tussy's pen when she wrote up this part of her family history. 'Hundreds of refugees – all more or less destitute – were now in London. There followed years of horrible poverty, of bitter suffering – such suffering as can only be known to the penniless stranger in a strange land.'[8] They were German Jews and revolutionary exiles in a tough city that with studied British indifference neither welcomed nor repelled them.

Möhme's next baby was born on 5 November 1849 in Chelsea. She laboured whilst outside all was in uproar and small masked boys shouted, 'Guy Fawkes for ever!' In honour of the great conspirator they called the new baby boy Heinrich Guido: 'Little Fawkes', or 'Fawksey'. He seemed weak and sickly from the start.

In the spring of 1850 the family was evicted from Chelsea by bailiffs who impounded their furniture and the children's toys. Hans Röckle was losing his possessions to the devil. Respite in a German hotel in Leicester Square lasted only a week. The family were ejected on to the street when the hotelier discovered they couldn't pay their bill. 'One morning,' wrote Jenny, 'our worthy host refused to serve us our breakfast and we were forced to look for other lodgings.'[9]

Aided by yet another small emergency handout from Möhme's mother, the Marxes found rooms in the house of a Jewish lace dealer in nearby Soho and spent a miserable summer there with the four children. Caroline, Möhme's mother, sent money for her daughter to come home to Trier with the baby so she could take care of her, and told her to leave Lenchen in London to look after the other children and Marx.

Fawksey proved as doomed as the gunpowder plot. He died from meningitis in November 1850, a year after his birth. Jenny feared that she'd transmitted her anxieties to Little Fawkes through her breast milk; he 'drank in so much sorrow and secret worries with the milk . . . that he was continually fretting, and in violent pain day and night'.[10] She was already about six months pregnant again.

Shortly after, they moved up the road to the two-roomed lodgings at 28 Dean Street where Franziska, named for her mother's youngest sister, was born in March 1851. Twelve weeks later there was another arrival in the household – Lenchen gave birth to her first and only child. There was no space for either of these newborns and Möhme was exhausted and unable to breastfeed, so both Jenny and Lenchen's babies were put out to a wet nurse.

All efforts to save Franziska failed; a year later in April 1852 she died of pneumonia. The family laid out her little body in the back room. 'Our three living children lay down by us,' Möhme recalled, 'and we all wept to the little angel whose livid, lifeless body was in the next room.'[11] Jenny had to borrow two pounds from a friend to pay for the coffin and Franziska's funeral.

These were events as lamentable, as terrible as any of Hoffmann's tales. In September Marx wrote to Engels in despair: 'My wife is sick, Jennychen is sick, Lenchen has a sort of nervous fever. I cannot and could not call the doctor, because I have no money for medicine. For the last eight or ten days I have fed my family on bread and potatoes, and it is still doubtful whether I can procure these to-day.'[12]

Engels had recently left London. He'd given up trying to get literary and journalistic work and moved to Manchester 'to go, under very disadvantageous conditions, into his father's firm, as a clerk'.[13] Someone, Engels realised, had to earn money to subsidise Marx's unique but unprofitable genius. His new job as clerk and general assistant at Ermen & Engels earned him an annual salary of £100 plus 10 per cent of the firm's profits, all of which he shared with the Marxes.

From the moment he arrived in London in 1849 Marx had a mountain of political work to address, all of it unpaid. Setting up a new headquarters for the Communist League at the London offices of the German Workers' Educational Society and running a committee for the aid of German refugees were amongst his most time-consuming tasks. He also attended regular meetings at the German Workers' Educational Society clubroom above the Red Lion pub on the corner of Great Windmill Street and Archer Street, where he gave lectures and classes to young refugees in subjects ranging from languages to philosophy and political economy. In November 1849 he began a long multi-part lecture series entitled, 'What is Bourgeois Property?' Well might he ask, since he had none.

In 1850 Marx turned 28 Dean Street into the temporary head office of the Communist League and filled it with volunteers campaigning for the support of the Cologne trialists, adding yet more pressure to the household. By the end of the year the Communist League was defunct, and Marx decided to refocus on his scholarly research on capital. However, he was instantly distracted by the relaunch in London of the *New Rhenish Gazette*. It was good journalism but, unable to pay for itself through subscription, it folded after five issues.

By the autumn of 1851 Marx was working as a regular correspondent for the *New York Daily Tribune*. As well as his wages from the *Tribune*, Marx pulled in some £50 from journalism for other publications. Yet despite an average income of £200 a year, of which just over 10 per cent (£22 p.a.) went on the rent for Dean Street, there was never enough to pay off his creditors or the new bills for essential provisions.

Whilst Marx, like Hans Röckle, could never meet his obligations either to the devil or to the butcher, he laboured under these stressful conditions to investigate the workings of capitalism. This work was constantly interrupted by the temptations of timely, 'essential' pamphleteering. In December 1851 he began writing *The Eighteenth Brumaire of Louis Bonaparte*, commissioned by an American publication written in German, *Die Revolution*. He wasted several months of 1852 writing a satire of the 'noteworthy jackasses' and 'democratic scallywags' on the dispersed socialist fraternity, gleefully entitled *The Great Men of Exile*. Fortunately, the manuscript was sold fraudulently to the Prussian secret services by the scamp who was supposed to deliver it to the publisher, and consequently wasn't published until a century later. More germane, he wrote a sound reflection on the *Revelations Concerning the Communist Trial in Cologne*. But he and Engels knew he was merely producing 'miniature dunghills', and should get on with writing his analysis of political economy, a fact that further aggravated his now constant, uncomfortable carbuncles.

Such was the context of the years immediately preceding Tussy's birth and narrated in fable form through the tales of Hans Röckle. 'It was a terrible time,' Library – Wilhelm Liebknecht – told Eleanor many years later, 'but it was grand nevertheless.'[14] Revolutionary socialist, member of the Reichstag and constantly migrating jailbird, Library was a loyal friend and political ally, a sometimes exasperatingly optimistic idealist, and a very important figure in Tussy's life. He arrived in London in 1850 and lived with his first wife at Model Lodging House in Old Compton Street. He applied to be vetted for membership of the Communist League, and Marx and Engels gave him a thoroughly hard time in checking his credentials.[15]

Liebknecht was dubbed Library by the Marx children, and all the adults accepted the title, though no one – including Library himself – was ever sure why he earned this nickname from the youngsters.[16] Having met her on the day of her birth, Library was fond of Tussy from the beginning. He loved her alertness, inquisitiveness and argumentativeness as a child, 'restless, curious, wanting to know everything, and constantly widening the horizon of her mind'.[17] Marx was fond of observing that children should educate their parents. However, he gave Tussy a decisive education through the process of writing *Capital* during her formative childhood.

'What', Engels asked Marx in 1851, 'will happen to all the gibble-gabble which the whole émigré gang can make at your cost if you answer them with a work on economics?'[18] Engels urged him to write down his economic analyses and explain his theory of historical materialism. Marx responded by finally settling down seriously to his great work on political economy that became *Capital*, the most influential piece of writing since the Bible, Quran, Talmud and the works of Shakespeare.

To say that Eleanor Marx grew up living and breathing historical materialism and socialism is therefore a literal description and not a metaphor. *Capital* was Marx's attempt to produce a coherent study of social, political and economic history from classical times to his present day. His quest was to discover the laws that govern history. Tussy couldn't understand the subject of her father's big project from an adult perspective, but as he amassed the evidence from which he formed his theory, he extracted examples and narratives that could be turned into enjoyable stories and useful instruction for his little girl.

When Mohr was studying the legislation against the poor and expropriated from the end of the fifteenth century that forced down wages by Acts of Parliament,[19] he explained this aspect of British history to the attentive Tussy. He shared with her the factual contexts for Shakespeare's history plays and tragedies that she loved. Tussy's childhood intimacy with Mohr whilst he wrote the first volume of *Capital* provided her with a thorough grounding in British economic, political and social history. Tussy and *Capital* grew up together.

Book-worming

In November 1860 Möhme erupted with smallpox. Sixty years after Jenner pioneered his vaccine, this contagious disease was still potentially life-threatening. Parliament had introduced compulsory smallpox vaccination in 1853, so Tussy was vaccinated. She and her sisters were packed up and delivered to the Liebknechts, now living nearby in Kentish Town, where they stayed until Christmas.

Five-year-old Tussy made herself at home with Library and Ernestine, but missed her parents. Seeing her father in the street one day from Library's windows Tussy yelled a raucous hunting call; 'Halloo old boy!' Clearly the Victorian dictum that children should be seen and not heard was not her style.

Living with the Liebknechts meant Tussy could play day and night with her best friend Alice. Tussy and Alice's friendship lasted into adulthood, mirroring the intimacy between their mothers.

When the sisters returned home at Christmas the atmosphere was subdued. Möhme was depressed by her illness, believing the smallpox scars had profoundly altered her looks and destroyed her previously youthful beauty. Outwardly she quipped about it, writing to Louise Weydemeyer that her face was still 'disfigured by pockmarks and of a red which is just the "magenta" that is now in fashion'.[1]

To brighten Tussy's sixth birthday amidst the general dejection her father gave her a special present. Mohr always said that

'book-worming'[2] was his favourite occupation. He now passed this
gift on to Eleanor. On Wednesday 16 January she eagerly unwrapped
the complete volumes of *Peter Simple* by Captain Marryat. It was
her very first novel. Seized immediately by the adventure, Tussy
sailed away from a gloomy north London winter with Midshipman
Simple to fight in the Napoleonic Wars. Her imagination voyaged
with ships of the line, square-rigged brigs, salty vernacular, cannons
and broadsides, weevils, ship's biscuits, cutlasses and tots of grog.
Immersed in this Victorian bestseller, Tussy was frequently heard
bursting into laughter at the preposterous, compulsive exaggera-
tions of Captain Kearney, Peter Simple's Munchausen-afflicted
naval master.

Marryat, the father of the seafaring adventure novel from which
all others followed, from C. S. Forester's Horatio Hornblower to
Patrick O'Brian's Jack Aubrey and Stephen Maturin, was the writer
from whom Tussy discovered not only her sea legs, but her inner
cross-dressed sailor:

> And when that little girl, fired by Marryat's tales of the sea, declared
> she would become a Post-Captain (whatever that may be) and
> consulted her father as to whether it would not be possible for her
> to 'dress up as a boy' and 'run away to join a man-of-war' he
> assured her he thought it might very well be done, only they must
> say nothing about it to anyone until all plans were well matured.[3]

Marryat held out the allure of life at sea fighting the French fleet and
profiteers. Tussy's next literary adventures transported her to the
new frontier of the American West. Responding to her enthusiasm
for Marryat, Marx introduced his daughter to James Fenimore
Cooper, whom she called the American Scott. Now Tussy plunged
into life under the wigwam, riding astride beside Natty Bumppo and
Chingachgook, following his incarnations through the serial editions
of his life – as Leatherstocking, Pathfinder and Deerslayer. Here
were Red Indians, hand-to-hand combat, scalping, luciferous Magua,
the exemplary Chingachgook, loquacious Creoles and quadroons.

And to her sharp, instinctive childhood observation, was there
something in the immortal friendship of Chingachgook and Natty

Bumppo reminiscent of her Dada and Engels? This unison of two men, as D. H. Lawrence put it, was imagined as the nucleus of a new society, their relationship 'deeper than property, deeper than father-hood, deeper than marriage, deeper than love'.[4] The rapport between Marx and Engels was as important to Tussy's childhood develop-ment as that which existed between her parents.

With the few exceptions of American 'Amazonians', Cooper's women are mostly saintly, shrinking, beige-blonde lilies or faintly smouldering, brunette would-be seductresses cut from stock patterns of young ladyhood, satirised memorably by James Lowell in his *Fable for Critics*:

> And the women he draws from one model don't vary,
> All sappy as maples and flat as a prairie.[5]

The sappy maples were of no interest to Tussy; focusing on the trou-ser roles, she barely noticed them.[6] As Lawrence dryly observed, of course it never rains in Cooper's Wild West: it's never cold, muddy or dreary; no one has wet feet or toothache and no one ever feels filthy, even when they can't wash for a week. 'God knows,' Lawrence speculates, 'what the women would really have looked like, for they fled through the wilds without soap, comb, or towel. They break-fasted off a chunk of meat, or nothing, lunched the same and supped the same.'[7]

This was a mode of existence that seemed very agreeable to Tussy, fiercely resistant as she was to brushing her hair or taking heed of Lenchen's instructions to sit down to lunch. Lenchen complained that Tussy could only be persuaded to gulp down a mug of milk and accept a piece of bread, clutched in her hand as she ran out into the street to play with her friends, all of whom she afterwards cordially invited back to her home to spread further misrule.

Neither Mohr nor Möhme were concerned about enforcing conventional formalities. Contrary to the received historical opinion that has misrepresented her as socially and sexually conservative, Jenny Marx was a liberal mother who had no patience for mannered affectation. She wrote to Ernestine about her disapproval of the constraints placed on some of their friends' offspring: 'the children are constantly watched and called to order: they must eat correctly, they must speak correctly; the only thing that is not done according to rule is drinking; to my great astonishment there was neither beer nor wine on the table . . . The children have never yet tasted spirits.'[8] She felt compassion for a little boy who just wanted to enjoy his dinner, but 'was in a fearful state over an unmanageable duck's leg. He very much wanted to get the little bit of meat off it, but he did not dare lay a finger on the bone (the governesses eye never leaves the children).'[9]

Not a single day's schooling had yet interfered with Tussy's busy childhood. From her sisters she picked up French and some musical notation, and from her mother knowledge of contemporary theatre. Books and her father's study became her classroom, Marx her personal tutor. After consuming Marryat and Cooper,[10] Tussy's plans to run away to sea or to America were diverted by the advent of her Scott mania, bringing plots for rousing the Highlands and reviving the Jacobite 'Forty-Five'. She was, however, horrified when Marx teased her with the suggestion that she might partly belong to the detested clan of Campbell.[11]

Marx passed on his love and admiration of Scott, Balzac and Fielding to Eleanor. It was an intense home-schooling of the most entertaining form, with her father a subtle educator:

> And while he talked about these and many other books he would, all unconscious though she was of it, show his little girl where to look for all that was finest and best in the works, teach her – though she never thought she was being taught, to that she would have objected – to try and think, to try and understand for herself.[12]

In later life Tussy would complain that very little was spent on her formal education. In fact her home-schooling with her father was much better than that of her two older sisters, who attended a variety of unlicensed teaching establishments for girls. Whilst Laura and Jenny spent a disproportionate amount of their schooling learning to sing, sew, paint, play the piano and be ladylike, Tussy read widely and deeply, debating everything, in detail, with one of the greatest minds of the age.

After Laura and Jenny left South Hampstead College they continued to take classes in French, Italian, drawing and music. The
academic shortcomings of the Misses Boynell and Rentsch's school
were typical of the mid-nineteenth-century British education system.
The best on offer were private establishments, accessible only to the
fee-paying middle classes, run by dedicated semi-professionals who
did their best to provide some kind of structured education to young
women in a context where there were no required teaching qualifica-
tions or defined curriculum. The first reforms making education for
women possible were still a decade away. Tussy would be fifteen
when the Education Act (Forster's Act) was passed in 1870. This was
the first legal reform attempting to provide elementary education for
all children, including girls. Fees of a few pennies per week were
charged, with exemption for poorer parents. In the same year the
London School Board was established to provide elementary schools
in London. In 1869 suffragist Emily Davies and educationalist and
human rights campaigner Barbara Leigh Smith Bodichon established
Girton College at Cambridge, the first residential women's college in
England. Oxford University allowed the first graduation of a woman
a decade later in 1879. Cambridge was founded in 1223 and Oxford
in 1187: thus it took both establishments nearly seven centuries to
grasp the startling concept that women were also human beings,
entitled to education.

Like so many of the great artists, writers, intellectuals and politicians who followed her into the next century, such as Virginia Woolf,
Tussy had no access to formal schooling. However, by contrast with
Woolf, whose wealthy scholarly historian father Sir Leslie Stephen
did not believe in investing in the education of his daughters, Tussy's
impoverished historian philosopher father was committed to the
education of women. Where the rich and entitled Leslie Stephen –
with his successful sons – lost no sleep over his daughter's struggle
for an education, penurious intellectual immigrant Marx recognised
the material constraints on educational development experienced by
the daughters of all classes. Part bluestocking, part leatherstocking,
part hoyden, wholly bohemian-in-the-making, Tussy had an unconventional, rigorous intellectual education in freedom of thought
critical to her later attitude to life.

Tussy started writing as well as reading novels at the age of six. She wrote her first letters to her sisters, filching their stationery and pens and leaving elaborately addressed envelopes to 'Miss L Marx from E Marx' on their writing desks.[13] Beyond the circle of her immediate family, Tussy had august correspondents. Few six-year-old children had the opportunity to write with such verve and ease to some of the most formidable men of their century. One of her first letters was a neighbourly note to Library, signed teasingly 'Niemand' (nobody).

Her first international letter was posted to her Uncle Lion Philips in 1861, thanking him for the gift of a Dutch doll sent from the Netherlands, and enclosing a missive in elaborate and unintelligible ideograms that she claimed were Chinese characters. Uncle Lion was married to Marx's Aunt Sophie, sister to his mother Henriette. Uncle Lion administered widowed Henriette's estate on her behalf. He was a hugely successful tobacco merchant and trader, primogenitor of what became the Royal Philips Electronics commercial empire – and very fond of Tussy.

Eleanor's invented ideograms were part of her craze for all things Chinese, brought about in 1861 by the coalescence of a bout of jaundice with her father and Engels's writing continually about the Celestial Empire. 'I remember well, that seeing myself quite yellow I declared I had become a Chinaman and insisted on my curls being made into a little pigtail.'[14] From 1853 Marx and Engels had covered the politics, economics and society of the great empire and its role in the world, mostly for the *Tribune*. All matters Chinese were the focus of discussion in the Marx home. Tussy's curls captured and smoothed into a queue, her little arms draped in improvised Chinese box sleeves, she succeeded her sister Jenny to the imperial throne as Successor to the Empress of China. Writing to his wife, Marx paid tribute to Tussy's supreme power as ruler of the household: 'Above all and in particular, please give the Chinese Successor a thousand kisses on my behalf.'[15]

Her Sinophilia lasted. Eight years after her jaundice had led to her ascendance to Empress, Tussy asked Engels for a big ball of Chinese thread from Manchester, as 'the little humbug loves all Chinese formalities'.[16]

Aside from her invented ideograms, Tussy's first letters were written primarily in English. Uniquely in her family, English was her first language. She could speak and read German well, and write it rather badly. She could speak, read and write French, learned from her Paris- and Belgium-born and raised older sisters. She was interested in learning Dutch, so she could better get to know her family in Holland. As a teenager, due to Engels' influence, she was to develop a literary interest in Old Icelandic, Old Norse, Danish and classical Arabic.

Tussy's early writing carries the acoustics and vibrations of her childhood voice and the realms of her imagination. An early example of this is audible in a letter to her Uncle Lion Philips written sometime during the winter of 1863:

My dear uncle,

Although I have never seen you I have heard so much about you that I almost fancy I know you, and as there is no chance of my seeing you I just write these lines to ask you how you are. Are you enjoying yourself? I am, and always do at Christmas time which I think is the jolliest in the year. I wish you a very happy new year, and daresay you are as glad to get rid of the old one as I am. I heard from papa that you are a great politician so we are sure to agree. How do you think Poland is getting on? I always hold up a finger for the Poles those brave little fellows. Do you like A.B. [Auguste Blanqui]? He is a great friend of mine.

But I must say goodbye now, but dare say you will hear from me again.

Give my love to my cousin Nettchen and to Dada.

Goodbye, dear uncle

I am
Your affectionate
Eleanor Marx[17]

The letter is written in a free-flowing, forward-sloping hand, with stylish capital letters. Tussy's reference to holding up a finger for the Poles is a reminder that from 1863 a general insurrection in Poland

had been violently repressed by the Russians. At the time the uprising had not been definitively crushed. Tussy firmly took the side of
Poland in its resistance against the Russian occupation. During
November 1863 the London Trades Council campaigned on behalf
of Polish emancipation, calling on the governments of England and
France to support Poland's fight for freedom. Marx's Inaugural
Address to the International Working Men's Association of October
1864 condemned 'the shameless approval, mock sympathy, or idiotic
indifference with which the upper classes of Europe have witnessed
heroic Poland being assassinated by Russia'.[18] Marx's writings on the
subject of Poland remained in unpublished manuscript form for
nearly a hundred years; Tussy was already writing about them at the
age of eight.

Brittle paper, drier ink; Tussy's 150-year-old letters, held in the
hand, still seem to crackle with energy. Her script is generous in size
and forthright in proportion. Paper and ink, we get the sense, were
not items in short supply in this household. Tussy treated them as
toys and tools, not a luxury. Her family home was often short of
food, fuel, clothing, shoes, furniture and medicines, but nowhere can
be found a lament for lack of paper or ink. Growing up in a trilingual
household, she had an acute ear, whilst her erratic spelling as a youngster made her sensitive to the puns, multiple meanings and poetic
transpositions revealed by slips and malapropisms.

At the beginning of 1861 the *New York Daily Tribune* turned its
attention to the impending American Civil War. Reducing its cover-
age of Europe, it halved its commissions from Marx, immediately
cutting the family income by 50 per cent. Marx went to visit Uncle
Lion in Zaltbommel and his mother in Trier to try and raise loans
against his inheritance. Henriette refused to help him. She was unwa-
vering in her complaint that her son would do better to earn money
rather than to keep writing about it unprofitably. Uncle Lion resolved
Marx's cash-flow problem by agreeing to a bridging loan for his
nephew against his future inheritance.

Her father's absence for nearly three months prompted Tussy's
curiosity about the Dutch relatives who were keeping her beloved
Dada away for so long. 'My grandmother,' she wrote later in an
account of her Dutch ancestry, 'belonged by descent to an old

Hungarian Jewish family driven by persecution to Holland . . . known by the name of Pressburg, really the town from which they came. These Pressburgs, of course, intermarried, and my grandmother's family name was afterwards Philips.'[19]

In 1879 Uncle Lion's grandsons, the brothers Gerard and Anton Philips, were fascinated by the incandescent lamps demonstrated by Thomas Edison; they started experimenting with electric light with a view to developing it commercially. Financed by their inheritance from their magnate grandfather, the brothers set up the first Philips factory. In 1891 the family founded the company of Philips Lamps in Eindhoven to meet the growing demand for light bulbs following the commercialisation of electricity. The company remains known as Philips to this day, the multinational electronics company worked on and established by Tussy's Dutch cousins during her twenties and thirties.

The going at home was tough whilst Mohr was away. Lenchen fell ill, and Möhme ran out of money. Ashamed, she had to ask Engels for help until Marx returned, an episode witnessed by the perceptive Tussy. Their economic situation worsened in 1862 when Marx's work for the *Tribune* ceased altogether. Tussy burrowed into her adventure novels and wondered at the hushed discussions between her mother and Lenchen about Marianne Kreuz, their maidservant. Marianne, thought to be Lenchen's younger sister or cousin, had joined the Grafton Terrace household in 1860. In their present circumstances, a maidservant was an unaffordable luxury. In fact, they were helping Marianne conceal an unwanted pregnancy. The rent was a year in arrears. Möhme was battling a clinical depression tactfully diagnosed by Dr Allen as a stress-related illness, producing tension between her and Marx.

Despite domestic problems, Marx's work on the draft of the first volume of *Capital* seemed to be progressing well. But even he had to admit that this time they were sliding too close to penury. Much to Engels's amusement he received a letter from Marx telling him that he had just applied for a clerical job with an English railway company. His mother's nagging that he find a proper job to provide for his family seemed to have prodded his conscience. Fortunately, *Capital* avoided the fate of being shunted into the sidings of history thanks to its author's illegible handwriting. The railway company rejected Marx's submission because they couldn't read his application for the job.

Unlike the hiring committee of the English railway company, Tussy could decipher her father's handwriting. This unremarkable aspect of the relationship between father and daughter might appear insignificant, had it not changed the course of history. The only other people who could reliably transcribe Marx's writing were his wife and Engels. In the meantime Marx's most valuable asset, which Engels called his mighty 'brainbox', was functioning highly effectively, and he was making what Möhme optimistically described as 'gigantic strides towards completion',[20] despite his persistent liver trouble. Laura started going with Mohr to the British Museum to help him with his research. Meanwhile her sister Jenny's health caused great concern. She was rapidly losing weight, and her obstinate cough wouldn't go away. It didn't occur to anyone that Marx's smoking had anything to do with it.

Dr Allen insisted that Jennychen needed sea air and bathing to restore her health, but there was no money for trips to resorts. In early July an unexpected windfall arrived from their friend Berta Markheim. Berta, Jenny and Karl had become friends in 1852, when the German writer spent some time in London. At that time she was still Berta Levy, sister to the well-known poet, novelist and librettist Julius Rodenberg. In 1854 Berta married businessman and gymnastics pioneer Joseph Markheim. Hearing of the Marx family's financial straits, Berta dispatched a kind letter and postal order to Jenny, who was surprised that Berta had been thinking of her 'with love, loyalty and sympathy, without so much as a reminder on my part'.[21] Berta's generosity enabled Jenny to take the children for a holiday to Ramsgate whilst Mohr went on another fundraising expedition to the Netherlands and Rhineland. Jenny never knew that her husband had secretly prompted the Markheims' act of generosity.

This was Tussy's second seaside visit. Her first had been a rainy fortnight in Hastings when she was five. Built in the 1840s, and one of the earliest railways in England, the London to Ramsgate line made quick, cheap travel to the coast possible for southern urbanites. The Ramsgate line terminated at the harbour – a working port and pleasureground. Tussy's first views were of trim-skiffs (paddle steamers), tugs, boatmen and the lighthouse, framed by clifftops and enticing seascapes topped with tall-ship masts. Popular since the Napoleonic period when it served as a garrison town, Ramsgate, 'a delightful and beautifully situated spot'[22] according to Tussy's mother, attracted holiday makers of all classes and notable visitors such as Coleridge, Queen Victoria, Prime Minister Lord Liverpool and George Canning.

Lenchen encouraged Jenny to bathe her smallpox scars in the healing salty sea.[23] 'We spent our time,' Jenny wrote to Berta, 'either *beside, upon* or *in* the sea.'[24] The five women enjoyed three blissful weeks of swimming, reading, walking, shell-seeking, munching paper cones of cockles and clams and ice cream, and people-watching. Jennychen stopped coughing and gained weight. The Ramsgate holiday was the high point of 1862. In August Library, Ernestine and little Alice returned to Germany after twelve years in exile. Tussy and Alice became penfriends, but missed each other.

Möhme went to Paris to try and secure a loan from Monsieur Arbabanel, a banker she and Karl had got to know when they lived there. Monsieur Arbabanel was paralysed by a stroke a few hours before she arrived and she returned home empty-handed on 23 December, to learn that Marianne Kreuz had died the same day from a heart condition diagnosed earlier in the year by Dr Allen. As she could not be buried until after Christmas, her body stayed at Grafton Terrace until her funeral on 27 December. With a corpse in the parlour and money tight, it was a glum Christmas.

During the night of 6 January 1863 Mary Burns, Engels's beloved, died suddenly. In shock, Engels wrote the next day from their shared home in Manchester:

Dear Moor,
    Mary is dead. Last night she went to bed early and, when Lizzy wanted to go to bed shortly before midnight, she found her already dead. Quite suddenly. Heart failure or an apoplectic stroke. I wasn't told till this morning; on Monday evening she was still quite well. I simply can't convey what I feel. The poor girl loved me with all her heart.

So ended their relationship of two decades, begun in 1842 when Engels was twenty-two and his father sent him to England to learn the textile business. Engels admired Mary for her inborn, passionate feeling for her class and her staunch loyalty: she 'stood by me in all critical moments more strongly than all the aesthetic nicey-niceness and wiseacreism of the "eddicated" and "senty-mental" daughters of the bourgeoisie could have done'.[25]

How Mary and Engels met is unconfirmed, but it seems that she and her sister Lydia (Lizzy) were working as mill-hands in an Ermen & Engels factory in Manchester. 'She was,' Tussy later recalled, 'a very pretty, witty, and altogether charming girl . . . a Manchester (Irish) factory girl, quite uneducated, though she could read, and write a little.'[26] Tussy said that her parents were 'very fond' of Mary, and spoke of her with the 'greatest affection'.[27]

Recent work by Roy Whitfield and Tristram Hunt[28] has done much to reconstruct the life of Mary Burns and restore her significance to history. Her role in politicising Engels is proven. Engels took Mary to bed; Mary took Engels to the tenements and to the heart of the Irish immigrant community of Manchester. She showed and explained to him the conditions of factory and domestic workers. Her role was directive and Socratic.[29]

Two years after meeting Mary Burns, in 1844, Engels produced *The Condition of the Working Class in England*. This detailed social survey of the 'condition, sufferings and struggles of the working classes of Britain and their middle-class opponents'[30] produced a critique of 'the cause of contemporary class antagonisms'[31] and his condemnation of capitalism. Engels left England with his political consciousness awakened by Mary Burns and revolutionised by his experience of the world into which she had initiated and guided him. This was not exactly what Engels *père* had had in mind when he sent his greenhorn son to Manchester to study the family business.

Mary later joined Engels and the Marxes in Brussels. The couples lived in adjoining apartments and Jenny and Mary became friends. Möhme liked Mary, and respected her free union with Engels. Contemptuous of the sexual double standards of 'bourgeois nicey-niceyness', Jenny refused to acknowledge or greet any of the

mistresses, chatelaines and latest passing fancies the jovial philandering Engels had a habit of bringing to public social events. Jenny
was as unbending in her loyalty to Mary as Engels was to Marx, and
Engels knew better than to expect Jenny to act the polite hypocrite
in these circumstances. When Engels and Lizzy Burns later moved
to London, it was Jenny who househunted and found a home for
them, located as close to her own family as possible. The relationship between Engels, Mary and subsequently Lizzy Burns played a
crucial role in Tussy's development.[32]

Engels famously received a breathtakingly insensitive response
from Marx to the news of Mary's death. Mohr sent a letter prefixed
with only the most abrupt commiseration, 'She was so good-natured,
witty and closely attached to you.'[33] Without further solace Mohr
launched into a detailed list of his own current calamities – lack of
money, inability to get credit, school fees, rent, impossibility of
getting on with work, unpaid bills, lack of presentable clothes, shoes
in hock – concluding with the great flourish that surely it would have
been preferable for his own mother, who 'has had her fair share of
life',[34] to die rather than Mary. 'It is dreadfully selfish of me to tell
you about these *horreurs* at this time,' Marx acknowledges. 'But it is
a homeopathic remedy. One calamity is a distraction from the other.
And, in the final reckoning, what else can I do?'[35] Like all mumbo-
jumbo homeopathic remedies, Marx's prescription was useless.
Inexcusable as his letter was, it's odd that Marx's postscript is never
remarked upon. 'What arrangements will you now make about your
establishment? It's terribly hard for you, since with Mary you had a
home to which you were at liberty to retreat from the human imbro-
glio, whenever you chose.'[36]

Engels waited nearly a week before replying. As the friends
usually corresponded daily, his silence was eloquent, as was his
unusually formal address:

Dear Marx
    You will find it quite in order that, this time, my own misfor-
tune and the frosty view you took of it should have made it
positively impossible for me to reply to you any sooner. All my
friends, including philistine acquaintances, have on this occasion,

which in all conscience must needs affect me deeply, given me proof of greater sympathy and friendship than I could have looked for. You thought it a fit moment to assert the superiority of your 'dispassionate turn of mind'. So be it, then![37]

Contrite, Marx wrote a penitent response, a rare apology that the big-hearted Engels readily accepted, confirming their friendship saved and restored, and signifying business was as usual by sending a cheque for £100 that averted Marx's imminent bankruptcy. Engels was cash-strapped at the time, so stole a cheque from Ermen & Engels and made it over to Marx, 'an exceedingly daring move on my part'.[38] This was the first and last time there was a threat of a rift between the two.

As children do, Tussy played a vital role in tempering the desolation Engels experienced following Mary's sudden death. Like many other youngsters of the 1860s, Tussy was seized by the new craze for stamp-collecting. Engels sent her new additions for her album and enjoyed her enthusiastic thank-you letters. When he wrote to Marx, he enclosed more stamps for her, revealing the source of his supply: 'A great deal of thieving in this article is going on at the office just now.'[39]

In this way, Mary's death at the beginning of Tussy's eighth year strengthened her relationship with Engels, her 'second father'. It was the substantive beginning of an intimate relationship that shaped both of their lives, and political history.

On 30 November Henriette Marx died, bequeathing £600 to her indigent son, the remainder of his legacy. Marx was now an orphan, and Tussy without grandparents.

Abraham Lincoln's Adviser

One cold Saturday in early 1864 Jenny took 'the whole gang'[1] to the West End to see the American actress Kate Bateman in *Leah the Forsaken*, the role that was making her famous on both sides of the Atlantic. The previous year Bateman had become the first actress to play a Jewish woman on the American stage.[2] The twenty-one-year-old, Baltimore-born actress was the daughter of a theatrical manager and started her career touring with P. T. Barnum. New York critics panned the play but theatregoers loved it; it became an instant hit, transferring to London in the winter of 1863.

Eleanor was mesmerised by *Leah the Forsaken*. This was one of her very first experiences of a new drama. Kate Bateman sounded and looked to Tussy like her sisters. And, perhaps, a version of her possible future self. Tussy knew the biblical story of the sisters Leah and Rachel, wives of Jacob, and recognised instinctively the play's depiction of virulent anti-Semitism. She already knew by heart Shylock's speech from *The Merchant of Venice*.

The role of Leah became a popular star vehicle for leading actresses and held the stage for the next three decades. There were to be four productions of the play in London during Tussy's life and she would see all of them – most memorably in 1892 when the lead role was played by the Jewish star Sarah Bernhardt.

George Curtis, political editor of *Harper's Weekly*, drew an analogy between the depiction of the persecution of the Jews in the drama and the persecution of black people in the Confederacy. Mid-war, Curtis wrote, 'Go and see *Leah* and have the lesson burned in upon your mind, which may help to save the national health and mind.'[3] This analogy between anti-Semitism and slavery is unlikely to have occurred to Tussy as she sat captivated at the London premiere of *Leah*, but she absorbed much of the zeitgeist from family trips to the theatre.

This happy outing ended with the rare treat of a cab home. It was the highlight of an otherwise tough, freezing winter for the women. Tussy celebrated both Christmas and her ninth birthday without her father, who was away for nearly two months settling his mother's estate with Uncle Lion and condoling with his aunts. Tussy missed her father and eagerly anticipated his homecoming, as Möhme described to Mohr:

> The little one can scarcely wait for you to return and says daily, my dada is coming today. She enjoys her holidays thoroughly and since she did not have a Christmas tree, her sisters made her more than 20 dolls in all sorts of costumes. Amongst the grotesque figures one fencer is Ruy Blas and an excellent Chinaman with a long train that the children made from Tussy's hair and glued on to the bald Kui Kui.[4]

In Victor Hugo's tragic drama set in the reign of Charles II, Ruy Blas is a lowborn poet who dares to love the Queen of Spain. As he's an indentured commoner, his love is wildly inappropriate. Even Tussy's dolls were radicals.

Spring did its job and delivered new beginnings. In March 1864 Henriette's legacy floated the family into a new house, 1 Modena Villas,[5] in Maitland Park Road, Hampstead. It was a large, detached home with the previously unimaginable luxuries of a big garden, conservatory and a study with a park view for Mohr. Möhme was energised by the upturn in their fortunes and the excitement of setting up what she beamingly called the palace. She overspent on new furnishing and interior decorations and became a regular at the local auctions. Jennychen decked out the conservatory with flowers and climbing plants which flourished beneath her green fingers. Best of all, 'the Medina of the emigration' or 'Maidena Villas', as Engels laughingly dubbed it, was sufficiently spacious for each of the three sisters to have a separate bedroom. Tussy now had her very first room of her own.

A menagerie of puppies, kittens and birds also took up residence at the new palace. Being the youngest, Tussy was the final arbiter of their names. As if growing into the new space she 'shot up' in height and, as her complacent mother reported to Ernestine Liebknecht, 'engages in a host of unprofitable pursuits'.[6] In this as in so many other areas, then, she was clearly emulating her father.

Chief amongst her unprofitable pursuits at nine years old was her love of chess and gymnastics. Founded by the Swedish, the popularity of gymnastics spread throughout Europe primarily as a physical training method for the military. From the 1820s pioneers of gymnastics campaigned for the benefits of physical training for girls as well as for boys. German immigrants opened the first gym club in Britain in 1860. British interest in gymnastics grew in the 1860s after the Crimean War revealed how grossly unfit British soldiers were. Calisthenics, a feminised version of gymnastics, was invented to deal with the argument that physical exercise was inappropriate for girls. Eleanor was clearly doing more than handstands, forward rolls and cartwheels in the garden; in 1868 her father asked Engels to pay the £1 5s fee for Tussy's gymnastic course at the German Gymnasium which opened nearby in St Pancras in 1865.

At chess, she excelled. In Mohr's study there was always a game on the go between them. 'She is', Möhme boasted, 'a first-rate chess player and Mr Wilhelm Pieper came off so badly against his opponent that he lost his temper.'[7] Möhme's impatience with the ineffectual Pieper must have made Tussy's victory all the sweeter. To her delight, her father also grouched at her chess prowess. 'I am getting on very well with my chess,' she reported to Uncle Lion, 'I nearly always win and when I do Papa is *so* cross.'[8] Tussy had clearly picked up some Mohr-beating moves from Lenchen.

Tussy's love of fairy stories, histories and adventure novels teeming with military campaigns, guerrilla combat and piracy combined with her love of Shakespeare's history plays ably equipped her to understand the strategies of the chess board. From Engels she knew the story of the origins of chess.[9] He loaned her Firdousi's *Sháh-Námah – Lives of the Kings* – teasing that she would have a job getting through such a long, multi-canto work. Chess, Tussy learned from Firdousi's preamble to the tale, was introduced into Persia from India. Like China, the Middle East and Indian subcontinent were established early in the geography of Tussy's imagination. All of these parts of the world would play key roles in the politics and passions of her adulthood, but it was the Middle East and Palestine that would figure most distinctly.

But in 1864 Tussy was looking west. Her father and Engels had been writing extensively about the American Civil War since its outbreak in 1861. Now Tussy joined in, feeling strongly that she needed to share her opinions directly with the president. 'I remember, I felt absolutely convinced that Abraham Lincoln badly needed my advice as to the war, and long letters would I indite to him, all of which Mohr, of course, had to read and post.'[10] In fact, Mohr never posted the letters, but kept them to show to Engels, to the great amusement of them both.

Abraham Lincoln's self-appointed Special Adviser in London also shared her views on the conduct of war with Lion Philips: 'My dear Uncle . . . What do you think of affairs in America? I think the Federals are safe, and though the Confederates drive them back every now and then, I am sure they will win in the end.'[11] Six days after USS *Kearsage* sank the British-backed Confederate commerce-raider CSS *Alabama*[12] off Cherbourg, a jubilant Tussy further remarked to her uncle, 'Were you not delighted about the *Alabama*? Of course you had known all about it; at all events a Politician like you ought to.'[13]

Tussy's letters to Lion Philips illustrate how clearly her young mind has grasped Britain's complicity in the slave trade and her natural allegiance to the Union cause. The seafaring adventure of the *Alabama* incident united two of her favourite themes: the American blood-brother theme of Fenimore Cooper, and the lusty sea-battles between merchant, mercenary and naval ships of Captain Marryat.

Along with her growing interest in the American war, Tussy was fascinated by the visit to London in the spring of Giuseppe Garibaldi, republican leader of the Italian Risorgimento. Following his month-long stay in Tyneside in 1854 on his way back from South America and New York, Garibaldi was already a popular figure with working men and women in northern British cities; now the working classes of London received the great Italian with ecstatic enthusiasm. Half a million republican Londoners poured on to the capital's streets, marshalled, as the *New York Times* sneered, by 'the refuse of the trade societies' and 'noisy, blaring bands'.[14]

Marx and Engels followed Garibaldi's progress systematically from his conquest of Sicily with his volunteer Redshirt army in May 1860 and wrote political journalism on this and his campaign to take Rome in 1862: *Roma o Morte* – Rome or death. The quintessential romantic hero, Garibaldi was Tussy's first revolutionary idol. Given her support for Abraham Lincoln and the Union cause, she doubtless approved of Garibaldi's public offer to fight in the US Army.

Whilst Tussy improved her chess game, dished out political advice to Abe Lincoln and practised her gymnastics, Möhme continued to decorate Modena Villas. She was nesting, 'and instead of being obliged to furnish as before in the most sparing fashion,' as she told Ernestine, 'this time we set aside something more for the furniture and the decorations, so that we can receive anyone without embarrassment. I thought it better to put the money to this use,' she adds endearingly, 'than to fritter it away piecemeal on trifles.'[15] Their parents seemed to be trying to compensate Laura and Jennychen for their childhood privations.

Jenny and Karl were determined to expand the social horizons of their now nineteen- and twenty-year-old elder daughters. They proposed holding a proper 'ball' at Modena Villas. Invitations were sent to about fifty of their friends and, on 12 October, they threw open the new house with a great party for the young people, who danced until breakfast time. Tussy got to throw her own impromptu children's gathering for all her friends the next day, feasting on the leftovers – though doubtless she'd been up all night with the grown-ups too. Jenny's intentions in organising this party were clear, as she explained to Ernestine: 'It has become possible to provide the girls with a pleasant and respectable setting, so appointed that now and again they can receive their English friends without fear or shame, we had placed them in a false position and the young are still thin-skinned and sensitive.'[16]

This fun revived the spirits and health of the whole family. Practically speaking Modena Villas was in a healthier, elevated position, freestanding and with a well-laid-out garden and clear view directly on to Hampstead Heath. The air was fresher than in Kentish Town and Soho. However, all their spending, not to mention the three-year lease on the new house, exceeded the actual sum of Marx's maternal legacy. Had it not been for the unexpected death of their dear friend Lupus – Wilhelm Wolff – they would have been on their uppers once again before the year was out.

A farmer's son and student revolutionary from Silesia who spent four years in a Prussian prison for his defence of freedom of speech and the press, Lupus met the Marxes through the Communist League in Brussels in 1845 and remained 'on the closest terms' with them and Engels until his death from a cerebral haemorrhage on 9 May 1864. 'With him,' Engels wrote in his biography of Lupus, 'Marx and I lost our most faithful friend, and the German revolution a man of irreplaceable worth.'[17]

A committed believer in liberation through education, Lupus dedicated his post-activist life to private tutoring in Blackburn, to where he moved in the 1850s after failing to raise the means to emigrate to America. Fond of children and without his own, Lupus cared particularly for the Marx sisters and was greatly cheered by the letters Tussy wrote to him through what turned out to be his final illness.

Lupus continued teaching up to the end and bequeathed the parsimonious savings from his annual salary of £60 per year to the Marxes. He left a handsome estate of £825 to the family – almost a third greater than the £580 Marx inherited from his mother. Volume I of *Capital* is dedicated to Wolff, 'My unforgettable friend; intrepid, faithful, noble protagonist of the proletariat.' It was appropriate acknowledgment that Lupus's generosity ensured the completion of the book by supporting the Marx family at a critical time.

Eleanor expressed an instinctive empathy with Lupus when he was dying, just as she had been concerned about Engels when Mary died the previous year. Aged nine, her ready force of feeling for other people starts to take distinct shape as a defining characteristic of her personality. Here was the dynamic contradiction of one of Tussy's

greatest strengths combined with a potentially perilous weakness –
an overdeveloped ability to empathise, too much feeling. The
weakness of her primary instinct for self-preservation and good old
Darwinian self-interest was badly aligned to the contemporary
historical conditions of a culture enforcing self-sacrifice and self-
abnegation in women. Her father and mother probably realised this
long before she did.

But although she was naturally too nice, Tussy was neither a
simpering nor a saccharine child. Physically robust and fearlessly
brave to the point of risk, her empathy was direct, big-hearted and
entirely sincere. She hated to see things suffer and was carefully
protective of her set of dolls and the family's seven pets.

What prevented Tussy from the immense dullness of being too
good and tempered her unrestrained emotional nature was her fine
humour and sense of the comedic. No possible joke could be left
unexplored. Every opportunity for a pun should be pursued, and her
poor spelling gave rise to a steady stream of malapropisms and unintentionally poetic turns of phrase. She played with words as easily as
she played with her kittens, puppies, dolls and stamp collection.

Tussy was quick to sniff out posers and didn't suffer fools. Her
droll response to the death of Mohr's erstwhile friend Ferdinand
Lassalle is a case in point. Lassalle was a longtime comrade and family
friend who had been very generous with financial assistance, but he
and Marx fell out irrevocably in 1862 over growing political differences and what Marx regarded as Lassalle's absurd self-interest and
ambition. He nevertheless regretted the news that Lassalle had been
wounded fatally in yet another of his many duels over women.
Lassalle's serial romances were well known in the family; as Laura
remarked, he *would* declare to *every* lady that he could love her only
for six weeks. To which the sanguine Tussy retorted, 'So he is
warranted for six weeks.'[18]

Lassalle's nationalistic egomania was utterly opposed to Marx and
Engels's belief in the urgent need to establish an international organi-
sation of workers in order to oppose the forces of nationalism and
capitalism. On 28 September 1864 Marx went to St Martin's Hall in
Long Acre to attend the founding meeting of the International
Working Men's Association (IWMA). The gathering elected a

committee that was directed to prepare provisional rules and a constitution. The committee comprised twenty-one Englishmen, ten Germans, nine French, six Italians, two Poles and two Swiss.

Marx wrote the First International's Provisional Rules, approved by the Provisional Committee on 1 November 1864 and published as a pamphlet and in the press the same month. He wrote them in English, and they are a concise statement of the purpose and objectives of the organisation:

> Considering, That the emancipation of the working classes must be conquered by the working class themselves; That the struggle for the emancipation of the working classes means not a struggle for class privileges and monopolies, but for equal rights and duties, and the abolition of all class rule; That the economical subjection of the man of labour to the monopoliser of the means of labour, that is, the sources of life, lies at the bottom of servitude in all its forms of all social misery, mental degradation, and political dependence; That the economical emancipation of the working classes is therefore the great end to which every political movement ought to be subordinate as a means; That all efforts aiming at the great end have hitherto failed from the want of solidarity between the manifold divisions of labour in each country, and from the absence of a fraternal bond of union between the working classes of different countries; That the emancipation of labour is neither a local nor a national, but a social problem, embracing all countries in which modern society exists, and depending for its solution on the concurrence, practical and theoretical, of the most advanced countries; That the present revival of the working classes in all the most industrious countries of Europe, while it raises a new hope, gives solemn warning against a relapse into the old errors and calls for the immediate combination of all disconnected movements; For these reasons – The undersigned members of the committee, holding its powers by resolution of the public meeting held on September 28, 1864, at St Martin's Hall, London, have taken the steps necessary for founding the Working Men's International Association; They declare that this International Association and all societies and individuals adhering to it, will acknowledge

truth, justice, and morality, as the basis of their conduct towards each other, and towards all men, without regard to colour, creed or nationality; They hold it the duty of a man to claim the rights of a man and a citizen, not only for himself, but for every man who does his duty. No rights without duties; no duties without rights.[19]

Fine words to live by. Or to rebel against, if written by your own father.

The programme of the International 'is not a mere improvement that is contemplated,' said a leader in *The Times* of London four years later, 'but nothing less than a regeneration, and that not of one nation only, but of mankind. This is certainly the most extensive aim ever contemplated by any institution, with the exception, perhaps, of the Christian Church.'[20] Tussy, as we have already seen, dispensed with Christianity at the age of six. These provisional rules of the International were the articles of faith by which she was to try and lead her life.

The principle of internationalism in a socialist form was to be at the heart of Eleanor's existence. In the 1860s the proletariat regrouped all over the industrialised world. Proletariat, at that time, meant the people – everyone who was not gentry, aristocrat or, in a nutshell, amongst the ruling classes. As the principles of the IWMA written by Marx lay out, the social and economic problems suffered by the labouring underclasses were neither just local nor national, but included all societies in which modern industrialisation existed. Between the 1840s and 1860s modern capitalism had developed into an international force, therefore socialist organisation to manage and resist its consequences needed to be international too. There could not be capitalism in one country; nor could there be socialism in one country, or city states of socialism. The capitalist economy changed in several substantial ways in this period.[21] The first industrial revolution was driven by new forms of power: electricity, oil, turbines and the internal combustion engine. From the 1860s this was superseded by a new technological era, with machinery based on new materials such as steel and alloys and new science-based industries like the organic chemical industry. Domestic consumer markets emerged, driven by sheer demographic growth and rising mass incomes in the United States. This was the beginning of the age of mass production: consumer capitalism and market globalisation had arrived.

Proletarians and their supporters in all industrial countries needed to coordinate their efforts and organise collectively. As 1848 showed everyone, disconnected national movements could not succeed. In Britain, many people from previous socialist-inspired campaigns joined this new attempt to create an international socialist movement. British Chartists and Forty-Eighters from the European revolutions were key amongst them, and Eleanor's father was their leader – as an organisation the IWMA became known as Karl Marx's First International. Leaders of the English working-class movement were frequent visitors to the Marx home, including journalist Ernest Jones; Chartist, socialist and old family friend from the 1840s Julian Harney; and 'the aged patriarch of socialism', the great Robert Owen.[22]

There is no neat story of the origins and rise of British socialism qua socialism in Britain because by character socialism was a combustion of widespread social, political and industrial activism and cultural engagement, made up of broad alliances of radicalism from industrial unionists and pro-statist democrats to anti-statist anarchists. As a general overview, British Chartism grew into socialism. The beginnings of unionism lay partly in the early co-operative movements of socialist idealism, but were not confined to it. Mass urbanisation of the former peasantry and appalling conditions in unregulated modern factories brought many different interest groups into what, in the 1860s, were still nationally uncoordinated trade union campaigns. British Trade Unionism became a unified movement from the 1860s to the 1880s because of the transnational European 'socialist international' and its filial relations with American and colonial organisation, such as in India and Australia.

'The proletariat, like the bourgeoisie, existed only conceptually as an international fact.'[23] Marx and Engels wrote in *The Communist Manifesto* that 'working men have no country',[24] but for many people, political consciousness was always in some way or another nationally defined. However, there were many practical aspects of labour and market organisation that could be addressed and tackled.

Many of the issues that led to the unions are famously depicted in Dickens's *Hard Times*, published the year before Eleanor's birth. Despite the collapse of British Chartism in the 1840s and the failure of the Communist League in the 1850s, Britain had one of the strongest traditions of working-class organisation in the world. Outside of Britain, the United States and Australia, trade unions and strikes were legally prohibited – banned by the state – in most of Europe and its colonies. As a result, if workers in Britain and America went on strike to improve pay and conditions, employers and shareholders would ship in pressed labour from continental Europe and the colonies, where strikes were banned. This successfully undermined industrial action in the countries where it was most organised – Britain and America. One of the very workable and practical objectives of the IWMA and the First International was to put an end to this divide and rule attitude to the global labour force.

The founding of the IWMA, the First International and the rise of the new trade unions movements around the world were a political progression from the experiences of the 1848 nationalist revolutions, driven largely by Forty-Eighters who, like the Marxes, were refugees and exiles of this earlier failed social uprising. Nine years old when her father went off to the founding meeting of the IWMA, Tussy soaked up the atmosphere, conversations and events around her during these formative years. She was a child of the age of collectivism and internationalism. These precepts did not only shape the external events of her life, they directly shaped her mind and personality. Eleanor's internationalism started in her family.

There is an intriguing photograph dating from this time of the founding of the First International. The image captures Tussy, Jennychen, Laura, Marx and Engels posed in front of a background garden scene of trees and a white picket fence. Whilst both Mohr and Tussy's 'second father' are present, neither of her mothers appears in the picture. The family portrait seems incomplete without them. How incomplete would not be visible to Tussy for another thirty years, when this rare image revealed secrets obscured by the framing of the photograph.

Tussy sits centre stage in a jaunty straw boater between her sisters, who are dressed in matching crinolines and awful flowery hats. Marx and Engels stand behind them. Marx, Jennychen and Laura look directly at the camera shutter; Tussy and Engels look away. She looks only fleetingly poised; Laura clasps her hand, as if restraining her. Tussy's summer dress reveals bare legs and ankle boots. She wears a too-big hand-me-down jacket over her sundress. The outsize arm seam slips over her shoulder clownishly and the wide cuff flaps around her thin wrist. It might of course be a jacket adapted for the ceremonial wardrobe of the Empress of China. Tussy's face has an expression of lively amusement and unmistakable impishness.

She looks like trouble.

The only known surviving photograph of the three siblings together, this image illustrates strikingly the age difference of a decade between Tussy and her now grown-up sisters. Finding gainful employment was now amongst the questions uppermost in Jennychen's mind. Secretly, she sought opportunities for work as a governess or personal secretary. As the oldest of the three sisters, she was anxious to help her parents; she was the most acutely aware of the financial brinkmanship on which the family constantly teetered. Jennychen was by this time accompanying her father and Laura to the Reading Room at the British Museum to help them with research and transcription. It was work for which she volunteered and she enjoyed it.

Despite his own obsessions, Marx never compelled any of his children to follow in the family business, though all of them did. He may also have hoped that Jennychen's book-worming with him at the library would broaden the scope of her social life, the limitation of which was all too evident at her twenty-first birthday party on 1 May, where the majority of guests were her parents' friends and political contemporaries, mostly from the IWMA. Gallingly, her younger sister Laura received her first marriage proposal – instantly rejected – at the party.

The Marx daughters were a catch. You'd wonder why, given their unconventional upbringing and absence of any dowry prospects. No one outside their inner circle knew until much later the extent of financial commitment by Engels and their other friends to supporting the family. Jenny and Laura were not beauties in the way that their mother had been, but they were striking and self-composed and had inherited the charm, wit and vivacity of their parents. They were both well read and highly intelligent and they were the offspring of Europe's most inspiring and calumniated revolutionary thinker. Depending on where you stood, these attributes were either intriguing or rendered them totally unmarriageable.

Given that they'd met each other as children, Mohr and Möhme didn't have much useful experience with which to equip Laura and Jenny for dealing with these circumstances. They were anxious that their daughters did not repeat the errors of their own wayward youth. If they hoped that well-meaning attempts at social engineering like the October party at Modena Villas would put their daughters in the way of a future more secure than their own, they were roundly disappointed. Mohr and Möhme miscalculated on one very crucial point: they were soulmates who set a very fine example of that elusive human state – a truly successful marriage.

In February 1865 Tussy wrote in confidence to Engels asking him to please send a few bottles of hock and claret for a surprise belated party she and her sisters were planning for Möhme's birthday, 'as we are going to give the party ourselves without any help from mama we want it to go off very grandly'.[25] Cutely, Eleanor asked Engels for this secret delivery of provisions for her mother in lieu of her own Valentine from him. Engels dispatched the wine immediately and Tussy wrote him a thank-you letter the following day: 'now we have wine and everything ready for tonight we shall have a jolly time of it.'[26]

Throughout 1865 Marx was seriously ill, his health and nerves straining under the pressure of completing the first volume of *Capital*. He'd been at it for over a decade. What started as a thirty- to fifty-page essay had long ago developed into his life's work. He was determined to finish the first part by the end of the year and despite his physical infirmity, his 'brainbox' was working overtime, fuelled by passion, adrenalin, tobacco, insomnia and the rousing encouragement of his family.

In December he announced that the first volume was finished. There was no money, therefore no Christmas but the completion of 'that damned book' was as fine an advent in their lives as they could wish for. Concurrent with his full draft of the first instalment of *Capital*, Marx had also started developing his address to the General Council of the IWMA given in June of that year, a speech that later became *Value, Price and Profit*. These two milestones in the progress of her father's work accompanied Tussy's tenth year. She and Volume I of *Capital* had spent a decade growing up together.

The year had brought another significant development in the form of a fiancé for Laura. In mid-February 1865 Paul Lafargue, a debonair, wild-haired young French medical student, sailed from France for England. He arrived in London in time to join in the 24 February anniversary of the 1848 revolution with fellow émigrés and exiles, and presented a report on the development of the working-class movement in France to the committee of the IWMA. Six months later he was Tussy's prospective brother-in-law.

Born 16 June 1842 in Santiago de Cuba, Paul Lafargue was the only child of a wealthy coffee planter. In the language of the day, the Lafargues were *mestizos* – of mixed ancestry, excluded from access to higher education and socially marginalised. His family emigrated to France in 1851, where his father became a *rentier* and wine merchant in Bordeaux. François Lafargue moved to France largely to provide greater opportunity for his son. Paul went to school in Toulouse and enrolled to study medicine at the University of Paris. The Faculty of Medicine was conveniently located in the Latin Quarter, where Paul soon fell in with radical student politics and opposition to the Second Empire.

Paul was at the centre of a group influenced by the social critic Pierre-Joseph Proudhon and the revolutionary Auguste Blanqui. Mostly medical and law students, they made Blanqui their mentor, like him rejecting a comfortable academic career, identifying themselves with the 'damned of history' and becoming active revolutionaries. Paul wrote for a prestigious student newspaper, *La Rive Gauche*, edited by a senior student, Charles Longuet.

Lafargue arrived in London in early March 1865. Proposed by watchmaker and council member Eugene Dupont, he was elected to the International General Council. His fellow student activist, Charles Longuet, was also on the council. Lafargue focused on the

Spanish labour movement and wanted to establish a section of the International there. Fluent in Spanish, he wrote for *El Obrero* – organ of the recently founded Spanish workers' federation – and by the end of the month was Secretary of the International for Spain, a post he held until 1870.[27]

Soon after his arrival in London,[28] Lafargue visited Marx at Maitland Park Road. 'I was then 24 years of age. As long as I live,' he wrote later, 'I shall remember the impression that first visit made on me.'[29] The unforgettable impressions of that first visit included his first encounter with Laura. Captivation struck twice in one day. Lafargue left the Marx home 'seduced and conquered'.[30] Six months later, Laura and Paul announced they were half-engaged, prompting Engels – who sent them a celebratory £50 – to inquire if he should offer half or the whole of his congratulations. Perhaps if they'd been fully engaged he would have sent £100.

In the autumn of 1865 Lafargue was expelled from the University of Paris for his role in the first Students' International Congress in Liège. He relocated to London, where he enrolled at Barts – St Bartholomew's, one of the oldest hospitals in the world – in the hope of taking an English medical degree. His tutor, Dr Carrière, was a revolutionary refugee.

Tussy was an instant hit with the outgoing Lafargue, who declared her 'a charming child with a sunny disposition'.[31] She was equally charmed and allowed Paul to join the elect who contributed to her stamp collection. The two became firm friends and Tussy an important go-between, mediating the sometimes rocky road of Paul and Laura's courtship.

As well as providing Tussy with the attentions of a charming older brother and sharing her love of her pets, Paul's political engagement in all things Spanish and Latin-American would prove decisive in the not-too-distant future in Tussy's initiation into political activism and, excitingly, espionage.

For the meantime, Paul dedicated as much energy to seducing Laura as he did to political activism. It's a moot point how much time he devoted to studying physics and chemistry at Barts. Tussy soon identified a shared love of popular fiction with Paul, quizzing him for his opinions of Walter Scott, Paul de Kock and Alexandre

Dumas senior, and reading with him on the sofa in her father's study when Mohr was away. Paul was generous with his father's allowance and loved treating the appreciative Tussy to new books. Writing to her father away in Germany, she told him:

> Paul has been keeping me in books, he got me Cooper's *Deer-slayer, Homeward Bound, The Eppingham*[32] . . . Good Friday I eat [*sic*] 16 hot cross buns, Laura and Jenny ate 8. Tommy, Blacky and Whisky send their compliments. Paul and Laura have had three riding lessons. Laura looks very nice in her riding habit, and Paul looks a little shaky.[33]

Receiving this letter, Marx was probably less worried about Tussy's record-breaking consumption of hot cross buns than he was about Lafargue taking up residence in his home in his absence. Aware of how much Paul was adored by the women of his family, he knew he would be indulged. Marx observed, 'The young man first attached himself to me, but soon transferred his attention from the Old Man to the daughter.'[34]

With the completion of the first part of *Capital* and the arrival of Lafargue in their lives, 1865 was a good year for the still carefree Tussy. Two months after her birthday, in March, she played the popular party game Confession with her family. Her game sheet provides a telling self-assessment of herself at ten. Time would show how many of these preferences would continue or change into her adulthood. Confident in all other categories, it's intriguing that the only category tomboy Tussy failed to complete was her favourite virtue in woman.

Your favourite virtue: Truth
Your favourite virtue in man: Courage
Your favourite virtue in woman: [left blank]
Your chief characteristic: Curiosity
Your idea of happiness: Champagne
Your idea of misery: The Toothache
The vice you excuse most: Playing the truant
The vice you detest most: Eve's Examiner

Your aversion: Cold Mutton
Your favourite occupation: Gymnastics
Your favourite poet: Shakespeare
Your favourite prose writer: Captain Marryat
Your favourite hero: Garibaldi
Your favourite heroine: Lady Jane Grey
Your favourite flower: All flowers
Your favourite colour: White
Your favourite names: Percy, Henry, Charles, Edward
Your favourite maxim and motto: 'Go ahead'[35]

Fenian Sister

And go ahead she did.

To her great annoyance, in 1866, at the age of eleven, Tussy started attending school regularly. It's endearing that Tussy cheekily confessed to truancy as the vice she most excused and school exams the vice she most detested. The disliked 'Eve's Examiner' in her Confession was not a witty reference by the young atheist to either God or the Devil, but more prosaically to Charles Eve's unfortunately bestselling textbook *The School Examiner*, published in 1852 and containing 4,000 examination exercises in the subjects of Sacred History, Geography, Arithmetic and English Grammar.

In 1866 Paul thrilled Tussy with a great surprise – he built her 'a *delicious* swing'[1] in the back garden of Modena Villas, with seat and handles hand-stitched in soft white leather. As she kicked up her heels and swung higher she could see the wild abundance of Hampstead Heath over the fence, in harmony with her own ungovernable nature. She wrote to Alice excitedly to tell her about the swing, 'on which I would willingly forget school and everything else'.[2]

Misses Boynell and Rentsch who ran South Hampstead College for Ladies found they had their work cut out with the unbiddable youngest Miss Marx. Tussy grumbled to Alice that she had too little time now, 'as I have so much to do at school'.[3]

Regular schooling weighed uneasily on Tussy. She was already functionally numerate, highly literate – although her spelling was sometimes erratic – and a dedicated enthusiast for her chess and gymnastics. South Hampstead College placed more emphasis on the required upright deportment and decorum of young ladies – who were not meant to tumble, leap, do handstands, cartwheels, headstands, forward rolls or have firm opinions on political matters.

The concept of a young lady was in itself worrying and questionable to gypsy-spirited Tussy, excluding as it did the possibility of being taught the skills required to pursue a life at sea, in frontier exploration or international politics.

Tussy liked her peers, and her sense of fun and disregard for hierarchy made her a popular ringleader and playmate, but academically she was bored and her teachers made easy targets. She disliked authority. On the upside, the school was non-denominational and taught comparative religion and history to its diverse pupils. She evidently enjoyed the handwriting and spelling drills. Her exercise books – all second-hand, pasted over and repurposed from her father's study – are full of doodling marginalia alongside disciplined ranks of neatly executed spelling exercises marching across the pages.

'Benediction'. 'Cheerfulness'. 'Improvements'. 'Temperate'. 'Fashionable'. These were inspiring words. Restraint, needlework and the bland poetic homilies on the general accomplishments of femaleness were not. These she instantly dispensed with. They were in too marked a contrast to her home schooling and mentoring by her mother, father and Engels, who now took an increasingly active role in her education, continuing to send her books and discuss them with her. In 1866 her class were set an assignment to practise their longhand by transcribing an annoying poem by David Bates, a saccharine lozenge beloved of Victorian schoolteachers tasked with cultivating the dulcet tones and murmuring conformity of conventional femininity:

> Speak gently! it is better far
> To rule by love than fear
> Speak gently! let no harsh words
> Mar the good we might do here.[4]

And so on, continuing in the same vein for too many stanzas. Tussy much preferred Lewis Carroll's send-up of this poem, 'Speak Roughly!', in *Alice's Adventures in Wonderland*, the popular new bestseller published in 1865 that sold out instantly on its first appearance. The Duchess's song to the pig baby offers a more rigorous parenting model:

> Speak roughly to your little boy
> And beat him when he sneezes
> He only does it to annoy
> Because he knows it teases.[5]

Tussy's school exercise books from this period are filled with sketches of her sisters, usually in profile, with wedding veils and fashionable accessories. These marginalia reflect the family preoccupations of the period between 1866 and 1870, during which Jenny and Laura matured and left home; one to become a governess, the other a wife, the most conventional of outcomes for the daughters of a very unconventional family. On the cusp of puberty, Tussy watched the shaping of her sisters' lives and wondered what her own might be.

Less constraining than copying out homilies on the proper behaviour of children was writing letters to her father in Margate, where he was buffing up the manuscript of the first volume of *Capital* and, on the advice of his doctor, recuperating for a month from the exertion of finishing it. Tussy recalled him imperiously to London, reminding him of his promise to attend a party she and her sisters had arranged for 22 March. 'Now, Dr Karl Marx of bad philosophy, I hope you will keep your promise and come on Thursday.'[6] How could he refuse?

After the party, Tussy and her elder sister went back to Margate with Mohr. Tussy spent a blissful ten days walking, eating rock candy and ice cream, and playing with her father, liberated briefly from his study and in impish mood.[7]

The whole matter of formal schooling was made worse in August, when Laura and Tussy were sent to Hastings to board for a month at the establishment of a Miss Davies. Their parents were eager to get them out of London for a while. There was unrest in the city, a result of the 23 July Hyde Park Riot over the Reform Bill and the cholera epidemic. Naturally, it was the risk of cholera and not the popular demonstrations that concerned Möhme and Mohr. Although it was only a circumscribed move towards universal male suffrage in the United Kingdom, the Marxes strongly supported the gradualist 1866 Reform Bill.

Möhme and Mohr also wanted to separate Laura and Paul Lafargue – they didn't like the intimacy between them and Paul had, without being invited, effectively moved in. Marx complained to Engels that 'Lafargue is as good as living with us, which perceptibly increases expenses.'[8] Paul's father had written from Bordeaux asking Marx to give his consent for Laura's hand in marriage to his only son Paul. Despite the kindly tone of the letter, Marx did not respond directly to Lafargue *père* but to the young man himself, with a firm and pompous refusal.

Laura likened the regular recurrence of meals at Miss Davies's boarding school for young ladies to the march of destiny. The food haunted them; 'like ghouls – the four monsters – breakfast, dinner, tea and supper . . . cast shadows before them and behind.'[9] Prisoners of perpetual rain, they were stuck indoors behind closed, shuttered windows and subjected to the sensory torture of listening to pupils banging away all day on an out-of-tune piano.

The sisters rebelled. Laura informed Miss Davies that Tussy and she would neither attend church on Sundays nor observe the daily 9 p. m. curfew. Ignoring Miss Davies's threats to inform their parents, Tussy and Laura broke free and wandered the seafront of Hastings, spending their £5 pocket money on cab rides, fun fairs and sea-bathing; munching on spice biscuits from Lenchen and returning, when they felt like it, to an exasperated Miss Davies who had no choice but to let them in. When the £5 ran out, they asked their parents for some more and another £3 duly followed. They had clearly inherited the family talent for spending beyond their means.

Following this detention without trial, it is hardly surprising that Tussy was further put off organised education as an alternative to home schooling. Nor that Laura reviewed her options and on her return to London redoubled her efforts to persuade her father to relent and consent to her marrying Lafargue. She would try and escape into marriage; Tussy, to her swing.

Displeased by the couple's persistence, Marx goaded Paul for his ardour, overzealous nature and skittishness, putting this down to his 'Creole temperament' and – as he got more wound up – coming out with racist broadsides about Paul being blemished by the customary faults of 'the negro tribe – *no sense of shame,* by which I mean shame about making a fool of oneself'.[10] Marx seemed suddenly very forgetful of his own lamp-post-swinging youth and unbridled florescence of ardour for Jenny.[11]

> You know that I have sacrificed my whole fortune to the revolutionary struggle. I do not regret it. On the contrary. Had I my career to start again I should do the same. But I would not marry. As far as lies in my power I intend to save my daughter from the reefs upon which her mother's life had been wrecked . . . You, a man so practical that you would abolish poetry altogether, cannot wish to wax poetical at the expense of my child.[12]

This Oedipal outburst galvanised the young lovers. A month later, on her twenty-first birthday, Laura announced her formal engagement to Paul. Tussy was jubilant but troubled by the realisation that her sister would be leaving home. Möhme was rather taken with her future son-in-law's 'dark olive complexion and extra-ordinary eyes'[13] that reminded her of her little black boar of yesteryear.

Lafargue *père* wrote from Bordeaux assuring Marx that he would continue to support his son financially and that Paul must pass his medical school examinations before he could marry. Möhme was comforted and started building castles in the air for Laura; after all, Paul's parents were rich: they owned plantations and property in Santiago and Bordeaux, and Paul was their only child. They liked Laura, and welcomed her into their family with open arms.[14]

These are effusions far more suited to a Mrs Bennet than to Europe's most revolutionary mother. But how could she not hope that Laura would be spared her own suffering, endurance and quiet disappointments?

Laura showed signs of embarrassment at the bohemian behaviour of her unconventional parents. She told her elder sister that she was mortified when their mother wandered into the parlour where she was having tea with friends. 'Mama came in without her boots on and wearing just enough that one did not have to rely on the naked effect of nature and yet dressed in such a way that she showed more than she veiled . . . I simply closed my eyes and did not look where I could not look without blushing nor blanching.'[15]

But Möhme saw the importance of Laura and Paul's shared ideals, 'particularly concerning religion. Thus Laura will avoid the inevitable conflicts and sorrows that a girl with her convictions experiences in bourgeois society.'[16] And as Mrs Marx, she should know.

Laura and Paul's engagement opened up the borders of Tussy's world. Early in 1867, Paul's parents invited the three sisters to spend a summer holiday with them at the newly fashionable tourist resort of Royan. Tussy looked forward to her first holiday abroad with great expectations, as she'd had a lowering winter. Uncle Lion Philips had died at the end of 1866 and for her twelfth birthday she'd got the measles. The upside of being ill was, of course, that she didn't have to go to school – but her eyes were sore and she strained them reading. Her eyestrain shows in the few letters she wrote during her illness; the handwriting is spidery and awkward and the ink blotched. Sweetly, she copied out the Confession game for Alice so she could play it, signing off her letter with love to Alice's Mama and Papa, 'and tell them I will write a little letter to them soon'.[17] But she never had the chance – Alice's mother Ernestine died in April. The loss of a mother was unimaginable to Tussy.

For her father, 1867 was all about the publication of *Capital*, meaning that he was away for much of the year. Marx took the final proofs to the Hamburg publisher himself in April, where Tussy wrote him a pining note, 'I have not as I used to do looked in the bed for you, but I constantly sing, "Oh! Would I were a bird that I might fly to thee and breathe a loving word to one so dear to me".'[18] The same month, on 27 April, Engels announced that he was quitting filthy business in two years, perhaps prematurely confident that the publication of the first part of Marx's magnum opus would now enable his impecunious comrade to earn a stable living by his pen.

On 21 July the three sisters set sail for the French Atlantic coast.[19] They were away until 10 September. This was the first and last holiday the unmarried sisters spent all together without their parents. They swam, went beachcombing, browsed bookshops and explored the villages around the port. Strong in French, Tussy was able to keep up with the local and national newspapers and journals, following discussion of the celebrated new poet and future Communard, Paul Verlaine, whose first collection *Poèmes saturniens*, published the previous year, rocketed him to controversial literary stardom. The Lafargues were generous hosts – the sisters enjoyed Charentais melons and the local aperitif pineau, as well as its more august and world-famous elder brother, cognac. Best of all, they ate a lot of seafood – Tussy's favourite.

Four days after the sisters returned to London the first volume of *Capital* was published in Germany. Marx had drawn up the initial plan of *Capital* in 1857. His final plan was completed by 1866, based on nearly a decade of research. In the twentieth century Marx's great masterwork would become a bestseller, but in 1867 the publication of the first instalment of the book that has become as eponymous as the Bible and Shakespeare passed entirely unnoticed except by Marx's family, friends and immediate political circle. Although Engels dearly wanted a clear plan for the publication of the subsequent volumes, Marx's mode of production made it impossible to stick to a time-defined schedule. Marx owed delivery of Volumes II and III to his publisher before the end of 1867, but this transpired to be one of the most famously unmet deadlines in publishing history. Volume I was the only part of *Capital* to be published whilst he was alive and no English edition ever became available during his lifetime. Engels brought out Volume II in May 1885, almost two years after Marx's death, and the third and final Volume III followed in 1894.[20]

Laura and Paul married in the spring. Chivvied by Engels, who paid for their wedding, Marx relented. On 2 April Tussy watched eagerly out of the front parlour window of Modena Villas for the new Mr and Mrs Lafargue to return from St Pancras Register Office, where Marx and Engels had witnessed their civil marriage.

Möhme, Lenchen and Jenny prepared an extravagant lunch party at Modena Villas and Engels, in his cups, teased Laura about what he supposed to be the imminent loss of her virginity. Years later she remembered fondly how he 'cracked a lot of silly jokes at a very silly girl's expense and set her a-crying'.²¹ The newlyweds set off for a honeymoon in Paris, soon followed by a letter from Mohr celebrating 'the spring and sun and air and Paris jollities' that 'conjure in your favour'²² and attaching a long list of requests for books, articles and journals that he sheepishly asked Laura to find time to source whilst on honeymoon. He seemed amiably resigned to the match and was pleased when the couple returned in time to celebrate his fiftieth birthday with the family.

The new Mr and Mrs Lafargue left for Paris in October, only to discover on arrival that Paul's English medical degree was not recognised over the Channel and that he would have to sit a set of new exams in order to qualify to practise in France. This development kept the newlyweds economically dependent on their respective parents, forcing Jennychen to make haste finding paid work so she could contribute to the household.

The same month she secretly got a job as governess to the children of a Scottish family called Monroe. When they found out, Jennychen's clandestine move upset her parents. Dr Monroe was politically conservative, so Jennychen was reticent about the identity of her family. Even though *Capital* had only just been published in Germany and would take a long time to reach the awareness of a general readership in Britain, Marx was already well known by 1867 as the radical founder and leader of the International Working Men's Association and a journalist. Jennychen's governessing meant she no longer had as much time to assist her father with his book-worming in the Reading Room at the British Museum, so Tussy took her place, undertaking research and becoming his secretary. For the first six months Jennychen brought no additional income to the family, as the Monroes failed to pay her salary until Marx intervened and forced them to do so. Still they didn't work out who he was.

Conscious that Tussy might be missing Laura and Paul, Engels sent her a cheering letter with some stamps for her collection. He reported that he and Lizzy Burns had continued to celebrate her sister's nuptials with such great gusto when he got back to Manchester that, whilst drunk, he had accidentally sat on his pet hedgehog, the

Right Honourable, snoozing on the sofa. Tussy probably admonished Engels for being 'on the spree again',[23] and was sad that she would now only see the Right Honourable stuffed, on his return from the taxidermist.

In June, Tussy and her father, armed with a picnic from Lenchen, boarded the Great Northern Railway at King's Cross bound for Manchester. It was a day's journey. Through soot-flecked windows Tussy saw the smudged outlines of the Derbyshire peaks. They stayed with Engels and Lizzy Burns in Manchester for two weeks and, in that fortnight, Tussy became a Fenian.

Engels, Mary and Lizzy Burns had lived in amicable unity from 1850, when Engels and Mary agreed their free union and set up home together at Engels's 'unofficial' residence at 86 Mornington Street, Stockport Road, Ardwick, on the edge of the city. After Mary's death in 1863 her sister Lizzy, baptised Lydia, took her place as head of the household, and in Engels's bed. Two months before Tussy visited Manchester for the first time Engels quit his 'official' gentleman's lodgings in Dover Street and moved into Mornington Street lock, stock and a multitude of vintage barrels. The household consisted of Lizzy Burns, her eight-year-old niece Mary Ellen – known to all as Pumps – and a maidservant, Sarah Parker.

Like her sister, Lizzy Burns was a dedicated player in the Irish Republican movement, and 86 Mornington Street was a meeting place and a safe house for Fenian activists. Freedom-loving, uncorseted, fiercely political and sparkling with fun, Lizzy Burns was everything the Misses Boynell and Rentsch feared that Tussy might become without proper restraint.

The background to Tussy becoming a supporter of the Irish Republican cause was the Fenian Rising the previous year, 1867, in County Kerry and then Dublin. The Irish Republican Brotherhood, founded by James Stephens in 1858, organised veterans of the American Civil War to support the establishment of an Irish Republic. Led by Irish-American officers of the US Army, the uprising was brutally quashed. Following this defeat the exiled Colonel Thomas Kelly, now leader of the Republican Brotherhood, rallied the movement and made Manchester its headquarters. Almost immediately, he was seized and arrested by the English authorities. An operation to rescue him resulted in the death of a policeman, sparking outrage in both nations.

Tracked down and denounced by a crown spy, Fenian officers Thomas Kelly and Timothy Deasy had been remanded in Manchester city jail in September 1867. On 18 September they were brought before Bridge Street court and charged. They were driven back to Belle Vue prison in a horse-drawn Black Maria, followed by an escort of armed constables.

As the police van passed under the railway viaduct on Hyde Road a posse of armed men ambushed it, cut loose the horses, smashed open the roof of the carriage, fired at the locks on the doors and succeeded in liberating Kelly and Deasy, who escaped. Tragically, police sergeant Charles Brett caught a fatal bullet in the crossfire. The English authorities arrested more than thirty Irishmen, five of whom later stood trial.

The conviction of all five men on 1 November prompted national demonstrations in English cities, the raising of petitions and furious parliamentary debates. One man was conditionally pardoned; the sentence of another was commuted to penal servitude because he was an American citizen. The remaining three were hanged in Manchester on 23 November. All of them to the end refused to give up the name of their comrade Peter Rice, who fired the lethal shot that killed Brett.

Catholic priests in Manchester denounced the murder of the martyrs from their pulpits. Masses took place across England, and in Hyde Park a peaceful demonstration gathered. Engels was present at the hangings of the Manchester Martyrs, one of the last public executions to take place in England. As he predicted, these events put the Irish question at the heart of English national politics. The Fenians now had martyrs, and Irishwomen a story of comradely heroism to sing over the cradles of their children.

Marx thought the central importance of Irish liberation was profoundly misunderstood, and that Fenian radicalism, jailbreaks and martyrdom were unlikely to help clarify popular misconceptions. Later, in December, terrorist bombers blasted Clerkenwell prison in a failed attempt to release two Fenian detainees. All they managed to do was blow up some working-class houses and their inhabitants near the prison, tactics Marx condemned as melodramatic folly. Tussy's father and Engels both sympathised with the cause of the Irish Republican Brotherhood but strongly disapproved of the use of armed struggle, conspiracy and violence. She disagreed.

On her return to London from Manchester in 1868 she solemnly declared herself a partisan of what she called 'the convicted nation'.[24] When Jennychen told Tussy that she 'had turned from her former higher Chinese character into a LOCALISED (IRISH) BEING and was therefore no longer showing due respect to the EMPEROR', Tussy retorted, 'Formerly I clung to a man, now I cling to a nation.'[25]

She took to buying the *Irishman*, 'from a little Irish Catholic shop. The woman always gives me her blessing because she says I am "true to the auld countryee".'[26] The *Irishman* was the leading publication of the Irish nationalist movement.[27] Tussy had plenty of time to read journals. When she got back from Manchester she and Jennychen caught scarlet fever and were confined to bed. As good luck would have it, their physician and near neighbour Dr Korklow, an expert in the treatment of scarlet fever, was an Irishman of republican sympathies.[28] Dr Korklow prescribed a diet of Liebig's beef tea laced with port, the latter kept in generous supply by Engels.

Delighted to be off school with her nose stuck in novels, the *Irishman* and letter-writing, Tussy dashed off regular letters to Lizzy, signing herself, 'Eleanor, F. S.' [Fenian Sister]. Her family scoffed at this militant affectation and dubbed her with the new nickname of 'the Poor-Neglected-Nation', the phrase she now most repeated. Whilst the Poor Neglected Nation languished in bed, she read up on the history of her latest passion – everything she could lay her hands on, including her father's articles, journalism and reports to the IWMA on the Irish question. In the Marx family there was nothing out of the ordinary about their thirteen-year-old daughter sitting in bed sipping port during the day, reading radical nationalist publications and humming Fenian freedom songs whilst dashing off letters on current affairs.

Tussy wrote to Lizzy, knowing that Engels would read her the letters in his growlery – as he described his study-sitting room – presided over by the stuffed Right Honourable in his glass case. Tussy shared with Lizzy her amusement at the stamina required by the practice of democratic politics: 'The Fenians have been having a congress, at which they sat for *19* hours without interruption! I should think they were tired after that.'[29] She was delighted by new words for the British national anthem in the same edition, 'God save our flag of green, Soon may it bright be seen,' which 'you as a Fenian sister will appreciate'.[30] Her family were probably subjected to her loud renditions of this anti-monarchist version of the national anthem from her sickbed.

In August everyone but Mohr and Lenchen decamped to Ramsgate. Laura was three months pregnant and Paul had at last completed his MRCS degree and was, he thought, qualified to practise. Paul's parents joined the party from France. The news that Library had remarried reached the Marxes from Germany; little Alice now had a stepmother, the kindly Nathalie Liebknecht. The Marxes congratulated Library and warmly befriended Nathalie, who soon fell pregnant with the baby destined to become Karl Liebknecht, future co-leader of the Spartacus movement with Rosa Luxemburg.

Fully recovered by Christmas, Tussy was in a party mood and ready to enjoy all the festivities. She was disappointed when an invitation to spend Christmas with some French friends meant that 'we had neither goose nor turkey for our Christmas dinner, but a hare!!'[31]

Having briefly neglected the Poor Neglected Nation, Tussy returned to harping on her Irish theme. She told her sister about the Christmas presents she had made for Lizzy and her niece Mary Ellen. For Lizzy she had made 'a little satin collar, with a green ribbon in it, and pinned with a harp', and for Mary Ellen she worked together 'a very pretty steal [sic] cross in a green ribbon'.[32] Here emerged her mother's daughter: radical debutante Jenny von Westphalen had pinned the tricolour into her hair; for Tussy, it was green ribbons of Irish republicanism.

Tussy didn't know that the reason for the gooseless, turkeyless Christmas was that her parents were flat broke by the end of 1868. Marx had recently failed to pass a medical examination required in order to secure a loan. He was no more able to raise the cash for a large goose or turkey than Bob Cratchit. Engels was working on his upcoming departure from Ermen & Engels and discussed with Karl and Jenny whether they could survive on £350 a year. They readily agreed, despite the fact that the budget they prepared against their existing accounts was incomplete. Engels arranged to make quarterly deposits, beginning 1 January 1869, to the Union Bank of London, a large joint stock bank with branches in the City and Chancery Lane.

Tussy finished 1868 with a piece of theatre. She cast herself as the hero, with her close friends the Lormier brothers in supporting roles: 'Louis, Ludovic and I are going to act a little play. I think Beauty and the Beast. Louis to be the Beast, Ludovic the Beauty, I to be the Prince.'[33] The trouser role. Naturally. Tussy was director, producer, stage manager and lead. *Beauty and the Beast* at 1 Modena Villas on 29 December 1868 was Tussy's first full theatrical production before an invited audience. It was a fitting and significant end to her thirteenth year.[34]

On 1 January 1869 Tussy became an aunt. Charles Etienne Lafargue was born in Paris. Jennychen got leave from her governessing work for the Easter holidays and she and Tussy left London at the end of March to visit their sister and new nephew. Paris was in uproar over the revelations of Haussmann's financial malfeasance, under investigation by the Chamber of Deputies.

Though Haussmann's financial reputation was in question, his rebuilding and modernisation of the city centre made it a place of breathtaking beauty and splendour, whilst over half of the capital's population starved below the breadline in squalid, overcrowded slums in the outskirts of the city. Both Paris and her nephew seduced Tussy. She adored Schnaps – or Schnappy – declaring that she had 'never seen such a lovely child'[35] and admiring his good looks, intelligent forehead, amiable temper and early teething. As she was responsible for looking after him, it's a good thing that she was so enamoured. Jennychen returned to work in London in mid-April, but no one seemed to think it pressing for Tussy to go back to school.

Tussy nannied Schnappy in the small Lafargue apartment in the Rue du Cherche-Midi, but she also managed to have fun during her seven-week stay in Paris. She took herself 'bockomanning' in the city centre. This was a term invented by Laura to describe leisurely sightseeing on foot, punctuated by regular stops at bars and cafés for a small *pression*. Tussy started smoking regularly, no doubt lured by the satisfactions of sipping a small, cold beer and rolling a cigarette at a pavement café as she watched Paris life pass by. She sought out open-air puppet shows, enjoyed an outing to Sardou's *Séraphine* at the Gymnase and went to the fun fair – calling it 'the fair of the pain d'épis'.[36]

Marx missed her. He wrote regularly, assuring her that Lenchen would forward on her copies of the *Irishman* and sending updates on her pets, which were in his charge whilst she was away. Blacky, he reported, behaved like a very dull gentleman; Whisky, her dog, was suffering as only a lofty soul could in her absence; and Tommy had just produced a large litter, proving both the error of her name and, Mohr said, 'the truth of the Malthus theory'. He complained to her of auditory abuse from Dicky, her bird: he 'treats me like Luther treated the devil'.[37]

Möhme came to Paris in May and they returned home together. Barely a week later Tussy set off for Manchester with her father. Still there was no talk of her going back to school. They left London on 25 May from the new St Pancras station. An engineering feat of glass and steel, Sir George Gilbert Scott's ambitious design enclosed a 243-foot span, making this airy transparent flying vault the largest undivided space ever enclosed – a futuristic marvel of modern architecture in Gothic revival style and the biggest structure of its kind in the world. The sparkling concourse of this cathedral of the railways offered to passengers travelling north on the new Midland Railway flower-sellers, tea shops and a W. H. Smith stand selling magazines, journals and cheap popular books. Victor Hugo's latest serialisation, *By Order of the King*, in the *Gentleman's Magazine* (May 1869), had just hit the racks. They boarded one of the fastest trains in the country, the high-speed express to Manchester. Connecting passengers to the Metropolitan Railway via Kentish Town and Leicester, the nearly 100-mile track to Manchester was the longest non-stop railway run in the world.

Lizzy saw to Tussy's practical education in history and politics by introducing her to the working-class districts of Manchester. At Tussy's request, Lizzy led her around all the places of Fenian significance, as she told her eldest sister: 'Mrs Burns and I went to see the Market, and Mrs Burns showed me the stall where Kelly sold pots, and the house where he lived. It was really very amusing, and Mrs B. has been telling me a great many things about "Kelly and Daisy" [*sic*] whom Mrs B. knew quite well, having been to their house and seen them 3 or 4 times a week.'[38]

Engels put Eleanor on an intense course of literature, philosophy, political theory and poetry. He gave her an eclectic range of reading, including Goethe, the Icelandic *Edda*, Danish *Kjampeviser*, Firdousi, and Serbian folksongs in German translation.[39] He also made time for recreation, talking to her on their walks around Manchester and its greener outskirts, just as her maternal grandfather had done with her father years before in Trier. Uncle Angel, as she now called him, joined in the fun whenever he could get away from his Ermen & Engels business, in which he was in the process of winding up his interest:

> I walk about a good deal with Tussy and as many of the family, human and canine, as I can induce to go with us . . . Tussy, Lizzy, Mary Ellen [Pumps], myself and two dogs, and I am specially instructed to inform you that these amiable ladies had 2 glasses of beer apiece.[40]

This peripatetic education in the university of life was all very well, but what of school? She was, her father reported with satisfaction, 'blooming', and he thought 'a longer stay in Manchester would do her good'.[41] There is no record of the further discussions that must have taken place about the question of her necessary return to South Hampstead College. She simply didn't go back. It's clear that Mohr, Möhme and Engels made the assessment that Casa Engels had as much to usefully teach a wayward fifteen-year-old like Tussy as South Hampstead College. The investment in Jennychen and Laura's schooling hadn't altered the outcome of their pre-ordained lives as mid-Victorian women in any significant way: one married and baby-making, the other on the governessing treadmill at paltry wages.

At the beginning of June the whole party took off on a three-day jaunt to Bolton Abbey in Yorkshire, where they stayed at the famous Devonshire Arms. Flanked by her father and Engels, Lizzy, Pumps and Sarah, Tussy saw fireworks at Belle Vue prison and, fleetingly, the Prince and Princess of Wales at the Royal Agricultural Show at Old Trafford. Eleanor suggested that the youth of Manchester should greet the royal couple by singing, 'The Prince of Wales in Belle Vue jail for robbing a man of a pint of ale.'[42] The director of political theatre was in the making.

It was always open house at Uncle Angel and Lizzy's place. Here Tussy met Sam Moore and Karl Schorlemmer for the first time; the Marxes nicknamed the latter Jollymeier. Close friends and comrades of her father and Engels, both men were significant to the political patronage of her future life. Moore, a lawyer, brilliant translator and businessman, translated *The Communist Manifesto* into English, and later co-translated the first volume of *Capital* with Edward Aveling. Schorlemmer, after her father one of the most influential men in the European socialist movement, was a talented chemist and taught at Owens College in Manchester, where later a Chair in Organic Chemistry was created specifically for him.

Sam Moore and Jollymeier were eminent in their public lives but as with all these distinguished change-makers, Eleanor saw their human side. Chuckling, she reported to her sister that on one night of revelry Jollymeier 'got so "screwed" that we had to make a bed for him and he slept there too, for he couldn't get home'.[43] Inebriation was common. Uncle Angel staggered home on foot from a particularly good party 'as drunk as jelly',[44] and Lizzy and Tussy had to take off his boots and get him into bed.

Engels had good reason to be in a party mood. He'd settled his severance negotiations with his partner Gottfried. The terms were much to his disadvantage, but he didn't really care. Although he walked away a millionaire by today's capital values, Engels's settlement fell far short of what his share of the wildly successful international business was worth. He left the offices of Ermen & Engels on 1 July. Tussy recalled the momentous day in detail:

I was with Engels when he reached the end of his forced labour and I saw what he must have gone through all those years. I shall never forget the triumph with which he exclaimed, 'for the last time!' as he put on his boots in the morning to go to his office. A few hours later we were standing at the gate waiting for him. We saw him coming over the little field opposite the house where he lived. He was swinging his stick in the air and singing, his face beaming. Then we set the table for a celebration and drank champagne and were happy.[45]

The next day Uncle Angel confirmed his delight at liberation: 'Hurrah! Today *doux commerce* is at an end, and I am a free man . . . Tussy and I celebrated my first free day this morning with a long walk in the fields.'[46] The coincidence of Engels's final departure from *doux commerce* and what turned out to be Tussy's five-month stay in Manchester clearly settled the matter of her non-return to school. Engels now had time to spend with her and educate her for a substantial period, an arrangement that alleviated the financial pressure of paying tuition fees.

Thanks almost entirely to Engels, Eleanor grew up in a family where alcohol flowed quite freely. Lenchen and her parents were convinced of both the medicinal and convivial benefits of small beer, port, wine and – Tussy's favourite – champagne. In their Soho days it was certainly safer and preferable to drinking too much of the water from the street pumps. Möhme thought parents who did not give their children wine a little odd, rather mean and proscriptive.[47] Engels's motto, 'take it *aisy*', was ably abetted by the passionate and uninhibited Lizzy, who Engels, once released from the conventions of acting the businessman, now openly and lovingly referred to as 'my dear spouse'. Writing to 'My Dear Mrs Burns' in October 1868, Tussy added this postscript:

> Paul and Laura are going away tomorrow and we have just been drinking a bottle of champagne to their health, so you must excuse the smears in this letter, as the champagne has [ink blot] had a little effect [another ink blot] upon my head, and also on my hands for I can't write a bit.
> Good [blotch, blotch] bye.[48]

Preceded by a very fluent and chatty four pages, this letter demonstrates that Tussy had taken on her Uncle Angel's good habit of still seeing to his correspondence even if he was semi-inebriated.

By the time of Tussy's return to Manchester in 1869 'My Dear Mrs Burns' had become 'My Dear Lizzy'. Lizzy was Eleanor's first female mentor. Tussy responded to her bracing unladylikeness and her inborn, passionate feeling for her class.[49] Marx and Engels clearly conspired to ensure that Tussy was not subjected to becoming 'heddicated' and 'sensitive' by the second-rate education available to women.

Tussy helped Lizzy in turn by reading to her, suggesting they went to the theatre together and teaching her to play the piano. Eleanor was also resolute in her determination to educate everyone out of their deference to Karl Marx's daughter. Irritated by the absurdity of respectful submissiveness, she characteristically tackled the problem with humour. 'One evening,' she told her sister, 'they had all called me Miss Marx. So I made Auntie [Lizzy] and Moore and Jollymeier and Sarah all stand in a row and say Tussy 24 times . . . I've also made a rule that if anyone did not call me Tussy they had to stand on a chair and say Tussy 6 times & if I said Mrs Burns I had to say Auntie.'[50]

If she wasn't making them stand on chairs, she was up to other mischief. Engels returned one hot afternoon in July to discover his home taken over by a riotous petticoat party. Tussy, Lizzy and the housemaid Sarah had been superbly lazy, 'all lying', Tussy confessed, 'our full length on the floor the whole day drinking beer, claret etc . . . with no stays, no boots and one petticoat and a cotton dress on and that was all.'[51] Engels, delighted at his harem en deshabille, doubtless joined in.

Engels intended to write a book about the history of Ireland as his first post-capitalist project, and celebrated his liberation from business with a trip to Ireland with Lizzy and Eleanor. They travelled by sea from Liverpool. Eleanor's excitement at her first trip to the homeland of the Poor Neglected Nation was irrepressible. They visited the Wicklow Mountains, Killarney and Cork. They drank Guinness by peat fires, and told each other ghost stories in the Irish mists. Tussy was dazzled: by the sea, by the song, by Irish storytelling and stew.

Her first visit to Ireland took place at the same time as a new groundswell of support for the national liberation movement, prompted by the demand for amnesty for the Fenian prisoners. Nearly a quarter of a million people demonstrated in Dublin and

Limerick. The English government was petitioned for the release of the maltreated prisoners. Tussy, Engels and Lizzy found the country bristling with troops and the armed Royal Irish Constabulary. Field batteries patrolled the centre of Dublin and Ireland was effectively under military dictatorship.

Tussy returned to London in October. Eleanor, Fenian Sister, was beginning to hold sway over her family and bring them round to her way of thinking: 'Tussy has returned from Ireland a stauncher Irishman than ever.'[52] Fired up by her recent return from the Emerald Isle she was determined to go to a demonstration in Hyde Park on 22 October where 100,000 gathered to demand an amnesty for Fenian prisoners. Her family resisted but eventually relented. She 'did not rest,' Jennychen wrote to their family friend Dr Ludwig Kugelmann, a respected gynaecologist in Hanover, 'until she had persuaded Mohr, Mama and me to go with her.'[53]

Red, white and green banners rippled through the crowds, amidst a profusion of red Jacobin caps and placards proclaiming 'Disobedience to Tyrants is a Duty to God'. Tussy led her family in singing the Marseillaise. 'We are all of us downright Fenians,' Jennychen told Kugelmann, admitting that 'we all danced with joy' when they heard the news of the election of imprisoned Fenian Jeremiah O'Donovan Rossa to Parliament as member for Tipperary, a seat he was ineligible to take up. 'Tussy went quite wild!'[54] There was a valuable lesson for Tussy to learn from her support for O'Donovan Rossa, as Engels explained: 'It forces the Fenians to abandon their conspiratorial tactics and the staging of minor coups in favour of practical activities which, though seemingly legal, are far more revolutionary than anything they have done since their unsuccessful insurrection.'[55]

Most students join protest movements when they go to university; Tussy had returned from the University of Engels and Burns in Manchester a fully fledged youth protester. Less carried away by the political theatre, Marx optimistically identified the salient point: 'The main feature of the demonstration . . . was that at least a part of the English working-class had lost their prejudice against the Irish.'[56]

Towards the end of the year Tussy was an onlooker at a different type of protest. On Tuesday 6 November Queen Victoria opened the new Blackfriars Bridge and Holborn Viaduct, where, in Tussy's words, she 'stared fuming-mad and ultra-crabby'[57] from her coach at the crowd as she made her way from the South Bank to the north side of the Thames. 'Everywhere,' Tussy told her father, was 'over-run by police, as in France',[58] to prevent a threatened riot. In the weeks before the opening a few agitators had their fun circulating hoax handbills calling on the starving workers of the East End to present themselves en masse to the Queen at the opening and 'de ne pas laisser passer la reine [not let the Queen pass]'.[59]

'This week,' Marx reported to Engels in November, 'Tussy and I lost 3 days putting my workroom in order. It had become jumbled to the frontiers of possibility.'[60] By the end of 1869 it was accepted that Eleanor had taken Jennychen's place as Marx's secretary and research assistant. Engels wrote to her and asked her to work for him as researcher on his book on Ireland; 'I am very much obliged to you for sending that advertisement,' Tussy replied archly. 'The situation is one that will suit me very well, so I shall lose no time in applying for it. You will I am sure give me a reference.'[61] Her father suggested she start by combing Cobbett's *Political Register* for something there about Ireland.

Laura gave birth to her second child, named Jenny, on New Year's Day of 1870, exactly a year to the day after the birth of her first. In July 1870 France declared war on Prussia. Marx, Engels, Lafargue and the movements of the socialist left regarded the Franco-Prussian War as fratricidal. Marx hoped for victory for the Germans and 'the definite defeat of Bonaparte'[62] as the best outcome, as it was likely to provoke revolution in France, whereas German defeat would only extend the life of the ailing empire. This judgement proved correct.

This conflict had a considerable effect on Tussy's adolescence. Engels started writing a series of war notes in the *Pall Mall Gazette* where he famously and accurately predicted the outcome of the Battle of Sedan. When *Le Figaro*, quoting Engels, referred to the 'General Staff' as if it were an individual, Jennychen christened him 'the General'. Engels was the family expert on the military strategy of the Franco-Prussian War. As Tussy recalled, 'Engels, after 1870, became our "General".'[63] The *Pall Mall Gazette* sent Marx a cheque for the first article, which 'the ferocious girl' Tussy tried to appropriate, announcing that she and Jennychen 'should seize upon these first spoils of war as due to them for brokerage'.[64]

The family spent three weeks of August in Ramsgate. When they came back, Lenchen and Jenny worked very hard overseeing the renovations and interior decorating of Engels's new house for his move from Manchester. Möhme felt self-conscious that their home, subsidised by the General, was grand compared with the modesty of his: 'After all, we live in a veritable palace and, to my mind, far too large and expensive a house.'[65] On 20 September Engels, Lizzy and Pumps moved into 122 Regent's Park Road. The General loved this property and decided he never wanted to move again.

Across the Channel things were not good for the Lafargues. Their new baby daughter lived less than two months. Möhme despaired at her middle daughter's suffering. Laura was now pregnant again. The Lafargues were renting a small house in Levallois-Perret, close to the fortifications of Paris and scheduled for imminent demolition. They were in the direct firing line of the city's fortifications and Marx was anxious that they get out of the capital immediately. They arrived in Bordeaux early in September, where Paul launched a new magazine, *La Défense Nationale*, aiming 'to stir up the drowsy inhabitants of Bordeaux'.[66]

They got out just in time: Wilhelm I headquartered himself at the Rothschilds' chateau on the outskirts of Paris and in early October his troops started shelling the city. The capital was closed down from 7 November. No one was permitted to enter or leave and after a 135-day siege the city capitulated. Louis Napoleon's Second Empire, 'the reign of mediocrity, hypocrisy and profit', was now defeated.[67]

It was the beginning of one of the most contested periods of French history and Tussy was about to plunge headlong into the thick of it.

The Communards

The brief, heroic and doomed Paris Commune of March to May 1871 was the first and only attempt to make a proletarian revolution in nineteenth-century Europe. It was the first political event in which Tussy was personally involved. Governments, international press and the respectable classes scared out of their wits by the Commune claimed it was a workers' insurrection deliberately plotted by Karl Marx's First International (1864–72).[1] The Paris Commune was a Marx family matter.

On 16 January 1871 Tussy turned sixteen in London. In Paris, a week before, the Republican Central Committee of the Twenty Arrondissements issued the 'Red Poster', calling for the replacement of the French provisional government by a *Commune de Paris*. Two days after her birthday, the Proclamation of the German Empire was made at Versailles. Ten days later, the conservative French provisional government signed an armistice with the newly proclaimed Bismarckian German Empire. The armistice was the tipping point for the forces of French radical democracy. In Lyons, Toulouse and Marseilles communes were proclaimed and in Narbonne and Saint-Etienne they were attempted.

The citizens of Paris organised themselves against both the provisional government and the Prussian occupiers. The National Guard swung its support behind the masses of Paris on 18 March, and the political tide turned in favour of the common people. The majority of Parisians voted in the elections on 26 March and two days later the Paris Commune was declared. All sectors of the poor supported the Commune, but its leading activists were mainly skilled workers, craftsmen – and women. Adult men were the majority, but there were more women involved in the Paris Commune than in any revolution preceding it.

The Commune lasted for two months. In mid-May the Versailles army, in alliance with German forces, seized the moment to attack and, in *la Semaine Sanglante* – the Bloody Week – executed some 20,000 Communards and suspected sympathisers, more people than were slaughtered in Robespierre's 'Terror' during the first French Revolution of 1793–4. Some 8,000 people were jailed or deported to places like New Caledonia. Thousands of others fled to Belgium, England, Italy, Spain and the United States.

In the following year, 1872, stringent laws were passed that ruled out all possibilities of organising on the left. Not until 1880 was there a general amnesty for exiled and imprisoned Communards. Meanwhile, the Third Republic renewed Louis Napoleon's imperialist expansion – in Indochina, Africa and Oceania. Many French intellectuals and artists participated in the Commune or supported it, including Courbet, Rimbaud and Pissarro. The repression of 1871 and after alienated all who were persecuted by it from the Third Republic.

Alarming news came from Laura in Bordeaux in March 1871. Her baby Marc Laurent, born in February, was gravely ill and Paul Lafargue had gone missing. Paul had gone to Paris to request authority to organise 'the revolutionary army in Bordeaux',[2] but had not been heard from since he set out to return to Bordeaux. In the meantime, Schnappy, their elder son, had also become ill. Jennychen announced she was going to go and help, with or without Möhme and Mohr's permission. Inspired by her elder sister's determination, Tussy said that she was going too.

April 1871 was the highpoint of the Paris Commune. On 22 April the Foreign Office issued a passport to 'Miss Eleanor Marx (British Subject) accompanied by her sister, going to Bordeaux'. The following week the women of Paris established the Union des Femmes; abandoned factories and workshops were transferred to worker-owned co-operatives. In the same month empty housing stock was requisitioned for the people, employers were forbidden from deducting fines from workers' wages, bakery workers excused from working nights and municipal elections held all over the rest of France. This was the world into which Tussy enthusiastically thrust herself.

The railways were all either blocked or under secondment to the German or French armies, so the sisters travelled by steamer from Liverpool. On their arrival in Bordeaux on 1 May they went by the name of Williams, in what turned out to be a laughable attempt to conceal their true identities. They found Paul safely returned, but the children very ill. News from Paris was ominous. Reports of the atrocities of Bloody Week reached them shortly after 21 May. Street-fighting and horrific massacres continued. By the end of May the Versailles army had overpowered the Commune. It was all over – and Paul was a wanted man. It hadn't yet occurred to the Marx sisters that they might be not just under suspicion, but in danger.

Mohr sent an urgent coded letter telling them to get Paul and the children immediately to the Spanish side of the Pyrenees, where there was a 'better climate'.[3] They quickly started packing up in preparation for a discreet pre-dawn flight to the small resort town of Bagnères-de-Luchon in the Haute-Garonne. But the baby became sicker during the night and Paul and Laura refused to make the journey over the mountain footpath to Spain until he improved. The family laid low, Jennychen and Tussy maintaining their disguise as the Williams sisters.

Marc Laurent died on 26 July. News came that government spies were closing in on Paul; the sisters persuaded him to leave straight away for Spain whilst they buried the baby. A week later, on 6 August, the three sisters and Schnappy made the tricky journey over the border so that the Lafargue family could be safe together with Paul in Bosost in the Spanish Pyrenees. To cover their tracks as soon as possible, Jennychen and Tussy made the journey on foot back into France the same day. The arrangement was for the 'Williams' sisters to leave Bordeaux by ship as soon as possible. Everything was going according to plan until they crossed the border back into France.

The instant they put their feet back on French territory armed police seized them and, as Tussy described, they were 'conducted by 24 gendarmes right across the Pyrenees from Fos to Luchon',⁴ within French territory. Tussy protested throughout the journey that the police had no jurisdiction to apprehend a British citizen, but the armed guards ignored her.

The furious Marx sisters were delivered directly to the front door of the residence of the police chief Emile de Kératry, Prefect of the Department of the Haute-Garonne. Kératry had been Police President of Paris the previous year and knew the Marxes and the First International all too well. He wanted to interrogate the sisters personally, and made them wait under armed guard in a carriage outside his residence until he returned from a summer concert in the park.⁵

His concert over, Kératry finally arrived, accompanied by a judge, Monsieur Delpech.⁶ The sisters were separated and Jenny interrogated first, from 10 p. m. At midnight, it was Tussy's turn. She'd been up since 5 a.m., travelled nine hours in difficult mountain terrain on a crushingly hot August day, and last eaten a quick snack hours before when they left Bosost. Kératry told Tussy that Jenny had confessed all, and tried to get her to contradict her sister's version of events. 'It was a dirty trick, wasn't it,' she remarked in a letter to Library.⁷

Their ordeal continued for a further two days. They were placed under house arrest in the Lafargues' abandoned lodgings. As soon as they got back there the sisters discovered the apartment they had left neat and swept was in chaos, having been searched and turned upside down. The rooms were, Tussy said, 'already full of gendarmes, *mouchards* and agents of every description'.⁸ The police had interrogated both the landlady and the Lafargues' servant, and Eleanor felt guilty that the servant was badly shaken.

Poking through their mattresses and bed linen, the police asked the sisters where the bomb-making equipment and munitions were hidden. They saw the lamps 'in which we had warmed the milk for the poor little baby who died', Tussy wrote, and thought they were filled with 'petrole'.⁹ It's easy to have some sympathy with the *mouchards* on this point. Meeting the Marx sisters in person tended to confirm, not allay, their reputation amongst conservatives of being dangerous *petroleuses*: the legendary women street-fighters of the Paris Commune, led by the formidable Union des Femmes. It is likely that spies had already told the French authorities that Elisabeth Demetrioff, founder and leader of the women's union, was a personal family friend of the Marxes in general and Eleanor in particular.

Tussy had met the brilliant nineteen-year-old Russian Elisabeth Demetrioff the previous year, when she came to London on a fact-finding mission and turned up at Modena Villas with a letter of introduction to Marx. Born Elizabeta Luknichna Tomanovskya, the daughter of a tsarist civil servant, feminist and actress, she was the co-founder of the Russian section of the First International. Tussy and Elisabeth struck up an instant friendship and spent a great deal of time in each other's company until Elisabeth was dispatched to Paris in March as a Russian envoy to the Paris Commune.

Just before Tussy left for her adventures in Bordeaux in April, she heard that Elisabeth had set up the Union des Femmes in Paris with Nathalie Lemel at a memorable public meeting at the Grand Café de Nation. The Union des Femmes chose representatives from each of the arrondissements and Elisabeth organised the women's committees in each district. She fought on the barricades during Bloody Week and managed to elude her impending death sentence and escape to Geneva.

Demetrioff's story is a reminder that, above all else, the Paris Commune was a great gender event. The dominance of political and activist women in the Commune was seen as one of the key reasons for its awfulness, bloodthirstiness and failure. Spectacular misogyny is never very far from anti-Communard accounts. 'The weaker sex', fulminated one commentator, 'behaved scandalously during these deplorable days':

> Those females who dedicated themselves to the Commune – and there were many – had but a single ambition: to raise themselves above the level of man by exaggerating his vices . . . They were all there, agitating and squawking . . . the gentleman's seamstresses; the gentleman's shirtmakers; the teachers of grown-up schoolboys; the maids-of-all-work . . . What was profoundly comic was that

these absconders from the workhouse unfailingly invoked Joan of Arc, and were not above comparing themselves to her. During the final days, all of these bellicose viragos held out longer than the men did behind the barricades.[10]

The correspondent of *The Times* of London concurred: 'If the French nation were composed only of French women, what a terrible nation it would be.'[11] These and several similar expressions of anti-feminist antagonism were collated and in some cases translated by Eleanor herself for the most famous book ever written about the Paris Commune, a project with which she was shortly to become intimately involved.

Back in Bordeaux, twenty-four hours of further searches and interrogation revealed nothing from the bellicose virago daughters of Karl Marx. Tussy and Jennychen expected to have their passports returned and to be escorted to the docks and put on the next steamer back to England. Instead, they were taken to the gendarmerie, locked up overnight and refused permission to let anyone know where they were. They were released the following morning and placed under house arrest without the return of their passports. After a week confined to the Lafargues' former apartment under the watchful eye of agents who accompanied them to the shops to buy bread, coffee and tobacco, they were suddenly ordered to pack up immediately, shoved in a carriage and shooed over the Spanish border as their passports were slapped back into their hands.

The Marx sisters had won the game. Since their arrest, Jennychen had successfully concealed an incriminating letter to Marx and Lafargue from Gustave Flourens, a famed leader of the Paris Commune. Flourens, who had been captured by gendarmes and butchered during Bloody Week, was one of Karl Marx's oldest friends.

Undetected by all except Tussy, Jennychen slipped the letter from her sleeve into a ledger on the booking officer's desk when they were brought into the gendarmerie. Whilst the *mouchards* continued to search their apartment, the letter was safely hidden in plain view, interleaved in the police station detention register. As Engels observed, if discovered, this incendiary letter would have provided 'a sure passport for the two girls to go to New Caledonia'.[12]

Shortly after Eleanor and Jennychen's return to London Tussy's father wrote to Charles Dana, editor of the New York *Sun*, reporting on the daily increase of Communard refugees arriving in London: 'Our means of supporting them is daily on the decrease, so that men find themselves in a very deplorable state . . . We shall,' he added, 'make an appeal for assistance to the Americans.'[13] To illustrate the poor state of things in France under Louis Thiers' repression of the Commune, Marx says, 'I will tell you what has happened to my own daughters.' Hilariously, the right-wing press incorrectly assumed the troublesome 'insurgents' hotly pursued through France, over the border into Spain and back again were three *brothers* of Karl Marx, 'well known and dangerous agents of the International Propaganda, though I have no brothers'.[14] Or sons.

The Paris Commune was a brave failed attempt at a proletarian revolution. The ripples lasted far, far longer than the event itself and influenced and coloured the view of many people for years to come, not least Tussy. It also strongly affected Tussy's choice of her first lover.

Tussy helped with the organisation of the International Working Men's Association London Congress, held during the third week of September. She joined the open sessions of the conference and subcommittee sessions held in her father's study at Modena Villas to deal with the problem of Bakuninist opposition. Tussy was, Library observed, growing into 'the International Working Men's Association personified'.[15]

As indicated by its name, the role of women within the International was contested. At the founding of the First International in 1864 the General Council, led by Marx, voted to admit women as members. The French delegation opposed this on the grounds that women 'belonged by the hearth, not at the Forum'.[16] Following Pierre Proudhon's misogynist policy, the French chapter proclaimed that, 'To men belong labour and the study of human problems; to women child care and adornment of the worker's home.'[17] This view was disproved by the leading role of women in organising and leading the Paris Commune. The problem was resolved by allowing each national delegation to determine the constitution of its own membership.

The Marxes put up as many international visitors as they could fit in their house for the IWMA London Congress in September, and Tussy was ever helpful. When Spanish delegate Anselmo Lorenzo needed to send a telegram to Valencia, Tussy volunteered to show him the way:

> I was most surprised and touched by the alacrity with which the young lady helped a foreigner whom she did not know, this being contrary to the customs of the Spanish bourgeoisie. This young lady, or rather girl, as beautiful, merry and smiling as the very personification of youth and happiness, did not know Spanish. She could speak English and German well but was not very proficient in French, in which language I could make myself understood. Every time one of us made a blunder we both laughed as heartily as if we had been friends all our life.[18]

Lorenzo described to Tussy his journey from Spain across France. He'd passed through Paris 'when the persecution of the Communards was at its highest and courts-martial were sitting without interruption, passing death and deportation sentences wholesale . . . I saw the Hotel de Ville in ruins . . . part of the Louvre burnt out, the pedestal from which the column had been knocked down in Place de Vendôme and various buildings and houses showed traces of the week of bloodshed.'[19]

The IWMA London Congress buzzed with reports and gossip about missing Communards, shot, deported, exiled, on the run or disappeared. Eleanor heard that Elisabeth Demetrioff had made it back to St Petersburg and chosen a new fiancé, leaving her forlorn lover Leo Frankel, Hungarian Communard, stranded, heartbroken and glumly contemplating his broken dreams. Frankel, also under a death sentence in France, joined the leadership of the First International in London and comforted himself by turning his rebounded attentions on Tussy.

By December, in addition to conducting Mohr's correspondence, Eleanor had the official role of assisting refugees by coordinating the Relief Committee for Communards, giving Frankel ample opportunity to put himself in her way. The refugees, Tussy wrote to Library, 'suffer frightfully and they have none of them any money and you can't think how difficult it is for them to get work'.[20] In the same letter to Library about her work on the relief committee she remarks archly that she wishes the Communards *had* 'taken some of the millions they're accused of having stolen'.[21]

Frankel tried to advance his cause. Tussy enjoyed flirting with him; he was intelligent and entertaining, but that's as far as her interest extended. Her mother had a much firmer grasp on Tussy's development at this time, describing her as 'eine Politikerin von top to bottom'.[22] Möhme identified this as the point at which her youngest daughter emerged into adulthood: she was Eleanor, with a public political identity, no longer only Tussy the family tearaway. And it is her direct engagement with the Paris Commune and some of its key players – both men and women – that made her so.

Exiled Communard refugees starved on the streets of London. Those discovered to have changed their names in order to get work were sacked immediately. English mainstream press opinion was hostile to the political exiles. Reflecting years later on the potency of anti-Communard feeling in her homeland at the time, Tussy recalled,

> . . . that it was proposed – quite seriously – that the Communards who had taken refuge in England should be handed over to the doctors and the hospitals for purposes of vivisection . . . this proposition . . . largely expressed the feelings of the whole of respectable society. Saddest of all is the fact that in England the workers also, with rare exceptions . . . were as bitterly hostile to the Commune as their exploiters.[23]

Tussy experienced this first hand when she organised the first anniversary meeting to celebrate the memory of the Commune at St George's Hall, Upper Regent Street in London. The Communards and their English supporters arrived at the venue to find it barricaded against them and the landlord demanding the return of his deposit. He preferred to pay the penalty for breach of contract rather than allow 'such a set of "ruffians" in his highly respectable Hall'.[24] Said ruffians instead adjourned to the Cercle d'Etudes on Tottenham Court Road, where 'despite . . . so much suffering . . . we were a merry party . . . gay with the gaiety of perfect faith.'[25] Brave words. In truth, the surviving Communards were, according to Engels, 'hideously demoralised'. The General lamented the extent of their trauma and inability to regroup efficiently: 'only sheer hard necessity can bring a disorganised Frenchman to his senses.'[26]

Meanwhile, Leo Frankel persisted in trying to bring his senses to bear on Tussy. He had by now made some headway with her, appealing to her easily awakened sympathies for his plight as a Communard and engaging her attention with his new perspectives on art and politics. She seemed more responsive; Frankel hoped to catch her in party mood at the Commune anniversary celebration and propose to her. Worse luck for him, this was the very moment that Hippolyte Prosper-Olivier Lissagaray strode into Tussy's life.

As the party turned away from St George's Hall and they all walked together from Upper Regent's Street to Tottenham Court Road, Frankel tried to take Tussy's arm. But he found her already talking easily with the legendary Communard Lissagaray. It was a conversation that Frankel was never able to interrupt.

Whilst Tussy was in Bordeaux during Bloody Week at the end of May 1871, Lissagaray had been fighting on the barricades, defending Paris from the Versailles army, who aimed to recapture the city and shoot every man, woman and child who resisted. By 26 May the Versailles army was in control of the city centre and only the worker districts had not been overpowered. In these working-class arrondissements of Paris the army fired on the populace with heavy artillery, shot captured prisoners and piled up the bodies in public buildings.

The defeated Communards fought on at ridiculous odds, refusing to surrender. Their military organisation and discipline were shambolic. They no longer had any strategic plan or central command. Two hundred Communards fought their last battle in Père Lachaise Cemetery, where 147 of them were lined up, shot and buried in a communal pit in front of one of the cemetery walls.

Prosper Lissagaray fought singlehandedly for a quarter of an hour on the last manned barricade of the Commune on the Rue Ramponeau, until he ran out of ammunition. With a death sentence on his head, he escaped from Paris and made his way, circuitously, to London.

Lissa, as Tussy called him, was quite literally a tall, dark and handsome stranger, a Basque from the Midi-Pyrenees in south-west France. A journalist and activist turned street-fighter, he was seventeen years older than seventeen-year-old Tussy. At thirty-four, he had the energy and alert, nervous anxiety of those Communards involved in hand-to-hand combat who had fought and survived the day. He took no prisoners in his politics, writing, journalism, or on the barricades. Dashing and flamboyant, experience of extremity and realpolitik had made him also gentle-mannered and good-humoured. Legendary for his physical bravery, political adventures and serious intellectual mindset, he was as yet unmarried. Marx admired his thinking and activism. But he didn't like his attentions to Tussy.

A more saturnine disposition lurked beneath Lissa's élan, but for now this was obscured from Eleanor's view by sexual naivety and the flush of first attraction – instant and mutual. Tussy, blooming at seventeen, already had some of her own adventures to recount, shone intellectually in any situation and – for a man who had just outwitted death – had the charm of bold, unfettered youth. She laughed a lot and she argued continuously. Physically striking, with her father's flashing coal-black eyes, and unconventional in the stylish simplicity of her dress, Tussy at seventeen was elemental and mercurial, far from the gauze and velvet of vapid romantic love. She was boisterous, passionate and, to Lissa, unlike any other woman he had yet met.

They made a striking couple, enchanted with each other's company. Tussy's close friend Clara Collet recorded that Tussy in love was 'prettier than ever' but she missed their former intimacy: 'I wish he would commit forgery and suicide. It would be such a relief.'[27]

At the end of 1871 Lissa had published a pamphlet about his experiences in the Commune. Entitled *Les huit journées de mai derrière les barricades*, this was the beginning of what would become – and remains to this day – the primary first-hand historical account and source of Communard history. He read early extracts to Tussy, and the two decided to both expand and translate the pamphlet together. Lissa's project was a hook for Tussy that Frankel could not hope to match. The rest of her family were preoccupied with Jennychen's

wedding plans and busy preparing for the last congress of the First
International at The Hague, scheduled for September.

Jenny had become engaged to Charles Félix César Longuet in
March 1872. Longuet was a university friend of Paul Lafargue; the
two had been student radicals together in Paris and worked together
for the Commune. Communards were in romantic favour with the
Marx sisters, though not with their mother or the General.

Initially Möhme thought Longuet a 'good, fine, proper man',[28] but
wished her eldest daughter's choice had 'fallen on an Englishman
rather than a Frenchman, who, combined with the national qualities of
charm, is naturally not without their weakness and irresponsibility'.[29]
Her regrets proved well-founded as Longuet's constitutional laziness
became evident. Möhme grumbled that she was fed up with his 'pack
of lies', national chauvinism and 'French fiddlededee'.[30] Her Prussian
prejudice was naturally mixed up with her maternal anxiety about the
future security of daughters married to impecunious revolutionaries, a
concern – entertainingly – shared by her husband.

When Schnappy died in Spain in July, Jennychen's marriage was
postponed. Tussy's parents and the General set off for Spain to
comfort Laura and Paul, and then proceeded directly on to The
Hague congress. Tussy stayed in London to attend to her work on
the Refugee Relief Committee, allowing her – conveniently – to
spend time with Lissa.

In October Jennychen married Longuet at St Pancras Register
Office. Marx and Engels were preoccupied with settling the fate of
the First International. Tussy, meanwhile, had to calm Lissa when he
became jealous of Frankel. Both men then discovered that another
Communard refugee, with the initials JJ, was furious with Frankel
for cutting in on *his* approaches to Tussy. Tussy tried to untangle
these complications with the help of a friend, Maggie, about whom
little is known except that she lived on Harley Street and liked
romantic intrigue. Maggie urged Tussy to tackle Lissa head on, 'try
and pump my dear – all is fair in love and war – I hope you are no
longer miserable'.[31]

Tussy's practical solution to reassuring Lissagaray was to give him
her virginity. She was not the sort of girl to lose it, as if by accident.
Likely as not, this agreeable sexual initiation happened whilst the

rest of the family were abroad. Of course the instant the couple got themselves sorted out, Eleanor's family objected to the relationship.

Lissa was another Frenchman. Marx had just married off his eldest daughter to a disappointed, broke Communard. Now here was another one. To make matters more tricky, Lissagaray and Lafargue had fallen out over political differences concerning the future of the International. Laura sided with her husband and on a family visit to Modena Villas in 1872 the Lafargues cold-shouldered Lissa. Furious about this snub, Tussy complained to Jennychen about 'this really unladylike behaviour on Laura's part'.³² A rich criticism, coming from the champion of the unladylike.

On the cusp of her eighteenth birthday, Tussy was headstrong, a force of nature for the first time truly in love with someone as well as her father but, uncomfortably, very much like him. Marx admired Lissa for his politics and his mind but had no intention of allowing his favourite to throw away her life as her sisters had now done without discovering the unrealised value in herself. That Lissa was twice her age was not, by contemporary standards, a matter of much concern to anyone.

From the outset of their relationship, Tussy acted as the far too dutiful amanuensis, translating, transcribing and editing Lissa's history of the Commune and bolstering his ego. Her relationship with him brought a huge improvement in her French. She entered a phase of long struggle, breaking away from her father's dominance with a charming, talented older man who was in many points reminiscent of Marx. Tussy was resolute and determined to stand her ground. Her father was the most stubborn man in Europe. A titanic clash between father and daughter was brewing. Daddy's little girl might now break both of their hearts.

In an attempt to quell the tension, Marx took Eleanor to Brighton for a fortnight. However, less than a week later, on April Fools' Day, Marx came home alone, without prior warning and with a face like thunder.

The previous day Tussy had informed her father that she had decided to stay in Brighton and earn her own living. The ensuing twenty-four-hour row failed to alter her decision. Marx sulked in his study at Modena Villas and wrote complaining letters to Engels about the confounded Lissagaray. 'I want nothing from him except that he would give proofs instead of phrases, that he would be better than his reputation, and that one could have certain right to rely on him. You will see from [Tussy's] answer how the man continues to act. The damned thing is that I have to proceed with much consideration for the child's sake.'[33]

The child, meanwhile, set herself up in private lodgings at 2 Manchester Street, very near the seafront and Brighton Pavilion, signed up with an employment agency recommended to her by family friend Arnold Ruge and asked some French friends living in Brighton to help her find private pupils to teach whilst she sought a more permanent position.

It was no small thing in early 1870s England for an eighteen-year-old without her own money or formal education to strike an act of independence like this from her family. Tussy did not want to continue living off the General's bounty. She knew her parents depended on Engels for the mainstay of their annual income and that her married sisters relied on his financial support for their new households. It was the General who taught her the value of self-sufficiency; her bid for economic freedom was out of respect for him as much as it was for her parents – but primarily, it was for her own self-respect.

Five months after Jennychen married and left home, the pitfalls of being the last remaining daughter in the Marx household were now clear to Tussy. She was as much running away from the spectre of becoming the stay-at-home daughter on whom her parents depended as she was running towards the lover of her choice.

Counting on the General to mollify Marx, Möhme gave Tussy's decision her practical and unqualified support. Eleanor had a firm ally in her mother. The Jenny Marx who was once a young female radical firebrand empathised with Tussy's decision. Almost immediately after her husband's furious return to London Jenny sent her youngest daughter 'a little outfit'[34] to tide her over for the first week or so until she found a job. In the accompanying note she also advised Tussy to buy a few extra pairs of stockings from the Brighton shops. 'I alone understand how dearly you long for work and independence, the only two things that can help one over the sorrows and cares of present day society.'[35] Sound feminist advice from a mother who had neither. Tussy received many reassuring letters from her mother: 'Believe me, despite appearances to the contrary, nobody understands your position, your conflict, your embitterment better than I do. Let your young heart triumph . . . Forgive me if at times you have felt that I hurt you.'[36] Jenny recognised her own youth in Tussy, in which her natural instinct for liberty from the absurdities of patriarchy and class-based social expectation were cast as rebellious provocation. The reference to 'embitterment' is to Eleanor and Laura's feud over the discord between Lissa and Lafargue. Jenny tried to repair the rift, to no effect. Tussy and Laura remained at loggerheads.

Tussy's French friends quickly referred some pupils to her and in the month of April 1873 she earned ten shillings a week from private tuition. She needed every penny to cover her rent and subsistence. Brighton and independence were expensive.

Möhme packed up and sent her clothes from London, along with detailed notes and practical advice about all manner of things including accessories, keeping warm and eating regularly. She apologised to Tussy that all this fuss over clothes and self-presentation would doubtless try her patience: 'I know how little store you set by such things and how lacking in vanity and a love of finery you are.'[37] Her mother was quite right to be more concerned about the state of Tussy's stockings than her ability to find work.

Early in May the agency found her a salaried part-time teaching post at a seminary for young ladies run by the Misses Hall in Sussex Square. She was to start in the new academic term. Eleanor upgraded her lodgings to 6 Vernon Terrace and prepared for her new job.

On 3 May Tussy wrote a breezy birthday letter to her father, describing all that she had achieved in the past month and making no allusion to the argument between them. She told him that she'd read Pythagoras and asked him to send her some history books. Nothing could have further flattered or reassured Marx that he had done a good job with the apple of his eye: she was coping magnificently, and as well as securing herself two sources of income she was applying herself to continuing study. Mohr reacted to this eloquent olive branch by sulking: Tussy was not making the hour-long train journey from Brighton to London to come home and see him for his birthday.

Quite aside from Mohr's Lear-like fatherly solipsism, the manner in which Tussy organised these first weeks of her independence demonstrate her self-motivation and intellectual discipline. By a combination of nature and culture, she was a tireless autodidact. Had she been a boy, she could have aspired to university and socially sanctioned study like her father. Without that option, like many gifted women before her, she had to set about educating herself. As Mary Wollstonecraft observed, if woman 'be not prepared by education to become the companion of man, she will stop the progress of knowledge, for truth must be common to all, or it will be inefficacious with respect to its influence on general practice.'[38]

The history books she requested came in her mother's parcels containing some clothes and accessories for her new job, complete with detailed instructions on how to assemble and wear them attractively. Möhme's vicarious embrace of Tussy's independence is palpable. In opposite, inverse proportion to her husband's fit of pique, Jenny Marx, about to turn sixty, enjoyed the life her younger self might have led through Tussy.

Resisting Mohr's silence, Tussy threw herself into her first professional teaching job. Of the limited options available for women to earn their own living in 1870s Britain, governessing and teaching were crucial means to hard-won independence. The narrative of Tussy's life begins to take shape like that of a feminist anti-heroine of the great Victorian novels. Except that she is real, not the aspirational projection of a frustrated intellect that longs to express itself through the actualisation of contested freedom.

Tussy was immediately interested in her pupils, particularly the individuals with active political inquisitiveness. A teenager with an 'immense interest'[39] in the Commune and the International quickly attached herself to her inspiring new history teacher, Miss Marx. 'Is it not odd that I should always hit on such girls?'[40] Tussy asked her mother with a charming lack of awareness that she might be a role model for younger women.

For the first time mistress of her own routine, working hard at a double teaching load, carrying her own salary in her purse, Tussy was challenged and exhilarated. Lissa caught the train from London and visited her regularly at the weekends. They took long walks arm in arm along the Brighton and Hove seafront, munching fish and chips, eels, clams and whelks on the pier, chain-smoking, talking, debating what they were reading. They rambled over the Sussex Downs with picnics of bread, cheese and wine, discussing the fate of the International now that Marx had ensured the relocation of its head of operations to New York, bitching about the Lafargues, his writing, her teaching, ending the day in lamplit country pubs with pies and pints of ale. As far as Tussy's landlady and friends in Brighton understood, Lissa was Tussy's fiancé.

She was, in her mother's view, working too much and eating too little. But what tipped Möhme's anxiety was her discovery that in Brighton Lissa seemed to be accepted by all as Tussy's betrothed – allowing the couple free rein to wander around unchaperoned. Möhme learned from Tussy's employers that Lissa had been visiting her at the school. The Misses Hall concluded these visits were appropriate as they understood that Tussy and Lissa were engaged.

Following a visit to Brighton in late May, Möhme developed serious reservations about Tussy's welfare. With all the very best of maternal intentions, she fussed over Tussy's health and interfered with her professional life. She wanted Tussy to take a short mid-term break from work to accompany Lenchen on a trip home to the funeral of her sister in the Rhineland, and was put out when Tussy, of course, firmly rejected the proposal explaining that she couldn't just suddenly take unscheduled holidays. Tussy was deeply embarrassed when her mother, thinking her direct request would resolve the matter, bypassed her and wrote directly to the Misses Hall instructing them to release Tussy from her duties so she could go to Germany. In a hilariously bad-tempered exchange of letters between mother and headmistress, the school refused – to Tussy's relief.

Her bid for independence had initially seemed successful but her parents combined got the better of her. Now fighting against their allied forces, Eleanor lost the battle in her first war of independence. Under pressure from her mother and father, she became stressed and anorexic. Reluctantly, she gave up her teaching job and returned to Modena Villas in September, deeply disappointed, extremely thin, and in a state of nervous collapse. Mohr had got his secretary back in his study and his favourite by his hearth, but she was resentful at her return, and physically unwell.

The ongoing dispute between Lissa and Lafargue escalated still further and Tussy – confronted with her 'secret' engagement to Lissa – was forbidden from seeing him at all. Her parents proposed that father and daughter 'take the waters' in Harrogate for three weeks of mineral baths, cleansing Kissingen waters, reading and early nights, so in November Marx took her with him to chilly Yorkshire. Smarting from her recent defeat Tussy spent afternoons of watery sunlight in the spa gardens reading Saint-Beuve and sipping her sixteen glasses of sulphurous water per day swathed in damp mist and a fog of smoke from the cigarettes she puffed between each glass. Her chain-smoking didn't annoy her father but she hoped that reading Saint-Beuve did – a pathetic twitch of resistance against her loving paternal tyrant.

It was a tough call for anyone who loved Mohr to resist his nervous hypochondria and emotional blackmail. Unlike her mother and the General, Tussy had less experience of how to manage her father's domineering nature. She put up a spirited resistance to his possessiveness, but she had inherited his propensity for stretches of intense, concentrated productivity punctuated by stress-related exhaustion.

This was the great age of nervous anxiety and feverish repression labelled 'hysteria'. Tussy contracted the whole infuriating syndrome of Victorian feminine neurosis so brilliantly depicted by Wilkie Collins, that great expressionist of the effects of patriarchal repression and thwarted desire on intelligent, ambitious daughters. For every stress-related carbuncle, ulcer, swollen foot and bout of intense depression acutely suffered by her father, Tussy could answer with her own particular array of feminine nervous symptoms. Forgetting to eat, preoccupied with proving herself in her job, Lissa, smoking and burning the midnight oil in order to understand the world, Tussy broke down. Fainting and anaemic, she was torn between her father, her lover and her independence.

Tussy had lost the first battle, but stuck to her campaign. In March 1874 she wrote, 'quite entre nous', to her dearest Mohr:

I am going to ask you something, but first I want you to promise me that you will not be very angry. I want to know, dear
Mohr, when I may see L. again. It is so *very* hard *never* to see
him. I have been doing my best to be patient, but it is so difficult and I don't feel as if I could be much longer. I do not expect
you to say that he can come here. I should not even wish it, but
could I not, now and then, go for a little walk with him? You let
me go out with Outine [another Russian revolutionary admirer],
with Frankel, why not with him? No one moreover will be
astonished to see us together, as everybody knows we are
engaged . . .

When I was so very ill at Brighton . . . L came to see me, and
each time left me stronger and happier; and more able to bear the
rather heavy load laid on my shoulders. It is *so* long since I saw him
and I am beginning to feel so very miserable notwithstanding all
my efforts to keep up, for I have tried hard to be merry and cheer-
ful. I cannot much longer. Believe me, dear Mohr, if I could see him
now and then, it would do me more good than all Mrs Anderson's
prescriptions put together – I know that by experience.

At any rate, dearest Mohr, if I may not see him now, could you
not say when I may. It would be something to look forward to,
and if the time were not so indefinite it would be less wearisome
to wait.

My dearest Mohr, please don't be angry with me for writing
this, but forgive me for being selfish enough to worry you again.

Your

Tussy[41]

Striking information from this beseeching letter is that the great
Elizabeth Garrett Anderson is now Eleanor's doctor. Born in
Whitechapel in 1836 and brought up in Aldeburgh, Garrett Anderson
was the first woman to qualify in England as a doctor, appearing on
the Medical Register for the first time in 1866. Her sister was the
suffragette Millicent Garrett Fawcett. Elizabeth Blackwell, who
preceded Garrett Anderson, had to train in America. Garrett
Anderson was admitted to the British Medical Association in 1873
and for two decades was its only female member.

Tussy's health was poor for most of 1874 and Garrett Anderson did a great deal to restore her to her robust self by the end of the year. The strain she experienced was compounded by the death of her eleven-month-old nephew, Jennychen's son Charles Félicien, who was weak and sickly from the start. Eleanor nursed him day and night without a break – to Jennychen's eternal gratitude.

When he died, as he had been born, in his grandparents' home at Modena Villas, Tussy collapsed completely. For nearly a month she was attended daily by Dr Garrett Anderson, who was under no illusion about the nature of Tussy's ailments. She focused primarily on Tussy's need to eat and build up her weight and strength, rather than living driven by cigarettes, air and repressed nervous energy. With firm diplomacy, Tussy's woman doctor also focussed on her need for occupation. Tussy's father was impressed by Garrett Anderson and influenced deeply by her practical diagnosis of the causes of so-called 'hysteria' that characterised so many specifically female complaints.

Garrett Anderson sensed Marx's contribution to Tussy's weak health in unintentionally thwarting her youthful ambition and desires, but judiciously withheld comment and encouraged the whole family to build up Tussy's appetite, which improved in 'geometric proportions'[42] according to her relieved and delighted father.

Dr Garrett Anderson recommended that Tussy would benefit from a recuperative trip to the famous waters at Karlsbad. Marx's own physician Dr Gumpert had ordered him to go to Karlsbad the previous year, an instruction that Marx, unwilling to leave England whilst Tussy was unwell, had ignored. Subsidised by Engels, daughter and father set off in August 1874 for the famous Bohemian spa resort where they stayed at the Hotel Germania. Marx applied for British citizenship shortly before they travelled, but as he'd heard nothing back from the Home Office before they left, he set off without the protection of a British passport. To avoid drawing attention to himself he took the precaution of registering at the hotel under the alias of Mr Charles Marx, Private Gentleman.

The legendary health-giving waters at Karlsbad had made the resort popular with monarchs, millionaires and such artists as could afford it. Bach, Goethe, Schiller and Turgenev were visitors, as well as Beethoven, Leibniz, Paganini and Mozart.

Tussy was enthusiastic about Karlsbad and enchanted by the 'admirable scenery'.[43] She told Jennychen that, 'We are very exact indeed in all our duties. We take long walks, and altogether get on very well here.'[44] No doubt, with the thorn of Lissa temporarily removed from Mohr's side. They combined strict adherence to their medical programme with socialising. Their eclectic, noisy companions included painters, old fellow exiles, writers and aristocrats.

Tussy was less enthusiastic about their old family friends the Kugelmanns, who joined them on the trip to Karlsbad. 'An impossible man'[45] was how she described Kugelmann, agreeing with her father that he was an overly pedantic, small-minded, petit-bourgeois Philistine. And that was just for starters. What offended Tussy the most was how Kugelmann mistreated his 'charming'[46] wife and daughter, Franziska, with whom she became 'very intimate'.[47] Franziska confided to Tussy that her father verbally and physically abused both her mother and herself, and that she had longed for Karlsbad as a brief respite from their miserable lives at home in Hamburg under his tyranny.

'It is a hard thing,' Eleanor wrote to Jenny, 'when a woman has no money of her own and her husband tells her every minute that she is ungrateful for all his "Wohltaten" to her and the child. You cannot imagine how brutish Kugel is and how shameless.'[48] Initially allocated adjoining rooms, one night Marx heard appalling scenes through the hotel walls that left him in no doubt of Kugelmann's behaviour. He asked to be moved to another room, and Kugelmann forbade his wife and daughter to speak to Tussy or her father.

This episode sharpened Tussy's awareness of the dangers of economic dependency for women within marriage. Here, along with her consciousness of the growing unhappiness and struggle of both of her sisters, are the first explicit signs of her nascent feminism.

On their return journey they went to Leipzig to visit the Liebknechts for three days, which Tussy described as 'a bright and joyous souvenir'.[49] She and Alice were delighted to see each other and for the first time Tussy met Nathalie, Library's second wife, and their growing family. The newest addition Karl Liebknecht was three years old and he and Tante Tussy struck up an instant and lasting rapport.

Tussy confided her difficulties to Library. He was quietly sympathetic to her struggle with Mohr and her family's opposition to Lissa. They agreed to work together on reciprocal briefings between the socialist movement in Germany and France, with Eleanor reporting on the progress of socialism in England. Library and August Bebel had founded the German Social Democratic Party on Marxist principles in 1869. Library's *Volksstaat* was the publication for this German workers' party. Lissa was about to launch a new weekly review of politics, *Rouge et Noir*, and Tussy in turn invited Library to contribute. Their reunion was a turning point in her restoration to full health. 'I could not find words to tell you ... how happy I was to see you all. It has been one of my dearest wishes to see you again, for ... I have grown up with the remembrance of many a happy day spent with you.'[50]

For the rest of 1874 Tussy worked on the first two editions of *Rouge et Noir*, for which she translated from German into French Library's rather tiresome Reichstag speech demanding the lifting of the sentences of imprisoned Social Democrats and a review of the judicial process set to try them. Tussy agreed with Library's position but not his didactic rhetoric, 'Qu'est-ce que la bourgeoisie? – Tout. Que doit-elle être? – Rien.'[51] She would have preferred clear analysis and persuasion. *Rouge et Noir* ran to just three editions, folding at the end of November. It turned out to be more a random review of Lissa's thinking than a comprehensive report on international socialism, but Marx did not miss the extent to which Lissagaray was now clearly influenced by his own thought. Perhaps the most entertaining items in the short-lived journal were the lampoons of contemporary politicians, including radical enthusiast Victor Hugo, spokesman of the Assembly, characterised as having a tongue like a Parisian running sluice.

Library's well-meaning but limited rhetoric and Lissa's generalised Marx-inspired Socialist sentiments in *Rouge et Noir* illuminate by contrast the sharp clarity of Tussy's political thought before the age of twenty. She saw the practical need for the journal. The French press she dismissed as 'thoroughly abject'[52] and useless,

That a socialistic movement is going on in Germany is a fact which the French people are quite ignorant of! It is necessary then for

France that some publication should take place in which the Social-istic movement in all countries will be spoken.[53]

Here is Tussy the ingrained internationalist, at nineteen. Here too in 1874 is Tussy making a brisk précis of the state of politics in England to her new frequent correspondent, Nathalie. The English worker movement is, she comments, at a complete standstill, overshadowed by the defeat of the Commune. Her visit to Germany, she tells Nathalie, has demonstrated to her what good work a repressive police force does 'to help our Cause'.[54] Revealing a strategic mindset of which the General would approve, Tussy expresses her great 'regret that the Prussian regime is not possible in England. It would do more than all the Trade Unions and Working Men's Societies put together to bring life into the movement here.'[55]

Depression overcome, appetite regained, engaged in matters of the world at large, Tussy had won the first round in the match with the Victorian feminine malady. Perhaps reflecting on Dr Garrett Anderson's role in her recovery, Tussy also told Nathalie about the launch of the first Medical School for Women, the initiative of Sophia Jex-Blake, supported by Garrett Anderson and Professor Huxley. Although, she observed, the Medical School would only help middle-class women, this was at least 'always something'.[56]

On her return to England in October, Tussy was in reflective mood on her recent past and immediate future. In the same missive she sent Nathalie a clipping from *The Times*: a personal advertise-ment from someone who, like Tussy and her eldest sister, sought to earn an independent living from teaching:

A young lady desires an engagement as governess. She can give good references and teaches German, French, music and drawing, learnt abroad. Terms six shillings a week.

Tussy wrote with the feeling of first-hand knowledge of how this advert demonstrated the absolutely 'horrible position of governesses'.[57] She had as examples her own recent experience and her eldest sister's miser-able servitude governessing to the Scottish Dr Monroe, who had summarily sacked her after three years' good service the instant 'he made the terrible discovery that I am the daughter of the petroleum chief who defended the iniquitous Communal movement'.[58]

By the end of 1874 both the Lafargues and the Longuets had moved back to London and were living nearby in Hampstead. Longuet got a job teaching French at King's College London and Jennychen secured a post at St Clement Danes Parochial School in central London. Jenny and Laura's marriages had got them out of their parental home but neither were happy seconded to the demands of motherhood and their husbands' careers.

For a few years Tussy's life had resembled that of the thwarted heroine of a Collins or Brontë novel. Now she was beginning to break the mould. She desisted from trying to beard her leonine father in his own den. She stopped asking for permission to continue with her liaison with Lissa and simply re-established the relationship in the open, daring anyone to challenge her directly.

Coming of age in the epoch of the Commune, encountering all its challenges and contradictions, Tussy was presented with alternative versions of femininity and the possibilities of the life of woman. As a general political event, the Commune was a failure, but as a gender event it was an extraordinary landmark in the history of the emancipation of women. Tussy teased and loosened the bonds of the struggling Victorian anti-heroine. Where she was going others could only follow or criticise. And without satisfactory role models in family, fact or fiction, she really didn't know the right direction herself.

Dogberries

'A slim attractive girl of the German type,' said the admiring Russian revolutionary Nikolai Alexandrovich Morozov, 'she reminded me of the romantic Gretchen, or Margaret, in Faust.'[1] The comparison with Goethe's tragic ingénue would make Tussy roar with laughter.

Morozov was just one of a large cast of colourful characters who visited the new Marx home at 41 Maitland Park Road, to where the family moved in March 1875. A new-build, four-storey, mid-terrace house just round the corner from their previous house, the rent was significantly cheaper. 'A very ordinary suburban villa' remarked Tussy's friend Marian Comyn. 'The charm of the household, however, was by no means ordinary.'[2] Another friend, the actress Virginia Bateman, thought it was 'a horrid little house'.[3] Maitland Park Road was convenient walking distance to Camden Chalk Farm station on the North London Line, which boasted a ladies waiting room on the bridge platform.

A cadre of Narodnaya Volya, the secret unit for revolutionary struggle against tsarist autocracy, Morozov was part of the combat team with Lev Hartmann and Sofya Perovskaya who in 1879 tried and failed to blow up Tsar Alexander II in his royal train. Morozov fled to France and was arrested when he returned to Russia in February 1881. A month later Narodnaya Volya tried again, and succeeded in assassinating Alexander in a mission led by Sofya Perovskaya. Tussy's interest was drawn to Russia's political upheaval and she contributed several articles on the subject to St James's Gazette.

As Comyn knew already and Morozov was about to discover, the unremarkable front door of the 'horrid little house' in fogbound, suburban London opened into a parallel universe. Tussy's friend Clara Collet described the crowded living room as 'full of people all talking French at the top of their voices most of whom were refugees from the crisis after the Paris Commune . . . a Frenchman told [me] that in the event of a revolution everyone in the room was under the sentence of death – presumably he excused himself from the sentiment.'[4] The Marxes at 41 Maitland Park Road became London's most homely radical bohemian salon between 1875 and 1883.

The day Morozov and Lev Hartmann first visited, London was enveloped in its notorious yellow fog. Lamps were lit in all the houses. Exiles under extradition orders, the men were potential terrorists against the British state. The constable tasked with tailing them had to loiter outside in the smoggy street whilst the subjects of his surveillance were pulled up cosily to the fire in Marx's study with coffee and Lenchen's home-made biscuits. Tussy welcomed and entertained them until Mohr returned from the British Museum. She switched to French when she noticed Morozov's hesitation with English. He noted her facility. Her much-improved French demonstrated the linguistic benefits of her liaison with Lissa.

Morozov remembered a detail: Marx's study lamp had a green shade that cast Tussy in soft light as she talked with them, sitting in her father's armchair, framed by the book-lined walls.[5] The effect of that green lampshade evoked Morozov's admiring comparisons of Eleanor with Goethe's Gretchen.

'The conversation,' Morozov recalls, 'was mainly on Narodnaya Volya matters, in which Karl and Eleanor showed a great interest. Marx said that he, like all other Europeans, imagined our struggle with autocracy as something fabulous, like a fantastic novel.'[6] It was a double-edged remark. Marx and Engels remained implacably opposed to terrorism and emphasised the necessity for a broad-based, representative, popular movement in Russia rather than Narodnaya Volya's clandestine, minority clique militia. Tussy, undecided on the question of armed struggle, was absorbed in the debate.

Morozov's comparison of Tussy with Goethe's famous heroine captures her aura: pan-European émigré citizen of the world. But

Tussy did not share Gretchen's preoccupation with counting petals on daisies or being hoodwinked into premarital pregnancies. Tussy turned her thoughts to the state of her nation and by extension her place within it: 'Who would think that in quiet respectable happy England millions of people are on the verge of starvation!'[7]

First-generation child of immigrant parents, British citizen, product of many cultures, by upbringing and temperament an internationalist, much travelled for her age, Tussy had grown into a metropolitan Londoner who batted for Britain in all its social and political struggles. During her twenties she became actively involved in the sharp edge of developing London education policy, the debate over Irish Home Rule, the evolution of the SPD (German Social Democratic Party), and the amnesty campaign for Communards. She wrote to Nathalie Liebknecht on New Year's Day of 1875, a fortnight before her twentieth birthday:

A kind of internal movement (strikes etc) never entirely ceased in England but John Bull has been accustomed for so long a while to behave himself that he goes the way he should go to an alarming extent . . . Not a day passed in which 'death from want' of some 'pauper' is not recorded. It passes all understanding how the thousands of men and women starving in the East End of London – and starving by the side of the greatest wealth and luxury – do not break forth into some wild struggle. Surely nothing could make their lot worse than it is now.[8]

International, national and local – given her background, father and predisposition, this was to be expected. When they moved to Maitland Park Road, Tussy, essence of radical Englishwoman alchemised with broad European cultural influences, became an equal draw to the Marx hearth with her father. Marian Comyn described the atmosphere:

I suppose it was Bohemian in its open-handed hospitality, its gracious welcome to strangers within its gates. And the strangers were numerous and shared the classic charm of great variety. There was one point of resemblance between them – for the most part they were impecunious. Shabby as to clothes, furtive in

movement, but interesting, always interesting...Dr Marx's
manners to his family were altogether delightful. A goodly number
had no doubt found their native land too hot to hold them – clever
conspirators to whom London was a chosen centre, political prisoners who had contrived to shake the shackles from their limbs,
young adventurers whose creed was of 'if-there's-a-government-
I'm-agen-it' order.[9]

Like many others Comyn was warmly invited to join the regular
Sunday open house at 41 Maitland Park Road. Tussy was at the helm
of these weekly 'At Homes'. An attempt to regularise the perpetual
flow of visitors whilst Mohr worked on his *Critique of the Gotha
Programme* and edited Lissagaray's *History of the Commune*, the
Sunday salons in effect just added to the house's bustling sociability.

Tussy wheedled Lenchen into preparing enough food for an inde-
terminate number of guests and Lenchen obliged with roasts, stews,
soups, dumplings and her renowned baking. 'Helen was an excellent
cook,' Comyn noted; as well as her German biscuits, 'her jam tarts
are a sweet and abiding memory to this day.'[10] Helen served the meal
in 'the semi-basement dining-room' and it 'seemed to be going on
more or less all the Sabbath day'.[11] All who joined the Marx At
Homes knew Lenchen, in her signature gold earrings and chenille
hairnet. Her kitchen was adjacent to the dining room – and her opinions were shared equally in dining room and kitchen. There was no
upstairs downstairs in the Marx family home. Lenchen 'reserved to
herself the right of speaking her mind, even to the august doctor. Her
mind was respectfully, even meekly, received by all the family, except
Eleanor, who frequently challenged it.'[12]

Eleanor stayed in London during the summer of 1875 whilst Mohr
once again took the sulphurous waters of Karlsbad and Möhme an
extended break in Lausanne until September. Whilst they were away
Lissa visited daily, or more to the point, nearly every evening, under
Lenchen's benevolent eye. She had facilitated the secret engagement
between Marx and Jenny in their youth and now obliged Tussy and
Lissa the same way.

Tussy's sexual relationship with Lissagaray raises the question of
her use of contraception. By the 1870s numerous birth control

devices were available for over-the-counter purchase in English pharmacies, including rubber condoms, diaphragms, chemical suppositories, vaginal sponges and medicated tampons. Contraception was advertised widely, in allusive language and images the implications of which were quite clear to the general public. Literate and urban, Eleanor had ample opportunity to take necessary measures; she also had an older, experienced partner who did not want children until he'd published his history of the Paris Commune.

Throughout the summer of 1875 Lissa toiled on his book. Tussy was his principal researcher, writing to Karl Hirsch with requests for facts from Paris on the final playing-out of the Commune. Frustrated about indefinite exile, Lissa's levity and brio slipped away into an overly solemn moodiness. 'Youth must be earnest and austere rather than light-hearted, for we have no time left to be young.'[13] This new fogeyishness unsettled and upset Tussy but she shoved her anxieties to the back of her mind, put Lissa's stress down to his book deadline and chivvied him along.

Karl Hirsch scrupulously supplied all the information Tussy requested on the Commune. Overscrupulously. As his correspondence with her demonstrates, Hirsch had fallen for Tussy at his first meeting with her in London in October 1875, shortly after his release from prison in Germany. Journalist and career politician, editor of a number of Social Democratic newspapers, Hirsch was a patient pragmatist, and not about to declare himself to Tussy and confront Lissagaray head on. Wisely, given the latter's willingness for armed combat. Hirsch committed himself to the longer game, setting about so formal and insinuating a courtship that Tussy was the last to recognise it. To her, Hirsch was a generous friend and charming correspondent with whom she loved discussing art and politics. Jennychen, more astute about the ulterior motives of 'the *unamoured* Hirsch',[14] dropped heavy hints to her little sister, who missed them all. Knowing herself to be any man's equal, Tussy's behaviour – regardless of age or station – was airily unencumbered by the social inhibitions of ladylikeness. Drawn to her flame, many men and women pined for Tussy at this stage of her life. Focused on Lissa, she let most of this attention pass her by completely.

Tussy's correspondence with Hirsch after he returned to Paris was concerned chiefly with French politics and the campaign for amnesty for the Communards, a subject close to her heart. She was sure that resolution on this issue would restore Lissa to his former self. Tussy and Hirsch wrote to each other in French. Writing in May 1876, Tussy supposes that Hirsch is very much occupied with the amnesty in Paris: 'At any rate the newspapers start talking about it. At last we shall know shortly who will be able to return to France. For I think the Assembly will be forced to give fairly numerous pardons.'[15] Her over-optimism was raised by the regime change in France over the winter of 1875–6, replacing the Conservative National Assembly with a Republican Chamber of Deputies that introduced the bill for full amnesty for the Communards. Kicked out of both chambers soon after Eleanor wrote this letter, the introduction of the bill nevertheless served to put the debate about peace and reconciliation with the former Communard rebels on the agenda.

Meanwhile Hirsch reflected on how he might secure an advantage in his attempt to win Tussy. Her twenty-first birthday offered the perfect opportunity.

He sent her a carton of cigarettes, mailed with a warm note congratulating her on her majority. Thanks to the police dutifully intercepting all their correspondence, we know that it was Hirsch who first introduced and supplied Tussy with the luxurious modern convenience of ready-made cigarettes to which she became as pestiferously addicted as her father to his cheap cigars. Up until now Tussy, like most people, had bought loose tobacco and papers and rolled her own. She was delighted, and thanked Hirsch fulsomely, who followed up just a few months later with another, even more successful present: a fashionable pair of pince-nez in the latest design.

A style of spectacles supported without earpieces, by pinching (*pincer*) the bridge of the nose (*nez*), pince-nez had been around since the 1500s. Developments in the engineering of lightweight steel and the manufacture of thinner glass during industrialisation made possible lighter, far more comfortable pince-nez that reached their height of popularity in the late 1800s. The styles were unisex and were carried in a snap-case or, for women, clipped to a muff-chain worn around the neck or attached to a customised hairpin. For Tussy's unruly hair, a hairpin was too fussy. She attached her pince-nez to a long, flat-link, pinchbeck chain, which can be seen in photographs taken from this period and ever after.

The pince-nez from Hirsch had a hard bridge that fitted her Marxian nose perfectly. The lenses weren't right, but she had them changed by a Soho optometrist and wrote to Hirsch, wearing his gift, expressing her gratitude and delight. Hirsch was quietly pleased to know he was providing her with practical comforts that Lissa had not thought about. The shortsightedness that she had developed in recent years was now much relieved by this superior German eyewear. Tussy, despite the dramatic improvement in the quality of her vision thanks to her new pince-nez, still failed to notice that Hirsch's attentiveness signified anything other than comradely friendship.

Ready-made cigarettes and the very latest pince-nez were amongst a host of new innovations and time-saving devices Tussy embraced with unhesitating enthusiasm. She was an early adopter of any practical technology that reduced or removed labour from domestic work and leisure. She ticked off her friend Marian Comyn when she dropped by unexpectedly to reclaim a book she had loaned her and discovered her, needle in hand, with the book on the table beside her – unfinished:

> This lapse was to her an indication of mental, if not moral, ineptitude, and she expressed her opinion with dramatic vigour. Upon the ladylike accomplishments of Victorian days she poured vials of contemptuous wrath. 'Fancy work' she scorned; plain sewing she looked upon as superfluous in view of the permanence of sewing machines.[16]

For Tussy was now an ardent enthusiast for theatre work not fancy work, and it was literary circles, not sewing circles, that were uppermost in her attentions.

'Since August 1877 the Dogberry Club has been established,'[17] Clara Collet recorded in her diary. Clara and Tussy were childhood friends. Their families became acquainted at the beginning of the 1870s when Marx started contributing to *The Free Press: A Diplomatic*

Review, founded and edited by Clara's father Collet Dobson Collet.[18] Tussy and Clara met at the Collet home in Hornsey Lane, Crouch End, and liked each other immediately. Clara remembered vividly this first meeting, where she was dazzled by Tussy's energy and 'frock of blue merino trimmed with white swan's down'.[19] The parents had a play-reading in the downstairs parlour whilst the girls roamed 'throughout the entire upper rooms of the house'.[20] Tussy made Clara's own home an adventure for her.

Seven years later, the two of them co-founded the Dogberry Club, dedicated to play-reading and all other thespian and cultural activities relating to Shakespeare. Named after Mr Dogberry, the self-important, egotistical constable in *Much Ado About Nothing* who fabulously misuses the English language, it was a cheekily apt title for a group of young British radicals who disapproved of the undemocratic monarchist state of England whose claim to authority they held in little regard. Like much else that happened at Maitland Park Road, the Dogberry meetings were under surveillance by Scotland Yard. There's nice wit in naming a Shakespeare reading club in honour of the hapless constable detectives who had to waste their time monitoring its membership and activities.

The original Dogberry-ites consisted of family and friends – including dramatists Edward Rose and Israel Zangwill, and actresses Theodora Wright and Virginia Bateman. Engels, Sir Henry Juta, and Eleanor and Clara's parents made up the regular adult cohort, augmented by passing visitors.[21]

As we know already, Tussy's love of Shakespeare took root in childhood. Now the family passion for 'the bible of our house, seldom out of our hands or mouths',[22] came in for a revival. Tussy was the leading spirit of the Dogberry-ites. She organised fortnightly play readings at Maitland Park Road, and outings to Henry Irving's premieres at the Lyceum Theatre.

Henry Irving was the stagename of John Brodribb, born in Somerset to a travelling salesman and a fire-and-brimstone Methodist mother who never forgave him a minute of the immoral damnation of his life on the stage.[23] Irving studied at commercial college and had no background in theatre but he went on to make himself the most successful celebrity actor-manager of the nineteenth-century English stage. Self-made, Irving demonstrated that the theatre was a professional world in which people could succeed regardless of where they came from.

Until Irving's sensationally successful *Hamlet* in October 1874, Shakespeare productions had long been box office poison.[24] Irving reinvented the idiom of Shakespearean performance. His new interpretations made the bard popular again with mid-Victorian audiences. Critics panned Irving's version of *Hamlet* for breaking with the traditional declamatory tradition of Shakespearean performance. Tussy and her parents pitched in vociferously on Irving's side in the press controversy over his modern, radical interpretation that followed the new psychological, humanising approach introduced by American actor Edwin Booth. Alfred Tennyson praised Irving for portraying the Prince of Denmark's 'method in his madness as well as the madness in his method'.[25] Irving's groundbreaking *Hamlet* in 1874 and *Macbeth* the following September rekindled Tussy's childhood Shakespeare mania and set her on the path towards a life in theatre. Or so she began to dream.

On opening nights the front row of the Dress Circle at the Lyceum was reserved for the Dogberries – a notable concession, given that it was London's leading theatre under Irving's management. Tussy probably secured the favour through Virginia Bateman, a Dogberry whose parents had managed the Lyceum prior to Irving. Virginia, stage name Virginia Francis, was the youngest of the four Bateman sisters, who were all actresses. Tussy, she recalled, was most anxious to make her take Shakespeare seriously.[26]

On one of these first club outings Tussy presented Irving with a laurel wreath on behalf of the Dogberries. He stagily kissed her hand in thanks. As Mr Dogberry might have remarked on seeing the rebel daughter of socialism introduced to the rags-to-riches superstar actor from humble origins in the achingly fashionable Lyceum, 'Our watch, sir, have indeed comprehended two auspicious persons.'

Following the move to Maitland Park Road, Möhme began to feel tired and beset by continuous niggling ailments. To try and cheer her, Eleanor encouraged her mother to go to the theatre often and to write reviews on Shakespeare that Hirsch published in the *Frankfurter Zeitung* at her request:

Mr Irving . . . interests us very much (although we do not know him personally) firstly because he is a man of rare talent and secondly because all the English press, in consequence of the most miserable intrigues, set itself furiously against him and has got up a cabal.[27]

Reinvigorated by her new 'writing mania', Möhme wrote several other reviews as well as a round-up report on the London theatre season of 1876, all of which were placed by Tussy and published by the *Frankfurter Zeitung*.[28] Mohr was content to take a supporting role in the Marx family Shakespeare revival. He encouraged Tussy's enthusiasm, sensing that it gave her a platform of her own to build on and a means of integrating with the culture of her birth. He rarely went out at night these days, and the Dogberries provided home entertainment. 'He never read a part', Marian Comyn observed,

. . . which, for the sake of the play, was perhaps quite as well, for he had a guttural voice and a decided German accent. He was interested in talking of Shakespeare's popularity in Germany and of how it had come about; Eleanor always maintained that the German dramatic ideal approximated much more closely to the English than the French, and waxed eloquent over Lessing and Wieland, who had done so much to make Shakespeare known in their own country.[29]

It wasn't all so highbrow. When the Dogberry-ites had finished their serious reading they played games and pastimes such as charades and the traditional English rhyming game of dumb-crambo – to the delight of Marx and Engels, who always entered into the spirit of any fun that was going on and laughed until the tears ran down their cheeks at anything comic, 'the oldest in years, but in spirit as young as any of us'.[30]

During this period Eleanor also got involved in more academic Shakespeare studies. She joined the New Shakespeare Society, established in 1874 by the philologist and early-English text scholar Frederick James Furnivall.

Furnivall was an interesting character who made an enormous contribution to founding the discipline of studying English literature. A free-thinking agnostic of strong Christian Socialist leanings, Furnivall had taught grammar and literature at the Working Men's College. He headed up the preliminary work on the *New Oxford English Dictionary*, a project of which he was editor. The *Concise Oxford Dictionary* was his idea, formulated when he realised that the *New OED* was going to be a lifetime labour. Furnivall was committed to both worker education and higher education for women. He also hugely enjoyed messing about in boats. One of his most charming projects was to organise a Ladies Rowing Club on the Thames for Harrods 'shop girls'.

The New Shakespeare Society gathered weekly at University College. Eleanor attended her first meeting in May 1876. Furnivall was unapologetic about the cultural nationalist intentions of his Shakespeare society. His opening speech reminded those present that it was 'the duty of Englishmen to study Shakespere [*sic*]' and that in his opinion it was both 'humiliating and lamentable' that 'not one in 20 – or shall we say 20,000' Englishmen had a 'real notion of the greatest author in the world'.[31] In joining Furnivall's society, Tussy was getting involved in emerging definitions of Englishness and the forging of 'English literature' as a subject of scholarly study.

When Marx arrived in England, he taught himself English by making systematic classifications of Shakespeare's original phrases that he then learnt by heart; in turn, he passed them on to Tussy, who absorbed them as part of her immigrant cultural inheritance. Now Tussy, in her turn, pitched herself into debate and textual investigation in a society dedicated to promoting the primacy of Shakespeare as purveyor of English, the greatest theatrical and poetic language in the world.

Eleanor volunteered to translate a hefty German essay by German philosopher Nikolaus Delius, a professor from Bonn University, on the epic element in Shakespeare's dramas, and was commended in the society minutes for her work. The society records of Eleanor's contributions demonstrate her particular interest in Shakespeare's representation of women characters and the relations between the sexes. She objects to John Ruskin's suggestion that Cordelia could not have been beautiful, for if she had been she would 'never have been so wilfully misunderstood'. Tussy, demonstrating a much firmer grip on female psychology, retorts that 'Cordelia must have been beautiful, or else her sisters would not have hated her so.'[32] Furnivall recognised that it was an advantage to have women in the society, because they identified fresh aspects of Shakespeare's work, particularly interpretations of his female characters, 'many points of which were new to him'.[33]

Furnivall had a gift for the light touch required to bring people excluded from higher education into learning contexts where they could feel comfortable with 'high culture' and ideas. His informal tea-and-buns gatherings in the ABC teashop in Bloomsbury, regularly attended by Eleanor, were a magnet for a diversity of people barred by class, gender, faith or atheism from the universities.

Even if they had been able to enter higher education, young women like Tussy could not study English literature and its illustrious history as a subject – because it did not yet exist. Furnivall and his followers, of whom Eleanor was amongst the most active, played the leading role in establishing the vernacular English literature as a subject worthy of scholarship and study, making a humanities education accessible.

Furnivall began by launching the Early English Text Society in 1864, followed by the Chaucer Society in 1868, the New Shakespeare Society in 1873 and the Sunday Shakespeare Society in 1874. The Browning and Shelley societies followed in 1881 and 1886 respectively. He was dedicated to promoting the production of reliable Shakespeare texts, drawing on his specialism in philology. In an age where there was as yet no concept of the study of English literature as a discipline in universities, Furnivall was a pioneer.

After 1876 Eleanor was active in all of these societies and started to do scholarly research directly for Furnivall, with whom she became friends. Disbarred by her sex from taking a degree from an English university, research work was, as for her female contemporaries, the only route to literary scholarship available to her. In this way Tussy effectively made up a university degree for herself, earning money along the way. She was, thanks to cutting her teeth with her father, a dedicated and tireless researcher of steamrolling efficiency who could gut and précis even the most mellifluous arguments on paper with clarity and economy.

Though she worked hard at them, these autodidactic studies were a subplot to the main theme: Tussy's key interest, to which her academic work was an adjunct, was in the craft and performance of theatre. Acting seemed to offer the possibility of exploring and defining her life beyond the narrow options of teaching, governessing or acting as handmaiden to Lissagaray's increasingly self-absorbed intellectual endeavours. The stage beckoned.

The Only Lady Candidate

In September 1878, Eleanor stood at Engels's side in Kensal Green Cemetery at the funeral of her 'Auntie' Lizzy Burns. The General was now bereft of both beloved Burns sisters and Eleanor had lost one of her most important mentors and friends. Lizzy and the General had lived together happily in unmarried amity since the death of Lizzy's sister Mary in 1863. Engels married Lizzy the night before she died, 'to please her . . . on her death bed', as Tussy put it. For her, 'Auntie's'[1] departure was loss of kin. Lizzy's great legacies to Tussy were inculcating her understanding of Irish politics and history and the urgency of the need to free women – economically, socially and sexually.

Lizzy and Möhme had become particularly close during recent years, drawn together by illness, menopause and a shared understanding of the oppression of women. Möhme reflected frankly on the difference between her and Lizzy's lives and those of their much-loved men:

> In all these battles we women have to bear the hardest, i.e. pettiest, part. In the battle with the world the man gets stronger, stronger too in the face of enemies, even if their number is legion; we sit at home and darn socks. That does not banish the worries, and little daily cares slowly gnaw away the courage to face life. I am talking from more than 30 years experience. I can say that I did not give up

courage easily. But I have grown too old to have much hope, and the last unfortunate events have shocked me greatly. I am afraid that we, we older ones, won't live to see many good things.[2]

Tussy was determined to escape this pettiest part. The start of her struggle to escape the predestination of playing the woman's part had already caused her desperation, frustrated rage, eating disorders and near breakdown, experiences she shared with many women of her generation.

Lizzy's death brought home to Tussy how the people she grew up with worked tirelessly for goals and values unlikely to be realised during their lifetimes. Her parents and Engels and Lizzy had come of age in the more revolutionary, optimistic era of the 1840s. Tussy's radical stance on Ireland owed much to what she had learned first-hand from Lizzy Burns. She followed closely the escalation in tension in the struggle for Irish Home Rule in the late 1870s, intensified by the effects of the slump in trade and agriculture. In 1879 the Irish National Land League was founded, with the aims of abolishing landlordism and improving conditions for impoverished tenant farmers. The government responded to the formation of the Land League with draconian repression, arresting leaders and gagging freedom of speech. Tussy wrote to Jennychen:

Never . . . even in '67 during the Fenian rising – has the government tried so hard to drive the people into a revolt. Therein lies the great danger – for an open rising would be crushed and the movement thrown back years. Notice the conduct of the police in Dublin, Limerick etc. It is simply outrageous. If only the people will keep firm but quiet the government will find its hands full.[3]

She's one to talk about keeping quiet. Earlier in the year Tussy joined a demonstration outside Bow Street Magistrates Court, where the arrested Land League leader Michael Davitt – the League's Irish republican founder – was detained in a holding cell. Showing no sign of 'keeping firm but quiet', she asked a policeman 'with a very hibernian countenance' if Davitt was still inside:

'No,' said he, 'it's meself put him in the van.' From his brogue I of course knew the man was Irish, so, as our American cousins say, I 'went for him.' I asked him if there weren't enough English-men to do such dirty work that an Irishman must help 'put in the van' a man who like Davitt had done so much for his country etc etc. Some other policemen present scowled at me, but said nothing.[4]

The prerogative at stake was the freedom of the British subject. In 1881 Gladstone's new cabinet implemented the Coercion Act, suspending habeas corpus in Ireland. Tussy deplored this restraint on freedom of expression, as she expressed to Library:

> After all, Library, we English people are thorough. Let Bismarck do what he will, even in his own field of despotism we beat him! . . . In utter meanness too I think we can – to say the least of it – hold our own. As an act of cowardly retaliation and petty spite the arrest of Michael Davitt is unparalleled. The House of Commons too is now most effectively gagged, and liberty of speech is a thing of the past . . . The English workmen – than whom (between you and me) a worse crew does not exist – even are beginning to think that Gladstone is 'coming it strong' – as a Yankee would say – and they are beginning to hold meetings all over London and the provinces to protest against the Irish Bill.[5]

Resistance to the Irish Coercion Act by working-class people inten-sified the mobilisation of radical British forces for democratic electoral representation – of working men. From the early 1880s a wide range of efforts were made to set up a social democratic party in England. Two workers from the London Trades Council launched a paper, the *Labour Standard*, to support the call for an independent working men's party, to which Engels contributed leading articles. Youthful Edinburgh socialist Robert Banner, acquainted with Marx and Engels, and disillusioned by the see-saw policy of reformist trade unions, became convinced the union route would never settle the labour question and turned his energies to founding the Scottish Labour Party.

In 1880 Tussy was invited, along with Marx, to dinner at the plush house of wealthy financier Henry Hyndman in Devonshire Street, Portland Place. Hyndman wanted to establish a new party for the direct representation of labour and, in March 1881, held a conference in London aimed at setting up this 'New Party'. Hyndman's stated intention was to launch 'a really democratic party in opposition to the monstrous tyranny of Mr Gladstone and his Whigs in Ireland and their equally abominable policy in Egypt, with the object of bringing about democratic changes in England'.[6] Hyndman and his wife Miranda, who Marx liked except for her adulatory attitude to her husband, became frequent though uninvited visitors to Maitland Park Road, and Marx complained of being 'invaded' by them.[7]

Tussy shared her father and Engels's scepticism about Hyndman. His Eton and Cambridge background and soft liberalism were not the cause of their objections; rather it was his determination to try and expunge the class struggle from the socialist movement. 'When the International was founded,' Marx and Engels wrote:

> we explicitly formulated the battle cry: The emancipation of the working classes must be brought about by the working classes themselves. We cannot therefore associate ourselves with people who openly state that the workers are too uneducated to emancipate themselves and must be freed from above by philanthropic big bourgeois and petty bourgeois . . . for which purpose the working-class must place itself under the leadership of the 'educated and propertied bourgeois' who alone possess the time and opportunity to acquaint themselves with what is good for the workers.[8]

Paternalistic down to his handmade Jermyn Street silk socks, Hyndman paid lip service to the essential need for grass-roots organisation, but in reality propagated what he saw as the necessity for a bourgeois elite:

> . . . that the emancipation of the workers must be brought about by the workers themselves is true in the sense that we cannot have Socialism without Socialists . . . But a slave cannot be freed by the

slaves themselves. The leadership, the initiative, the teaching, the organisation must come from those who are born into a different position and are trained to use their faculties in early life.[9]

There were several dinner discussions at Portland Place and repeated invasions of Maitland Park Road by the Hyndmans. Tussy reported to Jennychen a few months later, 'we've not heard much more about the newest "New Party", but I don't think it will come to much.'[10]

She was wrong. Two months later Hyndman launched the party of Democratic Federation, regarded to this day as one of the foundation stones of the late-nineteenth-century English socialist revival. His manifesto, 'England for All', bowdlerised two chapters of *Capital* without attribution or permission of its author and added numerous mistakes, but this was much in the way of things for political philosophers and was to be expected. The cause of the rift was Hyndman's betrayal of Marx and Engels's principle that democracy could only be brought about by broad-based grass-roots organisation from the ground up: the slaves must freed by the slaves themselves.

The Hyndmans were banned from Maitland Park Road and further dinner invitations to Portland Place declined. Tussy, still acting as her father's correspondence secretary, had to run the crossfire of these skirmishes between Marx and those allied to the Democratic Federation who tried to sidestep the central argument of *Capital* about the need for ground-up struggle. She dutifully composed calm letters summarising concisely the grounds of Marx's objections,[11] such as to the Scottish barrister, ethnographer and historian John Stuart Glennie, another person who wholly missed the point of *Capital*. Glennie wrote complainingly to Tussy, 'You say, "His only objection to your book rests on your treatment of his scientific theories." But, the special theories of Dr Marx's great work on *Capital* I have not treated at all.'[12] Precisely: 'not treated at all'.[13]

Hyndman and Glennie shared with many other well-educated liberal British men the bizarre view that democracy would be created if only working men were enfranchised and directly represented. Eleanor saw this for the nonsense it was. From her mid-twenties she started to question and challenge the exclusionary focus and insistence *only* on the rights of working men, not women, as the first step of socialist organisation in England.

This is the juncture at which Tussy's artistic and cultural pursuits forge the metal of her own worldview, which already included the more than half of the world that are women. Socialism for one sex didn't add up. It was as absurd as the notion of socialism in one country. Tussy had learned this from the example of the Commune. For all its other failings, the Commune maintained the centrality of women's emancipation as a necessary precondition of democracy.

Eleanor had before her the examples of the role of women in the Irish struggle, the International, the Commune and the early Russian revolutionary movement. Lizzy, Eleanor and Jennychen were the strongest Fenians in the family. Marx and Engels supported the Irish republican cause, but not the tactics. Lizzy and Eleanor were more ambivalent. Tussy wrote two articles about the Russian revolutionary movement for *Progress* in 1883, which illustrate that she was thinking about the uses of armed violence.[14] This analysis applied equally to her attitude to the emancipation of women as a class and to the Fenians and Russian revolutionaries.

Her father and the General were unbending in their opposition to the resort to terrorism under any circumstances; Tussy was not so sure. Was this just the impatience of hot-headed youth or did being a disenfranchised, second-class citizen give her, like Lizzy, a different perspective that eluded Mohr and the General's born entitlement as men?

Closer to home, she had also the local, familial examples of her mother, her sisters, Lenchen and Lizzy – all of whom, as they matured, became more self-critical and angry about how they'd allowed themselves to be short-changed by their political, intellectual men; and all of whom in their different ways expressed feelings of unfulfilment and disappointment.

Her sisters, the next generation, were now treading the same path as their mother. Jenny and Laura were clever, capable and talented women enchanted by charming, likeable, liberal Bluebeards who lassoed their desire with babies, domestic drudgery and censorious in-laws. Laura and Paul had three children, who, despite their tremendous care and effort, all died tragically in childhood. As a consequence Paul lost his faith in medicine, his chosen profession, and tried to earn his living as an engraver and photo-lithographer.[15] To empathise with Laura and Paul as they grew older, Tussy always had to remember that they had made and lost a family in the early years of their marriage.

Laura was bright and gregarious but could settle for pragmatic self-preservation. But Jennychen possessed a truly brilliant and original mind and, under different historical circumstances, would have made a distinguished businesswoman, politician, newspaper editor, publisher or economist. As it was, rose-tinted romance cost her her liberty and career. In the early days of her marriage to Longuet Jennychen believed, like her mother before her, that she could have both marriage and a career. Once children and the responsibility of running the household arrived, she discovered that, like her mother before her, she could not.

In the breathless early days of their falling in love, Jennychen threw down her bluestocking cap and lovingly invited the charming Longuet to tame her shrew. Teaching in Oxford, Longuet was depressed and 'ill at ease' in the 'small world of . . . hopelessly dull . . . English university men and professorial shopkeepers'.[16] Bolstering his self-confidence and gently stroking his ego, Jennychen foolishly assured him that 'you deserve the title of man of letters more than I do bluestocking.'[17] Marriage, babies and ten years later, Jennychen's letters to her sisters tell a different story. She now rues her mistake in succumbing to romance and marrying an indigent charmer, full of fascination with himself to the exclusion of all others. Where once Jennychen was happy to send Longuet her own money and tell him how wonderful he was, she now longed for the independence of her single life. She'd given birth to two more babies in prompt succession, Harry (Harra) in July 1878 and Edgar Marcel (Wolf) in April 1879. 'Those blessed babies,' Jennychen confides to Laura from rural France:

> . . . though really charming good-tempered little fellows, put such a strain on my nervous system by day and night that I often long for no matter what release from this ceaseless round of nursing, and think with a pang of the dark underground, to

Farringdon Street, where when I was not stifling with asthma, I could at least indulge in my morning daily, and on alighting could run down the muddy Strand and stare at the advertisements, which I miss more than I can say in this Argenteuil waste, where I hear and see nothing but the baker and butcher and cheesemonger and greengrocer. I do believe that even the dull routine of factory work is not more killing than are the endless duties of the ménage. To me at least, this is and always has been so. Some women I know, such as Mrs Lormier for instance, glory in this home drudgery – but we are not all made of the same stuff. You have always accused me of being somewhat of a misanthropist – now I have lost all my animal spirits – man delights not me nor woman either.[18]

With no immediate positive examples on which to model herself, Tussy nevertheless refused to contemplate a future of, in her mother's words, bearing the pettiest part, sitting at home and darning socks. She wanted to get stronger and be free. Men delighted her, and women too.

In 1876, the year before she formally joined the New Shakespeare Society, Tussy fought the first round in her lifelong battle for women's and worker education, representation and participation. For the London School Board election in November 1876 she joined the campaign for Alice Westlake, standing for the Marylebone division. Marylebone was Elizabeth Garrett Anderson's former seat, and she introduced Tussy to Alice Westlake as her chosen successor. Westlake, an artist whose work was exhibited at the Royal Academy and the Paris Salon, signed John Stuart Mill's women's suffrage petition in 1866 and was closely involved in Garrett Anderson's hospital for women. Garrett Anderson persuaded Westlake to stand for her seat, as did her husband John Westlake QC, founder of the Working Men's College, where Furnivall taught.

Marylebone was London's largest metropolitan division and, as was widely reported in the press, Westlake 'The Only Lady Candidate'. 'The Only Radical Candidate' in the entire London School Board elections, also standing in the Marylebone constituency, was Maltman Barry, a close family friend of the Marxes whom Tussy knew well from her father's early International days. Barry was a good journalist but a poor politician, little suited to leadership.

Tussy made an unhesitating choice to support the only woman candidate over the only male radical, disappointing Barry, who also approached her to help with his campaign. Tussy explains to Hirsch that Alice Westlake, 'though bourgeois at heart like almost all Englishwomen is at least very much of a freethinker and is in any case worthier than the men who offer themselves as candidates'.[19] 'Our aim,' she tells Hirsch, 'is above all to work against the self-styled Church Party who want absolutely to abolish compulsory instruction.'[20] This is tendentious: Westlake's stated policy was not, in fact, freethinking on religious instruction in compulsory education; but it's true she was very clearly the best of the seven constituency candidates and a woman to boot. The tone of Tussy's instinctive meritocracy and feminism ring clear: she ignores class, disregards family allegiance and pitches for the best candidate. The slaves will be freed by the slaves themselves.

She signed up at the Westlake campaign headquarters at 157 Camden Road and quickly proved herself a champion door-to-door canvasser. Her first real grass-roots activism, it was a terrific blooding in London politics and an eye-opener. 'You cannot imagine,' she marvels to the admiring Hirsch, 'the strange things which I see and hear':

> In one house they ask that religion above all other things should be taught – in another house I am told 'education is the curse of the country' and 'education will be our ruin' etc. Finally it is amusing but also sad now and then when you go to the house of a working man who tells you that he wants to 'consult his boss' first.[21]

Westlake carried the day, polling 20,231 votes, and Tussy came out clearly on the side of women's entry into public office. Westlake held the seat until 1888 and did a very good job. By 1882 she was on the Central Committee of the National Society for Women's Suffrage, and remained an active suffragette for the rest of her life.

Tussy's uncompromising act of feminist independence in striking out from men-only radicalism and the silliness of the notion of socialism in one gender impressed the General, the only member of the extended family who practised free love as well as preaching it. He knew very well that the struggles for political change so far fell woefully short of his own theorisations in *Origins of Private Property, Family and the State*. Now Tussy, as steeped in this great attempt to analyse the gendered basis of history and economics as she was in her father's *Capital*, was putting the theories to practical test. 'When we take power,' Engels remarked to a friend about Tussy's participation in the campaign, 'not only will women vote, but they will be voted for and make speeches, which last has already come to pass on the London School Boards . . . the ladies on these School Boards distinguish themselves by talking very little and working very hard, each of them doing on average as much as three men.'[22]

Tussy, Engels would acknowledge, worked very hard and now did the work of three or more men – although she also talked a great deal. On 22 October 1877 she registered for her first Reader's Ticket at the Reading Room of the British Museum. 'My whole day is taken up with work at the Museum,' she told Hirsch.[23] Eduard Bernstein met her at this time and recalled her combination of vivacity and labour, 'a lively young girl of slender build with beautiful black hair and fine dark eyes . . . At that time she was already working hard at the British Museum partly for her father, partly "devilling" that is, taking excerpts or doing research for a pittance to save well-to-do people who wanted to write books the trouble of looking things up for themselves.'[24] Bernstein was to play a pivotal role in Tussy's adult life. Born in 1850, the son of a Jewish railway engineer, Bernstein famously formulated evolutionary socialism and became a key founder and leader of the German Social Democratic Party (SPD).

Eleanor refused to take an allowance or any money from Engels, whereas Jennychen and Laura depended on him to support their husbands and families. His support was willingly and freely given – he had no children and regarded Marx's as his own – and Tussy was always welcome to her portion. But she didn't want money she hadn't earned.

Socialist feminist activist, intellectual, budding woman of letters, secretly aspiring actress, Tussy also shouldered the concurrent responsibilities of a parental carer, secretary, unpaid nanny to her nephews and Lissa's dutiful, unpaid researcher. She also encouraged and supported him through his trauma of surviving the Commune, which became more pronounced as time went on. She knew exactly the female feat of acting in a supporting role in family and personal life.

Tussy's sprint away from the dangers of imprisonment as a Victorian angel of the house drove her towards the composite, contested lifestyle of the New Woman. Unmarried and childless, Tussy was exposed to the dependency of her ageing parents and to being nanny to her sister's children. It was the dilemma of every woman of her ilk. To fulfil her aspirations for a life as an artist and activist, intellectual and community leader, she needed to learn how to murder the self-sacrificing, eternally good, dutiful, boiling with resentment, angelic youngest daughter. This is not to praise Tussy for some kind of multi-tasking heroism for her capacity to cope with competing responsibilities, but rather to raise the alert on the multiple pressures bearing down on her: pressures that brought stress, neurosis and nervous breakdown.

More important for Tussy than the drama of her personal struggle between duty and independence was the knowledge this brought of the pinched narrowness of the majority of middle-class women's lives, confined solely within the suffocating walls of domesticity. And so within her own family Tussy found herself at the crossroads of the opposition between the two socialisms that shaped the history of the British left: one prioritising the liberation of women from the get-go, the other seeking first the freedom of the people, from which definition women were, apparently, excluded. To Tussy's way of thinking, this was an illogical dichotomy and against natural justice. Either men and women both are free, or no one is.

However, she didn't only sit in the British Museum Reading Room analysing this dilemma. She lived it. Her working life and self-education progressed at a brisk rate, but her relationship with her family revolved in a continuous loop of companionship, care, duty and conscientious obligation. Being nice to children, nice to her parents, supporting the intellectual work of both her father and fiancé: the repetitive cycle of the one impeded the development of the full potential of the other. Tussy wanted, always, to 'Go ahead!' But in order to do this she had to take unthinkable action and abandon her family. This was not in her nature. She wouldn't be free unless they abandoned her. And that was not in *their* nature.

She knew now that it was only life outside her family that could lead to the opportunities for her to play unlived parts and explore her unimagined selves. Making a new family with Lissa would simply replace one form of captivity with another. Duty, genuine love and bewilderment at how to break free tethered her to the monotonous calls of domestic life. Loving others better than she loved herself was emerging as one of Tussy's key failings; by contradiction, it is also one of the characteristics that made her so human and likeable.

Throughout her twenties she continued to accompany her parents on their annual rest and recuperation cures and mini-holidays, together and separately. There was a return with her father to Karlsbad in August 1876, their twenty-eight-hour journey dogged by unanticipated adventures caused by the world premiere of Richard Wagner's *Ring of the Nibelung* from 13 to 17 August at his Bayreuth Festspielhaus, which drew audiences from around the world. Miss and Dr Marx must have been the only travellers to the region not clamouring for tickets to this fest of what Möhme described as 'Siegfrieds, Valkyries and Götterdämmerung heroes',[25] hogging every bed in the town and surroundings, and making it impossible for them to find accommodation en route to Karlsbad. Once they were there, the daily routine of water-drinking was the repetitious order of the day.

'Before continuing,' Tussy wrote to her mother from the Hotel Germania,

> I must however remind you how proverbially stupid one gets at Karlsbad – so don't be surprised if I seem rather incoherent. We go through exactly the same routine that you have heard me speak of so often . . . You cannot imagine how the time goes doing nothing.

What with drinking and eating, and walking, it is bedtime before one has well managed even to commence a letter.[26]

Tussy spiced the stupefying leisure with idle anthropological observation and gossiping about the state of other visitors' marriages and financial affairs, remarking, 'There are as many Jews as ever, and more anxious than ever to get as much water as possible. Still, an American has outdone them. He came to Karlsbad but being unable to stay more than two days took forty-two glasses a day! It's a marvel he didn't die of it.'[27]

The 'very witty' and hardworking young Dr Ferdinand Fleckles supplied much of this gossip. Tussy took a great shine to Fleckles and he, enraptured, endeavoured to spend as much time as he could in her company. Marx liked Fleckles, and encouraged Tussy's dalliance with this bright, light-hearted, youthful (German) doctor, a tonic after the now existentially tortured and world-weary (French) Lissagaray.

Tussy and Ferdinand must have been pleased when she conveniently came down with a sudden fever and became his primary patient, allowing him legitimately into her bedroom and to demonstrate his best bedside manner. Marx overdramatised this episode, praising Fleckles for his expert intervention that saved her from what he claimed would otherwise have been a long and dangerous illness. Fortuitously, Tussy's illness was potentially long and dangerous enough for Dr Fleckles to instantly prescribe a period of convalescence that required them to extend their stay in Karlsbad by a full fortnight, under his daily supervision.

On their way home Mohr took Tussy to Kreuznach to see the church where he'd married her mother thirty-three years earlier. After that they didn't go to Karlsbad any more. As Tussy later explained, the German and Austrian governments intended to deport her father and it was too far and expensive to travel there and risk expulsion on arrival. Their precaution was well founded. Tussy's Uncle Edgar von Westphalen wrote to tell them that 'the police visited our hotel – just one hour after we had left it'.[28]

The following year they tried the thermal springs at Bad Neuenahr on the Rhine. Unusually Möhme accompanied them and, after the rest cure, they went for a three-week holiday together in the Black Forest. Tussy remarked that her father missed Karlsbad, 'for he always felt like one born anew after his treatment there'.[29] But she mistook the source of her father's anxiety. As Marx finally forced himself to acknowledge, something was seriously wrong with the health of the woman he had known since infancy and loved his whole life. Naturally it was to Engels that he admitted his concern about Jenny's intense suffering 'from impaired digestion'.[30] At Neuenahr a reputable doctor assured her husband that Mrs Marx had arrived just in time for him to prevent her from becoming seriously ill. By November Möhme let go of this over-optimistic diagnosis and went to Manchester for a consultation and frank chat with their old friend Dr Gumpert. She wrote to Tussy, 'The head and feet are all-right, but the centre of the machine, where the brewing goes on, is not yet in working order.'[31] Gumpert diagnosed cancer of the liver, confirmed by a London consultant the following March. The large doses of belladonna prescribed as treatment were ineffective.

Jennychen and Laura had households, husbands, new babies and illnesses of their own to deal with; the chief responsibility for looking after her parents and assisting her sisters with childcare fell on Tussy. Whilst the Longuets lived in London, Jennychen was often forced to call on Tussy to look after the children or cover her teaching work: 'with great reluctance and regret . . . I send you these lines to ask you to replace me at Clement Danes tomorrow and Tuesday. I know you have already too much work on hand . . . it pains me . . . to burthen you with work of mine.'[32] Whilst Tussy's whole day was taken up with research work at the museum for Furnivall and the Philological, Chaucer and Shakespeare societies, she was also burning the midnight oil on her translation into English of Lissa's *History of the Commune*, 'at the express wish of the author'.[33] An unpaid labour of love, it was an ambitious project to undertake for her first major translation; the result, literal and unwieldy in style, nevertheless brought English readers the first authentic, personal memoir of the Paris Commune and, to this day, the starting point for all subsequent historians of this period of French history.

Jennychen and Möhme went on several holidays together to seaside and resort towns, leaving the little boys to stay with favourite

Aunt Tussy, Nym or Nymmy, as they called Lenchen, and Opi Karl, for whom the grandchildren were an inexhaustible source of joy. Tussy was on hand to nurse her nephews and nieces. Aged fourteen, she had tended Laura and Paul's first child, 'that little Turk of a Fouchtra' who, she wrote to her mother from Paris:

> . . . won't let one do anything but nurse him, or if he be asleep in his cradle admire his good looks . . . his forehead is immense! Just like Papa's . . . if he begins to cry, one need only let him suck your finger, or thump his little belly, and he quits in a minute. As to his teeth he really is cutting them; for you can see them quite plainly. I took him into bed with me for two hours this morning and he behaved beautifully.[34]

Following the birth of Wolf (Edgar Marcel) in August 1879 Tussy worried about the burden on Jennychen. 'Jenny expects another baby in March! This last expectation is not altogether a blessing . . . it is difficult to attend to three – one might almost say four babies, for of course Johnny is still only a baby.'[35] She loved the second boy best of all, Harry, '*my* boy'. Not pretty but the sweetest natured of the three, in need of extra love, she thought, because he had about him the air of a child 'who seemed destined to suffer'.[36] Competent at caring for infants from a young age Aunt Tussy was, according to her father, also 'an excellent disciplinarian'.[37]

After one of her trips away with Möhme, Jennychen thanked Tussy for having completely transformed Harry's behaviour and giving him good routine habits at night. In 1882 Tussy brought Johnny back to London after a visit to Argenteuil to relieve the burden on eight-months-pregnant Jennychen. Johnny had become an out-of-control hoyden. Longuet, who now didn't get out of bed until lunchtime and headed off to Paris every evening, let him run wild. Back in London Aunt Tussy put Johnny on a schedule of daily attendance at school, cold-water scrub-downs morning and evening, and compulsory early bedtimes. She kept his mother up to date: 'I have just put my boy (I am getting so used to and so fond of Jack I forget he is *your* boy) to bed.'[38] He is anxious, Tussy tells Jennychen, for news about his little sister, whilst Tussy is concerned about his terrible English: 'The way he speaks is awful, but I suppose in time he will grow out of it.'[39]

Tussy paints a clear picture of her typical evenings in. Johnny is tucked up in bed, Lenchen and Pumps (Mary Ellen Burns, Lizzy and Mary's troublesome niece) have gone to the theatre and Tussy is dashing off a quick line (four pages) to her sister 'before I begin my evening's work at the glossary'.[40] She didn't specify what or who the glossary was for; it seems to have been a commission from Furnivall for the Shakespeare or Chaucer Society.[41]

'London is the brain of the world,'[42] wrote Margaret McMillan, one of Eleanor's contemporaries, and Eleanor was one of its busiest brains. Simultaneous to her work as an emerging woman of letters, hack researcher, running the Dogberries, acting as Marx's correspondence secretary, translating Lissa's revisions of his ever-lengthening book, writing her first reviews and political articles, and a catholic range of reading from political economy to poetry to exposures of fraudulent spiritualists, Tussy dutifully and devotedly cares for her parents and her nephews.

Her dedication extends even to hated needlework. A sure sign of Möhme's decline, 'she can neither read nor write and her never-idle needle is beginning to rust at last.'[43] Tussy takes over, butchering some red flannel into badly bunched petticoats for Jennychen's little boys. 'I fear you won't find the making very brilliant – you know needlework is not my forte (entre nous it is not yours either) and you must take the will for the deed, remembering that if the buttonholes are weak the spirit has been willing.'[44] Contradicting her own experience of juggling the competing demands of intellectual wage labour and unpaid domestic labour in a pitched battle between duty and desire, Tussy tries to reassure her eldest sister that the hiatus in her career is only temporary:

Of course we know without telling what an awful time you must be having, in a strange house with three babies and no proper servant . . . It certainly would be a great pity if you had to give up writing but by and by when you've settled down and have a good servant you'll find more time. Just now naturally every moment is occupied with the house or the children, but that will only be for a time.[45]

As it turned out for Jennychen, the time that every moment was occupied with house and children was to be her lifetime. Even when the good servant finally arrived, Jennychen never again returned to her writing or active political engagement.

By the early 1880s both of Tussy's sisters had conclusively given up their working lives for children, husband and house. Möhme was incurably ill; Lizzy Burns dead. Amongst all the Marx women, Tussy was The Only Remaining Lady Candidate for emancipation from the damned future of the angel of the house.

A Line of Her Own

At the end of 1880 Tussy gave a public recital of the *Pied Piper of Hamelin* at a Communard benefit held in a north London concert hall. Marx, Engels, Hirsch, Leo Hartmann, August Bebel and Eduard Bernstein were present for her first performance of Robert Browning's retelling of the popular ballad, published in 1842. Bernstein praised her 'tremendous verve and wonderful voice', describing how she 'spoke with a great wealth of modulation and earned a great deal of applause'.[1] It was an encouraging start.

Two men who were in her audience that night proposed marriage to her around this time, neither of whom were Lissagaray. A decade after the Paris Commune the amnesty campaign for the exiled and banished Communards was won. The fight had gained new momentum from the founding of the French Workers' Party earlier in 1880, agreed in a motion passed at the third Socialist Congress in Marseilles in October 1879. Lissagaray and Longuet wrote in support of the motion on behalf of Communards in London. In March 1880 Paris openly celebrated the anniversary of the Commune for the first time and in July full pardons were finally implemented. Lissagaray left immediately for Paris.

It was clear to Tussy that he would not return permanently to London. Jennychen and Laura started to make plans to move their families back to France with their French husbands. Lissa may have assumed Tussy would follow him. For ten years, enforced exile had preoccupied him; freedom to return to France would, he seemed to expect, allow all the other elements in his life to fall into place – including his marriage to Tussy, deferred by his banishment and his book.

As Hartmann and Hirsch, both planning their proposals, watched Tussy's performance of *The Pied Piper* they must have wondered which piper was finally going to call the tune in Tussy and Lissa's longstanding betrothal:

> Brothers, sisters, husbands, wives –
> Followed the Piper for their lives.
> From street to street he piped advancing,
> And step for step they followed dancing.[2]

But Tussy, much as she cared for Lissa, wanted to lead, not follow. With Lissa in France and Tussy showing no signs of following promptly, Hartmann and Hirsch took their chances.

As for the subject of all this attention and desire, her passions lay elsewhere. Even though at twenty-five others might think she should be getting on with it, Tussy's thoughts were not of marriage, but of the stage. The Dogberries were at their zenith and the source of new friends and opportunities. In April 1881 Tussy discovered a new 'Wunderkind'[3] who joined the Dogberries: Ernest Radford, a young English barrister, poet and critic who despised the law and wanted to give it up for a life in the arts. Tussy and Mohr thought he looked like a cross between Irving and the late Ferdinand Lassalle. Another Dogberry and friend of Tussy's, the poet Caroline 'Dollie' Maitland, took a passionate interest in Edward and the threesome started to spend a great deal of time together, with Tussy as nominal chaperone. They went to the theatre as often as possible, including to see Irving in *Hamlet*. Edward, Tussy remarked to her sister, 'is a very nice young fellow . . . he is wonderfully like Irving!'[4]

Tussy, too, wanted to be wonderfully like Irving. He got all the best roles, after all. She identified with him rather than his brilliant stage 'wife' Ellen Terry because Irving was, like her, an outsider to the theatre world who worked his way on to the stage, whereas Ellen

Terry, daughter of a theatrical family, was born into it. Until the end
of the nineteenth century most actresses, like Terry, were stage children, brought up in theatreland. But Tussy was born and brought up
in the world of politics. Women did not have the freedom to choose
the stage as men did.[5]

As well as Irving, Wyndham, Kendal and Willis, and the later
generation of Beerbohm Tree, Maude, Bourchier and Hawtrey, many
other male actors started out completely unconnected to the theatre.
Conversely, Ellen Terry, Fanny Kemble, Madge Kendal, Marie
Bancroft, Mrs Charles Young (later Mrs Vezin) and Mrs John Wood
were born to the boards into acting families.

The Dogberries formed an ensemble, led by Tussy, Dollie and
Edward, and put on two one-act plays by Eugène Scribe, the father
of the 'well made play', at the Dilettante Club in Regent Street. *First
Love* was a vaudeville comedy and *At a Farm by the Sea* a drama.
Scribe, the leading French dramatist and librettist of the first half of
the nineteenth century, wrote some 300 plays and pioneered adeptly
structured studies of contemporary bourgeois existence – in short,
he was a modern.

Engels took a party of friends to the show on 5 July and sent a
prompt review to Marx and Möhme, away in Eastbourne under
doctor's orders. Tussy and Dollie, Engels reported, 'played very
well':

> Tussy was very good in the passionate scenes and it was easily
> perceived that she took Ellen Terry for model while Radford took
> Irving, yet she will soon use it up; if she wants to make a public
> impact, she must absolutely strike out a line of her own and there
> is no doubt that she will.[6]

There was the rub. Opposite Radford playing Irving, Tussy had no
choice but to play the woman's part. There couldn't be two Irvings
on stage. Tussy played Emmeline, who tests the maxim that the first
love is the true love and that a person only loves once – with surprising results. Søren Kierkegaard loved the play so much he saw it
repeatedly in Copenhagen and wrote one of his most famous essays
on love about it.

To develop her own style Eleanor first needed training – as well she knew. In the summer of 1881 Elizabeth and Hermann Vezin, amongst London's best-known theatrical couples, moved into the neighbourhood. Their coaching methods emphasised physiological approaches to elocution and theatrical performance. They credited their techniques to two influential contemporary pioneers of voice training, John Hullah and Emil Behnke. Hullah taught 'Public Reading' in the theology faculty at King's College London. His classic *The Speaking Voice* (1870) summarises his approach to physical stance, deportment, modulation, structure of delivery and techniques for managing audiences – especially rowdy ones. Behnke focused on physical aspects, including diet, breathing and – especially for women – loose clothing.[7]

Impressed by seeing Tussy perform, Elizabeth Vezin told her she had talent and suggested she come to her for professional coaching. Tussy explained her plan to take elocution and performance lessons so she could give professional recitals. Vezin opposed this, telling Tussy she was underestimating her talents and should aim for the full scope of an acting career. 'Even if,' Tussy wrote to Jennychen, 'as I fancy will be the case, Mrs Vezin finds she has much overrated my powers, the lessons will still be useful to me, and I can always make the recitation venture.'[8]

Nervously, she approached her father and asked him to help her pay for the tuition. Engels would have invested willingly in her training but as ever she refused to ask him for money – though Marx probably got it from him anyway. Her father had misgivings about her new choice of career direction. Her mother hedged and Jennychen, who Tussy looked up to, encouraged her ambition but tempered her support with cautions about the economic and practical obstacles.

Tussy was fully aware that she needed to seek out her part in the world. 'I feel sorry to cost Papa so much, but after all very small sums were expended on my education – compared at least to what is <u>now</u> demanded of girls – and I think if I do succeed it will have been a good investment. I shall try, too, to get as much work as I can so that I may have a little money by the time I need it.'[9] Considerably more money had been put into Jennychen and Laura's schooling and extramural accomplishments than into hers. She never had the music or art lessons dedicated to her elder sisters, both of whom also stayed at school for four years longer than she did. That said, when she did have opportunities for formal education she had in truth shown more desire to run away from school than to attend regularly. Her comment that it is imperative she continue earning and put by what she can is telling. Both of her sisters owed a large proportion of their livelihood and security to their husbands, in-laws and Engels. The first of these two she didn't have and she wouldn't take from the latter.

Thanks to a chance encounter with John Mayall on an omnibus, Tussy picked up some regular work as a précis writer for a scientific journal at the handsome regular rate of £2 per week. She hoped this might release her from some of the other freelance work that sucked up so much of her time and create space for her theatrical training. 'I have never tried it and don't know if I can do it,' she confided to Jennychen. 'Well, I'll try anyway – if I fail, I fail. You see, dear, I've a goodly number of irons in the fire, but I feel I've wasted quite enough of my life, and it is high time I did something.'[10]

This is a concise expression of the condition of the odd woman, in George Gissing's apposite formulation. The strain of nearly a decade of unpaid labour as dutiful daughter, correspondence secretary, parental companion, carer, and nanny to nephews and nieces were beginning to show. She desired romance, marriage and children but deferred, prompted by the still small voice that warned they were potential roads to future unfreedom. As a little girl she had written a loving letter to her 'dear Dady' [sic] – signing herself 'Your UNdutiful daughter Eleanor.'[11] How to recapture the unbounded optimism of the little girl bold enough to be an undutiful daughter?

The urgency of Tussy's need to 'strike out on a line of her own', as Engels elegantly put it, is not just a question of finding an original voice and style for her potential theatrical career – it is the need to find a voice of independence on the bigger stage of life beyond the extended Marx family. 'Strike' is the perfect verb for soul-socialist Tussy; 'a line of her own' the exact description of her rights and needs. Engels's suggestion that Tussy needed to persue line of her own anticipates Virginia Woolf's later proposition that a woman needs a room of her own and £50 a year in order to make a bid for a life of artistic freedom.

Once settled into their new home, the Vezins went away until mid-August. Tussy forced a tense agreement from her father that she could start her training when they returned. Action being always the thing for Tussy, this deferral precipitated the nervous collapse her assertion of a definite life plan aimed to avert. Mohr, Möhme and Lenchen planned to be away all of the summer. They spent July in Eastbourne and then went to France to visit Jennychen and the children in Argenteuil. Lenchen went with them – she now never left Möhme's side during her waking hours and when Möhme rested provided welcome companionship and support for Mohr.

Tussy was left to the pleasure of her own devices for six weeks, working continuously, chain-smoking, forgetting to eat, sleeping very little and fretfully counting the days until she could start her tuition and open the door on a possible new life. Absorbed in her work, fuelled by nicotine, coffee, alcohol and sleeping draughts, she didn't notice her body calling the game.

A fortnight after their arrival in France her parents received an urgent telegram from Dollie Maitland telling them Tussy was seriously ill but wouldn't let Dollie help her or call a doctor.

Marx rushed back to London immediately to find Tussy in a state of nervous collapse. 'For some weeks she has eaten nothing (literally),' he wrote to Jennychen. 'Her nervous system is in a pitiable state, whence continual insomnia, tremblings of hands, neuralgic convulsions of the face, etc.'[12] Dr Donkin said there was no organic disease present, except for 'a perfect derangement of the action of her stomach'[13] due to her lack of interest in eating – based, implicitly, on a perfect derangement of the action of her brain to take proper care of herself. Tussy's disastrous self-management was the mirror of her exemplary capacity to look after others.

Dr Freud would have recognised the symptoms directly: he and Dr Marx would have concurred on the causes of her acute, 'hysteric' symptoms – the twitching, the shaking, the lack of appetite. Use of too many stimulants. Insomnia. Depression. Frustrated desire. Surfeit of unchannelled ambition, intellectual talent and energy. Resentment at being for so long a repressed, obedient daughter fighting her contrapuntal desire to break free and strike out on a line of her own. Passionate will to live her own life. Underpinning the intensity of her reaction: guilt, regret, foreboding, self-doubt, insecurity. And in the shared case notes might be a mention of her awareness – conscious, unconscious or mixture by turns of acknowledgement and denial – that she was losing her mother. Grief.

Added to the mix was the fact of Lissa's return to Paris and how to deal with her realisation that she would never follow him.

Tussy was annoyed with Dollie for notifying her parents. Poor practical Dollie got short shrift from her workaholic, anorexic friend for trying to help her. Tussy agreed to follow Dr Donkin's prescription for recovery, and the combination of regular eating, sleep and the assurance from her father that she could start her acting lessons as soon as she was recovered put her back on an even keel.

It was a brief respite. Whilst Marx supervised Tussy's recovery Möhme and Lenchen returned by slow stages from France, travelling first class and stopping at Amiens and Boulogne. Möhme now endured chronic pain and constant exhaustion. Lenchen managed their travel, gently nurtured, and administered her medication and morphine for what both sensed might be their last journey together. These two women had shared their lives since childhood, always lived together in the same homes, shared the flights of exile, brought their children into the world together, looked after Marx together, cooked and sewed, mended and made do in the hungry years, gone to the theatre and music recitals in each other's company. Their longest period of separation in six decades was seven months in 1851, when Jenny went home to Trier for an extended visit and Lenchen stayed in London to look after Marx. When Jenny returned, there had been a great row and temporary rift between them but they resolved the difference and never after revealed the cause. They had nursed each other through illness, fought and resolved the arguments of true friendship and now, both in their sixties, shared secrets that remained their own.

For every hundred meals they cooked, Marx and Engels expressed an idea; for every basket of petticoats, bibs and curtains they sewed together, Marx and Engels wrote an article. For every pregnancy, childbirth and labour-intensive period of raising an infant, Marx and Engels wrote a book. Some years later the favourite daughter of these four friends postulated 'a general idea that has to do with all women. The life of woman does not coincide with that of man.'[14] In their lifetimes the friendship and comradeship between the inseparable Karl Marx and Friedrich Engels was legendary on at least three continents. Because, as Tussy puts it, the life of woman does not coincide with man, nor does her afterlife – or history. The comradeship between the inseparable Jenny von Westphalen and Helen Demuth is neither legendary nor generally well remembered. Yet at the heart of this female friendship rests the key to the secret of the Marx family household: the identity of the father of Lenchen's only child.

Tussy was physically recovered, ate and slept more regularly under her father's watchful eye, and was revived as always by the pleasure of his company. On Möhme and Lenchen's return, it was Marx's turn to be sick, knocked down by a bad attack of pleurisy.

With both parents now invalids and requiring round-the-clock care from Lenchen and herself, Tussy was once again grimly forced to defer the start of her professional coaching with Elizabeth Vezin. 'Since Saturday I have not left Papa's room – day or night,' she told Jennychen. 'Tonight however Helen will be with him as the doctor wants me to have a night's rest. There is of course continuously something to do.'[15] Alarmed, Jennychen wanted to come to London immediately to help, but Tussy had to discourage her as it caused Marx such great anxiety to countenance his grand-children being left in the random care of their slapdash father. Emotional anxiety intensified Marx's breathing difficulties, in turn increasing the frequency of Tussy's need to administer his inhalation treatments.

Having seen Jennychen recently, Mohr and Möhme also knew that she'd been having her own health problems that wouldn't be helped by a long journey. Tussy assured Jennychen that she and Lenchen had a great deal of support: 'Engels is of a kindness and devotion that baffle description. Truly there is not another like him in the world – in spite of his little weaknesses.'[16] Family friend

Madame Lormier wrote offering to come and help, and Tussy's friend Clementina sat up with Möhme to let Tussy and Lenchen get some sleep. 'Isn't it kind of people to take such an interest?'[17]

Starting her theatrical coaching, continuing her work at the British Museum, regular correspondence; all these melted into the shadows. Tussy kept going, stamina being one of her strong points when looking after others rather than herself. She was relieved when Laura arrived from Paris. Where Tussy colluded with her father in shielding Jennychen from the truth about the health of their parents, Laura was characteristically frank and brusque:

> Möhme is slowly growing worse. She can scarcely be thinner or weaker than she is, but her spirits are undying. You do wrong to fret so much about her separation from her grandchildren. At this time of day their presence here could do very little for her: she is unhappily too far gone to derive much comfort from the prattle and the pretty naughtiness of children.[18]

Undercurrents of the animosity Laura felt towards Tussy surface during these troubled times. What was probably Möhme's last letter failed to reach Jennychen: 'It had cost her such an effort to write and she had put so much into it to which she looked for an answer from you that the loss of the letter is irremediable.'[19] With sisterly spite, Laura implied that Tussy, 'into whose hands it was placed before being put into an envelope', was responsible for forgetting to post this important 'last letter'.[20]

Nevertheless Laura's extra pair of hands gave Tussy respite to look again to her own recovery. She took a course of iron prescribed by Dr Donkin and followed his orders to go more regularly for Turkish baths and get out more. Laura returned to France as soon as Marx was sufficiently improved to be up and out of bed for a few hours a day.

James Murray, general editor of the *Oxford New English Dictionary*, had contracted Tussy to do some work on the project just as Marx fell ill. A part-time maidservant, Sarah, was now taken on to help Lenchen, and on the days Sarah came to Maitland Park Road Tussy was able to grab two or three hours' work in the

Museum, working at great speed, and enjoying the walk there and back. She was grateful to Murray for waiting until she could resume work for the dictionary. 'You don't know how many people – most far better qualified to do the work than I am – try to get what I've been doing, and if I once give it up I may whistle for something else.'[21]

By November Möhme barely rose from her couch in the front room; 'in the small room next to it Mohr was also confined to his bed,' Tussy recalled, sorrowful to see 'these two, so much accustomed to one another, so closely allied to each other', no longer in each other's company as much as they wished to be.[22] Towards the end of November, Marx rallied. Tussy remembered very clearly the last time her parents were able to be together:

> Never shall I forget the morning when he felt strong enough to go into dear mother's room. They were young once more together – she a loving girl and he an adoring youth who together entered on their life – not an old man wrecked by sickness and a dying old woman who took leave of each other for life.[23]

Jenny Marx died on Friday 2 December 1881, with her husband, Tussy and Lenchen by her side. In her last hour she said many things, but they could not hear them. The last intelligible word she spoke was to Marx – 'good'. The General came immediately. When they were alone, he said to Tussy, 'Mohr is dead too.' She 'resented' these words, but recognised, 'it was really so'.[24]

Tussy and Lenchen washed Möhme's body and laid her out. Visitors came to say goodbye over the weekend. Through the midwinter chill of the Sunday night, Tussy kept lamplit vigil with her mother. In the silence of the dark hours, she wrote to her eldest sister as she gazed on their mother's corpse:

> Oh! Jenny, she looks so beautiful now. Dollie when she saw her said her face was quite transfigured – her brow was *absolutely smooth* – just as if some gentle hand had smoothed away every line and furrow, while the lovely hair seems to form a sort of glory round her head. Tomorrow her funeral will be. I do dread it – but

of course Papa cannot go. He must not yet leave the house, and I am glad of this in every way.[25]

Tussy enclosed a lock of her mother's glory in this requiem letter: 'It is as soft and beautiful as a girl's.'[26]

Möhme was buried at Highgate Cemetery on 5 December, near to her grandson Charles Longuet, in what Marx described as the section of the damned (unconsecrated).[27] The General delivered the eulogy and, in accordance with Jenny's wishes, there was no priest. A few days before she died the nurse had asked her 'if anything ceremonial had been neglected?' Möhme fixed the nurse with a steely look. There will be no ceremony, she answered, 'We are no such external people.'[28]

'If ever there was a woman whose greatest happiness lay in making others happy, this was she,'[29] said the General at her graveside. Letters of condolence streamed in from around the world, in chorus with their homage to this spirit of selflessness. Former friends and comrades now estranged or outright enemies put aside hostilities and sent their condolences as well. 'In her,' wrote a bitter opponent to his once-friend Marx, 'nature has destroyed its own masterpiece, for in my whole life I have never encountered another such spirited and amiable woman.'[30] Library, deeply shaken, wrote to Marx celebrating Jenny's 'gallantry': 'that I did not lose myself in London, body and soul, I owe in great measure to her.'[31]

Marx reflected on these expressions of appreciation of 'Möhmchen's spirit of truthfulness and deep sensitivity, rarely found in such conventional communications. I explain it on the ground that everything about her was natural and genuine, artless and unaffected; hence the impression she made on third persons as vital and luminous.'[32] Jenny von Westphalen and Karl Marx were the loves of each other's lives. Marx and Lenchen had lost their best friend.

On 29 December, instructed by Dr Donkin, Tussy and Marx set out for Ventnor on the Isle of Wight. It was colder than London and rained continually. Marx's health prevented him from venturing out. They had comfortable rooms, a soothing view of the sea and hills[33] and the landlady was a good cook, but both Tussy and Marx were sick and raw with grief. Sleep eluded her, and she was loath to try again the 'various drugs' she had taken recently; as she revealed to Jennychen: 'it is not much better, after all, than dram-drinking, and is almost if not quite as injurious.'[34]

Tussy felt too ill to read, write or do anything and, she admitted to Jennychen, 'seeing how anxious I am to be able to look after Papa . . . was terribly afraid of breaking down altogether',[35] as she had done before. Marx was anxious and scolding by turns, as well he might be. He wanted to buck her up; she felt guilty, 'as if I "indulged" in being ill at the expense of my family'.[36] Jennychen wished that Laura had gone with their father instead, as he needed a more even-tempered companion. Acutely ill and without childcare, Jennychen couldn't come herself.

Worried by the tone of Tussy's letters, Clementina Black, Ernest Radford and Dollie Maitland discussed how they could help her. Ernest rushed to Maitland Park Road and begged Lenchen to go to Ventnor – but she couldn't abandon the house and pets. Instead well-intentioned Dollie turned up uninvited. Ungrateful and annoyed by the intervention, Tussy dismissed the assistance: 'I wished they had let me alone.'[37] Bored, Dollie tried to gossip with Marx. 'She tells Papa that she believes me to be *secretly married* and a lot of other cock and bull stories, that do far more honour to her imagination than her veracity.'[38] Marx of course instantly shared this with Tussy, who was disappointed by Dollie's meddling. More distressing to Marx were Dollie's lurid descriptions of Tussy's 'horrible' hysterical symptoms at night, about which he wrote anxiously to Engels.[39] In fact Tussy was perfectly aware of the nature of her disorder:

> What neither Papa nor the doctors nor anyone will understand is that it is chiefly mental worry that affects me. Papa talks about me having 'rest' and 'getting strong' before I try anything and won't see that 'rest' is the last thing I need – and that I should be more likely to 'get strong' if I have some definite plan and work than to go on waiting and waiting.[40]

Deferral of starting her theatrical training, inaction, self-sacrifice to her family, lack of her own money and, above all, the recognition through grief that her mother's true talents were ultimately unrealised; all these were the cause of Tussy's nervous symptoms: 'I am not young enough to lose more time in waiting – and if I cannot do this <u>soon</u> it will be no use to try at all.'[41]

Dollie's seeming inopportuneness was perhaps more calculating than Tussy admitted. Her freethinking friends had a shrewd understanding of her feelings about her overlong engagement to the now absent Lissagaray. On the eve of her twenty-seventh birthday Tussy wrote an explanatory letter to Jennychen:

> For a long time I have tried to make up my mind to break off my engagement. I <u>could</u> not bring myself to do it – he has been very good, and gentle, and patient with me – but I have done it now. Not only that the burden had become too heavy – I had other reasons (I can't write them – it would take so long, but when I see you I will tell you) – and so at last I screwed my courage to the sticking place.[42]

Perhaps not the most tactful of her Shakespearean allusions.

Tussy stressed that Lissa was blameless and asked Jennychen to try and see him sometimes and treat him kindly as a family friend. For herself, Tussy hoped she and Lissa would continue the best of friends – there's a repetitive fiddling on this string of friendship that suggests deep guilt on Tussy's part for the break-up. Though it was 'a terrible struggle', Tussy was certain the decision was right: '. . . we must each of us, after all, live our own life – and much and hard as I have tried I could not crush out my desire to <u>try something</u>.'[43] She was optimistic that there was still time for her; on account of her lifelong intimacy with cats, she believed that she had nine lives instead of one.

Tussy was galvanised by the death of her mother. She'd reached the limit of her endurance of living her life for other people, and had made the stark realisation that her time could now be wholly consumed by looking after her father, much as she loved him. Where the letters of condolence praising Möhme for her exemplary selflessness were gentle consolation for Marx, they appalled and depressed Tussy, spurring her to choose uncertain independence over the loving subjection of marriage. She made herself an inventory of good resolutions for her twenty-seventh birthday and felt that if she kept but half of them for the coming years she would do well:

> I mean to try hard by dint of hard work to make something more and better of my life than it has heretofore been. After all <u>work</u> is the chief thing. To me at least it is a necessity. That's why I love even my dull Museum drudgery. You see I'm not clever enough to live a purely <u>intellectual</u> life, nor am I dull enough to be content to sit down and do nothing.[44]

Marx and Engels knew that she wasn't, in fact, dull enough to live a purely intellectual life. Tussy needed action and to put ideas to the practical test. She longed to be able to make all this understandable to her adored father – 'How I love him no-one can know' – but struggled with her guilt over a sense of abandoning him in his grief: 'I <u>can't</u> explain to him.'[45] Jennychen took the hint, and wrote to their father directly on Tussy's behalf, informing him clearly of the situation.

With the mediation of her elder sister, Marx came to understand Tussy's problem. He expressed his conviction to Engels that no medicine, change of scene or air could cure her sickness; as he now realised, what he could do for her was support and enable her 'to do as she wishes and let go through her theatrical lessons at Madame Jung' – his wry moniker for Elizabeth Vezin, formerly Mrs Young. Marx would not 'for anything in the world wish that the child should imagine herself to be sacrificed on the family altar in the form of the "nurse" of an old man'.[46] And it was easier for him to stand down now that he knew that Tussy was no longer going to sacrifice her future to another man. The end of Tussy's engagement to Lissagaray was to everyone's satisfaction. Tussy of course could not admit for a moment that her father had been right all along; he was loving enough not to say I told you so.

Laura and Paul had never liked Lissa, and Jennychen, who now heartily regretted her own marriage, thought Tussy had made the right decision: 'these Frenchmen at the best of times make pitiable husbands.'[47]

Tussy's new life resolutions got off to a flying start. On the day of her birthday she and Marx headed home so she could give a recital in London. Her performances of *Pied Piper* and Thomas Hood's *Bridge of Sighs* – the tragedy of a homeless young woman who loses hope and drowns herself – were a triumph. 'I must tell you that I got on capitally on Tuesday and was "called" after the *Pied Piper* but as that is very long – it takes 25 minutes to do and I only bowed and would not take an encore – but after the *Bridge of Sighs* I had to take one and did.'[48] Best of all, she earned a handsome £2 for her performance.

In February Tussy and Marx went to visit Jennychen and the grandchildren in Argenteuil, from where Marx went on to Algiers after a week – alone. On the day Tussy returned to London Lissa gallantly called at the Longuets and asked if he could please see her off at Gare St Lazare that evening. They had dinner at a station bistro. Lissa expressed his heartbreak and regret but understood he could not hold her and did not try to change her mind. They parted friends. Tussy had acted for the best, Jennychen said, and had 'a narrow escape' from marrying a man who, she was sure, would never have made her happy. She didn't miss the opportunity to harp on her old theme: 'French husbands are not worth much at the best of times – and at the worst – well, the less said the better.'[49] She sounded just like their mother.

Whatever Tussy's feelings about the end of her affair with Lissa when her train pulled away from Gare St Lazare that evening, any chance to brood was prevented by a colourful fellow passenger in the 'dames seules' compartment who distracted her for the journey home.[50] She asked to borrow a corkscrew from Tussy, who didn't happen to have one to hand. Her travelling companion then proceeded to gouge out the cork from her brandy bottle with a pair of manicure scissors, downing the whole contents tumbler by tumbler. As the train didn't stop between Rouen and Dieppe, the sot heartily 'relieved herself' in the carriage – leading Tussy to vow she would never again travel in a ladies-only compartment.

Back home, Eleanor energetically embraced her new freedom. She was busy once again with the New Shakespeare Society and devilling at the British Museum doing research and bibliographic work for Furnivall. At last, her eagerly anticipated training with Elizabeth Vezin began. She went to the theatre at every opportunity, queuing for cheap tickets to sit in the gods, studying intently the performances of women actors. She loved the new *Romeo and Juliet* at the Lyceum: 'I have never seen a Shakespearean play so satisfactorily played "all round".'[51] But she was very disappointed by Ellen Terry's Juliet, 'charming in the early scenes – comedy scenes to say – Ellen Terry gets weaker and weaker as the tragic element appears till in the potion scene she collapses altogether.'[52] The question of how to perform Juliet was of great interest to Tussy, 'as since my return from Paris I've been grinding at Juliet with Mrs Vezin. She seems extremely pleased with it – and says, despite my absolute ignorance of stage business she would like me to try it publicly.'[53]

But was it Ellen Terry or the absurdity of an adult woman at the height of her powers having to play a star-crossed pubescent teenager in love that so disappointed Tussy? Her criticisms of Terry reveal the accuracy of Vezin's observation on her absolute ignorance of the stage business – she didn't yet understand the challenges of being 'an actress'. Of having to act out subordination and secondary roles on stage as well as living them, daily, off-stage; of being visibly silenced on stage by the greater parts for male actors whilst having to make do with being given silly lines, madness, machinations and clichés to perform. On stage and off, man's role was hero or busy villain; woman's, sweet server or some variant of deranged or power-hungry lunatic. Ellen Terry understood her position perfectly well, famously remarking, ' "And one man in his time plays many parts." (And so does a woman!)' Terry knew what Tussy would discover: though many and varied, they were rarely the best parts.

Had they the opportunity to discuss Terry's career, Virginia Woolf might have explained to Eleanor that Terry was often subverting her roles and their 'silly words', gathering to her the resentful compliance of the women in her audience, who could detect the whispered presence of forbidden, bigger, stronger roles in their real lives. It was Ellen Terry who inspired Woolf's portrait of Edith Craig in *Between the Acts*:

'What a small part I've had to play! But you've made me feel I could have played . . . Cleopatra!' 'I might have been – Cleopatra,' Miss Le Troke [Edith Craig] repeated, 'You've stirred in me my unacted part, she meant.'[54]

She couldn't hear this voice from the future but Tussy, too, sought her unacted part. As yet, she did not realise that she would not find the part to suit her amongst Shakespeare's women.

She missed her father and fretted over their separation – 'How I do <u>long</u> for a sight of your face.'[55] Marx concealed his ill health from all but the General. Dissatisfied with her father's accounts of himself, Tussy wanted to go to him in Algiers but the General deterred her. Meanwhile, the news that Eleanor had broken off her engagement with Lissa reached the delighted Karl Hirsch, who wasted no time and immediately deputed his sister, 'the uncanny Frau Kaub', to visit Jennychen – repeatedly – and make his suit for Tussy's hand in marriage.

Jennychen had to sit through endless minutiae about Hirsch's solid financial position and comprehensive accounts of his prospects in a manner that any Marx sister would find comical. Brother and sister resisted Jennychen's polite but conclusive rebuttals that Tussy had no current interest in marriage. 'I have done all I could to explain to the enamoured Hirsch that his aspirations are doomed to remain unfulfilled, he insists upon hearing his doom from your own lips.'[56] Tussy wrote Hirsch a gentle and courteous refusal in settlement of the matter. It never even occurred to either sister that it might be judicious for Eleanor to marry for financial security.

Jennychen totally supported Tussy's rejection of Hirsch but was puzzled by why she was so angry with him for proposing marriage in the first place. She never expressed her anger to him, but Tussy was deeply offended. From her perspective Hirsch had betrayed a long-time political and intellectual friendship and misled her by not being open about his intentions. This was hardly fair, given that Hirsch honourably did not declare his hand until after her betrothal to Lissagaray ended conclusively.

Jennychen supported her little sister's pursuit of an independent career rather than marriage, confident that her 'ambition to live an artist's life' would succeed, 'and at the very worst should you never tread the boards, the fact of acquiring perfectly the art of elocution ... will be a great gain to you through life and will repay any outlay your lessons now will cost you.'[57] Through Tussy, Jennychen revived her own long-dead daydream, the 'prospect of living the only free life a woman can live – the artistic one'.[58]

Tussy was often alone at Maitland Park Road. Lenchen spent much time in France helping Jennychen with the children. Marx travelled from Algiers to Monte Carlo, Nice and Cannes, heading straight back to Argenteuil for the summer. Tussy wrote him letters filled with enthusiastic news of her many activities and chat about current events. She was scandalised by the fuss made by 'British Philistines' who were moved to tears and pity by the removal of an elephant from Regent's Park Zoo to a circus whilst they gazed dry-eyed on starvation and abject poverty amongst their fellow human beings in East London. 'Shakespeare', Tussy reminded her father, 'already declared that your Englishman would not "give a doit to relieve a lame beggar, but lay out ten to see a dead Indian."'[59]

She took in all the London entertainment she could cram in between her work at the British Museum for the New Shakespeare Society, lessons with Vezin and disciplined practice. She saw Polish actor Helen Modjeska in *Odette* and the Italian Adelaide Ristori as Lady Macbeth, the first time the actress performed in English. There was a picnic down the river with the Furnivalls, dinners with zoologist Edwin Ray Lankester and his family, and inspiring new friendships with South African writer Olive Schreiner and Alexandra Leighton (Mrs Sutherland Orr).

On 30 June Tussy shared top billing at the annual celebrations of the Browning Society held at University College London. She performed the chivalric adventure *Count Gismond* and, by popular demand, her *Pied Piper*. Exhilarated, first thing the next morning she wrote to Jennychen with her morning coffee:

> The place was crowded – and as all sorts of 'literary' and other 'swells' were there I felt ridiculously nervous – but got on capitally. Mrs Sutherland Orr (the sister of Sir Frederick Leighton, the President of the Royal Academy) wants to take me to see

Browning and recite his own poems to him! I have been asked to
go this afternoon to a 'crush' at Lady Wilde's. She is the mother of
that very limp and very nasty young man, Oscar Wilde, who has
been making such a d.d. ass of himself in America. As the son has
not yet returned and the mother is nice I may go – that is if I have
time . . . [60]

Tussy's snide comments about Wilde are prompted by pure envy at
the scale of his theatrical and literary success. Far from making an ass
of himself, Wilde was, in fact, becoming a 'd.d.' star on his lecture
tour of America and creating enormous publicity for Gilbert and
Sullivan's *Patience*. Tussy was jealous to her back teeth at the greater
success of a male peer. When Wilde was tried later amidst rumour
and revelation about his homosexuality, Tussy's envy turned to allegiance. She was publicly critical of the disgraceful hypocrisy of the
press and public who, formerly fêting him, turned against him
because of his alleged sexual preferences and the conduct of his
personal life. She singled out for particular opprobrium the venality
of the managers of the Haymarket and St James's theatres who
continued hugely profitable runs of Wilde's plays to packed houses
but erased Wilde's name from the bill, programme and entire production. When no British paper would publish her defence of Wilde, she
got it published in Russia.[61]

Another highlight of her summer of 1882 was the benefit for
famous Dickens actor John Toole at the Charing Cross Theatre, now
under his management and renamed Toole's Theatre in his own
honour. The 'beloved Henry' recited, as did Madge Kemble and
Ellen Terry, who did Thomas Hood's *Bridge of Sighs* which, Tussy
joked, 'I look upon as a personal injury, that being one of my stock
pieces.'[62] Unable to get tickets, Tussy, Lenchen and the Black sisters
watched from the pit – the show started at 1.30 p. m. and they had to
be at the theatre doors at 11 a.m., drinking tea from a street vendor
and chatting for two hours whilst they waited to get in. 'What a fine
thing enthusiasm is!'[63]

These outings were welcome punctuation to long working days.
'I'm rather hard at it just now,'[64] she told Jennychen. As Lenchen
was with her sister in France, there were puzzling chores on the

domestic front for the aspiring actress. Neither of Lenchen's sitting hens had stirred from their nests since her departure and Tussy had no idea what to do with them – apart from hand-feeding them all kinds of treats and consoling the amiable, pining cockerel that Lenchen would soon return. 'I positively dread next Monday – when some of the chicks are *supposed* to come out. What I'm to do with them goodness knows.'[65]

In Mohr's absence, the General kept a watchful paternal eye on her, expecting Tussy to spend Sundays with him when a feast was served up with generous quantities of claret. If her hectic schedule forced her to miss this weekly ritual, Tussy made it up and had dinner with the General during the week at a theatre or club, introducing him to her new friends.

At the end of July she was forced to interrupt her work and intensive coaching and go to Argenteuil at her father's urgent request, to look after 'poor Jennychen'. Her careworn sister had another baby on the way and was suffering excruciating pain from a persistent bladder infection. 'I am dead beaten,' she flatly confessed to Tussy.[66] Tussy returned to London in mid-August, bringing little Johnny (Jean) back with her. After a carefree seaside holiday with Engels at Great Yarmouth, she put Johnny back into day school in London and looked after him like any working London mother with a day job.

At the end of August 'the old man of the mountain',[67] as Marx now called himself, went on from France to Switzerland, accompanied at his express and confidential request by Laura. He appreciated the great improvement in Tussy and did not want to go back on his resolve not to make her the nurse of an ailing old man. Jennychen's only daughter, also named Jenny – Mémé – was born on 16 September. Marx met his new granddaughter briefly at the end of the month, but Jennychen hid the seriousness of her illness from him, passing it off as post-natal exhaustion. Marx went directly to Ventnor for further treatment for his persistent pleurisy and bronchitis. His bad health compounded his reasons for not returning to London. He knew he could not recover from losing his wife but must learn to carry her loss with him. Without Möhme, he found the family home and London life unbearable.

With Lenchen back from France and running the household again, there was more support for looking after little Johnny at Maitland Park Road. Whilst he was at school during the day Tussy spent as much time as she could catching up on her work. In the evenings after the child was put to bed with Tussy's own version of Hans Röckle, she cracked on with her night work on the glossary and Lenchen visited the General to play chess or went with Pumps to the theatre.

The first week of October was the annual Closed Week at the Reading Room, when it was shut to readers, books dusted and repaired, and archives checked. Tussy was extremely anxious about her deadline for the Early English Text Society. 'Now I am, as you know,' she told Jennychen, 'very hard pressed for time, so I asked Mr Bond, the Principal Librarian, to allow me to go all the same to work.'[68] George Bullen, Keeper of Printed Books, his assistant Richard Garnett[69] 'and some half dozen of the head men very kindly went to Mr Bond and also asked him to let me come'. Bond gave permission. 'It is an immense favour, which I was told today had been extended to no one since some years ago Gladstone was allowed to go and finish his pamphlet on the "Atrocities" there' – his essay 'Bulgarian Horrors and the Question of the East' (1876). She couldn't work 'in the turmoil of the cleaning in the Reading Room', so she worked with both Garnett and Bullen in their own offices. 'It's a great boon to me, as I was desperate at losing so many days.'[70] The favour extended to her by the men who ran the British Museum demonstrated that Eleanor Marx had now taken her father's seat in the British Museum Reading Room.

Needing money, Tussy took on another job teaching at a school for girls in Kensington. 'I am too hard at work to go anywhere or see anyone,' she wrote to Jennychen. After work she mostly stayed at home reading newspapers and periodicals and writing letters in her father's study, such as her reflections to Jennychen on the factional split of the Saint-Etienne congress into Possibilists and Marxists – the latter led by their brother-in-law Lafargue. 'What do you think of the rival Congresses? They are more suggestive to me of the Kilkenny Cats than of anything else.'[71] According to folklore, Tussy's Kilkenny cats fought until nothing was left of them but their tails. On 11 October she was able to go with the Dogberries to see the preview of the Lyceum's first production of *Much Ado About Nothing* starring Terry and Irving, which she thoroughly enjoyed. Ernest, Clementina and Dollie were pleased to see her out and about; they were missing greatly the formerly regular soirées at Tussy's home.

Tussy took Johnny to visit Marx in Ventnor for a weekend. He was anxious for news of Jennychen and believed she would not recover unless more children were taken off her hands. He asked Tussy to drop everything to go back to France to help out for a little and bring back Harra in order to give Jennychen relief to nurse Mémé. Jennychen put her foot down. Tussy was not to leave her work.

> The only bit of good news that I have had these many days is . . . of your literary enterprises. I congratulate you with all my heart and rejoice to think that one of us at least will not pass her life in watching over a *pot au feu*.[72]

Jennychen's own news was not good. The bladder inflammation she believed to be linked to her last pregnancy had not gone away but worsened after the birth: 'To no one in the world would I wish the tortures I have undergone now since eight months, they are indescribable and the nursing added thereto makes life a hell to me.'[73] There is a valuable raw eloquence in Jennychen's frankness about the realities of her maternal experience, and great love in her resistance to Tussy being constrained to help her.

Tussy, Marx, Lenchen and the General did all they could to make a bright Christmas for Johnny in London. Laura was unable to join them. In September, the Saint-Etienne congress had split. Paul Lafargue and Jules Guesde formed the Marxist Parti Ouvrier Français (French Workers' Party) and were immediately arrested for subversion and sedition. In this instance, Marx highly approved of his son-in-law's actions.

Whilst Johnny provided a reason for the return of the traditional family Christmas tree, Marx's gift was to be free finally from pleurisy and bronchitis. 'This, then, is very encouraging,' he crowed, 'considering that most of my *contemporaries*, I mean fellows of the same age, just now kick the bucket in gratifying numbers. There are enough young asses to keep the old ones alive.'[74] He returned to Ventnor in a better mood.

During the first week of January Marx received awful news from the Lafargues that Jennychen's condition was now hopeless. She was bedridden, haemorrhaging and sunk in a torpor broken only by nightmares and fantastic dreams. Marx woke the next day with a spasmodic coughing fit so acute that he thought he was suffocating. Tussy need look no further for the source of her genetic inheritance of nervous illness. Marx was convinced that mental anguish was biologically inseparable from bodily health and well-being.

The week before Tussy's twenty-eighth birthday a telegram arrived at Maitland Park Road. Jennychen had died suddenly on the afternoon of 11 January. She was thirty-eight. 'I immediately left for Ventnor,' Tussy recalled:

> I have lived many a sad hour, but none so sad as that. I felt that I was bringing my father his death sentence. I racked my brain all the long anxious way to find how I could break the news to him. But I did not need to, my face gave me away. Mohr said at once: 'Our Jennychen is dead.'[75]

Within half an hour of Tussy's arrival Marx put her on the next train back to London, commanding her to proceed directly to Argenteuil and look after the now-motherless children. Tussy found it unbearable to leave him alone in this darkest hour, but he 'brooked no resistance'.[76] Everything, he said, must be arranged for the sake of the children.

Marx left so hurriedly for London that he had to request his doctor to forward his bill to Maitland Park Road. Enclosing a note of gratitude with the onward address, he explained to Dr Williamson the cause of his sudden departure and remarked, 'Indeed, I find some relief in a grim headache. Physical pain is the only "stunner" of mental pain.'[77] This is believed to be the last letter he wrote.

Lenchen's attempts to cheer up Marx with new recipes failed. Milk – which he had never liked drinking before – and rum or brandy became his preferred diet. His 'reading' was limited to flicking through publishers' catalogues or interpreting the flames in the hearth in his study into which he gazed for long hours. In February he developed an abscess on the lung and was confined to his bed.

When Tussy returned from France she understood immediately that her father had come home to London to die. She brought Harra back with her but he was seriously ill; very upset, Tussy had to commit him to the children's hospital in Shadwell.

On Wednesday 14 March Engels arrived as usual at 2.30 p. m. for his daily visit. Lenchen came downstairs and told him that Mohr had left his bedroom and gone into his study, where he was dozing in his favourite armchair. By the time they got upstairs, he was gone. 'The General had that armchair until he died,' Tussy later wrote. 'Now I have got it.'[78]

Tussy signed the registration of death and she and Lenchen washed and laid Mohr out in his coffin for the many mourners who came to Maitland Park Road to say their last goodbyes. 'Mankind is shorter by a head, and by the most remarkable head of our time,' said his best friend.[79]

Tussy had lost her first love.

Eleven mourners gathered at Marx's funeral in Highgate Cemetery on 17 March 1883. Tussy, flanked by Engels and Lenchen, watched her father's coffin committed to the same plot as her mother's. The small company included the recently widowed Longuet, Library, Lessner, Schorleemer, Edwin Ray Lankester and Paul Lafargue. Though her husband was present, Laura was not. Tussy missed her sister. They had been estranged by her marriage to Lafargue, the old feud over Lissagaray, and Laura's sense of not being the most favoured child. But they were now each other's closest surviving blood relatives.

Engels delivered the eulogy, concluding that Marx's 'name and work will endure though the ages'.[80] The following week, Karl and Jenny Marx's grave was reopened, in Tussy's presence, for the interment of the little body of Harry Longuet, who died on 21 March aged four and a half in Shadwell children's hospital.

Karl Marx made it clear before he died that he regarded Eleanor and Engels as his natural heirs. 'Our natures were so exactly alike,' Tussy wrote after her father's death:

I remember his once saying a thing that at the time I did not understand and that even sounded rather paradoxical. But I know now what he meant . . . My father was talking of my eldest sister and of me and said: 'Jenny is most like me, but Tussy (my dear old home name) *is* me.' It was true – except that I shall never be good and unselfish as he was.[81]

With this legacy, she now had to strike out a line of her own.

The Reading Room

After the death of her parents and eldest sister, Eleanor's life changed tense. From living in the subjunctive she shifted to living in the present. The transition was stark and prompted by grief and her new understanding of mortality. No more did she say 'I want to be' or 'I would were it possible'. Instead, Eleanor inhabited 'I am', 'I will' and 'I do'.

Condolences flowed from every tributary of the globe as news of Marx's death spread around the world. Tussy and Engels replied personally to thousands of letters and telegrams. Many offers of support were extended – sometimes from unlikely quarters. Matilda Hyndman, wife of Henry, offered Eleanor a retreat under her roof and assured her that if she preferred, she would keep her husband out of her way.[1] Furnivall asked if Marx had made adequate provision for her. Knowing Eleanor's impulsive generosity, he urged her not to give up any legacy she received to others who she might mistakenly consider had need greater than her own.[2]

Marx's estate amounted to £250 cash. His literary legacy was of inestimably greater value. Eleanor was appointed his executor on 18 August, 'according to English law . . . the only person living who is the legal representative of Mohr, in England',[3] as the General explained to Laura, who was upset about the decision to make Tussy, legally, sole executor. Tussy's entitlement left Laura feeling abandoned. Engels shielded Tussy from Laura's angry accusatory letters.

He urged her to visit London, regretting that she had been unable to come since her father's death. Unaware of Laura's fury, Tussy wrote to her unreservedly about the labour now required:

> . . . *all* the private letters I shall put aside. They are of interest only to us, and can be looked to any time. The other papers – Mss., International correspondence etc. – is what we must look to now. Would you like me to send you all your and Lafargue's letters? If so as I find them I will put them together. This sorting of the papers will be terrible work. I hardly know how it is to be got through. I must give certain days in the week to it *entirely*. Of course I cannot sit down and do *only* that. I must keep up my lessons, and get all the work I can.[4]

Tussy returned to teaching at Mrs Bircham's school in Kensington, adding an innovative Literature Class to her courses. She had neither the time nor the money to continue regular coaching with Elizabeth Vezin.

Despite her aspirations, Eleanor was sufficiently pragmatic to face facts squarely. She now understood that she lacked the qualities it took to become a first-rate actor on the English stage. This had also become apparent to Elizabeth Vezin, who reluctantly told her she was very competent, but 'would never achieve real greatness on the boards – the glory would always fall short of the dream'.[5]

Eleanor's reasons for letting go of this hard-fought-for dream appear at first prosaic: family illness and multiple deaths diverted her time and energies. She needed to find a new home and, for the first time, pay all the rent and bills. On top of her paid work, she must allocate several days a week for sorting Mohr's papers. In its inimitable way, death clarified things for the maturing Eleanor. She couldn't afford financial recklessness. After all, did the world need another actor more than it needed Marx's intellectual legacy, secured by the one qualified, undaunted individual other than Engels with whom it could be trusted absolutely?

Interwoven with the practical, the ineffable, Eleanor discovered that she couldn't pretend to be anyone other than herself. Onstage and off, she seemed unable to be convincing as anyone other than

Eleanor Marx. This failure of aptitude for dissimulation was simultaneously one of her greatest assets and, given her aspirations, a significant disadvantage of her personality.

This aspect of her character sat uneasily with the context of the specific historical moment in which she lived, and where she was so often way ahead of her time. By temperament and aesthetic Tussy was a movie star rather than a stage actress;[6] modernist naturalism was far more her style. George Bernard Shaw, who had recently introduced himself to Tussy in the British Museum Reading Room, said of himself that he was born 'fifty years too soon'.[7] The same could be said of Tussy. Born fifty years later, she might have found cinema the natural environment for her talent.

The repertoire available to Tussy in the theatre of her time was a world apart from the unacted parts she *wanted* to play. Though they profoundly interested her intellectually, Shakespeare's women – Juliet, Lady Macbeth, Beatrice – constrained and frustrated her. From childhood it was always Shakespeare's great male characters who intrigued and inspired Eleanor. She wanted to play Romeo, not Juliet; Macbeth, not his wife; Hamlet, not Ophelia; Richard, not Lady Anne; Mark Antony, not Cleopatra.

If she'd had a different, less conventional teacher than Elizabeth Vezin, perhaps Tussy might have found her voice. Like many other actors of her era – whether successful, would-be or failed – she longed for female roles articulating more truly her own experience as a modern woman. She needed, in short, the new theatre. Helen Alving in Ibsen's *Ghosts*, not Lady Macbeth; Nora Helmer in *A Doll's House*, not Cleopatra. The prototypes for the roles Eleanor desired were emerging from the pens of her contemporaries. Some of these pens were held in the grip of her closest friends and Eleanor herself was their inspiration and model. Tussy lived along new lines and not only expressed but acted in her real life new ideas of what woman was, wanted and could be.

In the early 1880s Tussy gathered around her a cast of remarkable people who took centre stage in her life after Mohr's death. Had such a thing been possible for a woman in her era, Tussy would have made a brilliant theatre director. Instead, her theatre for creating a new cast of radical actors in English art and politics was the British Museum

Reading Room, its lofty dome a metaphor for the seat of the brain, workspace for writers and thinkers.

Her father, Arthur Conan-Doyle and Bram Stoker had been amongst the first to apply for readers' tickets to the new Reading Room when it was opened in May 1857; and it will be recalled that Eleanor had joined in October 1877, when she was twenty-two. Second in size only to the Pantheon, Sydney Smirke's Reading Room was constructed from cast-iron arches and concrete in the central courtyard of the British Museum and lit with skylights and windows. Inside, hot-water pipes ran along the ground as warming footrests for readers. There were roomy leather-covered desks for 350 readers, each equipped with bookstands, a ready supply of free paper, ink and blotters. At the epicentre of the Reading Room was situated a desk for the librarians and attendants, with concentric shelves housing the famous catalogue, endlessly updated by cut and paste.

The circular interior with its librarians perched hawkishly in the middle was a reminder that the Reading Room was designed as a panopticon, the structure so beloved of Victorian public institutions and every social philosopher's favourite architectural metaphor for the power of surveillance.[8]

It was here that Eleanor and her Victorian Bloomsbury group worked, flirted and subverted.

Those permitted access to the intellectual manufactory of the Reading Room included some of the leading dissidents of the Victorian age. The freely spacious, adventurous mind sat next to the pretentiously overcapacious; the intellectual fringe next to state- and lawmakers. Women and men sat side by side. The Reading Room was unusual for being a public place where men and women had equal status and, almost, equal access to all subjects and resources of the mind.

Except when the subject was sex.

Tussy discovered that different rules were applied to men and women even in the democracy of reading when she submitted a ticket request to study the Kama Sutra. She was permitted to read it only at a specially designated naughty table under the direct supervisory surveillance of the librarian.[9] Did the powers that be (whoever *they* might be) fear that the daughter of socialism would be inspired to make an impromptu, on-the-spot, practical demonstration of what she learned from its pages?

Mental and visual wandering was common in the charged, ambient hush. Women in the Reading Room were still a rare enough sight for their male peers to regard them as an oddity and, in the tradition of the library, to typecast them: 'the serious writer', 'the lady novelist', 'the giggling girl', 'the conscientious[10] scholar or researcher', 'the strident political battle-axe'. People knew each other by sight, if not by name.

Eleanor was easily recognisable. Her trademark pince-nez clipped to a long pinchbeck chain dangled over shapely breasts and waist that were, very clearly, as nature made them and not corseted. Her curls tumbled loosely and thickly to her waist – a style unusual for the time outside of factory, field, bedroom, brothel or dance hall. Tussy's attempts to pin back her tresses were perfunctory, absent-minded operations, and she shed pins on the desks and in the catalogues.

Special occasion photographs in which her hair was carefully ironed and dressed into submission for the formal pose before the camera are deceptive. Her radical dress sense and relaxed physical bearing announced her as unconventional and avant-garde without a word being spoken. Beatrice Potter recognised her immediately, as she recorded in her diary on 24 May 1883:

> In person she is comely, dressed in a slovenly picturesque way with curly black hair, flying about in all directions. Fine eyes full of life and sympathy, otherwise ugly features and expression and complexion showing signs of unhealthy excited life kept up with stimulants and tempered by narcotics.[11]

Beatrice Potter, later Mrs Sidney Webb, was one of Tussy's many passing acquaintances in the Reading Room at this time. Beatrice introduced herself and suggested tea in the refreshment room, curious to hear Eleanor's views on British secularist and journal editor George Foote's recent prosecution for blasphemous libel. Foote had set up *Freethinker* in May 1881. Its regular sections included

'Comic Bible Sketches' and 'Profane Jokes'. He was prosecuted for blasphemy in May 1882. When Foote's sentence of one year with hard labour was passed down from the bench by Judge North, a Catholic, he replied, 'My Lord, I thank you; it is worthy of your creed.'[12]

A fellow secularist campaigner called Edward Aveling, who contributed religious and scientific articles to the journal, was appointed acting editor during Foote's imprisonment. In his editorials Aveling robustly continued to defend the 'right to blaspheme'.[13] Eleanor had first heard Aveling speak with Michael Davitt in 1880 during the Irish agrarian war, when she was present at the National Secular Society meeting in London to demand land law reform. The Dogberries also noted Dr Aveling's lecture series on Shakespeare at the Hall of Science in 1881, and Eleanor was aware of him standing as a candidate for Westminster in the London School Board elections of 1882. As they talked about his acting editorship of *Freethinker*, Beatrice was unaware of any connection between Aveling and Miss Marx.

Beatrice asked Eleanor whether or not she thought Foote had exceeded the proper limits on freedom of expression by offending Christian believers. Eleanor replied she didn't find Foote's extracts particularly amusing, but could find nothing intrinsically wrong with them: 'Ridicule is quite a legitimate weapon. It is the weapon Voltaire used and did more good with it than any amount of serious argument.'[14] They discussed Christianity:

> She read the gospels as the gospel of damnation. Thought Christ, if he had existed, was a weak-minded individual with a good deal of character but quite lacking in heroism. 'Did he not,' Eleanor said, 'in the last moment, pray that the cup might pass from him?'[15]

To Potter's proposition of 'the beauty of the Christian religion' Tussy replied that Christianity is an immoral illusion. The debate continued – no doubt drawing an interested audience in the tearoom. 'The striking difference of this century and the last,' Eleanor continued, 'is that free thought was the privilege of the upper classes then and it is becoming the privilege of the working classes now.'[16]

Modern socialism, she put to Beatrice, aimed at educating people to 'disregard the mythical next world and live for this world and insist on having what will make it pleasant for them'.[17] And what, Beatrice asked Eleanor, was 'socialist progress'?

> She very sensibly remarked that I might as well ask her to give me in a short formula the whole theory of mechanics . . . I replied that from the little I knew about political economy (the only social science we English understood) the social philosophers seemed to limit themselves to describing forces that were more or less necessarious. She did not contradict this.[18]

Beatrice, of course, had to comment on the personal life that must surely accompany such revolutionary thinking:

> Lives alone, is much connected with the Bradlaugh set, evidently peculiar views on love, etc., and should think has somewhat 'natural' relations with men! Should fear that the chances were against her remaining long within the pale of 'respectable' society.[19]

It would amuse Eleanor to know she had ever been in danger of consideration for entry to respectable society. More still that she was assumed to be an adherent of Charles Bradlaugh, a vigorous opponent of socialism.[20] Tussy and Mohr disagreed on many things but one of the values they shared absolutely was religious unbelief. Yet it was true that a few years previously her mother and eldest sister had briefly tried out Bradlaugh's secularist Sunday services. Mohr disliked secularism, and told Möhme that if she sought 'edification or satisfaction of her metaphysical needs she would find them in the Jewish prophets rather than in Mr Bradlaugh's shallow reasonings'.[21] Edward Aveling was a prominent figure in the National Secular Society from 1880 and had seen – though never spoken with – Mrs Marx and her eldest daughter when they tried out Bradlaugh's Sunday meetings.

Aveling started using the British Museum Reading Room in 1882. It was here that he finally approached and introduced himself to Eleanor. Aveling was well versed in the opportunities provided for flirtation and potential liaison in this studious space. He wrote a comic article on 'the humours of the Reading Room' for *Progress*, finding it 'in equal degrees a menagerie and a lunatic asylum' and playfully recommending that sexual segregation would achieve 'less talking and fewer marriages'.[22] This article appeared in May 1883, shortly after Marx's death and at the same time that Eleanor began to speak publicly of her association with Edward Aveling.

Edward Bibbins Aveling was born in London on 29 November 1849 at 6 Nelson Terrace, a middle-class street in Stoke Newington, Hackney. Edward's mother was Mary Ann Goodall, and his father the God-fearing Reverend Thomas William Baxter Aveling, a Congregational minister who presided over the Independent Congregational Chapel in Kingsland High Street for nearly half a century. The Avelings had three servants. Adult Edward claimed an admixture of French and Irish ancestry. His mother and paternal grandmother were indeed Irish emigrants to England, but there is no evidence of his claims to French blood. His mother Mary Ann was the daughter of a Cambridgeshire farmer and innkeeper, a great wit and, by the time of Edward's birth, an alcoholic.

Reverend Thomas William Baxter Aveling was a distinguished Dissenter and republican who held honorary doctorates, chairmanships and leadership positions in Nonconformist organisations. It says something of Edward's father that within fifteen years he had built a ministry that required the building of a brand new Gothic edifice to accommodate his expanded congregation of over 2,000. The parishioners clubbed together to buy a hideous pulpit from the Great Exhibition of 1851 and dubbed their new place of worship the 'Cathedral of North London'.

Reverend Aveling advocated the establishment of schools for both sexes and was vocal about his belief in the rights of women to be educated. He didn't, however, believe in pleasure, and there was none of the frivolity and fun in the Aveling household that surrounded Eleanor's upbringing as a Marx.

Edward grew up in a large family of three elder brothers, two younger brothers and two sisters. A spine injury caused by a childhood accident gave adult Edward a slight stoop that contributed to his reptilian air. Sickliness resulting from this injury confined him to home for many of his early years, where he had the run of his father's excellent library, the shelves of which housed Bunyan, Shakespeare, Defoe, Fielding and any number of theological texts. He was free to read what he chose except on Sundays, when he was forbidden to read anything except *Pilgrim's Progress*.

In 1863 Edward and his younger brother Frederick were sent to board at the Dissenters' Proprietary School in Taunton. Edward and Frederick were the first of the Aveling boys to be fully educated. At the same age, their elder brothers had all started work as apprentices and clerks. The benefit of this superior education came to Edward as a result of his eldest sister Mary marrying a bullion agent, enriching the whole family.

Edward stayed at Taunton for two years, after which he was privately educated by a series of tutors. He decided on a medical profession and enrolled at University College, London in the Faculty of Medicine in 1867. He won an entrance scholarship for £25 and garnered medals, prizes and first certificates for excellent academic performance in chemistry, practical physiology, histology and botany. In 1869 he won a scholarship to specialise in zoology, in which he took his BSc. Edward was a hard worker and took a job as a lab assistant in Cambridge to eminent physiologist Michael Foster.

Edward's choice to study medicine at the 'Godless College' – as University College was known – was logical. Dissenters were banned from holding public office under the Crown and barred from entry to the old universities – Oxford, Cambridge and Durham – until 1871. Conversely, London University was open to all creeds.

Edward took up a teaching post at Miss Buss's North London Collegiate School for Girls in Camden Road, a pioneering institution for women's education of which, not coincidentally, Edward's father was a patron. Whilst studying for his undergraduate degree, Edward took on private coaching and published cheap editions of *Botanical Tables* and *Physiological Tables* for students. Various medical bodies, including the Department of Science and Art, subsidised the publication of these textbooks to prepare students for examination. The Department of Science and Art was set up to expand technical instruction and the training of qualified teachers, threatened by competition from foreign countries whose superior technical education was beginning to negatively affect British competence in trade, science and technology.

In 1875 Edward was appointed as a part-time lecturer in comparative anatomy and biology at the London Hospital; the following year, he obtained his DSc at University College, London, and was made a Fellow of the Linnean Society. In 1879 he applied for a vacant chair in comparative anatomy at King's College London but didn't get the job.

Edward Aveling was an intelligent, hard-working young academic with a promising career ahead of him. He showed no talent for original thinking but he was an excellent teacher and a highly competent scholarly writer. He was seriously committed to the public education of a mass, often working-class audience in atheism and Darwinian philosophy, through the popular platform of the National Secular Society.[23] He stuck to his political principles at the expense of continuing a respectable, successful progression within conventional academic institutions. That his politics had cost him his academic career went a long way with Tussy and the General towards establishing Edward as a man who would sacrifice personal gain for political principle.

Inevitably, Edward had a religious upbringing from his ambivalent father, who was very receptive to Darwin's theories. His education and training in the natural sciences coincided with the time when Darwin's theories, propagated primarily in his *On the Origin of Species*, challenged both religious and previous scientific mythologies about the evolution of species. Edward was an enthusiastic Darwinian. Orthodox theologians objected, but his dissenting father remarked that the word of God 'does not come to us to expound any science at all, except that of salvation'.[24]

Edward's passion for art and theatre, on the other hand, was a source of anxiety and discord with his father. Edward was a born showman, infused with passionate enthusiasm and belief in the power of his own performance – on and off stage – during which he became completely absorbed in the sound of his own voice and lost himself as he spoke.

While a student, Edward married Isabel Campbell Frank – known to all as Bell – daughter of a well-off Leadenhall chicken farmer who came with a handsome dowry. The couple married in a service conducted by Edward's father in the Union Chapel in Islington in July 1872. The marriage didn't last long. By Edward's various contradictory accounts, the – he claimed – 'adulterous Bell', who was religious, ran off with a priest and spread malicious gossip about her husband. Edward claimed to other people that they had parted amicably 'by mutual agreement'.[25] Edward's younger brother Frederick, however, provided a different account of the separation. He wrote of Edward that 'he married Bell Frank for her money (300 a year). She could only get half. He soon made her do that. When not able to get any more out of her, he left her.'[26]

In fact the dowry she brought to her marriage with Edward was a £1,000 legacy from her father, who had died four years previously, which was due to her when she either turned twenty-one or married. Frederick also pointed out that his brother's separation from his wife coincided exactly with a series of rumours about extra-curricular sexual dalliances with his female students.

Edward's mother Mary died of alcohol-related apoplexy in 1877, and his father, then sixty-three, remarried the sister of another Congregationalist minister. Edward adored his mother. It was after her death that he declared himself fully as an atheist. Charles Bradlaugh, President of the National Secular Society, in which Edward became extremely active, claimed that Edward's involvement in the freethought movement cost him many old friends and family ties. It was nearer the truth that his friends and family were appalled at his shameless treatment of Bell Frank, and objected to his attempts at a disreputable theatrical career.

Edward worked for a while as the manager of a travelling theatre company but, stuck in amateur repertory, he transferred his skills as a performer into his travelling public lecture series and appearances in secularist movement entertainments. Like Eleanor, he gave recitations of poetry and prose at campaign rallies and benefits, from Shakespeare to Edgar Allan Poe. He excelled at reciting his favourite piece, *The Bells* by Poe, the long poem in which bells are tolled by ghouls. In 1881 Henry Salt was very struck by Aveling's rendition of this piece at the Hall of Science, finding 'something rather uncanny and impish in his nature which doubtless made him a good interpreter of the weird'.[27]

London University made its degree courses available to women in 1878. It was the first university in Britain to open its doors to women on equal terms with men. Four female students achieved Bachelor of Arts degrees in 1880, and two gained Bachelor of Science degrees in 1881. Inspired by this precedent, Annie Besant enrolled at London University. Dr Aveling was her tutor. As well as becoming his pupil, the two became colleagues in the Secular Society.

Annie Besant was two years older than Aveling and separated from her husband, a clergyman, as a consequence of her scepticism and secularism. Besant and Charles Bradlaugh soon emerged as the leaders of the organised movement of British secularism, and evidently were in love. Aveling's arrival as their newest intellectual recruit who would bring scientific credibility to the work of the campaign also put the rather syrupy romantic Annie Besant in a position she liked and continually sought to reproduce – having her attentions fought over by (at least) two men simultaneously.

British secularism emerged as an organised movement in the mid-nineteenth century. Early freethinkers such as Jeremy Bentham, the father of utilitarianism, and Thomas Paine, author of *The Age of Reason*, led its thinking, inspired by the impact of the French Revolution. Publisher Richard Carlile was prosecuted and served a nine-year prison sentence for publishing Paine's book. In broadest terms the practice of scepticism or indifference, secularism takes the view that considerations of religion and faith should be excluded from public education and all civil affairs.[28]

At the beginning of 1879, shortly after he turned thirty, Aveling started a series in the Secular Society magazine the *National Reformer*, outlining Darwin's theory of natural selection. He published a statement in the *National Reformer* titled 'Credo Ergo Laborado' – 'I believe, therefore I shall work' – stating he had become a freethinker. 'I desire . . . to labour for freedom of thought, of word, of act, for all men and women . . . Beautiful Nature, the eternal comforter, is with us.'[29] Shortly afterwards, he successfully transcribed his lectures into a series of accessible, popular penny tracts published as *Student's Darwin* and *Darwin Made Easy* (1881).

Edward delivered his first public lecture in the Hall of Science on 10 August 1879, with Annie Besant chairing. Percy Bysshe Shelley was his subject, and the central idea that this poet's art demonstrated the unity of all forms of sensation and the kinship that exists between two related orders of thought, the scientific and the poetical. The argument was an expression of his thinking on materialism and efforts to integrate science and art. Besant gave a gushing vote of thanks from the chair, praising the 'music' and 'artistic charm' of Dr Aveling's 'exquisitely chosen' and 'polished' language.[30] This torrent of ego-enhancing admiration floated the pair away on a romantic interlude in the mountains of north Wales, where they penned explicit love poetry for each other.

There's no record of how Charles Bradlaugh reacted to the entry of Edward into his relationship with Annie but publicly they continued to work together as a triumvirate known as 'the great Trinity in Unity',[31] constantly extolling each other's talents. It was the arrival of Eleanor in Edward's affections that put the socialist cat amongst the secularist pigeons.

Passionately committed to the new cause, Edward toured all around Britain from Cornwall to Scotland, giving Sunday lectures on the subjects of secularism and science, problems with the Christian conception of God, and on evolution and Darwin's theories. Aveling ably explained to his audiences Darwin's contention that Christianity 'is not supported by evidence',[32] and reassured them that Darwin himself had confessed to not giving up Christianity until he was forty years of age. Darwin had searched for empirical evidence based on proof against illusions – and found none.

In one of his lectures, entitled 'Why I dare not to be a Christian', Aveling explained that one of his reasons for giving up Christianity was the acute pain and agony of moral uncertainty he had suffered when adhering to the faith. Secularism, on the other hand, provided him with a form of undiluted utilitarianism: the right to unlimited pleasure. 'In this, our creed, we have not to concern ourselves with the will of a hypothetical being . . . There is for us the simple question ever recurring, will this act, or word, or thought of mine add to the sum of human happiness or of human misery?'[33]

In the 1880 general election Charles Bradlaugh stood for the two-member constituency of Northampton and was elected with radical anti-monarchist Henry Labouchère. Forbidden from taking the parliamentary oath and from making affirmation, when Bradlaugh claimed the right to be sworn in and refused to withdraw when he was blocked, he was physically dragged out of the House of Commons by the Serjeant-at-Arms. This struggle went on for some years. Bradlaugh was re-elected five times by the voters of Northampton and five times forcibly removed from the House before the constitutional battle to take up his seat was finally won. The campaign prompted Aveling to write a lecture on 'Representation of the People', reflecting on British constitutional rights, and proved a political education for Edward in activist politics that was a prelude to his entry into socialism.

Aveling delivered his manifesto for secularist thinking in his essay *The Gospel of Evolution*, published in a journal called the *Atheistic Platform* in 1884. Here he explains evolution as the idea of unity and continuity of all phenomena; the unity of matter and motion, and life itself as essentially 'a mode of motion'. And who are the apostles of secularism?

> The preachers of this new gospel are nature herself and all her children. Thus the history of man, all science, all human lives, we that live and love, are the apostles of the new evangel. And its temples ... are the halls of universities, the state-schools, the science classes for our young men and maidens, the laboratories, and the studies of the philosophers, the hearts of all that seek truth.[34]

Aveling believed passionately in the importance of secular education. Education, he said, was the only means by which all people could be lifted above religious ignorance and exposed to the option of choosing atheist principles. His mission was explicitly evangelical: 'The Board Schools of this century will be to the generations that succeed us as the churches were to those before our time.'[35]

Aveling stood for the Westminster Division at the London School Board elections of November 1882, declaring himself in favour of 'free, secular, compulsory education'.[36] The Westminster branch of the National Secular Society and Henry Hyndman's Democratic Federation assisted his campaign. As well as Henry Hyndman, two veteran Chartists, the editor of the *Labour News* and several other members of the Democratic Federation worked for his nomination and election. He was returned with 4,720 votes.

As his speeches after his election make clear, Edward was now well on the road to socialism, explicitly supporting the cause of higher education and technical education as a rightful entitlement of the working classes. Westminster, his constituency, included 'Soho, Peabody Buildings, Seven Dials, and the voices of the dwellers in such places as these are faintly heard; for over-work and under-pay, hardship and sickness, stifle them. I want to speak especially for such as these. The poor, the wronged, the untaught are, above all, my constituents.'[37] Henry Hyndman declared of Aveling, 'I did not like the man from the first',[38] but recognised his political usefulness and agreed with Annie Besant that Aveling's election to the Westminster School Board struck 'a sore blow to the Church and Tory party'.[39]

Edward was a prolific jobbing reviewer and critic of literature, history, theatre and music. He took over the Art Corner columns of *Our Corner*, the secularist magazine founded by Annie Besant in January 1883, and wrote many yards of copy on Irving at the Lyceum. With Bell Frank's dowry to spend, Edward took boxes at the Lyceum for his friends and also treated them to shows and dinner at the fashionable Criterion Restaurant and Theatre in Piccadilly. Aveling suited his liberation from Christian morality to his predilection for self-gratifying hedonism. For Tussy, this was both an intriguing and a dangerous combination. According to Aveling's self-portrait of the atheist, he was:

> ... not inclined to be miserable in this his only life. He loves it, joys in it, revels in it. He is not blind to its pains and sorrows. Bearing these as cheerfully as he may, he concentrates his attention on the pleasures and sweetness of life, and on ... the task of lessening the aggregate of the world's misery.[40]

And so Aveling was an attractive, clever cad who played a significant role in popularising Darwin and steering British secularists towards socialism.[41] It's easy to see why his anti-establishment, anti-religious, anti-materialist turn of mind appealed to Eleanor. And equally easy to understand how she failed to recognise that his character was the projection of a consummate actor.

Aveling claimed later to have known Marx before his death: 'I stood by the side of his corpse, hand in hand with my wife,'[42] by which he meant Eleanor. A touching conceit, though entirely untrue. Aveling was canny enough to lure Eleanor through her intellect. Just as the way to many a man's heart might be through his stomach, the surest way to Eleanor's heart was through her head. Offering his condolence on her father's death, Aveling suggested she might like to write two articles about him for *Progress*, a monthly magazine 'of advanced thought' launched in January 1883 by Foote, with Aveling as co-editor.

To the satisfaction of both, this commission provided ample pretext for them to spend time together in the Reading Room and around its Bloomsbury precincts. Within weeks, Eleanor agreed to Aveling's request that she assist him with the general editing of *Progress* – and thus arose more opportunities for them to put their heads together.

From the beginning to the end of their relationship, Edward almost always called her Eleanor. Amongst family and friends who knew her as Tussy this was unusual, and somehow a bit ponderous. Those close to her remarked on it immediately. There were occasions when Edward called her Tussy, but they were rare enough to be notable. Sam Moore and Jollymeier remembered her childhood rule, 'that if anyone did not call me Tussy they had to stand on a chair and say Tussy 6 times'.[43] Clearly the rules were different for Edward Aveling.

Eleanor's articles about her father appeared in the May and June editions of *Progress*. The first was a biographical and historical account of Marx's life, the second a concise explanation of the theory of surplus value. Thus Eleanor Marx became her father's first biographer and posthumous exponent of his economic theory. The first essay was a personal human story; the second a clear, rigorous, macroeconomic exposition:

There is no time so little fitted for writing the biography of a great man as that immediately after his death, and the task is doubly difficult when it falls to one who knew and loved him. It is impossible for me to do more at present than give the briefest sketch of my father's life. I shall confine myself to a simple statement of facts, and I shall not even attempt an exposition of his great theories and discoveries; theories that are the very foundation of Modern Socialism – discoveries that are revolutionising the whole science of Political Economy. I hope, however, to give in a future number of *Progress* an analysis of my father's chief work – *Das Kapital*, and of the truths set forth in it.

Karl Marx was born at Trier, on May 1818, of Jewish parents . . . [44]

And so ever since have all biographers of Marx followed suit, basing their account on the primary sources supplied by Eleanor immediately after her father's death.

Moving from this succinct narrative of Marx's life to the core of his thought, the second *Progress* article delivers, as promised, an explanation of the theory of surplus value. Undaunted by the task, Eleanor grasps the reader firmly by the hand and situates her father's work within its longer tradition of economic analysis:

David Ricardo begins his great work, *Principles of Political Economy and Taxation*, with these words: 'The value of a commodity, or the quantity of any other commodity for which it will exchange, depends upon the relative quantity of *labour* necessary for its production, and not on the greater or less *compensation* which is paid for that labour.' This great discovery of Ricardo's, that there is but one real standard of value, *labour*, forms the starting-point of Marx's *Das Kapital* . . . Marx completes, and partly corrects, Ricardo's theory of value, and develops, out of it, a theory of that fearfully contested subject, currency, which . . . has carried conviction even into the heads of many political economists of the ordinary stamp.[45]

Eleanor proceeds to explain clearly and succinctly 'the mode, based upon his theory of value, by which Marx explains the origin and the continued accumulation of capital in the hands of a, thereby, privileged class'.[46] At this time only the first volume of *Capital* had been published, so Eleanor was working also from unpublished manuscript materials. Her biographical narrative was collated, in part, from the mass of papers, correspondence and interminable lucky-dip muddled-up boxes and files she, the General and Lenchen were painstakingly trying to sort into some sort of archival order in the move from Maitland Park Road.

It was during this period that George Bernard Shaw introduced himself to Tussy in the Reading Room. Imagining himself a suitor, he was initially unaware of the shadow of Edward Aveling hovering in the bookstacks, keeping a watchful eye on everyone Eleanor talked to. Shaw's interest in politics was developing at the time he met her. His passionate newfound interest in socialism and her father's work led him to read *Capital*, an experience he described as 'the turning point in my career'.[47]

Shaw first studied *Capital* in Deville's abridged translation, approved by Marx before his death and Engels after, and published in August 1883. He read it in the place where much of it was written, the Reading Room, the only library where the publication was accessible to him. From poring over the book that changed his life, it was only a short step for Shaw (GBS) to introduce himself to Eleanor and invite her to a nearby Bloomsbury teashop.

Tussy and GBS shared a love of both socialism and the stage. A year younger than her, Shaw came to England in 1876 at the age of twenty. His Irishness, of course, was a point of great recommendation to Tussy, as presumably was his admiration of her father's work. Undoubtedly he was correct in his claim to be the only member of Hyndman's Democratic Federation who had actually read *Capital*. They 'chatted about this [*Capital*], death, sex, and a lot of things'.[48] They went to shows together and Shaw urged her to pursue her theatrical ambitions – as he did most of the women he fell for.

In September Tussy went to Eastbourne on holiday with the General, Lenchen and Pumps. Helen was in a funk of grief and exhausted from the labour of sorting out the family home. Deeply concerned, Tussy wrote to Laura asking if Lenchen might visit Paris for a few weeks' holiday and change of scene, and perhaps see the

Longuet children. Laura didn't reply. It was a devastating time for
Lenchen. She'd shared her life with Jenny and Karl since childhood.
She'd delivered all their children, and buried with them the many
that died. They were family. Lenchen shared all their secrets and
would take them with her to their communal grave. Engels was the
only other survivor who shared the same intimacies.

Eastbourne provided a welcome rest. As always, Tussy and the
General went for long and rambling talking walks, and on dry days
sat on the seafront reading together. Eleanor showed the General a
review of Ralph Iron's startling new novel, *The Story of an African
Farm*, in the latest edition of *Progress*, written by Edward Aveling
and headlined, approvingly, 'A Notable Book'. First published by
Chapman & Hall at the end of January in two volumes, each with an
ostrich on the spine evoking the story's Karoo setting, this extraordinary debut went to a second larger edition in July. Tussy told the
General that the remarkable South African author of this groundbreaking new novel, 'Ralph Iron', was in fact a new friend of hers,
Olive Schreiner.

The General was aware that, since writing her memorial articles
on Marx for its May and June editions, Tussy had been doing a great
deal of work for *Progress*, and was now co-editing the journal with
Aveling. Eleanor spoke about 'Edward' frequently and he came to
visit her in Eastbourne, causing amused exchanges of meaningful
looks between the General and Lenchen.

After the holiday in Eastbourne, Maitland Park Road was broken
up and Tussy went to live on her own for the first time at 122 Great
Coram Street in the heart of Bloomsbury, with a lot of books, a box
of crockery and a few bits of furniture from the family home.
Lenchen went to live at Regent's Park Road as the General's house-
keeper, where the ebullient Pumps had to learn quickly to defer to
Lenchen's undisputed authority. Mohr's armchair went to Regent's
Park Road for the General.

The General and Lenchen started sorting Marx's letters together
and enjoyed a regular mid-morning tipple, gossiping about politics
and Marx's daughters and grandchildren.

After she moved into Regent's Park Road, Lenchen's son Freddy
and her grandson Harry began to visit her regularly for the first time.

Henry Frederick Demuth, born in Dean Street on 3 June 1851, grew up in foster care with minimal education. He firmly grasped the limited opportunities available to him for learning numeracy and literacy, and his letters have a clear and fluent though painfully humble voice.

Freddy served an engineering apprenticeship and became a skilled fitter and turner by profession, later joining the King's Cross branch of the Amalgamated Society of Engineers and the Hackney Labour Party. By the early 1880s he lived in Hackney with his wife and son, Harry. Adult Harry later recalled using the tradesman's entrance on his visits to Regent's Park Road with his father, and remembered his grandmother Lenchen as 'a motherly sort of person'.[49]

Though it's unclear when and how they first met, Tussy and Freddy had known each other for some time. Correspondence dated May 1882 between Jennychen and Laura makes it clear both of Tussy's elder sisters were involved in Freddy's life. 'You cannot imagine what it is to me to think that I still owe poor Freddy his money, and that it is probably my insolvency which prevents our dear Lenchen from carrying out her projects of going to Germany,'[50] Jennychen wrote to Laura. Engels looked after them; in turn, they believed they were supporting Engels's undeclared son, conceived with Lenchen in the old Soho days.

Eleanor was shocked but not puzzled by the General's indifferent, aloof attitude towards Freddy. Usually warm and genial to all extended family and friends, the General avoided close interaction with Freddy and usually went out or hid in his study when he and little Harry visited. This behaviour confirmed Tussy's long-held surmise that the General was the father of Lenchen's only child, and named for him. 'Freddy has behaved admirably in all respects and Engels' irritation against him is as unfair as it is comprehensible. We should none of us like to meet our pasts, I guess, in flesh and blood.'[51]

Eleanor began to think about the different impact of reproduction on women and men. She reflected on the lives of her mother and sisters, her friends and the women she met through her activism, both in England through the worker movement and abroad through the International. Reading extensively, Tussy began to compile research notes reflecting broadly on the position of women in human societies. She explored how political and economic philosophies approached sexual inequality – if at all – and began to systematically order her thoughts and inquiry into the woman question.

She returned to the founding texts of socialism to review what they had to say about sexual oppression and the equality of women, including the pioneering work of Charles Fourier, who argued that 'the extention of the privileges of women is the fundamental cause of all social progress'.[52] Gradually and thoroughly Eleanor was building the foundations of a work of feminist political philosophy.

Tussy and her sisters had learned from their mother not to ask Lenchen questions about Freddy. Tussy, warned off the subject, wouldn't dream of raising the question with Lenchen, though she longed to. As the General wouldn't talk to her about it either, Tussy had nowhere to take her questions except into thinking, writing and discussion with her close friends. 'Only when men and women pure-minded, or, at least, striving after purity, discuss the sexual question in all its bearings as free human beings, looking frankly into each other's faces, will there be any hope of its solution.'[53]

Whilst Tussy worried about the unspoken secret of Freddy's paternity, the tensions within the emerging socialist political family came out into the open. In 1884 a factional rift divided British socialists who had associated themselves with the Democratic Federation. Those who leaned to militant internationalism were in one division, represented by philosopher and journalist Ernest Belfort Bax; in another, the nationalistic democrats, led by Henry Hyndman. A third group, including designer, writer and libertarian socialist William Morris, was undecided between the two and so for the meantime supported both. Engels deeply opposed Hyndman and refused to work with him. But he did contribute to the journal *Today*, the monthly 'magazine of scientific socialism' that Bax co-edited and to which Eleanor and Edward were also regular contributors. Eleanor initially liked Bax, though she disagreed with him ideologically.

The gloves came off in March 1884 over a demonstration scheduled at Highgate Cemetery for the commemoration of Marx's death and the proclamation of the Paris Commune. Hyndman was invited to speak at Marx's graveside but declined, saying that an English working-man was the proper person to speak. Aveling was chosen instead.

Challenged head on by Eleanor to declare in favour of the demonstration, Hyndman supported it and endorsed Aveling as the preferred speaker. The event was a great success. A crowd of nearly 5,000 bearing red flags and singing the Marseillaise gathered outside the gates of the cemetery. The Highgate Cemetery Company would not allow them entrance. The 500 policemen deployed to 'defend' the gate seemed a little excessive. Eleanor and a group of women requested permission to enter the cemetery and place flowers on her father's grave. They were refused. So the demonstrators marched to the top of the hill at Dartmouth Park, where Aveling delivered a 'splendid speech' that, according to Eleanor, touched the hearts of all who heard it. He was a good speaker so we've no reason to doubt her, but some of the marchers had rather hoped to hear her speak.

Hyndman soon got his revenge. Four months later in July he drove Bax out of *Today* and replaced him with socialist activist and journalist Henry Hyde Champion. Eleanor declared Champion 'just a tool of Hyndman's, albeit a talented, and I think honest young fellow . . . I shall, of course, not go on writing for *Today* under these circumstances',[54] and made Aveling and Lafargue withdraw their labour too. Her conclusion on Hyndman was uncompromising:

So far he has things here much his own way, but he is playing his cards very badly – irritating everyone, and his little game will soon be played out. The sooner the better for our movement. It has every chance here at this present time if only we had better leaders than Hyndman and his henchmen.[55]

Tussy mobilised assiduously to encourage new leaders. She had a great facility for getting people in position, what she called 'working' them.[56]

In the same month she was involved in a spat over the new International, and drawn into the centre of the dispute between the two leading socialist factions in France: the reformist Possibilists, led by Paul Brousse, and the revolutionary Marxists led by Jules Guesde and Lafargue. The issue at the top of the agenda between the Possibilists and Marxists was the growing demand amongst European workers for an international eight-hour movement. Eleanor became one of the first socialist activists to take up the lead of the International's worker movement for the eight-hour working day.

Interwoven with Tussy's move into a prominent position in socialist organisation was her growing engagement with political feminism. Crucial to radicalising Eleanor's developing thought on the woman question was her new friendship with the South African writer Olive Schreiner. Tussy's new lodgings at Great Coram Street were a few minutes' walk from the British Museum Reading Room. This Bloomsbury neighbourhood was a heterodox place, 'in the midst of eager pulsing life . . . streets . . . crowded with artists, adventurers, Bohemians of many lands . . . people who lived an anxious, eager and perilous life'.[57] Pleasingly for both women, Olive Schreiner was one of these bohemian Bloomsbury artists and adventurers.

It was Tussy, of course, who had passed her copy of Schreiner's *The Story of an African Farm* to Aveling, urging him to review it for *Progress*. Aveling admired the book for being 'cosmopolitan and human',[58] qualities that equally describe its author. 'With all life-relationships this writer deals in the same bluntly honest, far-seeing, outspoken way,'[59] is an equally efficient summary of the twenty-eight-year-old Schreiner's character. Born two months later than Tussy in 1855, Olive was an immediate, like-minded contemporary, from 6,000 miles away on the other side of the world, with a heavy South African accent and – like Tussy – a German father.

A Wesleyan Wittebergen mission station on the edge of colonial Basutoland was the birthplace of Olive Emilie Albertina Schreiner on 24 March 1855. She was the ninth child of the Reverend Gottlob Schreiner and his wife Rebecca Lyndall. In 1865 her father resigned his ministry and turned his hand, unsuccessfully, to trading. The older Schreiner children, who were mostly a tough bunch, brought up little Olive. Inquisitive, a bookworm and ferocious autodidact, Olive became dissatisfied with answers to her questions about the ways of God to man at a very young age. She wandered alone in the

bush, sometimes sleeping out under the stars all night. She scruti-
nised the natural environment and considered the heavens. Like
Darwin, Olive found that what she observed did not equate satisfactorily with the account of creation in the Bible. So she asked difficult
questions that no one in her family would answer. Olive lost her
faith between the ages of eight and ten. Her mother was furious and
reacted punitively. Her siblings resented and feared her. Despite
mental and physical punishment for her rational unbelief, Olive held
fast to her scepticism.

She started work at the age of fifteen as a governess to children on
remote Karoo farms. For a time she lived with her brother, Theo, in
the harsh cowboy environment of a prospectors' camp at the newly
proclaimed New Rush (Kimberley) diamond fields where, in a damp
muddy tent surrounded by dust, digging and drunks, she first started
writing seriously. After a short period trying to live with her sister,
Alice, at the remote outpost of Fraserburg, Olive earned her living
through a succession of jobs in the small Cape towns of Dordrecht
and Colesberg and a number of isolated Great Karoo farms in the
Cradock district.

It was here that Olive conceived *The Story of an African Farm*, the
novel that established her reputation. She wrote by candle- and
moonlight after her day's teaching, at a small wooden table in her
quarters, a lean-to with a stamped earth floor and no ceiling. During
the heavy winter rains when the roof leaked, she dug a trench in the
floor to make an outflow and held an umbrella over her head with
one hand whilst writing with the other.

In March 1881 Olive sailed for England with the intention of
fulfilling her long-cherished ambition to study medicine and become
a doctor. She also hoped to get her novel published. Bad health and
lack of genuine vocation quickly put paid to her medical career. She
spent the winter in Ventnor in the Isle of Wight, redrafting her
manuscript as she had done many times before. Tussy also was in
Ventnor with Mohr during the winter of 1881, but the two women
did not meet.

Olive walked her book around most of the major London publishers, the handwritten manuscript bulging underneath her thin coat as
she tried to protect it from rain and mud. The novel was repeatedly

rejected and Olive was giving up hope of its publication when it was finally accepted and published by Chapman & Hall in early 1883 under the male pseudonym Ralph Iron. The immediate success of *The Story of an African Farm* shot the unknown South African to the heart of the proto-socialist circle that congregated in and around the Reading Room.

Aveling commended the novel's outspoken eloquence on atheism and feminism:

> The relations between men and women are discussed in a fearless, open, righteous fashion, altogether different from the hanging upon the outskirts of the question and pecking at it that are characteristic of your average person. The word of society today is to men 'work,' to women 'seem.' How different is the position of men and of women, how irrational is the difference is her constant theme.[60]

Eleanor and Olive were like magnets. They spent time together every day that they were in the Reading Room and within a year of meeting were intimate friends and political allies. Henry Havelock Ellis said that when he first met Olive in May 1884, Eleanor Marx was her 'chief friend' in England.[61] In the same month Olive moved to Fitzroy Street, in large part to be nearer to Eleanor.

From childhood Schreiner suffered from chronic asthma and Eleanor recommended the surgeon Bryan Donkin, her mother's doctor. Lovestruck Donkin wanted to marry Schreiner and when she refused, continued to yearn for her. Olive was at this time fascinated with Henry Havelock Ellis, who had written an admiring and critical appreciation of *The Story of an African Farm* shortly after its publication, leading to an enthusiastic correspondence between them. They fell in love by post. By the time they met in person, each had great expectations of the other. Ellis was not disappointed; Olive was, initially. The admiring young man was good-looking, erudite and eager to please but his physical presence was very different to the impression created by his strong, forcefully argued letters and determined opinions. Ellis was shy and awkward with a weedy high voice and he avoided eye contact.

However, the crisis had passed by the end of their first evening together, at a lecture on Swinburne at the Progressive Association. As Ellis puts it, there was 'an instinctive movement of approach on both sides'[62] and the two embarked on a serious love affair.[63] Olive and Henry were like-minded opposites who attracted.

Ellis remembered clearly first meeting Tussy at a meeting of the Progressive Association, a group of freethinkers, co-operative pioneers and ethical socialists who met on Sunday nights at Islington Hall, a favoured venue for radical organisations. Ellis became secretary of the Progressive Association, and recalled that he would 'every Sunday faithfully make the dreary journey from my home in the south of London',[64] with all the resignation of a supplicant wishing he didn't have to leave home to go to church. During the meeting his place was at a table near the door to answer enquiries and enrol new members. 'It was here that, one Sunday evening . . . early in 1884, I first met Eleanor Marx. She had dropped in for a short time but could not stay. I can still see her, with the radiant face and the expansive figure, seated on the edge of my secretarial table, though I recall nothing that was said.'[65] It's a perfect snapshot of Tussy and her political style. Informally perched on the table, no doubt smoking, taking time to engage with the pivotal organiser and administrator without whom the meeting wouldn't happen. And from this encounter, an acquaintance carried over into the sociability of the Reading Room.

Henry Havelock Ellis, born in Croydon in 1859, was the son of a merchant seaman and a strict evangelical Christian who, like Olive's mother, was the dominant parent in the household. Henry missed his father but had a relatively stable childhood. He was a shy, dreamy, frail boy who read obsessively. At seven he went on his first sea voyage with his father and was delighted by the books he discovered in the ship's library. He developed the persistent habit of collecting data that he tabulated and annotated in exercise books. Like Olive, Ellis experienced a loss of religious faith early in life, which left him feeling alienated in an 'empty and mechanical world'.[66]

Henry left school at sixteen, puzzled as to what to do with his future. His father took him on what was supposed to be a voyage around the world but he remained in Australia, worked as an assistant schoolmaster and matriculated at Sydney University. During this time he took two jobs tutoring with families in the bush, where he experienced what he described as a conversion.[67] These extended periods of rural solitude, teaching in isolation in tough farmland, resonated with Olive Schreiner's teaching experiences in the South African outback. Like her, he read voraciously, kept a journal and thought and walked extensively.

Inspired by reading the work of James Hinton, Ellis decided to study medicine so that he could lay bare the truth of human nature, including sexual behaviour, as he could not develop any 'new conception of sex without studying the established conventions of medical science.'[68] He returned to England in 1880 and enrolled as a medical student at St Thomas's Hospital in London.

Ellis pursued his other interests throughout his medical training, writing literary criticism for the *Westminster Review*, *The Indian Review* and *Modern Review*, planning a series on contemporary science, and editing Hinton's new work, *The Lawbreaker* (1884). Ellis's legacy tends to be overshadowed by his monumental and controversial *Psychology of Sex*, but his contribution to the field of literature was considerable. He was the first to translate Émile Zola's *Germinal* into English (1894), and forcefully directed attention in England outwards to new international writers such as Leo Tolstoy, Henrik Ibsen and Walt Whitman. He was a very good and copious literary reviewer.

Ellis's commitment to researching female sexuality and desire, his acknowledgment of its existence, force and power, was not motivated entirely by objectification or prurience. He constantly stressed the great beauty and pleasures of the body and its functions and he fought boldly against sexual prejudice and ignorance all his life. He demanded compassion, not condemnation, and demonstrated that many confused, antiquated notions about the sins or evils of the human body – particularly those of women – were merely biological occurrences within the laws of nature. In this progressive, sexual freethinking he met the minds and shared common cause with Eleanor and Olive.

Feminism and the struggle for the emancipation of women from patriarchy, as they emerged in Europe from the eighteenth-century

Enlightenment, and as Eleanor and her contemporaries inherited their philosophical, economic and political traditions, were always understood to be an imperative for all people. It was logically assumed and expected that as sexual inequality structured the whole of the functioning of all societies, it concerned men and women equally. This is the argument and assumption of Mary Wollstonecraft's *Vindication of the Rights of Women* (1792), as it is the argument of John Stuart Mill's *Subjection of Women* (1869), August Bebel's *Woman and Socialism* (1879), and Engels's *The Origin of the Family, Private Property and the State* (1884). Eleanor was studying all of these works in depth and detail during the early 1880s. In the case of *The Origin of the Family, Private Property and the State* she participated in its production, and read and discussed the manuscript with the General as he wrote it. Moreover, she was one of the women its author loved who inspired it. Hers was the case for the role of free love in radical social movements, hers the struggle for emancipation from patriarchy.

The necessity for women's emancipation as a primary requisite for free and equal societies is also a foundational precept of Marx's own work.[69] Grieving for Marx and concerned about the future of his friend's daughters, Engels was prompted to explore the most fundamental form of patriarchy that begins close to home: the father–daughter relationship, and how mothers are co-opted to its cause.

The relationships between Eleanor and her bohemian Bloomsbury circle (including Schreiner, Havelock Ellis, Shaw, Aveling), and their healthy enmities with worthy opponents such as Annie Besant and Charles Bradlaugh, demonstrate, shockingly, the degree to which the active inclusion and participation of men in feminism later got lost, or went missing, after the First World War.

Havelock Ellis, Engels and Shaw were amongst a talented cohort of men who thought deeply about their relationships with women, worked together professionally and politically with women, and made major contributions to feminism in the nineteenth century. However wrongheaded some of their conclusions, these were men genuinely interested in challenging universal patriarchy, and willing to roll up their sleeves to actively participate in a struggle for emancipation they regarded as necessary to their own well-being as that of women. In different ways these were also men who understood profoundly the demands patriarchy made on them to become and remain emotionally underdeveloped and hypocrites in their own homes. Sexual revolution had to begin at home; as long as women were unfree, so were men.

Peculiar Views on Love, etc.

'It is a curious fact,' wrote Engels:

> that with every great revolutionary movement the question of 'free
> love' comes into the foreground. With one set of people as a revo-
> lutionary progress, as a shaking off of old traditional fetters, no
> longer necessary; with others as a welcome doctrine, comfortably
> covering all sorts of free and easy practices between man and
> woman.[1]

The latter, in Engels's view, is indulgent philistinism; the former, an
attempt to loosen the bounds of convention, unfetter love and make
women and men free of the double standards of patriarchy. One
promises a radical rearrangement of relations between men and
women, holding out the promise of empowering those excluded
from the privileges of influence and wealth; the other is a reactionary
rerun of existing convention, masquerading as morality, working in
the interests of those already in power.

In 1884, when she was twenty-nine, the question of free love came
into the foreground of Eleanor's life. In June, she wrote to Laura:

> I must give you some other news – unless Engels has forestalled
> me – You must have known, I fancy, for some time that I am very
> fond of Edward Aveling – and he says he is fond of me – so we are

going to 'set up' together . . . I need not say that this resolution has been no easy one for me to arrive at. But I think it for the best. I should be <u>very</u> anxious to hear from you. Do not misjudge us – He is very good – and you must not think too badly of either of us.[2]

By July Eleanor and Edward had found rooms to rent at 55 Great Russell Street, directly opposite the entrance gates to the British Museum. They signed the lease and moved in on 18 July. With characteristic generosity the General gave them a handsome £50 as a 'wedding present' towards their new home and a honeymoon.

Edward had also just come into a modest legacy from his father, who died on 3 July. It was a busy week: six days after they moved into their new lodgings Eleanor and Edward joined the launch of the Westminster branch of the Democratic Federation. Tussy told her sister that she and Edward were going to Derbyshire in the middle of July by way of a honeymoon, 'then we return to London – and will give our "friends" a chance of cutting us or not, just as they please. <u>Do write soon, Laura, and don't misunderstand him</u>. If you knew what his position is, I <u>know</u> you would not . . . I shall await a line from you and Paul very anxiously.'[3]

Edward's 'position', he told Tussy, was that he was a married man separated from his difficult wife Bell, who refused to agree to a divorce because of her religious beliefs. Tussy put the case openly to her friends. Ellis commented, 'I think we regarded the free union which was open and public as based on principle.'[4] Tussy was anxious not to compromise her women friends. She wrote to Dollie, now Mrs Radford since she and Ernest had married, conventionally, in July 1883:

Well then this is it – I am going to live with Edward Aveling as his wife. You know he is married, and that I cannot be his wife <u>legally</u>, but it will be a <u>true</u> marriage to me – just as much as if a dozen registrars had officiated . . . E had not <u>seen</u> his wife for many, many years when I met him, and that he was not unjustified in leaving her you will best understand when I tell you that Mr Engels, my father's oldest friend, and Helen who has been as a mother to us, approve of what I am about to do – and are

<u>perfectly</u> satisfied . . . In three weeks we are going away for some little time . . . when we return we shall set up housekeeping together, and if love, a perfect sympathy in taste and work and a striving for the same ends can make people happy, we shall be so . . . I shall <u>quite</u> understand if you think the position one you cannot accept, and I shall think of you both with no less affection if we do not any longer count you amongst our immediate friends.[5]

Tussy told Dollie that while she felt she was doing nothing wrong, she could understand that people brought up differently, 'with all the old ideas and prejudices',[6] might think her very immoral. 'You know I have the power very strongly developed of seeing things from the "other side".'[7] Her power of seeing things from the other side made Tussy careful to try not to cause offence. She had recently become friends with kindred soul Edith Nesbit (Mrs Bland), poet and author of children's books, married to Hubert Bland. When Edith invited Eleanor to visit her home, Tussy replied:

I feel it is only right that before I avail myself of your very kind invitation I should make my present position quite clear to you . . . I am . . . with Edward Aveling, and henceforth we are going to be together – true husband and true wife, I hope, though I cannot be his wife legally. – He is, you probably know, a married man. I could not bear that one I feel such deep sympathy for as yourself should think ill of, or misunderstand us. I have not come between husband and wife.[8]

In this case, Eleanor's prudence was comically misplaced. Mr and Mrs Bland's unconventional domestic arrangements and sexually complicated marriage were notorious and Edith was the last person to judge harshly Eleanor's dilemma. Elsewhere, her concern was well founded. Eleanor's invitation to Beatrice Potter to visit her at home was politely declined, as Potter recorded in her diary: 'Asked me to come and see her. Exactly the life and character I should like to study. Unfortunately one cannot mix with human beings without becoming more or less <u>connected</u> with them.'[9]

Eleanor's decision to live openly with Aveling was not lightly taken, nor did she underestimate the difficulties of the position. Like George Eliot (Marian Evans), Eleanor formally informed her friends of her decision and gave them the option to withdraw from social connection with her. But there the likeness ends. Tussy was more robust, and didn't suffer from the excruciating anxiety about what other people thought of her that turned Eliot into a virtual recluse when she set up with George Henry Lewes.

Unremarkable today, these were radical actions in the 1880s. What Eleanor did share with George Eliot was the principle that other people should not be compelled to accept her moral choices. Aveling, on the other hand, didn't have to send a single letter to anybody to explain or justify his position. That the same social conventions did not apply to him only underlined the double standards of patriarchal convention.

Eleanor was justly anxious about how her decision might affect her political reputation. She knew the opponents of socialism, and women's emancipation, could and would use her self-avowedly feminist free-love union as negative publicity. Tussy had also experienced first-hand the strong tendency towards social conservatism in Christian socialism. Her decision to live with Edward as his wife opened her to criticism and attack from political left, right and centre; from without and within her own movement.

Eleanor's correspondence with Scottish engineer and activist John Mahon illustrates the vulnerability to which she was exposing her public life. Mahon, a decade younger than Tussy, co-founded the Scottish Land and Labour League:

It seems only right that I should acquaint you, both . . . as a friend and fellow-worker in the good cause, with the important step I have just taken . . . We are doing no human being the smallest wrong. Dr Aveling is <u>morally</u> as free as if the bond that tied him years ago, and that had been severed for years before I ever met him, had never existed. We have both felt that we were justified in setting aside all the false and really immoral bourgeois convention-alities . . . May I hope that you will be amongst those who have not misunderstood our motives? Anyhow, it is only right that as one of our most active and useful Scottish propagandists you should know.[10]

Engels worried that Tussy underestimated the force of social opprobrium that her decision might attract from her socialist allies, never mind political opponents. He wrote to Laura describing how Tussy had, finally, brought Edward to Regent's Park Road to make a formal declaration of her relationship to him and Lenchen, *in loco parentis*:

> Of course . . . [we] have been fully aware of what was going on for a considerable time and had a good laugh at these poor innocents who thought all the time that we had no eyes, and who did not approach the quart d'heure de Rabelais [moment of confession] without a certain funk. However, we soon got them over that. In fact, had Tussy asked my advice before she leaped, I might have considered it my duty to expatiate upon the various possible and unavoidable consequences of this step, but when it was all settled, the best thing for them was to have it out at once before other people could take advantage of its being kept in the dark . . . [11]

Engels understood that as a man patriarchy allowed him sexual double standards that would not be tolerated in a woman, as he demonstrated in his writings. Whilst reflecting on Tussy's predicament and trying to protect and publicly support her, Engels was completing *The Origin of the Family, Private Property and the State*, published in October 1884.

Grief at losing Marx prompted the General to write this book. Lost and miserable without his soulmate, glumly sifting through the jumbles of papers, driven to distraction by the disorder in which Marx had left his work, the General stumbled upon Marx's annotations and notes on the work of American anthropologist Lewis Henry Morgan on the origins of ancient society. He immediately cheered up. 'There is a definitive book,' he wrote enthusiastically, 'as definitive as Darwin's was in the case of biology – on the primitive state of society.'[12]

The General's class and social contradictions as a socialist man would and could play out differently in Eleanor as a socialist woman.

Marx and Morgan's was the theory; Eleanor's life was the practice. Engels studied the historical sources with his usual scholarly rigour, but it was observing at close quarters the modern lives of Eleanor and her friends that inspired him to think about sex, socialism, free love and revolution in the early 1880s.

The demands of being a father protective of his daughter's sexuality in a patriarchal society had prevented Marx from properly engaging with Tussy on the question of the relationships between her political, public, private and sexual lives. He'd thought only to keep her, wisely it might be argued, away from an early marriage; and he succeeded. Others, like economist and historian Max Beer, thought Marx a sexual conservative who tolerated but did not approve of the General's domestic arrangements:

> Marx, one of the greatest revolutionists that ever lived, was in point of moral rectitude as conservative and punctilious as his Rabbinic forebears. Breeding tells. I once asked my old friend Eduard Bernstein about these relations and he replied, 'In the home of the Marxes they used to speak about Engels' family life as in the home of Friedrich Schiller about Goethe's amorous adventures.[13]

The General wrote frankly to fellow German socialist Eduard Bernstein about the new living arrangements of the youngest, chosen Marx: 'My London is a little Paris' – which Bernstein interpreted a bit stiffly to mean that, 'A somewhat free conception of life had perhaps permeated certain circles of London society.'[14]

Now that her father was dead, the ceiling was lifted from Tussy's sky. There was acute grief but also new possibility. Released from Marx's protectiveness, the General could play a different role for Tussy, that of a paternal figure without the complications of being her real father. Her father and the General theorised about the emancipation of women and the possible future forms of free love. They made some significant experiments with these ideas in their personal lives but, as Victorian patriarchs, were largely immune from criticism.

Eleanor's historical role was to put free love to the practical test of evidence-based experience. 'The woman question' was in fact a multiplicity of questions. How should freethinkers, atheists and socialists measure their new ways of living against principle? How could equality be achieved in the workplace and the home? What constituted equality in marriage, bearing and raising children and running households together? Couples wanted to know what was the right thing to do and how to do it. Was there, for example, an ideal socialist home? Marjorie Davidson said to Shaw, 'I don't think we should have servants,' and wondered if it was 'an open question'.[15]

The General hoped for the best and prepared for the worst. Since Mohr's death, the General and Laura had become frequent correspondents. This began as a consequence of the need to settle Marx's estate and the future of the manuscripts, but the General also felt a great duty of care to look after the sisters. 'I hope,' he wrote to Laura,

> they will continue as happy as they seem now; I like Edward very much and think it will be a good thing for him to come more into contact with other people besides the literary and lecturing circle in which he moved; he has a good foundation of solid studies and felt himself out of place amongst the extremely superficial lot amongst whom fate had thrown him.

Annie Besant, one of Aveling's previous circle, might well object to being called one of this extremely superficial lot. Tenacious in all things, she wasn't going to let socialism take Aveling without a fight. Mahon sent Tussy a clipping from the *National Reformer* by Besant, published at the end of December 1883: 'My name is being used by a Miss Eleanor Marx . . . to give authority to a gross and scandalous libel on Dr Edward Aveling . . . Warning should be given of strangers who try and creep into our movement with the object of treacherously sowing discord therein.'[16] Eleanor warmed to the fight, welcoming attack from 'Mrs Besant, from whom I consider it the best compliment'. The reason for her animosity was evident:

> The one clear thinker and scientific student whose popularity *in the Secularist Party* almost equals Mr Bradlaugh's – Dr Edward Aveling, has joined the ranks of the Socialists, & Mrs Besant does

me the honour to make me responsible for this. I am very proud of
Dr Aveling's friendship for myself, but I hope I need not tell you
that his conversion to Socialism is due to a study of my Father's
book & not to me.[17]

This was entertaining humbug. Edward Aveling's 'study' was most
earthily of Tussy and not of transcendent socialism. The spat between
Tussy and Annie was a good old-fashioned catfight: Edward had
abandoned Annie's romantic affections for Tussy's, and spurned
Annie was cross. Writing to her sister, Tussy heartily expresses her
wish that she could deal with the matter in a masculine rather than
feminine manner. She thinks 'Mrs Besant's chaste style' utterly
absurd, and as to Bradlaugh, 'I've more than once of late wished like
Beatrice that "I were a man"; and that I could inflict on Mr Bradlaugh
the sound thrashing he deserves.'[18]

The rambunctious verbal punch-up between Tussy and Annie
was amusing as long as it lasted – which was not long at all. The
following year Annie met Shaw and the two began a love affair, the
consummation of which was Annie's political conversion to socialism and sporting reconciliation with Eleanor. Their argument over
who shared Edward's bed was long outlasted by their shared feminist bond.

On the whole Tussy's family and friendships stood the test of her
free-love union with Aveling. Although Laura didn't know him, she
wanted to be supportive of Tussy and her desires. In the years
following their father's death, the two sisters progressively drew
closer, as their frequent correspondence shows. Tussy's separation
from Lissagaray had removed him as a sore point between her and
the Lafargues. They suffered together in losing their eldest sister.
Laura, initially upset in the aftermath of Marx's death by Eleanor's
position as their father's legal executor, had been brought round by
Engels's patient clarifications and mediation. The two sisters were
now friends again.

'Everyone almost has been far kinder than I ever expected,'[19] Tussy
admitted to Laura about the announcement of her free union with
Aveling. Initially, Tussy encountered almost no objection to her
cohabitation with a still-married man. It was only when people got

to meet and know Edward Aveling better that their doubts were raised about the wisdom of her choice.

At five o'clock on the morning of 8 July 1884, Eleanor and Edward left London by train for Derbyshire and what the General laughingly called 'honeymoon No. 1'. They booked into the Nelson Arms in the village of Middleton, just outside of Wirksworth, as Mrs and Mrs Marx-Aveling. Tussy had suggested to Olive Schreiner that she and Henry join them on a 'joint honeymoon', and Olive had already arrived and was staying a mile away at a farmhouse at Bole Hill. Henry was due to arrive a week later.

The joint honeymoon-holiday in the Peak District symbolised an experiment in sexual freedom and quest for the answers to 'the woman question'. It turned out, of course, to be a comic *mise en scène* of the anticipated idyll.

When Eleanor and Edward arrived they went to see Olive in her bright little four-room cottage on the side of a hill overlooking Wirksworth. Olive expected to see Tussy joyous and ebullient at the brand new beginning of her 'marriage'. However, the instant they left, Olive wrote to Henry, 'Dr Aveling and Miss Marx have just come to see me. She is now to be called Mrs Aveling. I was glad to see her face. I love her. But she looks so miserable.'[20] By the following week, Olive's observations had hardened into an unshakeable dislike for Edward:

I am beginning to have such a horror of Aveling . . . To say I dislike him doesn't express it at all, I have a fear, a horror of him when I am near. Every time I see him this shrinking grows stronger . . . I love her, but he makes me so unhappy. He is so selfish, but that doesn't account for the feeling of dread . . . I had it when I first saw him. I fought it down for Eleanor's sake, but here it is stronger than ever.[21]

Henry's responses were more prosaic. He found Edward an agreeable companion, if a little boorish. He recalled later, 'Aveling's complications with women, however, became clear to us at an early stage.'[22] Henry, ever the sociologist, noticed that Edward was self-consciously watchful of his place in the group, especially when Tussy and Olive locked in a powerful mental embrace that left the men temporarily forgotten. Henry enjoyed sitting back and watching the lightshow between these two inspiring women, but their easy intimacy made Edward jealous. Though sexually confident, Aveling was emotionally insecure and an egoist, and thus, Henry observed, uneasy when not the centre of attention. By comparison, Henry's response to Eleanor was of unqualified delight and admiration. The worst he could find to say of her, amusingly, was that she had unfeminine body odour:

> Eleanor was then in full physical, mental and emotional maturity, a vigorous and radiant personality. It is perhaps a bodily trait of her powerful personality that I have never known a woman who on a long summer's day ramble diffused so potent an axillary fragrance. She was none the less always a delightful personality, intelligent, eager, full of enjoyment, whatever the moods and melancholy she may privately have been subject to. The alleged resemblance in mind and body to her famous father certainly included no trace of his dogmatic and domineering temper.[23]

It being a honeymoon, sexual desire and satisfaction were priorities. Olive and Henry had some knotty issues to untie in this regard, but for Tussy and Edward sex was an aspect of their relationship that came very easily, and frequently. Eleanor and Olive chatted freely together about all aspects of their sexuality and bodily functions – and how they connected to their mental and emotional lives. They discussed their sexual desire, periods, premenstrual tension, the effects of their monthly cycle on their work and moods, and wondered about the equivalents in their men. Olive shared these discussions with Henry:

> Speaking of the effect sexual feeling has on the mind, it is very clearly proved in the case of women. I must make more inquiries amongst other women, my friends who will have noticed and been able to analyse their feelings . . . Of course one may easily exaggerate what I have been talking about, but there is no doubt there is some truth in it . . . With myself <u>while</u> I am unwell every month

my feelings are particularly sensitive and strong. A little word that would not pain me at another time causes me acute agony. I cannot help feeling, and a little word of tenderness is so precious to me. (Especially the man who loves you ought to be tender with you then.) The time of greatest and most wonderful mental activity is just after, and perhaps the last two days of the time, too. Eleanor . . . the only woman I have spoken to on the subject feels much the same.[24]

Inspired by her frank conversation with Eleanor, Olive decided to address these subjects with some of her other intimate women friends and asked Henry to ask his sister Louie how she felt about them. 'I should like to know the man's side of the question too. I should think the relationship (between the power of the purely physical-sexual and the power of the mental-sexual) must be almost as close . . . Do you carefully observe . . . the interaction of your manly upon your mental nature?'[25] Henry, who was deeply interested in the psychology of sex, observed the relationship between Olive and Eleanor closely, and thought about all their questions.

Those who knew her often observed Olive's acute sensitivity to the emotions and behaviour of other people. She was possessed of an extraordinary ability to accurately size up and assess another individual. She felt personalities viscerally. A footloose colonial brought up unshackled by the constraints of English imperial politeness, Olive was also unversed in the dissimulating conventions of nice behaviour.

Eleanor told Olive and Henry that the reason Edward did not marry her was simply because he couldn't. Once she'd spent some time in his company, Olive became sceptical of Edward's story. She tried to caution Tussy, as did Edward's own brother Frederick, who had always disliked him, but at this preliminary stage of lovestruck infatuation Tussy paid no heed.

Olive's attitude was different. Like Eleanor, she enjoyed and was very interested in sex and curious about love. Unlike Eleanor, she clearly perceived marriage to be an oppressive social institution. Both women had been bethrothed at the age of seventeen, then thought better of it and got disengaged. At twenty-three, Olive said that unless someone were to 'absorb me and make me lose myself utterly . . . I should never marry. In fact I am married now, to my books! I love them better every day, and find them more satisfying. I would not change lots with anyone in the world, and my old sorrows look very foolish to me now.'[26] Had Tussy been less optimistic about human relationships at this stage of her life, she too would have seen that her books and writing were already her most faithful and supportive intimates.

One evening on their Peak District honeymoon, Tussy arranged a reading of part of Ibsen's *Ghosts*. Written in 1881, *Ghosts* was first performed by a Danish touring company in Chicago in May 1882. Its performance was banned throughout most of Europe, including England. Henrietta Francis Lord was working on her translation and Tussy, who was fascinated by the new drama of Ibsen, got hold of a part of the as yet unpublished manuscript version. Edward read the play. He had a good voice and read with much power of dramatic expression. 'It is one of the most wonderful and great things that has long, long been written,'[27] wrote Olive.

Ghosts terrified the Scandinavian press when it was published in December 1881. Every day Ibsen received letters decrying it. He was accused of blasphemy, freethinking and nihilism. The play called forth howls from camps of what Ibsen called the 'stagnationists' and 'so-called Liberals', appalled by his attack on conventional morality:

> They say that the book preaches Nihilism. Not at all. It is not concerned to preach anything whatsoever. It merely points to the ferment of Nihilism going on under the surface, at home as elsewhere . . . It may well be, that the play is in several respects rather daring. But it seemed to me that the time had come for moving some boundary posts.[28]

Ibsen was modest. The play didn't just move some boundary posts; it completely relocated the field of engagement.

There are uncanny resonances between Ibsen's *Ghosts* and the emotional underworld of Eleanor and Edward's free-love union. Helen Alving is the anti-heroine of the drama. The name Helen shares its semantic root with Eleanor, and Alving is Aveling minus a vowel. In the disastrous marriage plot, Captain Alving is damaged goods before Helen marries him. There's a brief period of hope for redemption and new beginnings, but when the revenants of the past return, all fails. Helen tolerates Alving's serial philandering, lies and venality as a disease for which he is not morally responsible. She becomes a woman who stays in a marriage in order to try and make a bad man good. She suppresses the call of her own desires. When Helen hears disembodied voices coming from the dining room she thinks they are ghosts but she can't hear what they are saying.

For Eleanor in love, Ibsen's *Ghosts*, performed so well by Edward on their Peak District honeymoon, were just fascinating theatrical shades. But Olive heard something else in Aveling's consummate reading and it haunted her.

Unexpectedly, Eleanor and Edward suddenly cut the holiday short and returned to London early, pleading demands of work. Henry heard that Edward, who lived extravagantly at the Nelson Arms, freely ordering food and drinks, 'had quietly decamped without settling the bill'.[29] Olive's feelings of 'horror' and 'dread' of Aveling returned stronger than ever. 'I have an "intuition" that they are in trouble,'[30] she wrote.

Olive's 'intuition' always proved correct.

Proof Against Illusions

'Is *that* your husband?' blurted out the incredulous Max Beer to Tussy when first introduced to Edward Aveling at the Communist Club in London.

Beer, who defined himself as a socialist Jew, had heard about Eleanor's open marriage and was curious to meet her spouse. Shortly after his arrival in London in 1894, Beer gave a lecture at the German Workers' Educational Society, known also as the Communist Club, at 49 Tottenham Court Road to a hall crowded with Germans, Austrians, Hungarians, Scandinavians and Jewish working people from Whitechapel.

Beer didn't know that in the adjoining room Eleanor and Edward were holding a meeting of the executive of the Bloomsbury Socialist Society. After his lecture Eleanor appeared and introduced herself and Edward. Beer was elated to find himself unexpectedly face to face with the daughter of Karl Marx. He recalls that there was certainly no reason whatever for him to stand in awe before Eleanor Marx, who he described as 'a middle-aged lady of great charm, radiating intelligence and loving-kindness':

None the less, I did stand on that evening in awe before her. Moreover, I felt that she ought to have married some very great man, and not Aveling, who my intuition told me, was a low comedian, and looked it, so I blurted out to her in German: 'Is *that* your husband?' But he, after all, had English manners, and said quite cheerfully, 'Comrade, let us go with Eleanor to the Horse Shoe and have a glass of English ale.'[1]

Beer found the English ale as unpalatable as Dr Aveling, describing it as tasting like 'some nasty medicine'.[2] Like Olive Schreiner's, Beer's intuition prompted immediate feelings of foreboding about Aveling from the moment he met him.

There must have been people other than Tussy who liked Edward, but apart from Engels their reports are lost to the historical record. The General respected Edward on Tussy's account, and was affectionate towards his foibles. 'The fact is,' he explained to Bernstein, 'Aveling has a lawful wife whom he cannot get rid of *de jure* although he has for years been rid of her *de facto*.'[3]

Aveling had a self-conscious demeanour that provoked extreme reactions.[4] George Bernard Shaw, who considered himself physically unattractive, wrote of his sometime rival, 'Though no woman seemed able to resist him, he was short, with the face and eyes of a lizard, and no physical charm except a voice like a euphonium.'[5] Karl Kautsky found Aveling simply 'repulsive', but stomached his aversion for Eleanor's sake.[6] Henry Hyndman shared GBS's amazement at Edward's desirability for women: 'Aveling was one of those men, who have an attraction for women quite inexplicable to the male sex . . . ugly and repulsive to some extent, as he looked, he needed but half an hour's start of the handsomest man in London.'[7] Hyndman, who worked extensively with him politically, tried to allay his unease about Aveling's true nature by telling himself that 'nobody can be as bad as Aveling looks'.[8]

Not all women, as is evident from Olive's reaction, found Edward attractive. Like Shaw, Eleanor's friend May Morris sensed something reptilian about Edward, describing him as 'a little lizard of a man'.[9] To his own brother Frederick, Edward was just a liar and 'unprincipled windbag'[10]. The dubious impression created by these negative descriptions of Edward's appearance seem to imply that had he been better-looking people would have been more tolerant of his appalling behaviour.

Campaigns mounted against his secular activism, vilification by ideological opponents and public calumny created an aura of victimisation around Edward that prompted Tussy and the General's instinctive tendencies to succour the underdog. But it was the General's limitations in being able to manage the different impact that sexual freedom had on men and women in practice and not just in theory that let Tussy down most where she needed a guardian and mentor. All three believed in free love. Engels could afford it. Aveling borrowed interest-free from women to fund it. For Eleanor, a woman, free love was the most expensive form of love in which she could possibly have chosen to invest.

Eleanor was a confirmed atheist and freethinker. If only she'd noticed that unconditional love and the faith it requires are too much like the requirements for believing in an unverifiable god. GBS saw this clearly and directly in relation to the dynamic between Eleanor and Edward. In 1906 he wrote a play based on their relationship, *The Doctor's Dilemma*:

> There is no harder scientific fact in the world than the fact that belief can be produced in practically unlimited quantity and intensity, without observation or reasoning, and even in defiance of both, by the simple desire to believe founded on a strong interest in believing. Everybody recognises this in the case of the amatory infatuations of the adolescents who see angels and heroes in obviously (to others) commonplace and even objectionable maidens and youths. But it holds good over the entire field of human activity. The hardest-headed materialist will become a consulter of table-rappers and slate-writers if he loses a child or a wife so beloved that the desire to revive and communicate with them becomes irresistible . . . Doctors are no more proof against such illusions than other men.[11]

For GBS, the doctor in question was the questionable Dr Aveling.

In June 1885, less than a year after their Derbyshire honeymoon, Eleanor confided to Olive her realisation of her illusions about Edward. With only cats and cigarettes for company at Great Russell Street, Tussy wrote to Olive:

> Edward is dining with Quilter and went off in the highest of spirits because several ladies are to be there (and it just occurs to me you

may be one! How odd that would be!) and I am alone, and while in some sense I am relieved to be alone, it is also very terrible; I can't help thinking and remembering, and then the solitude is more than I can bear.

I would give anything just now to be near you. You can always help me . . . The <u>constant</u> strain of appearing the same when nothing is the same, the constant effort not to break down, becomes intolerable. How natures like Edward's . . . are to be envied, who in an hour forget anything. If you had seen him, for example, today, going about like a happy child with never a sorrow in his life, you would have marvelled.[12]

Eleanor enjoyed Edward's intellectual and sexual energy, their tastes were much the same, they agreed on socialism, they both loved the theatre and they worked well together. These were all vitally important, positive aspects of their union, particularly along the scale of nineteenth-century marriage. More problematically, Eleanor wanted children but Edward prevaricated. She was resigned to housekeeping for both of them but hated it and was fairly bad at it.

They had enough money troubles to worry them both into early graves. 'I often don't know where to turn to or what to do. It is almost impossible for me now to get work that is even decently paid for, and Edward gets little enough.'[13] Shades of the penurious dog days of her mother and father, with the significant difference that, unlike her father, Edward simply didn't care, as she wrote to Olive:

And while I feel utterly desperate he is perfectly unconcerned! It is a continual source of wonder to me. I do not grow used to it, but always feel equally astounded at his absolute incapacity to feel anything – unless he is personally incommoded by it – for twenty-four consecutive hours. We, into whose hearts joy and sorrow sink more deeply, are better off after all. With all the pain and sorrow – and not even you, my Olive, know quite how unhappy I am, it is better to have these stronger feelings than to have practically no feelings at all. Write me a line in case I do not see you tomorrow or the next day. Just one line – say you love me. That will be such a joy, it will help me get through the long, miserable days, and longer, more miserable nights, with less heavy a heart.[14]

Her friends, uncomfortable around Edward or just downright disliking him, began to avoid their home and social invitations. Eleanor found herself alone more often. She worked constantly. The entire burden of housework fell to her.

Olive's 'intuition' that Eleanor and Edward's relationship was in trouble when they left their honeymoon early the year before in 1884 proved correct. Two months after Tussy wrote her miserable confessional letter to Olive, Shaw reported to his diary, 'Rumour of split between Avelings.'[15]

Tussy reviewed her options, trying to acknowledge head-on that Edward was not what he'd appeared to be and that the relationship wasn't working. In another letter to Olive, her confidante in this dilemma, she proposed:

> One alternative, is to leave Edward and live by myself. I can't do that; it would drive him to ruin and it wouldn't really help me . . . My father used to say that I was more like a boy than a girl. It was Edward who really brought out the feminine in me. I was irresistibly drawn to him.[16]

And here's the nub of it. Eleanor allowed Edward to reinforce the cage of her unresolved femininity, in its nineteenth-century embodiment.

When Marx said, 'Tussy *is* me', he was saying that she was more like a man than a woman. In so many ways that was true – her constant impetus to action, robust intellect, self-confidence, ability for leadership, camaraderie, original thinking, physical stamina, stomach for a fight; if these are characteristics that define masculinity, then Tussy was more like a boy than a girl.

If femininity was the posture of subordination, self-doubt, concession, servitude, secondary status to an unelected superior, then there was little of natural 'femininity' in Tussy. But her body, the house of her femininity, the muscles, pulleys, levers and hormones designed to produce further life,[17] combined with the social conditioning of her age, made her vulnerable to being caught in the trap of being more like a girl than a boy when it came to her own adult sexual relationships.

Max Beer, so incredulous at Tussy's choice of Edward, thought it was cultural compulsion that hobbled her. 'How', Beer said, 'she could go on living with this man . . . is a riddle which puzzled us all':[18]

> I, as a Jew, knowing the indestructible, age-long Jewish reverence for the sacred bond of wedded life, explain it by her Jewishness. She tried indefatigably to mend him, but, alas! he was past mending. Yet she clung to him with all the loyalty and devotion inherited from a long line of famous Rabbis on her father's side.[19]

It was a sharp insight. As Beer suggested, Eleanor was under the influence of her cultural ancestry, which presented the questionable example of loyal, dutiful wives and mothers. The formative examples of her Möhme and 'second mother' Lenchen, both utterly devoted to her father, shaped her attitude to Edward. But Aveling was no Marx. Unintentionally, Tussy's mothers were dangerous, unhelpful role models, ill-equipping their daughter for freedom from subordination to romantic illusions.

14

Educate, Agitate, Organise

'If scrubbing "is my vexation", cleaning knives is "twice as bad",
joints "puzzle me", and "potatoes drive me mad",' quipped Tussy.
She resented domestic labour. 'Who is the fiend who invented house-
keeping? I hope his invention may plague him in another world.'¹
There was no need for Eleanor and Edward to discuss the ethics of
employing a servant; even if they wanted to they couldn't afford one.
Nor did it occur to Edward to share the domestic labour. He was,
Tussy grouched to her sister, 'the very devil for untidiness . . . and
I'm a good second . . . I swear at myself all day.'²

To Tussy's delight, Laura came to visit in October 1884 for the
first time since their father's death. The visit confirmed their reconciliation. Eleanor enjoyed introducing her sophisticated French
political sister to her new circle. Laura liked Olive, who became a
friend. She reserved her views on Edward. Both sisters wanted a
rapprochement and to rebuild their relationship. The Lafargues
shared political common ground with Aveling, if not personal, and
given their prominence in the socialist movement he was keen to
curry their favour.

Laura observed that, alongside her unpaid activism, Tussy was
working harder than ever, writing, researching, teaching and translating. Encouraged by Edward, she had offered a course in the early
summer on 'The Reading and Study of Shakespeare' at the Highgate
Literary and Scientific Institution. Her twelve-lesson programme on

As You Like It was fully subscribed. She offered students sitting the Cambridge Higher Local Examinations instruction in close textual study of the play. 'Difficult references, archaic forms, and the dramatic construction of the play will be explained and discussed.' Her students were women of all classes and working men excluded from the public and private education systems by gender, class, race, or all three. The cost of this Shakespeare course was £1 1s. Students who couldn't afford the fees were subsidised by trade unions and other progressive organisations. And for those who couldn't raise the money by any means, Eleanor just quietly overlooked the lack of payment. She recommended students borrow or buy the Clarendon Press edition of the comedy published by Macmillan, costing one shilling and sixpence (1s 6d).

Eleanor's course began with a group reading of the play and students continued to perform scenes and speeches throughout the programme. Her accessible teaching methods evolved from the Marx family Shakespeare readings and the Dogberry Club. Eleanor also delivered a series of lectures on economic and political subjects to her local Westminster branch of the Social Democratic Federation.

Tussy spent a great deal of time voluntarily tutoring organisers and emerging leaders within the socialist and worker movement whose numeracy and literacy were rudimentary. Few working-class activists in the 1880s had the opportunity of more than a basic education, if any. Access to equal education was one of the rights for which they struggled. A score of memoirs by working-class leaders of the late nineteenth and early twentieth centuries bear testimony to Eleanor, who tutored them in reading, writing, accountancy, and political and economic theory, as well as speech writing and public speaking. Tussy's passion and sometime train-ing for theatre and performance were now playing out on the political stage. Marx demonstrated definitively the relationship between public life, performance, theatre and state politics in *The Eighteenth Brumaire*, one of his most brilliant and enduring works about Louis Napoleon Bonaparte's coup d'état. Once again, the dynamic pattern between philosopher father and political daugh-ter shows itself clearly: Karl Marx was the theory; Eleanor Marx was the practice.

Whilst Eleanor grafted, Edward was embroiled in public allegations of financial mismanagement of monies belonging to the
National Secular Society, of which he was vice-president. Charles
Bradlaugh alleged that Aveling had made personal use of campaign
funds and not repaid them. The Democratic Federation – recently
renamed the Social Democratic Federation – was annoyed that
Aveling brought the organisation into disrepute. Hyndman thought
that as Aveling was much disliked and Bradlaugh too careful to make
unfounded allegations, the charges were likely to stick. Edward
resigned his vice-presidency of the National Secular Society, making
sure he was gone before the proposal to remove him from office was
put to discussion and vote. He defended himself in an open letter to
Justice in September:

> I am at the present time indebted in many sums to many persons.
> I am using every endeavour to clear myself of this indebtedness.
> But I wish to say that to the best of my knowledge and belief all
> monies received by me as funds in trust for others have been fully
> accounted for. My monetary difficulties have to do with my
> poverty and my want of business habits alone.[3]

Eleanor took up a leadership role in the renamed Social Democratic
Federation (SDF). In August, both Eleanor and Edward had been
elected to the twenty-strong executive council at the SDF annual
congress. William Morris, Ernest Bax, John Burns, and Henry and
Matilda Hyndman were amongst the other members. From August
1884 to January 1885 Eleanor attended every meeting of the executive council, frequently taking the chair.

Marx and Engels were sceptical about the Democratic Federation
in its early days and disliked Hyndman. But the times were changing. In 1883 the SDF presented a clear socialist manifesto and in
January 1884 it adopted an explicit socialist programme. The SDF
was evolving into a new kind of political party. January 1884 was
the same month in which the Fabian Society of London was
founded, in which Shaw took a leading role. The Fabians, all men
under thirty, dissociated themselves from other socialist organisations and opposed economic theories based on class struggle and

political revolution. In the next century, GBS reflected back on the early Fabian eggheads, including himself. Not a working man or woman amongst them, 'They paraded their cleverness ... and spoke of ordinary Socialism as a sort of dentition fever which a man had to pass through before he was intellectually mature enough to become a Fabian.'4 However, GBS's younger self was a committed Fabian gradualist. Billed as 'Comrade Shaw' to speak against the war in Sudan he tartly retaliated, 'I am G. Bernard Shaw, of the Fabian Society, member of an individualist state, and therefore nobody's comrade.'5

The SDF was a broad church, as represented by the variety of different approaches to revolutionary politics amongst its council members. All agreed, however, for the meantime on the principal aims of the new SDF: universal suffrage, an eight-hour day for industrial workers, and the introduction of salaries for British MPs to enable representation of working-class people in parliament.

The 1880s was a period of schism, fraction, split and regrouping in the socialist movement. Eleanor had to strategise on several fronts. First, there were increasing numbers of would-be Marxists who claimed their version of her father's scientific philosophy to explain the processes by which societies develop as *the* ultimate, correct interpretation. Because they diverged from the fundamental principles of his analysis, Marx had firmly opposed these self-styled Marxist revolutionaries in his lifetime.

Eleanor inherited the burgeoning problems of those amongst her father's followers who either didn't read his work properly, or were constantly at war with each other, or both. Secondly, Eleanor was sucked into the vortex of hostility between Hyndman and Engels. Hyndman's hatred of Engels took in anyone associated with him, including and especially Eleanor, fellow elected member of the executive council of the SDF. This, combined with Hyndman's doctrinaire, simplistic Marxism placed him and Eleanor at loggerheads. They moved and counter-moved against each other: she accused Hyndman and his henchmen of petty intriguing and foul play; he accused her of manoeuvring and exploiting the dubious clique of the 'Old International' that made one unholy family of British and continental European socialists. Engels, Hyndman claimed, was the devil behind the un-English aims of internationalism and the devil behind Eleanor.

As an outsider, Shaw cast a sharp observational eye on the infighting in the SDF executive. He wrote to socialist activist Andreas Scheu telling him about the bad blood between 'the Marx-Aveling party and the Hyndman party':

> What we have got at Palace Chambers now is a great deal of agitating, very little organising (if any), no educating, and vague speculations as to the world turning upside down in the course of a fortnight or so. Aveling . . . is on for educating, but he is hard up, heavily handicapped by his old associations and his defiance of Mrs Grundy in the matter of Eleanor Marx, personally not a favourite with the world at large . . . [6]

The SDF schism happened at the end of 1885. Hyndman puffed himself up and treated the SDF as his personal vehicle, exacerbating internal conflict. A faction organised against him within the executive council. William Morris reluctantly understood that he had to reconcile himself to the split and step up to the plate. 'More than two or three of us distrust Hyndman thoroughly,' he wrote privately to a friend:

> I have done my best to trust him, but cannot any longer. Practically it comes to a contest between him and me . . . I don't think intrigue or ambition are amongst my many faults; but here I am driven to thrusting myself forward and making a party within a party. However I say I foresaw it, and 'tis part of the day's work, but I begin to wish the day were over. [7]

Eleanor and William Morris led the cabal of ten secessionists, who met at her home on 16 December 1884. They were a good combination. Morris was aware of his shortcomings as an economist and political theorist: 'I want statistics terribly,' he confessed to Scheu. 'You see I am but a poet and artist, good for nothing but sentiment.' [8] Shorter on sentiment and long on statistics, with a formidable grasp of economics, organisation and strategy, Eleanor was Morris's perfect political partner. She explained the fundamental causes of the split to Library:

> One of our chief points of conflict with Hyndman is that whereas we wish to make this a really international movement . . . Mr Hyndman . . . has endeavoured to set English workmen against 'foreigners'. Now it is absolutely necessary we show the enemy a united front – and that we may do this our German friends must lend us a helping hand. If you want anything to come of the movement here; if you want to help on the really Socialist, as distinct from the Soc Democrat – jingo – Possibilist – Party – now is the time to it.[9]

A vote was taken on 27 December and the resolution passed in favour of the internationalists against Hyndman's 'Jingo faction' – as Eleanor called them – by a majority of ten to eight. Ten signatories, including Eleanor, Edward, Morris, Bax and Robert Banner, then handed in their resignation from the SDF. Given the narrowness of their majority, and Hyndman's voracious political careerism, this was a sensible move. As Tussy told Laura, 'Hyndman forced things to such a condition that it was impossible to go on working with him.'[10]

Two days later, on 29 December, this small group of ten internationalists opposed to Hyndman's attempts at autocratic mastery founded the Socialist League. Its principles were commendable but its prospects poor. The General was sceptical, as he wrote to Laura: 'There is this to be said in their favour: that three more unpractical men for a political organisation than Aveling, Bax and Morris are not to be found in all England. But they are sincere.'[11] To Bernstein he stated his concern at the well-meaning, predominantly middle-class leadership of the Socialist League: 'Those who resigned were Aveling, Bax, and Morris, the only honest men amongst the intellectuals – but men as unpractical (two poets and a philosopher) as you could possibly find.'[12] Though Tussy was irritated by Hyndman's personal sniping, this was not the issue at stake:

> The personal question – inevitable personal questions will be mixed up in all such movements as these – is after all very

secondary to the principal one – that of whether we were to sink into a merely Tory-democratic Party or go on working on the lines of the German Socialists and the French Parti Ouvrier . . . Our majority was too small to make it possible for us to really get rid of the Jingo faction, and so, after due consideration with Engels we decided to go out, and form a new organisation . . . Oh dear! Is not all this wearisome and stupid! But I suppose it must be gone through . . . I suppose this kind of thing is inevitable in the beginning of any movement.[13]

Eleanor's long view of history and its knack for repeating itself equipped her well for the political scrum. Dispute and intrigue were tiresome but to be expected. She deployed the General to round up international support from the old revolutionary émigrés of the 1848 revolutions and the Paris Commune. Her letters rallying support claimed repeatedly, 'Our friend Engels is entirely with us.'[14] She overstated the case; as the General told Laura, he thought the secessionists had moved too soon. Eleanor's invocation of the name of Engels created, exactly as she intended, the impression that he was orchestrating events from behind the scenes, strengthening her call for support from old internationalists who knew and had worked with him. Having taught her strategy, he admired her use of it.

Three days before Tussy's thirtieth birthday the Socialist League issued its manifesto from its headquarters in Farringdon Road. *To Socialists* laid out the reasons for the split from the SDF and the formation of the new Socialist League. The manifesto was sent out to all SDF branches and Eleanor enclosed copies of it in all her correspondence to potential allies. *To Socialists* is a position paper that identifies a number of determining factors, such as opposition over questions of leadership, party structure and process, but essentially this founding statement boils down to the principle of internationalism. Under the 'skilful and shifty' leadership of Hyndman and his followers, 'there was a tendency towards national assertion, the persistent foe of Socialism: and it is easy to see how dangerous this might become in times like the present.'[15] Eleanor's political foundations, to which the Paris Commune and the Irish Republican movement were so central, show through clearly at this defining moment in British political history.

Eleanor was the only woman amongst the ten founding signatories of the Socialist League. And of those ten, she was the most committed and forceful internationalist. Eleanor entered her thirtieth year at the vanguard of the emerging British socialist movement. Political from top to bottom, had been her mother's descriptive refrain. Had Jenny Marx lived to see this moment in Tussy's life, she would not have been surprised.

However, the published manifesto of the Socialist League substantially diverged from the draft constitution drawn up earlier in the year by Eleanor, William Morris and Edward in consultation with Engels. The draft incorporated key aspects of socialist policy, such as support of trade unions, co-operatives and other forms of representative working-class organisation. It also adopted the policy of entering into political power by elective means through administrative, civil, state and parliamentary bodies. Eleanor blamed the disjuncture between the draft constitution and the published manifesto on the anarchist members of the provisional council. Eleanor expressed this view to Paul Lafargue:

> The Anarchists here will be our chief difficulty. We have many on our Council, and by and by it will be the devil to pay. Neither Morris, nor Bax, nor any of our people know really what these Anarchists are: till they <u>do</u> find out it is a hard struggle to make head against them – the more that many of our Englishmen taken in by the foreign Anarchists (half of whom I <u>suspect</u> to be police agents) are unquestionably the best men we have.[16]

The Socialist League started its monthly newspaper *Commonweal* at the end of January 1885, with William Morris as editor and Aveling as sub-editor. *Commonweal* declared its support for revolutionary international socialism, working for education, organisation and party democracy through the parliamentary process in order to achieve the aims of the Socialist League. Editorially, it strongly opposed national-level politicking and rejected outright 'incomplete schemes of social reform' like co-operation, nationalisation of land and state-imposed social and political restructuring.

Groups of revolutionary socialists set up branches of the Socialist League around the country and in February Eleanor, Aveling and Morris went to Oxford to address undergraduate students at a hall in Holywell Street. Filled with vocal opponents, the meeting began in a disorderly fashion. The students heckled Morris into silence but Aveling swiftly stepped in and won the audience over with a dramatic opening, after which they listened fairly attentively to him until the meeting was cut short by a student letting off a stink-bomb. Eleanor, Edward and William escaped the rumpus to New College, where they were hosted by a group of socialist-sympathising students who, as a result of this encounter, launched the Oxford Socialist Association as a branch of the Socialist League, and later also established a Marx Club. The opponents of the socialist students were so furious with the failure of their stink-bombing ringleader to effectively disrupt the success of the evening that they smashed the windows of his rooms that night for not making a better job of it.

From the cloisters of Oxford University Eleanor went to address the Mile End and other London branches of the Socialist League. Her speech at Mile End in the second week of February was her first of this sort, as she told Peter Lavrov: 'Next Sunday I shall be giving a public lecture for the first time in my life (and perhaps the last?). The subject is "The Factory Acts in England".'[17] She also gave this lecture at her own local Bloomsbury branch in a meeting room above the Eagle and Child Coffee-House on Old Compton Street, and in March delivered it to the Southwark branch of the Socialist League.

Eleanor's deep knowledge of British factory conditions, history and legislation was grounded in her knowledge of her father and Engels's work. Engels asked her to start archival research for the English translation of *Capital*. For this she spent long hours in the Reading Room of the British Museum and London law libraries tracing back the sources Marx used to write *Capital*. Marx had used English sources, translating them himself into German. Tussy therefore had to translate her father's German translations back into English as the first step to locating the originals.

With painstaking attention to detail, she found these in the reports of factory inspectors, medical officers on public health, government select committees and commissions enquiring into children's employ-ment, the housing of the poor, mines, railways, bakeries and the adulteration of food. This research was probably a better grounding in social and economic policy than that received by many of her university-educated male contemporaries. It's hard to identify anyone else of her epoch so well equipped to speak on the dangers to industrial workers, the shortfalls of existing legislation and the unim-aginably appalling labour conditions in English factory workshops up and down the country.

Tussy's research into factory conditions and legislation was detailed, empirical and specific. From this bedrock of fact she drew clear, decisive analyses. Eleanor developed her public lectures on the Factory Acts in England with Edward into a one-penny pamphlet entitled *The Factory Hell*. Published in April 1885 by the Socialist League, the pamphlet appeared for the first time in the joint names of 'Edward Aveling & Eleanor Marx Aveling'.[18]

Reading a factory report of 1884, Eleanor pointed out, it might as well 'be that of 1864. The same disease, accidents, prosecu-tions ... Our factory-chimnies that Radical politicians call "the glory of England" are in truth, the curse of England.'[19] Meanwhile, Edward's philandering and neediness due to ill health became the curse of Eleanor.

In March 1884 Edward was diagnosed with kidney stones and by April was seriously ill. Dr Donkin prescribed a break from work and Edward went to Ventnor to recuperate. Paul Lafargue offered to cover some of Edward's work on translating *Capital*, to Eleanor's immense gratitude, 'for help means the rest for Edward that Donkin declares "absolutely necessary" (Doctors are such "absolute" knaves!).'[20] As they couldn't both afford to go, Edward went alone. Eleanor stayed in London and anyway, as she told her sister, 'I am up to my neck in work of all kinds (not alas! very remunerative)':[21]

> Apart from the necessary work for getting a living – *tant bien que mal* [somehow or other] – there is the constant worry from the Socialist League. From childhood we have known what it is to devote oneself to the proletaire. It is superfluous to explain this to you.[22]

Olive Schreiner was concerned. 'If he gets dangerously ill I must go,' she wrote to Havelock Ellis. 'If the Avelings are very hard-up I must try to send them something.'[23] Olive of course did not give a fig for Edward – Tussy was her concern.

Tussy took advantage of Edward's absence to try and spring clean their apartment, re-blacking the grates, rinsing out the curtains and whitewashing the walls. The process infuriated her. 'How I wish people didn't live in houses and didn't cook, and bake, and wash and clean! I fear I shall never, despite efforts, develop into a decent Hausfrau! I am horribly Bohemian in my tastes!'[24]

Aveling was under a considerable amount of public scrutiny so, painfully real as his kidney stones were, his retreat into illness and to the Isle of Wight was timely. There was an accumulating trail of complaints about the financial management of any project he touched. His personal finances also seemed questionable. Henry Lee, secretary of the Westminster branch of the SDF, who worked closely with Aveling during this period, described him as 'utterly unscrupulous about the way in which he satisfied his desires . . . The best was good enough for him – at no matter whose expense.'[25] A Soho tailor, who was a member of the Communist Workers' Educational Association, couldn't get Aveling to pay his account for clothes he made for him, and was further infuriated when he saw Edward in the stalls of the Lyceum Theatre 'attired in the unpaid for velvet jacket and waistcoat, and accompanied by a lady'.[26] A lady who was not Eleanor.

Eleanor confided to Olive that although it made her emotionally lonely, she now accepted Edward's dalliances. They were both, after all, proponents of free love. Problematically, the freedom was all on his side. The net result was that Tussy took the aspect of conventional stoical wife and Edward of conventional philandering husband. His little affairs were usually with young actresses or his female students and he usually came home afterwards. As far as Tussy knew, he didn't set up mistresses. She'd grown up within the ambit of the highly successful open ménage common-law marriage between Engels and the Burns sisters. The General played away but Mary and Lizzy were keepers of his home, hearth, heart and head. The difference being that where the General paid for his peccadilloes out of his own pocket, Edward used Eleanor's income as well as his own to subsidise his wining, dining and gift-giving to students and actresses.

Like Helen Alving in Ibsen's *Ghosts*, Eleanor kept up appearances. To family and friends she emphasised Edward's ill health, whilst working furiously to try and pay off as many of his outstanding debts as she knew about – if Engels hadn't got there first. 'Edward is very seriously ill and has not yet recovered,' she wrote to the activist writer and thinker Sergei Stepniak (Sergey Mikhaylovich Stepnyak-Kravchinksy), for whom she had recently translated a two-part article on conditions in Russian political prisons from Russian into French, 'the very devil to do, being the translation of a translation'.[27] She told Stepniak that Edward had gone away, 'but will return tomorrow, and I fear no better. I need not tell you how worried I am. You will understand this.'[28]

Eleanor's translations for Stepniak were published in *Today*, for which she wrote a regular feature as international correspondent. From February 1885 she transferred this column to the pages of *Commonweal*, gathering international news items under the unwieldy title of 'Record of the Revolutionary International Movement'.

Aveling's unconscious had a psychosomatic knack of developing physical ailments at moments of acute emotional distress. Only in retrospect would it become clear that his sexual infidelities and financial mismanagement coincided with illness or sudden collapses in his health. Too afraid to tell Eleanor the truth, too invested in his own self-delusion, he retreated behind the screen of sudden, dramatic afflictions to throw her off the scent of his relationship juggling. It was much easier to position himself as a victim of either ill health or other people – or her.

Tussy fell for it repeatedly; she should have known better. Love made her stupid, distracting her into anxiety and pity. Eleanor's 'chronic state of hard-up-ness', as she described it, was due almost entirely to Edward's extravagance. Anything that came in was already spoken for. Unfortunately, her childhood experience had lulled her into the illusion that this was a normal state of domestic affairs. The clear difference, of course, was that where her parents had borrowed at interest and pawned in order to clear their constant debts, as poor people do, Edward had no intention of honouring his obligations to others. His financial exploitation, of Eleanor and anyone else he could take advantage of, is revealing, not for what it indicates about his attitude to money but for what it tells us about his pronounced egotism. Where Tussy was a natural egalitarian, Edward lacked any ability to see others as his natural equals. He profoundly believed in his own exceptional abilities but was insecure and oversensitive.

Amidst all these domestic pressures, Eleanor managed to organise a public meeting to protest against the war in Sudan. She called the assembly for 23 April, 'but of course this Russian business rather complicates matters' – a reference to the dispute between Britain and Russia over the north-west frontier of Afghanistan. British troops had been in the Sudan since 1883, when Gladstone's government sent a convoy of warships to suppress a national uprising. British forces occupied Khartoum under the command of General Gordon and expeditionary troops arrived to relieve them by August. Further large army battalions and the naval fleet, meanwhile, congregated in Egypt, with an eye to the interests of the Russians in Afghanistan.

Gordon was killed at Khartoum on 26 January, prompting an outpouring of furious nationalistic sentiment and anti-Arab vitriol from grieving imperialists. The Socialist League, as an internationalist organisation, fundamentally opposed British imperialism and thus the war in Sudan. The Leaguers made common cause with the peace movement and other opponents of the war but were critical of the unwillingness of other organisations to understand the shared interests of government and the 'market-hunters . . . capitalists and stock-jobbers'[29] who together drove colonial imperialism. This position is illustrated in the Socialist League's amendment to the general peace solution proposed at a stop-the-war gathering in February:

> That this meeting, consisting mainly of working men, is convinced that the war in the Sudan was prompted by the capitalist class, with a view to the extension of their fields of exploitation. And we admit that the victory gained by the Sudanese was a triumph of right over wrong by a people struggling for their freedom.[30]

No nationalistic sentiment here for the death of General Gordon. Eleanor drafted a policy leaflet tracing the origins of the war and explaining the position of the Socialist League in opposing this and other imperialist wars. William Morris commissioned artist Walter Crane to illustrate the pamphlet and design its cover. Crane, a committed socialist, later became principal of the Royal College of Art. This publication, signed by Eleanor and all of the other twenty members of the provisional council, was distributed at and after the meeting on 23 April. It made clear the perspectives of the Socialist Leaguers towards imperialism. The language used to describe Arab civilisations – 'the children of the desert' – was paternalistic and orientalist but the critique of economic imperialism was nevertheless sound.

> Fellow Citizens.
>   Tens of millions wrung from the labour of workmen of this country are being squandered on Arab slaughtering; and for what:
> 1) that Eastern Africa may be 'opened up' to the purveyor of 'shoddy' wares, bad spirits, venereal disease, cheap bibles and missionaries;
> 2) that a fresh supply of sinecure Government posts may be obtained for the occupation of the younger sons of the official classes;
> 3) as a minor consideration may be added that a new and happy hunting ground be provided for military sportsmen, who find life boring at home and are always ready for a little Arab shooting when the occasion arises.
> Citizens, you are the dupes of a plot.

The leaflet then documents the history of the war in the Sudan, explaining its relationship to Egypt, and ends by asking 'you to consider who it is that have to do the fighting on this and similar occasions':

> Is it the market-hunting classes themselves? Is it they who form the rank and file of the army? NO! But the sons and brothers of the working classes at home. They it is who for a miserable pittance

are compelled to serve in these commercial wars. They it is who conquer, for the wealthy middle and upper classes, new lands for exploitation, fresh populations for pillage, as these classes require them, and who have, as their reward, the assurance of their masters that they are nobly fighting for their Queen and country.[31]

Tussy seemed tireless. It is impossible to find her slacking or napping, let alone holidaying. Her correspondence from 1885 onwards is like an administrative and organisational machine, each missive fuelling her steam engine of activism. 'Please check there are plenty of papers up at the Athenaeum tonight; also all the pamphlets,'[32] she writes to Mahon. She collects addresses for distributing manifestos and leaflets, and writes postcards for mailshots ('I told Edward to copy them for me yesterday, but he forgot . . . ')[33] She finds, negotiates and books venues and organises for the windows to be cleaned with the Window Cleaning Association of Oxford Street. She chairs, she minutes meetings and writes up reports. She collects subscriptions and delivers them to the Socialist League offices. She arranges for the distribution of manifestos, letters and leaflets all over the UK and beyond, to Holland, France, Germany, Belgium. Meanwhile, Tussy asks, can someone else go to a big restaurant and ask how much it will cost to hire one hundred plates, knives, forks, glasses, cups and saucers? 'I'm asking too,' she says, 'but want to compare prices.' Oh, and can a colleague please send her half a dozen tickets for an entertainment to distribute amongst potential funders?[34]

'Go ahead!' urges Tussy's favourite motto. And she does. She hopes heartily that the fiend who invented housekeeping may be plagued by his invention in another world, but when it comes to political organisation, no task is too menial or laborious for Tussy to undertake willingly and execute with superb efficiency.

As if there wasn't enough drama in the rough and tumble of her daily political life, Tussy threw herself into a busy schedule of amateur dramatics from the winter of 1884 to the summer of 1886. As her fellow performers made up more than half of the leadership of the new Socialist League, it's clear that the Leaguers thought of art and entertainment as integral to their political project.

Eleanor's precepts on art were clear. Everybody was entitled to enjoy good quality, challenging culture and entertainment. This is demonstrated in her debates with her fellow members of the Socialist League over art and education. 'Surely education to a Socialist means also Art Education?' she wrote to the Secretary of the Socialist League in March 1886.

This was a letter of complaint about the programme for a free variety concert recently put on by the Leaguers, organised by musician Theodore Reuss, who was a member of the executive council. Eleanor took exception to the choice of some of the content programmed for the evening:

> I really cannot think that he, a musician, <u>could</u> be responsible for the 'comic songs' sung. I am perfectly certain Comrade Reuss would never dream of having such songs sung at one of his own concerts, and I do not think he would say that was 'good enough' for mere Socialists, which he would not judge 'good enough' for a bourgeois audience.

Tussy says that she feels utterly ashamed that the League should ask people to come and be inflicted with dull vulgarity. She cites the audience's great enjoyment of the readings from Dickens's *Pickwick Papers* and other good quality comedy as evidence of their appreciation of genuine fun, but deplores the low-grade 'comic effusions':

> I like fun – any fun no matter how rough so it be wholesome – as well as any, but I fail to see fun in pure (or impure) and simple vulgarity. Brainless middle class cads may like this sort of thing: I don't believe working men who have a real sense of humour do . . . I know, alas! that we can't pretend to give grand Concerts: but let what we do give at least be of such a kind that we need not be ashamed of it, and do not let us say 'anything will do' for an audience because it is a poor and working-class one.[35]

Eleanor championed good education and art as everyone's entitlement. No one should talk down to another, in culture or in politics. She regularly objected to bread-and-circuses mentality, acting swiftly

to try and root out and expose it when it appeared within the fraternal leadership. Eleanor was by dint of birth of the radical political
elite, but she did not have an elite education. She knew the extent to
which the majority of people were dependent upon the opportunities provided by public culture and entertainment to develop their
artistic knowledge, pleasure and education.

In November 1884 Eleanor and Edward collaborated with Bax,
Morris and (new Fabian) GBS to put on a fundraising 'Art Evening'
of entertainment at the Neumeyer Hall in Bloomsbury. Shaw
played an opening Mendelssohn duet with Katherine Ina, Aveling
recited from Shelley's *Masque of Anarchy* and Morris read from his
own poetic reworking of *The Passing of Brynhild*. The programme
also included Fabian and amateur actress Theodora Wright reading
from Eliot's *Adam Bede*, and an overlong recital of Schumann's
Carnival by Bax that sent most of the audience to sleep before the
interval.

The rest of the evening's programme was given over to Eleanor
and Edward's performance of *In Honour Bound*, a dramatic piece by
a young playwright called Sydney Grundy. Lenchen, who was in the
audience – as she was at all Tussy's performances – reported to the
General when she got home that the short play was a rather stylistically conventional piece that told 'more or less their own history'.[36]
Telling, this compulsion of Eleanor's to try and represent – explain
publicly – her relationship with Edward, as if she sensed the concern
and disapproval of others and as if she was defending Edward from
the allegations of financial malpractice. Unseeing faith led her to
think that others misunderstood who Edward Aveling really was,
rather than realise her own self-delusional misunderstanding of the
man with whom she thought she shared her life.

At the end of January 1885 Eleanor, Edward and GBS again
performed together at a fundraiser held at the Ladbroke Hall in
Notting Hill. After a first half of music and recital, the second half of
the programme featured Eleanor, Shaw and Edward taking the leads
in a three-act play entitled *Alone*, co-written by John Simpson and
Herman Merivale.

Whilst getting up these amateur fundraiser performances in public
halls around London, the Leaguers also took to open-air platforms

for the more serious business of taking the fight for free speech to the streets. In good-humoured rivalry, the new Socialist League vied with the SDF over who could keep open the most open-air pitches in London.[37] In order to draw good crowds, great attention was paid by both sides to programming these free speech events: good quality speakers, regularity, relevant topics of interest to the public were essential. Persistent hecklers and a police presence were a bonus. Open-air propaganda was vital for drumming up public support and debate and Eleanor, her colleagues quickly realised, was a gifted outdoor speaker with an ability to draw large, attentive crowds.

As movement and momentum grew, so too did state interference. Dod Street in Limehouse, an old open-air site used for centuries by radicals and religious sects and now favoured by the SDF, became a focus of police harassment. Several SDF speakers were prosecuted for obstruction. One of these, Jack Williams, refused to pay his fine and was sentenced to a month's hard labour. The League formally offered its support to the SDF and other radical organisations followed suit, including the Fabian Society, represented on this issue by Annie Besant. On 20 September 1885 a mass gathering at Dod Street moved a resolution protesting over the prosecutions against free speech. Eleanor was one of the twenty-seven speakers, 'greatly applauded' when she declared herself sure that this large assembly 'would show the upper classes an example in the way of orderly conduct'.[38] But as she spoke, police moved stealthily along the side of the street. Just as the meeting was closed and the crowds were dispersing, the police unexpectedly attacked, seizing banners, arresting banner-bearers and several other protesters, including William Morris.

The following day, the eight detained were brought before Magistrate Saunders in the Thames Police Court, charged with obstruction or resisting arrest. Eleanor appeared as a witness for the defence, asserting the rights of free speech and stating that she intended to go to and speak at further meetings. Saunders reprimanded her for 'impertinence'; Eleanor brushed him off and stated that of the many meetings in which she had participated, this had been one of the most orderly and quiet. The police, she said, had acted with great brutality without provocation.

Saunders's summing-up dished out sentences of hard labour and steep fines on all the defendants. Havoc broke out at these draconian sentences, spectators shouting 'Shame' from the gallery. The police suddenly charged at the people in court. Edward reported that the police 'commenced an assault on all and sundry', and that Eleanor and Morris were singled out for a particularly brutal thumping. The punch-up ended with Morris being re-arrested and Eleanor, who joined in the fighting, nevertheless appalled by the use of physical violence in the court.

In July *Commonweal* started running advertisements for a summer series of 'free evenings for the people'. Eleanor and Edward appeared on the bill of all these nights that Morris usually introduced with his prologue, *Socialists at Play*. Come autumn, Tussy suggested the Leaguers also put together a programme of free events and entertainment for children.

She dreamed of being able to go and see Laura and the family in Paris for Christmas but she couldn't afford it. Consolation for this disappointment arrived in the welcome form of her nine-year-old nephew Johnny Longuet, son of her dead sister Jennychen. It had taken Tussy nearly two years to persuade his father Charles to let him come for an extended visit and she was delighted. Prompted by having Johnny in her care, Tussy planned a Christmas that the motherless little boy could enjoy with hundreds of other children. She wrote to the League's council with her proposal for the Christmas tree fund and a festival of light, reminding them that the origin of the Christmas festival pre-dated Christianity: 'the beautiful old Pagan feast that celebrated the birth of light . . . is not Socialism the real "new birth" and with its light will not the old darkness of the earth disappear?'[39]

Eleanor loved having Johnny staying with them at Great Russell Street but Edward showed no interest in the boy. He was irritated at no longer being the centre of Eleanor's attention. The General and Lenchen, now both sixty-five (having been born just a month apart in 1820), thoroughly enjoyed Johnny's visits to Regent's Park Road. Just as he had done with Tussy as a child, the General gave Johnny lots of books to read and took him for long talking walks. Aunt Tussy established a routine of daily washing, school, homework and early nights with bedtime reading, none of which Johnny had at home.

'We cannot too soon make children understand that Socialism means *happiness*,'[40] Eleanor told the League council when describing her Christmas festival. Out of context this sounds a little absurd and very ideological, but when read in the context of Tussy's simultaneous preoccupation with Ibsen's new play *A Doll's House*, it makes startlingly good sense. Simultaneous to becoming treasurer of the 'Tree Committee' and working on the children's light festival and Christmas party, Tussy was deeply immersed in organising the first performed reading of *A Doll's House* in England.

By agreement of all, Eleanor was to take the lead role as Nora Helmer and Edward would play her husband, Torvald Helmer. Famously, the play opens with a Christmas tree as the consummate symbol of Nora's lightness of being and the unbearable heaviness of financial hardship in her foundering marriage.

Nora enters in her outdoor winter coat, humming a tune and in high spirits, laden with parcels:

Nora: Hide the Christmas Tree carefully, Helen. Be sure the children do not see it till this evening, when it is dressed.[42]

Nora is summoned by Torvald, who calls her his 'little squirrel', 'lark twittering', 'featherhead', caging her firmly within flighty feminine diminutives before their conversation begins. A minute later husband and wife are engaged in a seemingly light-hearted marital argument about the need to economise. Torvald reprimands Nora for being spendthrift. She retorts that the children should have light and happiness for Christmas:

Helmer: That is like a woman! But seriously, Nora, you know what I think about that. No debt, no borrowing. There can be no freedom or beauty about a home life that depends on borrowing and debt.[42]

Eleanor and Edward had recently started drafting their treatise on the woman question from a socialist point of view. These words that Torvald says to Nora found their way into this pioneering work.

On 26 December a group of London children who would otherwise have been without Christmas celebrations enjoyed a festival of
food, light and fun at 13 Farringdon Hall, all raised on donations.
The event was oversubscribed but, despite logistical pressures, Tussy
was resolved that it was all worthwhile, 'the fact that some 200 little
ones enjoyed themselves is quite enough satisfaction.'[43]

Nora Helmer would have agreed.

Nora Helmer, Emma Bovary and 'The Woman Question'

'Laziness is the root of all evil,' said Tussy frequently.[1] In this regard, she seemed to practise what she preached. Within the twelve months between the summers of 1885 and 1886 Tussy started and finished the first English translation of Gustave Flaubert's *Madame Bovary*; revised a new edition of Lissagaray's *History of the Paris Commune*; put on the first performance of Ibsen's *A Doll's House* in England; championed the programming of art and education in the Socialist League; produced a body of journalistic work on prostitution and sex slavery; became a ghostwriter and finally completed the English translation of the first volume of *Capital* with Samuel Moore, Engels, Aveling, Lafargue and Longuet. If this were not sufficient, she and Edward completed and published 'The Woman Question: From a Socialist Point of View'.

Novelist and Francophile George Moore commissioned Eleanor to translate *Madame Bovary* for the radical English publisher Henry Vizetelly in the summer of 1885.[2] She started in the autumn and delivered it to the publisher complete with introduction in May 1886. The original publication of the novel in France thirty years earlier had been the occasion of an obscenity trial at which Flaubert was acquitted. The dauntless Vizetelly published Flaubert, Maupassant, Baudelaire and Edgar Allan Poe in Britain, running the twin risks of commercial flops and prosecution under the Obscene

Publications Act of 1857. A few years later, in 1888, Vizetelly was to be tried for obscenity for publishing three Zola novels and served a three-month sentence in Holloway Prison. He died shortly afterwards.

Famously, it took Flaubert a large part of his life to produce *Madame Bovary*; innumerable years of gestation and then five years writing at the rate of approximately a page a week. Eleanor had just shy of six months to produce her complete translation and she was unable to devote all her time to it. In her introduction, Tussy identifies three possible methods of translation: 'genius', 'hack' and 'conscientious worker'. She puts herself in the last category, and then adumbrates 'the weaknesses, shortcomings, the failures of my work':[3]

> ... but at least ... I have neither suppressed nor added a line, a word ... My work ... I know is ... pale and feeble by the side of the original ... But ... I do not regret having done this work; it is the best I could do.

Having declared comprehensively its 'faults', Tussy concludes her introduction with satisfaction: 'Yet if it induces some readers to go to that original, if it helps to make known to those who cannot study this work of one of the greatest French novelists after Balzac, I am content.'[4] She was just pleased to get it done, as she wrote to Laura in April 1886: 'I have (Lord be praised!) finished my translation of *Madame Bovary*. It *has* been work!'[5] Work indeed to translate a novel where the lead character does not open her mouth to speak, to her dog, until the seventh chapter: 'Pourquoi, mon Dieu! Me suis-je mariée?' A question Eleanor might well have asked her own pets, now numbering several cats and a dog.

Tussy's challenge was to translate, to a tight deadline, a writer who himself spent whole days – sometimes weeks – seeking a single word to get the right one, and whose masterpiece is structured through ironic cliché, banality and romantic convention. Then there was the question of how to translate *le style indirect libre* – free indirect speech – in a way that made this radical new style of writing aesthetically meaningful to English readers.

The character of Emma Bovary haunted Tussy. 'But for her surroundings,' she wrote in her introduction, 'she would be a monster and an impossibility.' Tussy is thoughtfully ambivalent about her assessment of Emma: 'She is foolish, but there is a certain nobleness about her too. She is never mercenary.'[6] Of course, Tussy would never judge harshly a person who gave her last sou to a blind beggar. Emma's problem of self-deception and falsification of her personality fascinated Tussy:

> Her life is idle, useless. And this strong woman feels there *must* be something to do – and she dreams. Life is so unreal to her that she marries Bovary thinking she loves him . . . She does her best to love 'this poor wretch.' In all literature there is perhaps nothing more pathetic than her hopeless effort to 'make herself in love.' And even after she has been false, how she yearns to go back to him, to something real, to a healthier, better love than she has known.[7]

We can only imagine what Olive thought when she read this introduction and reflected on Tussy's parallel self-delusion about her failing relationship with Edward, in which she felt inescapably trapped. *Madame Bovary* was an echo chamber in Tussy's life. Flaubert famously identified himself with his novel's heroine – 'Madame Bovary, c'est moi.' The construction uncannily mirrors Karl Marx's dictum, 'Tussy *is* me.'[8]

The critical reception of Eleanor's translation when it was published in August 1886 was, as ever, varied. Some reviewers forgot their objectivity on sight of her surname; others gave vent to their anti-French xenophobia. The *Saturday Review* referred contemptuously to 'Mrs Aveling's friends in France',[9] a jibe at both Tussy's family and her well-known socialist internationalism. The *Athenaeum* summarised her effort as done 'with more zeal than discretion'.[10] In the twentieth century Vladimir Nabokov fulminated at excessive length about Eleanor's version, as he did about all the others, but then chose hers as his set text when teaching the novel – perhaps an acknowledgement of Eleanor's hope that her work helped to make a great French writer accessible to those unable to read it in the original. And for many years it remained the only English version available.

Writer William Sharp was amongst significant critics who judged Eleanor to have done a highly creditable job. Reviewing her translation in the *Academy*, Sharp reminded readers that Flaubert was a 'pre-eminently ... untranslatable writer',[11] and praised Eleanor for producing a 'translation that is at once faithful and entirely natural'.[12]

Tussy did most of the work on *Madame Bovary* and Lissagaray's *History of the Commune* in a house she and Edward rented temporarily in Kingston-upon-Thames. They first went to Kingston the previous December, in 1885, leaving Johnny Longuet behind to spend the rest of the holiday at Regent's Park Road. Lenchen and the General were surprised that Tussy left her Johnny behind – she'd fought with her brother-in-law Charles for two years to get him to agree to her nephew's visit. The reason emerged over the next few months: Edward didn't want the boy around any longer. Tussy remonstrated. They fought and Edward threatened to leave her; Tussy sadly relented, and Johnny was sent to Uncle Engels and Lenchen. Children had become a vexed subject between Eleanor and Edward, as she confided to Olive. Edward didn't feel ready to have children. Tussy did. Children, Edward reassured her, would happen – like their legal marriage – in the future.

'We get more work done here really than in London, and get some fresh air besides,'[13] Tussy wrote of Kingston. Her revision of Lissagaray's *History of the Commune*, by now acknowledged as the definitive eyewitness account of this period of French history, was deftly done. She still had a good rapport with Lissa and understood intimately his relationship to his book. Lissa's lifework, which remains to this day the ur text of French Communard history, was the place where he tried to come to terms with his trauma at the failure of the Commune and his own role in the killing.

In so many understandable ways Lissa could never quite move beyond those fifteen minutes of fear and horror alone on the last barricade, as his ammunition ran out and he was left, finally, with only a bayonet to defend himself. Lissa was a formidable soldier of the Commune but had the courage and honesty to speak the truth about all sides. He clearly highlighted the errors of his party and exposed the fatal weaknesses and failures of the revolution whilst supporting its aims.

Consequently Eleanor proposed, 'Lissagaray's *History of the Commune* is the only authentic and reliable history as yet written of the most memorable movement of modern times.'[14] Eleanor's preface to this edition is a clear statement of her internationalism in the 1880s. She follows her father's interpretation of the Commune as 'the first attempt of the proletariat to govern itself' and its potential for 'the substitution of true co-operative, ie. Communistic, for capitalistic production', but departs from and develops her analysis further by proposing international collectivism: 'the participation in this Revolution of workers of all countries meant the internationalising, not only the nationalizing of the land and of private property.'[15]

Revising Lissagaray's book was familiar territory but later in the year Tussy revealed to Peter Lavrov her new venture into the world of ghostwriting, which she called 'hackwork'. 'I am writing a biography and critical sketch of the artist Alma Tadema for someone who will publish it under his own name, not mine!'[16] Invited as the side-bar wife, ghostwriting, speech-writing, underwriting articles she'd written with Edward's name when he'd never touched them: Tussy seemed to be getting into a habit of doing things in – or with – the name of a man. But this trouser-writing paid and she needed the money. Tussy was actually good at earning money, as her ability to juggle her paid freelance work demonstrates. She 'imagined herself to be in financial difficulties';[17] in fact, Aveling was her financial difficulty. As fast as she could earn money from journalism, translation, research, teaching and hackwork, he spent it. She was thrifty for herself and generous to others, he profligate. But she was the chief breadwinner and for Tussy this constituted a form of economic independence.

The year 1886 was Eleanor's thirty-first. She saw it in with a memorable birthday. Over the Christmas season Tussy's friends received invitations to a performance of Ibsen's *A Doll's House* – or *Nora*, as the play was called at the time – to be given in Tussy and Edward's living room at 55 Great Russell Street on 15 January. It was a Friday, so the plan was to party through the night in celebration of her birthday after the staged reading. Tussy urged Havelock Ellis to try and come. 'I feel,' she wrote to him, 'I *must* do something to make people understand our Ibsen a little more than they do, and I know by experience that a play read to them often affects people more than when they read by themselves.' Fifty years later Shaw recalled that:

> at the first performance of A Doll's House in England, on a first floor in a Bloomsbury lodging house, Karl Marx's youngest daughter played Nora Helmer and I impersonated Krogstad at her request with a very vague notion of what it was all about.[18]

Eleanor's close friend May Morris, daughter of William, took the role of Christine Linde and Edward, inevitably, played Torvald Helmer. Shaw had pledged an unconventional 'Mystic Betrothal' to May Morris the previous year, adding frisson to their playing opposite each other as hard-won lovers.

May Morris was a brilliant textile designer with an extraordinary talent for the arts of embroidery and tapestry. She also secretly desired and adored Tussy, though no one knew it until many years later. May gave Tussy as many gifts as she would accept, and Tussy's lodgings were adorned with modern William Morris furnishings and fabrics.

May Morris studied at the National Art Training School (later Royal College of Art, South Kensington) and combined artistic flair with a good business sense and political commitment. In 1884 she joined the SDF Hammersmith branch, following her father and Tussy in the breakaway formation of the Socialist League in 1885. At the beginning of 1886 she was just about to be appointed head of embroidery at Morris & Co., as well as producing wallpaper designs, at which she also excelled. In time, she became general manager of her father's hugely successful interior design, furnishings and fabrics business run on collective principles. To William's satisfaction, May combined artistic ability with a capacity for the practical sides of commerce that far exceeded his own. As he cheerfully boasted, May was a far better businessman than he was.

Curiously, no one remembered who played Dr Rank on this occasion. Whatever the identity of Nora/Eleanor's loyal, undeclared admirer, this event was a landmark in Eleanor's declared passion for Ibsen in general and A Doll's House in particular. Eleanor's first written reference to the play is to her sister in June 1884. She'd recently been introduced to the Swedish writer Ann Edgren, at the time on a visit to England, and admired her short stories and novels. Edgren was about to visit Paris and Tussy asked Laura to meet her and introduce her to the Parisian socialist demi-monde:

> It is strange how immensely rich Scandinavia is just now in authors! . . . I send you an English translation of the Norwegian (this is rather Irish!) Ibsen's splendid play *Nora*. I don't say anything about it, because I know <u>how</u> you will appreciate it.[19]

Edward was also a firm admirer, stating in his *Today* column that Ibsen 'sees our lop-sided modern society suffering from too much man, and he has been born the women's poet'.[20] Ibsen's aim, Edward claims, is to revolutionise the marriage relationship – an ambition with which he identifies. Indeed.

The intense conflict and contradictions of contemporary marriage that Ibsen gave life to on the stage mirrored the struggles between Eleanor and Edward. Writing to Shaw and telling him he had to take the role of Krogstad, Tussy stressed how much Ibsen's new naturalism brought the magnitude of private personal themes into the public realm of the modern stage:

> I wish some really <u>great</u> actors would try Ibsen. The more I study the greater I think him. How odd it is that people complain that his plays 'have no end' but just leave you where you were, that he gives no <u>solution</u> to the problem he has set you! As if in life things 'ended' off either comfortably or uncomfortably. We play through our little dramas, and comedies, and tragedies, and farces and then begin it all over again. If we <u>could</u> find solutions to the problems of our lives things would be easier in this weary world.[21]

Tussy continued to twin her interest in modern theatre with political performance. In March the anniversary of the Paris Commune was celebrated in Moorgate, drawing a bigger audience than ever before. The SL, SDF and anarchists suspended animosities to make it a collective event. Eleanor spoke alongside Tom Mann of the SDF, fellow Leaguer Frank Kitz and Peter Kropotkin, the Russian anarchist released that year from prison in France and now living in London. Hyndman, Morris, John Burns, Kautsky and Charlotte Wilson also spoke. By unanimous agreement Eleanor's was the best speech of the evening and the finest of her political career so far. Her opponents praised the excellence of this address, including Hyndman, who described it as 'one of the finest speeches I ever heard':[22]

> The woman seemed inspired with some of the eloquence of the old prophets of her race as she spoke of the eternal life gained by those who fought and fell in the great cause of the uplifting of humanity: an eternal life in the material and intellectual improvement of countless generations of mankind.[23]

But it was the role of womankind Eleanor spoke about. Matilda Hyndman, always a quiet ally of Eleanor's politics, must have inwardly cheered her on this occasion as she made the central role of women in the Paris Commune and socialism the subject of her speech. This was the first time women's leadership of the Commune was the subject of an anniversary address.

Eleanor drew a confident portrait of Communard women and the women's unions and, from their example, raised the need for women's emancipation as necessary to achieving the aims of the socialist movement. Not just integral or desirable, but a precondition for the progress of meaningful social change. She was the only person on the platform that night to address the questions of sexual difference and gender inequality but, resoundingly, the most well-received speaker. The audience, from many different classes and walks of life, did not feel hectored or lectured, or hear her assertive, confident and persuasive opinions on the revolutionary force of feminism as strident, brash or aggressive. Tussy was pitch perfect.

Eleanor's speech at the Commune anniversary drew on her and Edward's essay 'The Woman Question: From a Socialist Point of View', co-written in 1885 and published in both of their names in *Westminster Review* in the first quarterly edition of 1886.[24] Eleanor had argued consistently throughout her political life so far that it was essential for women and men to work together in order to effectively address the question of women's oppression in society. This thesis of co-operation was central to 'The Woman Question', both in its collaborative form of production and in its philosophical content. 'The Woman Question' was the first of several key projects they worked on together over the next decade. The division of labour varied over time but Aveling generally claimed that Eleanor did the lion's share.[25]

Marx and Aveling[26] propose that two of the greatest curses that ruin the relations between man and woman 'are the treatment of men and women as different beings, and the want of truth'.[27] It's worth pausing to consider the implications of this. The publication of 'The Woman Question' opens up a significant new perspective on why Eleanor persisted in trying to make her relationship with Edward work. Her vision, apparently shared by Edward, of how women and men might resolve their differences is all laid out clearly and uncompromisingly in this essay:

> And first, a general idea that has to do with all women. The life of woman does not coincide with that of man. Their lives do not intersect; in many cases do not even touch. Hence the life of the race is stunted.[28]

The first answer to the woman question is that the oppression of women has a disastrous effect on men. It hampers the development of the whole of humanity. If both sexes are incomplete, both are damaged, 'and when, as a rule, neither of them comes into real, thorough, habitual, free contact, mind to mind, with the other, the being is neither whole nor entire'. So far, so Kant, but Eleanor and Edward are not seeking to reconcile materialism (objective reality) and idealism. They start with far more practical, everyday experiences: sex, desire, marriage, earning a livelihood, property ownership, the bringing up of children, the impact of consumer capitalism.

They both believed, like Marx and Engels, that the existing social contracts between women and men were corrupt. It wouldn't, therefore, surprise them to encounter common difficulties about property, economics and sexual infidelity in their own relationship. In their collaborative work, they tried to tackle and work out some of these all-too-familiar and thorny issues. They understood how things were in the concrete. They looked towards how they might be re-envisioned in the abstract future. It helps a great deal to keep this in view when reflecting on the question of why Tussy stuck by Edward.

The specific moment of 'The Woman Question: From a Socialist Point of View' was, in part, prompted by August Bebel's *Women and Socialism*. Produced in Germany in 1879, Bebel's book was, famously, banned from publication in Bismarck's Germany under the anti-socialist laws. The English translation was published in 1885, providing an opportunity for Eleanor and Edward to bring the ideas of the role of the woman question in socialism to English-speaking audiences. With this objective to introduce socialist feminism to Britain held firmly in mind, it's important to note the full title of their essay: 'The Woman Question: From a Socialist Point of View'. Important, because subsequent reprints of the essay in English during the twentieth century persisted in dropping the subtitle – which so clearly states both the perspective and intent of this groundbreaking treatise.

The Marx-Aveling essay tested Bebel's analysis in *Women and Socialism* that there could be no emancipation of humanity without the social independence and equality of the sexes. Therefore the abolition of sexual inequality was integral to the working-class movement. Bebel's thesis, which Tussy studied closely, resonated with Engels's book *The Origin of the Family, Private Property and the State*, published just two years previously. The General's book was another key influence on Eleanor to produce her statement on the relationship between feminism and socialism. Described by Lenin as 'one of the fundamental works of modern socialism',[29] *The Origin of the Family* did not appear in English translation until 1902. Eleanor had discussed it with the General whilst he was writing it and read it in its draft stages.

As we already know, Engels sorted through Marx's papers after he died, and found the notes his friend had made on the contribution of Lewis Henry Morgan, the American anthropologist, to the discussion of the origins and future of the family. Immediately seized by inspiration, Engels channelled his desolation at losing Marx into writing *The Origin of the Family, Private Property and the State*. In doing so, he developed and far exceeded both Morgan's and Marx's findings. As made clear by his title, Engels drew on Darwin's theory of natural selection and anthropological studies of matriarchal societies. For the present and future of the family, he drew on the living examples around him: his own life, the Burns sisters, Lenchen, Pumps, and Marx's daughters.

Crucially, Engels introduced Herbert Spencer's juxtaposition of the forces of production and reproduction into thinking about the family, sex and economics. This absolutely fundamental philosophical, political and economic realisation made a transformational impact on Eleanor. Engels had achieved what her father's work did not; he had made the crucial step of identifying the relationship between the theory of historical materialism and feminism. This was the equivalent of Galileo's discovery that the earth revolved around the sun and not, as had always been believed, the other way round. And as a theory it was greeted with just as much scepticism.

Bebel's and Engels's work enabled Eleanor to bring together her materialist, Darwinian understanding of history and economics with her reading of feminist thinkers, most particularly Mary Wollstonecraft and Mary Shelley. Eleanor always supported the campaigns for women's suffrage and rights-based arguments but knew that their application was politically limited: creating access to the ballot box and education for bourgeois women was a partial intervention that would not address the broad, underlying structural problem of sexual inequality. Women were an economic and social class, globally oppressed. Working-class and middle-class women were conjoined by the inseparability of production and the reproduction required to replenish the work force. From this perspective, patriarchy and capitalism were not just blood brothers but twins. She was clear, like Clara Zetkin, that women were divided by economic class. Bourgeois women's resistance tended to be reactive – they challenged their men – whereas working women had to be radical and challenge the whole society:

Here comes the true struggle *against* man. Here the educated woman – the doctor, the clerk, the lawyer, is the antagonist of man. The women of this class are sick of their moral and intellectual subjugation. They are Noras rebelling against their doll's homes. They want to live their own lives, and economically and intellectually the demands of the middle-class women are fully justified.[30]

The position of the working woman was different. The proletarian woman was drawn into the vortex of capitalist production because her labour was cheap to buy. But her position was not merely reactionary; it was also revolutionary. As a worker, the proletarian woman had a different kind of independence to the housebound middle-class woman, 'but truly she paid the price!':

And that is why the working woman cannot be like the bourgeois woman who has to fight against the man of her own class . . . The objections of the bourgeois man to the rights of women are only a matter of competition . . . With the proletarian women, on the contrary, it is a struggle of the woman *with* the man of her own class against the capitalist class . . . For her . . . it is a necessity to build up new barriers against the exploitation of the proletarian woman, and to secure her rights as wife, and as mother. Her end and aim are not the right of free competition with men, but to obtain the political power of the proletariat. Truly the working woman approves the demand of the middle-class women's movement . . . But only as means to the end that she may be fully armed for entering into the working-class struggle along with the man of her class.[31]

Eleanor was impatient with the caution within socialist organisations about how to treat the question of the equality of the sexes. Her and Edward's objectives in 'The Woman Question' were to show that feminism was an integral necessity, not just a single aspect or issue of the socialist working-class movement, and that sexual inequality was fundamentally a question of economics. 'The Woman Question' was the first treatise of its sort written by a woman active in the working-class movement and the first manifesto by a woman on the woman question in the socialist international. Published on the eve of the founding of the Second International in Paris, where both Eleanor and Clara Zetkin spoke on women and labour, 'The

Woman Question' is the founding text of socialist feminism and offers a concrete plan of action as well as theoretical abstraction. The necessity for women of all classes to work together, and for men and women to work together, were two of Eleanor's key precepts. To this end, the collaborative writing of the essay was exemplary. They made it clear that theirs were the independent opinions of two individual socialists, and that they did not speak on behalf of any party or sect.

In the essay, Eleanor and Edward linked the oppression of women within patriarchal societies with that of the proletariat – arguing, like Wollstonecraft, Engels and Bebel, that the causes of women's oppression within capitalist society were economic and social, not inevitably governed by instinct or nature. 'The Woman Question' explores all the key aspects of sexual inequality debated in the nineteenth century across the ideological spectrum: mercenary marriage; unregulated prostitution; segregation of the sexes; lack of health care; inadequate medical research into how women's bodies function; lack of sex education for both sexes; different systems of moral judgement imposed on men and women's behaviour; and the unnaturalness and hypocrisy of social expectations for the chastity of women. Many forms of sexual inequality, they suggest, transcend existing economic class divisions, making middle-class (bourgeois) women proletarians in their own homes. Eleanor and Edward argue therefore that, whilst they are wholly sympathetic to the impulse underlying the limited aim of campaigns for women's suffrage and legal constraint on prostitution, the call for civil and parliamentary participation and representation are only a narrow approach to a broader problem. Women should be forming a united feminist front, challenging across class divisions the divide and rule that regulates production and reproduction.

Engels's *Origin of the Family* has been studied and written about since the beginning of the twentieth century. Yet 'The Woman Question', written from its explicitly socialist point of view, contains, unlike Engels's work, a clear programme for the emancipation of women and men. The few interpretations of the essay to date have suggested that Eleanor and Edward argue that the overthrow by the proletariat of the capitalist system of production will lead to the end of women's oppression. In other words, equality of women and men will follow after the revolution that will bring about a classless society. However, this argument appears nowhere in the essay. In fact, Eleanor and Edward advance the diametrical – or rather, dialectical – opposite. Eleanor and Edward's landmark essay makes it absolutely clear that the struggle for women's emancipation and the equality of the sexes is a prerequisite for any effective form of progressive social revolution.

Engels hints that feminism was probably a necessary *a priori* to socialist revolution but he didn't quite get there in proposing a practical programme. His economic and political support of all the women around him was unstinting, but he would have been the first to admit that his vision was restricted by his position of entitlement in the world as a man.

Anticipating the usual weariness and hostility with which calls for feminist transformation are traditionally greeted by patriarchal society, Eleanor and Edward begin by saying that to treat the position of women at the present time in detail, 'is to repeat a thousand-times-told-tale'.[32] The story of women's oppression, and the correlative effect it has on oppressing men's capacities, is no more respected if told by men than by women. The new English translation of Bebel's latest work, they point out, was met in certain quarters with 'a vituperative reception'.[33] 'The thousand-times-told same old story is that "women are the creatures of an organised tyranny of men, as the workers are the creatures of an organised tyranny of men."'[34] This applies to women across all classes. The notion that women's lives are defined by their 'natural calling' is convention and ideology:

> There is no more a 'natural calling' of woman than there is a 'natural' law of capitalistic production, or a 'natural' limit to the amount of the labourer's product that goes to him for means of subsistence. That in the first case, woman's 'calling' is supposed to be only the tending of children, the maintenance of household conditions and a general obedience to her lord; that, in the second, the production of surplus value is a necessary preliminary in the production of capital; that, in the third, the amount the labourer receives for his means of subsistence is so much as will keep him only just above starvation

point: these are not natural laws in the same sense as are the laws of motion. They are only certain temporary conventions of society, like the convention that French is the language of diplomacy.[35]

Positioning itself in relation to current campaigns, 'The Woman Question' states its critical allegiance to revisionist forms of women's suffrage within existing capitalist and colonial societies. It warns that the sectors of the women's suffrage movement who work for class-restricted reform will fail. Eleanor and Edward honour the 'excellent and hard-working folk who agitate for that perfectly just aim, woman suffrage':

> for the repeal of the Contagious Diseases Act, a monstrosity begotten of male cowardice and brutality; for the higher education of women; for the opening to them of universities, the learned professions, and all callings, from that of teacher to that of bagman.

In all this work – good as far as it goes – they identify three notable characteristics. First, those concerned in the women's suffrage movement 'are of the well-to-do classes, as a rule. With the single and only partial exception of the Contagious Diseases agitation, scarcely any of the women taking a prominent part in these various movements belong to the working class.'[36] Second, ideas of advancing women through suffrage and human rights are based either on property, or on sentimental or professional questions: 'Not one of them gets down through these to the bedrock of the economic basis, not only of each of these three, but of society itself.'[37] Exclusively suffrage-based women's advocates, Eleanor and Edward argue, show demonstrable ignorance of both economics and the proper study of the evolution of society. 'Even the orthodox political economy, which is, as we think, misleading in its statements and inaccurate in its conclusions, does not appear to have been mastered generally.'[38]

The third problem Marx-Aveling identify with women's suffrage is that its limited aims confine it to working within existing society. It fails to encompass the broad-scale social revolution required to achieve a democratic civil society. There is no vision of a future, different society:

We will support all women, not only those having property, enabled to vote; the Contagious Diseases Act repealed; every calling thrown open to both sexes. The actual position of women in respect to men would not be very vitally touched . . . For not one of these things, save indirectly the Contagious Diseases Act, touches them in their sex relations . . . Without larger social change women will never be free.[39]

Demanding the vote for only middle-class, educated, moneyed women and not for the majority of their working-class sisters and disenfranchised working men perpetuated existing undemocracy. Eleanor, like Clara Zetkin, could see clearly the political appeal of the women's campaign for the bourgeois vote in England, the USA, France, Germany and Russia. Both realised that the Second International needed to take account of the fact that the demand for women's rights articulated by middle-class women was being heard first, above those of working women. The Second International needed to raise the voice of a transnational feminist movement. Just as there could not be socialism in one country, there could not be feminism in one country.

Critically, women 'must understand that their emancipation will come from themselves'.[40] Women will find allies amongst the better sorts of men, just as workers find allies amongst philosophers, artists and poets, 'but the one has nothing to hope from man as a whole, and the other has nothing to hope from the middle class as a whole'.[41] In this regard, 'The Woman Question' respects and honours the valuable civil rights won recently in England, 'due to the action of women themselves'.[42]

By comparison, the situation of women in Germany was far worse: women were legal minors with regard to men, legally physically punished, and disallowed from owning either earnings or property; men decided when babies were weaned, and women were prohibited from entering into contracts or joining political organisations. The essay also makes further fascinating comparisons with the status of women in France and Russia:

It is unnecessary for us to point out how much better, within the last few years, these things have been managed in England . . . But it is necessary to remind them that with all these added civil rights English women, married and unmarried alike, are morally dependent on man, and are badly treated by him.[43]

Eleanor and Edward argue that emancipation from sexual oppression cannot be brought about only by legislation and through political organisation. From the socialist point of view, feminism has to begin in the family, home and community. Crucially, modern society needs to talk openly about sex:

> Our children are constantly silenced when they ask about the begetting and the birth of offspring. The question is as natural as one about the beats of the heart or the movements of respiration ... As our boys and girls grow up, the whole subject of sex relations is made a mystery and a shame. This is the reason why an undue and unhealthy curiosity is begotten to them. The mind becomes excessively concentrated upon them, remains long unsatisfied, or incompletely satisfied – passes into a morbid condition. To us, it seems that the reproductive organs ought to be discussed as frankly, as freely, between parents and children as the digestive. The objection to this is but a form of the vulgar prejudice against the teaching of physiology.[44]

Marx-Aveling, in 1886, are here firmly in the terrain of the psychological and physiological construction of human sexuality. Eleanor has brought Freud and the fledgling discipline of psychoanalysis into discussion with a materialist analysis.

From the outset, the essay is clear that it is impossible to understand inequality between men and women without seeing the economics that underpin it: 'those who attack the present treatment of women without seeking for the cause of this in the economics of our latter-day society are like doctors who treat a local affection without inquiring into the general bodily health.'[45] But at no point do Eleanor and Edward argue that sexual oppression can be resolved merely with an economic answer: 'The woman question is one of the organisation of society as a whole.'[46] For every aspect of the question they raise, they explore answers from a range of perspectives – economic, psychological, emotional and scientific. For example, they state 'that the conditions of divorce should be the same for the two sexes',[47] and demonstrate the economic inequalities that determine the impact of divorce on men and women: different relations to property, the means of livelihood, responsibility for childcare. But reform of these factors alone, Eleanor and Edward argue, would not eradicate women's oppression; the whole of social attitudes to sex, desire and sexuality also have to be taken into account. Women need the same opportunities accorded to men to become 'sound in mind and body'.[48] This is far from a reductive economistic approach to understanding the proposition of socialist feminism.

Though thoroughly analytical, 'The Woman Question' is not a didactic or propagandist tract. Tussy was the child of a collective age and the child of Marx. The polyphony of voices in 'The Woman Question' makes it a rich and pleasing read. Ibsen's Nora Helmer, Olive Schreiner's Lyndall Gordon, Shakespeare's Rosalind, Miranda and Helena are all conjured to address the subject. Mary Wollstonecraft, John Stuart Mill, Harriet Taylor and Helen Taylor, Isabella Beecher Hooker, Demosthenes, Francis Bacon, Kant, Coleridge, Tennyson and Shelley all make contributions to the argument.

When Eleanor and Edward hold up for scrutiny the marriage contract as an institution, they avoid dry economistic analysis. Instead, they call on modern theatre. 'As Ibsen makes Helmer say to Nora, "Home life ceases to be free and beautiful directly its foundations are borrowing and debts." '[49] When writing with great probity and sensitivity about sex, chastity, reproduction and the hypocrisy that bedevils how society deals with the 'sex instinct', they give voice to Olive Schreiner's searing condemnation of systemic sexual inequality:

With the false shame and false secrecy, against which we protest, goes the unhealthy separation of the sexes that begins as children quit the nursery, and only ends when the dead men and women are laid in the common ground. In *The Story of an African Farm* the girl Lyndall cries out, 'We were equals once, when we lay new-born babies on our nurses' knees. We shall be equals again when they tie up our jaws for the last sleep.'[50]

Eleanor understood profoundly that the woman question, and the relations between men and women, began in the family. Men and women were made, not born. How children were brought up and treated was as determining to sexual inequality and the oppression of women as the generation of surplus value at any social cost was to capitalism. And the two were linked directly: 'Our marriages, like our morals, are based upon commercialism.'[51] Socialist feminism, like historical materialism, was for Tussy a family affair.

At the beginning of 1886, when Tussy scrupulously tidied up her accounts before her birthday, she found a small surplus from the Christmas Tree Fund. Donations of toys continued to arrive at the Socialist League offices in the months after the festival. Poor people made toys and games and delivered their donations on foot to Farringdon; rich people had deliveries sent from William Hamley's toy store at 200 Regent Street. To deal with both the surplus and the toys, Tussy proposed that 'we could give the little ones an outing'.[52] May Morris and women members of the SL offered to help organise a children's summer beanfeast.

The picnic party took place in June, the same week that Eleanor wrote the introduction to her completed translation of *Madame Bovary*. Vizetelly published the book just as Eleanor and Edward set sail for New York. Already going ahead to the next thing, she wasn't in England to see the reviews.

Lady Liberty

Eleanor and Edward steamed out of Liverpool bound for the New World on the *City of Chicago,* an Inman liner, on Tuesday 31 August 1886. The Socialistic Labor Party (SLP) of America had invited them to give a four-month speaking tour of fifteen states. Eleanor came up with the idea of a lecture tour in 1880, and suggested it to Library – Wilhelm Liebknecht – and the Social Democratic Party of Germany (SPD), of which he was one of the founders.

There were close kinship ties with European emigrants to America in the developing international socialist movement. Exiles from the 1848 uprisings, the Paris Commune and the ongoing Irish revolution congregated in republican America. Overall, socialist organisation in America remained too narrowly German in membership, leadership, language and influence. It needed to internationalise, and this was one of the primary objectives of the lecture tour. Library's English was not fluent, so he would speak in German. Multilingual Eleanor and well-spoken Edward could bring together different organisations and put socialist ideas to English speakers in America for the first time in their own tongue.

Fundraising was another motivation for the trip. Bismarck's anti-socialist legislation had led to persecution and privation for social democracy organisations in Germany and had a domino effect on the rest of Europe. The movement needed money and, as Tussy pointed out to Library, Charles Stewart Parnell had made 'thousands and thousands'[1] for the Irish cause in America.

In 1886 the American SLP made a formal invitation to Liebknecht and Aveling, subsuming the invitation to his wife within his. Never mind the fact that the tour was her idea in the first place. What brought the speaking tour into its right moment was the so-called year of 'great upheaval' of American labour. On 1 May 1886 there was a nationwide strike for the eight-hour day called by the Knights of Labor, the largest American union of unskilled workers. The Socialistic Labor Party, however, was hampered by the same teething troubles experienced in England as a consequence of the ideological rifts between socialists and anarchists. As in Europe, American socialists believed in pro-state solutions to social revolution based on social democracy, universal suffrage and respect for the rule of law; anarchists were anti-statist and disregarded the authority of the rule of law.

Johann Most, declared leader of an anarchist faction which broke away from the SLP, had led his wing into the heart of the campaign for the eight-hour day in Chicago. A bomb exploded in the city on 4 May 1886, killing and wounding several policemen. The bomb was attributed to Most's anarchists and employers used the violence as an opportunity to launch a forceful strategy of state-backed retaliation against the striking workers.

Industrial action firmly quashed as a consequence, American workers turned their interest away from anti-statist anarchism to organised political struggle to pursue electoral means of representation. They regrouped into the independent United Labor Party, which included socialists and unionists. Their first initiative was to put up Henry George as socialist candidate for the upcoming New York mayoral election in the autumn of 1886. In this context the Socialistic Labor Party, predominantly German in origin and language, agreed it was a good idea to invite Liebknecht and the Marx-Avelings on a countrywide consciousness-raising lecture tour as part of the national campaign to strengthen the collectivism of the labour movement in America and bring together a united democratic front of socialist organisations.

The Avelings had a double-berth cabin, costing £24 return. Liebknecht, more flush, travelled on the *Servia*, a Cunarder. 'The Cunard is the dearest line of all and no better than many others, and is dear because "swells" go by it,' Tussy wrote to Library. 'On the Cunard in order to be together ... we shd. have to pay *£18 each*,' plus, she noted, a deposit of £5 to secure the booking.[2] Although it was taken as a given by the SLP that Eleanor would speak alongside the men, their expenses were covered entirely and hers were not – it being assumed her husband would pay for his wife. She explained this gendered economy to Laura: 'You know I am bound to "keep myself" as the Party only pays for Edward.'[3] Both of them took on journalism to subsidise the trip and gave up their tenancy at their first shared home at 55 Great Russell Street as they could not afford to cover the rent whilst they were away.

SS *City of Chicago*, built at Glasgow by Charles Connell & Co. in 1883, weighed 5,202 tons, was 430 feet long with a beam of 45 feet, and boasted a modern three-cylinder compound steam engine that guaranteed passengers a ten-day crossing from Liverpool to New York. Tussy, on her first transatlantic voyage, was fascinated by life at sea.

A woman on her way to be reunited with her husband died unexpectedly on board and her body was committed to the ocean. Eleanor saw her burial 'in the early morning, at daybreak – the simplest, and most impressive funeral I have ever witnessed'.[4] She was unimpressed by the wealthy passengers, who 'could laughingly look at the poor emigrants lying on the deck in their wretched clothes ... without the least sign of sympathy'.[5] Edward disparaged the travelling American. 'He is too palpably the creator of commerce, she is too palpably its creature. It's all business and success, business and success.'[6] Spotting whales and porpoises caused much excitement but otherwise the voyage was an opportunity for a welcome change after an extraordinarily busy and productive year.

Eleanor stood on the deck dressed in a white summer blouse and skirt as *City of Chicago* arrived in New York harbour under a clear blue sky on 9 September. Her light gown had a bodice and sleeves but she never wore a corset. She must have enjoyed the breeze through the Hudson more than the other women on deck, who stood stuffed into their stays on the hot late summer day.

'The entrance up the bay to the harbour is a marvellous sight,'[7] Tussy wrote. Passing Bedoe's Island, as it was known then, she admired the towering construction site of Auguste Bartholdi's *Statue of Liberty*, its gigantic steel supports girded with scaffolding and canvas and the little island surrounded by sturdy tug boats ferrying supplies and workers to the build. Red-gold glimpses of Liberty's bright copper sheeting flashed in the sun. Tussy knew of this gift of friendship from republican France to the people of the United States to welcome immigrants on their arrival and hoped to see it unveiled before she left. The imminent completion of *Liberty Enlightening the World*, as she was originally known before America sensibly gave her a shorter name, combined with the Democratic presidency of Grover Cleveland appeared to be good omens for Tussy's first arrival in the New World.

The visitors were met by a delegation of 'red ribboned gentlemen', and a hungry press pack of 'reporters were down on us like wolves on the fold'[8] before they'd even stepped ashore. The journalist from *New Yorker Volkszeitung* came aboard in the scrum of journalists, and was struck by their unusual appearance:

The man wore a grey travelling costume and a broad, black felt hat . . . he made the impression of a Quaker. Briskly flashed his dark eyes. The young lady, who leaned on his arm, had rich glossy black hair, dark brown eyes and a not unlovely oval face. Her complexion was heavily browned by the sun during the voyage. The cotton garment which the young lady wore was gathered together at the waist by a black girdle, above which a kind of blouse with delicate creases fell and from there a steel watch-chain stretched towards the girdle. The intelligent face of the lady was covered by a large, white straw hat with a white bow.[9]

Asked about the voyage Eleanor, wearing as always her favourite cool white, was firmly critical of the 'rudeness' and 'brutality' of 'the so-called better classes on board', and, she said, being herself the daughter of immigrants, felt indignation at how badly the poor emigrants on the voyage to America were treated by rich tourists.

Their welcoming delegation from the National Executive Committee of the Socialistic Labor Party took them to a hotel in the German quarter. 'I rather regret this,' Eleanor said in a note to Laura, 'for the Vaterland like the poor is always with us here.'[10] It was a ready reminder that their job was to internationalise American socialism.

They gave their first lectures at Bridgeport in Connecticut on 14 September. Bridgeport was a stronghold of the German-dominated SLP, but Edward ploughed right in and urged the mass audience to work with the Knights of Labor and trade unions. Eleanor, in her first American address, focused on feminism and urged women to join the socialist movement. Two days later Eleanor fascinated the audience at New Haven, which included students and professors from Yale University, with her exposition of socialist modernity to a largely middle-class, moneyed audience. Americans, Tussy quickly grasped, had an entirely different conception of questions of class and self-betterment. Aveling subjected the gathering to an hour-long, bone-dry exposition of scientific historical materialism but Eleanor re-awoke them by tackling head-on the bogeyman for the bourgeoisie: fear of losing private property.

People feared, Eleanor said, that the abolition of private property meant that no one would be allowed to say 'my coat', or 'my watch', for example. On the contrary, thousands of dispossessed people who today possessed absolutely nothing would under socialism be able to say 'my coat' and 'my watch' for the very first time in their lives. Rather, no individual or group of individuals would be able to say '*my* factory' or '*my* land' – and above all, no man could any longer say of another, '*my* hands'.

She then turned to the question of law and order and the problem of the use of armed resistance to achieve political freedom. No socialist, she said, should wish to use physical force. However, as Americans had fought to abolish slavery, so they might have to take up arms to abolish wage-slavery.[11] In all her key speeches in America over the coming months, Eleanor spoke directly and clearly on this theme of property and production:

One of the first things you are told is that we socialists want to abolish private property; that we do not admit the 'sacred rights

Eleanor Marx, 'Tussy' to the family, in 1871, aged about sixteen.

Helene Demuth and Jenny von Westphalen: best friends from childhood to the grave. 'Lenchen had the dictatorship in the house, Mrs Marx the supremacy,' wrote Wilhelm Liebknecht.

The most dangerous family in the world. Family portrait taken in London, 1864: Frederick Engels (*standing, left*) and Karl Marx, with his daughters (*from left to right*) Jenny, Eleanor and Laura.

Eleanor's big sisters: Jenny and Laura Marx in the 1860s,
when they still lived at home.

Wilhelm Liebknecht,
Eleanor's dearest 'Library', as
the Marx children knew him.

Paul Lafargue, Tussy's
brother-in-law and leader
of the French left.

Hippolyte Prosper-
Olivier Lissagaray or
'Lissa': Communard and
revolutionary, to whom
Tussy gave her virginity.

Irish Republican, putative *pétroleuse*, internationalist, feminist, writer, translator, aspiring actor – Tussy comes into her own in her early twenties.

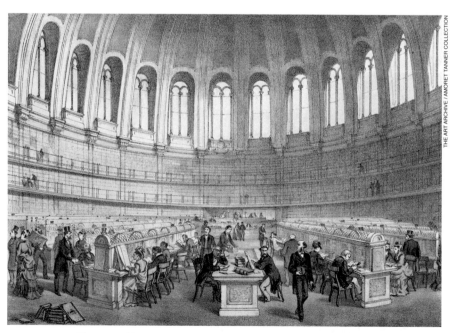

Eleanor and her Victorian Bloomsbury group working, flirting and subverting in the Reading Room at the British Museum.

'This International Association and all societies and individuals adhering to it, will acknowledge truth, justice, and morality, as the basis of their conduct towards each other, and towards all men, without regard to colour, creed or nationality; They hold it the duty of a man to claim the rights of man and a citizen, not only for himself, but for every man who does his duty. No rights without duties; no duties without rights.' The Founding of the International Working Men's Association, St Martin's Hall, London, 28 September 1864.

The Paris Commune of March to May 1871, the first and only attempt to make a proletarian revolution in nineteenth-century Europe, and the first political event in which Tussy was personally involved.

Eleanor's soulmate, Olive Schreiner, the great South African writer.

Elizabeth Garrett Anderson, scientist, activist, feminist, the first Englishwoman to qualify as a physician and surgeon in Britain as well as close Marx family friend and Tussy's doctor.

Havelock Ellis, writer, socialist and sexologist, who saved Tussy's life when she attempted suicide in 1888.

George Bernard Shaw, who loved Eleanor and said that reading Marx's *Capital* changed his life.

William Morris, romantic, revolutionary
and father of English arts and crafts
movement; together he and Eleanor
established Socialist League.

William Morris's daughter May, artist and
designer, businesswoman and for many years
Tussy's yearning, unspoken admirer.

Edward Aveling, Eleanor's 'husband'.
Socialist educator and would-be playwright.

Will Thorne, trade unionist and one of the
first Labour MPs. Firm friends as well as
political comrades, Tussy coached him from
bare literacy to eloquence and oratory.

Brooklyn Bridge, 1880s. Liebknecht, Tussy and Edward sailed into New York harbour on 9 September 1886 aboard the SS *City of Chicago*, which docked close to Brooklyn Bridge. The Socialistic Labor Party (SLP) of America had invited them to give a four-month speaking tour of fifteen states.

Tussy in America in 1886, with Liebknecht and Aveling, champion of the Chicago anarchists: 'It was our duty, and we made it our business, to speak out at every meeting we held in America in favour of a new trial for the condemned Anarchists of Chicago.'

A page from the *National Police Gazette*, 24th April 1886, depicting the great railway strike of 1886. Eleanor interviewed workers, unionists, strikers, the poor and unemployed across fifteen states for the book that became *The Working Class Movement in America*, one of her finest works.

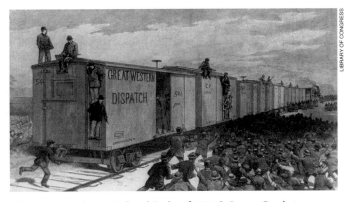

The great Southwest Railroad Strike of 1886, St Louis. On their tour, Eleanor, Edward and Library travelled around America primarily by train.

Shakespeare's home in Stratford. Eleanor and Edward returned from America
and took country lodgings, first in Stratford and later in the heart of Warwickshire:
'Now that I have been in this sleepy little Stratford and met the Stratfordians I
know where all the Dogberries and Bottoms and Snugs come from…'

Bidford, a village close to the hamlet of Dodwell ('pronounced Dad'll by the
"natives"') where Tussy spotted two stone cottages on a farm, one with a sign
to let. The surprised farmer told them it was two shillings a week.

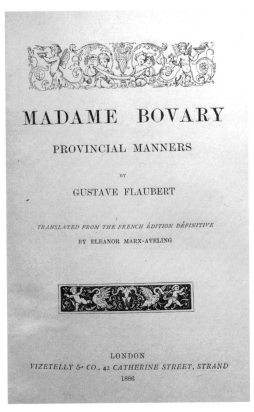

The title page of Eleanor's translation of *Madame Bovary*, published by Vizetelly & Co., 1886.

Eleanor translated Amy Levy's *Reuben Sachs* from English into German. 'The novel', Tussy said, 'had used the last of Amy's reserves, and, left her "a disembodied spirit".'

Eleanor and Israel Zangwill co-wrote the lampoon *A Doll's House Repaired* to answer Ibsen's scathing British critics. Many believed Zangwill longed for her romantic attentions.

Socialist politician John Burns addresses a
dockers' rally on Tower Hill during the
great strike of 1889.

An 1889 trade union meeting of the
National Gas Workers' society.

The London Dock Strike of 1889.

EIGHT HOURS LEGAL
WORKING DAY
DEMONSTRATION !
HYDE PARK

ON MAY 4th 1890

In favor of Reduction by Act of Parliament of the Working Day to Eight Hours.

All Unions, Clubs, and Societies, with the exception of those coming from the West (North of the Thames) will assemble on the Thames Embankment at 2 p.m., and form in Procession, Six abreast, facing East, the head of the Procession at Blackfriars Bridge. At 2.30 punctually the Procession will March by Bridge Street, Bride Street, Holborn, and Oxford Street, and by the Marble Arch into Hyde Park.

The Western Contingents will fall in with the main Procession at the Marble Arch.

Assembling Places.

FOR THE NORTH. No. 1. At Fitzroy square at 12.30. No. 2 at St. Pancras Arches at 12.30, will meet at the corner of Pancras road and Euston road at 1. They will then march by King's Cross road and Farringdon road, where they will meet the Clerkenwell Green contingent at 1.30. No. 3, the Mildmay Radical Club, Newington Green road at 12.15, will march to Clerkenwell Green & arrive there at 1.15

THE EASTERN CENTRAL. Assemble on Clerkenwell Green at 1, wait for Northern Contingent, No. 3, march with them into Farringdon road, to meet the Northern Contingents Nos. 1 and 2, at 1.30, and march with them by Bridge street to the Embankment.
For the NORTH-EAST. Assemble at the Triangle Hackney, at 12.45.
For the EAST. No 1 from Stratford Broadway at 1 ; from Bow Church 12.30 ; from Mile End Waste at 1 ; at Gardner's Commercial road, where they meet Contingents Nos 2 and 3. No. 2 from Barking Broadway at 10.30 ; from East Ham at 11 ; from Canning Town Station at 11.15 ; from East India Dock Gates at 11.45 ; at Gardner's Commercial road, at 1.30. Other East Contingents to meet at Mile End Waste at 12.15, and fall in with Column No 1, at 1, marching to Gardner's Commercial road. These Contingents, Nos 1 2 & 3, to march from Gardner's, Commercial road, at 1.30, by Aldgate, Leadenhall street Cornhill, Queen Victoria street to the Embankment.
FOR THE SOUTH-WEST. Meet at the Plain, Wandsworth Marsh, at 11.30, Princess Head, Battersea, Park Road, by 12.30, arrive at Battersea Park Gates at 1 at Albert Embankment at 1.30, thence by York Road, Stamford Street, Blackfriars Bridge to the Embankment.
FOR THE SOUTH EAST. No. 1. The Dartford Erith and Belvedere Contingents falls in at the Arsenal Square, Woolwich at 10, reach Deptford Broadway by 12. Bromley (Market Head) 10 a.m. Catford (Fire Bridge Station) 11 a.m. March to the Obelisk Lewisham Road 11.30. Chislehurst Common 10 a.m. Foot's Cray (Railway Bridge) 1.30, March to Obelisk Lewisham and meet the General Body in the New Cross Road No. 2 The East Greenwich Contingents reach Deptford Broadway also by 12. Thence No. 1 and 2 Column march at 12 by New Cross Road, Old Kent Road to Canal Bridge by 12.45, thence by New Kent road and London Road to the Obelisk by 1.30 to meet contingents 3 and 4.
No. 3. At Peckham Rye, march at 12 to the Obelisk arrive by 1.30. No. 4, Rotherhithe at Gladstone Club, Pages Walk march at 1 to the Obelisk, to arrive at 1.30. No 1, 2, 3 and 4 march at 1.30 from the Obelisk by Blackfriars Bridge to Embankment.
FOR THE WEST, NORTH OF THAMES. No. 1 leave Kew Bridge at 11.30, reach Hammersmith Broadway by 12.30. No. 2 Fulham, leave Bellbrook Common at 12, reach Hammersmith Broadway at 12.30. No. 3 other western contingents assemble at Hammersmith broad'ay by 12.30.
No 1, 2, and 3 leave Hammersmith Broadway at 1 march by its eleventh road, High street Kensington, Church street, Uxbridge Road, to the corner of Edgware Road; then to meet contingent No. 4 & 5
No. 4 Assemble at Kensal Green, to meet at 1.30 by Harrow road, Portchester road, the Royal Oak, Bishops road, arrive at Paddington green by 2.15, to meet Contingent No. 5
No. 5 Assemble at Paddington Green, at 2 wait for No. 4 contingent, march together at 2.15 along Edgware road, to meet contingents 1 2 3.
The whole of the Western contingents No. 1, 2, 3, 4, and 5, to wait at the corner of Edgware road, for the main procession from the East, and to march together into the Park by Marble Arch.

ORGANISATIONS

The following Organisations will take part in the Demonstration : The Gasworkers and General Labourers' Union : Horse-Hair and Fibre Workers' Union : Amalgamated Union of Electrical Operatives : London Carmen's Trade Union : Amalgamated Union of Operative Baker : Spitalfields Market Porters Union : International Boot Finishers Society : International Wallers Section Federation of Trades : Metropolitan and Provincial Piano-forte Makers : National Labour Union : Postmen's Union : Coach, Bus and Van Union : Labour League : Umbrella Makers and Mounters Union : International Stick and Cane Dressers Society : Millers National Union : National Federation of Labour Union : London and Southern Counties Labour League and Kent and Sussex Labourers Union : Photographic Cabinet Makers Union : Women's Union : Printers Warehousemen and Cutters Union : Coal Porters Union : United Cap Makers Society : Hebrew Cabinet Makers Society : Stick and Cane Dressers United Fancy Box Makers : Covent Garden Porters : House Painters and Decorators Union : Shop Assistants Union : Bloomsbury Socialist society : Printers Labourers Union : Stone Masons and Pavitors : Amalgamated Protective Union of Hammermen Enginesmen Helpers and General Labourers : Tramways and Omnibus Employees Union : South Norwood Labour Union : National Federation of all Trades and Industries : Clickers Union : Pitman Society : Mill Sawyers Union : Working Machinists Navvies Union : Box Makers : Fulham Branch Luxterseams and General Labourers Union : the following Radical Clubs : Cobden (Kensal Road), Acton, Stratford, Mildmay, Newington, Rotherhithe, Spitalfield, East Finsbury, Central Finsbury, North Lambeth, Star Fulham, Patriotic, North Camberwell, Communistic Holborn Gladstonian, Borough of Marylebone, Borough of Battersea, New Road, Woolwich, Croydon, Bow & Bromley, Bermondsey, Gladstone, Borough of Shoreditch, Hackney, Deptford, Rotherhithe, Goldhurne, Peckham : the South London and Battersea Demonstration Committee, and the following Branches of the Social Democratic Federation : Battersea, Wandsworth, Greenwich.

MARSHALS.   Chief - W. THORNE

The Head Marshals for each district will wear a Red Sash with the words, "Legal Eight Hours," on it. The assistants will wear Red Armlets on the left arm. Head Marshals for North: G. Smith, Noakes, Simmonds, and T. Shore. East-Central Borgia. North-East : Copsey. East: Holby, Whiting and Thorne. South-West: Oatley. South-East: Banner and Canty. West: Browning and Williams.

SPEAKERS.

JOHN BURNS   CUNINGHAME GRAHAM M.P.

Will Thorne, W. De Mattos, W. Willis, Edward Aveling, Eleanor Marx Aveling,
J. J. Chapman, W. W. Bartlett, T. E. Wardle, Annie Taylor, Borgia, J. Williams,
B. Hudson, Mac Hugh (Liverpool Dockers), Lawler, Sutherst, Curran, J. Ward,
G. B. Shaw Stockbridge, Bernstein, O'Conor, Lee, Copsey, Finley, Mrs. Schaack, Miss Robertson, Dell,
G. B. SHAW, J. M. DAVIDSON, W. H. WARD, G. LANSBURY, BENNETT BURLEIGH, JOHN ROY, HORNIGOLD
Watkinson, Collinson, Rev. W. A. Morris, Stepniak, and Others.

H. PETERKEN, Trades' Union Printer, 33, Rathbone St., Canning Town, and High Street, Poplar, London, E.

Poster advertising a demonstration for the eight-hour working day,
at which Eleanor and Edward were speakers.

Putting aside personal rivalries,
Eleanor helped Annie Besant
organise the successful Bryant
& May match-girl strike.

Strikers at the Bryant & May match factory:
Eleanor's political life was dedicated to the
unionisation of girl and women workers.

Congrès International socialiste, de Bruxelles, 1891. Eleanor and Edward
are just visible three rows from the front, third and fourth from the left.

Frederick Demuth, Helene Demuth's only child. Skilled
engineer, union steward of the Amalgamated Engineering
Union, founder member of the Hackney Labour party, and
single father. Eleanor said of him, 'I can't help feeling that
Freddy has had great injustice all through his life.'

The tomb of Karl Marx in Highgate Cemetery, where his wife Jenny Marx and Helene Demuth are also buried with him. 'My dear Dada, Oh! Would I were a bird that I might fly to thee and breathe a loving word to one so dear to me, Now dear Daddy, goodbye. Believe me, Your UNdutyful daughter, Eleanor', wrote Eleanor to Karl Marx, 26 April 1867.

of property'. On the contrary, the capitalistic class today is confiscating your private property, and it is because we believe in your 'sacred right' to your own that we want you to possess what today is taken from you ... all wealth, all we today call capital is produced by your labour ... out of the unpaid labour of the people a small class grows rich, and ... we want to put an end to this by abolishing all private property in land, machinery, factories, mines, railways etc.; in a word, in all means of production and distribution. But this is not abolishing private property; it means giving property to the thousands and millions who today have none.[12]

Their next stop was Meridien, where they met with leaders from the Knights of Labor and came away with assurances that the Knights would very shortly unite with the SLP – which of course never happened. Eleanor was concerned about the more conservative elements amongst leaders of the Knights but nevertheless regarded the organisation as 'the first spontaneous expression by the American working people of their consciousness of themselves as a class'.[13]

Eleanor and Edward published a remarkable collaborative account of this tour, *The Working Class Movement in America*, first published by Swan Sonnenschein in 1888 and reprinted in an enlarged edition in 1891. In chapter eight, they describe how at Thanksgiving in 1869 a Philadelphia tailor, Uriah Stephens, called together eight friends and formed the secret order of the Knights of Labor, known only by its cabbalistic five stars until June 1878 when it felt strong enough to declare itself a public organisation. By 1886 its national membership was estimated conservatively at half a million.

On Sunday 19 September 25,000 people assembled at Brommer's Union Park at 133rd Street. Liebknecht, who had just arrived, led the address by fulsomely thanking the German comrades who had invited him; he then moved swiftly to the urgency for the movement to grow beyond German-speaking Americans to include all labour organisations and American working people of all languages and origins. Eleanor and Edward followed suit, putting into action the strategy agreed with Engels in London before their departure.

The Brommer's Union Park rally was the largest public gathering ever to have taken place in New York's history, and, although it was orderly and well disciplined, heavy and rather intrusive policing inevitably led to some jostling and rough handling. Eleanor, as ever, was at the centre of the fray and was pushed over by a couple of policemen. One independent newspaper declared itself mortified and published an apology on behalf of 'the land of the free' that Eleanor Marx should be subjected to 'such wanton interference on the part of police with the liberty of the subject'.[14]

The following day, Monday 20 September, and again on Wednesday 22, there were two further mass meetings held at Cooper Union in Cooper Square in the East Village, focusing on the role of trade unionism as a step in the process towards social-ism. By now, Eleanor's presence had seized the imagination of the east coast, particularly since her beguiling address in New Haven, dressed again all in white, gracefully highlighting the shortcom-ings of private property and ownership of the means of production within a capitalist system. The *New York Herald* was threatened by this living, breathing Lady Liberty, apparently so much more forbidding than the silent statue under construction in the harbour:

SOCIALISTIC PLEADINGS. COOPER UNION CROWDED.
SPURRED ON BY A WOMAN

The *Herald* deplored the 'Sozialistische Frauenbund' crowding the platform. It gave Eleanor a matronly tone – 'CARL MARX'S DAUGHTER BOOMS' – and described her, hilariously, as 'a German looking lady with eyeglasses'.[15]

Shortly before they left New York Edward and Eleanor had dinner with the Democratic mayoral candidate, Henry George. George shared Eleanor's views on Ireland, and had a bedrock of support amongst the New York Republican Irish. He was also popu-lar amongst black New Yorkers for his radical views on what was then described as 'the negro question' – a subject about which Tussy became much better informed during her visit to America. They agreed on much, but not the most important question:

He does not, like the Socialist, regard the mode of the production and distribution of commodities, with its private property in the means (of which land is but one) of that production and distribution, as the basis of modern society, and therefore of the ills of that organisation.[16]

Rather, George believed the land question to be at the bottom of everything. Just nationalise the land and all else will follow. Eleanor got on well with him but predicted correctly that he wouldn't stay in the socialist fold for very long. George won the mayoral election with a third of the total vote, beating the Republican candidate Theodore Roosevelt by a majority of almost 8,000. Within a year he had declared against socialism. 'As far as a real working-class movement is concerned, he is a ruined man,' Eleanor concluded, though she liked him personally as a friend and stayed in touch with him as a progressive thinker.

On 2 October Eleanor and Edward set out on a three-month whistle-stop itinerary that took in thirty-five towns in fifteen states. Eleanor dubbed it the 'agitation tour'.[17] In Manchester, New Hampshire she was appalled to see women millworkers who looked even more famished and degraded than their sisters in Lancashire.

Perhaps the most important achievement of the American SLP was its success in founding the Central Labor Union (CLU) of New York in 1882, to organise foreign workers from amongst the nearly six million penniless immigrants who arrived in America during the 1880s from Ireland, Germany, France, Italy, Scandinavia, Hungary, Bohemia, England, Russia and Poland. CLU organisations spread beyond New York, springing up in other large cities on the eastern seaboard, joined by both black and white Americans, including cowboys.

Many cowboys were in discussion about establishing a Cowboy Union or Assembly of their own, as Tussy discovered in Cincinnati, as she said, in 'a sufficiently odd way'.[18] Their German-American hosts took them on a sightseeing tour of the city, including a dime museum. The chief attraction at the show was a group of cowboys, 'sitting in twos and threes on various little raised platforms, clad in their picturesque garb and looking terribly bored'.[19] A spruce museum guard, in ordinary clothes, made 'stereotyped speeches about them in a voice metallic enough for stereotyping', but at one platform he mercifully stopped short and told the visitors that Mr John Sullivan, alias Broncho John, would speak for himself:

> Thereupon, a cowboy of singularly handsome face and figure, with the frankest of blue eyes, rose and spoke a piece. To our great astonishment he plunged at once into a great denunciation of capitalists in general and ranch-owners in particular . . . Broncho John evidently knew what he was talking about, and felt what he said.[20]

He described cogently the hard work and poor conditions endured by cowboys as a non-unionised class of workers and the despotism of the ranch owners, including orders that the men 'must not read books or newspapers'.[21] Their horses belonged to the ranch owners, who deducted the cost of their outfit – including saddle, spurs, hat, chaps, oilskin, boots, whip and gun – from their monthly wages. The working season on the plains was six to eight months, but cowboys were not paid during the off time and had to get other jobs to keep themselves and their families.

During the season they were in the saddle all day and mostly through the night, looking after the huge Western herds of cattle, preventing milling and stampeding. 'I have been with a party when we were obliged to ride 200 miles before we got the cattle under . . . in all that time not one of us took a moment's rest or bit to eat!'[22] Drowning was common as cattle were moved across streams and rivers. Tussy was surprised to learn that it was not uncommon for it to take three weeks to a month getting a herd of 4,000 cattle across a river.

Then there were innumerable dangers from bands of marauders, Native Americans and prairie fires. 'Into the bargain,' Broncho John pointed out, 'the herd must not only be delivered safe and all told, but they must have increased in weight since leaving the ranch. The rule is, the cowboy must fatten the cattle on the trail, *no matter how thin he may grow himself.*'[23]

So much for Tussy's childhood delight with Natty Bumppo and Chingachgook singing round the campfire with baked beans, tin mugs of coffee and starlight. Fenimore Cooper's grand romantic adventures that Tussy had loved to read as a child proved to be romantic fiction.

Eleanor immediately arranged to meet Broncho John privately the next day. He told her and Edward that any cowboy, including himself, who tried to organise a union for fairer pay and working conditions was immediately discharged and branded by the ranch owner, who sent his name to every other member of the Rancher's Society around America: 'the name is turned to in the books of each ranch and a black mark placed opposite it. This is called "black-listing" the cowboy. He might as well leave the country at once.'[24]

Broncho John gave Eleanor and Edward a pamphlet he and fellow cowboys had put together in their effort to unionise and they published its contents in *The Working Class Movement in America*, devoting a chapter to 'The Cowboys' and deploring 'the terrorist regime of the ranchers . . . who are all staunch upholders of the sacred rights of property'.[25]

At Hartford, Connecticut Eleanor and Edward were the guests of Isabella Beecher Hooker, the half-sister of Harriet Beecher Stowe and Henry Ward Beecher. Isabella was an outspoken abolitionist, suffrage activist and committed spiritualist.[26] Eleanor, who rarely visited homes of wealthy people, admired Isabella's 'delectable mansion' and said that with Isabella and her friends 'we spent perhaps the most happy and assuredly the most peaceful hours of our stay in America.'[27]

Eleanor was introduced to Isabella Beecher Hooker's work by August Bebel, who wrote about her in his book *Women and Socialism* (1879), reprinted in a revised and expanded version as *Woman in the Past, the Present and the Future* in 1883. Censored and banned in Germany under Bismarck's anti-socialist laws, the book was circulated underground and was viciously attacked in the press, despite the absence of a public edition.

Bebel sent Engels a copy in January 1884 and Eleanor read it immediately, corresponding with Bebel about the English translation by Harriet Adams Walther. Modern Press published the English edition in 1885 in its International Library of Social Science imprint – and the British press generally gave the book as hostile a reception as it had received in Germany.

Eleanor was one of the few critics to review Bebel's book favourably, in the August 1885 supplement to *Commonweal*. After years of gestation, she was ready to give birth to her own work on feminism. When she did, she approvingly referenced Beecher Hooker's approach to speaking honestly to children about sex and reproduction, interweaving the words of Olive Schreiner's anti-heroine Lyndall Gordon previously cited:

> With the false shame and false secrecy, against which we protest, goes the unhealthy separation of the sexes that begins as children quit the nursery, and only ends when the dead men and women are laid in the common earth.

Eleanor was very impressed by Isabella in person and they discussed at length the need for a women's movement in America. This was a central theme of Eleanor's speeches on the tour and she raised it regardless of audience, to worker meetings and middle-class gatherings alike. Eleanor summarised her views on the woman suffragists of America in *The Working Class Movement in America*:

> They appear to be like and yet unlike their English sisters labouring in the same field. They are like them in their nonunderstanding of the fact that the woman question is one of economics and not of mere sentiment. The present position of women rests, as everything else in our complex modern society rests, upon an economic basis. The woman question is one of the organisation of society as a whole. American woman-suffragists are like the English in the fact that they are, as a rule, well to do. And they are like them in that they make no suggestion for change that is outside the limits of the society of today.[28]

However, Eleanor found that American suffragists differed from their English sisters in two vital particulars. She found them far more open-minded and 'much more outspoken', unafraid of 'being thought improper'.[29] 'They are beginning to understand that this special question is only part of a much larger one.'[30] Suffragette activist Mrs Devereux Blake and Isabella Beecher Hooker listened eagerly, Eleanor found, to any attempts at defining practical methods for finding a solution to the problem, and were:

> ready to engage in the more far-reaching struggle for the emancipation of the workers as well as that for their own sex. And in this wider view of the contest for liberty there is of course no narrowing of the view as to the woman question especially nor does anyone lose the womanlike in the larger mind.[31]

Eleanor's experience of America broadened, educated and confirmed her critical assessment of the political possibilities of an integrated socialist and feminist programme for revolution. 'The Woman Question: From a Socialist Point of View' and Eleanor's study of both working-class feminist women and well-to-do suffragists in *The Working Class Movement in America* are the first statements of socialist feminism in Western thought, and the first on both sides of the Atlantic.

The inseparability of the socialist project from feminism continued to be one of Eleanor's key themes all over America, exemplified in a speech she gave in Chicago:

> We are told that 'socialists want to have women in common'. Such an idea is possible only in a state of society that looks upon woman as a commodity. Today, woman, alas, is only that. She has only too often to sell her womanhood for bread. But to the socialist a woman is a human being, and can no more be 'held' in common than a socialistic society could recognise slavery. And these virtuous men who speak of our wanting to hold women in common, who are they? The very men who debauch your wives and sisters and daughters. Have you ever reflected, you working men, that the very wealth you create is used to debauch your own sisters and daughters, even your little children? That is to me the most terrible of all the miseries of our modern society: that poor men should

create the very wealth that is used by the man of 'family and order' to ruin the women of your class. We socialists, then, want common property in all means of production and distribution, and as woman is not a machine, but a human being, she will have her profits and her duties like men, but cannot be held by anyone as a piece of property.[32]

Everywhere they travelled in America, Eleanor met and interviewed working-class women and children about their lives and labour conditions. She also talked with factory owners, foremen and labour superintendents. She found that capitalists preferred to employ women and children. Women took lower wages and were perceived as being easier to bully and subdue if they tried to organise or strike. Children, even more so.

In Fall River, she found entire communities of young men supported by their sisters and mothers because there was so little work in the mills for men. In New Jersey, woman and child labour was more than usually drastically lower-priced than that of men, the hours longer and agitation more violently suppressed. These women, Eleanor observed, 'merely toil and scrimp, and bear'.[33]

In Pennsylvania, women were permitted to perform heavy manual labour generally reserved for men in order to save on wages. In Utica, New York State, the factory owners saved money by getting young girls to clean the running looms, 'at the risk of getting their hands taken off'.[34] Other women had poisoned hands from the toxins in the paint used for making artificial flowers and were no longer able to work – they were laid off without support or compensation. Women and children with industrial diseases and injuries had to resort to unregulated prostitution in and around the factories.

On a positive note, in Vineland, New Jersey, women had organised and joined the Knights of Labor, which had agreed to their participation. Working together, they succeeded in securing the same wages for women as for men – but this was a rare victory.

Conditions for textile workers and cigar-makers were particularly shocking. Expert crocheters earned 12.5 cents a day for making beautiful, highly-crafted shawls. Half-starved, overworked seamstresses had to pay for the machines on which they made jeans for

$1.50 a dozen. Collar- and cuff-makers had to pay for thread. Shirt-ironers, glove-makers and milliners were paid a few cents a day and received their wages received only once every fortnight. Women workers were fined for reading newspapers, or for going to the toilet, drinking water or sitting on a stool whilst working.

In America, as in England, sweaters – Eleanor grimly remarks – are so named because the sweater 'lives on the woman's earnings, literally on her sweat and blood'.[35] Cloakmakers in New York worked from six in the morning to one o'clock at night for 25 cents a day, sharing a piece of bread and small bowl of soup between four of them for the entire shift. Like the women cloakmakers, cigar-makers also slept by the machine:

> These women also, with their families, work, eat and sleep in these rooms ... surrounded by filth with children waddling in it, and having sores on their hands and faces and various parts of the body ... They are all the time handling this tobacco they make into cigars.[36]

Diseases of the womb, miscarriages, stillbirths and nervous depression inevitably resulted.

The extent and degradation of child labour drove Eleanor wild with fury and despair. As in England, child labour was gradually ousting adult male labour, when not in turn ousted by machinery. Parents were forced to send children to the mills at an early age to earn subsistence for the family. With many families dependent for survival on wages earned by children, young ones were regularly taken out of school as soon as they were strong enough for manual labour, on average at twelve or fourteen years old. Parents and employers lied about the ages of children to evade laws regulating child labour, which existed but were not enforced.

Many states enacted compulsory education laws in 1879 and there was an admirable provision of publicly-funded state schools available to working-class children of both genders but, as Eleanor described:

> When people are starving the children must get bread before they get teaching. In all the Eastern factory towns, in all the lumber

districts, even in many a Western city, we heard the same story. 'The children must work; they can't go to school.'[37]

After a long day's labour, thousands of young men and women of sixteen and upwards strove to combine their factory jobs with trying to get some education at night schools. Young agricultural workers grew up without any chance of learning. Eleanor goes into minute and exact detail on the pay, conditions and lives of children in the labour system – conditions for children in the tobacco and telegraph industries were particularly horrendous, in her view: simply slave labour. These children were not educated, they didn't play and often barely had homes to go to. Less able to organise than adults, child labourers were the most vulnerable sector.

Eleanor ended her analysis of woman and child labour 'by calling attention to the three chief points as to which, according to the reports, intelligent labour is unanimous: abolition of child labour, eight-hour working day, organisation.'[38]

Aveling went to the theatre at every opportunity. Tussy joined him when she could get away from meetings and work in the evenings, which was not often. As his expenses were covered and hers were not this was, on the face of it, fair enough. Except that whilst Edward kept all his theatre tickets to reclaim on expenses, it later turned out that he had attended most shows on complimentary press tickets by claiming that he was a drama critic for the *Saturday Review* and other arts periodicals.

Edward certainly took well to the opportunities for fine living in America, at others' expense. He argued for upgrades in hotels and on Pullman trains wherever he could, and took huge delight in flouting abstinence laws in Prohibition states. In Rhode Island he mischievously ordered a bottle of champagne and 'in ten minutes a bottle of Heidsieck was before me and, soon after, within'.[39] On the Pullman through Prohibition Iowa Edward both amused and discomforted Tussy by uncorking a bottle of white wine he had hoarded up and drinking it, with great deliberation, in front of fellow passengers, whilst she gazed out of the window and made notes on the price of land, 'so wickedly exorbitant that the shanties are mortgaged up to the roof'.[40]

In profligate mood, Edward bought Tussy good Virginia tobacco to smoke – probably produced by the child labourers she had interviewed. On one occasion when she accompanied him to the theatre, he presented her with an elaborate floral corsage, far from her usual understated taste but welcome as a mark of his attention.

Library joined them and at the beginning of November the three-some arrived in the Midwest. Edward and Library visited the condemned Chicago anarchists in Cook County Jail. Their visit was hosted by the 'physical and mental giant' Captain William Perkins Black and his 'indomitable' little wife (little, as Tussy remarked, only in stature, not spirit).[41] Decorated Civil War veteran and hero Black, a successful corporate lawyer with his own practice, was now repre-senting the Haymarket riot case. During their four-day stay in the city hosted by the Blacks, Tussy came to understand in detail the seismic events that had rocked Chicago over the course of this momentous year.

The first of May 1886 had been proclaimed a nationwide workers' strike to enforce the eight-hour working day in America, under the leadership of the Federation of Organised Trades and Labor Unions led by Samuel Gompers. The decision was ratified and supported by the Knights of Labor, with the agreement that those unions which did not decide to strike would do everything possible to help their brothers. Up until this point the Knights, in principle, discouraged open conflict with employers and their rules forbade political discus-sion, but now they reconsidered.

On Saturday 1 May more than 300,000 workers from 11,000 trades and businesses demonstrated on the streets of America. Forty thou-sand in Chicago, 11,000 in Detroit and in New York 25,000 marched in torchlit procession through central Manhattan led by the city's bakers. The New York Times declared the Eight Hour Movement 'un-American',[42] and alarmed industrialists and pro-capitalist media screamed that 1 May was in fact the date for Communist working-class insurrection and America's 'Paris Commune'.

The successful outcome of this May Day action was to secure an eight-hour day for approximately 200,000 American workers. To prevent large numbers of their employees joining the strike, some employers had made the concession in advance of the action. Trade union membership increased dramatically, as did solidarity and social networking between different worker organisations. Police, pro-capitalist press and the Pinkerton Detective Agency were dismayed at the nationwide ferment, particularly in the socialist stronghold of Chicago where on 1 May the city had come to a standstill.

An opportunity for retaliation presented itself on 3 May, at the gates of the McCormick Harvester reaper factory, where the workers struck against an unjust piecework system. On that evening, the strikers waited at the gates in a picket line that had been crossed by 300 blacklegs escorted into the works that morning under police and Pinkerton's protection. As the strike-breakers emerged flanked by armed Pinkerton's men, the crowd heckled and jostled them. The Pinkertons opened fire and, as the strikers fled, seven men were killed. Furious Chicago citizens – men, women and children – convened in the Haymarket Square the following evening to protest against the killing of strikers. Carter Harrison, the anti-socialist mayor of Chicago, attended the demonstration and, before leaving to go home for his dinner, told the police that they should disband and withdraw as it was a peaceful and calm affair.

They ignored him. Some 200 armed police stormed the centre of the crowd and ordered the meeting to stop. Sam Fielden, a British immigrant who was the final speaker of the evening, objected from the platform that this was a peaceful assembly. As he said this, a bomb exploded and policeman Mathias Degan was killed instantly. A further six police officers were mortally wounded and fifty more badly injured. The police opened fire, shooting directly into the crowd and at those running away. Many protesters sustained serious injuries and, controversially, an unknown number were killed.

Panic, mass arrests and detention without trial followed all over the city that night. Suspects were beaten and tortured and, finally, eight men were charged with Degan's murder. Of these eight, Sam Fielden and August Spies, the editor of the anarchist German language newspaper *Arbeiter Zeitung*, were the only two men present when the bomb was thrown.

The grand jury trial in June was a farce. Judge Joseph Gary didn't even maintain the pretence that the eight defendants were on trial for Degan's murder. Defendants were charged with producing anarchist literature in languages they could neither speak nor read. In the summing up and sentencing of seven of the men to be hanged on 3 December, the state prosecutor spelled it out: 'Anarchy is on trial.'[43] The eighth man, who was proved not to have been present at the Haymarket meeting on the evening in question, was sentenced to fifteen years' penal servitude.

These were the men that Aveling and Liebknecht visited in Cook County Jail, and whose case William Perkins Black presented so convincingly to Eleanor, who had followed the case from London since the events of May. At the time of their visit in November, the defendants had just received the news that their first application for an appeal had been disallowed. Undeterred, Black pushed for a retrial.

Eleanor's view was that anarchism had proved as much a hindrance to the development of a programme for social and economic democracy in America as it had to the English movement. She was 'entirely opposed to the methods and aims of Anarchism'.[44] However, the Chicago anarchists were now famously the victims of an appalling corruption of the justice system and Eleanor, despite political differences, was uncompromising in her support:

> It was our duty, and we made it our business, to speak out at every meeting we held in America in favour of a new trial for the condemned Anarchists of Chicago.[45]

From the beginning of their 'agitation' tour of America, Eleanor had encouraged her audiences to 'throw three bombs amongst the masses: agitation, education, organisation'.[46] She precisely defined the fundamental difference between socialism and anarchism:

> It is true both anarchists and socialists attack the present capitalist system. But the anarchist attacks it from the individualist, conservative, reactionary point of view, the socialist from the communist, progressive standpoint . . . The socialist believes in

organisation; he believes in political action, in the seizure of political power by the working class as the only means of attaining that complete economic emancipation which is the final aim.[47]

In a speech in New York on 19 September Eleanor pointed out how characteristic it was that the most violent attacks made on her, Aveling and Liebknecht since their arrival in the US had come from anarchist writers and speakers. 'The Chicago capitalist press wanted us to be hanged after we had landed; Herr Most's[48] paper, *Die Freiheit*, was for shooting us on sight, before we landed.'[49] But justice, Eleanor said, was the point here, not antagonism between socialism and anarchism.

From the moment she set foot on American soil, Tussy demanded justice for the Chicago anarchists. She continued to speak in support of a new trial for the condemned men at every meeting in America. She laid out her case with precision and mastery of the requirements of the rule of law.[50]

Eleanor deplored anarchism. In her judgement it 'ruined the International movement . . . threw back the Spanish, Italian, and French movements for many years . . . proved a hindrance in America; and . . . in England . . . is a decided nuisance'.[51] But she was unstinting both politically and personally in her support and activism on behalf of the Chicago anarchists. Justice must be done.

On Thanksgiving Day, 25 November, William Black secured a stay of execution, ensuring the men would not be hanged on 3 December. With Henry George, leader of the new Labor Party, in the New York mayoralty, things were looking more hopeful by the time Eleanor and Edward's tour concluded in December.

Ending in New York where they began, Tussy and Edward joined a mass meeting on 21 December to object to the establishment of a workhouse for tramps. Edward went to the theatre and, between her meetings, Tussy met suffragists and browsed the bookshops. On 23 December they presented a report on their agitation tour to a general meeting of their hosts, the Socialistic Labor Party. Eleanor's address emphasised the need for a women's organisation as an integral part of the social movement.

American working women, she found, suffered worse conditions than those in England. The problem of the wages of women and children was the general problem of all labour and industrial conditions, and women's organisation was not and must not be a separate political body. Women should attend meetings, run for leadership and bring their mostly working children with them to meetings too, and encourage them to have a voice in youth councils. All working men, Tussy said, had a duty to give women a helping hand with children and the home to ensure their full ability to participate in the social and political movement.

Where Eleanor's closing speech in America was decisively a call to socialist-feminist arms, Aveling's was strategically controversial. Boldly and bravely, Edward declared that, 'The movement, if it were to succeed, must become American and pass from the hands of the German over to those of the English-speaking people.'[52] Directly challenging his hosts the party leadership, Aveling stated that on the basis of his experience of the past three months, 'If I were a worker settled here, I would join the Knights of Labor and the Central Labor Union to spread my socialist doctrines in those circles.' He drove his point home by stating that if the German party did not do this, it might as well give up and 'leave the scene'.[53]

Aveling's unwelcome recommendations prompted a barrage of hostile questions from the floor, deteriorating into a personal attack by Edward on 'the stupidity and egotism' of Wilhelm Rosenberg, the SLP party secretary. After this bad-blooded end to the public assembly Edward, accompanied by Tussy, went immediately into a meeting with the party executive to present his accounts and expenses. The timing could not have been more disastrous. Unbeknown to Tussy, Rosenberg had already advised Aveling earlier in the month that the expenses of the tour 'had swallowed up more than the SLP expected', and that consequently there was no money left to organise the conference of English-speaking socialists in New York proposed by Aveling and Liebknecht to the German leadership.

At the executive meeting to review the financial accounts from the tour, the gloves came off between Aveling and Rosenberg. The executive 'declaimed against my reckonings as excessive from end to end,' grumbled Aveling, 'and denounced us both as aristocrats living on the money of the workers, and not worthy to belong to the party, &c.'[54]

Edward lumped all his expenses together, failing to separate out costs for doing his journalistic work, theatre tickets and entertaining expenses for Library and his daughter when they were all together in Boston. The executive had agreed to pay Tussy's rail fares and include her on Edward's hotel tariff, but Edward had lazily bundled all the receipts and invoices together and sent them with a cover note to the SLP executive, asking 'it to decide for which it would feel the party was responsible'.[55] His expenditure was flamboyant, his bookkeeping slapdash – and he forgot he was dealing with Germans.

Rosenberg charged Aveling with financial mismanagement and Tussy sat mortified and mute throughout the whole debacle. The executive committee agreed to honour Aveling's submission of $1,300 for thirteen weeks' touring, but deplored his presumption at their expense. The crowning humiliation for Tussy was when Herman Walther pointed in a rage to a charge of $25 for corsage bouquets: 'Do you consider these legitimate expenses?' he roared at Edward. Tussy had received a corsage bouquet from Edward during the trip but nothing like the hothouse of flowers required to run up this bill, and could only silently conclude that Edward had bought these bouquets for other women.

They left New York on Christmas morning. Wrapped up against the winter cold on deck, Tussy looked up at the resplendent copper statue, 151 feet high, with her uplifted arm holding a torch. *Liberty Enlightening the World* had been unveiled on 28 October by President Cleveland. Eleanor had read in the press that Lady Liberty's pedestal was inscribed with 'The New Colossus', a sonnet by aptly named Emma Lazarus, an American poet, welcoming immigrants to the United States:

> Give me your tired, your poor
> Your huddled masses yearning to breathe free
> The wretched refuse of your teeming shore.

Send these, the homeless, tempest-tost to me
I lift my lamp beside the golden door.

America's contradictions – like Tussy's own – were enough to fill her thoughts for the entire journey home.

Essentially English

Professionally, Tussy's thirty-second year started well. The English translation of *Capital* came out in early January 1887 and Ernest Belfort Bax wrote an admiring review of Lissagaray's *History of the Paris Commune* in *Commonweal*, saying that it ought to be in the hand of every socialist, and 'the translation of the book . . . is excellent'.[1] Her professional success, however, was eclipsed by Edward's expenses scandal.

On New Year's Day, whilst Tussy and Edward were still at sea, the *Daily Telegraph* had picked up the story from the *New York Herald* and handed Hyndman a weapon to discredit Aveling in England. By the time the 'Costly Apostle'[2] made landfall in Liverpool on 4 January, the ambush of press and his political enemies was well set. 'Aveling's Idea of "Unpaid Labour", Corsage Bouquets and Theatre Tickets', 'A Deadhead at the Hotels' and 'Crisp Bills Flung in His Face' ran headlines in left- and right-wing press alike. Tussy's smoking habit was derided: 'The extraordinary bill had a round sum of $50 for cigars to the doctor and *cigarettes to his emancipated lady*.'[3] 'Altogether,' concluded the *Evening Standard*, 'delivering lectures on socialism seems a lucrative business.'[4]

Aveling's financial fiddling gave the SLP an opportunity to retaliate for their real grievance against him: his public recommendation, everywhere he went in America, that the SLP should unite with the Knights of Labor and other English-speaking, grass-roots American

socialist organisations. Whilst Hyndman pursued his political advantage, Tussy and Edward had to camp with the General and Lenchen
at 122 Regent's Park Road until they found somewhere to live. The
General was relieved to have Tussy under his protection. 'Poor
Edward's' reaction to the crisis was, as usual, to get sick, with quinsy
this time, requiring him to duck out of London to convalesce. 'He is
not over endowed with power of resistance to malady,' Engels dryly
remarked to Laura, 'and so this threw him back very much. He has
been off and on at Hastings.'⁵

Publicly Engels supported Aveling and rejected official requests to
boycott him. Although, he said, he had only known Aveling for four
years, he had no reason to doubt his character or believe he had
attempted to 'swindle' the party:

> How could he do that during all his tour without his wife being
> cognizant of it? And in that case the charge includes her too.
> And then it becomes utterly absurd, in my eyes at least. Her I
> have known from a child, and for the last seventeen years she has
> been constantly about me. And more than that, I have inherited
> from Marx the obligation to stand by his children as he would
> have done himself, and to see, as far as lies in my power, that
> they are not wronged. And that I shall do, in spite of fifteen
> Executives. The daughter of Marx swindling the working class –
> too rich indeed!⁶

The General's defence was all about Eleanor. There's no doubt that
Aveling crocked his accounts. He shrugged off the fraud with lame
special pleading that his 'artistic nature' precluded him from being
able to account or administer. Edward's studied incompetence made
the General worried about Tussy's security but he excused Edward
for being guilty only of witlessness, not political corruption:

> The youngster has brought it all on himself through his complete
> ignorance of life, people, and business, and through his weak-
> ness for poetic dreaming. But I have given him a good shaking
> up, and Tussy will do the rest. He is very gifted and useful, and
> thoroughly honest, but gushing as a boy, and always inclined to

some absurdity. Well, I still remember when I was just such a noodle.[7]

Eleanor was less forgiving. The General himself had taught her that financial and business competence were essential requirements of political probity. It wasn't the first time she'd noticed that there was more social latitude given to men for sexual and financial impropriety than to women in public life.

From the outset of 1888 much of Eleanor's time was taken up with public speaking. On 26 January and 2 February she gave lectures about America to packed meetings at Farringdon Hall. On 11 April she addressed an outdoor rally in Hyde Park of some 15,000 people, primarily working men, gathered to protest against the new criminal law for Ireland. By all accounts, Tussy was the most popular speaker. Even the reporter from the *Daily Telegraph* found himself seduced by Eleanor's siren socialism:

> Considerable interest was taken in the speech delivered by Mrs Marx Aveling, who wore beneath her brown cape, a dress of green plush with a broad hat trimmed to match. The lady has a winning and rather pretty way of putting forth revolutionary and Socialistic ideas as though they were quite the gentlest thoughts on earth.[8]

As another open-air meeting in Victoria Park, Hackney, around this time illustrated, Eleanor now came fully into her own as a popular public orator. She lectured on *Socialism in America* and *The Relative Position of English and American Workmen* at Socialist League branches all over London. She and Edward instigated what Engels described as 'a very successful agitation in the East End of London', speaking at the Radical Clubs – working-men's clubs – on the American movement, and proposing the formation of a new working-class party based on Marxian principles:

> . . . he and Tussy are very busy in the work. It is now an immediate question of organising an English Labour Party with an independent class programme. If it is successful, it will relegate to

a back seat both the Social Democratic Federation and the Socialist League, and that would be the most satisfactory end to the
present squabbles.[9]

Amongst the present squabbles were those between Eleanor, Edward,
William Morris and the anarchists in the Socialist League. Eleanor's
campaigning aimed to persuade members that socialism was the best
political framework and of the need for an independent labour party
that, contrary to the anarchist approach of the SL, would stand for
electoral representation within the existing parliamentary system
and respect the rule of law.

Her experience in America had confirmed her belief in the absolute necessity for a parliamentary workers' party. She travelled to
places and institutions beyond London's heartlands to spread this
message, including to the Central Croydon Liberal and Radical
Club, which she addressed on the subject of 'Working Men and
Politics'.

This mobilisation was contiguous with the gathering storm within
the Socialist League that finally broke at its Third Annual Conference
on 29 May. Whilst resolutely defending the condemned anarchists in
Chicago, Eleanor was deep in ideological battle with the anarchists
within the Socialist League. As she'd predicted from the outset, the
anarchist tendency was the stronger force in the SL and would ultimately prevail. Up until now they'd ridden their differences but now
came the crunch point, all ravelled up in Aveling's disrepute.

On 29 May, Morris proposed an amendment committing to 'the
policy of abstention from parliamentary action', carried by seventeen votes to eleven. Eleanor, representing the Bloomsbury branch,
voted against this anarchist resolution not to participate in representative parliamentary democracy. She resigned from the SL the
following morning, as did Aveling. The very same day, with disastrous timing, a sexual scandal broke over Aveling's head in the
indignant form of Gertrude Guillaume-Schack, a German anarchist
and feminist. Aveling, she asserted, was guilty of disreputable sexual
acts far more grave than his financial embezzlement in America and
had been 'slandering his own wife', Eleanor.[10] Tussy's political decision to split from Morris's now explicit anarchist policies and leave

the SL on a clear vote was overshadowed by gossip about Aveling's sexual philandering and disloyalty.

Tussy and Edward moved into New Stone Buildings at 65 Chancery Lane. Despite its name, there was nothing new about the tenement. Zinaida Vengerova visited Tussy in the tiny top-floor flat, describing 'the dim gaslight of the endless staircase,' which 'entirely preserved the Dickens spirit of commercial slums.' The flat was 'grey, unattractive and thoroughly poverty-stricken'.[11] Little wonder then that Tussy was thrilled when, later in the spring, a commission to write a series of articles on 'Shakespeare's Stratford'[12] led her and Edward to stumble across a bolthole in the heart of Warwickshire.[13]

Following one of the bard's favourite walks to Bidford, they passed through the hamlet of Dodwell ('pronounced Dad'll by the "natives"'[14]), just off the old Roman Road from Evesham to Warwick.[15] Tussy spotted two stone cottages on a farm, one with a sign to let. The surprised farmer told them it was two shillings a week, 'but at first tried to explain these were only cottages for labourers – he could not understand our wanting to come.'[16] They took up the tenancy immediately and brought their pets from London. Tussy was delighted to escape the pomp and circumstance of Queen Victoria's golden jubilee and the self-congratulation of British imperialism in London, what William Morris described as 'this vulgar Royal Upholstery procession'.[17]

Eleanor and Edward dug up potatoes and spent happy afternoons together sowing all sorts of vegetables and flowers: 'Next Spring our garden will be not only ornamental but useful!'[18] Dodwell and its neighbouring village had a combined population of 100 and boasted, as William Cobbett admiringly recorded, some of the richest soil in the kingdom. Until now urban to her bootlaces, Tussy was enchanted, outside and in. For the first time since leaving home she had her own kitchen, as well as a pantry, washhouse and quarter-acre garden. She invited Laura and Paul to come and stay:

> I can't tell you how charming this country life is after the hurry
> and worry and wear and tear of London. It is as Scott calls it – 'the
> beautiful county', essentially English of course, in character, as it

becomes Shakespeare's home to be. Think of it Laura, Shake-speare's home!'[19]

Tussy delighted in working a few days a week 'at his birthplace (by permission of the Librarian)', and, she continued with enthusiasm, 'we have been over his home, and seen the old guild Chapel . . . and the old grammar school – unchanged – whither he went "unwill-ingly to school"; and his grave in Trinity Church, and Ann Hathaway's cottage, still just as it was when Master Will went a-courting, and Mary Arden's cottage at Wilmecote – the prettiest place of all.'[20]

Tussy revised their articles on America, initially published in *Time*, for the forthcoming publication by Sonnenschein of *The Working Class Movement in America*. She enjoyed translating short stories by Norwegian writer Alexander Kielland, and having taught herself Norwegian with unassuming proficiency, determined to improve her understanding of Ibsen. 'It is . . . a real duty to spread such a great teaching as his and my little effort is just a poor beginning.'[21]

Edward's delay in delivering his work, a translation of Lev Aleksandrovich Tikhomirov's *Russia, Political and Social*, meant that Sonnenschein witheld the royalties owing from the successful sales of 'The Woman Question'. A nice irony. The last speech Tussy gave before leaving London for the summer had been to the Clerkenwell branch of the Socialist League, on 'The Woman Question', in which she described how the economic basis of gender oppression and exploitation cut across all classes of women. She knew what she was talking about.

Aveling was working on an adaptation of Hawthorne's *The Scarlet Letter* and a production of his own one-act play, with the unprepos-sessing title of *Dregs*. This required numerous trips back to London to consult with – he claimed – a popular rising young actress called Rose Norreys, of whom no one had ever heard. Edward's scope for dalliance in London whilst Tussy was tucked safely in the country was suddenly constrained when, not coincidentally, Olive rented rooms directly next door to them in Chancery Lane. Whilst Edward crept around with his young protégé elsewhere, beyond the watchful eye of Olive, Tussy, cheerfully oblivious, focused on Elizabethan drama:

> Now that I have been in this sleepy little Stratford and met the Stratfordians I know where all the Dogberries and Bottoms and Snugs come from. You'll meet them here today. Just near our 'Kastle' is a bank – many think it Titania's for it is covered with wild thyme and oxlips and violets . . . I never knew before how Stratfordian Shakespeare was. All the flowers are Stratford ones and Charlecote I would wager is Rosalind's Arden.[22]

Whilst midsummer-night-dreaming on Titania's bank, Tussy received a letter from Havelock Ellis with a welcome commission to edit a new collection of unexpurgated plays by Christopher Marlowe. He also asked her if she would work on a drama 'little known but of considerable interest, *A Warning for Fair Women*'.[23] Vizetelly had recently appointed Havelock Ellis general editor of a radical new project, called the Mermaid Series, to publish plays by Elizabethan dramatists.

Content though she was, the biological clock of early-thirties baby hunger ticked through Tussy's correspondence at this time. She yearned to see Johnny again, asked in great detail about her niece Mémé, Jenny's daughter, sent the children books and toys that she could ill afford and fretted about their futures. 'I wish I could have one with me. A house is so different that rings with a child's laughter.'[24]

From the oxlips and violets of Shakespeare country Tussy returned to the capital in October and marched straight back into the smoke and steam of political proselytising in East London. Though not before visiting Lenchen and the General to proudly present them with a large hamper of produce, including butter she'd churned herself, fruit she'd picked, and eggs from her own ducks and hens. She'd slaughtered, plucked and trussed a few of her flock for Lenchen to roast for one of the General's 'usual Sunday debauches',[25] as Tussy called them. Not bad progress, Lenchen noted approvingly, for the city girl who a few years previously had panicked when left in charge of a few laying hens.

Eleanor returned to a London in ferment over Irish Home Rule. The Radical Clubs, Irish National League and socialist organisations were orchestrating massive agitation. 'Everywhere large meetings are being held and for the first time the English working class is supporting Ireland,'[26] Tussy reported to her family in Paris. She spoke all over London in support of Irish Home Rule, between teaching and her usual 'devilling' hackwork. During this autumn she also campaigned on behalf of the Chicago Anarchists.

In September, the Supreme Court of Illinois had rejected the appeal and confirmed the death sentences of the accused. William Black asked Eleanor and Edward to mobilise working-men's clubs in London to pass resolutions protesting against the decision and to get up petitions to the US President and US Supreme Court. Many Radical Clubs subscribed to a cablegram petition asking for mercy, organised by Eleanor: 'we got – on the one day – 16,405 votes for the petition we cabled over.'[27] Other sympathisers in England organised similar petitions, including Henry Hyndman and Annie Besant.

In an interview with the *Pall Mall Gazette* Eleanor drew the attention of its middle-class readership to the flouting of the rule of law perpetrated against the trialists: 'There really was not enough evidence to hang a dog upon.'[28] She made the case in more explicit terms to the socialist readers of *Today*. The eight-hour movement, she reminded readers, was the root cause of the events in Chicago: 'the sentence is a class sentence; the execution will be a class-execution.'[29]

Petitions and calls for clemency failed to prevent the hangings. What Eleanor described as the 'legal murder' of the martyred Chicago Anarchists took place on 11 November. In the midst of the consternation over this outcome, Hyndman claimed publicly that one of the petition cablegrams had never been sent because Edward had trousered the subscriptions.

The issue over Irish Home Rule was but one part of the economic strife and political unrest that characterised Victoria's jubilee year. The discontent of the London unemployed accelerated throughout the spring and summer months, catching the rising tide of industrial struggles around Britain inspired by the miners' strikes in Lanarkshire and Northumberland earlier in the year. The Socialist League supported all the strike centres, evolving the slogan 'UNION amongst ALL workers' and proposing the necessity for education in socialism and a great federation of national and international labour. By 1887 large sections of workers had already found their own way to socialism, particularly in Scotland.

Just as they were beginning to analyse the possibilities for revolutionary social and economic change, the swelling movement of unemployed in London was left leaderless at a critical moment when John Burns and Henry Hyde Champion suddenly quit the Social Democratic Federation due to their discontent with Hyndman. People congregated in Trafalgar Square, holding public meetings, making speeches themselves, asking questions, discussing how to appoint new leaders and the viability of leaderless revolution. Trafalgar Square became a hub of daily democratic protest and free speech, within hearing distance of Parliament. The starving unemployed inconvenienced the shopkeepers, hoteliers and restaurateurs who paid high rents to be in the centre of the metropolis. Well-heeled day-trippers and tourists who came to London to spend money found their fun spoiled. After all, said the *Illustrated London News*, 'Who would bring a party of ladies and children to a hotel at Charing Cross with the chance of their exit being blockaded all the afternoon?'[30]

As their numbers increased, repeated attempts were made to clear the square. During October assaults and arrests were made on the protesters using mounted policemen, truncheons and staves. On 8 November, the government banned all further meetings in Trafalgar Square and overnight Londoners mobilised to protect their right of free assembly. The Metropolitan Federation of Radical Clubs, Irish National League and Socialist League called for a freedom of expression and anti-coercion demonstration to be held on Sunday 13 November, under the slogan, 'To the Square!'

Tussy and Edward marched at the front of the rally that started in the east of the city and converged with other processions on Trafalgar Square. They were greeted by armed military, foot and mounted police. The 300 Grenadier Guards and 250 Life Guards of the Household Brigade had twenty rounds of ammunition apiece and the total force awaiting the protesters, including the police, numbered 4,000.

Tussy threw herself into the frontline of demonstrators attempting to force themselves into the barricaded square. Fighting broke out. Many unarmed and frightened protesters fled in panic. Eleanor was dismayed at their cowardice: 'only after I had shouted myself hoarse calling on the men to stand and show fight, did a few Irishmen close round. These attracted others, as you will see from the papers, we on Westminster Bridge made a fair sight. But it was sickening to see the men run.'[31] She was horrified at the police brutality, kicking men and women where they had fallen, forcing people under their horses' hooves, and striking them with their staves. Hundreds were injured, arrested, charged and later sentenced. More than 200 were hospitalised and at least three died as a result of their injuries.

Two bobbies got hold of Eleanor and tried to run her in, but she escaped and made her way back on foot to the General's house in Regent's Park. She'd lost Edward, who evaporated from her side when the skirmish began. Tussy turned up on the General's doorstep with 'her coat in tatters, her hat bashed and slashed by a blow', as he told Lafargue, adding wryly, 'Edward saved his skin, the contingent with which he found himself having hopped it at the outset.'[32] George Bernard Shaw, who was in this group, cheerfully confirmed their manly cowardice. He described how he was paralysed with terror when the fighting broke out in Trafalgar Square and instantly ducked: 'you should have seen that high hearted host run. Running hardly expresses our collective action. We *skedaddled*, and never drew rein until we were safe on Hampstead Heath . . . I think it was the most abjectly disgraceful defeat ever suffered by a band of heroes outnumbering their foes a thousand to one.'[33]

Tussy did not run but prepared another offensive. After they'd been repelled from Trafalgar Square, she'd led her Clerkenwell crowd through the backstreets of Victoria Embankment and over Blackfriars Bridge to join the battle on Westminster Bridge with those who'd arrived from the south. 'I got pretty roughly used myself . . . I have a bad blow across the arm from a policeman's baton, and a blow on the head knocked me down . . . But this is *nothing* to what I saw done to others.'[34] The General was not persuaded by her version of events, as he wrote to Nathalie Liebknecht: 'Tussy . . . was not the attacked, but the attacker.'[35]

Overnight, Bloody Sunday, as it was named, became one of the most notorious attacks on civil liberties in British history. The following day the *Pall Mall Gazette* dedicated the entire issue to the episode. Eleanor was furious with William Stead for publishing without her permission a note she had written to him the previous evening. 'Karl Marx's daughter writes to us as follows: "I have never seen anything like the brutality of the police, and Germans and Austrians who know what police brutality can be, have said the same to me. I need not tell you that I was in the thick of the fight at Parliament Street."'[36] Stead set up a Law and Liberty League to assist victims of Bloody Sunday and subscribers put up funds for those who had been detained. Eleanor was amongst those who made bail for them.

Shocked and riled by the state aggression on Bloody Sunday, Eleanor revealed that she retained her militant instincts about the uses of violence. Reflecting on Bloody Sunday, she condemned the 'lack of fight in the working men' with as much scorn as she held for the police brutality. 'If only Radicals were not so many of them cowards we could [have carried] the Square. As it is, they are all "funking" more or less.'[37] Tussy thought state violence would do their political work for them by winning over better radical elements to socialism: 'Last Sunday the troops had ammunition ready and stood with fixed bayonets. Next Sunday I think it very possible they will actually fire. That would be very useful to the whole movement here.'[38]

She noted that 'our fire-eating Anarchists here as usual are getting frightened now that there really is a little danger', and criticised Morris for proclaiming that the revolution wouldn't be made until the people were armed: 'He doesn't seem capable of understanding that by the time all the people are armed, there will be no need for the Revolution (– with a very big R).'[39] Tussy's fearlessness is quite terrifying.

In May, at the Fourth Annual Conference of the Socialist League, the Bloomsbury branch, led by Eleanor and Edward, had been suspended for working together with the SDF to put up candidates for local elections. Morris remained resolute on his anti-parliamentary, anti-state position on electoral participation. The game was up at this conference anyway: the Bloomsbury branch put forward a motion to change the Socialist League's constitution so that individual branches might 'be empowered (if so disposed) to run or support candidates for all the representative bodies of the country'; it was defeated by a majority led by Morris. The Bloomsbury branch declared itself autonomous after the conference and announced to the League its intention to form a new organisation for the express purpose of running candidates at elections. Unsurprisingly, the branch was immediately expelled and dissolved.[40] The anarchist majority in the SL, led by Morris, would not tolerate this parliamentary socialism.

What underpinned Eleanor's ability to fight? Without context, she might seem like a blood-lusting scrapper, lacking pacifist constraint. Far from it. As a reflective letter to her sister written three days after Bloody Sunday reveals, Eleanor's motivation to fight was prompted by her recent first-hand experience of the conditions endured daily by unemployed Londoners. Eleanor was now immersed in working in East London. The suffering she witnessed amongst the struggling unemployed was worse than any thump from a policeman's baton:

To walk through the streets is heartrending. I know the East End well, and I know people who have lived there for years, both working men and people like Maggie Harkness, interested in the conditions of life in the East End, and all agree that they had <u>never</u> known anything approaching the distress this year. Thousands who usually can just keep going at any rate during the first months of the winter are this year starving . . . One feels almost desperate at the sight of it all . . . Is it not extraordinary that these people will lie down and die of hunger rather than join together and <u>take</u> what they need, and what there is abundance of ?[41]

It was meeting hungry people on the streets of London that made Eleanor wretched. Her response was not guilt, sentimentality or sticking-plaster philanthropy but to fight for justice.

In November Aveling put on a production of his play *By the Sea* at Ladbroke Hall. The play was an adaptation of a French piece based on an old Scottish folk ballad, 'Auld Robin Gray'. Edward cast Eleanor in the role of erring wife and himself as wronged husband. The *Dramatic Review* judged her performance as shockingly bad:

> small though the theatre was, she was frequently inaudible, even close to the stage, and never for a moment seemed to understand that she ought to be heard by anybody more than a few feet off. Some of her lines were prettily spoken, but she did not rise to the height either of the repentant wife, who grieves to have offended against her husband even in thought, or the loyal wife who repulses the still-loved lover of her childhood.[42]

So, Eleanor failed because she was utterly unable to perform the role of conventional wife convincingly. Could this cringing inaudible mouse possibly be the same woman who confidently commanded attentive audiences of workers in their tens of thousands at outdoor public meetings and in mass indoor meetings in packed, echoing halls with difficult acoustics?

And here was Aveling, so insecure in real life, convincingly strutting about the stage in the role of the wronged husband. The theatre press now spoke of him as Alec Nelson, the soubriquet Edward adopted in his stage work in order to separate his name from the financial and sexual scandals that had followed him.

Tussy was fed up. As a woman in public life there seemed to be no escape from being constantly sized up and evaluated by different criteria to men. Critical opinion that she was not cut out for the stage was old news; she'd long given up hopes of a theatrical career. It was rather the sense of weariness that everything a woman did in public life had to be sanctioned, or judged and found wanting.

Tussy ended the eventful year in gallows mood. She was depressed about the apparent world victory of capitalism, the cowardice of men, and her loneliness brought on by Edward's emotional abandonment. Edward spent most of December in Torquay rehearsing repertory productions of two of his plays, *By the Sea* and *The Love Philtre*. Tussy would have enjoyed a break in the seaside town but

Edward couldn't tell her that her presence would interfere with his current holiday plum pudding in the form of a young lead actress. *The Love Philtre* was a well-turned piece and justly garnered plaudits. Its ingenious plot featured a love potion that made a young woman besotted out of blind duty with its purveyor. Eerie, how effectively Edward sucked all his successful themes from the marrowbones of his troubled relationship with Eleanor.

Tussy found herself pretty much alone at Christmas, too proud to throw herself on the goodwill of Engels and Lenchen or the many other friends who invited and would have welcomed her. As she wrote to Dollie Radford, who'd recently had a second baby, 'Christmas without children is a mistake.'[43] Dollie and Ernest Radford tried to tell her it was her relationship with Edward that was the mistake but Eleanor had to learn her own lessons and couldn't hear them. As soon as Edward left town for Torquay, Tussy's friends called to visit. Seasonal invitations – to her alone – flew in thick and fast. Realisation dawned. Fiercely loyal, Tussy was offended.

In a brittle note to George Bernard Shaw, Eleanor let him know she was now aware how things stood. 'I am so used to being boycotted that it is no longer a novelty. I marvel much more now when I am not boycotted. You never come to see us now, and I have sometimes wondered if you were boycotting us too!'[44] Three boycotts in as many sentences, from a seasoned politico who regarded boycott as one of the most practical strategies available to encourage engagement on difficult, apparently intractable issues.

She busied herself over the holiday season by sprucing up the dull flat in Chancery Lane. 'I believe I have a genius for house painting,' she joked to her sister. 'We have a most splendid enamel here now . . . which I find invaluable. I enamel chairs, tables, floors, everything. If the climate only permitted I should enamel myself.'[45] She also reported to Laura that blank warrants had been put out against her and Edward, 'so that we can be "run in" whenever the police choose'.[46] She was much more preoccupied with painting over the cracks in her love life with modern enamel than the open police warrants.

Havelock Ellis claims that Eleanor made a suicide attempt early in 1888. He records that she took a large dose of opium and that he – and by implication Olive – saved her by administering strong coffee, forcing her to vomit and making her walk up and down the room. 'I never knew what special event it was in her domestic life which led to this attempt. Her friends were grieved; they were scarcely surprised.'[47] Edward was still away in Torquay. Olive now begged her friend to separate definitively from him, without success. Henry and Olive conspired to help Tussy by putting her to hard literary and intellectual work, which always transported her away from dwelling on 'the sense of the sadness of life' that 'comes upon us almost too painfully for endurance',[48] as she expressed it rawly to Dollie a week after her thirty-third birthday.

Vizetelly had just commissioned Ellis to edit the first volume of Ibsen's plays in English, and he immediately employed Eleanor to translate *An Enemy of the People*, or as she chose to translate idiomatically, '*En Folkfiende*' – '*An Enemy of Society*',[49] 'for the magnificent sum of £5'.[50] The two other works in the trilogy were *Ghosts* and *The Pillars of Society*. Tussy felt these plays 'a very unwise selection' and, whilst praising Henry for his excellent introduction, expressed frankly her great regret that *Nora* was not included in the collection. 'It should have been, I think, in any <u>first</u> volume of Ibsen.'[51] As Henry himself later admitted, the future success of *A Doll's House* proved her right.

The year 1888 was one of intense literary production. Tussy cracked on with editing *A Warning to Fair Women*, the Marlowe commission Ellis had promised the previous year. Vizetelly covered her ten-shilling return fare to Oxford so she could consult the original manuscript in the Bodleian – 'I fancy certain passages that seem corruptions may be simply due to the transcribers' mistakes.'[52] This scholarship would be unremarkable in someone trained to it but Eleanor had barely been to school, never mind had the benefit of a university education.

With a strong grasp of dramatic conventions, she structured the play into five acts, wrote stage directions on the locality of the scenes and recommended the printing of an old 1593 map along with the play: 'It makes it all so much more interesting and amusing.' She asked Ellis if he could give her another to do. 'I have become much more interested in the subject *as a whole*. I used to know the individual plays well enough. I don't think I before realised their value as "documents".'[53]

Ellis and Vizetelly were impressed and delighted with her work. But shortly after Eleanor submitted the completed manuscripts, Vizetelly was prosecuted for publishing Zola's novels in English and his trial, imprisonment and subsequent death stalled the publication of Eleanor's text. *A Warning to Fair Women* was delayed publication until the next century, when it lasted as the definitive edition until the 1950s.

During the first half of the year Eleanor spent a large proportion of her time with dock workers in East London, organising union committees and campaigns for the eight-hour day:

> To go to the docks is enough to drive one mad. The men fight and push and hustle like beasts – not men – and all to earn at best 3d or 4d an hour! So serious has the struggle become that the 'authorities' have had to replace certain iron palings with wooden ones – the weaker men got impaled in the crush! . . . You can't help thinking of all this when you've seen it and been in the midst of it.[54]

She hoped that returning to Dodwell for the summer would make her feel better, but after her experience of the bitter struggle for basic survival in the docklands, the groves of Shakespeare's pre-industrial imagination no longer soothed her. It rained constantly, and she now saw the privation of the small farmers and agricultural workers. The hay was spoilt, the potatoes rotted and the country tracks were full of 'men, women and children who have trudged weary miles to come for the hay making, and who have to therefore trudge back again, starving'.[55]

She couldn't turn away. She confided to Laura that she was suffering alternately from sleeplessness and nightmares: 'One room especially haunts me. Room! – cellar, dark underground. In it a woman lying on some sacking on a little straw, her breast half eaten away with cancer . . . The woman was naked but for the scraps of an old red handkerchief and sail over her legs, surrounded by four children and a baby, all howling for bread whilst her husband tried to pick up a few pence at the docks.'[56] Eleanor took the woman to hospital, only persuading her with great difficulty to leave her children in the care of neighbours, 'but it was too late – and that's only one out of thousands and thousands'.[57]

She appealed to her friends to give her some perspective, asking how they coped with the scale and pain of human suffering, apologising for her incoherence:

> It is a nightmare to me. I can't get rid of it. I see it by day despite our green fields and trees and all the flowers, and I dream of it o'nights. Sometimes I am inclined to wonder how one <u>can</u> go on living with all this suffering around.[58]

In a later age, Tussy, trying to articulate in rational terms why she felt so 'sore at heart',[59] might have been diagnosed as clinically depressed.

Buoyed up by the positive reception for his adaptation of *The Scarlet Letter*, Edward thought he'd try his luck at conquering the American stage. He told Eleanor he had been invited to put on three of his plays in New York, Chicago and 'God knows where else besides',[60] as the General put it. Edward promised Tussy that if he made it in the theatre, she could have the child for which she so ardently longed: 'If only Edward goes well with his plays we want to try and have Johnny with us for good.'[61]

Edward and Tussy's trip to America coincided with the General's own plans to take a holiday in the United States with his old friend Karl Schorlemmer, known to Tussy since childhood as Jollymeier. The General had rheumatism in his legs and acute eye trouble, mostly thanks to his labours transcribing Marx's manuscripts, and wanted a break. Though he and Marx had thought and written about it extensively, Engels had never been to America and he wanted to see it for himself. Especially, he said, as the American working classes were evolving towards class-consciousness[62] and organisation with greater 'vigour' than their British brothers and sisters:

> The last Bourgeois Paradise on earth is fast changing into a Purgatory, and can only be prevented from becoming like Europe, an Inferno, by the go-ahead pace at which the development of the newly fledged proletariat of America will take place. I only wish Marx could have lived to see it![63]

Engels and Schorlemmer kept their travel plans secret in order to avoid 'the delicate attention of the German Socialist Executive, etc. of New York'.[64] Engels said he wanted 'to see not to preach'.[65]

The foursome set sail from Queenstown on 9 August, once again on the Inman liner SS *City of Berlin*. 'We've <u>such</u> a lot of priests, and clergymen on board, and some babies and no end of Amurcen [*sic*] twang,' Tussy told Laura. 'Both our old men seem to be enjoying themselves and eat, drink and are as merry as possible.'[66] The General called Tussy in any weather to go for a walk on deck with him and have a glass of beer. 'It seemed to be one of his unshakeable principles never to go round an obstacle but always to jump or climb over it.'[67] She could have said the same of herself.

Their month-long trip to 'Yankee-land' was scheduled to take in New York, Boston, Niagara and Pittsburgh, then go on up to Canada. The General and Jollymeier would then return to Europe whilst Edward and Tussy stayed on to visit Chicago for the production of one of 'Alec Nelson's' plays. From the outset the trip took years off Engels, but didn't seem to cheer up Jollymeier: 'He is only Sad-meyer now,' wrote Tussy. 'He is terribly broken down, and I doubt if he will be the same again.'[68]

The Marx-Avelings, or rather Marx-Nelsons, had booked into a cheap boarding-house in New York whilst the General and the erstwhile Jollymeier stayed with friends. But Edward didn't think cheap digs suited his image and insisted they move to a better hotel near Broadway, more fitting for an up-and-coming dramaturge. He told Eleanor that his theatrical backers would pay the hotel costs. Whilst Edward disappeared all day to see to his rehearsals, Eleanor walked the city:

> The city of iniquities strikes me as more hideous than ever – and yet it might be so beautiful. I don't believe there is any large town in the world so exquisitely situated as New York – and commerce has made of it a very hell.[69]

These typical views of New York as the grandest site for the capital of Capitalist Production, as Engels put it,[70] sat alongside Eleanor's enthusiasm and admiration for American people in general and their use of the English language in particular.

'Alec Nelson', as he was known in New York, made much of bustling off 'to see to his rehearsals', and kept his family party waiting in the city some extra days in the cause of his theatrical work before they set off by steamer up the Hudson River to Albany, Lake George, and thence to Boston and Niagara Falls. Tussy and Engels were surprised that he was able to join them at all, given his hectic rehearsal schedule.

From 'that most wonderful of places Niagara', the foursome went by boat along the river into Lake Ontario and through the very rough Great Lakes to Toronto, 'a queer place, where all the people look English.'[71] Eleanor enjoyed the voyage along the St Lawrence River, 'of a size we in Europe have no conception of'.[72] She described how the lake was studded everywhere with islands, large and tiny: 'In the so-called thousand-island part rich Californians chiefly but millionaires from all over the States have summer houses, and at night these were all lit up by hundreds of lights and Chinese lamps, and the effect was very strange and very beautiful.'[73]

She was fascinated by the Frenchness of Montreal, and its unexpected roughness. 'It is the muddiest, most tumble-down town I ever saw . . . And the streets! Such holes and such mud, that one is struck by them even after American towns which are all of them unpaved and would be considered disgraceful in a European village.'[74] But she liked the setting of the town with the mountainous Adirondacks beyond, which she hiked to the top of the hills around Montreal to admire.

Something odd happened. Edward came along on this sightseeing trip and then stayed with them for the entire remainder of the holiday. No further reference was made to his rehearsals, plays or productions. The whole projected scheme, by which Tussy and the General had been for months so impressed in anticipation of Edward's rising success, simply evaporated. Before they came to America, in one of his many missives telling people how well Tussy's husband was doing and boasting about Edward's imminent American theatre tour, Engels remarked, 'If his dramatic success goes on at this rate, maybe he will have to go next year to Australia, at the expense of some theatrical impresario.'[75] Or on a convict ship when he was revealed to be a self-delusional conman? Is there a note of knowing irony twinkling in the General's ink here? Did Engels time his impromptu holiday to coincide with Edward's theatrical tour of America, making sure Tussy wasn't once more left alone and exposed by Edward's opportunism?

In the event, Edward tagged along with the others for the whole holiday and never set foot in Chicago. Contrary to his stated plans to remain in America for the run of his plays, he joined the others on the voyage home when they returned to England, leaving on 19 September on the new liner *City of New York*. Eleanor went totally silent on the subject of Edward's much-vaunted conquest of the American stage.

Engels and Eleanor might have asked themselves why a theatrical community about which Edward had only recently been so thoroughly contemptuous would suddenly do a volte-face and invite him with open arms. On his return from their first trip to the US, Edward had given an interview to the *Dramatic Review* in which he expressed his 'intense disgust for the American stage . . . He says dramatic work in the States is all imported, and that when the Yankees are left alone with their own plays, the result is too painful for contemplation.'[76] Evidently the Yankee stage preferred to be left to its own pain rather than import the work of Alec Nelson.

Tussy was refreshed and lighter-hearted after a month's proper holiday in the General's company. The trip drove away her depressive nightmares and hauntings and the General had put her back on her marching mettle. But a shadow clung to her on the voyage back to England. Edward had promised that when his plays did well in the United States they could have Johnny with them 'for good' if Longuet, as was now likely, would agree. Like all Edward's promises this failed to materialise. He promised to marry her eventually when his legal wife died; he promised that they would have children when the time was right; he constantly assured her that he would provide his full half-share of their joint income when he made it in the theatre or one of his academic textbooks hit the big time. Eleanor should have applied the same principles to her personal life as she did to her politics: actions not words; first-hand evidence; material proof; lack of sentimentality.

Edward was, as the General diagnosed, a charming feckless dreamer. Tussy made things work. The rent on Dodwell was £5 a year. In 1888 she sold £3-worth of potatoes and made up the £2 balance from her 'hacking'. Tussy recommended to Laura that she sell her French garden produce to pull in family income. Like their mother before them, both sisters were bridled by impecunious men. But whether by selling her potato crop or ghostwriting, Tussy supported both Edward and herself and got by. 'It's jolly hard though! I often think I'd rather be a kitten and cry mew than a woman trying to earn a living.'[77]

At Christmas 1890, just before her thirty-fifth birthday, Tussy told Laura:

> I am doing hack translations (very bad) for a new magazine . . . Edward writes all sorts of things – good, bad & indifferent. We both have meetings and work of that sort in every spare hour. There's really no time to consider whether life is worth living or is a most unmitigated nuisance.[78]

Work, as Olive Schreiner and Havelock Ellis had hoped, pulled Tussy back from depression's abyss. Poetry also helped. Percy Bysshe Shelley in particular was on Eleanor's mind and her close reading of his work at this critical time contributed to sorting out her head. Eleanor had joined the Shelley Society when it was founded by Furnivall in 1885 and Edward applied for membership shortly after. Henry Salt recalled the trouble Aveling's application caused, 'for the majority decided to refuse it – his marriage relations being similar to Shelley's – and it was only by the determination action of the Chairman, Mr W. M. Rossetti, who threatened to resign . . . that the difficulty was surmounted.'[79] Salt wondered if the name ought to be changed to the 'Respectable Society'.

As Salt and Rossetti argued, Aveling seemed unfairly judged in this matter. Their support seemed well placed when three years later Eleanor and Edward co-presented two talks at the society on 'Shelley's Socialism'. Commonly referred to as 'Two Lectures', they revised and self-published these lectures in a tiny single-volume edition of twenty-five copies in 1888. Eleanor and Edward's work on Shelley has subsequently been described as a 'Marxist evaluation' of Shelley's poetry. However, the Marx who gave it her name called it no such thing. Edward and Eleanor described the essay as a literary investigation into 'whether Shelley was or was not a socialist',[80] and the question of the revolutionary intent of his poetry.

Eleanor and Edward looked at Shelley's personality, his influences, his concept of tyranny and liberty in the abstract, and tyranny in the concrete. One of the most engaging parts of the essay is their discussion of Shelley's understanding of the real meaning of words, where they look at, for example, his use of 'anarchy', 'freedom', 'custom', 'crime' and 'property'.[81] Within the range of poems they explore there is particular focus on *Queen Mab* and *Laon and Cythna*. The latter is particularly indicative of Eleanor and Edward's feminist intent in this essay. They argue that whilst a great deal had been made of Godwin's influence on Shelley, 'Not enough has been made of the influence upon him of the two Marys; Mary Wollstonecraft and Mary Shelley.'[82]

Reminding their audience that it was one of Shelley's 'delusions that are not delusions'[83] that man and woman should be equal and united, they explore how much Shelley saw through the eyes of these two women and his relative recognition of the position of women in society: 'In a word, the world in general has treated the relative influences of Godwin on the one hand and of the two women on the other, pretty much as might have been expected with men for historians.' In 'Shelley's Socialism' Eleanor and Edward continue their experiments in collaborative work begun with 'The Woman Question' and continued, at least in spirit if not in action, in *The Working Class Movement in America*. 'Shelley's Socialism' opens with an intriguing description of their plan to co-write and present the paper:

That plan is based upon the co-operation of a man and woman, whose sympathies are kindred, but whose points of view and methods of looking at facts are as different as are the positions of the two sexes today, even in the most favourable conditions, under the compulsion of our artificial and unhealthy society.[84]

These valuable and apparently well-intentioned shared experiments in working together across openly acknowledged 'points of view and methods of looking at the facts' are a keen insight into one of the reasons why Tussy persisted in a relationship so few from the outside could understand. By mutual agreement,[85] Aveling read out the papers when they presented them at the Shelley Society, 'and although I am the reader, it must be understood that I am reading the work of my wife as well as, nay more than, of myself.'[86] When it came to these precious moments when their public and private lives meshed on the treatment of important subjects, the idea that Eleanor and Edward should be equal and united glimmered hopefully, looking and sounding very much like one of Shelley's 'delusions that are not delusions'.

Our Old Stoker!

The mighty Independent Labour Party emerged out of the battle-scarred terrain of the British left in the late 1880s and early 1890s. The formation of Britain's first democratic socialist parliamentary party is a story that, like many great founding narratives, begins with the birth and coming-of-age of non-identical twins: in this case the new trade unionism and the Second International. Other siblings, such as the Fabians, initially hung back with nervous trepidation and joined the party later.

Eleanor was midwife to the twins of trade unionism and socialist internationalism. She was far more influential, and thus more dangerous, than she appeared superficially. Records of the time reveal her always at the absolute seeing eye of the storm, the epicentre of strategy and organisation. She understood the power of the secretariat. Innumerable significant meetings with key political figures of the period took place in her smoky, gas-lit garret up the rickety staircase at Chancery Lane. Keir Hardie, Ben Tillett and Will Thorne were regular visitors to her home before anyone else had ever heard of them. Tussy convened, she caucused, she networked. She wrote policy and think pieces, budgeted, kept accounts, drafted reports and typed them up herself, and then quietly left the room, moving on to the next point of organisation – be it factory gates, East London rookery, pub, bourgeois club, or literary or artistic society.

Tussy is the feminist shade of socialism. Surviving photographs represent this graphically. Occasionally she is caught in full view, head and shoulders above an attentive gathering listening to her speak from a platform, dray wagon or industrial packing case – the focal point in a mass gathering. She's there, arms folded, leaning in the doorframe behind a crowd of men assembled outside for the group conference picture. Her image appears shoulder to shoulder in the crowd, then partially revealed in a scrum of assembled delegates: the flash of a smile in a throng, or a swing of that old brown cloak amongst demonstrators and protesters. Grainy reproductions of perished originals retain the unmistakeable combination of pince-nez and loosely piled-up hair atop squared shoulders.

From the start of 1889 to the end of 1893 Eleanor was immersed in strategy and mobilisation. At home and abroad she worked primarily in trade unions and transnationally led the design and building of a new international, soon known as the Second International. The new trade unionism and the Second International were the essential infrastructure that enabled British Socialists to coordinate the formation of a mass labour party. The Independent Labour Party (ILP) recruited its representatives and membership from the expanded and strengthened unions, supported and reinforced by the Second International.

The momentum for the establishment of an independent British labour party was set in motion by the force and open aggression of the counter-attack on trade unions by capitalist employers. The name of Eleanor Marx is ubiquitous in the story of how the people's party was forged. Her voice was in everyone's ear and her name on everybody's lips. In the 1890s, Tussy was given two new names by British socialists: 'Our Mother' and – when she took leadership of the gasworkers – 'Our Old Stoker!' By the final decade of the nineteenth century Eleanor had become a national figure – mother of the radical British nation to her friends and followers; fire-eating, rabble-rousing, class-warmongering, a dubious Jewish immigrant, witch, strident bluestocking and harridan to her enemies. As Eleanor observed, 'Those who denounce Socialists as mere firebrands and dynamitards used fire and sword to crush the people into submission.'[1] Loved or hated – and people rarely felt anything in between for her – by 1893 Tussy was one of Britain's leading orators and activists, at home and abroad.

Will Thorne, the Birmingham-born leader of the gas workers who became one of Britain's great labour leaders, remarked that, 'Strange to say, the historians hardly notice the revolution we created.'[2]

Socialism had gained strength throughout Western Europe during the 1880s. By country, the German Social Democrats were the largest socialist body. France was looked to as the path-breaker of revolutionary tradition, but was smaller in numbers than Germany. Italy, Holland, Switzerland and Belgium were the other nation states with broad enough bases to play an international role. Industrialisation was now so far developed in Western European countries that most governments were already considering the need for international labour legislation. In this context international meant Europe and its imperial colonies.

July 1889 was the centenary of the storming of the Bastille and the year of the famous Paris Exhibition to commemorate the revolution. Two rival congresses were held in Paris which ultimately led to the emergence of the Second International. Eleanor's role was to negotiate a compromise between the two and undo the schism. On the one hand were the French trade unionists, allied to the Marx-Engels-Liebknecht faction and supported by Paul Lafargue and Jules Guesde. On the other were the International trade unionists, allied with Hyndman, the SDF, some British trade unions, and supported by Paul Brousse and the Possibilists. Wrote Eleanor:

To play off the French Possibilists against the English Marxists . . . was a very clever dodge on the part of that most artful dodger, Hyndman. That the whole (practically) of the French provinces were Marxist didn't count. To the Englishman Paris is still France, and Paris in the hands of the Possibilists meant to them a Possibilist France.[3]

Numerous tactical errors on both sides made it seem that merger between the two factions was unworkable. Eleanor realised the imperative for a united congress and, to that end, rallied the trade unions, 'and as after all, a single Congress is desirable we must do our best for that'.[4] Hyndman, meanwhile, published some mischievous assaults on what he dubbed the 'Marxist clique'.

Engels wrote a pamphlet stating the Marxist case, countersigned by the leading German Social Democrat Bernstein. Three thousand copies were printed and distributed around England. Eleanor and Bernstein then visited Hyndman at his plush home to talk with him directly about the need for a single international congress:

> Hyndman looked green when he saw me, and knowing what an awful temper I have, did his best to irritate me. But though I've a bad temper I'm not a fool. I saw his game and would not play up to it. I remained quite polite and amiable, even when he began his usual calumnies against us and Paul. I only remarked . . . that if Lafargue was accused of all manner of sins to the party, he, Hyndman, too, was so accused, and that it all came to a question of personalities rather than facts . . . but what's that to do with the Congress? Then came up the old sore of our <u>family</u>. You and I should feel proud. <u>We're</u> supposed to be doing it all! About twenty times Hyndman informed Bernstein that I was a 'bitter partisan'. I am, and I'm not ashamed of it. However the upshot of it all is (you could trust me and Bernstein, Jews that we are, to drive a bargain) that Hyndman will, we think, do all he can to bring about some sort of 'conciliation'. He evidently was staggered when he heard that all Socialist Europe is practically with us.[5]

From opposing camps, Hyndman and Liebknecht both put pressure on the Possibilists to compromise, without success. Engels grumbled about Liebknecht's 'mania for unity'.[6] He thought that two rival congresses could comfortably sit alongside each other without any harm, 'one of Socialists and the other chiefly of <u>aspirants</u> to Socialism'.[7] Let people listen to both cases and decide for themselves. William Morris set himself and followers against the merger, though for different reasons, believing the Possibilists fostered only election opportunism and no real socialism. Tussy felt for him: 'His army is one that would have put even Falstaff to the blush. He himself blushes at it. Morris is personally liked, but you would not get half a dozen workmen to take him seriously.'[8]

Eleanor slaved in the political factory. 'I've today sent off 500 copies of the last invitation, and some hundred letters and post-cards, and am dead tired,'[9] she scrawled to Laura. And this was not the end of it. After sending off 600 pieces of handwritten corre-spondence since the morning, as well as cleaning the grate and getting food from Shepherd's Market for Edward's dinner, she still had 'to see half a dozen Trade Unionists tonight about the Congress'.[10]

Eleanor and Edward spoke frequently at Radical Clubs, effort that seemed to be paying off. 'Only last night I lectured to a capital audience, who, some three or four years ago, would have either laughed at my lecture or yelled at me . . . if the official Socialists are in a bad way, the real workers are getting on.'[11]

Once she arrived in Paris, Eleanor barely had time to step outside the conference venue, Salle des Fantaisies Parisiennes on rue Rochechouart. She was on a standing committee of the congress with Morris and other English representatives and, simultaneous to this executive position, was chief interpreter from French and German into English. She translated a long speech by an Italian professor on anarchism and was roundly attacked for unfair editing. Conversely, her translation of Clara Zetkin's speech on the question of female labour met with approbation, including from its author. Zetkin was a delegate for the women workers of Berlin and later the co-founder of International Women's Day. Eleanor and Clara struck up an instant rapport and became friends ever after.

Eleanor translated the main business of the congress: the resolu-tion in favour of international eight-hour legislation; the resolution in favour of disarmament to challenge the capitalist arms industry; and the resolution for the establishment of an international labour demonstration for 1 May, in which Eleanor played a vital role. Eduard Bernstein testified to Eleanor's labour:

> Some few of us were struck by the superhuman effort she put into this task [as interpreter]. She was ceaselessly busy, from morning to evening, generally interpreting in three languages. She gave herself no respite, missed no session. Despite the oppressive heat in the hall she stayed the course of the whole Congress doing this

thankless, gruelling work: in the truest sense of the word the 'proletarian' of the Congress.[12]

Tussy spent her few snatched breaks with Johnny (thirteen) and Edgar Longuet (nine). Edgar remembered her ever after as 'my loved Ant [sic] Tussy, who was so good to her nephews', taking them to the Paris Exhibition on the Champ de Mars to see the *son et lumière* show illuminating Gustave Eiffel's 300-metre-high ironwork tower, the centrepiece of the exhibition. At seventy, Edgar still remembered the taste in his mouth 'of a remarkable strawberry sirup [sic] she presented to me'[13] as they gazed up at Eiffel's tower. The General thought it a monstrosity and the whole exposition vulgar capitalist gimcrack.

Eleanor's prodigious work at the Paris congress was greatly facili-tated by her favourite piece of new technology: her typewriter, acquired four months previously on hire purchase. She taught herself how to use the 'machine', declaring it 'very easy',[14] and advertised her typing services. Typewriters had been mass-produced in America since the end of the 1870s, but took longer to penetrate the British retail market. Olive Schreiner sent the first chapter of her unfinished novel *From Man to Man* from South Africa and asked Tussy to type it up, for which she insisted on paying the full rate. Twelve copies of a lengthy pamphlet Eleanor typed for Swan Sonnenschein earned her two shillings.

Shocked at how badly the work was paid by hourly rate, Tussy did some investigative journalism into typists' wages and labour conditions, published as 'Sweating in Type-Writing Offices' in the *People's Press*.[15] Typists who needed to live by their labour 'must work at high pressure and a good many more hours than eight a day'.[16] She proposed that 'the unhappy human machine'[17] should form a union of those who typed in businesses and from home. Her own quick skill at typing was of course soon pressed into unpaid political service.

Like her father and Engels, Eleanor paid close attention to advances in technology and their impact on the time and motion of workers' jobs and employers' profits. Almost every sector of industry was now in the process of mechanisation. She calmly challenged the persistent misrepresentation of British workers as Luddites resistant to technological modernisation, a favourite propaganda theme of the political right, employers and shareholders.

The truth was that, from the worker's perspective, technological advance created the capacity to make the eight-hour day a reality, accelerating speed of production, providing greater safety and healthier working conditions, thus increasing efficiency. Instead of stumbling home exhausted in the middle of the night, an employee who could complete their daily labour in eight hours might realise the dream of a life with a little family and leisure time to live for themselves rather than alienated labour. Employers, however, viewed mechanisation as an opportunity to suck increased profit margins from the production process, not revitalise the lot of their wealth-producing workers.

Aunt Tussy brought her nephews back to London with her after the Paris congress. Outgoing Johnny and his shy, bookish little brother Edgar stayed for several months, treated with visits to the zoo, museums, walks on Hampstead Heath and trips to the theatre, including one of Edward's performances. The General and Lenchen loved having the Longuet boys to visit. The General entertained them and let them sit at his desk and use his ink, paper and blotter. Tussy once again silently wondered at his contrasting aloofness with Freddy Demuth, evidenced by Engels's entirely uncharacteristic withdrawal and avoidance of Freddy whenever he came to the house.

Shortly before they returned to France, Johnny and Edgar were at her side when Aunt Tussy addressed a massive crowd of 100,000 people at a rally in Hyde Park in support of the Dock Strike. The dockers struck on 14 August. Within a fortnight they successfully brought London commerce to a standstill. The great trading Thames was eerily silent, the familiar commercial river traffic that had busily plied its waters since Roman times hushed. Shipping magnates, bankers and investors in the city and Tories and Liberals in parliament were terrified. Never had industrial action brought mighty London trade to such a still point.

The famished, broken-down dock labourers from the East End docklands to the mouth of the industrial estuary endured appalling employment conditions. Eleanor had already written about how they were forced to physically fight each other every morning to get work for the day. Dock workers had to compete with each other for every farthing they earned. All the more significant therefore that the dockers collectivised and organised themselves into a consolidated group of 50,000 workers, planned and implemented a mass strike, and pulled in after them all and every trade and support service in London in any way connected with shipping, including even the fire services and river men.

The wealthy, powerful dock companies felt suddenly anxious and insecure. Much like a dock worker might every morning wake with the anxiety of whether he would be able to earn a subsistence wage for the day. The London Chamber of Commerce complained that the strike had a worse impact on trade in general than if 'a hostile fleet had held triumphant possession of the mouth of the Thames'.[18]

The dockers ultimately won some significant benefits and the new Dock, Wharf, Riverside and Labourers' Union of Great Britain, Ireland and the Netherlands was formed, with Ben Tillett at its helm as secretary. In 1921 it became the Transport and General Workers' Union, one of Britain's leading worker institutions.

Johnny and Edgar – accompanied by Lenchen, her grandson and Freddy – saw their Aunt Tussy in a new light that Sunday of the mass congregation in Hyde Park. MP Robert Cunninghame Graham described the event in the *Labour Elector*:

> And so speaker succeeds speaker. To Mann and Burns succeed Mrs Aveling, Tillett and MacDonald. Curious to see Mrs Aveling addressing the enormous crowd, curious to see the eyes of the women fixed upon her as she spoke of the miseries of the dockers' homes, pleasant to see her point her black-gloved finger at the oppression, and pleasant to hear the hearty cheer with which her elegant speech was greeted.[19]

The following day Eleanor and Edward went up to the Trades Union Congress in Dundee. The successes of the Dock Strike and the Gas Workers' Strike that preceded it buzzed in every meeting, conversation and corner of the annual congress. As Will Thorne, the gas workers' leader pointed out, these were the first strikes in over half a century to merit capital letters.

This was the era of gas as a main form of domestic and commercial energy. Electricity was still expensive and less used than gaslight. Gas was a public utility. The gas companies operated as a massive monopoly, their allocation profits regulated by parliamentary legislation. The work was seasonal. It required considerable skill and endurance in a hazardous environment, yet gas workers were considered unskilled labourers. They did not serve a formal apprenticeship and thus were not considered tradesmen. Fifty-two weeks of the year they worked like soldiers in a state of battle in a permanently combustible atmosphere. The carbonisers in the retort houses worked twelve-hour shifts, day and night, in infernal conditions – it was literally hot as hell and the works held enormously dangerous machinery.

For almost twenty years, gas workers had tried and failed to organise for better pay and conditions. Employers quickly stifled the first gas stokers' union, formed in 1872. Further attempts in 1884 and 1885 suffered similar defeat. Now the gas workers finally succeeded, taking the ground for new unionism. The gas workers were not alone. So-called 'unorganisable' unskilled workers were organising all over the country. The stirrings began in 1886 with the Bryant and May match-girls strike. This was followed by strikes of sailors and then tram-men, amongst other worker collectives which unionised.

The year 1889 was critical for new unionism. Earlier in the year the London gas workers won the eight-hour day, led by Will Thorne who had joined the Canning Town branch of the SDF in 1884. Eleanor, Edward, Tom Mann, John Burns and Ben Tillett gave their full support and helped Thorne form the National Union of Gas Workers and General Labourers. The new union was launched at the end of March with the aim of reducing the working day from twelve to eight hours and establishing double rates for Sundays, to recognise that Sunday work was overtime labour. On 7 June the National Union of Gas Workers and General Labourers of Great Britain and Ireland was formally registered, with the hopeful motto 'Love, Union and Fidelity'.

Will Thorne was born in Birmingham. He had no access to education in his childhood. His parents were illiterate. At the age of six he began his working career as a child labourer in a rope-spinning factory where he toiled a twelve-hour day, six days a week. He had to take his own dinner to work and there was no time for study or play. His introduction to numeracy and letters came from factory education groups. Later, Thorne attended all the evening classes he could at the institute of adult education on Barking Road, East London. Here he was taught physiology by Aveling, whom he admired, and literary courses by Shaw, whom he did not.

'It was a time when one Socialist, active and determined, giving assistance to the unskilled workers, was worth twenty discussing revolutionary tactics in their private clubrooms,'[20] wrote a historian of the epoch. Tussy was usually one of those few active and determined Socialists. Will Thorne and Ben Tillett were unequivocal about Eleanor's role in the sequential Gas Workers' Strike and the Dock Strike. Like Thorne, Tillett started his working life as a child labourer. His first job, aged eight, was as a labourer in a brickyard. These men recognised hard graft. Thorne observed that Eleanor worked long hours as a correspondent for the strike committee, walking home late at night or in the early hours of the morning when public transport was no longer running. Tillett remembered Eleanor:

> . . . doing the drudgery of clerical work as well as more responsible duties . . . Brilliant, devoted and beautiful . . . she lived all her life in the atmosphere of Social Revolution . . . during our great strike she worked unceasingly, literally day and night . . . a vivid and vital personality, with great force of character, courage and ability.[21]

Tillett regretted the 'very unhappy conditions' of Eleanor's life with Aveling, but observed that this 'did not, however, break her spirit, or cause her to waver in her devotion to the working-class cause'.[22]

Tom Mann recorded Eleanor's 'valuable service' as a volunteer in his memoirs. To him she was 'a most capable woman':

> Possessing a complete mastery of economics, she was able alike in conversation and on a public platform to hold her own with the

best. Furthermore, she was ever ready, as in this case [the London Dock Strike], to give close attention to detailed work, when by so doing she could help the movement.[23]

This work she did at the Wade's Arms pub at Poplar, the headquarters of the strike committee.

Tussy worked behind the scenes to educate and encourage proletarian leaders, men and women. Once appointed secretary of the National Union of Gas Workers and General Labourers, Thorne soon found himself struggling with the administration and accountability required by his office. He did not have the benefit of an education to equip him with these skills. Thorne raised his anxieties in confidence with Tussy and asked for her help, which she readily offered. Thorne, a formidable leader, acknowledged Tussy's role in educating him: she 'helped me more than anyone else to improve my very bad handwriting, my reading and my general knowledge'.[24]

Eleanor assisted Thorne in composing and drafting the rules and constitution of the union. She helped him do the accounts and write the half-year report from March to September 1889, circulated to 30,000 members around the country. In 1939, at the age of eighty, in an interview in the House of Commons, Thorne described Eleanor as the most intelligent woman he had ever known, who had an immeasurable influence on his life. He described her voluntary tuition and her help in teaching him to do his job in the early days. Eleanor never once mentioned it.

On Christmas Day of 1889 Tussy wrote a long letter to Laura, reviewing the year, before she and Edward headed off to Regent's Park Road for Christmas festivities with the General and Lenchen and their guests. Edward, Tussy reported, was happily busy writing plays, being a theatre critic and churning out short-order journalism. He still did some coaching but his union and Socialist League work now largely superseded his teaching.

For my own poor part, look you, life seems to be becoming one long strike. First there was the Dock Strike. No sooner was that over than I was summoned to Silvertown, and for 10 mortal weeks

I travelled daily to that out-of-the-world place; speaking every day – often twice a day, in all weathers in the open air. I began to hope for peace – when lo! the Gas Strike begins. For this, I have, so far, not had much to do (we both spouted in Hyde Park o'Sunday) but ... I may well be called at any minute to 'help' with the Committee work.[25]

That 'help', as Laura understood, was a euphemism for running it.

Silvertown took its name from the industrial compound and chemical factories that dominated the London docklands. Silver's India Rubber, Gutta Percha and Telegraph Works Ltd had been in West Ham in one form or another since 1852, when it started life as a small waterproofing works. By 1889 it had six factory departments for rubber, ebonite, gutta percha, electrical and chemical, and a sister factory in France. Silvertown supplied sales offices all over the United Kingdom, British colonies and to global trading partners. During the strike, management attempted – unsuccessfully – to ship in blackleg workers from the French factory.

Although so close to the city of London and Westminster, Silvertown was a circle of industrial hell unknown to those who never ventured east of the Square Mile. Due to its position on the estuary flatlands on the fringe of the metropolis the area was, by long tradition, the home of so-called 'offensive industries'. It produced every legal industrial chemical, compound and by-product on which commodity capitalism depended and shed its toxic, poisonous industrial effluent directly into the ancient river. The workers, many of them women, were badly paid, exposed to every industrial hazard imaginable, and worked a minimum of eighty hours a week for entirely unprotected pay regulated by an invidious, slave-like system of 'pass tickets'.

Silvertown struck in the third week of September 1889. The primary demand was that workers should be entitled to overtime pay for weekly shifts exceeding eighty hours. For the duration of the strike Tussy commuted daily to Silvertown from Chancery Lane. Between 6 a.m. and midnight she travelled by Underground, overground, buses or trams. When public transport closed at midnight she walked home, or just stayed through the night and kept on working.

She spoke every weekday and Saturday, sometimes several times a day, at the factory. On Sundays she spoke at mass rallies in Hyde Park (29 September), Victoria Park in Hackney (6 October), Clerkenwell Green (27 October), and again in Victoria Park the following Sunday, when 10,000 workers marched from the dock-lands to Hackney, led by Silver's workers, all with union tickets stuck in the bands of their hats.

The Silvertown strike pickets were pitched battles. Although picketing was legal under British law, the factory owners and police refused to allow it. Blacklegs were brought in under police escort. Once they were inside, they slept in the works, supplied with food driven in by government vans. 'The Blacklegs in the works are getting v unmanageable,' Tussy wrote:

> 132 were seriously burnt (through lack of skill) in one week; they had a fight yesterday and one Blackleg . . . stabbed another. Out of 45 men brought from Brighton 42 had had enough of it, and had not only 'given notice' but have promised to put 'a shilling a man' in our collection boxes. In many ways this fight is the most interesting we have had. It is distinctly on a question of princi-ple.[26]

Engels wrote to socialist leader Friedrich Sorge that 'Tussy leads the gasmen (under cover) and this union certainly seems to be by far the best.'[27] However, Tussy was not under cover in her leadership of the women gas workers. For nearly three months she led the women from the front. Eleanor climbed on chairs and tables to harangue workers in Silvertown pubs, gathering her skirt up briskly above her ankles and revealing a flash of red flannel petticoat.

Eleanor formed the first women's branch of the National Union of Gas Workers and General Labourers on 10 October 1889. On Sunday 27 October, the executive council formally admitted the Silvertown Women's Branch and its secretary, Mrs Eleanor Marx-Aveling, to the union. This new role, she told her sister, 'takes up no end of time'.[28] Tussy was now a public leader of a major union. The formation of the Silvertown Women's Union was critical to British labour history.

Eleanor knew that subsuming women within the male-led union would not work. Nor would ghettoising women's labour rights in a separate organisation. Women's participation and representation had to be incorporated in every aspect and at every level of organisation, action and process. A wrong done to one is a wrong done to all. This strike and all others would ultimately fail unless the women workers unionised and coordinated strategically with the men's unions. By dividing workers by gender, the employers kept everyone's wages down. If male workers accepted women's labour as being of less value than their own, they allowed employers to undercut their wages. Net result: lower pay for the entire workforce.

The division of labour into men, women and children, Eleanor explained, was simple long-division divide and rule. This was not clever economics or the natural law of markets; it was the unnatural law of patriarchal commodity capitalism. Adults of both sexes must refuse the co-option of minors into child labour and insist on the rights of working-class children to education and play. Women must take the lead in refusing to undercut the wages of their fathers, brothers, lovers and husbands. Men must insist on women's wages being equal to theirs.

Eleanor explained the structure of industrial capitalism in plain English. Inequality between men and women in the workplace did not just favour or support capitalism, *it made capitalism possible.* Each great strike of 1889 taught the union movement an important lesson. The crucial lesson of Silvertown was the necessity for men and women workers to work in unison.

The Silvertown strike ended in defeat on 14 December. When the first snow came, hungry workers could no longer hold out. Bailiffs hired by the employers started evicting families from factory-owned lodgings. Will Thorne, supported by the union executive, urged workers to return to the factory rather than starve themselves, their families and communities. They needed to live to fight another day. The remaining international relief funds were distributed amongst the 450 remaining locked-out workers.

But as Eleanor pointed out, the Silvertown defeat was chiefly due not to the actions of the employers but to the failure of skilled labourers to continue to support their unskilled colleagues. Some highly skilled labourers had the vote by the end of the 1890s. The Amalgamated Engineers' Society of skilled labourers scuppered the strike by returning to work.[29]

The Dock Strike had taught the necessity for skilled and unskilled labour to organise together. The Gas Strike succeeded in large part because it applied this principle. Silvertown failed because it did not. 'The great danger here in England is the spirit of compromise,' Tussy wrote. 'I am glad the Gas Workers are saved from the "patronage" of the bourgeois.'[30] So saying, she headed off with Edward to the General's distinctly bourgeois Christmas meal, crowned by the steaming glory of Lenchen's legendary plum pudding.

At the beginning of December Eleanor and Edward had been offered a new job editing *Time*, the monthly shilling journal recently bought by Bax. The day the Silvertown strike ended, Eleanor started writing and commissioning for the next issue. As she quipped, there was no reprieve after the end of her work in the docklands; now 'I have not . . . too little but . . . too much *Time*.'[31]

One of the most important resolutions of the 1889 Paris congress was to establish May Day as an annual demonstration of the international solidarity of labour in the demand for a legal eight-hour day. Eleanor spent the first months of her thirty-fifth year working to get this resolution implemented in Britain. At her instigation, the Bloomsbury Socialist Society campaigned to bring the broadest possible base of London workers to observe May Day at a mass rally in Hyde Park.

The Socialist League and the SDF distanced themselves from the May Day campaign, though their rank and file supported it. Morris and the Socialist League were in favour of May Day as a demonstration of general international socialist solidarity but opposed the specific call for the eight-hour day. They felt it was of peripheral importance.

Tussy rallied support for what she called the 'universal May Day demonstration' all over Britain. Unions subsidised her travel so she could speak at eight-hour demonstrations. The Bristol unions, for example, sent her thirty shillings to cover her return fare. After the meeting she handed back ten shillings to the treasurer with a typed account and her receipts. What a contrast between Tussy, who accounted for every ha'penny and farthing she spent, and Edward, who never accounted for any sum of money, however large or small.

Because of the Socialist League's refusal to back the call for the eight-hour day, there were two May Days in London in 1890. On 1 May about 3,000 people convened on Clerkenwell Green under the banner of the official Socialist League and were addressed by William Morris and others. On 4 May, upwards of 250,000 congregated in Hyde Park and were addressed by Eleanor and others. Nearby in Paris, the first official May Day attracted 100,000 supporters to the Place de la Concorde.

May 1890 was also the month of the first annual congress of the gas workers' union. Eleanor was elected to the national executive committee. The show of hands in the hall supporting her nomination was unanimous, and – embarrassingly – accompanied by members leaping to their feet and roaring cheers of approval.

As secretary of the women gas workers and serving member of the gas workers' national executive, Eleanor was a leader of one of the biggest emerging labour movements in the UK.

Tussy was now so much in demand that she had to ask the press not to publicise her name as a speaker in advertisements unless they had checked that she had agreed to appear. On several occasions where her name was billed without her agreement to speak, protest and disturbances ensued at meetings and rallies when she didn't turn up.

Inspired by her vision that women and men needed to coordinate and work together in order to restructure the labour market and stop the divide and rule of wage-undercutting, various organisations asked Eleanor to come and show them how to organise, strategise and take action. Amongst them were the fast-growing numbers of shop assistants in the expanding retail service industries. Women and men worked together closely in this sector, particularly since the advent of modern department stores.

In March 1890 the Hammersmith branch of the Shop Assistants' Union asked Tussy to address a meeting at the Hammersmith Palais – the music hall Palace of Varieties. They wanted her to endorse their campaign calling for a local boycott of shops that refused the union's demand to implement a fixed eight-hour day plus overtime. Tussy commended the union's good sense in involving local consumers in a retail boycott. She declared herself willing to sign the petition and support the action, but she recommended that the union might want to consider removing the word 'boycott', as this was an indictable offence under British law.

She suggested replacing the illegal 'boycott' with 'exclusive dealing', which was legal in contract law. So 'we will boycott' became 'we will go in for exclusive dealing'. With self-taught knowledge of the law and a two-word edit Tussy saved everyone who signed the petition from potential prosecution. There followed Sunday marches and mass meetings supported by shop assistants from all over the capital. 'Our Old Stoker' addressed most of the gatherings.

The retail employers threatened legal action but their lawyers advised them that the framing of the protest was technically legal. Eleanor had protected what was, indeed, an all-out boycott. Skirmish and negotiations ensued.

By 3 April all of the Hammersmith shopkeepers had capitulated and agreed to the eight-hour working day in order to reopen their hard-hit businesses. The shopkeepers had hired expensive lawyers from Chancery Lane. Tussy ensured the Shop Assistants' Union organised within the rule of law. David beat Goliath.

The onion-skinners at the Crosse & Blackwell factory in London's East Ham called on Our Old Stoker to help them organise industrial action. Onion-skinning was a hazardous job and the workforce comprised exclusively so-called 'unskilled' women workers. Women skilled with knives and cutters laboured twelve- to fourteen-hour shifts with their arms plunged elbow deep into noxious chemicals, inhaling lung-burning fumes in unventilated workrooms. They suffered from eye infections, and skin, respiratory and reproductive diseases, which in turn caused permanent disability and layoff without medical support or pension. Top wages for onion-skinners were two shillings and threepence for a fifteen-hour day – but most received only a shilling for a full day's work. Eleanor organised 400 women into a union. They set terms for an eight-hour day, minimum standard wage and improved work conditions, and struck.

Within a week, Crosse & Blackwell were unable to meet their orders to retailers. Management tried to bribe the women with selective pay rises and, in final desperation, free beer for all workers. These offers were rejected; the skinners won.

From onions to sweets. The factory girls (most of them under twenty) at Barratt's sweet-making factory in Tottenham invited Eleanor to come and address them and advise on their strike, prompted by the draconian system of fines imposed on them by management. To try to pacify them, the Barratt's board offered the young women a free party, described by Eleanor as 'a beanfeast'. She challenged them to dish out 'beans' to Barratt's in return and led a demonstration of 800 women and their male supporters through the streets of Tottenham. Their action was successful, but Eleanor convened a review meeting with the young strikers and discussed how they would have been more effective if they'd joined the union before being forced into action.

All-male labour forces, such as the railway workers, also asked Eleanor to work with them. Railway employees, Eleanor wrote, worked hard and were paid badly, yet they held the potential power to bring the industry of the entire country to a complete standstill.

A few weeks later, Tussy made history as the first woman to speak on West Drayton Green, a long-established public meeting place for democrats and radicals. One of the topics raised by the women at the meeting was the problems they encountered at home if their families or men refused to join unions. When the women organised strikes or unionised – or both – some of their boyfriends or husbands verbally and physically abused them, or threatened to throw them and their children out of their homes – even if it was the women's wages that paid the rent. Tussy suggested to these women that they insist potential lovers show them a fully paid-up union card and, if they would not, show *them* the door. She was only half-joking. Keir Hardie expressed the same view when he observed that men who were unable to be true to their co-workers and brothers would make bad lovers and husbands.

In a speech to the gasworkers' union gathered in Northampton market square on a Saturday morning, Eleanor stated that workers would brook no opposition to the continuing struggle for 'a legal eight-hour working day'. She reminded the mass gathering that unskilled workers were more vulnerable to unregulated working hours:

Up to the present time the Trades Councils and old Trades Unions have been not merely indifferent, but actually hostile to the union of the unskilled workers. But . . . there are hopes that . . . this suicidal opposition will cease and the skilled and 'unskilled' will row together. The latter sorely need organising. They work terribly long hours for wretched wages. Our Union has started and is being cordially helped by the Socialists.[32]

Much of the dissension within the union movement about legislating working hours stemmed from the fact that fixed working hours affected working women more than working men. Craftsmen, for example, rejected the call for the eight-hour day. However, there was one exception: there was majority support for the eight-hour day for miners – the one industry in which unskilled labour was absolutely dominated by men. The sexual division of labour in the industrial workplace under capitalism was laid bare by the eight-hour movement.

Tom Mann, Will Thorne and Ben Tillett were all sons of working mothers. All three insisted on the absolute necessity for legislation on working hours. Eleanor hammered home the point that the principle of overtime pay could not be established without first benchmarking what constituted a working day. Most women labourers were classified as unskilled and most were working mothers with the primary responsibility for childcare, home and – if they had one – a working husband. These women were the most vulnerable to the difficulties of undefined or unlimited working hours. Women worked and to them fell the burden of reproducing the labour force to feed the capitalist machine.

To many men women were, by definition, unskilled workers. Aware of the division and debate this caused in the union movement, Eleanor tackled this sexism head on. She started to refer to herself in her speeches, pointedly, as 'a more or less unskilled worker' who was nevertheless a leader on the union executive on which she had served almost since its foundation. As such, 'it is my duty to protest against the statement that the "unskilled" do not demand a legal right to the eight hour day.'[33]

Provoked by this intervention, her fellow – male – unionists and political allies cavilled, in hilariously misogynist terms, over whether or not Eleanor could fairly call herself an 'unskilled worker'. All agreed that she laboured very long hours but they refuted her argument that she was 'unskilled' as she came from the intellectual class. But Tussy's socialist sisters got her point: as a woman of any class she was, by legal and social definition, classified and regarded as 'unskilled'.[34]

There was no question that Tussy worked extremely hard. The turnout in Hyde Park that first May Day bore testimony to the effectiveness of her campaigning, alongside the other almost exclusively male union leaders. The General described the 4 May demonstration as 'nothing short of overwhelming, and even the bourgeois press had to admit it . . . the platform where Tussy was, had a brilliant reception.'[35]

Eleanor made a speech that first May Day of 1890 that encompassed her determined socialist internationalism, her commitment to British trade unionism and the need for a parliamentary labour party to represent working people:

> We have not come to do the work of political parties, but we have come here in the cause of labour, in its own defence, to demand its own rights. I can remember when we came in handfuls of a few dozen to Hyde Park to demand an Eight Hours Bill, but the dozens have grown to hundreds, and the hundreds to thousands, until we have this magnificent demonstration . . . Those of us who have gone through all the worry of the Dock Strike, and especially the Gas Workers' Strike and have seen the men, women and children stand round us, have had enough of strikes, and we are determined to secure an eight-hours day by legal enactment; unless we do so, it will be taken from us at the first opportunity. We will only have ourselves to blame if we do not achieve the victory which this great day could so easily give us.
>
> There is in the park this afternoon a man whom Mr Gladstone once imprisoned – Michael Davitt; but Mr Gladstone is now on the best of terms with him. What do you suppose is the reason for this change? Why has the Liberal Party been so suddenly converted to Home Rule? Simply because the Irish people sent eighty members of the House of Commons to support the Conservatives;

in the same way we must kick these Liberal and Radical members out if they refuse to support our programme.

I am speaking this afternoon not only as a Trade Unionist, but as a Socialist. Socialists believe that the eight hours' day is the first and most immediate step to be taken, and we aim at a time when there will no longer be one class supporting two others, but the unemployed both at the top and at the bottom of society will be got rid of. This is not the end but only the beginning of the struggle; it is not enough to come here to demonstrate in favour of an eight hours' day. We must not be like some Christians who sin for six days and go to church on the seventh, but we must speak for the cause daily, and make the men, and especially the women that we meet, come into the ranks to help us.[36]

At this concluding point Eleanor paused, then rolled out Shelley's great thunderous invocation to working-class Englishmen and women in *The Masque of Anarchy*:

> Rise like Lions after slumber
> In unvanquishable number,
> Shake your chains to earth like dew
> Which in sleep had fallen on you –
> Ye are many – they are few.[37]

19

Ibsenist Interlude

After two years unpunctuated by rest, Tussy was thrilled by an unexpected summer holiday in 1890. Her last break had been a few wet days in Cornwall with some 'rich folk' friends of Edward's. They were welcoming and charming but Tussy felt uncomfortable. Outspoken and argumentative on socially inappropriate subjects – all of which to her seemed to be the only things worth talking about – smoking, seamlessly comical and unconventionally dressed, Tussy was a tiresome guest in polite society – and she knew it. Ibsen would have recognised her predicament.

For over a decade, Tussy's most enjoyable leisure time had been spent with Olive but she had returned home to South Africa the previous October. They didn't know when they would see each other again. Her most intimate friend and confidante was now on the other side of the world and Tussy saw less of the heartbroken Havelock Ellis after Olive had left.

In July 1890, the General spent a few enjoyable weeks in Norway and wrote to Tussy urging her and Edward to do the same. It was time she took a break and, after all, he was 'amazed that such zealous Ibsenites could bear to wait so long before setting eyes on the new Promised Land'.[1] Tussy had recently been commissioned by the publisher Thomas Fisher Unwin to translate Ibsen's *The Lady from the Sea*, written in 1888. It was due out in a separate volume later in the year, with an introduction by writer Edmund Gosse. Eleanor and

Edward were also booked to co-produce the play in London at Terry's Theatre the following May. In the context of all this Ibsenism, the General was right – it was time Tussy made pilgrimage to Norway and the translation work could pay for it.

They took the prompt and set sail on 6 August. Tussy and Edward's three-week tour of Ibsen's Norway was in many ways a voyage around themselves and their troubled relationship. Tussy recognised in Ibsen's work what she struggled with in herself. The perception that monstrousness can be vanquished by beauty or love or good housekeeping or satisfactory sex or having children is one that has kept women in bad marriages since the beginning of time. Means of escape are available but the methods and opportunities for survival are uncertain.

This is one of Ibsen's key themes.

Ellida Wangel, protagonist of *The Lady from the Sea*, stays within the security of a marriage to which she finally becomes reconciled. Where Flaubert's Emma Bovary exercises the suicide option, in *A Doll's House* Nora Helmer, Ibsen implies, might get away without killing herself and even have a chance at forging a new existence. In her private, personal relationship with Edward there were many points of identification and resonance between Eleanor and Ibsen's Nora Helmer and Ellida Wangel.

The Lady from the Sea stages the dilemma of Ellida Wangel, who has to choose between a loving and devoted but boring, safe husband and a seductive but dangerous lover, a sailor who returns from her past to try and reclaim her. The lure of sexual desire is at the heart of the play. Ellida expresses her anguish over the presence of the unnamed stranger, the 'horrible, unfathomable power he has over my mind'.[2]

The audience experiences Dr Wangel's gathering apprehension of the dilemma his wife faces: 'I begin to understand little by little . . . Your longing and aching for the sea, your attraction towards this strange man, these were the expression of an awakening and growing desire for freedom; nothing else.'[3] Once Ellida's husband recognises and acknowledges to her that she is at liberty to make her own choice between them, she chooses him.

George Bernard Shaw, Havelock Ellis and many of her close friends thought Edward's hold over Tussy was predominantly sexual.

But this was simplistic. Eleanor loved Edward. Edward loved himself. Of the two, he was the more content. His selfishness and egotism appalled Tussy but also fascinated and impressed her. She saw that his way of being inoculated him against her own virus of depression and world-weariness contracted from persistent empathy and over-identification with others.

Edward's marvellous immunity highlighted questions that remained unanswered by her family upbringing. What influences and factors, apart from the great structural edifices of capitalism, patriarchy, class inequality and the abstract forces of historical materialism, make human beings prioritise self over others and, irrationally, individual over common good?

A Doll's House was Tussy's favourite of all Ibsen's plays. Edith Lees Ellis described its first public performance in Britain at the Novelty Theatre in London, on 7 June 1889:

> A few of us collected outside the theatre breathless with excitement. Olive Schreiner was there and Dollie Radford . . . and Eleanor Marx. We were restive and almost savage in our arguments. What did it mean? Was it life or death for women? Was it joy or sorrow for men? That a woman should demand her own emancipation and leave her husband and children in order to get it, savoured less of sacrifice than sorcery.[4]

Even a conservative like Clement Scott of the *Daily Telegraph*, hostile to Ibsen's 'immoral universe', acknowledged he was in the presence of great theatre: 'the interest was so intense last night that a pin might have been heard to drop. '[5]

A Doll's House had a more profound impact on British theatre than any other stage production of the late Victorian era. The actor Harley Granville-Barker described it as 'the most dramatic event of the decade'.[6] Ibsen's unsparing study of the marriage between infantilised Nora and tyrannical Torvald electrified middle-class audiences into shocked recognition. Social conservatives said it would corrupt women, destroy the quietude and rule of men, and hasten the end of decent British morality founded on hearth and home, where middle-class women knew their place as subordinate to husband and children.

Progressives saw the piece as holding out the possibility of social change if women could muster the courage to refuse their assigned domestic social roles. 'Ibsenism' was the label attached to new social movements – socialists, feminists, Marxists, Fabians – who interpreted Ibsen as a pioneer of the new theatre that radicalised classical theatrical forms and repertoire.

By and large, the British press objected to Ibsen's new vision by charging him with cheap obscenity. Ibsenism, declared the *Evening Standard*, was enjoyed only by 'lovers of prurience and dabblers in impropriety who are eager to gratify their illicit tastes under the pretence of art'.[7]

Shaw succinctly grasped the essential point of Ibsen. 'It is in the middle class itself that the revolt against middle class ideals breaks out . . . Neither peer nor labourer has ever hated the bourgeoisie as Marx hated it, or despised its ideals as Swift, Ibsen and Strindberg despised them.'[8] He saw that people driven from conventional theatre by the 'intolerable emptiness of the ordinary peformances' started to enjoy theatre again when they encountered Ibsen, whose work was without 'the conventional lies of the stage':[9]

> The woman's eyes are opened; and instantly her doll's dress is thrown off and her husband left staring at her, helpless, bound thenceforth either to do without her (an alternative which makes short work of his independence) or else treat her as a human being like himself, fully recognizing that he is not a creature of one superior species, Man, living with a creature of another and inferior species, Woman, but that Mankind is male and female.[10]

For Eleanor, *A Doll's House* encompassed what she loved about those moments in art when individual human stories intersected with social contradiction and ethical struggle, that place where freedom prompts the individual to think about how things might be made different in the future.

The Playgoers' Club, originally formed in 1884, reassembled to debate the 'Ibsen question'. Edward performed an excellent reading of *Ghosts* and Tussy gave a lecture on 'Immorality on the Stage'. She and GBS always sat together at club meetings, and disrupted the seriousness of the proceedings. As he recalled, 'Mrs Aveling and I being of course seasoned socialist mob orators, were much in the position of a pair of terriers dropped into a pit of rats.'[11]

Several writers penned parodic sequels to *A Doll's House*, Eleanor amongst them. In March 1891, *Time* magazine published *A Doll's House Repaired*, co-written by Eleanor and Israel Zangwill.

Zangwill, known as the 'Jewish Dickens', was born in London in 1864 to a Latvian father and a Polish mother. As a child, he attended the Jews' Free School in Spitalfields, where he became a pupil-teacher. Next, he was admitted to the University of London. Zangwill later became well known as a writer in Britain and America as the author of *Children of the Ghetto*, published in 1892. He coined the phrase 'the melting pot', the title of his hit play that stormed Broadway in 1908. He was a moderate pacifist and stead-fast supporter of the women's suffrage movement. His association with Zionism began in 1895, when he introduced his friend Theodor Herzl to potential sponsors amongst his Anglo-Jewish intellectual friends. When he and Tussy met, he was at the start of his career, working as a cartoonist, humorist and journalist and, being nearly a decade her junior, somewhat in awe of her. He introduced her to several of his intellectual circles, including the Jewish Wanderers of Kilburn, and many of his friends believed he pined for Tussy's romantic attentions.

Israel and Tussy's entertaining lampoon proposed modest altera-tions to the architecture of *A Doll's House*, in order to repair its 'manifestly impossible, nay, immoral conclusion':[12]

> how ridiculous and hateful the conception of a woman deliber-ately abandoning husband and children must be to an English audience. In accordance with these clean, wholesome ideas of morality we have slightly altered the third act ... alterations that ... cannot fail to satisfy the English sense of morality and decency.[13]

In their version Nora apologises for acting and thinking for herself, and admits to her error in having worked to earn money. Contrite, she stays on Torvald's terms, and resolves to mend her wilful ways.[14]

On their return from Norway, Tussy returned to lecturing, wage labour and political activism. She now experienced the patriarchal sexism within some sectors of the socialist movement that punished women who spoke up too loudly. Our Mother was becoming too powerful a public figure. She needed to be cut down to size. Eleanor's first realisation that she was being targeted specifically as a woman was when she was excluded from the Trades Union Congress of 1890.

By 1890, the Union of Gas Workers and General Labourers had a hundred branches around the UK and a paid-up membership of 60,000. The union sent nine delegates to the congress, from Bristol, Dublin, Leeds, Manchester, Birkenhead and Uxbridge. Eleanor was one of the three delegates elected by the membership to represent London. To her surprise, the national executive committee – of which she was a member – informed her that she would not be admitted as a delegate. She was even more shocked at the reason for the rejection. Her mandate, 'conferred upon me by the representatives of the whole union – is rejected on the grounds that I am not a working woman!'[15]

Clementina Black and Lady Emilia Dilke, the writer, art historian feminist and trade unionist, were both admitted to the TUC. 'Miss Black, who has never done a day's manual labour is admitted. I am boycotted!'[16] Clementina, a friend, confirmed to Tussy that she had not been asked to be a delegate, especially as 'I do not at the present time hold any position that would entitle me to have done so.' In fact, she reported, she and Lady Dilke were merely 'allowed by the special kindness of the president and vice-president to sit in a vacant place at one of the delegate's tables'.[17] This was exactly the evidence Tussy needed. 'Now, to begin with, I am a working woman – I work a typewriter; and secondly it is surely preposterous for anyone except the Congress itself to declare who shall sit and who shall not.'[18]

Will Thorne and other delegates brought the matter before congress on her behalf, without success. Tussy was stuck in a press seat, as reporter for four different international newspapers. Presumably being a journalist for four different publications in three languages didn't make her a working woman either.[19]

Due to Eleanor, the gas workers were so far the only union to have two women's branches. With her leadership on the national executive committee, the entire gas workers' union – not just the women's chapters – supported the demand for equal pay for women workers doing the same work as men. The intervention by officials to overrule the representational rules of Congress and ignore the gas workers' union mandate was an attempt to sabotage the challenge that equal pay for women brought to the predominantly skilled, worker-based, male-dominated TUC.

Eleanor went after them publicly. She pointed out that the same stonewalling of democratically mandated women delegates had been tried on Edith Simcox and Annie Besant at the 1888 International TUC. Simcox and Besant were president and secretary respectively of the Matchmaker's Union. The 'old unionists' were for keeping them out, but in that case were outvoted by new unionists Will Thorne, John Burns and – significantly – 'foreigners' from European unions. In the absence of universal male and female suffrage, the TUC was the labour parliament and the principle was one of labour representation:

> Passing over the fact that I am a worker, the important points are: – (1) That according to the standing orders any legal member of a trade union duly elected is eligible, this condition I fulfilled, having been elected not even (as most delegates) by a small Executive, but by a conference representing the whole Union. (2) A Union of men and women has the right to decide by whom it shall be represented, a principle recognized in Parliamentary representation.[20]

Denied her elected place amongst the delegates, Eleanor angrily joined the press corps, where Cunninghame Graham watched her, observing that she was thoughtful, shortsighted, eloquent of speech and pen.

The following year the executive of the French Workers' Party invited Eleanor and Cunninghame Graham to attend their Lille congress in October. Eleanor was the only recognised delegate from a foreign country and the only woman officially listed. On arrival she was bounced into an unanticipated event:

... think of my horror, General, when huge placards on the Lille walls calling for a meeting with a large white slip pasted across stared me in the face with the following announcement, 'Sous la présidence de Eleanor Marx-Aveling'! I felt mightily inclined to clear out – but couldn't very well, and the meeting went off all right under my 'présidence'.[21]

Her 'présidence' was, however short-lived. From Lille she took the overnight train to Halle in Germany to attend the German Social Democratic Congress. She got lumbered with three French delegates who, though charming, expected her – because she was the only woman – to look after them. She wrote to the General, 'If I ever travel in "foreign parts" with one [Frenchman] – let alone three – again, may I be damned. I would rather travel with two babies in arms and half a dozen others. They couldn't be more helpless and they wouldn't be nearly so troublesome.'[22] They nearly cried, she told the General, when they didn't get their meals soon enough.

In November Tussy was called to Lenchen's deathbed. Helen Demuth, her 'second mother', died aged seventy, from untreatable cancer, on 4 November 1890. Freddy Demuth was now motherless and, as far as Tussy knew, in the painful position of having a still-living father who, unaccountably, refused to openly acknowledge him or his grandson Harry.

No one pressed Lenchen for final confirmation of Freddy's paternity on her deathbed. Lenchen commanded a stoical silence that they dared not breach. It was obvious she would reveal nothing that might compromise the General whilst he was still alive. Yet here was a contradiction at the heart of her family that spoke directly to Eleanor's thinking on 'the woman question'. Engels was a freedom-loving libertarian who'd written more cogently than anyone she knew – including her own father – on bourgeois sexual hypocrisy. His refusal to acknowledge his paternity of Freddy seemed unfathomable.

The accounts for the Bloomsbury Socialist Society and Central Committee for the Eight-Hour Day show that Lenchen continually donated money to these campaigns and the May Day demonstrations. She remained a socialist until the end of her life.

Following Möhme's instructions, Lenchen was buried with Karl and Jenny in their Highgate grave, in which little Jean Longuet also rested. Whatever the genuine bonds of love, trust and mutual respect between this extraordinary triumvirate, there was always a hierarchy in the triangle: Karl at the pinnacle, served by Jenny and Lenchen, who also served Jenny. As Tussy observed, if a wife can love devotedly a husband who subordinates and constrains her, so too can a servant love a mistress or master who does the same.

Helen Demuth was history's housekeeper and, as Tussy knew, keeper of its secrets. She just didn't understand why Freddy's paternity had to be a secret.

I Am a Jewess

To everyone's alarm, Lenchen's death threw the usually unflappable General into a panic. The management of Regent's Park Road imploded. In an essay painting a portrait of 'Frederick Engels at Home' Aveling had described Lenchen as becoming for Engels what she'd been to Marx, 'his housekeeper and . . . his trusted counsellor and advisor, not only in the matters of daily life, but even in politics'.[1]

The General instinctively sought out a replacement.

Several years previously, Engels had met and taken a great shine to Louise Kautsky when she visited London with her then-husband Karl. Shortly afterwards, at an alpine conference, Karl met a young Fräulein with whom he fell instantly in lust. With considerable dignity and maturity, Louise set him free to marry her. The couple had since divorced. Confusingly, the second Mrs Kautsky was also called Luise; and the first Mrs Kautsky decided to retain her married name.

Louise started studying midwifery in Vienna. She maintained her involvement in the German Social Democratic Party independently of her ex-husband. Disregarding her studies, the General took up his pen and beseeched her to come and take care of a 'helpless' old man, rather than waste her energies on learning to bring new young ones into the world. Louise promptly accepted and arrived to take over the running of Regent's Park Road.

The 'redoubtable' Pumps, as Tussy called her, took great umbrage at the arrival of this Viennese interloper. Terrified of being 'Pumped', the General hid behind Tussy's skirts and told Pumps that Louise had come to take over the management of his household at *Tussy's* invitation, not his. Tussy was much amused by this, as well as by the vexed diplomacy of the 'head of the table question' at Regent's Park Road.[2] She was quick to empathise with Louise's predicament in what she dubbed the 'Pumpsiad' – a domestic drama of epic proportions:

> I am sorry for Louise. Bebel and all the others have told her it is her <u>duty</u> to the party to stop [with Engels]. It hardly seems fair to her. She was getting on so well at Vienna, and to sacrifice her whole career is no trivial matter – no one would ask a <u>man</u> to do that. She is still so young – only just thirty. It seems not right to shut her up, and keep her from every chance of a fuller and happier life. And you know what her life here will be.[3]

But Tussy's ready empathy with Louise Kautsky made her an easy mark. Louise's fortuitous availability at the General's hour of need was far from the convenient coincidence it appeared to be. August Bebel, Paul Singer and Victor Adler, all founders and leaders of the German Social Democratic Party, had put Louise up to making a play for Engels's attentions. The German party was anxious about the future of Marx's manuscripts and intellectual estate (known as the *Nachlass*). Unbeknown to Tussy and Engels, Louise had a specific mission. It was public knowledge that Marx had bequeathed exclusive rights to his intellectual property to Eleanor and Laura, to be held in trust by Engels for the duration of his lifetime. Bebel, Singer and Adler hoped to contravene Marx's wishes and to influence Engels to get him to divert all the Marxian manuscripts and correspondence to the German SPD. To this end, they persuaded Louise to ingratiate herself with Engels and get him to change his will in favour of the German party.

All three men came to London for Engels's seventieth birthday celebrations and were pleased to see that Louise was settling in and had won the trust of both Engels and Eleanor. As Bebel noted conspiratorially to Adler, 'Louise herself must know what she has to do.'[4] Louise embedded herself at the heart of the General's life and succeeded in insinuating herself into Tussy and Edward's lives as well.

Tussy should have paid heed to Pumps's forthright hostility to Louise. Pumps insisted that Louise's sole purpose was to displace her, Eleanor and Laura from Engels's affections and thus his will. Tussy, however, sensed no conspiracy, and was just pleased to see him happy and productive. 'The General is wonderfully well,' she wrote to Laura:

> Louise has him splendidly in hand. Pumpsia's nose is hopelessly (at present) out of joint . . . – It is good news . . . that the General is working at Volume III [of *Capital*] and that a very good portion of it will be sent off to Meissner immediately after Christmas – it would not be safe to send during the holiday traffic.[5]

Karl Kautsky tried repeatedly to alert them but his warnings sounded too much like the wounded griping of an ex-husband because Tussy and the General had taken Louise's part over their divorce.

Anyway, Tussy was too busy working to reflect on the details of what was happening at home.

Between 1890 and 1893 she was in perpetual motion. Activist life was full of mundane daily tasks like any other. Eleanor's speeches, campaigning, arbitration meetings, articles, reports, breaking of bread and beer after congress sessions required determination and great stamina. In the summer of 1891 she wrote to her sister from London, 'I go to Brussels for the Gas Workers – and I must come back here from the Congress. I see no possibility of a holiday this year! Holidays and I seem to have parted company.'[6]

Instead of a holiday, Tussy returned to London for more speaking, lecturing, union work and to what she called the 'Gillesiade' – Edward's inflamed tangle with the tricky journalist Ferdinand Gilles. Gilles had recently joined the SDF and become one of Hyndman's lackeys. At Hyndman's instruction, Gilles briefed against Aveling at the Brussels congress, spreading gossip about him amongst the delegates. That the stories were probably true made Aveling all the more indignant.

On their return to London Edward, accompanied by the oh-so-loyal Louise, went to Gilles's home in Islington and doorstepped him. The ensuing row resulted in Aveling punching Gilles in the head and the police being summoned. Aveling was fined forty shillings for assault. August Bebel, who despised Gilles, remarked to Eleanor that twenty shillings per box on the ear was temptingly cheap. The squabble continued in the pages of the *Workman's Times* and *Vorwärts*. Eleanor was keen to respond to Gilles's printed attacks but rightly cautious of British libel law: 'one never knows where one may be landed in a libel case, and every word of what we may say would be, in a sense, libellous.'[7] Louise's apparent partisanship during this dispute, and many others, strengthened her credibility as an ally.

Eleanor did notice that Louise started to fuss and bustle about the General's various ailments and what she characterised as the failing health of an old man. Tussy scoffed. Louise's solicitude about poor old Engels, who certainly was not poor and never acted old, initially amused Tussy, who believed the seasoned rogue was just toying with the gullible Louise: 'the dear old General is as jolly as a sandboy (what a sandboy is, or why he should be jolly I don't know) and seems to get younger and younger.'[8]

Edward's health, however, began to deteriorate. His illnesses were now manifestly real. 'Edward is far from well,' Eleanor anxiously told her sister. 'He is stopping with a friend in Brighton. He has had a very bad – and indeed still has, a very bad throat – quinsy.'[9]

Politics commanded Eleanor's full attention. The counter-attack on new unionism by employers and vested capitalist interests was strengthened by the economic recession of the early 1890s. By both principle and as the means to consolidate the momentum for a new independent labour party, Eleanor and Edward – when his health allowed – focused on forming international alliances. Their object was to forge transnational solidarity between worker movements in Europe and its colonies. Trade, finance, industry and capital organised itself internationally; so too, therefore, must opposition to it.

Eleanor's work became increasingly international. In her report to the delegates of the 1891 Brussels congress, she updated members on the financial support sent by Nottingham lace workers to their striking co-workers at Calais, by Austrian to English brick-makers, and by English glass-blowers to flint-glass workers in Lyons.[10] Eleanor acted as intermediary, setting up the processes for delivering these strike funds and ensuring their proper distribution. It was this money that provided subsistence – food, heat, shelter – for workers and their families so that they could undertake and survive industrial action.

In 1892 Eleanor served as both secretary and translator at the fourth congress of the International Glass Workers' Union. The following year she supported the sixteen-week lockout by Yorkshire and Lancashire glass workers, rapidly firing off volleys of correspondence to her sister, the French media and the Lyons glass workers:

> This fight means a life and death struggle here of the whole Glass Working industry. It is bound to last for months. What the end will be the Lord knows – and as Edward always says, the Lord is *so* incommunicative.[11]

Glass workers from Germany, France and Denmark subscribed to the strike fund from their own wages, and kept subsistence flowing to the Yorkshire and Lancashire workers so they could continue their action. They succeeded in forcing a capitulation from their employers in April 1892.

At the third International Miners' Congress in London in July 1892 Eleanor worked as secretary and translator by day and by night wrote full-length political and economic analyses for both the English and German press. She typed up her own reports in both languages.

Engels recorded in detail Eleanor's critical role in arbitrating in a potentially disastrous political dispute between German and Scottish coalminers. No mean feat. It was her intervention, Engels told August Bebel, which set the matter right. Tussy seemed indefatigable. Her own record was far more perfunctory: 'I left (I had to see some German miners) on the Thursday evening at 9:15; reached Cumnock about 9am; was hard at work all day, caught the 9:15 at Cumnock on the Friday evening and was back in London, considerably the worse for wear, at 8 on Saturday morning.'[12]

Congress suceeded congress. Tussy translated, interpreted, and kept verbatim reports, which she then copied from her own short-hand with 'the machine' – her much-loved typewriter. Though always in the midst of the fray, a refrain of solitude emerges during the years of the early 1890s – 'though I am always busy I am also very lonely'.[13] She was particularly upset in 1891 when her widowed brother-in-law Charles Longuet set up home in Caen with a new partner, a decorous eight years after Jennychen's death. Disappointed that her nephews would now never come to live with her as she'd hoped, Tussy was vicious about their new stepmother Marie, nastily dismissing Longuet's new arrangement as 'unspeakably disgusting'.[14]

At the gas workers' annual congress of June 1892, held in Plymouth, Eleanor described how the gas workers upheld the prin-ciple of fighting for economic justice through direct political engagement and participation. This may sound like highfalutin and idealist language, but in the contemporary context it was just the new language of practical action by workers for workers. The Plymouth congress unanimously resolved to put forward candi-dates for all municipal and parliamentary elections from all their district organisations and branches. A landmark vote: this was an explicit strategy to stand candidates for election in opposition to the old established parties.

Keir Hardie, now leader of the Scottish Labour Party founded in 1888, and unionist John Burns were selected as candidates for the 1892 general election. Eleanor campaigned for both of them. Burns, founder of the Battersea Labour League, was returned for Battersea with a thumping majority of 1,500 and Keir Hardie elected to represent South West Ham. Burns had form delivering impressive results in his work in the London County Council and was, like Tussy, a consistent supporter of unskilled labour. The gas workers' union, with Eleanor the driving force, ran Hardie's successful campaign. In a think piece for *Neue Zeit* Eleanor and Edward wrote that Burns and Hardie were the first Members of Parliament in Britain to be elected specifically 'on the ground of a definitely proletarian programme that will keep them distinct and separated from the two bourgeois parties'.[15] They were disappointed, however, that Robert Cunninghame Graham, the first socialist MP in the UK parliament and founder of the Scottish Labour Party, lost his Glasgow seat to a Liberal-Unionist. Eleanor quite understood Liberal complaints about the new Labour candidates splitting their votes. 'We consider it essential to knock the Liberal shadow-boxers out of the field, and so we split the Liberal Party . . . Let them feel our fangs.'[16]

Edward was wooed to stand as a candidate. Henry Hyde Champion, 'of all people!' Tussy exclaimed, 'wrote and offered to get Edward all the money necessary if he cared to "run" anywhere!!!'[17] Aveling had no desire whatsoever to run for office and said, very properly, that should he ever for a moment contemplate standing, he could of course only accept campaign money from a committee of his constituents.

After the 1892 TUC in Glasgow Keir Hardie chaired a meeting of delegates who supported the founding of an independent labour party to lead Britain towards industrial democracy. This historically decisive gathering mapped the journey to the formation of the new party early the following year.

Three days before Eleanor's thirty-eighth birthday, in 1893, the national conference to form the Independent Labour Party convened in Bradford. Shortly before this Eleanor delivered a speech on 'Socialism, at home and abroad'. She was critical of the old-style English trade unionist views of politics that still dominated the incumbent TUC leadership. Despite the clear fact that recent victories in industrial action had depended upon fraternal financial support from international workers in Europe and Australia, the TUC leadership displayed strongly nationalistic tendencies and propounded anti-European policies and rhetoric. A storm gathered between the old nationalist guard and supporters of the new international. And Eleanor, of course, was internationalism incarnate.

She spoke, wrote and campaigned hard to persuade all constituencies that the new labour party should embrace internationalist principles. But the TUC vanguard persisted in pursuing a foolhardy attempt to take control of the leadership of the international working-class movement. Ben Tillett's fulsome attack on the 'Continental Socialists' succinctly expressed the character of parochial cultural nationalism that hounded the thinking of old unionism at the time. 'English trade unionism', Tillett proposed pompously, is 'the best sort of Socialism and Labourism'. Tillett was glad to say, reported the *Workman's Times*:

> That if there were fifty such red revolutionary parties as there was in Germany, he would sooner have the solid, progressive, matter-of-fact, fighting trade unionism of England than all the hare-brained chatterers and magpies of Continental revolutionaries.[18]

To Eleanor this chauvinism was idiotic. Writing to her friend Anna Kuliscioff, the Italian revolutionary, she described the official TUC anti-internationalist stance as 'not only an imbecility, but a malice'.[19]

Eleanor educated and informed members and supporters of the new Independent Labour Party (ILP) about the bigger picture of international socialist solidarity. 'The English,' she wrote, 'are profoundly ignorant of all foreign movements.'[20] In a series for the *Workman's Times* on the 'International Working-Class Movement' she wrote articles about the Italian Workers' Party, the German general elections, and summaries of socialist political speeches delivered in European parliaments, including one by her recently elected brother-in-law Paul Lafargue in France.

After the Bradford TUC summit in January 1893 Eleanor and Edward toured the Black Country, including Dudley and Wolverhampton. It was here that Eleanor spent her thirty-eighth birthday. She sent her customary New Year letter to her old friend Dollie Radford, to whom she confessed her melancholy about the apathy and indifference of ground-down, exhausted, grossly impoverished workers. Their search for solace in religion depressed her even further:

> The Black Country is *too* horrible . . . They talk of 'Christian faith'. I don't know how anyone with only *Christian* faith can bear to see all this misery and not go mad. If I had not faith in Man and *this* life I could not bear to live.[21]

The newly formed ILP fought its first parliamentary seat at the Halifax by-election in February 1893. Edward assisted candidate

John Lister with his campaign. Lister was defeated, due to Protestant workers who voted against him on the grounds of his Catholicism.

Eleanor despaired of this mixing-up of religious sectarianism with politics. She shared her anxieties with the General about the close alliance between the ILP and the Christian churches. That Protestant Christianity should enjoy a dominant position in modern British socialism alarmed her, as it did all British workers and leaders who were not Christian.

On 22 January 1893 Eleanor gave two lectures in Aberdeen. William Diack, secretary of the Aberdeen Socialist Society where she spoke, recorded the day in enthusiastic detail. Diack describes how at the end of her second lecture:

> a Communist critic . . . ventured to take Mrs Aveling to task, and endeavoured to explain to her what Karl Marx really meant by Social Democracy. Eleanor Marx listened patiently to the luridly red exposition, then, rising from her seat, she said in tones of caustic solemnity, 'Heaven save Karl Marx from his friends!'[22]

If Karl Marx could observe her from beyond the grave, he might have asked if the heaven he didn't believe in might also save him from his radical daughter.

The most fundamental difference between Eleanor and her father was in their attitudes to their Jewishness:

> I am the only one of my family who felt drawn to Jewish people, and particularly to those who are socialistically inclined. My happiest moments are when I am in the East End amidst Jewish workpeople.[23]

Russian philosopher and sociologist Peter Lavrov, an old friend of her father's, got Tussy involved with 'Jewish workpeople'. A Russian Jew based in Paris, Lavrov was a Communard and self-professed secular Jewish Marxist whose followers in England established the International Working Men's Club (IWMC) in 1885 at 40 Berner Street, off Commercial Road in London's East End.

The 'Berner-Streeters' formed the IWMC out of frustration with the religious and cultural segregation in their own communities. Secular, radical and unorthodox, they opposed ghettoisation and challenged the veneration of class and financial success that set rich against poor Jews. The IWMC ran evening adult education classes in Yiddish for working-class Jews to learn English and study politics, economics and literature. Many of their members were garment and textile workers, seamstresses and tailors sub-contracted by the high-end bespoke gentlemen's and ladies' outfitters in Bond Street and Savile Row – 'the rag trade': from the rags of the East End to the riches of the West.

At the end of 1889 IWMC requested Eleanor to teach evening classes and speak at public meetings. She started studying Yiddish and began to teach and make speeches in it – haltingly at first, gradually gaining fluency. She read as many of the new Yiddish papers as she could, including *Fraye Velt* (*Free World*) and various Polish, German and Italian immigrant journals.

Tussy discussed learning Yiddish with the Russian critic and translator Zinaida Afanasievna Vengerova, who was in London to study English.[24] They shared an interest in philology, transition periods in language and folk dialects. Vengerova recalled Eleanor's focus on examining the relationship between Yiddish dialects and European languages. Tussy talked about picking up languages in the same way rich, leisured women might talk about acquiring hats. 'My latest linguistic acquisition is Yiddish,' she said. 'I deliver lectures in Yiddish and easily distort German grammar so that my audience should understand me better.'[25]

Vengerova was surprised that 'the language of the Jewish ghetto' still existed in 'enlightened England',[26] but Tussy informed her that many of the impoverished immigrants from Eastern Europe who fled to England from the tsarist Russian pogroms of 1881 had no opportunity to learn English. Targets of anti-Semitism and general hostility, thousands converged around Whitechapel, Mile End Road and Stepney Green, consolidating into self-contained communities in order to survive. The situation of these new refugees was aggravated by the rivalry between the millionaire oligarchs of Anglo-Jewry who fought for patronage and influence over them.

Roughly, these divided between the proponents of an adaptive form of anglicised Judaism led by the United Synagogue, endorsed by the chief rabbi and sponsored by the banker Lord Rothschild, and, distinguishing itself from this reformist approach, the Federation of Synagogues,[27] sponsored by bullion broker Samuel Montagu, which promoted adherence to a more strictly Talmudic approach familiar to those who had lately escaped brutal discrimination in Russia and Eastern Europe. However intense the schism over how the faith should be practised, religious leaders and patrons of both approaches were united in their opposition to apostasy.

Eleanor also gave personal reasons for learning Yiddish: 'the Jewish language is akin to my blood . . . In our family it is thought that I am like my paternal grandmother, who was the daughter of a learned Rabbi.'[28] Vengerova wrote:

One somehow felt from these words that Eleanor Marx set greater store on the heritage of the spiritual life of her forefathers, the Jewish Rabbis, than on the pure class arrogance of the aristocratic family to which her mother belonged.[29]

Vengerova's class chauvinism extended to racist typology. She found Eleanor 'rather plain though attractive', presenting 'intelligent, somewhat masculine features, with a big nose of the Jewish type'.[30] Tussy would retort with one of her favourite jokes: that unfortunately she had only inherited her father's nose and not his genius.[31] But Vengerova's comments illustrate that Tussy shared the common experience of anti-Semitism.

Many Jewish-based worker unions formed in the East End from the 1880s. Resistance from established capitalist Anglo-Jewry and religious leaders reinforced opposition to secular free thought at home within family, community and synagogue. At work, Jews found that some gentiles refused to labour alongside them, giving rise to the necessity to form their own unions. Jewish worker unions included the Hebrew Cabinet Makers' Society; Stick and Cane Dressers' Union; International Furriers' Society; Tailor-Machinists' Union; Tailors' and Pressers' Union; Amalgamated Lasters' Society; United Capmakers' Society; and International Journeyman

Boot-Finishers' Society.[32] In December 1889, all of these were amalgamated into the Federation of East London Labour Unions.

As reported by *Commonweal* in January 1890,[33] these unions congregated at a mass meeting of Jewish workers at the Great Assembly Hall to vote on inaugurating this Federation of East London Labour Unions. Jewish workers turned for support to existing British trade unions and the socialist movement – the Fabians, the SDF and the Socialist League. The Fabians and the SDF shunned them equally but for different reasons; the Socialist League welcomed alliance, but primarily through factions with shared anarchist tendencies.

By the following year, 1891, the anarchists, in militant mood, had taken over the Berner Street Club and pushed out its Jewish Marxist founders. The original Berner-Streeters, including Eleanor, recongregated around their new paper, *Fraye Velt*.

In October 1890 Eleanor accepted an invitation to speak at the Great Assembly Hall to this new federation of Jewish unions, with a clear assertion of her father's ancestry:

> Dear Comrade
> I shall be very glad to speak at the meeting of November 1st, the more glad, that my father was a Jew.[34]

Eleanor was invited to speak to Jewish unions in Leeds and Bradford, which drew her attention to the latent cultural and religious nationalism within the Independent Labour Party. She saw the evidence of anti-Semitic attitudes within the ranks of the ILP and the TUC. Eleanor consistently identified herself as a Jew at public meetings. A story about a memorable incident at the Leeds Hall Institute is unsubstantiated, but indicative. Eleanor was invited to speak, but on arrival was prevented. She began to speak from where she was standing, shouting out, 'I am a Jewess!'[35] Many years later Eduard Bernstein described Eleanor as 'nearly Zionistic', but there's no evidence to support this view. Certainly, the tenets of early socialist Zionism that promoted the interests of the collective above the individual spoke to Eleanor's beliefs. But her internationalism and economic philosophy made all forms of ethnic nationalism wholly unacceptable in her world-view. Berstein's questionable conflation of Tussy's ardent cultural Jewishness with proto-Zionism reveals his own tendencies, not hers.[36]

Simultaneously, the Second International also revealed its refusal to deal with anti-Semitism. Despite the large membership of Jewish socialists in the Second International, the Brussels congress of the International in 1891 carelessly dismissed anti-Semitism, in the words of its official report, as originating 'from the hatred of the Christian capitalist against the Jewish capitalist, cleverer than him'.[37] This was an opinion Eleanor initially seemed to share. Writing about the Dreyfus affair in *Justice* in November 1897, she reductively attributed the motivation for the controversy to 'a Christian jealousy of superior Jewish money making'.[38] But as her experience developed, so did her thinking.

During the early 1890s Eleanor became aware of the anti-Semitism experienced by socialist Jews within the international labour movement. East End journalist, poet and radical leader Ben Vinchevsky, born Benzion Novochovits, had been exiled from Germany in 1879 under the Anti-Socialist Law. In 1884 he launched the first socialist journal in Yiddish published in London, *Die Tsukunft* – The Future.[39] When Eleanor met him he was publishing *Arbeter Fraint* (Worker's Friend) from Berner Street.

Eleanor and Vinchevsky travelled together on the train to Zurich for the International congress in 1893. Vinchevsky told Eleanor that many socialists were unaware of the existence of Jewish workers, 'that is, a Jew engaged in manual labour, let alone organised Jewish workers'.[40] The congress was inaugurated with a bright pageant that took over the streets of Zurich. As delegates lined up in the procession, Tussy saw Vinchevksy hanging back on the pavement, uncertain of where he should take a place in the ranks. 'Eleanor ran up to me in great haste. She placed me next to herself with Will Thorne on one side and Edward on the other. "We Jews must stick together," she said.'[41]

One of about a dozen Jewish delegates at the congress, Vinchevsky soon encountered difficulty in getting himself tabled to speak. Repeatedly blocked at the daily speaker allocations, he presented his dilemma to Tussy. She told him to write down the names of his unions and their membership numbers, 'and as translator I will somehow smuggle this into the Congress.' When the congress session reconvened an hour later, she announced in German, French and English that real Jewish workers organised in eight unions had their representative present, and he should be allowed to speak.[42] According to Vinchevsky's account, this information was greeted by the congress with 'tumultuous applause', and 'Eleanor's face was radiant with pride.'[43]

The marginalisation of Jewish unions was confirmed two years later in 1895 when the TUC passed a resolution calling on the British government to control the immigration of 'alien workers'. In response, ten Jewish unions called for thousands to attend a mass meeting at the Great Assembly Hall, to protest against the xenophobic anti-internationalism taking hold of the TUC executive at national level. Eleanor spoke, alongside other leaders, including Stepniak and Kropotkin:

> Jews! The English anti-Semites have come to the point where the English workers' organisation calls on the government to close England's doors to the poor alien, that is, in the main, to the Jew. You must no longer keep silent.

Tussy's personal friendships also influenced her. Olive Schreiner, Israel Zangwill and Amy Levy were all Jewish, and writers. Tussy had known Israel since Dogberry days, and they had co-written *A Doll's House Repaired*. Their mutual friend, Clementina Black, introduced Eleanor to Amy in the mid-1880s; in turn, Eleanor introduced Amy to Olive.

Amy was born in London in 1861. Her father, Lewis, was a stockbroker and believed in educating women. Amy shone intellectually and became one of the first women, and one of the first Jews, to attend Cambridge University, where she published her first volume of poetry, *Xantippe and Other Verse*. Jews had only been admitted for the first time to Cambridge in 1872, a mere seven years before Amy took her place at Newnham. She left college early to pursue her literary career but not before becoming the first Jewish woman to pass the Higher Local Examination in 1881. She wrote regularly for the *Jewish Chronicle* and other magazines, and was part of the group of Bloomsbury women intellectuals who congregated in and around the British Museum.

In 1888, Macmillan published Amy's new novel *Reuben Sachs*. Eleanor was commissioned by Amy to translate the book into German. The German edition appeared in 1889 and shortly afterwards Amy, aged twenty-eight, committed suicide. Tussy said that Amy was always frail, very often depressed and inclined to hopeless melancholy, 'an infallible symptom of nervous exhaustion'.[44] The novel, Tussy said, had used the last of Amy's reserves and left her 'a disembodied spirit'.[45]

Levy wasn't a socialist but she was a trenchant critic of social and religious life, materialist obsessions with status and class and what she saw as the moral turpitude and patriarchal constraints of her own well-heeled Anglo-Jewish background. These are the themes of *Reuben Sachs*, a novel that fascinated Eleanor as much as *Madame Bovary*. The Reuben Sachses satirised by Amy Levy were of the aspirant materialist type prodded by Marx in his controversial essay 'On the Jewish Question', written in 1843.

Tussy's writing shows that she empathised with Emma Bovary's plight, but did not identify with her. Conversely, she identified strongly with Amy Levy's portrait of the complexity of being a British Jewish woman in *Reuben Sachs*. Emma Bovary fascinated her because she was Tussy's petit bourgeois, resolutely gentile antithesis; on the other hand Judith Quixano, the anti-heroine of *Reuben Sachs*, was a figure much closer to home: a woman whose struggles Tussy shared across class differences. Because Gustave Flaubert is better remembered in the literary canon than Amy Levy, so too is Eleanor's translation of *Madame Bovary*. Yet *Reuben Sachs* is a novel, and Judith Quixano a character, much closer to Eleanor's life.

Marx said, 'Tussy *is* me.' Flaubert said, 'Madame Bovary, c'est moi.' But Eleanor never made these identifications. She did, however, state that, like Judith Quixano, 'I *am* a Jewess,' a statement she made in response to the Dreyfus affair.

When Emile Zola published his well-known indictment of the miscarriage of justice experienced by Dreyfus, Eleanor wrote to Nathalie Liebknecht expressing her disgust at the silence of the French left in supporting Dreyfus. Witness the fact that 'the one clear, honest note has been struck not by one of our party, but by

Zola! ... What *does* it matter if Dreyfus is "sympathique" or not? The only question is: was he even according to accepted standards *fairly tried?*[46] She suspected French socialists of being motivated by anti-Semitism. This is a significant development from her previous position of blaming anti-Semitism on Christian capitalists. Disregarding political differences, she wrote again for *Justice*, according 'honour to whom honour is due – even if we do not find these persons "sympathetic". And so all honour to Clemenceau, and above all to Zola.'[47]

What would Marx make of all this? Eleanor remarked that in later life her father hardly ever spoke about religion, 'neither for nor against'.[48] Marx never denied his Jewish origins – he just didn't regard them as of particular interest. He was famously critical of the tyranny of all religions but he was sympathetic to the spiritual impulse.[49] As he put it in his essay 'Towards a Critique of Hegel's Philosophy of Right' (1844): 'Religious suffering is at one and the same time the expression of real suffering and a protest against real suffering. Religion is the sigh of the oppressed creature, the heart of a heartless world and the soul of soulless conditions. It is the opium of the people.' Religion was not Eleanor's chosen opiate. She preferred to stick to her chain-smoking. Resolute secularist and atheist, for Eleanor the human spirit embodied and encompassed in earthbound form all that she took to be the essence of life. People were answerable and accountable to each other, not an absent, unseen arbiter – including her own dead father.

'Oh! for a Balzac to paint it!'

At the end of 1892 Louise Kautsky introduced Engels and Eleanor to a young Viennese doctor she'd met whilst on holiday in Austria during the summer, who had just arrived in London. Dr Ludwig Freyberger was a fresh-faced, twenty-seven-year-old physician who had graduated with distinction from the University of Vienna, specialising in anatomical dissection, physiology and pathology.

Tussy paid scant heed to Louise's chatter about the marvellous ministrations of her new doctor. Whilst Louise flirted with Freyberger, she and Edward were marshalling a mass demonstration by unemployed workers that assembled on New Year's Day in Trafalgar Square and marched to St Paul's Cathedral. Recommending Freyberger's skills, Louise encouraged Engels to consult him. The only doctor the General trusted was his old friend Edward Gumpert, but he became gravely ill and died in April 1893, leaving the glum Engels to brood on the loss of two of his greatest friends within a year. The once-Jollymeier, Karl Schorlemmer, had died of lung cancer in Manchester the previous June, a sad event Eleanor described as 'a very great blow' to the General,[1] who spent much time at Jollymeier's bedside, though he was no longer recognised by him.

Whilst Freyberger's popularity grew at Regent's Park Road, Tussy and Edward moved to quieter lodgings at 7 Gray's Inn Square. This move coincided with three simultaneous anniversaries: the tenth anniversary of her father's death, the fourth birthday of the gas work-ers' union, and Laura and Paul's silver wedding anniversary, which they spent, as promised, in London. Engels, Tussy knew, was work-ing intensively on completing the third volume of *Capital* as a suitable commemoration to Marx.

Several months later Tussy noticed properly that Freyberger had become the General's indispensable personal physician and ubiqui-tous presence at Regent's Park Road. She wasn't much impressed; something about him drew her spitfire. 'I *can't* see how anyone can stand Freyberger,'[2] Tussy grumped to her sister. Engels, conversely, brimmed with enthusiasm for Freyberger's modern medical know-ledge and the 'splendid scientific career'[3] that doubtless lay before the young man, willingly writing the references that enabled his relo-cation to London.

Gumpert had been one of Engels's executors, so he had to redraw his will. On 29 July Frederick Lessner and Ludwig Freyberger witnessed this new testament. Engels appointed the barrister Samuel Moore, journalist Eduard Bernstein and Louise Kautsky as his exec-utors. He left generous bequests to Pumps and the election funds of the German Social Democratic Party. All the books in his posses-sion or control, including those originally belonging to Marx, were bequeathed to the German SPD, along with Engels's copyrights. His correspondence and manuscripts went to Bebel and Bernstein. All 'manuscripts of a literary nature in the handwriting of my deceased friend Karl Marx and all family letters written by or addressed to him shall be given by my executors to Eleanor.'[4] His house, furniture and effects, except where otherwise specified, were to go to Louise Kautsky, with a quarter of his residue estate. The remaining three-quarters were divided equally between Eleanor, Laura and Longuet's children.

Eleanor was not named as an executor or informed by Engels of provisions that determined the destiny of her father's literary estate. The General may have been trying to shield Tussy from the anxiety of being exposed to the pressures he was under from the leaders of the German SPD to bequeath the entire Marxian *Nachlass* to the party. Practically speaking, Marx's will left all his papers to Tussy, to be kept in trust by Engels until his decease. Under English law, Eleanor had rightful inheritance of her father's manuscripts and letters.

Eleanor didn't see the General until they were reunited in Zurich at the 1893 International Congress. She represented the British gas workers at the congress, translating, organising and chairing. She numbered one of five women amongst the sixty-five-strong British delegation, which also included her old friend May Morris who was there on behalf of the Hammersmith Socialist Society. There was a grand extended family reunion for Engels with Eleanor, Edward, the Liebknechts, Louise Kautsky, Freyberger, Bernstein, Adler and Karl Kautsky, who brought the second Luise.[5]

Eleanor's friend Anna Kulishov, who represented the Milan Working Girls' Union, chaired the closing session. The congress voted for its next assembly to be held in London in 1896, then Kulishov announced the surprise appearance of Friedrich Engels, 'the intellectual pioneer of International Social Democracy'.[6] From the front row, Tussy watched the General take the platform as the hall and public galleries rose to their feet and greeted him with tumultuous and continued applause. Standing underneath the giant portrait of her father, painted by Margaret Greulich, bordered by red flags, Engels thanked the congress for their 'unexpectedly magnificent welcome', [7]

> which I receive with deep emotion. I accept not in my personal capacity but as the collaborator of the great man whose portrait you have here. It is just 50 years ago that Marx and I came into the movement . . . From the small sects of that time, Socialism has since developed into a powerful Party making the officials of the whole world tremble. Marx has died, but were he still alive there would be no one in Europe and America who could look back upon his life's work with such justifiable pride.[8]

What were Tussy's thoughts as the General continued in this grandly rhetorical vein? She was generally sceptical of the presentation of her father as an ideologue. The end of the General's speech was met with cheering, an ovation and a rousing rendition of the Marseillaise. For the excellence of her English, French and German translation Eleanor was presented with a gold watch by the British delegation. Whatever her thoughts on the lionisation of her father by Engels, no one knew this would be his last public address in mainland Europe.

Johnny Longuet came to stay for September – now 'a great laughing lad of 17!'[9] – entertaining her with his natty views on Clemenceau and reading aloud to her from all the French newspapers he went out to buy daily. Tussy loved her eldest nephew's visits and never felt lonely when Johnny was staying. His departure, combined with a depressing defeat at a suffragette meeting in November, lowered Tussy's mood. Asked to speak at this meeting in St James's Hall, Eleanor eloquently seconded an amendment to enfranchise all adult women, regardless of class or education. The motion was resoundingly defeated. Tussy left feeling weary and frustrated at once again encountering the opposition from the socially elite factions of the suffragette movement to the enfranchisement of their working-class, activist suffragette sisters.

The long shadows of the melancholy to which she'd been intermittently prey since her twenties cast a deeper darkness on the shortening winter days in November. Edward's frequent absence exacerbated Eleanor's depression. His only constant source of income was from coaching, a now fashionable occupation, and from writing introductory science textbooks, a form for which he had a true talent. Edward's introductions to natural philosophy, mechanics and experimental science, botany and geology were solidly successful, and gave him plenty of happy hours dallying with his young student researchers in the Reading Room at the British Museum. Eleanor felt Edward's disappointments as her own, and tried to compensate by indulging his spendthrift, pleasure-loving predispositions, however lonely – and broke – they left her. Her friend Max Beer was driven to distraction by Eleanor's unshakeable loyalty to Aveling:

He was a fine speaker, an impressive elocutionist, and a man of considerable scientific attainments, but struck with moral blindness, utterly failing to perceive the difference between right and wrong. How she could go on living with this man for over fourteen years is a riddle which puzzled us all.[10]

Beer, like so many of her friends, wanted to visit and spend more time with Tussy, who extended many invitations, 'but my unconquerable dislike of Dr Aveling made me decline it'.[11]

By the end of the year, Tussy wished she could run away to Laura for Christmas and make the festivities a real holiday. But she hadn't the cash and felt unwell. 'I'm fearfully dull and stupid, and I would not write except that I hope by doing so to get a line from you,' she confesses to her sister. 'I've been very seedy the last few days. Indeed, I feel so thoroughly ill without being ill – if you can understand that bull, that I fancy I must be enjoying a little bout of influenza.'[12]

Tussy signs off her pre-Christmas letter to her sister remarking that Edward is 'out supping with some theatrical friends . . . as it is nearly 1 and my fire is out, I shall say goodnight.'[13] She's long given up waiting for him to come home. It's a dismal image of unwanted aloneness in a vital, naturally gregarious spirit, but Tussy's dynamism and spark was precisely the problem. Aveling knew very well that if Tussy joined him supping with theatrical friends, she would light up and fill the room – all attention would be on her and deflected from him.

Early in 1894 Tussy headed off to Lancashire to deliver an intense series of eight lectures in seven days to as many SDF branches. To her astonishment, she received a delightedly scandalised note from Edward reporting the sudden marriage of Louise Kautsky and Ludwig Freyberger. The wedding took place in secret, with Engels as witness, and the new Dr and Mrs Freyberger sent out cards notifying friends of their marriage after they returned from their fortnight's honeymoon spent in Eastbourne, Engels's favourite resort, at his expense. 'But it <u>does</u> seem queer to take the General a-Honeymooning with them,' Tussy wrote to Laura. 'You can imagine the delicacy of his jokes on such an occasion.'[14]

Tussy, like everyone else, was surprised at the abrupt manner of the marriage. 'It's all very well to say that all tastes are in nature. This taste seems to me a very abnormal one,'[15] she said to Laura, expressing a view identical to so many made by others about her own choice of Aveling. But Tussy knew something else: Louise had confided in her the previous year that she was having an ongoing affair with August Bebel.

Tussy received a self-justifiying missive from Louise, constructing an elaborate digressional tale about how she and Ludwig had, coincidentally and completely unexpectedly, decided to get married 'that Monday, you went to the North'. On and on the letter ran, Louise claiming that no one was more surprised by their unplanned marriage than herself and Ludwig – and that nothing at all had happened between them prior to this sudden event. She also said she'd told Ludwig about her clandestine relationship with Bebel. 'That dear girl is the simple story.'[16] Nothing simple in so convoluted a story.

'The whole affair has been "wrop in mistry",' said Tussy, admitting that she could with the benefit of hindsight now see the Freyberger match being a foregone conclusion.[17] Added to Louise's embarrassment that she knew the inconvenient truth about Bebel was also Tussy's characteristic frankness in telling Louise upfront that she thought Freyberger an opportunist and fraud:

> I fancy I've rather put my foot into it because I'm such a poor hand at pretending, & I never could pretend to admire the profound sagacity & wit of the new bridegroom. Well, on the whole I'm glad Louise is married. She was too young for the rather dreary life at the General's, & no doubt Karl [Kautsky] will be delighted.[18]

'Poor Louise', she felt, had dropped from the overused cliché of the frying pan into the fire. 'But then with us women it is generally a question of the frying pan or the fire & it is hard to say wh. is the worse. At the best our state is parlous.'[19]

The formerly revered Pumps was dethroned and Louise raised in her place as the new queen who could do no wrong in the General's view. This much was to be expected from inveterately glad-eyed Engels. Pragmatically, Tussy was anxious to know what the household arrangements were to be, 'for frankly it will be intolerable if Freyberger permanently installs himself at Regent's Park Road. It was unpleasant enough to constantly meet him there, but to know him always there!'[20]

Tussy returned home from her Lancashire tour to unwelcome confirmation of this disagreeable premonition. Now genuinely alarmed, she sat down and quickly scribbled to Laura 'the latest news from the ménage of Regent's Park Road':

> (Oh! for a Balzac to paint it!) . . . She [Louise] informed me that she – & he – were to remain with the General!!! . . . That Freyberger shd hold 'at homes' at the General's is certainly coming it strong . . . personally I confess that invitations to the General's from a man like Freyberger are a little queer, &, in my opinion, bode no good for the future . . . I question much if the Freyberger influence is likely to be a good one for the party. Anyone who has the slightest knowledge of human nature must know this gentleman is playing his own game alone.[21]

Engels attempted to make light of the matter by joking about this entirely matriarchal new marriage in which the husband had become his wife's boarder. He claimed initially to be delighted that the newlyweds had decided to remain under his roof. But Louise's all-too-soon evident pregnancy quickly caused the General great anxiety when he had to start making arrangements for them all to move into a bigger house on the other side of the street.

In August Engels and the Freebooters – as Eleanor now aptly called them – went to Eastbourne for a holiday, during which the General suffered a mild stroke. Eleanor's distrust of Ludwig now proved conclusive. 'I wd not trust a fly to his tender mercies,' she wrote to Laura. 'He is an adventurer pure and simple, & I am heartily sorry for Louise.'[22]

Tussy was now convinced that the security of all the papers and manuscripts at the General's was in jeopardy. The impending move from 122 to 41 Regent's Park Road, with Engels semi-invalided, made her suspicious that a deliberate plan was under way to steal the Marx cultural capital. 'Freyberger is quite capable of getting hold of anything he can & selling it!'[23] The Bernsteins visited London and, after observing the situation, confirmed they shared Eleanor's apprehensions. Sam Moore also seemed alarmed and doubtful, which made Tussy all the more anxious as she knew Moore to be one of the General's executors.

She was still unaware that Engels had revised his will the previous year, making Louise an executor, as witnessed by Dr Freebooter. The likelihood of Freyberger stealing and selling the manuscripts now obsessed her. Feeling vulnerable and exposed, she appealed to Laura and Paul to come to London and help her intercede with Engels:

> For you must remember Freyberger is simply an anti-Semite (tho' I wd wager my Jewish head that he's a Jew) & has nothing to do with the movement. It is no joking matter I can assure you, for you know very well that anyone living with the General can manipu- late him to any extent . . . Mohr's MSS etc are things we can't be too careful about.[24]

Sam Moore said he would try and discuss the matter with Engels, probably with the added intention of quietly urging him to inform Tussy about his revised will, in order to allay her fears and remind Engels of his legal obligations.

It took another adept pretender to unmask Louise. Aveling's present and future economic security depended upon Eleanor's inheritance. Edward found an unexpected opportunity to cause mischief for Louise when Tussy carelessly shared with him Louise's confidence about her affair with Bebel. Edward set to work spread- ing the news. Louise knew that Aveling was the source of this awkward gossip. Knowing Tussy responsible for this betrayal of feminine confidence, she wrote her a furious letter challenging her with a breach of faith in their friendship.

'All this *klatsch* (gossip) showed me that I have to step in,'[25] Louise whined. Tussy was not fooled by all this hand-wringing. She began to suspect that the intimate web of relationships between all the play- ers might indicate that Louise, in league with Bebel and Freyberger, had ulterior motives to divert possession of the *Nachlass* for the German party, and their own ends.

The breakpoint came later in 1894, when Louise clumsily tried to persuade Eleanor to sign a document that made her, the new Mrs Freebooter, responsible owner of all the papers and manuscripts for fear, Louise claimed, that Pumps should get hold of them. This was a step too far. Pumps had no shortage of flaws and failings but Tussy knew she was not a thief, nor had she ever attempted to supplant the Marx sisters in the General's affections.

Tussy's fury at Louise's deception was implacable. She now saw that she'd been duped. She pleaded with her sister and Paul to come to London and intercede with the General. The game was up. 'Pumps *is* got rid of,' she wrote to Laura in a tone of shocked disbelief, '& it is a positive pain to go to the General's. When he sees me alone – which is only for a moment, he seems glad enough – & then when the two others appear, he becomes like them, & in all but words I am told de trop. '[26] No longer maintaining any pretence of alliance with Tussy, the Freebooters set about sticking their combined boots in everywhere they could. She was made to feel unwelcome at 41 Regent's Park Road, and Louise and Ludwig hovered at her elbow, refusing to leave her alone with the General when she visited. Her sense that the now vulnerable Engels was being bullied by his erstwhile protégé turtle doves seemed accurate.

The General had a miserable winter, hinting in his correspondence with Laura at the mistakes he'd made. He wanted to celebrate his approaching seventy-fourth birthday in peace but the coal cellar was flooded, the condensation in the wine cellar threatening to ruin his best vintages, the kitchen renovation still incomplete, and most of his books still packed in crates, slowing down his work. There was no point in turning to Louise for assistance, as she'd just given birth to a daughter. For once, Engels expressed no enthusiasm about the arrival of a new baby. Instead, he locked himself in his new study, trying to sort out his library, although 'more than once I felt inclined to throw all my books into the fire, and house and all, such a bother it was.'[27] Dr Freebooter screwed his brass nameplate on the front door and a nursemaid and two further additional servants were employed to look after the Freybergers, not Engels. The takeover was complete.

Tussy needed Laura's solidarity: 'Alone I can do nothing. Together we might do something.'[28] The poor General, she told Laura, has come to the condition where he is a mere child in the hands of this 'monstrous pair'. 'If you knew all the wire-pulling of the F.s you wd understand':

If you don't want to see the F's as *sole literary* executors you must act, & that promptly. You will remember that Bebel wrote the papers wd be in the right hands. I think you & I shd know *whose* hands. If outsiders know we shd, for when all is said & done this is *our* business & no one else's. The papers – especially all the private papers – are our concern; they belong to us – not even to Engels.[29]

Laura failed to respond to this and subsequent, increasingly frantic, appeals from her sister. This was a terrible time for Tussy. Estranged from the General, unsupported by Laura, furious at herself for finding Louise credible, she didn't know how best to act alone, or who to turn to. Edward was no use. Having lobbed in the incendiary about Louise's affair with Bebel, he ducked to the Scilly Isles for seven weeks, with the plausible justification that he needed to convalesce from another bout of kidney disease. Fortunately his need to recuperate was not so acute that it prevented him from researching and writing a series of travel articles for *Clarion* about the pleasures of the islands, accompanied by his new holiday amour, a fair-haired, blue-eyed girl who he'd chatted up on the boat. 'I had seen her the day before in the Penzance Post-office, and invented a telegram that I might stick a stamp on her hands and touch her. She was as easy and frank as she was beautiful.'[30]

Meanwhile, Eleanor held the frontline in the escalating war with the Freebooters and looked forward to Edward coming home from playing at Alec Nelson, 'for I am rather lonely – in spite of my many four-footed friends'.[31] Could they speak, her four-footed friends might have suggested she was better off sticking to their company. Freddy and his son Harry Demuth alleviated Tussy's loneliness. Tussy and Freddy spent more and more time together, chatting and eating together by each other's firesides in Holborn and Hackney and taking the twelve-year-old Harry out for long rambles. As Freddy was a shop steward, socialist and active unionist, they had much in common politically. Both had chosen their partners poorly. Father and son lived alone together in Hackney, as they had done since Harry's mother had absconded overnight two years previously, leaving Freddy to raise his son as a single parent, which he did very successfully. Freddy's wife had not only stolen his heart when she ran away but most of his possessions and a £29 cash benefit fund trusted to his keeping by his fellow workmen. Out of consideration for Tussy, and perhaps sensing the potential danger in Edward, Freddy was ever courteous towards him. Harry recalled, 'Eleanor was always very nice, but I didn't like Aveling . . . He was very educated and that, but he wasn't nice.'[32]

Freddy had a 'rough childhood',[33] leaving the home of his foster parents the Lewises as soon as he was of legal age. He had no further communication with them but he never lost touch with his mother Lenchen. Hard-working, self-reliant, interested in everything, Freddy was a resolute autodidact. 'He hadn't much schooling,' Harry reported, 'but he taught himself everything. Wonderful what he knew.'[34] Harry recalled the two of them of an evening sitting either side of the table with an oil lamp, reading to each other: 'Shakespeare it was – and I helped him with his pronunciation. He couldn't pronounce all the words as well as I could.'[35]

In this period in 1894, when Tussy's relations with the General were strained for the first time in their shared lives, she must have felt more acutely the frightening chill of being outside his life-warming circle of sunshine. Children, she knew, invariably pay for their parents' mistakes. Yet Engels of all people did not believe that mistakes were irreparable. So why – again that question for Tussy – did Engels, otherwise so often on the side of the angels, behave like a tetchy demon towards his only son, whom he refused to acknowledge?

Eleanor never hesitated to jump in to try and bridge Freddy's parental gap. When his wife stole the union fund in 1892 and abandoned her son, Eleanor had persuaded Laura, Lafargue and Longuet to discreetly accept financial responsibility for Freddy. Without asking the General for money, they put together as much as they could to help him repay the stolen cash. More than ever before, Eleanor felt it was a 'bad business' that Freddy couldn't count on the support of his father when her family had been financially supported by him their whole lives. It was the one aspect of the General's behaviour she could not square. She wrote to Laura, 'It may be that I am very sentimental',

– but I can't help feeling that Freddy has had great injustice all through his life. Is it not wonderful when you come to look things squarely in the face, how rarely we seem to practise all the fine things we preach – to others?[36]

The estrangement between Tussy and the General was resolved when his health deteriorated towards the end of the year. Engels sensed he was now mortally ill. He confided in Eleanor and Louise, swearing them to secrecy. Tussy kept her counsel. Louise trotted off immediately and spilled the bad news to Victor Adler, thus giving the German SPD notice to gather its vultures. The future of the Marx papers and manuscripts was now, as far as Eleanor knew, definitively at risk. Neither Engels nor Tussy imagined his death to be imminent but it was clearly possible that he might become incapacitated, vulnerable to losing control of exercising power over his wishes, as he had over his household. Edward, returned from his sojourn as Alec Nelson, rejoined the fray, adding a dramatic postscript to one of Tussy's pleading letters to Laura:

> Dear Laura, Come, *come*, COME. You have no idea of the imme-diate importance of it. The General is in this mood. He will brook no interference from <u>any</u> but you two women, whose right to demand account of your father's papers he must admit. You have to make that demand and declare point-blank your reason, that you do not trust the Fs. Believe me, this is the only way to save the M.S.[37]

But all were mistaken. Confronted by the final fact of his mortality, Engels acted swiftly to take additional measures to secure the papers and manuscripts in accordance with Marx's wishes and his own good conscience. During November he drew up a series of signed docu-ments supplementary and explanatory to his will. He added a supplementary clause that had a significant bearing on Tussy:

> All papers in Karl Marx's handwriting except his letters to me and all letters addressed to him except those written by me to him are to be restored to Eleanor Marx-Aveling as the legal representative of Karl Marx's heirs.[38]

This was unambiguous. Engels secured these supplementary documents in a drawer of his writing desk, along with a letter for Tussy and Laura to be given to them after his death, written in his own hand.

The aspect of the General's will that was to have the most impact on Tussy and Marxist literary history was his decision to separate his own manuscripts from everything in Marx's handwriting. Everything in Marx's hand went to Eleanor and stayed with her in England. If she died, the papers went to Laura in France. Engels's own manuscripts went to the leaders of the German party, Bebel and Bernstein. Critically, the correspondence between Marx and Engels went to the German SPD. This division of the *Nachlass* would make it impossible for Tussy to compile her father's letters for publication. This was a difficult position in which to place Eleanor as Marx's official literary executor.

Eleanor misjudged Engels over the Freebooters fiasco. He was hurt by her lack of confidence in him but there's sufficient evidence to demonstrate that he also recognised his own lack of judgement in indulging Louise and Ludwig so unguardedly. Engels may also have felt that he was protecting Tussy from further exploitation by her own adventurer. Publicly, the General remained benign about Aveling but he was no fool – Tussy might love where she would, but Engels had the measure of Edward. Well might the General think that Tussy had better look to the hoodwinking going on in her own home before investing all her energies in what was going on in his.

'Poor Edward', who had gone to St Mary's to convalesce, returned sick and exhausted from his excesses. 'When I looked I found he had an enormous abscess – twice the size of my fist! I at once sent for the doctor.'[39] If only Eleanor had removed her rose-tinted pince-nez when inspecting Edward, she would have seen that his enormous abscess was a moral turpitude that might have been far more efficiently treated by two punches with her fist rather than calling the doctor.

It was unfair to suggest, as she did, that the General had been convinced that 'like Pumps, I am only speculating on him, and am only jealous of Louise being in his house, etc.'[40]

The great denouement of the Marxes v Freebooters came over Christmas, as many of the best family crises do. Edward played a helpful role in precipitating the drama. Tussy suggested to Laura that she write to her and suggest that she was prepared to volunteer to help her copy out the manuscripts for Volume IV of *Capital*, which Tussy had recently discovered were not as far progressed as she had thought. Further, she would like to know clearly about the status of the future of Mohr's papers and their treatment in the case of Engels's death. Tussy would show this letter to Engels, providing her with an opening to engage him directly on the matter. Engels would trust and accept Laura's assistance where he was rejecting offers from others he knew he couldn't rely on to undertake the work effectively, like Eduard Bernstein. Bernstein was of the opinion that the Marx sisters were the proper persons to undertake the transcription. So, Tussy suggested to Laura, 'You cd offer to fetch the MSS you wd copy, & Bonnier, who so often goes across cd take them back. We cd both work at it, & so, at least establish some claim.'[41]

Laura agreed to the plan and wrote to the General. Four days before Christmas, Tussy went to Salford to give three lectures to SDF branch members on the questionably seasonable subjects of 'The International Socialist Movement', 'Socialism, Scientific and Otherwise' and 'Women and the Socialist Movement'. Hardly easy-going fare for the holidays – but it was precisely because it was the holidays that workers were able to get the time off to attend intense lecture programmes.

On her way to the station Tussy called in on the General, and found him entirely alone, left to 'shift for himself'.[42] Tussy had had enough. 'C'est la guerre,' she announced to Laura. Well, the General understood war. It was time to have it out. The Freebooters were as their names suggested. 'In a word, my dear, it's war, and we've got to fight.'[43]

Laura's letter arrived after Tussy left for Manchester. Edward, visiting Regent's Park Road for lunch, delivered it on her behalf and so witnessed the drama it precipitated. Engels read Laura's letter aloud, in the presence of the Freebooters. He immediately agreed that Eleanor and, if she needed assistance, Laura, should transcribe the manuscript for the fourth volume of *Capital*. Then, quietly and in a very dignified manner, he confirmed that 'of course Marx's MS & the papers were held in safe charge for his daughters and could have no other destination.'[44] There was no question about this: it was clear and definite. Thus far, all appeared calm. Aveling withdrew for his post-prandial nap – and pretended to be asleep.

During his 'nap' he heard raised voices coming from the General's rooms upstairs, followed by Louise rushing downstairs on gushing rapids of tears and heaving sobs. Engels followed and shook Edward, probably telling him to stop pretending to be a sleeping dog. Engels, enraged, said there was a conspiracy – in fact there had been endless conspiracies since he took the new house. Laura had been put up to writing the letter and Eleanor, of all people, should know better than to mistrust him. Aveling's war bulletin to the Lafargues described the General's most military manner, marching up and down, spluttering, and revealing a yeasty conscience. But the truth of it was that Engels was truly hurt. It was painfully obvious that the letter was a fit-up and the bitter truth hit Engels hard: if Tussy didn't trust him any more he had let down the people he most loved and failed in his duty of care to his best friend's daughters.

Tussy knew the General was struck and her heart went out to him. But the incendiary letter had achieved her aim; it opened a direct line of communication:

> It seems impossible you cd *really* believe Laura and I mistrust you. Whom on earth cd we trust but you? . . . I shall say no more now, except that if you had not been very much poisoned against us you cd never have thought so meanly of Mohr's children as to think they cd mistrust <u>you</u>.[45]

Letters flew between Engels, Laura and Tussy. Tussy presented herself four-square at Regent's Park Road for what turned out to be a 'Bad Christmas Day' for the Freybergers. Tussy and the General agreed they would talk together, alone, before the festivities began. 'As an appetiser for the festive meal,' she described to Laura, 'the General took me off to his "droring-room" & we proceeded to our first round.' He expressed his anger at Tussy's want of tact in setting up Laura's letter but had nothing to gainsay the accuracy of its contents.

> After a certain amount of sparring – during wh. I told him he had not been angry until others had made him so . . . we came to the point: the MSS. He said these were ours & wd, of course, come to us. I said if I had his assurance of that I was quite satisfied & knew you wd. be.[46]

Tussy then told the General for the first time that Louise was pestering her and Laura to sign a legal document she'd had drawn up making Louise the responsible owner of the papers, and that her stated reason for doing this was because she feared Pumps intended to steal them. Engels was clearly shaken by this and Louise – when confronted – was unable to deny the truth of it.

A few days later the General went to Tussy's for lunch. It was the first time he'd visited Gray's Inn Road since she'd moved in and he came on his own. They went over the same ground again, in detail, and had what Tussy described as their 'final round' in the dispute. Eleanor said everything she had to say about the Freybergers and her and Laura's concern about Mohr's papers and manuscripts. Engels was conciliatory and yet still didn't tell Tussy about the legal arrangements. Wisely, she took him on trust. 'He again said he <u>wd see</u> all papers of Mohr came to us, but said nothing of his will. Of course I said I was quite satisfied & that for the rest, I shd say nothing more about it.'[47]

The upshot of these two parleys was that Engels guaranteed to make sure about the fate of the papers and, with some bravado, declared his hope that two 'such "famose Frauenzimmer" as Louise & I – tho' I am not so "noble" as she is – must agree. Well, we – i.e. the noble one & I, will no doubt have a stormy interview – & then all will be peace – on the surface!'[48] And that is exactly what happened.

Tussy spent her fortieth birthday in January 1895 grateful that the 'ghastly festivities'[49] were over. Engels was also greatly relieved. 'Tussy and I had an explanation, which, as far as I know,' he assured

Laura, 'settled everything connected with the subject and left us as good friends as before.'[50] Resolution of this dispute was all the birthday present she needed.

In March Eleanor and Edward went to Hastings for a holiday – to improve Edward's health. He worked on *Clarion*, which he now edited, and Tussy looked after him and saw to her correspondence for the gas workers' union. She wrote to Library, asking him to agree to Will Thorne's request that he speak to the gas workers in West Ham, and reporting that a few hours of fresh air every day were doing Edward some good, 'Still, he is not very strong yet.'[51] When was he ever, around Tussy?

Whatever their birthday wishes, Tussy's friends must have hoped that the now forty-year-old powerhouse who'd successfully taken on pretenders to her father's legacy and inheritance might also reward her adult self by breaking from her tired relationship with the ever-needy, manipulative Aveling. On the anniversary of their father's death, Tussy wrote to Library from their guesthouse, looking out over the pebbled beachfront and roiling March sea at Hastings, 'Today it is twelve years since Mohr died – and I think I miss him and my mother and Jenny more to-day even than when we lost them.'[52]

Whilst she and Edward were in Hastings, Engels was diagnosed with throat cancer. Freyberger didn't tell him the exact pathology; if the General suspected, he didn't let on. But at the end of the month he composed a long codicil to his will, witnessed by the house cook and his live-in nurse. This codicil made substantive changes to his previous will. Overall, it shifted the bequest of the bulk of his capital wealth and assets to Louise.

But the General's material wealth was not Tussy's interest or concern. Significantly, Engels revoked all his previous directions about the Marx family letters. Excepting only the letters between himself and Marx, all letters written by or addressed to Karl Marx were to be given by his executors to Eleanor, 'the legal representative of Karl Marx's heirs'.[53] This revision made Eleanor sole heir to her father's manuscripts and all letters written by or to Marx, except between him and the General. The cash legacies for the Marx daughters and family were sufficient to make them financially secure for the rest of their lives but this probably mattered more to Engels than it did to Eleanor. In the great struggle over Engels's legacy, Tussy's inheritance was as secure as he could make it.

Had she known, Louise would have been delighted at the fortune she stood to inherit. But this boon of inherited material wealth would stand as nothing compared with the weight of responsibility placed on Tussy as guardian of so rich a portfolio of cultural capital. As Engels no doubt anticipated, worrying that the pressures on Eleanor as keeper of the Marxian *Nachlass* and her father's voluminous correspondence would be immense.

By May the pain and swelling in Engels's neck was intolerable. He needed an operation, followed by recuperation at the seaside. He asked Tussy if she and Edward would join him there for a week or so and told her that he'd also written to Laura and Paul inviting them to come and see him. For once, the Lafargues promptly agreed to come to England. As matters transpired, the trip to Eastbourne didn't happen until the end of June.

Tussy and the General shared eggnog and oysters and discussed Edward's nomination as a parliamentary candidate by the Independent Labour Party. The nomination came from the Glasgow Central branch of the ILP. Engels asked Tussy for all the papers and information and read them assiduously. He advised Edward to refuse the nomination as he surmised, correctly, that it was a political trap. They joked about the General's new addiction to anaesthetics and he tried, fruitlessly, to broker a final peace deal between Tussy and Louise.

He teased her about her Russian friend George Plekhanov's request to translate his monograph on *Anarchism and Socialism* from German into English. The General roared with laughter at the news – 'There indeed I do pity you,' he teased. 'Where is the poor girl to have picked up the necessary knowledge for such work?'[54] Tussy knew the subject almost by heredity and wished she didn't. It was a gag only the two of them could have shared. Tussy liked Russians and abhorred anarchists. Like Plekhanov, she was sensitive to the rising popularity of anarchist tendencies and critical of their promotion of terrorism and desire to 'make the whole world a playground for reaction and international spydom'.[55]

Immediately after returning to the city from Eastbourne, Eleanor packed up Gray's Inn Square and moved herself and Edward to Orpington in Kent. Their tenancy at Green Street Green started on 1 July and Tussy eagerly anticipated the novelty of an English country summer. She invited family and friends to visit, including Freddy and Harry, who she was sure would enjoy the opportunity of a great outdoors holiday.

Tussy had spent much of the year so far optimistic of a rapprochement between Engels and his alienated son. Her hopes were founded on the unprecedented fact that Freddy had been invited to Engels's seventy-fourth birthday celebrations at the end of the previous year. Freddy and Harry's appearance at the General's birthday party had attracted much attention from the other guests, foregathered from all over the world. Tussy stood by Freddy's side throughout the party. Those who subsequently dared to try and draw her into discussion of the meaning of Freddy Demuth's presence at the General's festivities were stared down. Eleanor's implacable silence – all the more noticeable from a usually voluble individual – was fearsome. There was no shame in the General's secret for Tussy – but it was not hers to tell. Removing herself from the wearying gossip of the London hothouse was another of the many pleasures Tussy felt in those first few weeks at Green Street Green.

Expecting her sister, or Freddy and Harry, to visit soon, Tussy was astonished to find herself greeting Sam Moore as her first visitor through the picket gate of her country cottage. A few days previously she had received an anxious letter from him, scribbled in haste from Lincoln's Inn on 21 July. In it he told her that the General had arranged to return to London with his two doctors: 'His state is precarious . . . He may go on for some weeks if pneumonia does not intervene, but if it does then it will be a question of a few hours . . . so that if you want to see him you had better go to 41 R.P. R. on Thursday.'[56]

When Sam turned up unexpectedly at Green Street Green to see her at a few hours' notice, Tussy wondered if he had come to tell her personally that the General was dead. But the news Sam brought was entirely unexpected. Tussy was thunderstruck. The time from Sam's arrival, the cups of tea, whisky and long, long conversation folded in on itself, compressed into a dazing flash. In that moment of shock, the axis of Tussy's world lurched to an angle so sickening that she couldn't regain her balance or bearings. She tried to make sense of the story Sam was telling her. It couldn't, just couldn't be true.

Mohr was Freddy's father. Not Engels.

Tussy's immediate and total psychological resistance to this revelation was a measure of the blow. Her denial was swift and easy: the cause of the revelation was Louise Freyberger. Lies, more lies. It had to be. Tussy seized on their enmity to dismiss the news as more Freebooting calumny against the Marx family. Sam took her hand, and gently, with reluctance, handed her the statement he had witnessed, signed in his presence by Engels.

Sam explained how Louise, encouraged by Bebel, her husband and others, challenged Engels to reveal the truth about Freddy's parenthood. Inveigling was always her mode. Why should Engels die with his name besmirched by the accusation that he had abandoned a son to foster parents and given him none of the opportunities his great wealth could buy? Surely Freddy deserved to have the truth known about him and to take his rightful place as one of Marx's children – his only son. Louise assured Engels she had only his and Freddy's best interests at heart. But her intentions were irrelevant. Amongst Engels's last thoughts was the knowledge that Louise had outmanoeuvred him and would reveal the secret. The story was out and he had to respond.

Aveling, standing behind Eleanor's chair, looked on with interest.

Eleanor went immediately to London and straight to the General's bedside. The story was a gross lie and she would hear Engels say so himself. But it was too late. By the time she arrived the General could no longer speak. His throat swollen, in agonising pain, Engels answered Tussy's question by writing on a slate, with great effort, in the affirmative. Both beyond the power of speech, they stared at each other, mute with grief and tears. All Engels could do was confirm the truth. He couldn't tell her anything more.

This was Tussy's last meeting with the General – her second father and only remaining parent. She left in shock and returned to Kent. The next day Engels became unconscious. Two nights later, on the evening of 5 August, he died. To Louise's credit she wrote immediately to Tussy that night, telling her that she had left his room briefly, 'was not away for 5 minutes, and when I came back, all was over.'[57] But all was very far from over.

Tussy and Edward joined the mourners at the Waterloo Necropolis on the morning of Saturday 10 August. Following the General's instruction, his funeral was private and attended only by personal friends, 'or such political representatives as were also his personal friends'.[58] Eleanor wrote many of the eighty or so invitations. Amongst the short speeches, Aveling and Lafargue gave tributes. Eleanor and Laura did not give eulogies. Nor did Freddy Demuth, who stood with Tussy, Johnny Longuet and the Lafargues as the hearse steam train bearing Engels's simple coffin pulled out of Waterloo's platform number 1. This single track owned by the London and South Western Railway ran to the single destination of Brookwood Cemetery and the Woking Crematorium, where Engels was cremated.

No one knows what passed between Tussy, Freddy and Laura that day or in the weeks following. If Louise Freyberger hadn't forced the situation, Engels might well have taken the secret of Freddy's paternity to his grave. Some said he wanted to clear his name of the imputation that he had abandoned the son he fathered with Helen Demuth in their youthful Soho heydays. Others believed that he was angry with Marx for saddling him with the lie. Both claims are persuasive but entirely misjudge Engels's lifework and his love for Marx and all his family. If Jenny, Karl and Helen had kept the secret, so could he. Engels never deviated from his dedication to Marx, in life or death, or from his belief that true greatness belonged to Marx alone.

He was completely wrong of course. Without Friedrich Engels, there would have been no Karl Marx, and vice versa. This was the true intellectual and economic dialectic, as Marx well knew. Looked at from this perspective, both were father to the ideas of Marxism. Besides the magnitude of sharing this creation, what was the difficulty with exchanging responsibility for the awkward paternity of a son? Men who were great friends did it all the time. The fatal error made by both benign patriarchs was to imagine that their concealment of Freddy's true paternity would protect their daughters – Eleanor, Laura and Jenny.

Simultaneously, Tussy lost both Engels and her idealisation of her father. It was the fact of not knowing, not the deed, that stunned her. If Freddy's paternity had not been kept a secret, it would just have been a part of who her father Karl Marx was. Instead, Tussy was confronted by one of the tattiest clichés in the misunderstanding of morality: the truth brushed under the carpet.

On the morning of 27 August Tussy, Bernstein, Lessner and Aveling boarded the train to Eastbourne with the urn containing Engels's ashes. They hired a rowing boat and pilot and, in accordance with the General's wishes, rowed some miles out to sea from Beachy Head and released his ashes to the wind and the waves.

Tussy stepped ashore to a life where the past now seemed another country. She'd lost two fathers and gained a half-brother.

22

The Den

In answer to the request that she write an obituary of Engels for the French journal *Devenir Social*, Eleanor swiftly revised the memoir she'd written for his seventieth birthday and sent it off. In consultation with Laura, she made arrangements with Engels's lawyer, Arthur Wilson Crosse, to work through innumerable matters of financial administration that were pending after the probate of the General's will was granted on 28 August.

After Engels died, Eleanor and Laura issued a public call for Marx's correspondence. They adopted the public letter form used by the sons of Darwin and Ernest Jones, which Tussy said was 'the best for England'. She sent the letter to all the British papers and to the Press Association. It was published in almost every country in the world, in many languages:

> May we appeal through your columns to all those who may have any correspondence of Karl Marx? We are anxious to get as complete a collection of our father's letters as possible with a view to publication. Any letters or documents that may be sent will, of course, be taken the utmost care of, and if the senders wish it, returned as soon as they have been copied. We should carry out any instruction that the possessors and senders of the letters might give us as to the omission of any passage they might desire not to have published.[1]

Eleanor then steamed up to Burnley for a few days to honour a longstanding engagement to give three lectures. Tussy spent much time
meeting, speaking and lecturing around Lancashire in 1895 and the
years following. Lancashire was a heartland of progressive union
organisation, a reaction to what Germans called 'Manchesterismus'
– the free-trade orthodoxy of Victorian Britain.[2] Manchester was
also known as Cottonopolis, reflecting the dominance of the cotton
textile industry in Lancashire. In Yorkshire, wool production dominated, but the county also had more collieries. Male workers
predominated in coal mining, women and children in the textile
industry. Consequently, Lancashire had a proportionately higher
number of women and children in the workforce than Yorkshire.
The Lancashire women textile workers were radical and organised
and as a result Tussy was in demand in the county.

Tussy's reputation now rode ahead of her. She wrote to William
Diack teasing him about his admission that he'd been nervous about
meeting her: 'You said you were afraid of me. I didn't know I had
such a formidable reputation . . . ([James] Leatham said he expected
an "intellectual iceberg", and seemed relieved to find I wasn't an
iceberg, or intellectual.)'[3] She imprinted on Diack with the intensity
experienced by so many others who met her: 'I can see again in my
mind's eye her slightly Jewish cast of features, and her fine dark eyes
glowing with the enthusiasm of perfervid faith.'[4] Her lectures, he
said, were 'as sound in the "fundamentals" as the Rocks of Rubislaw
themselves'.[5]

The Burnley lecture series was followed soon after by a week-long
speaking tour around Scotland, accompanied by Aveling, where they
addressed SDF and ILP branches in Edinburgh, Dundee, Glasgow,
Blantyre and Greenock. 'Edinburgh is assuredly, with the possible
exception of Prague, the most beautiful town I have seen (the *ville
lumière* included).'[6] The day of their return Tussy sent off a hasty
note in shortform to Louise:

> What h u d abt the bk cases etc. Are they with u? Or h u, as WA
> suggested transferred Ø to country? In former case I'll get Ø
> moved at once; v. latter, let me know & wht 2 pay & who 2=Cr
> or who.[7]

Her urgent mail to Louise about the bookcases was just one of hundreds of disputatious notes and letters flying between them since probate was granted on the General's will. Louise sent letters to Eleanor on matters so diverse as the inadequacy of her receipt for the handing-over of Marx's manuscripts, accusing her of failing to return the originals of letters she had been commissioned to type and, crucially, asking what she was to do about Eleanor's third of the General's wine collection? Should it be forwarded to the country, stored at the wine merchant's cellars or sold outright? Eleanor must pay for transporation and/or storage.

Six days later, Ludwig wrote to Tussy informing her that she would greatly oblige himself and his wife by removing immediately 'from our house . . . those articles which belong to you, viz. one armchair, three bookshelves, one bookcase, one newspaper shelf and seven framed photos and drawings'. If she couldn't do this at once, Ludwig went on, they would deposit the items listed in her name at the Regent's Park depository, at her expense.[8] The armchair in question was the one Mohr had died in that Engels inherited. Now it was hers. Tussy had no space for this stuff in the tiny cottage at Orpington. Grumbling to Laura that Dr Freebooter now proved himself the 'unmitigated cad' she'd always thought him to be, she told her, 'I'm having them stored until we find a house.'[9]

She'd been living there for barely two months but Green Street Green wasn't working. It is 'very pleasant', Tussy told Karl Kautsky, but Orpington was 'too far away from everyone and everything',[10] and the cottage damp and uninsulated. The rift with the Freebooters had drawn Eleanor and Kautsky back into their old intimacy and both welcomed the renewal of a friendship they had missed. She wanted to live closer to London, in 'some *convenient* suburb', but also daydreamed of building a commune of old friends. As she mused to Kautsky, 'I have a grand scheme for you and the Bernsteins & ourselves to . . . live near one another.'[11]

Tussy and Edward 'trudged mile upon mile'[12] house-hunting. 'We find that all the nice houses are either let or too dear and the "noble residences" we go to see are more often than not in some unspeakable slum.'[13] Spoken like a true aspirant petit bourgeois. Often when a small house seemed suitable it turned out to be cheap and nastily built, 'Or else a railway train ran through the garden'[14] – or it was practically inaccessible from London. 'Rents here,' she complained to Laura, 'are something fearful':

> If, however, we can find any really nice place, Crosse strongly advises *buying* instead of paying rent. Sometimes I feel like investing in a caravan (like Dr Gordon Stables) and living gipsy-like, anywhere.[15]

It's a relief to catch this flash of Tussy's nomadic gypsy disposition reasserting itself after all the snobby kvetching about nasty neighbourhoods and unspeakable slums. Dr Gordon Stables in his *Leaves from the Log of a Gentleman Gipsy: in Wayside Camp and Caravan*, published in 1891, recommended caravans as offering 'the most healthful and fascinating of all modes of travel'. Stables wrote on a range of subjects, including dog-breeding, and health and happiness for wives – Tussy's reference is an interesting insight into her browsing of popular books and magazines.

Arthur Wilson Crosse was the London lawyer who dealt with the probate of the General's will, in consequence of which Eleanor took him on as her legal adviser. It took Crosse to point out to Tussy that with her portion of the capital legacy bequeathed by Engels she could now afford to buy her own house. Laura had worked this out immediately and was already looking for houses to buy in the suburbs of Paris, suited to Lafargue's political profile and their desire for gardening and small-scale domestic farming. After death duties, distribution of bequests and all the other usual disbursements, Eleanor and Laura inherited approximately £7,645 each, a third of which they received on trust for Jenny's children. This left them with a phenomenal £5,000 apiece.[16] Everyone understood that the bulk of this legacy was to pay for Tussy and Laura's time to archive the *Nachlass*, publish their father's manuscripts and, in Tussy's case, manage all aspects of his literary estate. Engels expected that Aveling and Lafargue would also contribute to this endeavour, their intellectual labours financially supported by his legacy. It was more money than Tussy had ever commanded. Managed judiciously, it was an inheritance sufficient to form the basis of her – and

Edward's – financial security for the rest of their lives. As the General intended, it would enable Eleanor to give up her British Museum hack work and clear her desk for the full-time work of transcribing, ordering, editing and publishing her father's letters, papers and manuscripts.

No one understood the nature of capital better than Eleanor. She'd been weaned on its workings. Her father's Great Book on the subject had been the formative foundational scripture of her childhood, alongside the Shakespeare family bible. Her parents, radical Forty-Eighters shaking off the shackles of their social upbringing, had no truck with accumulating their own capital. Fortunately, they had Engels who was willing to get his hands dirty doing that for them. They spent everything that ever came to them and never saved or invested. Property ownership never occurred to them. But Tussy was English and fathered by Engels as much as Marx. She didn't go shopping for new clothes or shoes or handbags, or on extravagant spending sprees in new department stores buying the latest in furniture and interior design, eating at expensive, flashy restaurants and going on holidays and to European opera houses – all of which the Freebooters did conspicuously. Tussy looked for a house to buy, gave up her poorly paid freelance work and banked the rest until she had time to think and plan out its management properly. Edward, however, got what he asked for and, considering the money shared, she kept no account on him.

Alongside adjusting to the opportunity of private property ownership Tussy and Laura, much to their shared ironic amusement, had to make decisions about the selling of stocks and securities for the first time in their lives, in order to turn holdings into cash for the four Longuet children. Both Sam Moore and Crosse advised that liquidating to cash would be safer than transferring the holdings, as the Freybergers were raising objections and obstructing estimates of asset values on all of Engels's bequests. The Duke and Duchess Freebooter, as Tussy now called them, were on a spree.

Whilst savagely arguing with Hermann Engels over whether he would be permitted to keep £300 of his brother's money in Germany, the Duchess threw out all of the furniture Engels had bought them less than two years earlier for the new house and spent more than

£300 on new furniture. They are 'launching out in grand style', Tussy told her sister, and 'speak only with contempt' of the General and what they made him pay.[17]

The legal arguments and pettifogging over Engels's estate, of which Louise received the bulk as main beneficiary, was interminable. Moreover, although it was Louise who forced the issue of Freddy Demuth's true paternity, claiming she felt so sorry for him, she made no provision whatsoever or acts of simple generosity – emotional or material – to alleviate Freddy's exposure. As soon as Engels died, her apparently solicitous friendship for Freddy and Harry evaporated and they were never again invited to the house. Engels's close friends and comrades, like Bernstein, were dismissed in similar fashion.

Tussy shared financial responsibility for her Longuet nephews and niece with Laura but the administration of publishers' royalties, trust deeds and everything else related to Marx's literary remains fell to her. As the General had taught her (these habits certainly did not come from her father), Tussy executed all this paperwork and accounting with prompt efficiency. She also took the precaution of muscling her way into the new Fort Freebooter on Regent's Park Road and packing up Marx's papers in two large chests that she took immediately by cab to the safe depository in Chancery Lane. Here they were stored in a strongroom, locked with bespoke keys held only by Eleanor. The plan was that Laura would come over as soon as possible to start helping her sort and transcribe them.

Eleanor's lecturing and touring commitments for the rest of 1895 took her on another trip around Lancashire towns, as well as Aberdeen, Bristol, Crewe and Lincoln. She kept her journalism going whilst on the road. At the invitation of George Plekhanov and Vera Zasulich, Tussy had become the British correspondent for the liberal-leaning Russian journal *Russkoye Bogatstvo* – Russian Wealth. She thoroughly enjoyed contributing reports on Britain, covering political parties, social life and new trends in literature, arts and science. Her lively, concise and informative reportages included wide-ranging pieces on the Tories and the Liberal Unionists, the Factory Acts, unemployment, the May Day demonstration, current data on alcoholism, London poverty, the Oscar Wilde trial, and

Clementina Black's suffragette political novel *The Agitator*. She wrote also about the London County Council and the London School Boards and a mischievous piece on the lives and loves of her old sparring partner Annie Besant.

By early November, Laura had discovered and bought a house at auction. Situated at 20 Grande-Rue, Draveil (Seine-et-Oise), it was derelict and in need of massive renovation but boasted thirty rooms, outbuildings, an orange grove and a garden that stretched right into the fôret de Sénart. Tussy was still pounding the streets, finding 'all the *nice* houses are too dear, and all the cheap ones are shoddy in shoddy neighbourhoods.'[18] Just as she was feeling most glum about her fruitless house-hunting, she found her heart's desire. It was the address that caught her eye and made her trek to the suburbs of south-east London. She joked with Laura: 'the house we are about to buy . . . (Edward swears this is my only reason for buying it) is in JEWS Walk, Sydenham.'[19]

On 29 November Eleanor signed the purchase and paid £525. A fortnight later, on 14 December, she and Aveling moved in. On the borders of Lewisham, then West Kent, the house had a garden and good overground train and bus links into London. Yet despite its resolutely suburban location, there was something eerie and Romantic (with a capital R, as Tussy would say) about 7 Jew's Walk. Built in the 1870s in high Gothic Revival style, the semi-detatched double-storey house had a large front door with a stone arch and stained-glass panels comfortably in keeping with the architecture of the Castle of Otranto. Four stone gargoyles, winged like vampire bats, kept sentry on the parapet of the large bay window downstairs. Rose bushes in dire need of pruning and shaping straggled around the garden path like images from a fairy tale and unpruned trees cast shadows over the frontage.

Practical Tussy noticed nothing of these ominous aspects and Crosse thought it a bargain. 'It is big for us (but I *do* hate small rooms),' she wrote to Laura, 'and Paul will turn up his nose at our little garden, wh. however, will be quite big enough for us.'[20] And that is why the uncanny Gothic exterior signified nothing to Tussy. The small rooms that she hated were exactly what she'd been brought up in and lived in most of her life, always packing up, moving on, never able to put down roots or say, definitively, 'home'.

Discovering Freddy was her half-brother meant Mohr was not the father she'd thought him; nor were the relationships between her mother, Lenchen and Engels quite what they seemed. The General's forced revelation shook the foundations of her life. Building herself some security with bricks and mortar was a phlegmatic reaction. As if underlining the point, Tussy immediately named 7 Jew's Walk 'The Den'. Here she would nest, work from home in a study of her own and welcome old friends.

As a proportion, £525 was 10.5 per cent of Eleanor's inheritance from the General. Pound-for-pound historical conversions postulate absolute values and are wildly inaccurate, because they fail to account for the relative values of things and how those change over time; for example, the rise in cost of housing from the nineteenth to the twentieth century and the impact of new technology on individual and family budgets. Of course, Marx wrote about all this in *Capital*, so Tussy knew it well. Better than her father, in fact, since she lived it. Heritage conservationists might remark on the ugliness of her house but architectural aesthetics were of no interest to Tussy. She chose 7 Jew's Walk for the number and size of the rooms and for all the amazing modern technologies with which it was equipped, that made it affordable to run. Envisioning for the first time a family New Year in her own home, she wrote to the Lafargues inviting them for a holiday and took them on a virtual tour in anticipation of their visit:

> As to our house (I am Jewishly proud of my house in Jew's Walk), voilà. Ground floor: Large room (Edward's study and general room combined); dining room (opens on back garden), kitchen, scullery, pantry, coal and wine cellars, cupboards, large entrance hall. One flight of stairs (easy), bedroom, spare bedroom (*yours*), servant's room, bathroom (large enough to be another spare room on special occasions). My <u>study</u>!!! [Original is triple underlined.] Everywhere we have electric light – which is far cheaper, as we are near the (Crystal) Palace, than gas, though gas is laid in too, and I have a gas cooking stove and gas fires in most of the upper rooms.[21]

Laura, who had bought a grand *cache misère* that didn't boast any of the modern amenities of suburban Sydenham, praised her sister's choice: 'a *crystal* Den it must be, what with gas and electricity, that would make us villagers stare.'[22]

And, above all, Tussy had her own triple-underlined study. If she and Edward budgeted to live jointly on £90–£100 a year, they could bank on getting by to their dotage and the General's legacy could support Eleanor to devote herself to her political work, her writing and Marx's manuscripts. The General was subsidising her to do what she was best at – changing the world.

Eleanor ended the year with a thumping great public row with SDF activist Ernest Bax over sex and the woman question. Engels famously described Bax's 'womenphobia'[23] – Bax made a public case of his manic misogyny. Thus, when he passed public judgement on the personal life and behaviour of suffragette Edith Lanchester, he drew Eleanor's fire. Eleanor knew Edith and their lives were drawing closer together personally and politically during this period. On 16 November *Justice* published a public letter from Eleanor to Ernest Bax, challenging him to open debate on the woman question:

> DEAR COMRADE, – As JUSTICE, 'the Organ of the Social-Democracy', appears to adopt comrade Bax as the exponent of its views on the *sex* (*not* woman) question, and as the subject is certainly one worthy of consideration and debate, I desire, through your columns, to challenge my friend Bax to a public debate with me on the subject. The debate to take place in some hall in London before the end of the year, so that the proceeds of it . . . may be handed over to H. Quelch, hon. treasurer of the Zurich Committee (of the International Trades Union and Socialist Workers Congress, 1896). The debate to follow the usual lines, say 30 minutes on each side, and then two quarters of an hour for each speaker consecutively. Bax, as propounder of the general proposition, to open. Chairman to be mutually agreed upon. – Fraternally yours,
> Eleanor Marx Aveling.[24]

Bax responded, from his men-only gentlemen's club in Whitehall, that he was perfectly ready to undertake a debate on the woman question in writing but refused public debate, as he was 'too little *au fait* with oratorical tricks and platform claptrap to be able to success-fully defend the most simple and obvious propositions under the conditions proposed even if there were no shrieking crowd against which my voice would find it impossible to contend.'[25] Eleanor replied by reminding him that 'tricks' and 'claptrap' are not confined to the platform and that there are 'literary tricks and journalistic claptrap'. Then she hauled him in on his misogynistic characterisa-tion of women. 'With a fair and able chairman there would be no shrieking crowd; and you have no more right to assume that those holding the views I should attempt to put forward would "shriek" than I have to assume that your supporters would howl.'[26] She then took him to task on his wilful, liberal misunderstanding of what was at stake in the social revolution required to free women, and men, from capitalist patriarchy:

> I am, of course, as a Socialist, not a representative of 'Woman's Rights.' It is the Sex Question and its economic basis that I proposed to discuss with you. The so-called 'Woman's Rights' question (which appears to be the only one you understand) is a bourgeois idea. I proposed to deal with the Sex Question from the point of view of the working class and the class struggle.[27]

Bax replied by rubbishing Eleanor's 'dwelling on the class wrongs suffered by the working woman (in common with the working man) as though they were sex wrongs!' and once again refused her chal-lenge to public debate. He hoped her 'shrieking' supporters would enjoy 'the victory of aggressive womanhood over an absent antago-nist'.[28] Bax proved himself truly worthy of Engels and Eleanor's description of him as womanphobic.

Eleanor and Laura quietly made financial provision for Freddy and Harry from their inheritance. Crosse and Sam Moore knew that the sisters repaid in full loans Engels had made to Freddy from their portions of the estate. They knew nothing of these loans until after the General's death. Although Engels had written off these loans to Freddy, Louise insisted that the debts were owed. She calculated, correctly, how sensitive the Marx daughters and Freddy felt on this matter and knew they'd pay up rather than contest it.

Aveling and Lafargue knew about the financial arrangements Tussy and Laura made with Freddy but, aside from Crosse and Moore, no one else did. The significant capital value of Freddy's estate when he died in 1929 was far greater than he could have saved from his annual salary, suggesting that the Marx sisters did the one material thing they could to try and compensate Freddy a little for their mother and father's abandonment. But that remained a matter between the sisters and their new adult half-brother.

Aside from sharing their material gains, Tussy shared everything else she had with Freddy and, from the day she moved into the Den on 14 December, her home and heart were always open to him. What conversations took place between them about their now-shared father and the lifelong, unbroken friendship between their mothers, neither Tussy nor Freddy ever recorded.

To Tussy's disappointment, the Lafargues were unable to visit for the New Year because they were too busy renovating their dilapidated villa. The year 1895 ended with two unrelated events that added to its general strangeness and distinct sense of it being a fundamental turning point in Eleanor's life. First of all, she unexpectedly revealed, as if in passing, to the Lafargues and some of her intimate friends that Edward had for some time owned a share in a property in Austin Friars in the City. Eleanor told Laura and Paul it would be very unfair for them to think that she was paying for everything involved in setting up the Den. The value of Edward's share in 'the Austin Friars property,' she told Laura, 'has gone up so much that he has been able to get a very good mortgage (without of course, losing his rights in the property) on it and he is buying all the furniture that unluckily one can't do without.'[29] It was an extraordinary revelation to everyone that Edward owned a property and, moreover, had never before leveraged his interest in it in order to get him and Tussy decent lodgings or their own home. Baffled by this information, the Lafargues concluded that Edward had until now concealed his property interests from Eleanor and she was too shamed to admit it.

From this moment on, Laura kept a much closer eye on her little sister, writing frequently, arranging mutual visits and, now she could afford to, being generous with money and gifts for Tussy.

The second depressing incident of the Christmas season was the shocking death of Tussy's friend Sergei Stepniak, longtime comrade and confidant of her father and the General. Two days before Christmas Stepniak was hit by an oncoming train as he stepped across the railway line in Acton, reading a book as walked, as was his usual habit. It was a gruesome death, and Tussy's year ended by going to Woking for Stepniak's funeral.

In the New Year she fell prey to 'the Influenza Demon', writing glumly to her sister two days before her forty-first birthday, 'I now undertand why so many people have committed suicide when in the Demon's clutches.'[30] But she fought off the blues when Harry and Freddy came to visit for a birthday celebration and she received a generous cheque from Laura that she delightedly spent on 'getting all sorts of things I have long hankered after'.[31] She bought the complete five volumes of the immensely popular *Paston Letters*, 'and some other historical works I've much wanted'.[32] She considered buying some decorative pigeons for pets, like the ones Paul kept so expertly, and was thrilled by his gift, 'the delightful Hachette (most marvellous of books)'[33] that arrived by post.

Diligent swot that she was, and tasked with her new literary responsibilities, Tussy carefully planned her work on Marx's manuscripts, essays and letters for the year. She decided also that she would begin research in earnest by compiling materials to write her father's biography. She had started playing with this idea in 'Karl Marx, Stray Notes', her first stab at a biographical essay the previous year, written for the *Austrian Workers' Calendar*. After Engels died she and Laura had published their public call for Marx letters and Tussy also wrote personally to literally hundreds of people she thought might have letters from her father, asking them to send them to her or Laura and offering to transcribe them and return the originals.

Momentously, she decided to employ a domestic servant. She'd never been much of a cook, after all – and she hoped its electricity and gas fire would make the Den attractive accommodation. Tussy mused on what Lenchen would have made of her indoor kitchen with its hygienic meat safe and temperature-regulated gas cooker with oven for baking. In these ways, she made a meaningful New Year for herself. Edward appears to have been absent. She sat in her father's armchair by the fire in her study and read up on the 'wonderful' financial scandals sweeping France, including the exposure of capitalist manufacturers and moneymen for blackmail, tax fraud and insider trading. Mohr had died in the armchair and the General had spent his last good days sitting in it before finally being confined to bed. Tussy drew great comfort from the continuity of that armchair in which so much reading and thinking had taken place.

Her 'four-footers' sat on her lap as she read all the reports on 'our own little troubles – the Transvaal, Jameson's filibustering, the German Emperor, Venezuela'.[34] Her correspondence shows that she was thinking about her Dutch family again in 1896, and the Jameson Raid and focus on Kruger and Rhodes in the press must have got her wondering about her aunt who had married into the Juta family, who lived in Cape Town and ran an expanding legal publishing house in South Africa.

The Den became the headquarters of Tussy's intellectual and literary operations from the beginning of 1896. From her desk she corresponded with Kautsky over the fourth volume of *Capital*, on which she asked him to resume work as soon as she discovered that Engels had, unaccountably, made Kautsky stop work on it not long before he died. She tussled over publishers for this new companion volume to Marx's masterwork and corresponded with Kautsky and others about its preparation.

Eleanor continued editing all her father's essays and journalism written in English. Much difficulty was added to the task by Engels's decision to split everything in Marx's handwriting from his own manuscripts, causing problems with attribution for generations to come. She completed editing a series of essays published under Marx's name in the *New York Tribune*, for which she'd found the original manuscripts in the Chancery Lane strongboxes. Tussy compiled these 'eighteen articles on Germany'[35] into a collection titled *Revolution and Counter-Revolution*, for which she wrote a fascinating prefatory 'Note by the Editor', written at the Den in

April 1896. The compilation, she enthusiastically told Laura, would provide readers with 'a wonderfully interesting history of '48.'[36] Louise Freyberger and Bebel, representing the German Social Democratic Party, refused to allow Eleanor access to the Marx-Engels correspondence at this time. Therefore, she was under the impression that her father had written these articles during the years of 1851–2. In fact, Engels had written the bulk of them in Manchester and sent them to Marx in London for final edit, approval and postage by mailship to New York. Without the correspondence between them, Eleanor had no means of knowing that the articles, written in her father's style and tone, were in fact the work of Engels.

Imagining that Mohr had written these essays at the kitchen table in Dean Street before she was born, Tussy drew on her mother's autobiographical essay and her own memories of stories of family and friends to reconstruct the Marx family life in Soho in the years before her birth. There is a deep and resonant Freudian tale tangled with this Marx family narrative, for Freddy Demuth was born to Helen Demuth at Dean Street on 23 June 1851. The tempestuous family drama that raged in her family during 1851–2 coincided *exactly* with the period that Marx was supposed to be writing his regular essays for the *Tribune*. If Tussy had been given the access she wished to have to the correspondence between her father and Engels at the time, what would she have made of the following exchange between them in the new light of Freddy's paternity?

Engels, concerned that he had heard nothing from Marx for a fortnight after Lenchen gave birth, wrote and asked if he was all right – and how was he doing with his *Tribune* deadlines? Mohr's panicked response would have clarified for Tussy one of the reasons *why* her all-too-human father had been unable to deliver his journalism on time. 'For about 14 days I have not been able to write, for I was hunted like a dog all the time when I was not in the library.'[37] Engels didn't only give Jenny and Karl the enormous gift of friendship in covering for Freddy's true paternity to the outside world, but he ghosted the paternity of Marx's fine essays that made up the volume that became, under Tussy's hand, *Revolution and Counter-Revolution*, so that Marx could sort out his personal problems.

During 1896 Tussy also worked on editing Marx's articles on Palmerston, the Crimean War and his pieces on the secret diplomatic history of the eighteenth century. 'Marx's' articles for the *Tribune*, again in reality penned by Engels, were scheduled for publication as a single volume at the beginning of 1897 under the title of *The Eastern Question*. Aveling worked hard and assisted ably in preparing this compilation for press, providing broad historical context and summarising where there was too much local detail. Eleanor was pleased the material was to be published but regretted the publisher: 'I tried – for Sonnenschein is <u>such</u> a thief – to get another publisher: I have tried Methuen, Macmillan, Unwin (the only *likely* ones) and failed. I will make a last effort with Longman.'[38]

Archivist, editor, agent: Eleanor had turned the Den into a one-stop literary factory and clearance house producing newly published works of Marx and, by default, Engels at an extraordinary rate of productivity. Her ethos of modern industrial socialism, harnessing every new technology to her human cause, anticipated the zeitgeist of a future age of which she paved the way. Marx and Engels wrote longhand by candle and gaslight. Tussy had electricity to light her way, and her typewriter – which she regarded as the most marvellous technical innovation for the world of letters since the printing press. Tussy knew she'd done good work on 'The Story of the Life of Lord Palmerston' and 'Secret Diplomatic History of the Eighteenth Century'. Unaware she would not live to see them published, she could never know that both, produced from her father's idiosyncratic notes and cryptic shorthand, would be ranked highly by literary posterity.

And so Tussy worked on, producing some of the great urtexts of Marxism. More manuscripts by Mohr were on the bench. She had a series of her own lectures to write for her spring lecture tours, as well as piles of correspondence to deal with in preparation for the Fourth Congress of the Second International, due to take place in London in July.

With more money in his pockets, Edward tried to resurrect his career as a dramatist – a return to his old interests that had been rekindled in June 1895, when he organised a fundraiser at the SDF Hall on the Strand. Actors and entertainers had volunteered their talents for free, including a young actress, stage name of Lilian Richardson, who played a grieving widow to Aveling's seducer in his one-act play *In the Train*. Will Thorne, chair of the entertainment committee, noticed with disapproval that Aveling 'became very familiar' with his leading lady off stage as well as on.

Eleanor shot off on a whistlestop lecture tour raising awareness for the SDF in Edinburgh, Bristol and Aberdeen. She left on a Saturday and was back by Tuesday night – steam trains and the telegraph worked wonders to speed up the transmission of socialist ideas. As ever, Tussy was managing multiple demands on her hard-pressed time. There was the lecturing and the work on the *Nachlass*. 'Then the accumulated correspondence and housework take another day! *And* the Congress! That takes no end of time one way or another, too.'[39] During March and April Eleanor found herself at the helm of negotiating 'a very useful "reconciliation" between us & the SDF as part of the preparatory work for the Congress':

> For years we have (to the General's distress) been on good terms with the SDF *members*. Now we are *officially* to work together. You know what such 'official' friendship means – Edward & Hyndman no more love one another than do Paul & Brousse – but it is useful for the movement, & especially for the forthcoming congress.[40]

Realpolitiker to the tips of her boots – to paraphrase her mother. Parochial political skirmishes had to be held in respectful tension with the long-term political objective. Anarchist tendencies needed to be blocked. To opt out of the struggle to radically democratise the state was to render the worker movement, the trade unions and all forms of collective action and bargaining defenceless and voiceless. Throughout his life Engels had warned Eleanor that the relative passivity of English workers (clearly distinguished from the Irish, Welsh and Scots) was the Achilles heel the anarchists could exploit to bring down British socialism. Tragically, she realised, his prediction was proving correct.

Factions jostled for their position under different names, manifestos and banners, but Eleanor understood profoundly that this momentous London congress would effectively be a struggle between the forces of anarchism and socialism. The primary political issue in question was that of the relationship between parliamentarians and anti-parliamentarians. Tussy believed in, and practised, political fair play and tolerance; but when it came to practical organisation and effective political and social programmes, there was no way of squaring anti-democratic anarchism with democratic socialism and its commitment to work within a representative parliamentary system. George Plekhanov, whose important though stylistically wooden work *Anarchism and Socialism* Tussy translated, argued that anarchism was a force of reaction. Anarchism benefited from its shared language, style and aesthetic with thrilling espionage and Sherlock Holmes-like brilliant antic individualism, but it had nothing to do with the more mundane practice of everyday democratic life and the less glamorous struggle for social justice and an open society.

These primal ideological forces armed themselves for combat at the London congress in July. To rally support for democratic socialism and impress English workers with the political effectiveness of the parliamentary German party, Liebknecht travelled around Britain during May and June on a consciousness-raising tour. Eleanor and Aveling joined him on as many platforms as possible, Aveling often chairing and Eleanor speaking on British trade unionism, the woman question and economics. The venerable Liebknecht, reported *Justice* fondly, had 'the appearance of an old English gentleman farmer'.[41] Now an old political warhorse who in his day had gone into armed combat, Library was a figure well positioned to remind the modern generation of socialists that the old 'days of romantic fighting had gone by'.[42]

At the end of May Eleanor and Edward joined Library at the Mosley Hotel in Manchester for a reception held in his honour by the Independent Labour Party. The speaker who gave Liebknecht the vote of thanks was the barrister and legal reformer Dr Richard Pankhurst, husband of Emmeline Pankhurst, founder of the Women's Social and Political Union. Sylvia, one of their three daughters, accompanied him to the reception. The thirteen-year-old was fascinated by Eleanor's 'attractive personality' and, apparently, her dusky complexion, 'with dark brows and strong, vivid colouring'.[43] Sylvia thought Eleanor Marx marvellous, but 'beside her' the figure of Edward Aveling was 'repellent'. The celebrated leader of the women gas workers, Sylvia Pankhurst saw, was attentive and engaged but her husband shifted about in his chair, grumbling about 'that confounded draught' and complaining that he was cold. At which Eleanor smiled at him and turned up the collar of his coat.[44] The sharp-eyed Sylvia took in the whole scene and ever after remembered the impact Eleanor Marx made on her as a young woman.

Library's speaking tour ended in London in the middle of June. He stayed on for a while with Tussy and Edward at the Den and the three of them took some time out to go on an expedition into the past. As research for his memoir of Marx, Liebknecht wanted to go back to the part of the city where they had all lived as young immigrants and especially to see the places where the family had lived.

On Monday 8 June Tussy, Edward and Library set out from Sydenham to Tottenham Court Road. They started their search from Soho Square. 'We went about it methodically,' Library wrote, 'like Schliemann, who carried out the Troy excavations. It was by no means an easy job. He wanted to unearth Troy as it was in the time of Priam and Hector; our wish was to "excavate" the London of the emigrants from the end of the forties to the fifties and sixties.'[45] They went to his former lodgings in Old Compton Street, his one-time home on Church Street, and round the corner to the General's first London digs on Macclesfield Street; and then on to 28 Dean Street, the place of Tussy's birth, which they only found with some difficulty because the house numbers had been changed.

They rang the bell and asked the young woman who answered if they might go up and have a look. The two rooms on the second floor were locked, but the staircase was familiar and the layout exactly as Library remembered:

> Yes, that was the house that I had been in thousands of times, the
> house where Marx, assailed, tortured and worn out by the misery
> of emigration and the furious hatred of enemies . . . wrote his

Eighteenth Brumaire, his Herr Vogt and his correspondence for
the *New York Tribune* . . . where he did the enormous preparatory
work for *Capital*.[46]

And where he seduced Lenchen whilst his wife was away, leaving
her pregnant with Freddy Demuth, born at Dean Street nine
months later amidst storms and recriminations from which the
great philosopher hid in the British Museum Reading Room, writing to his best friend in Manchester that he was scared of going
home.

This latter part, of course, did not form part of Library's memoir.
But Tussy knew Freddy's birth date and had worked out that the
great rift between Mohr, her mother and Lenchen had taken place,
and been resolved for ever, behind those now locked doors. Soon
after this trip down memory lane with Library, Tussy decided to
start work on writing her father's biography. 'After all,' she wrote to
Laura, 'Marx the "Politiker" and "Denker" can take his chance,
while Marx the man is less likely to fare as well.'[47] These were not the
words of the wide-eyed, idolatrous, favoured daughter who gazed
up in admiration at a flawless father.

The secret of Marx the man had been taken to his shared grave.
Engels, too, would have stayed silent if the opportunistic Freebooters
hadn't interfered. There was no question of her exposing Freddy and
Harry to public scandal but the truth was now hers.

From Dean Street, the intrepid threesome hopped on an omnibus
to Kentish Town, where they visited three of the graves of Tussy's
dead brothers and sisters who had died in infancy, including Edgar,
with whom her life so briefly coincided. They were surprised by
how built-up Kentish Town had become. By the time they had been
to Maitland Park Road, where Jenny and Karl died, and wandered
about the old haunts on Hampstead Heath, they were beginning to
feel depressed by the pursuit of ghosts. So they went to Jack Straw's
Castle and got happily drunk: 'How often we had been there in days
of old! In the very room in which we sat I had sat dozens of times
with Marx, Mrs Marx, the children, Lenchen and others . . . '[48]

Whatever really happened between Karl, Jenny and Lenchen over
his infidelity and Freddy's birth, it hadn't broken the bond between

Jenny and Lenchen, or Jenny and her husband. All of them had known each other from their earliest years. After the short-lived storm, they were able to go out to the pub together, children in tow. Except, of course, Freddy, who paid the price for his parents' behaviour, as children always must.

The famous Fourth Congress of the Second International opened on 27 July at the Queen's Hall in Langham Place, preceded by a mass gathering in Hyde Park the day before. All legitimate socialist organisations in Britain were represented, including the Social Democratic Federation, the Independent Labour Party, the Fabian Society and the trade unions. James Ramsay MacDonald was delegated for the Fabians, and Charlotte Despard, Bernard Shaw and the Webbs were also present for the whole congress. Rosa Luxemburg, a contemporary of Library's son Karl, was also a delegate, much to Tussy's approval, since Luxemburg's credentials had not been accepted by the 1893 Zurich congress. Eleanor, her friend Clara Zetkin, Charlotte Despard and Rosa Luxemburg were natural allies amongst the many socialist women participating in the congress.

Eleanor represented the London gas workers, and led the team of translators that included Zetkin, Liebknecht, Bernstein, Luxemburg, the Swiss Johann Sigg – and everyone's favourite misinterpreter, the notorious radical journalist Adolphe Smith.

The mudslinging between socialists and anarchists started immediately. The British and German sections had, after lengthy argument and negotiation, agreed to exclude the anarchist factions from the congress. The French delegates, however, were divided on the issue. Matters were further complicated by the fact that, although the British had agreed to endorse the resolution, Tom Mann and Keir Hardie broke the agreement and organised demonstrations in favour of the 'Anti-Parliamentarians', i.e., as Tussy put it, clearly in favour of the anarchists. The argument over the resolution for exclusion was so loud and bad-tempered that Eleanor complained that she couldn't hear to translate properly. Tolerance and, in Eleanor's words, 'fair play', were debated. Hyndman kept a cool head, pointing out that, as the anarchists had stated over and over again that they didn't believe in congresses or formal representational political organisation, why were they making a fuss about being excluded?

Tussy, Edward and other congress organisers were on watch for an outbreak of anarchist violence. The sturdy secretary of the congress, Will Thorne, led a body of stalwart doorkeepers to bounce any insurgency. Once the resolution for exclusion was passed, the Fourth Congress of the Second International settled down to business. It was an eventful, productive and significant congress. The next big firework display was at the closing festival, held, conveniently for Tussy and Edward, at the Crystal Palace. Aveling MC'd the banquet, and after much singing of the Marseillaise, Auld Lang Syne and the Carmagnole, the congress disbanded until its next meeting, scheduled to be held in Berlin in 1899.

Tussy was grateful for the opportunity to return to her desk after these events and particularly enjoyed writing her weekly column for *Justice*. Eleanor's 'International Notes' are amongst her finest journalism. She covered the St Petersburg strikes throughout their duration from 1896 to 1897, bringing her reportage to life from her first-hand experience of serving on the Zurich Committee that organised international financial support and political solidarity for the St Petersburg strikers. In another series of articles Eleanor reflected critically on the development of the German SPD and also wrote a precise and critically sharp account of the famous Gotha congress of the German party in October. She wrote elegantly and forcefully about the controversy sparked by Bax's theory of revisionism, which notoriously sought to separate Marxism from its revolutionary aspects. Who better to write a critique of Marxist revisionism than Eleanor Marx?

More optimistically, Eleanor wrote columns on the evolution of French socialism in the public sphere, reporting on the impact of the socialist communes, free school meals, scholarships for poor children and theatre subsidies. However, when the French socialists supported the Greek invasion of Crete, she criticised them without hesitation:

France, even Socialist France, seems quite – I mean Crete – mad. As the French Socialists ... consider the Polish movement as 'Chauvinist', it is a little difficult to understand their present enthusiasm for the Greeks. And, personally, I must say I should be far more impressed by their diatribes against that much-damned Sultan if the French had even mildly damned the hideous Franco-Russian alliance.[49]

As previously noted, Eleanor was highly critical of the spineless-ness of the socialists in the French Chamber of Deputies who refused to take sides in supporting Dreyfus on the grounds that the affair was merely a skirmish between rival groups within bourgeois society. When Clemenceau and Zola came out for Dreyfus, she saluted them.[50]

On balance Eleanor completed an impressive proportion of her birthday plan of action for 1896. After the Second International's fourth congress she took up teaching at the Battersea socialist Sunday school and joined the local socialist choir, telling Kautsky how much she enjoyed singing with her 'dear Lewishamers'.[51] In September she began teaching weekly French and German language and debating classes on Friday evenings for SDF members, a volun-tary job she was to continue with barely a few weeks' interruption until January 1898.

Eleanor was struck by how very few of the British delegates at the Fourth Congress of the Second International in London had any knowledge of foreign languages or the rules of debate followed in European political organisations. This prompted her to start the classes. Within a few months Eleanor's advanced evening classes were reading and debating *The Communist Manifesto* in the original German and the manifesto of the *Parti Ouvrir* in French. What fun it must have been for the students to have the enlivening quality of Eleanor's first-hand experience and knowledge of the authors – mostly her family – thrown into the mix of rigorous, demanding learning. She showed them how the rules of debate enabled freedom of expression and individual opinion, and created a safe, encouraging space for criticism and self-criticism.

Edward offered to join the initiative by teaching science classes and preparing students for entry to the public Art and Science Examination. Their courses ran at the SDF Hall on the Strand. Tussy taught on Fridays, Edward on Wednesdays. As the Strand is so conveniently positioned in the heart of West End theatreland, Aveling naturally went to shows or dinner with his theatre folk after his Wednesday classes or individual tutoring sessions on other days. Or so Tussy believed.

Towards the end of the year she advertised for a live-in servant, and hired Gertrude Gentry, who immediately – to Tussy's wonder – removed from her the responsibility of a thousand necessary daily chores, freeing her up to spend long hours in her study, just as her mother and Lenchen had done for her father and Engels. As yet, no records have been discovered about Gerty's background before she came to work for Eleanor. In the early days of their mistress-and-servant relationship, Tussy referred to her unkindly as 'my very excellent but rather stupid Gerty',[52] but she revised and rescinded this condescending view as she got to know Gerty better. It was no special mark of honour to be called stupid by Tussy. It was a word she used freely and fondly about her friends, such as Library, when they demonstrated poor judgement or got distracted by ephemera, or spoke before thinking.

Gertrude Gentry, who had basic literacy when she arrived at the Den, expressed much interest in the books, journals, newspapers, play scripts, song sheets, leaflets and magazines that overspilled the furniture in most of the rooms she was tasked to keep clean and tidy. Reacting immediately to this curiosity, Tussy and Gerty started working together to improve her reading, writing and account-keeping. Maid and madam soon bonded in humour over Tussy's poor cooking skills and some of Edward's fussy foibles and masculine eccentricities. Eleanor imagined her cooking was merely mediocre until Gerty set her right and deemed her efforts generally inedible. In this regard alone, Dr Aveling was to be pitied: Lenchen had succeeded in teaching Tussy to play chess brilliantly, but had been far less effective in passing on her baking skills. Aveling was away a great deal but, when at the Den, he appears to have been a genial and generally undemanding master by the standards of the time. Yet for all that he appeared to be decent to her, Gerty never warmed to him.

Conversely, she devoted extra attention to Tussy – who, after all, paid her wages – and did a great deal to make the Den a welcoming place for visitors. Gerty was also a keen follower of fashion. Her interest in matters faddish concerning clothes, hair, cosmetics and accessories was probably what earned her the appellation of stupid from Tussy who, as a child, poked fun at her mother for strutting around like a peacock when she received the unexpected gift of an over-fancy new hat. Tussy hated fuss about matters of dress and personal toilette – a word and concept she found rather absurd. Nevertheless, Gerty clearly succeeded in exerting a subtle influence over Tussy's hitherto unruly hair and comfortably absent-minded dress sense – or rather lack of it. There was a visible improvement in the neatness and fashion of Tussy's clothes and hair that coincided with Gerty's arrival at the Den.

Tussy had never cared much about what she wore. Now she could afford a servant because of the General's legacy. Gerty, in turn, probably pointed out that she could also afford to replace some of her exhausted, frayed and much-turned and trimmed wardrobe. Why wouldn't Eleanor buy new clothes if she could afford them? Another exasperatingly 'stupid' line of thinking, in Tussy's view, to whom commodity capitalism was simply the emperor's new clothes. Eleanor hated shopping for anything except books, typewriters and nerdy time-saving gadgets but Gerty nudged and pestered her about her dated bohemian wardrobe and put some fashion magazines advertising department-store dresses under Tussy's nose.

Her new acquisitions included a dark blue velvet dress that became her favourite for winter, a brown skirt-suit for English summer and autumn, and a white silk cotton dress for when the sun really came out; this was also to be worn on happy days at home. White remained Tussy's favourite colour, just as it had been when she was a little girl – the colour of the unwritten page, of possibility, and the bolts of bleached cotton Engels had shown her as a child in Manchester.

In November Tussy was miserable when she was revisited by the Influenza Demon. She grumbled to Kautsky that she was 'quite hors de combat',[53] but cheered up immensely when, in defiance of her doctor's orders, she gargled salt and bicarbonate and headed off to Burnley with Aveling where they both gave lectures followed by a two-hander entertainment. Tussy lectured on the subject of anarchism and gave a turn of her popular *Pied Piper of Hamelin*; Aveling lectured on evolution and gave a recitation of his poem 'Tramp of the Workers', whose metre matches its flat-footed title. The two then gave a reading of *By the Sea*, Aveling's 1887 adaptation of the French love story *Jean-Marie* by André Theuriet, about which the *Dramatic Review* had written so disparagingly after Tussy's original performance. Tussy returned to London for Christmas in much higher spirits, telling Kautsky that 'a week of hard work in Lancashire . . . has done wonders . . . If I had followed the doctor's advice I should be quite a confirmed invalid now!'[54]

Liebknecht's memoir of Marx was published in December 1896. Much as she loved him, Tussy thought Library's book 'muddled finely' and 'disappointing in many ways'. But it was well intentioned and she thought it harmless, telling Kautsky he was wrong and alarmist to claim it would do Marx 'infinite harm'.[55] She asked Laura her opinion and acknowledged that it was hardly fair of her to criticise Library's attempt to get the ball rolling on the biography of Marx without devoting more attention to getting on with her own. She wrote to Kautsky to assure him that she was now setting out on the project in earnest. Tussy's anxieties will be recognisable to all biographers, as will her recognition that history is a collective project:

The *man* is least known, most misunderstood. And Marx as a *whole* . . . was so very many sided that many sides of him will have to be considered . . . Not only science appealed to him – but Art and Literature. Mohr's sympathy with *every* form of work was so perfect that it will take many men to deal with him from their own point of view. I only despair when I think of the task of gathering together all these loose threads and weaving them into a whole. Yet it must be done, though it is work to give the boldest pause.[56]

The Boldest Pause

In April 1897 the National Union of Gas Workers and General Labourers gathered in Battersea Park in London to celebrate their eighth anniversary. The reporter from the *Labour Leader* layered on thick description of 'a cutting east wind', 'dull sky' and 'fringe of dark trees' in which to set the aspirations of the assembled gas workers:

> . . . under the platform a shock of upturned, anxious, toil-scarred faces. Around are the trade union banners gay with silk and paint. On the platform stands Marx's daughter, as youthful and strenuous as ever.[1]

Youthful and strenuous as ever, Tussy began 1897 in a pugnacious mood. The week before her forty-third birthday she chivvied the Social Democratic Federation (SDF) to up its game, claiming mischievously in *Justice* that capitalist society was digging its own grave so rapidly she was afraid it would tumble into it before the Social Democrats were ready.[2]

The week after her birthday she condemned the 'horrible fact' that 'the great mass of the workers in the north are devouring their children.'[3] This gruesome Goya-esque image was conjured from her shock at seeing worker parents from Lancashire mills protesting against a proposal to raise the age of child labour. Everyone, Eleanor argued, was failing children on this crucial issue: 'not only the great mass of the workers, but a majority of the Socialists, are as bad as can be on this question.'⁴ The SDF needed to launch an immediate campaign for child workers in northern factories.

As she had recently rejoined the SDF and was rapidly becoming one of its most prominent leaders, she had good cause to drive it hard. Eleanor had resigned from the SDF in December 1884 in opposition to Hyndman's anti-internationalist 'Jingo faction'. For nearly a decade they'd found it impossible to work together. As political conditions changed during the 1890s, they resolved their differences. In 1895, the year he died, Engels said that whilst the socialist instinct grew stronger amongst the masses in England, as soon as it came to translating this into clear demands and action, everyone fell apart. Some went to the SDF, some to the Independent Labour Party and others stayed with their trade union organisations – all amounting to a lot of uncoordinated sects and a muddled ILP. The General also told Eleanor frequently that he was anxious that she was on too-good terms with SDF members. Eleanor responded that she shared his concern that the SDF leadership was for, rather than with, and of, the working class, but that the SDF grass-roots membership was moving towards more explicit internationalism and a socialist programme. A policy she played a significant role in encouraging.

The alliance formed for the 1896 Fourth Congress of the Second International, which Eleanor played a leading part in brokering, strengthened the rapprochement between Eleanor and Hyndman. The SDF evolved into a more socialist organisation, 'useful to the movement'.⁵ Another factor that bound them together politically was the worsening relationship with the German party: Bernstein's belligerent Marxist revisionism in Germany, supported by Ernest Bax, drew Eleanor, Hyndman and Library closer together. Bernstein led the German SPD in the view that Marx's analysis of capitalist society was no longer correct for the end of the nineteenth century. Eleanor suggested that all parties debate the case; Bernstein, in breathtakingly patronising and sexist terms, refused.

The Freebooters briefed furiously against her in support of Bernstein and he started to behave badly, acting the sulking tyrant and being 'terribly irritable'.⁶ He blew up at every imagined slight or sign of criticism. One evening at a dinner at the Den, when Library and Tussy supported Hyndman's authority on the subject of India, Bernstein exploded into a state of almost frantic rage.

Eleanor was intimate enough with her father's work to argue Bernstein point for point, a knowledge that sparked his irritation. She was delighted to tell Kautsky that she was editing 'a simply *magnificent* paper' of her father's that she'd found shuffled into his manuscripts, read by him to the Council of the International Working Men's Association in 1865 – '(Oh! the work that man did!)'[7] Entitled 'Value, Price and Profit', it was judged by Tussy 'an admirable exposition',[8] which she edited with great care, intending to write a preface for its publication. Bernstein, the Freebooters and those within their faction knew that Eleanor was an insuperable obstruction to their desire to rewrite 'Marxism' to their own convenience.

Democratic socialism in Britain was in a dilemma. Eleanor worried that Hyndman lacked the strength to stand up to it alone. The popular propagandising of revisionism under the guise of orthodoxy led by the irritable, bullying and petulant Bernstein required someone with the aptitude of an Engels to manage it. Someone, for example, like her. Eleanor also wasn't as good at harbouring old political grudges as Marx and Engels. Slander and slurs from within the SDF continued against Marx, Engels and herself but she ignored them. The new alliance was useful. The Hyndmans became family friends and regular visitors to the Den for lunch and dinner. Eleanor was far less emotional and more forgiving about personal feuds than Mohr and the General, which made her rather more dangerous in the realms of realpolitik.

Hence by 1897 the SDF and its organ, *Justice*, and the newly launched monthly journal *Social Democrat*, were Eleanor's official platforms. She continued to lead the gas workers and to be deeply involved in broad-based union work. The first issue of *Social Democrat* came out in January 1897, edited by Eleanor and Edward. In early editions she published a revised version of her biographical essay on her father written shortly after his death and published years earlier in *Progress*. She translated a section of Liebknecht's memoir of Marx to offer a different biographical perspective on her father, and translated European dramatists and writers, such as

Alexander Kielland, whose work she continued to follow. Aveling reviewed Olive's brilliant, controversial new novel, *Trooper Peter Halket of Mashonaland*. His review, entitled 'Filibuster Cecil Rhodes and His Chartered Company', was one of the best pieces of literary journalism Edward ever wrote.

The SDF and its allies took the lead in organised political opposition to British imperialist policy. In February Tussy weighed in on the SDF campaigns against imperialism in South Africa and what she defined as 'British capitalist misrule in India'.[9]

In the same month, Eleanor publicly welcomed South African activist Harriette Colenso in the pages of *Justice*. Colenso came to Britain for the first time on a tour speaking out against British foreign policy and informing people about the truth of the war atrocities taking place in South Africa in their name. Well known in South Africa for her anti-racist campaigning against British colonial policy, Harriette Colenso was the daughter of the late missionary Bishop of Natal, rumoured to have run wild with militant Zulus in 'native' Africa. Olive put Eleanor and Harriette directly in touch.

Eleanor urged members of the SDF to take every opportunity to listen to what this resolute and brave campaigner had to say about the 'horrors perpetuated in South Africa by the British forces and Mr Rhodes'.[10] The same Mr Rhodes whom Olive Schreiner had cause to fall out with on the same issue. Tussy compared Colenso favourably with Hyndman, who was simultaneously campaigning robustly against the continued British occupation and economic exploitation of India.

The appalling famine in India, Tussy concurred with Hyndman, was caused not by so-called underdevelopment but by colonial capitalism that unbalanced the world economies. For her lecture series of 1897 Eleanor chose most frequently the subjects of imperialism and colonialism in India and South Africa, often giving variations on her lecture ironically entitled 'Our Glorious Empire'.

Harriette visited the Den in July 1897 to meet Library, who was in England for the annual conference of the SDF in Northampton due to take place at the beginning of August. Tussy explained, 'He is very specially interested in the question of South Africa and most anxious

to learn something of the real facts of the case.'[11] Harriette came early
so they could take advantage of the decent weather and chat in the
garden before they ate. At this gathering Library offered Colenso a
platform for her views in 'the great daily paper *Vorwärts*', of which
he was editor.[12] What tales Gertrude Gentry could tell of the people
she cooked dinners for at the Den.

Visitors flowed through the door of the Den during the summer
of 1897 – 'Come to the Jews and the Den,'[13] Tussy wrote to Kautsky.
Bernstein, for all his exasperation with her, never lost his fondness
for Tussy and recalled how her face would beam with pleasure as she
welcomed friends to her home.[14] Freddy and Harry visited regularly
and stayed over more frequently as Aveling was away at St Margaret's
Bay on the Kent coast, convalescing from a recurrence of his
abscesses. Eleanor was preoccupied with the International Miners'
Congress at St Martin's Hall.

It was an enormously busy year. Eleanor's new role in the SDF
added further public speaking to her schedule – she was more in
demand to speak than any other leader in the organisation. Henry
Hyndman was as thrilled by her popularity within the SDF as he'd
been furious when she was outside it. His wife Matilda, who never
stopped secretly supporting Eleanor, was just as delighted. By June
Tussy had delivered forty-one lectures and spoken or taken the chair
at ten meetings in the past eight months, discounting the week's
lecturing in Holland in February. Her voice was giving out. She had
to publish a public letter in *Justice*:

BRANCHES TAKE NOTE

. . . in order to save time and trouble, *and* postage stamps, will you
let me tell the many SDF branches that are so kindly asking me to
lecture for them that I am obliged to decline, for the present at any
rate, all open-air work? My throat unfortunately will not stand up
to the strain. Those who know me will not suspect me of shirking
work . . . When the indoor propaganda begins again I shall, as
always, be at the service of my comrades and of the cause.[15]

As well as the physical demands of all this public speaking, Tussy
found it increasingly difficult to manage her office, appointments,

schedule, editing, research and correspondence. Gerty organised the Den on the domestic front but Tussy needed a professional secretary and researcher. To the mutual satisfaction of both, she employed Edith Lanchester for the job.

Aristocratically born Edith Lanchester, who broke away from her privileged background and became a radical, self-defined New Woman, was an executive member of the SDF, where she met and fell in love with working-class James Sullivan, an active representative of the Battersea SDF. The couple announced they would live together in what they called a 'free love union'. Their 'marriage' would begin on 26 October. Edith's wealthy, upper-class family were appalled. Edith's plan to live openly with a working-class man outside of matrimony clearly confirmed their suspicions that she was insane.

On 25 October, as Edith packed up her possessions to move in with James, her father and three brothers turned up unexpectedly at her lodgings with a psychiatric doctor, who certified her as mad on the spot. They dragged her away to a secure psychiatric asylum. When Edith tried to resist, her father handcuffed her.

The SDF attempted legal interventions to release her. All failed. James Sullivan and other SDFers stood outside the asylum wall beneath Edith's barred window and sang 'The People's Flag' to reassure her.[16] She was subjected to disgusting physical, mental and sexual torture. Edith was perfectly sane when she was incarcerated; given the abuse she received it is remarkable she wasn't driven mad by her imprisonment.

Edith Lanchester emerged from her ordeal further resolved to live her life according to her own principles and to break the silence on her appalling treatment. And break the silence she did. She retrained in typing and shorthand after her incarceration but her notoriety made it difficult for her to find work.

Eleanor took her on. Edith did Eleanor's secretarial work at the Den, typed up her manuscripts and did research at the British Museum Reading Room for Eleanor. This was work Tussy had done unpaid for her father for years. Now, in her turn, she was able to pay Edith the proper wage due to a skilled secretary and researcher ensuring her financial independence from her tyrannical relatives.

Betrayed by her own family, Edith desperately needed feminist sisters. Tussy gave Edith paid employment and nurtured, encouraged and protected her. The two became friends for the rest of Eleanor's life.

In June 1897, Edith and James had their first baby. It was a difficult pregnancy and birth, coupled with the added social pressures resulting from their openly having a love child. Eleanor invited Edith, 'who is very ill after her confinement', to stay at the Den 'for a few weeks' nursing'.[17] Eleanor and Gerty looked after Edith and protected her, James and the baby from Edith's family and social opprobrium. Gerty liked the couple and was a fierce champion of their cross-class love match, becoming very attached to their baby boy.

Edward seemed more genial and kinder during 1897. Tussy felt they had at last settled into amicable companionship, fostered by making a permanent home in Sydenham. He was away a lot but so was she; there was nothing new in that. Edward's spending took them constantly over budget but he assured her that the money was being put to good use towards his work with the SDF and new fund-raiser entertainments he was devising. As Eleanor had made clear in 'The Woman Question', woman needed to free herself from economic dependence on man. Tussy had achieved this; it mattered far more to her that she was economically independent than it did that her 'husband' was her financial dependant.

What Tussy didn't know, however, was that Aveling was now in considerable interest-free debt to George Bernard Shaw, the Radfords and many more of her friends in England and France. Nor did she know that he'd never repaid what he owed to William Morris before his death in 1896, though Tussy's friend May Morris did. Had Tussy known, she would have instantly settled his debts in full, if she could, from the Engels legacy and her own income. Quite aware that this would be her predictable reaction, Edward had no intention of allowing Eleanor to disburse their capital by repaying bad debts that he could continue to dodge, interest free. Shaw, who knew very well by now that he would never get any of it back, continued to lend Edward money; he said, for the purposes of soci-ological observation. He planned to write a play about moral degeneration and how men abuse women in relationships, with the lead character based on Edward. The play became *The Doctor's Dilemma* (1906). Shaw would not have been surprised to learn that his proto-moral degenerate protagonist Aveling was also 'borrowing' hush money from Freddy Demuth, on the threat of revealing his true paternity. How was Freddy going to tell Tussy that Edward was blackmailing him?

Eleanor's misperception that she and Edward had finally achieved a firm base for their shared future could not have been further from the truth. Unfortunately, as Edward, the consummate actor, was proficient at leading a double life, trusting Tussy had no idea how completely she was being duped.

In January 1897 Aveling – under his theatrical pseudonym Alec Nelson – organised a fundraiser of 'Dramatic Entertainment' at the Wandsworth Social Hall. Alec Nelson took the lead role in his comedy, *The Landlady*, playing opposite Miss Eva Frye, the twenty-two-year-old daughter of a music teacher and one of Aveling's students. Eva sang 'Love's Old Sweet Song' very prettily, to the evident delight of her co-actor. Eva Frye was the same charming talent who, under the name of Miss Richardson, had played opposite Alec Nelson in his one-act drama *In the Train* at the SDF Hall in the Strand on 15 June 1895, drawing the observation from Will Thorne that Miss Frye and 'Dr Aveling became very familiar'.[18]

Edward had had flirtatious affairs with students before, as Tussy knew, but she was not aware that Eva Frye was unusually persistent. Their trysts continued intermittently from 1895. Eva was a student on Aveling's Wednesday night classes in the Strand, providing a useful cover for their after-class meetings. Edward dined the excited Eva at West End restaurants, and she prettily invited him to go to Shakespeare plays with her, where she dreamily cast herself as the romantic heroine and listened uncritically to his literary views in the intervals.

Eva wanted a relationship with Edward, but Aveling saw no necessity of giving up all the material, cultural, social and political benefits of his relationship with Tussy whilst they still served him so well. He was also flattered by Eva's feminine neediness, in such marked contrast to Eleanor's self-sufficiency. Eva sent Edward clandestine little notes: when could they have dinner again? She had some tickets for a Shakespeare production, would he come? She was simply *hopeless* without him – and similar enticing appeals. On the other hand, Eleanor, as Edward once vehemently remarked, was 'as strong as a horse'.[19] And there it was – Edward's envy of Eleanor, her intellectual capacities, robust brilliance, the warmth of her sunny disposition, her resilience and ingenuity. He and Eleanor had both hugely underestimated the impact of masculine insecurity when they discussed 'The Woman Question' in the 1880s. Men were brought up to be the centre of attention and with the sense of entitlement of being top dog. Edward needed to play the lead.

June 1897 marked Queen Victoria's Diamond Jubilee. Eleanor was in the final stages of completing the manuscript for *The Eastern Question* and had to push herself through the crowds in central London to get to the Reading Room at the British Museum. She grumbled to Kautsky about the anachronism of monarchy, attracting 'idiots of sightseers – seeing "sights" that don't exist, for anything shabbier or meaner than the London "decorations" you cd not dream in a nightmare'.[20] She was wrong. A sight far shabbier and meaner had taken place the previous week. It was, however, a tawdry decoration to Aveling's duplicity that Tussy could not have envisioned in a nightmare.

Tussy was 'very much worried' about Edward's health, as she'd confided to Library on 2 June. She took him to one of London's best surgeons,[21] who diagnosed that 'the abscess in his side (open now for over 2 ½ years) *may* necessitate an operation (though we hope not), which would be a serious one.'[22] Just a few days after this consultation, on 7 June, the Eighth Miners' International Congress opened at St Martin's Town Hall, opposite the recently opened National Gallery. Eleanor, as usual, was speaking, chairing and acting as an official interpreter. Edward was supposed to be resting at home. However, on 8 June Alec Nelson married Eva Frye at the Chelsea Register Office, a few miles west of St Martin's Lane. Aveling doctored his age, faked his father's name and borrowed someone else's residential address on the marriage registration.[23]

Understandably, the new Mrs Nelson expected a honeymoon. The following week on 19 June, Aveling set off, ostensibly alone, 'by doctors' orders'[24] to 'convalesce' from his abscesses at St Margaret's

Bay at the Kent seaside. He was there with his new bride for a fort-night. Whilst Edward was away on his convalescent nuptials, Eleanor wrote the introduction to *The Eastern Question*, which was never-theless published as a co-authored piece in both their names.

Aveling was back in London for Library's arrival in July and at the Den on Saturday 16th when the Hyndmans came to visit for lunch and a lazy afternoon that stretched long into the night as the party debated the harness of English capitalism on India. Hyndman complimented twenty-one-year-old Johnny Longuet, who was visiting Aunt Tussy, on his translation of an article of his on India published in *Petit République*. Johnny was a cause of concern to Tussy. She thought him hopelessly lazy, incapable of real work or sustained effort. As Johnny's translation for the *Petit République* piece contained some fairly exact-ing economic analysis, it seems Aunt Tussy was perhaps being a little unfair to represent her nephew as a complete layabout – or indicates her hard-to-match standards of output.

Eleanor, Aveling and Library attended the annual congress of the SDF in Northampton together on 1 August, where the revived and jaunty Aveling was elected to the executive council of the SDF at the top of the poll. He persuasively sponsored a resolution for co-operation between trade unionists and SDF members and, after the conference, toured South Wales on a lecture tour for SDF branches.

Edward was sufficiently recovered to resume lecturing, speaking and teaching. On 22 August he gave a speech at a mass rally in Trafalgar Square. Sometime during the following week, he walked out of the Den without explanation, pocketing all the cash, money orders and movable valuables he could find.

Tussy turned to Freddy for help. Apart from him, she discussed these events with no one. Gertrude Gentry, the other permanent member of the household, was the only person who might have known what was going on. Edward refused to offer any explanation for his departure. Eleanor was not to know his address. She was 'permitted' to write to him via 'M—', one of his actor friends.

Shocked and confused, Tussy asked Freddy to intervene with Edward on her behalf. Freddy tried to find Edward. Although by now he might have dearly wished that Eleanor would just let Edward go, Freddy was also scared: Eleanor's faithless partner knew the family secret.

Aveling didn't reply. On 30 August Freddy received a painful letter from Tussy:

> My dear Freddy,
>   Of course not a line this morning! I have at once sent on your letter. How can I thank you for all your goodness and kindness to me? But, indeed, I do thank you from the bottom of my heart. I wrote once more to Edward this morning. No doubt it is weak, but one can't wipe out 14 years of one's life as if they had not been. I think anyone with the least sense of honour, not to mention any feeling of kindness and gratitude, would answer that letter. Will he? I almost fear he will not.[25]

If only Tussy could have called on George Bernard Shaw, or if Olive had been closer to hand in England rather than in South Africa. Pride and confusion prevented Tussy from seeking Shaw's assistance and distance prevented her turning to Olive, who no doubt would have been of enormous practical assistance to her at this critical moment in her life.

Eleanor asked Freddy to find Edward and bring him home to the Den or arrange for them to meet. At the very least she deserved to know why he had so suddenly abandoned their relationship without explanation. She thought that if Edward was in London he was likely to be around his West End theatre haunts. The following evening was an executive meeting of the SDF, which she and Edward were supposed to be chairing. Eleanor couldn't face going, 'because if he is not there I can't explain'. And if he was there, how could she pretend in public that everything was fine between them? 'I hate to give you all this trouble,' she apologised to Freddy, 'but could you go . . . and find out if he is there?'[26]

There is another aspect of this dispatch to Freddy as troubling as Tussy's emotional anguish. Enclosed with it was a letter she had just received from Crosse. She wanted Freddy to read it and then return it to her. 'I am now writing to Crosse to say I shall be there, but should like to see him before Edward – in the *very improbable* event of Edward turning up. '[27] As Freddy was to read it himself, there was no further explanation of the contents of Crosse's unexpected letter. Most worrying, why had Edward independently been in touch with Eleanor's lawyer? In turmoil, Eleanor failed to take sufficient note of Crosse's sudden and unprecedented involvement in her private relationship.

Much put-upon but valiant Freddy proved worthy of his name-sake in his unflinching support of a Marx but to no avail. Edward was not to be found. Forty-eight sleepless hours later, Tussy received a note in the morning post: 'Have returned. Shall be home early to-morrow.' A few hours later a telegram arrived: 'Home for good, 1.30pm.'[28] Were these communications to be trusted? If only Tussy had refused to see him then. But she was still in shock and not think-ing clearly. Her emotional reaction to stay and be at home that day for Edward's possible return was one of the worst decisions she made in her life. Tussy still responded to an unwritten bond of love and responsibility towards Aveling and their relationship that he had long since abandoned. Tussy wrote to Freddy describing Edward's return:

> I was working – for even with all the heartbreak one has to work
> – in my room – and Edward seemed surprised and quite 'offended'
> I did not rush into his arms. He has so far made no apology and
> offered no explanation. I – after waiting for him to begin – there-
> fore said one *must* consider the business position – and that I
> should never forget the treatment I had been subjected to. He said
> nothing.[29]

Aveling didn't need to say anything. He'd already won the game: Tussy had let him back into the house. It was the oldest story of emotional abuse between man and woman in the book. Thanking Freddy again for all his support, Tussy ended her letter thus: 'When I see you I will tell you what Crosse said.'[30]

It can only have been property and his legal position relative to Eleanor that brought Aveling back. Whatever transpired between Mr and Mrs Nelson and Crosse in those fraught few days, Aveling quickly discovered that he stood to lose all his material and capital interests in the relationship with Eleanor unless they came to a mutual agreement. He had probably also misled poor Eva Frye about the financial security and interesting society Mrs Alec Nelson could expect to enjoy. Always living it large, Edward passed off Eleanor's money, friends and connections as his own, borrowing light from Eleanor's star.

Within a few hours of that terrible afternoon Tussy understood clearly that Edward had not come back for her but for her money and a deal that they would be 'friends' in public, as they moved in the same circles. They argued all night. In the morning Tussy sent a hurried note to Freddy:

> Come, if you possibly can, this evening. It is a shame to trouble you; but I am so alone, and I am face to face with a most horrible position: *utter* ruin – everything to the last penny, or utter, open disgrace. It is awful; worse than even I fancied it was. And I want someone to consult with. I know I must finally decide and be responsible; but a little counsel and friendly help would be invaluable. So, dear, dear Freddy, come. I am heartbroken.[31]

We don't know what story Aveling told Eleanor when he came home; all that is clear is that it was not the truth. Eleanor still did not know that Aveling had recently married a mistress he'd been seeing for several years, of whose existence she was still unaware. Aveling held two trump cards: Eleanor's shame at having misplaced her faith in him and defended him to people who warned her otherwise; and the answer to the true paternity of Freddy Demuth. Both mattered a great deal more to Tussy than they did to the rest of the world and, knowing this, Edward played her well. The world already held Aveling in disrepute as damaged goods; only Tussy's good faith had stood between him and the cheap conman he really was. No one would be surprised.

As to her father, most of the world knew that a 'great' man in private was a man like any other. An illegitimate son would hardly be unexpected. But Marx valued the good opinion of children, a view Tussy shared. Childhood past and adult present were inseparably enfolded in these affairs of heart, home, sex and family.

Eleanor persisted in her loyalty to Marx, Engels and Aveling. All three men, whom she loved in different ways, lied to her about personal matters that had a substantive impact on her life. Freddy despaired at Eleanor's refusal to judge Edward but, for all her emotional vulnerabilities, Eleanor was – annoyingly – consistent in her application of logic. As she withheld judgement on her father, mother and Lenchen on their sexual conduct, how could she fairly judge Edward?

An incident concerning a private letter from Marx to his father, written on 10 November 1837, illustrates the dilemma. The previous year in 1897, Eleanor received a letter from her cousin Lina (Caroline) Smith, daughter of Mohr's sister Sophie. Lina, who lived in Maastricht, had found this letter from her uncle to her grandfather when she was sorting through her late mother's papers. Lina wrote Tussy a long letter bringing her up to date on all the news of her Dutch family and enclosed young Marx's letter, in which he earnestly defended his recent engagement to Jenny von Westphalen and declared his inviolable love for her. This 'extraordinary human document'[32] struck Tussy deeply. As she wrote in her introductory remarks to the letter, it spoke from the past in the voices of these 'two lifelong friends and lovers' who 'never faltered, never doubted', and 'were faithful till death. And death has not separated them.'[33] Eleanor told Kautsky that she could hardly bring herself to physically copy the letter. After much vacillation, she finally decided to agree to Eduard Bernstein's suggestion that the letter be published in a special edition of *Neue Zeit* but, as she told Kautsky, she changed her mind repeatedly, and writing the introduction 'was worse than having a tooth out!'[34] Unsurprising, given the perjury she committed in the introduction. She knew she had 'a real duty to Mohr to show him to the world in "his habit as he really lived"'.[35] How did she resolve that with the truth the General had revealed about Freddy? Tussy was torn:

> At the same time it is very painful to me, because I know – no one knows as well as I – how Mohr <u>hated</u> to have his private life dragged into public . . . So while I <u>do</u> feel this letter shd be published, I at the same time feel half a traitor in giving it to the world.[36]

Half a traitor to her father, to Freddy and to herself. Eleanor agonised about what she should do – or not – about the family secret. Coupled with this problem, familiar to every biographer, was the fact that she could not gain access to the correspondence between Mohr and the General. That fatal clause in Engels's will, 'except my letters to him and his letters to me', was making her biographical project seemingly impossible. In the midst of this, she had discovered that Edward was living a double life.

Edward's deceit began, of seeming necessity, at the beginning of their relationship. The story he told Tussy was that his first wife Bell – Isabel Campbell Frank – was emotionally unstable, difficult, vindictive and refused to divorce him. Therefore he couldn't marry Tussy unless Bell died. In fact, Edward had walked out on Bell when he had run through the dowry she received from her father on their marriage. She was more than willing to divorce; he refused. As long as they remained married he stood to inherit her estate in the event of her death. Edward's brother Frederick, who respected Tussy, tried to tell her that his brother wasn't telling the truth. Lovestruck Tussy didn't listen.

Bell died intestate in 1892. Three weeks later, her 'lawful husband' Edward Aveling was granted administration of her estate and promptly collected the £126 15s 4d Bell had left. Within a few months, unbeknown to anyone else, he invested in a residential property in Austin Friars. Edward maintained the fiction that Bell was still alive for several years. When it came out accidentally that she was dead, Eleanor is said to have told Frederick, 'Now Edward will marry me.' To which his brother responded, 'Oh no he won't. I know Edward.'[37] Again, Tussy paid no heed.

Tussy was now confronted by the fact that Edward, after all his fine words about free love and open unions being as morally and emotionally binding as marriage under the law, was simply a liar. And she was a gull, a fool who had willingly suspended her disbelief – because she loved him. It was laughable. Tussy knew this dialectic. History repeated itself first as tragedy then as farce. So much for Edward's radical politics, free love and the feminist-inspired 'woman question' – Tussy was merely Edward's cash-cow and passport to cultural capital.

A fortnight after Edward's return to the Den, he went with Tussy to visit her sister and Lafargue at Draveil. It was the first time Tussy had been to their 'magnificent', forest-fringed home on the banks of the Seine. Neither of the Lafargues seemed to notice any signs of trouble between the Marx-Avelings. Laura was happily absorbed in showing Tussy the house and grounds and Paul enjoyed showing off his vegetable gardens, orchards and livestock. Tussy thought Laura and Paul had found a 'wonderful place – really a "propriété"',[38] but felt uncomfortable with its grandeur. She suggested the huge 'orangerie' could be more usefully turned into a lecture and meeting hall for the local community, and the gardens and grounds opened as a public park. 'I don't think I would exchange my little Den with this palace,' she told Kautsky; for all that it was 'exquisite' it also made her worry about the future of Marxism in France.[39]

Tussy said nothing to Laura about the recent dramas in her personal life. Nor did she confide in anyone else. Only Freddy knew what had taken place over those stormy weeks in early August and why, superficially, Eleanor and Edward were reunited. Personal difficulties did not seem to throw Tussy off the forward march of her political work. She corrected the proofs for 'The Story of the Life of Lord Palmerston' and 'The Secret Diplomatic History of the Eighteenth Century', two highly achieved pieces of editing. At the same time, the engineering workers requested her help with their strike.

The Engineering Employers' Federation (EEF) was established in July 1897, with Siemens taking the presidency. Their aim, the Siemens spokesman told the press, was to get rid of trade unionism altogether'. In shortform, the EEF derailed negotiations with the eight-hour-day movement, the dispute intensified and a lockout began against workers who refused to submit.

As soon as she and Edward returned from France in September, Eleanor went to work long hours at the head office of the Amalgamated Society of Engineers (ASE) in Blackfriars. She was appointed foreign correspondent, fundraiser and campaign secretary for George Barnes, general secretary of the ASE. She dealt with all Barnes's correspondence, wrote his speeches and statements and handled the media and liaison with all the international organisations

THE BOLDEST PAUSE

supporting the British engineers. The ASE chose well. As foreign fundraiser Eleanor managed to bring in a staggering £29,000 to support the workers and their families over six months. This critical fund made the engineers' lockout survivable. Tussy admitted that she found it 'pretty heavy work . . . but this movement is worth the work'.[40] The engineers' fight for an eight-hour day proved to be the most protracted industrial dispute of 1897.

Whatever compromise they reached enabled Edward to continue to base himself at the Den with Tussy and, without her knowledge, maintain his double life with his new wife until November, when he caught debilitating flu. Tussy interpreted this sickness as a symptom of his moral disease, for which he should not be judged:

> Dear Freddy,
>   I know how kindly your feeling to me is, and how truly you care for me. But I don't think you quite understand – I am only <u>beginning</u> to. But I do see more and more that wrongdoing is just a moral disease, and the morally healthy (like yourself) are not fit to judge of the condition of the morally diseased; just as the physically healthy person can hardly realise the condition of the physically diseased.[41]

Eleanor tried to persuade Edward to stay behind and recover from his flu whilst she went on a speaking tour of Lancashire. Edward, reassuringly, insisted on coming with her to take his place on the hustings. The Burnley School Board election was due at the end of the month and they went to rally support, successfully, for the SDF candidate, Dan Irving. 'We had "real" Lancashire weather,' Tussy told Kautsky:

> What <u>that</u> is only those who have experienced it can say. But certainly if Dante cd have dreamed a Lancashire factory town in bad weather he wd have added circles to his hell, & to his 'lowest depth a lower deep'.[42]

They got wet through every day. Not, as Eleanor observed, weather 'to cure an invalid'.[43] By the time they got back to Sydenham

Edward's neglected influenza had 'developed into congestion of the lungs and a touch of pneumonia',[44] as Eleanor, channelling her inner Jewish mother, reported in detail to the Liebknechts on Christmas Eve. Eleanor spent an unseasonal December 'busy looking after Edward and after Barnes' correspondence. In both cases it is a labour of love.'[45] Or, in both cases, love's labours lost. The bitter winter and pressure on the strike subsistence funds weakened the engineers' 'great Lock-out'.[46] It looked like Aveling wouldn't hold out much longer either. Tussy anxiously reported to Laura that

> the doctor told me Edward might at any moment (his temperature was up to 103 at times) 'take a turn for the worse' and that I 'ought' at once to communicate with his relations. Of course I did not, because (except perhaps sister, now living in Devonshire) there is not a relation he wd want to see at any time.[47]

Not for the first time, both sisters wished they were a little nearer to each other.

It was a muted festive season. Edward – seemingly – invalided, Tussy couldn't go to France, and Library was serving a four-month prison sentence in Charlottenburg Prison under what Tussy jestingly called the 'Little Anti-Socialist Law' of 1897. On Christmas Eve she wrote a long letter to Library, designed to cheer him up. She put her best face forward on the engineers' action, making no mention of her troubles with Edward. She recalled a previous Christmas at Grafton Terrace, shared with Library

> ... and others who have now finished their work. Or rather their share of the work, for that is immortal, and lives more vigorously today than then. You are still at work and your magnificent courage, invincible good humour, and splendid cheerfulness are an example and a lesson to us all. 'Stone walls do not a prison make/Nor iron bars a cage', and the prison has not been built, nor the iron forged that could hold your spirit captive. I do not even feel it incongruous to wish to you a 'Merry' Xmas! A happy New Year I know awaits you, because work for others awaits you.

Our love to you, dear Library, my kind, dear friend and friend of Mohr and Möhme and Helen and Jenny.[48]

For reasons no one could foresee, a happy New Year did not await Library, nor anyone who knew and loved Tussy.

White Dress in Winter

In the first week of January 1898 actress Ellen Terry wrote to George Bernard Shaw in confidence telling him that Edward Aveling had asked her for a loan. 'His exploits as a borrower have grown into Homeric legend,' GBS replied, informing Terry that for some years past Aveling had 'been behaving well because Marx's friend Engels left Eleanor £9,000 . . . But the other day he tried the old familiar post-dated cheque on Sidney Webb – in vain. And then, I suppose, he tried you. Must I really not tell anyone? If you only knew how utterly your delicacy is wasted!'[1]

A few weeks later Tussy wrote to Laura thanking her for sending loving greetings and cash as an advance birthday present. 'It was very welcome, for, as I hardly need tell you, illness means immense expense in every way. Doctors' visits at 5/ a time, & sometimes twice a day – are no joke.'[2] She made no mention of planning any celebration for her forty-third birthday.

Eleanor was preoccupied with the engineers' ongoing struggle for an eight-hour day and the horrendous suffering amongst the workers. She marvelled to Kautsky that how some of the families survived was a mystery to her and confided to Nathalie Liebknecht that, 'unless much help is forthcoming (this of course entre nous) we are hopelessly beaten.'[3] Everyone had given as much as they could; the funds to support the workers' struggle against their immovable employers had run dry. They'd been starved out.

She thought the SDF 'pretty stupid in this matter',[4] and correctly anticipated that the Amalgamated Society of Engineers would be forced to withdraw their demands before the end of the month. Eleanor hoped this defeat might, in the long run, be more useful than a half-hearted victory. She observed that socialist feeling had grown rapidly amongst the engineering workforce as a consequence of the protracted dispute. 'If only', she mused to Kautsky,

> . . . we could now spread our Socialist nets properly we should get a splendid haul – but I fear our fishes slip away. <u>You</u> want to be in London – but sometimes I wish I could be, like you, in a country where there <u>is</u> a live movement. I suppose we shall move here one of these days – & this lock-out is helping to give what football players call a fine 'kick-off.'[5]

Tussy would have been better off sticking with fishing rather than football metaphors. When it came to sport, football was Edward's first love. And come the New Year, he was kicking off again:

> Edward <u>is</u> better. Indeed, he is working again, though I wish he wouldn't. But I did not exaggerate the danger . . . he is still terribly weak and terribly emaciated. He is a very skeleton – mere skin and bones. The slightest chill wd, the doctors say, be absolutely fatal – & Edward is a most unmanageable person. I write freely because he is in bed asleep (thank goodness he *does* sleep well!) & except in a letter to <u>me alone</u> you must not let him know there is still such cause for anxiety.[6]

Tussy had no idea that, as she wrote this letter to her sister, Edward was once again trying to borrow money from her friends and was leaning again on Freddy. Encouraging him to rest and get away from the winter fogs that settled over the Thames Estuary, Tussy persuaded Edward's doctor to send him to Hastings. 'I am anxious at having to let him go alone, though the people he is with – we have lodged there before – will, I know, look after him . . . But I really <u>could</u> not go with him: these four weeks have cost too much to make this possible.'⁷ Aveling needed no persuading. Tussy wrote to Freddy:

> Yes – I sometimes feel like you, Freddy, that poor Jenny had her full share of sorrow and trouble, and Laura lost her children. But Jenny was fortunate enough to die, and sad as that was for her children, there are times when I think it fortunate. I would not have wished Jenny to have lived through what I have done. I don't think you and I have been very wicked people – and yet, dear Freddy, it does seem as if we get all the punishment.⁸

Aveling returned from Hastings at the end of January. His pneumonia had cleared up, but the old kidney disease had returned, accompanied by his recurrent abscesses. He was impatient and in a foul temper. Eleanor put it down to his illness, which he persuaded her was probably fatal. Eleanor didn't know that Edward's new wife had joined him at Hastings, where they came up with another plan, with which Edward returned to London. Tussy appealed once again to Freddy:

> I have to face such great trouble, and <u>quite</u> without help (for Edward does not help <u>even now</u>), and I hardly know what to do. I am daily getting demands for money, and how to meet them, AND the operation and all else, I don't know. I feel I am a brute to trouble you, but, dear Freddy, you <u>know</u> the situation; and I say to you what I would not say to anyone now. I would have told my dear old Lenchen, but as I have not her, I have only you. So forgive my being selfish, and <u>do</u> come if you can.⁹

At the beginning of February Edward went to London, ostensibly for medical consultations. He refused to let Eleanor go with him. The old doubts returned. She told Freddy, 'Edward has gone to London today. He is to see doctors, and so on. <u>He would not let me go with him</u>! That is sheer <u>cruelty,</u> <u>and</u> there are things he does not want to tell me. Dear Freddy – you have your boy – I have nothing; and I see nothing worth living for.'¹⁰

Alarmed by this nihilistic expression of desperation, Freddy finally dug in his heels and acted with purposeful resolve. Aveling be damned. She had to throw him out and cut off any further communication with him, come what may. Given Freddy's social and economic vulnerabilities, this was a great act of solidarity. Hoping to bring her to her senses, Freddy finally spelled out to Eleanor the truth that Edward was blackmailing him and wanted more. Infuriatingly, Eleanor deflected Freddy and instead wrote him a rambling philosophical disquisition on forgiveness. She also promised that Edward had 'no idea of asking you again for money'.[11] She was sure Freddy didn't understand how ill Edward was and that he would not see him again after his forthcoming operation.[12] 'In some,' she confided to Freddy,

> a certain moral sense is wanting, just as some are deaf, or have bad sight, or are otherwise unhealthy. And I begin to understand that one has no more right to blame the one disease than the other. We must try and cure, and, if no cure is possible, do our best. I have learnt this through long suffering – suffering in ways I would not tell even you; but I have learnt, and so I am trying to bear all this trouble as best I can.[13]

Two days later Edward was admitted to University College Hospital for surgery. Tussy wrote to Freddy, 'There is a French saying that to understand is to forgive. Much suffering has taught me to understand – and so I have no need to forgive. I can only love.'[14] Tussy's forgiving love had become insufferable. She stayed in a bed and breakfast nearby the hospital in Gower Street. Edward had his operation on Wednesday 9 February. Twenty-four hours later it was clear that, though weak, he would survive. Tussy wrote to Kautsky to inform him of the news: 'If you see any friends let them know.'[15]

Judging by the drama Edward made of it, it would be fair to assume that his surgery was life-threatening. Tussy told Library that the thirty minutes that Edward had been in the theatre was 'like the "toilette" of the condemned prisoner to me' and that she 'wd gladly have changed places with Edward and have counted myself happy'.[16]

To Kautsky, she exaggerated the medical diagnosis: 'There is just a possibility (remote) of the abscess healing. If – as is likely – it does not, it will mean doing nothing and just waiting, or the terrible operation of removing one kidney.'[17] The day after, Edward's surgeon, Dr Heath, told Eleanor that Edward's procedure had been merely exploratory.

Echoes of conversations between women suggest a different version of events. Edward had several visitors while in hospital. Some of his students and theatre friends came to see him; possibly Mrs Eva Nelson slipped herself in amongst them. Eleanor asked Matilda Hyndman to come for a cup of tea and, as they walked the ward corridor, confided in her. Matilda shared Eleanor's confidence with her husband:

> The story Mrs Aveling told was most depressing . . . she evidently had to open her heart to somebody, and the tale she told of the misery and humiliation she had to undergo induced my wife to implore her to leave the man directly he was out of danger, and to come for a time to stay with us. She said she would gladly do so.[18]

Clearly, Eleanor no longer kept Edward's behaviour a secret from her friends. She brought Edward home to the Den a week later, Thursday 17 February, by carriage – the most expensive conveyance possible. The doctors, keen for him to avoid further infection, thought Aveling would have a better chance of recovery at home. Better still, if they could afford it, Eleanor should take him to Margate to convalesce.

Eleanor booked rooms at a hotel recommended by the Hyndmans and the day after his release from hospital they went to Margate. All of this involved further expense, but Tussy was throwing everything she had at the problem. She clearly believed Edward, like so many other people she loved, was going to die. As she put it to Freddy, 'It is all so surely going to the one thing that I am giving up all the little I have left. You will understand – I can get on anyway, and I must now see to him. Dear Freddy, do not blame me. But I think you will not. You are so good and so true.'[19]

Eleanor felt the financial pressures were now overwhelming. She confessed to Library that her current expenses were enormous: 'Doctors, chemists' bills, "bath chairs" for going out, and so forth, added to the home that must be kept up – all this means a very great deal. I speak so frankly because I know you will understand.'[20] For the first time, Eleanor was counting the financial cost of having Edward in her life. There could be no surer sign that she had, finally, reached the end of the line with him.

Tussy was ready to leave Margate, and Edward. 'It is a bad time for me,' she wrote to Freddy. 'I fear there is little hope, and there is much pain and suffering. Why we go on is the mystery to me. I am ready to go, and would gladly. But while he <u>wants</u> help I am bound to stay.'[21] She was duty-bound to care for him whilst he was sick – that was all. The tone of Eleanor's correspondence changes during these weeks. Her letters express her growing conviction that Edward would probably die and she survive. '<u>I</u> can get on anyway, and I must now see to <u>him.</u>' Tussy never doubted that she was the stronger party. If she could just do her duty, she might be free. 'I fear there is very little hope of ultimate recovery,' she told Kautsky, whose heart might have lifted a little at the news. 'Today he did – leaning on my arm & a stick – walk a little.'[22] She sent Hyndman a series of letters from Margate detailing the work she had programmed for the SDF for the forthcoming year. Aveling continued to shuffle, determined to break her. Edward didn't want Eleanor to survive; that would hurt his ego. He needed her money for his new marriage, and Eva Nelson, understandably, was impatient.

They returned to the Den on Sunday 27 March. Aveling's illness had forced Tussy to cancel her recent speaking engagements, but now she was keen to get back fully to work. She'd promised Library an in-depth account of the end of the engineers' lockout, and, as soon as she got back, made the final arrangements with Sonnenschein for the publication of *Value, Price and Profit*, promising that her preface, which she was currently writing, would follow within the next few weeks. She sorted through her correspondence with Edith and accepted a number of invitations, including a request to attend a gala dinner in Hyndman's honour in May. Significantly, Tussy was back to business as usual.

Tussy was delighted that Library had been released from prison and looked forward to seeing him as soon as possible. She caught up on a raft of correspondence and work, and enjoyed using her new stylographic pen, sent to her by the Miners' Federation and the Miners' Union with a matching writing case. She'd refused to accept wages for her translation work at the International Miners' Congress in June 1897, so the miners clubbed together to raise the money for the handsome gift, appropriately marking their recognition of the value of her writing and language skills. Eleanor glowed with pleasure: '(it was work!),' she preened to Freddy. 'I am ashamed to accept such a gift, but I can't help doing so. And it <u>does</u> please me!'[23] There's a sense of brisk optimism on Tussy's return to London at the beginning of March, pleasure at returning to work and the company of Gerty, Edith, her friends and her cats, and making plans for the future.

The days became a little warmer but, in the last week of March 1898, spring still just held off. Sometime between their return to the Den on Sunday 27 March and the morning of Thursday 31 March, Eleanor discovered that Edward had married another woman. No record survives of how she found out. Perhaps Eva Nelson had had enough of waiting and made Eleanor aware of what Edward couldn't square himself to tell her. Maybe Edward made the revelation, hoping it would break her. Or she found out by accident.

However the news came to her, Eleanor reacted by immediately changing her will and wrote a long covering letter to Crosse.

On the morning of Thursday 31 March Gertrude Gentry heard Eleanor and Edward arguing. Aveling said he was going to London, but he was still under doctor's orders to convalesce, and Eleanor objected. The previous afternoon he had to be wheeled in his bath chair just a few yards from the house into the garden, so she appeared to have a point. A row ensued, then silence.

Shortly before 10 a.m., Tussy called Gerty to her study and asked her to run an errand. She gave her an envelope to take to Mr Dale at the pharmacy nearby on Kirkdale Street. Gerty was a familiar face to George Dale – she'd been running prescriptions for Dr Aveling to the end of the street and back again regularly. Sealed inside the envelope Gerty presented to Dale was a script reading, 'Please give bearer chloroform and small quantity of prussic acid for dog.'[24] The prescription was initialled 'E.A.', and Edward Aveling's card was clipped to the corner of the note. Gerty returned to the Den with a packet and the poison book for signature. She was unaware of the lethal contents of the parcel she carried: two ounces of chloroform and an eighth of an ounce of prussic acid. Needing a signature for the poison book was not unusual; Dr Aveling often needed strong medicines.

Aveling was still in the house when Gerty left once again for the pharmacy to return the poison book to Mr Dale. When she returned to the Den the only sound in the house came from Tussy's cats, mewing in her bedroom. Her mistress was normally always in her study during the day. Gerty sensed something was terribly wrong.

Gerty found Tussy in bed, motionless. Her long, dark hair was loose, her eyes fixed open. Her face and body had changed colour, to a lurid mottled indigo. Gerty saw that Eleanor was wearing her favourite white muslin summer dress. It was unseasonal. Gerty had washed, ironed and starched it herself, then laid it away in lavender and tissue paper for the winter.

As there was no telephone in the house Gerty ran, shouting, out on to the street and to their next-door neighbour Mrs Kell, who called for the nearest doctor, a friend of her husband, who lived at the top end of Jew's Walk. His name was Dr Henry Shackleton, and he had a twenty-four-year-old son called Ernest who wanted to explore the Antarctic. By the time Dr Shackleton arrived, Tussy had been dead for two hours. Her face, hands and feet bloomed the purplish-blue associated with poisoning by prussic acid. The scent of bitter almonds lingered around her corpse.

Eleanor Marx was dead. And where was Edward Aveling?

Until the inquest, no one would know. Aveling, apparently, returned home from London around 5 p. m., to find a police constable stationed outside their front door. On being told the news, hearsay claimed, he was either distraught with tears and hysterical grief, or utterly removed and indifferent. As Aveling was known to be an accomplished actor, which was true is irrelevant.

Gerty washed and laid Tussy out, shrouding her in her white muslin dress. Her body was removed to the morgue and the inquest took place two days later, on the evening of Saturday 2 April, at Park

Hall in Sydenham. The presiding coroner was Edward Wood, Deputy Coroner for West Kent and South East London.

Aveling was the first witness, introduced to the court as 'an author residing at The Den':

CORONER: Was the deceased your wife?

AVELING: Legally or not do you mean?

CORONER: You are a most difficult man to deal with. Were you married to the deceased?

AVELING: Not legally.

CORONER: She lived with you as your wife do you mean?

AVELING: Yes.

CORONER: What was her age?

AVELING: I believe about 40, but I am not quite sure.

CORONER: Was her health usually good?

AVELING: Very.[25]

The inquest inquired into Aveling's movements on the day of Eleanor's death. His statements contradicted those of all the other witnesses. Gertrude Gentry was clear that Aveling was in the house when she returned from her errand to the pharmacy with the package and poison book. Aveling said Gerty was mistaken; he was adamant that he'd already left for London before Tussy sent Gerty to the pharmacy. Aveling's family, convinced from the moment they heard the news that Edward had murdered Eleanor by engineering her suicide, claimed that he walked up and down Jew's Walk until he knew the poison would have done its work, re-entered the Den to sort through the letters Tussy had left, and then quickly went up to London.

The crucial letter Aveling had to find and destroy was Tussy's new signed codicil to Crosse, just written, making Jenny's children and her sister Laura beneficiaries of her estate. Edward knew that under Tussy's previous will of 16 October 1895 he was sole executor and chief beneficiary. Under that will, the *Nachlass* manuscripts and royalties were to be divided equally between the children of her late sister Jenny. Everything else came to him. 'I give and bequeath the residue of my estate and effects to my said husband but in the event of my said husband dying in my lifetime then I give and bequeath the same . . . unto and equally between the children of my said sister.'[26] In the event of the death of her 'husband', her will named Eduard Bernstein her executor. In this will, she bequeathed Bernstein all her books, and £25 for the trouble of implementing her wishes.

A year later, on 28 November 1896, Gertrude Gentry and John Smith, the gardener and general handyman, had witnessed a new codicil to Eleanor's will of 1895 that substantively increased Aveling's share of the estate. Not only would he now get the house, all the capital and her effects, but in his lifetime he would receive the royalties and any other income due from the *Nachlass*. Anyone interested in the financial benefits due to Edward on Eleanor's death, up until she changed her will in the last days of her life, needed to look closely at the date of this amendment as it was coincident with Aveling starting his affair with Eva Frye. At that time, Aveling told Eleanor that the work he was doing on editing and translating Marx's works earned him the right to a share of the literary estate. Tussy amended her 1895 will accordingly: 'all my interests of whatever nature the same may be in the works of my late father Karl Marx and all the sums payable as royalties or otherwise . . . unto my husband the said Edward Aveling during his life and upon his death the said sums to be paid to the children of my said sister.'[27]

From November 1896 to the last week of March 1898, therefore, Aveling stood to inherit everything if he outlived Eleanor. 'Was her health usually good?' the Coroner asked. 'Very,' Edward replied. As strong as a horse.

It is certain that on the morning of Eleanor's death Aveling caught the train from Sydenham to London Bridge and arrived at the offices of the SDF in Maiden Lane about 11 a.m. As he sat down to his meeting with Henry William Lee, secretary of the SDF, Aveling called particular attention to the exact time: 11.15 a.m. He returned to the Den around five in the afternoon, to find the policeman stationed outside.

CORONER: Had you any idea that she would destroy herself?
AVELING: She has threatened to do it several times.

CORONER: Did you consider that the threats used were intentional?
AVELING: I regarded them as idle, because they were so frequently repeated.
CORONER: Had you any quarrel before you left in the morning?
AVELING: None whatever.

Gerty wondered at Aveling's barefaced lies. On behalf of the jury, the foreman asked further questions about the state of Eleanor and Edward's relationship. The summary of Aveling's statements under cross-questioning was that 'they had slight differences, but had never had any serious quarrel. The deceased was of a morbid disposition and several times suggested that they commit suicide together. When they had difficulties it was not infrequent for her to say, "Let us end all these difficulties together."'

CORONER: Do you mean pecuniary difficulties?
AVELING: Yes, pecuniary, not, however recently as in the past.

Another lie, as all Eleanor's correspondence with Laura, Library and Freddy of the past year demonstrated. Edward's clandestine marriage to Eva Frye in July 1897, a material fact he did not disclose to the court, might fairly have been regarded as constituting more than a 'slight difference' between them. At this stage no one knew about 'Alec Nelson's' marriage to Eva Frye; this only emerged later, after Eleanor's inheritance had been paid out to him. Asked about his legal marital status, Aveling said that he was not married to the deceased because he had been married before.

The coroner's court returned a verdict of 'Suicide by swallowing prussic acid at the time labouring under mental derangement.' Eleanor's death was registered in Sydenham, sub-district of Lewisham, on 4 April 1898: 'Eleanor Marx, aged 40, a single woman.' Her age was forty-three. Whether she was single was debatable.

The court returned Eleanor's letter to Crosse and the codicil enclosure to Aveling without further investigation. Of the letters she wrote in the last hours of her life, only three survived. The letter to Crosse was returned to Aveling. Another to Aveling himself, reiterating, pathetically, that her last word to him was the same she had said during all the long, sad years – 'love'. The third, to her nephew Johnny Longuet, instructed him: 'Try to be worthy of your grand-father.'[28] None of her other letters written shortly before her death were accounted for.

George Dale, the pharmacist, came off the worst at the inquest. He was reprimanded for selling deadly poison to a man who was not even a doctor. Dale explained that he had always thought 'Dr Aveling' a physician, as he presented himself as a medical man, though not in practice. The coroner ruled Dale in breach of the Pharmacy Act of 1869. Noting the discrepancy between the initials on the prescription and in the poison book, the coroner asked whether or not Eleanor was ever known to sign herself by the initials 'EMA'. Aveling said yes. The other witnesses said they didn't know. The correct answer was that Eleanor signed herself EMA in her print journalism, such as for *Justice*, did not use this signature in personal or administrative correspondence.

Laura collapsed on hearing the news and was sedated; Paul Lafargue and Johnny Longuet had to go to London for Tussy's funeral without her. Library, Hyndman and Bernstein felt respon-sible and desperately guilty for not trying much harder to persuade Tussy to separate from Edward. All three wrote about it for the rest of their lives. Olive would have told them that she'd tried, and failed.

On Tuesday 5 April 1898 a large crowd of mourners gathered at the Necropolis Station in Waterloo, the same place where Eleanor had stood by the side of Engels's casket three years earlier. Tussy's coffin and train hearse-carriage to Woking Crematorium were heaped with wreaths. Flower tributes came from all over Britain, Germany, France, Holland, America, Australia, Russia, Austria, Italy, India, South Africa and further afield. There were many wreaths of red roses. Those like Lafargue and the Hyndmans, who knew Tussy's favourite colour, brought garlands of white flowers. There were floral tributes and specially stitched banners from the Union of Gas Workers and General Labourers, the SDF, the Hammersmith Socialist Society, the French Workers' Party, the German Social Democratic Party and several American socialist organisations. The staffs of *Justice*, the *Hamburger Echo*, *Vorwärts* and *Twentieth Century Press* also sent homages, amongst many others.

According to several mourners present, Aveling tried to make conversation by talking about the football match he had been to on the Saturday afternoon before her inquest. Those present who knew of his recent, apparently near-fatal illness commented on his miraculous recovery.

Freddy Demuth came alone and shunned Aveling. Bernstein spoke for the German party. Peter Curran, the trade union leader who later became the first Labour MP for north-east England, was one of several who spoke for the gas workers, and Henry Hyndman for the SDF. Will Thorne, one of socialism's strongest speakers, broke down during his speech and completed it in a tearful whisper. He spoke of his friendship with Tussy, and how she had quietly tutored him and other working-class men and women who were now leaders.

Eleanor's body was taken to Woking Crematorium on the cemetery railway line from Waterloo station, platform number 1. It seems strange that no record could be found of Eleanor's wishes for her remains. Especially as so much about her life suggests that on her death she might have wished for her ashes to be interred in the family grave containing her parents, Helen Demuth and her nephew in Highgate Cemetery.

Aveling never claimed her ashes, but he moved swiftly to secure probate of Eleanor's will, granted on 16 April. The net estate after death duties, disbursements and funeral expenses was £1,467 7s 8d, excluding 7 Jew's Walk and contents, which also went to Aveling. Crosse told Bernstein that less than a quarter of the money bequeathed by Engels was left by the time of Eleanor's death. 'I do not know how much of it was spent on hush-money to cloak his infamies with women or children, but it must have been very much,'[29] Bernstein wrote to Adler on the day of Tussy's funeral.

Crosse's involvement started to look suspicious when it was revealed shortly after Eleanor's death that he was now the key beneficiary from Aveling's will after his new wife, Eva Nelson. Bernstein pointed out that Crosse knew of the letter and signed codicil Eleanor had written to him during the last days of her life, retained by the coroner's court and then returned to Aveling after the verdict of suicide. Why did Crosse not make Edward hand over the letter addressed to him?

Aveling's new will bequeathed the bulk of his estate to Mrs Alec

Nelson, with whom he moved in at 2 Stafford Mansions, Albert Bridge Road in May, after Gertrude Gentry had packed up the Den, with the assistance of John Smith. Aveling and Eva went on a spending spree, redecorating the apartment and enjoying going to shows and eating out. There was nothing Aveling could do about his interest in Marx's literary remains, which would revert to the Longuet children on his death. However, he worked fast to push out any edited work, as yet unpublished, from which he could get the royalties. He got a nice return from *Value, Price and Profit*, for which he composed a quick preface. In Bernstein's opinion, 'After her death one thing of hers only was of value to him: her property, her money.'[30]

Hearing that Aveling had failed to collect Eleanor's ashes from Woking Crematorium, Frederick Lessner interceded and took responsibility. Lessner put a signed and dated card inside the urn identifying them as 'the ashes of Eleanor Marx', and took them to the SDF offices on Maiden Lane. The same offices Aveling had come to for his 11.15 a.m. meeting on the morning of her death, as Tussy burned up from prussic acid.

The general secretary of the SDF, Albert Inkpin, placed the urn in a glass-fronted cupboard and here it remained for twenty-three years. In 1912 these premises became the offices of the new British Socialist Party and in 1920, of the British Communist Party. A year later the Communist Party moved offices to 16 King Street in Covent Garden and Albert Inkpin, now general secretary of the British Communist Party, took the urn with him and put it back in the glass-fronted cabinet, now in his office.

Shortly after the move, on 7 May 1921, there was a police raid on the Communist Party headquarters. Filing cabinets were looted, cupboards pulled over and, as reported by the *Communist* on 21 May, 'The Editorial office was sacked. The scene ... was one of complete devastation.' Inkpin was arrested, as were the other leaders of the Communist Party and most of the central committee around England and in Scotland in parallel operations. None were granted bail.

> A tragic note was sounded when the detectives were begged not to disturb the ashes of Eleanor Marx Aveling, reposing in an urn ready to be conveyed to Moscow. They were left in peace.[31]

The claim that Tussy's ashes awaited transport to Moscow was pure journalistic embellishment – but one that Tussy might quite have liked, as she was fond of Russia and Russians.

The Marx Memorial Library in Clerkenwell Green was opened in 1933, fifty years after Karl Marx's death. Eleanor's ashes were placed prominently on a bookshelf in the Lenin Room. During the Second World War they were stored temporarily in the basement of 16 King Street and then went back on display upstairs in the same old glass-fronted cupboard, adorned with a new red ribbon.

In 1956 the family grave of Karl and Jenny Marx, their grandson and Helen Demuth in Highgate Cemetery was exhumed. Their remains were re-interred in a monumental new tomb and the urn containing Eleanor's ashes finally buried with them. Her name was added to those of her family carved on the tomb, recording, in error, her birthdate as 16 January 1856 and, correctly, her death as 31 March 1898.

Poor Eva didn't really have the best of it. She discovered that she had a sick man on her hands. By the end of April, three weeks after her death, Eleanor's friends, family, political allies and the press were alleging that Aveling was a murderer, thief and fraud, and that he should be brought to criminal trial. If he hadn't died four months after Eleanor, on Wednesday 2 August, of his old kidney disease, Bernstein, Library, Hyndman and the Lafargues would have brought a civil case against him. He was cremated on 5 August, in the presence of his new wife and five other friends. Not a single member of his family or representative of the socialist movement or literary world attended. Mrs Eva Nelson, 'a young lady attired in deep mourning', was seen collapsing, unable to send the body off. It was such a sad outcome for twenty-three-year-old Eva, she could hardly be begrudged for the £852 of Eleanor's remaining estate that she inherited after probate of Aveling's will was granted. He had burned through over a thousand pounds of his inheritance from Tussy in just under four months.

For years afterwards letters of lamentation flew around the world between Eleanor's friends about her sudden and tragic death. The volume of this correspondence and the broad range of people who wrote it illustrate how much Eleanor was admired and how far-reaching was her influence. The obituaries published in almost every country of the world would run to several bound volumes, in languages so innumerable that even multilingual Tussy might not have heard of some of them. Obituaries flowed from printing presses in England, Scotland, Ireland, Wales, the Americas, Canada, Germany, France, Holland, Poland, Spain, Italy, Russia and Australia – to name just a few. The gas workers' unions, SDF, ILP, May Day Committee, German SPD and French socialists were amongst the many organisations that issued formal resolutions mourning her departure.

Anyone might feel pride from beyond the grave to be honoured in these ways. Yet none of this memorialising matches the quiet eloquence of two letters written by working-class women, Leah Roth and Gertrude Gentry, published here for the first time.

Gerty is well known to us as Eleanor's housekeeper. Leah Roth was one of the innumerable working-class women who, as Eleanor wrote in 'The Woman Question', were world-changers and history-makers. Leah Roth wrote to Eleanor and Edward from 42 Stepney Green Dwellings on 19 January 1898, in a laboured, careful hand:

> Great honerable [sic] Lady and Gentleman I am begging of you that you should not take this as a [sic] insulting and to help me out a little of our trouble as we are starving day by day and especially a baby from a year and a half which I have nothing to give her but just to save her life so I am feeding her on a bottle of pure water so I am begging of you dear lady and gentleman you should have pity on me and on my poor eight starving children and you should help me out a little with any thing that I should be able to buy some food for the children and I myself dear lady don't know what to do with them I am only 7 weeks after my confinement and my husband is out of work these 3 months an [sic] we have not broke our fast these three days and if the kind lady would be good enough and to help me a little with a few old clothes I shall be very thankful to her.
>
> I am yours [sic] humble servant, Leah Roth
> (Pity us)[32]

Eleanor regularly received individual requests for help. She assisted with money and care packages and put women like Leah Roth in touch with their local branch of the SDF, trade union or women's organisation. A handful of these missives survive, unitemised, in the archive of Eleanor's miscellaneous correspondence. They are the last trail of an aspect of Eleanor's life that is otherwise hidden from history.

The second letter is from Gertrude Gentry to Edith Lanchester, written – elegiacally – on 1 May 1898 from the Den, a few days before Edward closed up the house and moved to Battersea with his new wife.

Dear Miss Lanchester,

Thank you very much for your kind letter. I am so glad you liked the Pen. I thought you would like to have some little thing in remembrance of our dear Mrs Aveling and that you would like to have the Pen she used so much. Oh how we do miss her, and it nearly breaks our hearts when we go out into the garden and see all the flowers coming out that she was so fond of. I don't know what we shall do when we leave it for good. I think it will quite break our hearts then. For while we are here we feel she must be coming back.

We have had Dr Aveling very ill we did not know what to think of him at one time but he is better again now. How is your dear little boy, I should like to see him. Minnie's babies are getting quite big children now, they will soon be able to go away. Dr Aveling has conscented [sic] to have dear Mrs Aveling's last wish carried out about the cats as soon as the babies are ready to go. I think I must close now with love to you and heaps of kisses to dear baby trusting you are well.

Yours very sincerely,
G.M. Gentry[33]

And so it was Gertrude Gentry who took on Aveling to make sure Tussy's last wishes were carried out regarding her beloved four-footers. Gerty also made sure that Edith received a proper, appropriate memento – Tussy's cherished writing pen.

Gertrude bore a heavy burden. She was the unwitting bearer of the chloroform and prussic acid that killed Eleanor. It was Gerty who found her dead body in shocking rictus. Edith knew very well that Gerty never liked Aveling. Gerty's observation that 'we did not know what to think of him at one time but he is better again now' seemed very pointed. Gertrude Gentry was powerless to act on her own but she could hope that Eleanor's friends and family might take action.

There was outrage at the verdict of the inquest, which did nothing except establish the 'fact' of suicide. Kautsky wrote to Adler from Berlin that he was in favour of taking immediate legal action against Aveling and of 'proceeding relentlessly against the scoundrel'.[34] Robert Banner, devastated by the news, looked closely at the order of the facts, and pursued Aveling in the press for an answer to why Eleanor's letter to Crosse had not been delivered. As well as Aveling offering an explanation of why he intercepted this letter to her lawyer, Banner wanted him to explain publicly why his version of events differed in every point to Gertrude Gentry's.

Eduard Bernstein decided to take legal action against Aveling and blamed himself until the end of his life for not dealing with him before. The outcry for Aveling to be brought to criminal trial continued for the rest of his short life. As Bernstein bitterly observed, 'If there were no party interest to take into consideration, the people would have torn Aveling to pieces.'[35] Aveling's death put an end to the call for justice – and his blood.

Olive Schreiner wrote to Dollie Radford from South Africa, with unerring prescience:

> I have little doubt in my mind she discovered a fresh infidelity of Aveling and that ended it all. I had thought of writing a short notice of her in one of the monthly reviews. Then I felt that as I could not speak the truth about him I could not write of her. It would have hurt her to have him blamed . . . I am so glad Eleanor is dead. It is such a mercy she has escaped from him.[36]

Olive had never doubted her first instinct that Aveling was a conman who would be the death of Eleanor if she didn't leave him. She asked

Dollie if there were any further details. 'I have felt,' she wrote, 'that if I was in England I would find the servant who was the last person with her and get her to tell me all she knew.'[37]

If only she had done it.

Afterword

Death can help people discover who they are.

What forces drove Eleanor Marx to her death?[1] asked Eduard Bernstein in an article published just four months after it happened. Bernstein believed that Edward Aveling was culpable, either morally, or criminally – or both. Only the law could decide if Aveling bore criminal responsibility, for which he should be brought to trial. Bernstein rather focused on the question of Aveling's moral accountability.

Bernstein's piece was a response to anti-socialist press using the 'opportunity' of Eleanor's suicide as an example of the 'life-failure'[2] of socialism as a way of living. Popular accounts of the story ran as follows: Aveling had decided to return to his first wife Bell Frank and their children and wanted Eleanor to join them in a 'marriage of three'.[3] Appalled, Eleanor preferred death to this free-love union. The fact that Bell had been dead for several years and no children existed from that marriage exposed the absurdity of this version of events.

It's important to hold in mind that at this stage, July 1898, very few people knew of the existence of Eva Frye, apart from a few complicit friends of Edward and Eva's who went to their wedding party the year before in June 1897 – and even they weren't exactly clear on the true circumstances of the marriage they witnessed.

Bernstein's speculation of what drove Eleanor to her death is full of supposition, leaning heavily on what he calls the 'psychological enigma'[4] of Eleanor's attachment to Edward and her tragic belief that by sticking by him she could cure what she called his 'moral disease'.[5] 'It was from the moral point of view the life of Ibsen's *Frau Alving*,'[6] Bernstein summarises. His questions, however, are substantively pertinent: 'Did Dr Aveling desire or have any interest in the suicide of Eleanor Marx?'[7]

For *Labour Leader*, the 'ingratitude, injustice and hardness' that Aveling displayed at the inquest spoke for themselves. Aveling publicly repudiated Eleanor Marx; he would be judged accordingly.

Bernstein's article stands for many similar ones written immediately and in the years after Tussy's death by close friends and political comrades – including Havelock Ellis and the heartbroken Library. Like Bernstein, all Tussy's close intimates had experienced her absolute delight in her new home: 'An ideal existence seemed to open out before her; her face would beam with pleasure as she welcomed her friends to the "Den".'[8] Aveling was unable simply to leave, take only what was fairly his and start a new life. He seemed compelled to try and destroy Eleanor's contentment and security, as well as her legal entitlement to her own property. This was his psychological tragedy.

However, the most striking aspect of this piece is its telling focus on Freddy Demuth. Bernstein publishes nine letters Eleanor wrote to Freddy from August 1897 to March 1898, correspondence directly concerning tumultuous events in her personal life with Edward. Bernstein introduces Freddy as 'the son of Helen Demuth . . . who was a second mother to the children of Marx':

and in brotherly fidelity stood Frederick Demuth to Eleanor Marx. He is a simple workman, to whom life has not been too kind, and I have strong grounds for believing that in the documents left by Eleanor Marx for her legal advisor his name stood in a prominent position.[9]

Documents retained and destroyed by Aveling.

Cherchez les femmes. Two women, Helen Demuth and Jenny Marx, lifelong friends. They lived together, delivered and raised children together from their own childhoods to death. Tussy's two mothers, who both had relationships with the same man. A 'marriage of three'?[10] These three intermeshed selves inseparable from Friedrich Engels, as he was from them. Each in relation to the other a friendship quartet. Each one kept secrets – for each other but also, for different reasons, for themselves. [11]

In brotherly fidelity stood Frederick Demuth to Eleanor. Freddy, whose physical likeness to Karl Marx in every point was, as Louise Kautsky brusquely put it, almost comical. Even without the father philosopher's signature beard.

Edward Aveling died three days after Bernstein's article was published. Within weeks, Bernstein found himself confronted by new revelations as he worked on the settlement of Aveling's estate with August Bebel. Freddy Demuth stayed in contact with Laura Lafargue and Eduard Bernstein for the remainder of their lives.[12]

Bernstein wrote that Eleanor's friends had a double duty to clear up the crime committed against her: the maintenance of personal responsibility as a shared, common interest of social existence, and the responsibility of friendship.

And what of Eleanor's personal responsibility to the common interest?

There are as many theories of suicide as there are suicides. Aveling claimed at the inquest that Eleanor had several times suggested they end it together and he paid no attention to her threats of suicide, since she made them so frequently. Yet Eleanor was dead, apparently having agreed to the novel idea of a unilateral suicide pact.

No theory will unravel a death so complex in motivation. Each case of suicide is fixed in the human particular: the individual story. Suicide takes place at moments of great crisis. It may be chaotic and anguished; it may be perfectly ordered and rational. It may be a form of murder.

Ethical arguments continue over whether individuals have the moral right to take their own lives. In the end, all the argument and analysis and case studies and psychological profiling condenses into a clear set of choices. Ultimately, there are two kinds of suicide: one for the outside world; one for yourself.

Suicide is not making a point; it's making sense.

It is an act of control over the body. Self-control if entered into voluntarily. Control by another if an act of coercion or concealed murder. The instinct for human survival is so strong that any experience overriding the control of the body takes hold and leaves a strong memory. Anorexia. Depression. Miscarriage. Physical and emotional violence. Extreme bodily exploitation. These were common experiences amongst women of all classes in the nineteenth century.

Aaron Rosebury recalled that Tussy admitted to being sometimes tired of life. But who in her line of work wouldn't be, sometimes? For every example of her despair at life and humanity there is a counter-example of Tussy's stamina and joie de vivre. Her gloom at the global victory of capitalism and man's inhumanity to man could be dispelled by a bus ride through London, a new book, or an evening in the company of friends at the Den.

At the end of 1845, Karl Marx wrote an article on Jacques Peuchet's memoirs, entitled 'Peuchet: On Suicide'.[13] In it, Marx observed that French criticism of society had 'at least, the great merit of having shown up the contradictions and unnaturalness of modern life not only in the relationships of particular classes, but in all circles and forms of modern intercourse'.[14] A decade before her birth Eleanor's future father selected and highlighted the following passage written by Peuchet:

> Amongst the reasons for the despair which leads very sensitive persons to seek death . . . I [Peuchet] have uncovered as a dominant factor the bad treatment, the injustices, the secret punishments which severe parents and superiors visit on people dependent on them. The Revolution has not overthrown all tyrannies; the evils which were charged against despotic power continue to exist in the family; here they are the cause of crises analogous to those of revolutions.[15]

Marx and Engels, and Eleanor after them, thought, wrote and spoke extensively about tyranny and contradiction within the family and the forms of social revolution required to adequately address them. Eleanor, however, was clear on the question of personal responsibility. In her darkest hour, she did not blame the sins of the fathers for her own predicament but took the measure of the situation from within herself. In September 1897 she wrote to Freddy urgently asking him to come and assist her:

> I am so lonely, and I am face to face with a most dreadful situation: Absolute ruin – everything, even to the last penny, or deepest shame before the whole world. It is frightful. It presents itself to me even worse than it is. And I need someone with whom I can take counsel. I know that the final decision and responsibility will rest with me – but a little counsel and friendly assistance will be of immeasurable value.[16]

Eleanor Marx the woman leaves us with the contradictions of her life to consider. Eleanor Marx the politician, thinker, feminist and activist leaves us with our own question of personal responsibility to the common interest that is essential to social existence.

Many of the freedoms and benefits of modern democracy Britain inherited for the twentieth century and beyond into our own new millennium were a direct result of the work done by Eleanor Marx and women and men like her. The eight-hour day. The outlawing of child labour. Access to equal education. Freedoms of expression. Trade unions. Universal suffrage. Democratically selected parliamentary representation, regardless of class, religion, gender or ethnicity. Feminism.

To live with Eleanor for a while is to have an opportunity to remember how we got here, where the democratic liberties we enjoy came from. And at what price we let them go.

Undermining employment rights, socially stigmatising the poor, blaming the sick, demonising immigrants, betraying child labourers, polluting the environment in the name of surplus value and incentivising families to send women home to make babies: all of these contribute to the re-creation of an economic underclass – and all of them are happening now.

There is a deletion of historical memory under way. Ideational conditions have changed; it's almost as if we have convinced ourselves that inequality, consumerism and global commodity capitalism are a naturally inbuilt economic system to which there is no viable alternative.

Tussy's life is a reflection on the methods and values that got us to the forms of liberty, education, job protection, reproductive rights and access to healthcare that underpin social democracy and a strong civil society. If we don't remember how we got here, we won't know how to fix it.

This tale of Tussy's life is a remembering, not a recuperation. As she would be the first to say, all work is just a small contribution towards the next thing. Eleanor was the child of a lost collectivist age. But there are signs in the new collective impulses towards social democracy around the world that radicalism is being rethought and struggled over anew, from within a different set of historical conditions.

Eleanor outlived the classic dialectic invented by her revolutionary family: thesis, antithesis, synthesis. She named the next stage, with characteristic humour, 'the sequel'.[17]

Above all else, Eleanor knew that without bringing the question of feminism to the centre and heart of every imaginative act and movement for social and economic change, the sequel would remain indefinitely in the making. Eleanor took the longer view of history, so would not be surprised to know the sequel is still in the process of being written and would no doubt remark encouragingly, 'Go ahead!'

Tussy's life stirs memory and desire. As Gerty wrote to Edith from the Den on 1 May 1898, 'For while we are here we feel she might be coming back.'[18]

NOTES

Abbreviations for names and sources
EA – Edward Aveling
EM – Eleanor Marx
FE – Friedrich Engels
GBS – George Bernard Shaw
IISH – International Institute for Social History
IML – Institute of Marxism–Leninism
JL – Jenny Longuet
KM – Karl Marx
LL – Laura Lafargue
MEC – Marx–Engels Correspondence
MECW – *Marx–Engels Collected Works*
MML – Marx Memorial Library
PRO – Public Record Office

Preface

1 Eric Hobsbawm, *The Age of Capital 1848–1875*, Weidenfeld & Nicolson, London, 1996, p. 108.
2 Eleanor Marx and Edward Aveling, *The Woman Question: From a Socialist Point of View*, first published in *Westminster Review*, No. 125, London, January–April 1886; first printed as separate stand-alone edition by Swan Sonnenschein, London, 1886. Reprinted by Verlag für die Frau, Leipzig, 1986, p. 13. All page references are taken from the Verlag für die Frau edition.
3 EM to Karl Kautsky, 28 December 1896, IISH.
4 Eleanor Marx, in *Justice*, 31 October 1896, p. 5.
5 Ibid.
6 *Justice*, 23 November 1895, p. 8.
7 EM to Karl Kautsky, 3 June 1897, IISH.
8 EM to Laura Lafargue, 24 December 1896, IISH.
9 Karl Marx, in Friedrich Engels, *The Origin of the Family, Private Property and the State* (1884), Penguin Classics, London, 2010, with a new introduction by Tristram Hunt, p. 88.
10 Henry Havelock Ellis, 'Eleanor Marx', in Adelphi, Vol. 11, No. 1, 1935, pp. 33–4.

Chapter 1 – Global Citizen

1 Wilhelm Liebknecht, *Karl Marx: Biographical Memoirs*, translated by E. Untermann, Journeyman Press, London, 1975, p. 134.

2 KM to Ferdinand Lassalle, 23 January 1855, *MECW*, Vol. 39, Lawrence & Wishart, London, 1983, p. 511.

3 Liebknecht, *Karl Marx*, p. 134. 'Surely as the churning of milk bringeth forth butter, and the wringing of the nose bringeth forth blood: so the forcing of wrath bringeth forth strife.' Proverbs 30:33, *King James Bible*.

4 Engels ended up writing the piece, as he did most of the others on Crimea published under Marx's name between 1851 and 1855. The leader for 22 January, 1855, a week after Eleanor's birth, was entitled 'British Disaster in the Crimea' and later published as part of *The Eastern Question*, edited by EM, S. Sonnenschein & Co., London, 1885.

5 KM to FE, 17 January 1855, *MECW*, Vol. 39, p. 508.

6 Karl Marx and Friedrich Engels, *The Communist Manifesto* (1848), translated by Samuel Moore (1888), with an introduction by Gareth Stedman Jones, Penguin, London, 2002, p. 240.

7 Heinz Frederick Peters, *Red Jenny: A Life with Karl Marx*, Allen & Unwin, London, 1986, p. 6.

8 KM to FE, 12 April 1855, *MECW*, Vol. 39, p. 533.

9 Jenny Marx junior to KM, undated letter, September 1855, IISH.

10 And still is in many parts of Britain and the USA.

11 'Eleanor Marx, Karl Marx: A Few Stray Notes', in *Reminiscences of Marx and Engels*, Foreign Languages Publishing House, Moscow, 1957, p. 251.

12 Wilhelm Liebknecht, 'Reminiscences of Marx', in *Reminiscences*, p. 116.

13 Paul Lafargue, 'Reminiscences of Marx', in *Reminiscences*, pp. 82-3.

14 Liebknecht, 'Reminiscences of Marx', in *Reminiscences*, p. 123.

15 Ibid., p. 117.

16 Ibid.

17 Peters, *Red Jenny*, p. 100.

18 Friedrich Engels, 'On the History of the Communist League', in *Social Democrat*, 12–26 November 1885, and *Marx & Engels Selected Works*, Vol. 3, Progress Publishers, Moscow, 1970, http://www.marxists.org/archive/marx/works/1847/communist-league/1885hist.htm

19 Edgar Longuet, in *Reminiscences*, p. 261.

20 Jenny Marx junior to KM, undated letter, September 1855, IISH.

21 Mrs Jenny Marx to Louise Weydemeyer, 11 March 1861, in *Reminiscences*, p. 245.

22 Ibid.

23 Now 36 Grafton Terrace. I am enormously grateful to Bee and William Rowlatt for their research trip and contemporary photographs of Tussy's Kentish Town home.

24 Mrs Jenny Marx to Louise Weydemeyer, 11 March 1861, in *Reminiscences*, p. 245.

25 Peters, *Red Jenny*, p. 120.

26 Jenny Marx, in *Reminiscences*, p. 244.

27 Ibid., p. 228.

28 KM to FE, 23 April 1857, *MECW*, Vol. 40, p. 125.

29 EM, in *Reminiscences*, p. 250.

30 Ibid.

31 EM to Karl Kautsky, 19 June 1897, IISH.

32 KM to FE, 24 January 1863, *MECW*, Vol. 41, p. 444.

33 EM, in *Reminiscences*, p. 251.

34 Ibid.

35 Jenny Marx quoted in Edna Healey, *Wives of Fame: Mary Livingstone, Jenny Marx, Emma Darwin*, Sidgwick & Jackson, London, 1986, p. 102.

36 EM, in *Reminiscences*, p. 250.

37 Jenny Marx, in *Reminiscences*, p. 245.

38 If Tussy's adult sexual relationships are anything to go by, her childish unconscious may have interpreted these narrative propositions too literally.

39 Letter from Jenny Marx to Ernestine Liebknecht, 18 July 1864, IISH.

40 Paul Lafargue, cited in Lee Baxendall and Stefan Morawski, eds., *Marx and Engels on Literature and Art*, International General, New York, 1974, p. 152.

41 EM, in *Reminiscences*, p. 252.

42 EM to Karl Kautsky, 1 January 1898, IISH.

43 EM, in *Reminiscences*, p. 253.

44 Ibid.

45 Ibid.

46 Ibid.

47 Ibid.

48 EM, in *Reminiscences*, p. 251.

49 'How Sigfried Came To Wurms', verse 99, *Das Nibelungenlied (Song of the Nibelungs)*, translated from the Middle High German by Burton Raffel, Yale University Press, New Haven & London, 2006.

50 EM, in *Reminiscences*, p. 251.

51 Ibid., p. 252.

Chapter 2 – The Tussies

1 Peters, *Red Jenny*, p. 10.

2 For a uniquely detailed account of the politics and thought of Hirschel/Heinrich Marx, see Boris Nicolaevsky and (trans.) Otto Maenchen-Helfen's investigation of his political ideas in *Karl Marx: Man & Fighter*, Methuen, London, 1936.

3 See Francis Wheen, *Karl Marx*, Fourth Estate, London, 1999, p. 10.

4 Peters, *Red Jenny*, p. 13.

5 Paul Lafargue, in *Reminiscences*, pp. 81–2.

6 EM, in *Reminiscences*, p. 17.

7 Mazzini, dubbed 'the Soul of Italy', was the republican leader of the Risorgimento, the radical movement for Italian unification and popular democracy. Exiled first to Geneva and then Marseilles, Mazzini founded Young Italy in 1831. A clandestine society dedicated to the promotion of popular uprising as the means to unify Italy, it provided the spark for a European-wide republican revolutionary movement. In 1834 Mazzini and a group of refugees from Eastern and Western Europe formed a new international organisation called Young Europe. By the end of the 1830s Mazzini was in London, from where he set up a number of sister associations under the umbrella of Young Europe, aimed at the unification or democratisation of other countries – Young Switzerland, Young Poland and Young Germany. The movement later provided a blueprint for a collective of Turkish students and army cadets who organised themselves under the title of the Young Turks. Advocating middle-class republicanism, enlightened nation building and a 'cosmopolitanism' of nations, Mazzini foresaw the continent's evolution into a United States of Europe as a logical correlative to Italian liberation and unification.

8 Heinrich Marx to KM, May or June 1836, *MECW*, Vol. 1, pp. 653

9 Henriette Marx to KM, beginning of 1836, *MECW*, Vol. 1, pp. 649–52.

10 KM to Jenny Marx, 15 December 1863, IISH.

11 Peters, *Red Jenny*, p. 22.

12 Cited in Peters, *Red Jenny*, p. 24, translated from the original by Mollie Peters.

13 EM, in *Reminiscences*, p. 254.

14 Eleanor Marx, 'Remarks on a letter by the young Marx', in *Reminiscences*, p. 256.
15 Peters, *Red Jenny*, p. 28.

Chapter 3 – Hans Röckle's Toyshop

1 Peters, *Red Jenny*, p. 60.
2 Ibid., p. 40.
3 Peter Oborne, cited in Terry Eagleton, *Why Marx Was Right*, Yale University Press, New Haven and London, 2011, p. x.
4 Eleanor Marx, Note by the Editor on 'Revolution and Counter-Revolution', April 1896, Sydenham, http://www.marxists.org/archive/marx/works/1852/germany/note.htm
5 Eleanor combined her father's Hans Röckle with a series of autobiographical notes penned by her mother. These memoirs are published in Tussy's prefatory essay to the series of articles she edited in 1896 under the title *Revolution and Counter-Revolution*. They recount her family history in the decade or so preceding her birth, when her parents and siblings were 'driven from pillar to post' around Europe (in the crucible of its bourgeois republican revolutions). Tussy takes up the story of the real adventures of Karl Marx and his young family with his expulsion from his first editorship of the *New Rhenish Gazette*, charting briskly the energetic pace of their zigzag heave-ho across Europe as the engine of history heated towards the revolutions of 1848–49.
6 Hobsbawm, *The Age of Capital*, p. 108.
7 Wheen, *Karl Marx*, p. 184.
8 Eleanor Marx, Note by the Editor on 'Revolution and Counter-Revolution'.
9 Jenny Marx, 'Short Sketch of an Eventful Life', in *Reminiscences*, p. 226.
10 Peters, *Red Jenny*, p. 96.
11 Jenny Marx, 'Short Sketch of an Eventful Life', in *Reminiscences*, p. 226.
12 Wheen, *Karl Marx*, pp. 179–80.
13 Eleanor Marx, Note by the Editor on 'Revolution and Counter-Revolution'.
14 Ibid.
15 Wheen, *Karl Marx*, p. 154.
16 Wilhelm Liebknecht, *Karl Marx: Biographical Memoirs*, Journeyman Press, London, 1975, p. 121.
17 Wilhelm Liebknecht, 'Eleanor Marx', *Social Democrat*, Vol. 2, No. 9, 15 September 1898.
18 FE to KM, 13 February 1851, *MECW*, Vol. 38, 1982, p. 289.
19 Karl Marx, *Capital*, Vol. I, Penguin Classics, London, 1990, p. 896.

Chapter 4 – Book-worming

1 Jenny Marx to Louise Weydemeyer, 11 March 1861, *MECW*, Vol. 41, p. 569.
2 KM, 'Confessions', in *Reminiscences*, p. 267.
3 EM, in *Reminiscences*, p. 252. It's indicative that when Tussy declares that she wants to be a Post-Captain, she gets it from Marryat, not Austen. Lovers of *Mansfield Park* will remember that Fanny Price's beloved brother William is a Post-Captain. Had Tussy read the novel, Miss Crawford's great condescension towards this 'inferior rank' would no doubt have alerted her to it being a meritocratic naval position, and sharpened all the more her desire to don breeches and attain the rank herself.
4 D. H. Lawrence, *Studies in Classic American Literature*, Vol. 2, 1923, Ezra Greenspan, Lindeth Vasey and John Worthen (eds), Cambridge University Press, 2002, p. 58.

5 James Lowell, *Fable for Critics: Complete Poetical Works of James Russell Lowell,* Kessinger Publishing, Montana, 2005, p. 135.
6 Cooper for a period sported ink petticoats, writing romances for women readers under the nom de plume of Jane Morgan. But by the time Tussy encountered his work he was back in trousers, producing his leatherstocking tales.
7 Lawrence, *Studies in Classic American Literature,* p. 63.
8 Jenny Marx to Ernestine Liebknecht, 10 December 1864, IISH.
9 Ibid.
10 EM, in *Reminiscences,* p. 252.
11 Ibid.
12 Ibid.
13 These envelopes and folded letters are in the IISH.
14 EM to Karl Kautsky, 19 June 1897, IISH.
15 KM to Mrs Jenny Marx, Wednesday 15 December 1863, IISH.
16 KM to FE, 11 January 1868, MECW, Vol. 42, 1987, p. 519.
17 Eleanor Marx to Lion Philips, letter undated (contextual event chronology places this letter as having been written sometime during late December 1863), IISH.
18 Karl Marx, Inaugural Address to the International Working Men's Association, 21–27 October 1864. Printed as a pamphlet in *Inaugural Address and Provisional Rules of the International Working Men's Association,* along with the 'General Rules'. Original pamphlet, MML, and in *MECW,* Vol. 20, 1985, pp. 14–15.
19 EM to Frank Van Der Goes, 31 October 1893, IISH.
20 Jenny Marx to Berta Markheim, 6 July 1863, London, *MECW,* Vol. 41, 1985, p. 581, http://www.marxists.org/archive/marx/letters/jenny/63_07_06.htm
21 Ibid.
22 Mrs Jenny Marx to Berta Markheim, 12 October 1863, *MECW,* Vol. 41, 1985, p. 583.
23 Tussy recollected in later years that this was the last holiday when they were able to legally swim naked in the sea. Nude swimming for both sexes was common until the 1860s, popularised particularly during the Regency era for its health and sanitary benefits – and for making people smell better. Skinny swimming was made fashionable by the Prince Regent, whose favourite pastime it was. But in 1863 a law was passed segregating male and female bathers by a statutory 60 feet and requiring the proprietors of bathing machines to supply females with flannel gowns or shifts and males with drawers or trousers for swimming. This increased the cost of hiring a bathing machine and effectively segregated the upper from the lower classes as much as it separated the sexes.
24 Mrs Jenny Marx to Berta Markheim, 12 October 1863, *MECW,* Vol. 41, 1985, p. 583.
25 FE, in *MECW,* Vol. 47, 1995, p. 355.
26 EM to Karl Kautsky, 15 March 1898, Karl Kautsky papers, IISH.
27 Ibid.
28 Tristram Hunt identifies Burns as Engels's 'underworld Persephone, profoundly enriching [his] appreciation of capitalist society . . . Mary helped to provide Engels with the material reality for his communist theory.' Tristram Hunt, *The Frock-Coated Communist: The Revolutionary Life of Friedrich Engels,* Penguin, London, 2009, pp. 100–1.
29 See Roy Whitfield, *Engels in Manchester: The Search for a Shadow,* Working Class Movement Library Salford, 1988, p. 21, and Hunt, *The Frock-Coated Communist,* pp. 100–1.
30 Friedrich Engels, *Condition of the Working Class in England in 1844,* translated by Florence Kelley Wischnewetzky, http://www.gutenberg.org/files/17306/17306-h/17306-h.htm, The Project Gutenberg eBook, accessed 13 December 2005, e-book #17306.

31 Ibid.
32 See for example EM to Karl Kautsky, 15 March 1898, IISH.
33 KM to FE, 8 January 1863, *MECW*, Vol. 41, 1985, p. 442.
34 Ibid.
35 Ibid.
36 Ibid.
37 FE to KM, 13 January 1863, *MECW*, Vol. 41, 1985, p. 442.
38 FE to KM, 26 January 1863, *MECW*, Vol. 4, 1975, pp. 441–7.
39 FE to KM, 20 May 1863, *MECW*, Vol. 41, 1985, p. 472.

Chapter 5 – Abraham Lincoln's Adviser

1 Jenny Marx to KM, December 1863–January 1864, IISH.
2 Adapted by Augustine Daly from a melodrama by Salomon von Mosenthal that was currently popular in Vienna, the play, set in seventeenth-century Germany, tells the story of a Jewish girl (Leah) in love with a Christian farmer (Rudolph).
3 George William Curtis, in *Harper's Weekly*, 7 March 1863.
4 Jenny Marx to KM, December 1863–January 1864, IISH.
5 Modena Villas was also spelt Medina on contemporary London streetmaps.
6 Jenny Marx to KM, December 1863–January 1864, IISH.
7 Ibid.
8 EM to Lion Philips, 25 June 1864, IISH.
9 In Firdousi's account of the origins of chess, two warring brother-princes cannot accept their mother's instruction that they have equal shares of everything and rule the kindom together. Distraught at the civil war that breaks out between them the queen mother burns her palace to the ground and threatens to burn herself to death according to custom. The victorious, compromising Gav devises the game to avert her self-immolation and console her. He makes a board of ebony in the likeness of a battlefield, traced into one hundred squares, with two armies of teak and ivory, both on horse and foot, each moving after a different manner until the king is hemmed in with foemen and all escape cut off according to the rules of the game. At which point it is ordered that he should die – Sháh-mát (the King is dead) – checkmate.
10 Eleanor Marx, 'Karl Marx: A Few Stray Notes', in *Reminiscences*, p. 253.
11 EM to Lion Philips, 25 June 1864, IISH.
12 A popular sea-shanty of the time tells the story of the controversial British-built *Alabama* and her notorious demise in the English Channel on 19 June 1864:
    When the Alabama's Keel was Laid
    Roll, Alabama, Roll!
    'Twas laid in the yard of Jonathan Laird
    Roll, roll Alabama, roll!
    'Twas laid in the yard of Jonathan Laird,
    'Twas laid in the town of Birkenhead.
    Down the Mersey way she rolled then,
    And Liverpool fitted her with guns and men.
    From the western isle she sailed forth,
    To destroy the commerce of the north.
    To Cherbourg port she sailed one day,
    For to take her count of prize money.
    Many a sailor laddie saw his doom
    When the Kearsage it hove in view
    When a ball from the forward pivot that day,
    Shot the Alabama's stern away.
    Off the three-mile limit in '64,
    The Alabama was seen no more.

13 EM to Lion Philips, 25 June 1864, IISH.
14 *New York Times*, 30 April 1864.
15 Jenny Marx to Ernestine Liebknecht, 10 December 1864, IISH.
16 Ibid.
17 Friedrich Engels, *A Wilhelm Wolff Biography*, Die Neue Welt, July 1, 8, 22, 29; Sept. 30; Oct. 7, 14, 21, 28; Nov. 4, 25, 187.
18 Laura Marx to KM, nd, August 1864, IISH.
19 Marx, Provisional Rules of the International Working Men's Association in *MECW*, Vol. 20, 1985, pp. 14–15.
20 *The Times* leader, 9 September 1868.
21 See Hobsbawm, *The Age of Capital*, pp. 303–4 .
22 Wilhelm Liebknecht, in *Reminiscences of Marx*, p. 111.
23 Hobsbawm, *The Age of Capital*, p. 94.
24 Marx and Engels, *The Communist Manifesto*, p. 241.
25 EM to FE, 13 February 1865, IISH.
26 Ibid.
27 Leslie Derfler, *Paul Lafargue and the Founding of French Marxism, 1842–1882*, Harvard University Press, Cambridge MA, 1991, p. 34. Derfler's work provides the most comprehensive account of Lafargue's life and career to date, and corrects a large number of factual errors previously in circulation, including those he generated himself.
28 Lafargue said in his memoirs that he first met Marx in February 1865. His memory was faulty; in fact it was March.
29 Paul Lafargue, in *Reminiscences*, p. 71.
30 Derfler, *Paul Lafargue*, p. 33.
31 Paul Lafargue, in *Reminiscences*, p. 82.
32 She meant *The Effinghams*.
33 EM to KM, 26 April 1867, IISH.
34 Derfler, *Paul Lafargue*, p. 39.
35 Tussy's 'Confession', 20 March 1865, IISH.

Chapter 6 – Fenian Sister

1 EM to Alice Liebknecht, 14 October 1866, IISH.
2 Ibid.
3 Ibid.
4 David Bates (1809–1870), 'Speak Gently' – see http://rpo.library.utoron to.ca/poem/132.html
5 Lewis Carroll, *Alice's Adventures in Wonderland*, Lee & Shepard, Boston, 1869, p. 85.
6 EM to KM, 19 March 1866, IISH, and in Faith Evans and Olga Meier, with introduction by Sheila Rowbotham, *The Daughters of Karl Marx: Family Correspondence 1866–1898*, Andre Deutsch, London, 1982, p. 5.
7 Eleanor recalled this Margate holiday in detail in the last month of her life, in a letter to Natalie Liebknecht, 1 March 1898, IISH.
8 KM to FE, 6 March 1868, *MECW*, Vol. 42, p. 542
9 Laura Marx to Mrs Jenny Marx, nd, August 1866, IISH.
10 KM to FE, 11 November 1882, *MECW*, Vol. 46, p. 374.
11 KM to Paul Lafargue, 13 August 1866, MML, Lafargue correspondence.
12 Ibid.
13 Jenny Marx to Ernestine Liebknecht, 14 October 1866, IISH.
14 Peters, *Red Jenny*, p. 146.
15 Laura Marx to Jenny Marx junior, in *Die Töchter von Karl Marx*, Unveröffentlichte Briefe, Cologne, 1981, p. 6.
16 Ibid.

17 EM to Alice Liebknecht, nd, January/February 1867, IISH.

18 EM to KM, 26 April 1867, *MECW*, Vol. 42, 1987, p. 359.

19 Royan is situated on the French Atlantic coast, at the mouth of the Gironde estuary at the confluence of the Dordogne, Lot and Garenne rivers. Until the arrival of the railway in 1875 it was accessible from inland only by river and road. At the time of Tussy's visit, steamboat was the most common way of arriving from Bordeaux. By the end of the nineteenth century this sleepy, pretty port with its wide sandy cove would be a fashionable belle époque playground of grand villas, visited by Picasso, Sarah Bernhardt and Emile Zola. For now, it was a gem for the well-heeled of Bordeaux who, like the Lafargues, could afford the luxury of summer holidays. Tussy might have liked the historical fact that the settlement had been under English jurisdiction during the reign of Henry II, by his marriage to Eleanor of Aquitaine.

20 For a detailed and comprehensive account of the publication plan and history of *Capital*, see Ernest Mandel, Introduction, *Capital, Volume I*, Penguin, London, 1990, pp. 11–86.

21 Laura Lafargue to FE, 6 March 1893, in *Frederick Engels, Paul and Laura Lafargue: Correspondence Vol. 3, 1891–1895*, London, Lawrence and Wishart, 1959–63, Vol. 3, p. 247.

22 Ibid.

23 EM to FE, 13 February 1865, IISH.

24 KM to FE, 14 December 1868, *MECW*, Vol. 43, 1988, p. 184.

25 KM to FE, 26 June 1868, *MECW*, Vol. 43, 1988, pp. 49–50.

26 EM to Lizzy Burns, 14 October 1868, IISH.

27 The *Irishman* was launched in Belfast in 1852 by the journalist Denis Holland, under the name of the *Ulsterman*. Holland and his co-editor Richard Piggott moved the weekly paper to Dublin in 1858, renaming it the *Irishman*. Constant lawsuits and harassment made it necessary to have two managers to keep the publication going. Former members of Young Ireland numbered amongst its contributors. Holland sold out his interest to Piggott in 1863; by 1865 it had a circulation of 50,000 copies a week. Piggott's support for the Fenian Brotherhood landed him with lawsuits and, in 1867, imprisonment for his support of the uprising.

28 Lizzy fretted to Fred, as she called him, that Tussy had contracted the illness with them in Manchester. In fact she caught it from a school friend, daughter of Sir Edward Frankland, FRS, Professor of Organic Chemistry at the Royal Institution.

29 EM to Lizzy Burns, 14 October 1868, IISH.

30 Ibid.

31 EM to LL, 29 December 1868, IISH.

32 Ibid.

33 Ibid.

34 This was not Tussy's only theatrical escapade with the Lormier brothers. In 1869 she started writing 'A Drama in IV Acts' in French for Eugene and Ludovic Lormier and herself; only the cast list remains, IISH.

35 EM to Jenny Marx senior, 31 March 1869, IISH.

36 Ibid.

37 KM to EM, 26 April 1869, IISH.

38 EM and KM to Jennychen, 2 June 1869, IISH.

39 FE to KM, letters, 22 June, 6 July, 25 July, 30 July; Engels sent regular letters to Marx between June and the end of July, keeping him up to date on her reading; see *MECW*, Vol. 4, pp. 234, 244, 255 and 258.

40 FE to KM, 27 June 1869, *MECW*, Vol. 43, p. 298.

41 KM to Jenny Marx senior, 10 June 1869, IISH.

42 EM to Jennychen, 2 June 1869, IISH.

43 EM to Jennychen, 19/20 July 1869, IISH.

44 Ibid.

45 Eleanor Marx, 'Frederick Engels', in *Reminiscences*, pp. 185–6.
46 FE to KM, 1 July 1869, Vol. 43, 1988, p. 55.
47 See for example Mrs Jenny Marx to Ernestine Liebknecht, 10 December 1864, IISH.
48 EM to Lizzy Burns, 14 October 1868, IISH.
49 FE to Julie Bebel, 8 March 1892, in MECW, Vol. 49, 2001, p. 377.
50 EM to Jenny Marx junior, 20 July 1869, IISH, and Evans and Meier, *Daughters of Karl Marx*, p. 52.
51 Ibid.
52 Jenny Marx to Dr Ludwig Kugelmann, cited in Chushichi Tsuzuki, *The Life of Eleanor Marx, 1855–1898*, Clarendon Press, Oxford, 1967, p. 25.
53 Ibid.
54 Ibid.
55 FE to KM, 29 November 1869, Vol. 43, 1988, p. 387.
56 Karl Marx, *Documents of the First International*, Lawrence & Wishart, London, 1963–8, Vol. 4.
57 EM to KM, 7 November 1869, IISH.
58 Ibid.
59 KM to FE, 6 November 1869, *MECW*, Vol. 43, 1988, p. 367.
60 Ibid.
61 Eleanor postscript to letter from KM to FE, 10 February 1870.
62 KM to Paul and Laura Lafargue, 20 July 1870, IISH.
63 EM, in *Reminiscences*, p. 251.
64 KM to FE, 3 August 1870, *MECW*, Vol. 44, p. 30.
65 Jenny Marx to Frederick Engels, 13 September 1870, IISH.
66 Jenny Marx to Ludwig Kugelmann, 19 November 1870, IISH.
67 Hobsbawm, *The Age of Capital*, p. 298.

Chapter 7 – The Communards

1 Hobsbawm, *The Age of Capital*, p. 167.
2 Mrs Jenny Marx to Ludwig Kugelmann, 19 November 1870, IISH.
3 KM to Eleanor, Jenny and Laura, 13 June 1871, IISH.
4 EM to Wilhelm Liebknecht, 29 December 1871, IISH.
5 Ibid.
6 Ibid.
7 Ibid.
8 Ibid.
9 Ibid.
10 Prosper Lissagaray, *History of the Paris Commune*, New Park Publications, London, 1976, p. 419.
11 *The Times*, 19 May 1871, cited in Lissagaray, *History of the Paris Commune*, note p. 397
12 FE, in *Social Democrat*, 18 January 1884.
13 Karl Marx, in *The Sun*, 9 September 1871.
14 Ibid.
15 Wilhelm Liebknecht, Eleanor Marx, *Social Democrat*, Vol. 2, No. 9, 15 September 1898.
16 *Documents of the First International. The General Council of the First International, 1864–1866. The London Conference 1865. Minutes*, Foreign Languages Publishing House, Moscow, for the Centenary of the First International in 1964, http://www.marxists.org/archive/marx/iwma/documents/minutes/index.htm
17 Ibid.
18 Anselmo Lorenzo, 'Reminiscences of the First International', in *Reminiscences*, p. 291.
19 Ibid., p. 290.

20 EM to Wilhelm Liebknecht, 29 December 1871, IISH.
21 Ibid.
22 Mrs Jenny Marx to Wilhelm Liebknecht, 26 May 1872, IISH.
23 EM, letter to Aberdeen Socialist Society, 17 March 1893, in *Labour Monthly*, March 1940, p. 158.
24 Ibid.
25 Ibid.
26 FE to Frederick Adolph Sorge, 17 March 1872, *MECW*, Vol. 44, 1989, p. 342.
27 Cited in Deborah McDonald, *Clara Collet: 1860–1948: An Educated Working Woman*, Frank Cass, London, 2004, p. 21.
28 Mrs Jenny Marx to Wilhelm Liebknecht, 26 May 1872, IISH.
29 Ibid.
30 Ibid., and Mrs Jenny Marx to Johann Philip Becker, 7 November 1872, IISH.
31 Maggie to EM, 18 September 1872, cited in Tsuzuki, *The Life of Eleanor Marx*, p. 32.
32 EM to Jenny Marx, 7 July 1872, IISH.
33 KM to FE, 31 May 1873, *MECW*, Vol. 44, 1989, p. 504.
34 Mrs Jenny Marx to EM, 3 April 1873, IISH.
35 Mrs Jenny Marx to EM, nd, May 1873, IISH.
36 Mrs Jenny Marx to EM, 3 April 1873, IISH.
37 Mrs Jenny Marx EM, nd, April 1873, IISH.
38 Mary Wollstonecraft, *Vindication of the Rights of Woman*, Scott, London, 1891, pp. xxvi–xxix.
39 EM to Mrs Jenny Marx, 31 May 1873, IISH.
40 Ibid.
41 EM to KM, 23 March 1874, IISH.
42 KM to Ludwig Kugelmann, 4 August 1874, in *Letters to Dr Kugelmann*, *Lenin Collected Works*, Foreign Languages Publishing House, Moscow, 1962 Vol. 12, pp. 104–12.
43 EM to JL, 5 September 1874, IISH.
44 Ibid.
45 Ibid.
46 Ibid.
47 Ibid.
48 Ibid.
49 EM to Wilhelm Liebknecht, 13 October 1874, IISH.
50 Ibid.
51 *Rouge et Noir*, 24 October 1874.
52 EM to Wilhelm Liebknecht, 13 October 1874, IISH.
53 Ibid.
54 EM to Nathalie Liebknecht, 23 October 1874, IISH.
55 Ibid.
56 Ibid.
57 Ibid.
58 Jenny Marx junior to Ludwig Kugelmann, 21 December 1871, IISH.

Chapter 8 – Dogberries

1 Nikolai Morozov, 'Visits to Karl Marx', in *Reminiscences*, p. 302.
2 Marian Comyn, 'My Recollections of Karl Marx', *Nineteenth Century and After*, Vol. 91, January 1922, pp. 161–9, and *The Times of London*, 4 October 1938 and 30 January 1941. By today's standards, 41 Maitland Park Road is a large, elegant townhouse.
3 Compton Mackenzie, *My Life and Times*, Octave 7, 1931–38, London, Chatto, 1968. Virginia Bateman became the mother of Compton Mackenzie.

4 Cited in McDonald, *Clara Collet*, pp. 22–3.
5 Comyn, 'My Recollections of Karl Marx', and *The Times* of London, 4 October 1938 and 30 January 1941.
6 Nikolai Morozov, 'Visits to Karl Marx', in *Reminiscences*, p. 303.
7 EM to Nathalie Liebknecht, 1 January 1875, IISH.
8 Ibid.
9 Comyn, 'My Recollections of Karl Marx', and *The Times* of London, 4 October 1938 and 30 January 1941.
10 Ibid.
11 Ibid.
12 Ibid.
13 Yvonne Kapp, *Eleanor Marx, Vol. I: Family Life*, Lawrence and Wishart, London, 1972, p. 155.
14 JL to EM, 23 March 1882, IISH.
15 EM to Karl Hirsch, 12 May 1876, IISH.
16 Comyn, 'My Recollections of Karl Marx', and *The Times of London*, 4 October 1938 and 30 January 1941.
17 See McDonald, *Clara Collet*, p. 22.
18 Ibid., p. 6.
19 Ibid.
20 The founding of the Dogberry is still commonly attributed, in error, to Marx. As with so many other initiatives put down to Marx that were in fact Eleanor's, checking primary archival sources rather than crediting popular belief quickly corrects these historical errors.
21 McDonald, *Clara Collet*, p. 22.
22 EM, 'Karl Marx: A Few Stray Notes', in *Reminiscences*, 1957, p. 252.
23 See Nina Auerbach, *Ellen Terry: Player in Her Time*, Norton, New York, 1987, p. 176.
24 Michael Booth, *Theatre in the Victorian Age*, Cambridge University Press, Cambridge, 1991.
25 Hallam Tennyson, *Alfred Lord Tennyson: A Memoir by His Son*, Vol. 2, New York, Macmillan, 1897, p. 543.
26 Mackenzie, *My Life and Times*, Octave 7, 1931–38, London, Chatto, 1968.
27 EM to Karl Hirsch, 25 October 1875, IISH.
28 The titles of these articles tell their own story of Shakespeare's popularity in Germany: 'Shakespearean Studies in England', 'Shakespeare's *Richard III* at the Lyceum Theatre London', 'The London Theatre World' and 'The London Season'. Most memorable is her striking piece on *Richard III* in 1877. She relates the performance to contemporary politics, using the piece as an opportunity to highlight the disastrous International Conference in Constantinople, scuppered by Turkey's withholding of autonomy for Hercegovina and Bulgaria. 'The trumpet of war is silent and the philistine blathering about politics, quietly puts his fearful mind at rest, slumbers peacefully and lulls himself into golden dreams of peace and prosperity.' Irving claimed this to be the first unexpurgated performance of the play since Shakespeare's death. Whatever the truth of this claim, promoting this production of *Richard III* 'as it was written' was clever marketing. As Jenny Marx reported, 'The great mass of people who besieged the doors of the Lyceum last Monday, proved how successful the experiment was. Immediately after the first monologue of Gloucester, "Now is the winter of our discontent/Made glorious summer by this sun of York," the silence was breathless and even the gods of paradise listened in magic enchantment.'
29 Comyn, 'My Recollections of Karl Marx' and *The Times of London*, 4 October 1938 and 30 January 1941.
30 Ibid.

31 See Gail Marshall, 'Eleanor Marx and Shakespeare', in John Stokes (ed.), *Eleanor Marx: Life, Work, Contacts*, Ashgate, Farnham, 2000, p. 72.
32 Ibid., p. 73.
33 Ibid.

Chapter 9 – The Only Lady Candidate

1   EM to Jenny Marx junior, 20 July 1869, in Evans and Meier, *Daughters of Karl Marx*, p. 51.
2   Cited in Peters, *Red Jenny*, p. 158.
3   EM to JL, 18 October 1881, IISH.
4   EM to Wilhelm Liebknecht, 12 February 1881, IISH.
5   Ibid.
6   Henry Hyndman, *The Record of an Adventurous Life*, London, Macmillan, 1911, p. 226.
7   Wheen, *Karl Marx*, p. 371.
8   Marx and Engels, open letter to the German Social Democratic Party, http://www.marxists.org/archive/marx/works/1879/letters/79_09_15.htm
9   Henry Hyndman, *England for All*, Gilbert & Rivington, London, June 1881, http://www.marxists.org/archive/hyndman/1881/england/index.html
10 EM to JL, 7 April 1881, IISH.
11 See for example John Stuart Glennie, *Europe and Asia: Discussions of the Eastern Question in Travels Through Independent Turkish & Austrian Illyria*, London, Chapman & Hall, 1879.
12 John Stuart Glennie to EM, 27 November 1881, IISH.
13 Ibid.
14 'Underground Russia', in *Progress*, August & September 1883.
15 Olga Meier, commentary, in Evans and Meier, *Daughters of Karl Marx*, p. 109.
16 Jenny Marx junior to Charles Longuet, letter undated, April 1872, in Evans and Meier, *Daughters of Karl Marx*, p. 110.
17 Ibid.
18 Jenny Marx junior to LL, end March 1882, in Evans and Meier, *Daughters of Karl Marx*, p. 152.
19 EM to Karl Hirsch, 25 November 1876, in *Society for the Study of Labour History*, spring 1964.
20 Ibid.
21 Ibid.
22 FE to Ida Pauli, 14 February 1877, *MECW*, Vol. 45, 1991, p. 197.
23 EM to Karl Hirsch, nd, June 1878, IISH.
24 Eduard Bernstein, obituary of Eleanor Marx, in *Neue Zeitung*, No. 30, 1897–98, IISH.
25 Jenny Marx senior to Johann Philip Becker, nd, August 1867, *MECW*, Vol. 20, 1985, p. 439.
26 EM to Jenny Marx senior, 19 August 1876, IISH.
27 Ibid.
28 Tussy in Liebknecht, *Karl Marx: Biographical Memoirs*, p. 158.
29 Ibid., p. 157.
30 Peters, *Red Jenny*, p. 163.
31 Jenny Marx Mrs to EM, nd, November 1877, IISH.
32 Jennychen to EM, 23 September 1877, IISH.
33 EM introduction to Lissagaray, *History of the Commune of 1871*, trans. Eleanor Marx, Reeves & Turner, London, 1886.
34 EM to Jenny Marx senior, 31 March 1869, IISH, and see Evans and Meier, *Daughters of Karl Marx*, p. 45.

35 EM to Nathalie Liebknecht, 12 February 1881, IISH.
36 Ibid.
37 KM to FE, 3 August 1882, *MECW*, 1975, Vol. 47, p. 652.
38 EM to Jennychen, 2 October 1882, IISH.
39 Ibid.
40 Ibid.
41 Ibid.
42 Margaret McMillan, 'How I Became a Socialist', in *Labour Leader*, 11 July 1912.
43 Laura to Jennychen, letter undated, October 1881, in Evans and Meier, *Daughters of Karl Marx*, p. 139.
44 EM to Jennychen, 25 March 1882, IISH, and Evans and Meier, *Daughters of Karl Marx*, p. 150.
45 EM to Jennychen, 7 April 1881, in Evans and Meier, *Daughters of Karl Marx*, p. 129.

Chapter 10 – A Line of Her Own

1   Bernstein, obituary of EM, in *Neue Zeitung*, No. 30, 1897–98, IISH.
2   Robert Browning, *The Pied Piper of Hamelin* (1842), in *Selected Poems*, ed. Daniel Karlin, Penguin, London, 2004.
3   KM to JL, 11 April 1881, in *Marx–Engels Selected Correspondence*, International Publishers, New York, 1936, pp. 389–90.
4   EM to JL, 18 June 1881, IISH.
5   See Auerbach, *Ellen Terry*, pp. 173–83.
6   FE to KM, *Marx–Engels Selected Correspondence*, p. 590.
7   See Stokes (ed.), *Eleanor Marx*, p. 6.
8   EM to Jennychen, 18 June 1881, IISH.
9   Ibid.
10 Ibid.
11 EM to KM, 14 October 1866, IISH.
12 KM to JL, 18 August 1881, IISH.
13 Ibid.
14 Eleanor Marx and Edward Aveling, *The Woman Question*, p. 16.
15 EM to JL, 18 August 1881, IISH.
16 Ibid.
17 Ibid.
18 LL to JL, nd, October 1881, IISH.
19 Ibid.
20 LL to JL, nd, October 1881, IISH.
21 EM to JL, 31 October 1881, IISH.
22 EM in Liebknecht, *Karl Marx: Biographical Memoirs*, p. 158.
23 Ibid.
24 Ibid.
25 EM to JL, 4 December 1881, IISH.
26 Ibid.
27 Peters, *Red Jenny*, p. 164.
28 EM to JL, 4 December 1881, IISH.
29 Engels's eulogy for Jenny Marx, *MECW*, Vol. 24, p. 420.
30 Edna Healey, *Wives of Fame*, Sidgwick & Jackson, London, 1986, p. 127.
31 Liebknecht: *Karl Marx: Biographical Memoirs*, p. 118.
32 KM to JL, nd, December 1881, IISH.
33 EM to JL, 8 January 1882, IISH, and Evans and Meier, *Daughters of Karl Marx*, pp. 144–46.
34 EM to JL, 8 January 1882, IISH.

35 Ibid.
36 Ibid.
37 Ibid.
38 EM to JL, 15 January 1882, IISH.
39 KM to FE, 12 January 1882, *MECW*, Vol. 46, 1992, p. 176.
40 EM to JL, 8 January 1882, IISH.
41 Ibid.
42 EM to JL, 15 January 1882, IISH.
43 Ibid.
44 Ibid.
45 EM to JL, 8 January 1882, IISH.
46 KM to FE, 12 January 1882, *MECW*, Vol. 46, 1992, p. 176.
47 JL to EM, nd, January 1881, IISH.
48 EM to JL, 23 January 1882, IISH.
49 JL to KM, 24 February 1882, IISH.
50 EM to JL, 21 February 1882, IISH.
51 EM to JL, 25 March 1882, IISH.
52 Ibid.
53 Ibid.
54 Virginia Woolf, *Between the Acts*, Vintage, London, 1992, p. 95, and see Auerbach, *Ellen Terry*, 1987.
55 EM to KM, 3 April 1882, IISH.
56 JL to EM, 10 April 1882, IISH.
57 JL to EM, 7 March 1882, IISH.
58 JL to EM, 12–13 April 1882, IISH.
59 EM to KM, 23 March 1882, IISH.
60 EM to JL, 1 July 1882, IISH.
61 EM, 'Missive from England', *Russkoye Bogatsvo (Russian Wealth)*, No. 5, 1895.
62 EM to JL, 1 July 1882, IISH.
63 Ibid.
64 Ibid.
65 Ibid.
66 JL to EM, 3 May 1882, IISH.
67 KM to LL, nd, June 1882, IISH.
68 EM to JL, 2 October 1882, IISH.
69 Richard Garnett later followed Bullen as Keeper of Printed Books.
70 EM to JL, 2 October 1882, IISH.
71 EM to JL, 2 November 1882, IISH.
72 JL to EM, 8 November 1882, IISH.
73 Ibid.
74 KM to LL, 14 December 1882, IISH.
75 Eleanor Marx, 'Illness and Death of Marx', in *Reminiscences*, p. 128.
76 Ibid.
77 See Wheen, *Karl Marx*, p. 381.
78 EM, 'Illness and Death of Marx,' *Reminiscences*, p. 128.
79 FE to Friedrich Adolph Sorge, 15 March 1883, *MECW*, Vol. 46, 1992, p. 460.
80 Engels's speech at Karl Marx's graveside, 'Karl Marx's Funeral', in *Social Democrat*, 22 March 1883.
81 EM to Olive Schreiner, 16 June 1884, National English Literary Museum, Grahamstown, South Africa, and in Ellis, EM obituary in *Adelphi*, Vol. 6, September 1935.

Chapter 11 – The Reading Room

1 Matilda Hyndman to EM, 17 March 1883, IISH.
2 Frederick James Furnivall to EM, nd, March 1883, IISH.

3 FE to LL, 24 June 1883, IISH.

4 EM to LL, 26 March 1883, IISH.

5 Comyn, 'My Recollections of Karl Marx'.

6 I am indebted to Josie Rourke for this and many other insights that helped me understand the position and role of women and their relation to men in the history of British theatre and performance.

7 Michael Holroyd, *Bernard Shaw*, Vintage, London, 1998, p. 7.

8 Following English philosopher Jeremy Bentham's model, the design of the panopticon enabled watchmen to observe all inmates of an institution from a central point of surveillance without their knowing whether or not they were being watched.

9 Ruth Brandon, *The New Women and the Old Men: Love, Sex and the Woman Question*, Secker & Warburg, London, 2000, p. 18.

10 See Jennifer Juszkiewicz's entertaining MA thesis on the history of the Reading Room, *The Iron Library: Victorian England and the British Museum Library*, University of Notre Dame, Indiana, 2009.

11 Beatrice Webb (née Potter), 24 May 1883, *The Diary of Beatrice Webb, Vol. 1, 1873–92: Glitter around the Darkness Within*, Virago, London, 1982.

12 *The Times of London*, 6 March 1883, p. 12.

13 Edward Aveling, in *Freethinker*, 30 July 1882.

14 Webb, 24 May 1883, *The Diary of Beatrice Webb*.

15 Ibid.

16 Ibid.

17 Ibid.

18 Ibid.

19 Ibid.

20 The entire Marx family had distrusted and distanced themselves from Bradlaugh since a political dispute during the Paris Commune. Marx attacked Bradlaugh as 'a courtesan of Plon Plon [Prince Napoleon, leader of the 'left' Bonapartists]', was appalled at his 'utter meanness' and for being a noisy demagogue. See Tsuzuki, *The Life of Eleanor Marx*, Oxford University Press, Oxford, 1967, pp. 94–5.

21 Max Beer, *Fifty Years of International Socialism*, Allen & Unwin, London, 1935, p. 74.

22 Edward Aveling, 'Some Humors of the Reading Room', in *Progress*, May 1883, pp. 311–14.

23 Hunt, *The Frock-Coated Communist*, p. 328.

24 Cited in Tsuzuki, *The Life of Eleanor Marx*, p. 78.

25 Brandon, *The New Women and the Old Men*, p. 20.

26 Cited from unpublished Aveling family papers in Kapp, *Eleanor Marx*, Vol. 1, p. 257

27 Henry Salt, in *National Reformer*, 20 February 1881.

28 The Secular Society still exists, see http://www.secularism.org.uk/history.html

29 Edward Aveling, in *National Reformer*, 6 July 1879.

30 Cited in Tsuzuki, *The Life of Eleanor Marx*, p. 82.

31 Ibid.

32 Edward Aveling, *The Religious Views of Charles Darwin*, Freethought Publishing Company, London, 1884.

33 Ibid., p. 83.

34 Edward Aveling, *The Gospel of Evolution*, Freethought Publishing Company, London, 1884, p. 48.

35 Tsuzuki, *The Life of Eleanor Marx*, pp. 89–90.

36 Ibid., p. 90.

37 Ibid.

38 Ibid.

39 Ibid.
40 Edward Aveling, in *Modern Thought*, January 1882.
41 William Greenslade, 'Revisiting Edward Aveling', in Stokes (ed.), *Eleanor Marx*, p. 42.
42 Edward Aveling, 'Charles Darwin and Karl Marx', in *New Century Review*, April 1897.
43 Eleanor Marx, in Evans and Meier, *The Daughters of Karl Marx*, p. 52.
44 Eleanor Marx, 'Karl Marx I', in *Progress*, May 1883, pp. 288–94.
45 Eleanor Marx, 'Karl Marx II', in *Progress*, June 1883, pp. 362–6.
46 Ibid.
47 Hesketh Pearson, *Bernard Shaw, His Life and Personality*, Methuen, London, 1961, quoted in Holroyd, *Bernard Shaw*, p. 7.
48 GBS diary, 28 February 1885, cited in Holroyd, *Bernard Shaw*, p. 90.
49 See Hunt, *The Frock-Coated Communist,* p. 204.
50 JL to LL, 17 May 1882, IISH.
51 EM to LL, 26 July 1892, IISH.
52 Jonathan Beecher, *Charles Fourier: The Visionary and His World*, University of California Press, Berkeley, 1986, p. 208.
53 Eleanor Marx and Edward Aveling, *The Woman Question (Verlag für die Frau)*, p. 23.
54 EM to LL, 21 July 1884, IISH.
55 EM to LL, 21 July 1884, IISH, and Evans and Meier, *The Daughters of Karl Marx*, p. 180.
56 See Tsuzuki, *Eleanor Marx*, p. 112: 'I can always "work" some of the Committee', and 'I "worked" Sheu who seconded Murray's position' – she's a good strategist.
57 Margaret McMillan, *The Life of Rachel McMillan*, Dent, London, 1927, p. 34, quoted in Carolyn Steedman, 'Fictions of Engagement: Eleanor Marx, Biographical Space', pp. 23–39, in Stokes (ed.), *Eleanor Marx*, p. 28.
58 Edward Aveling, 'A Notable Book', in *Progress*, September 1883, p. 156.
59 Ibid., p. 163.
60 Ibid., p. 162.
61 Henry Havelock Ellis, *My Life*, William Heinemann, London, 1940, p. 183.
62 Cited in Ruth First and Ann Scott, *Olive Schreiner*, The Women's Press, London, 1989, p. 131.
63 'The intimate Olive,' wrote Arthur Calder-Marshall, 'the woman who never needed to drink because she was always in the sort of state that other people get into after a bottle of champagne, a woman as violently over-demonstrative in her feelings as he [Ellis] was undemonstrative, who could react so quickly to her environment that half an hour in a place she did not like would lay her low with what she called "asthma".' Cited in Johannes Meintjes, *Olive Schreiner: Portrait of a South African Woman*, Hugh Keartland Pubishers, Johannesburg, 1965, p. 68.
64 Ellis, 'Eleanor Marx', in *Adelphi*, September 1935.
65 Ibid.
66 Cited in First and Scott, *Olive Schreiner*, p. 125.
67 Meintjes, *Olive Schreiner*, p. 64.
68 Cited in First and Scott, *Olive Schreiner*, p. 127.
69 Terry Eagleton, *Why Marx Was Right*, Yale University Press, New Haven and London, 2011, p. 239.

Chapter 12 – Peculiar Views on Love, etc.

1 Friedrich Engels, 'The Book of Revelation' (1883), in Karl Marx and Friedrich Engels, *On Religion*, Scholars Press, 1964, p. 206.
2 EM to LL, 18 June 1884, IISH.

3 Ibid.
4 Ellis, 'Eleanor Marx', in *Adelphi*, September 1935.
5 EM to Dollie Radford (formerly Maitland), 30 June 1884, Radford Archive, British Library.
6 Ibid.
7 Ibid.
8 EM to Edith Nesbit (Bland), 25 July 1884, Edith Nesbit archive, McFarlin Library, University of Tulsa.
9 Webb, *The Diary of Beatrice Webb*, Vol. 1, pp. 87–8.
10 EM to John Lincoln Mahon, 1 August 1884, IISH.
11 FE to LL, 22 July 1884, *MECW*, Vol. 47, 1995, p. 166.
12 Cited in Tristram Hunt, introduction to Friedrich Engels, *The Origin of the Family, Private Property and the State*, Penguin, London, 2010, p. 3.
13 Beer, *Fifty Years of International Socialism*, p. 78.
14 Eduard Bernstein, *My Years of Exile: Reminiscences of a Socialist*, Leonard Parsons, London, 1921, p. 162.
15 Quoted in Brandon, *The New Women and the Old Men*, p. 23.
16 Annie Besant, in *National Reformer*, 23 December 1883.
17 EM to J. L. Mahon, 8 May 1884, IISH.
18 EM to LL, 13 February 1884, IISH. The reference is to Shakespeare's *Much Ado About Nothing*, Act IV, scene i.
19 EM to LL, 22 September 1884, IISH.
20 Olive Schreiner to Havelock Ellis, 16 July 1884, in S. C. Cronwright-Schreiner (ed.), The *Letters of Olive Schreiner 1876–1920*, T. Fisher Unwin, London, 1924, p. 19.
21 Ibid.
22 Ellis, 'Eleanor Marx', in *Adelphi*, September 1935.
23 Ellis, *My Life*, p. 186.
24 Olive Schreiner to Havelock Ellis, 16 July 1884, in Cronwright-Schreiner (ed.), *Letters*, pp. 51–2.
25 Ibid.
26 Olive Schreiner to Erilda Cawood, 24 April 1878, in Richard Rive (ed.), *Olive Schreiner Letters 1871–99*, David Philip, Cape Town & Johannesburg, 1987, p. 22.
27 Olive Schreiner to Havelock Ellis, 29 July 1884, in Cronwright-Schreiner (ed.), *Letters*, p. 53.
28 Henrik Ibsen, cited in introduction to *Ghosts*, translated and with an introduction by William Archer, Kindle edition, Location Marker 27.
29 Ellis, 'Eleanor Marx', in *Adelphi*, September 1935.
30 Cited in Brandon, *The New Women and the Old Men*, p. 34.

Chapter 13 – Proof Against Illusions

1 Beer, *Fifty Years of International Socialism*, p. 71.
2 Ibid.
3 Cited in Hunt, *The Frock-Coated Communist*, p. 329.
4 William Greenslade, 'Revisiting Edward Aveling', in Stokes (ed.), *Eleanor Marx*, p. 41.
5 Holroyd, *Bernard Shaw*, p. 90.
6 EM to Karl Kautsky, 4 December 1883, IISH.
7 Hyndman, *Further Reminiscences*, pp. 140–2.
8 Ibid.
9 May Morris & Bernard Shaw, *William Morris: Artist, Writer, Socialist, Vol. 2, Morris as Socialist*, Russell & Russell, New York, 1966, p. 226.
10 Correspondence of Reverend Frederick William Aveling; Aveling family papers

seen by Yvonne Kapp. See Yvonne Kapp, *Eleanor Marx: Vol. 2, The Crowded Years*, Lawrence & Wishart, London, 1976, p. 468n.

11 George Bernard Shaw, *The Doctor's Dilemma*, Penguin, London, 1946, p. 18.
12 EM to Olive Schreiner, 15 June 1885, IISH.
13 Ibid.
14 Ibid.
15 Holroyd, *Bernard Shaw*, p. 90.
16 EM cited in Aaron Rosebury, 'Eleanor, Daughter of Karl Marx', *Monthly Review*, New York, January 1973, Vol. 24, No. 8, pp. 45–6.
17 Zadie Smith, *NW*, Penguin, London, 2012, p. 123 – inspired by and borrowed entirely from Smith's novel.
18 Beer, *Fifty Years of International Socialism*, p. 74.
19 Ibid.

Chapter 14 – Educate, Agitate, Organise

1 EM to LL, 22 September 1884, IISH.
2 Ibid.
3 Edward Aveling in *Justice*, 27 September 1884.
4 GBS, cited in Kapp, *Eleanor Marx*, Vol. 2, p. 46.
5 GBS, 13 April 1885. See Sally Peters, *Bernard Shaw: The Ascent of the Superman*, Yale University Press, New Haven and London, 1998, p. 101.
6 George Bernard Shaw, cited in E. P. Thompson, *William Morris: Romantic to Revolutionary*, Lawrence & Wishart, London, 1955, p. 402.
7 Ibid., p. 384.
8 William Morris, cited in Thompson, *William Morris*, 1955, p. 411.
9 EM to Wilhelm Liebknecht, 1 January 1885, IISH.
10 EM to LL, 31 December 1884, IISH.
11 FE to LL, 1 January 1885, IISH.
12 FE to Bernstein, 29 December 1884, in *Labour Monthly*, October 1933.
13 EM to LL, 31 December 1884, IISH.
14 EM to Peter (Pyotry Lavrovich) Lavrov, 31 December 1884, IISH.
15 Socialist League Manifesto, 13 January 1885, IISH.
16 EM to LL, 12 April 1885, IISH.
17 EM to Peter Lavrov, 2 February 1885, IISH.
18 Edward Aveling and Eleanor Marx Aveling, 'The Factory Hell', *Socialist Platform*, No. 3, London, 1885.
19 Ibid.
20 EM to LL, 12 April 1885, IISH.
21 Ibid.
22 Ibid.
23 Olive Schreiner to Henry Havelock Ellis, 8 April 1885, in Cronwright-Schreiner (ed.), *Letters*, 1924, p. 69.
24 EM to LL, 12 April 1885, IISH.
25 Cited in Tsuzuki, *The Life of Eleanor Marx*, p. 117.
26 Ibid.
27 EM to LL, 9 May 1884, IISH.
28 EM to Sergei Stepniak, 15 April 1885, IISH.
29 Thompson, *William Morris*, p. 387.
30 *Commonweal*, April 1885.
31 Socialist League, 2 March 1885, Socialist League (UK) Archives, http://www.iisg.nl/archives/en/files/s/ARCH01344full.php
32 EM to Mahon, 25 June 1885, Socialist League (UK) Archives, IISH.
33 EM to unknown, 17 December 1885, Socialist League (UK) Archives, IISH.
34 Records of the Socialist League, 1884, 1885, 1886, IISH.

35 EM to secretary of the Socialist League, 1 March 1886, Socialist League (UK) Archives, IISH, http://www.iisg.nl/archives/en/files/s/ARCH01344full.php

36 FE to LL, 23 November 1884, IISH.

37 Thompson, *William Morris*, p. 393.

38 *East End Gazette*, 20 September 1885.

39 EM to council of the Socialist League, 5 October 1885.

40 Ibid.

41 Henrik Ibsen, *A Doll's House*, Act I, scene i.

42 Ibid.

43 EM cited in Kapp, *Eleanor Marx*, Vol. 2 p. 73.

Chapter 15 – Nora Helmer, Emma Bovary and 'The Woman Question'

1 Her first written use of the phrase is in a letter to her elder sister Jenny on 7 November 1872, aged seventeen. After that she uses it consistently until the end of her life.

2 'You know he [George Moore] got me the order for translating *Mme. Bovary*'; EM to LL, 27 April 1886, IISH.

3 Eleanor Marx, Introduction to *Madame Bovary*, Vizetelly, London, 1886, p. xxii.

4 Ibid.

5 EM to LL, 23 April 1886, IISH.

6 EM, Introduction to *Madame Bovary*, and EM to LL, 27 April 1886, IISH.

7 Ibid.

8 British novelist Julian Barnes brilliantly identifies Eleanor Marx and Emma Bovary in the playful opening to *Flaubert's Parrot* (Jonathan Cape, London, 1984). Poking fun at Nabokov, Barnes devises an examination paper:
    E1 was born in 1855.
    E2 was partly born in 1855.
    E1 had an unclouded childhood but emerged into adulthood inclined to nervous crisis.
    E2 had an unclouded childhood but emerged into adulthood inclined to nervous crisis.
    E1 led a life of sexual irregularity in the eyes of right-thinking people.
    E2 led a life of sexual irregularity in the eyes of right-thinking people.
    E1 imagined herself to be in financial difficulties.
    E2 knew herself to be in financial difficulties.
    E1 committed suicide by swallowing prussic acid.
    E2 committed suicide by swallowing arsenic.
    E1 was Eleanor Marx.
    E2 was Emma Bovary.
    The first English translation of *Madame Bovary* to be published was by Eleanor Marx. Discuss.

9 *Saturday Review*, 25 September 1886.

10 *Athaeneum*, No. 3075, 2 October 1886.

11 William Sharp, in *Academy*, 25 September 1886.

12 Ibid.

13 EM to LL, 23 April 1886, IISH.

14 EM introduction to *History of the Paris Commune*, June 1886.

15 EM preface to *History of the Paris Commune*, June 1886.

16 EM to Peter Lavrov, 7 June 1886, IISH.

17 Barnes, *Flaubert's Parrot*, p. 176.

18 GBS cited in Holroyd, *Bernard Shaw*, p. 179.

19 EM to LL, 18 June 1884, IISH.
20 Edward Aveling, *Today*, June 1884.
21 EM to GBS, 2 June 1885, IISH.
22 And this decades later when there was no longer any political advantage to him doing so. Hyndman, *Record of an Adventurous Life*, pp. 346–7.
23 Ibid.
24 Eleanor Marx and Edward Aveling, 'The Woman Question: From A Socialist Point of View', *Westminster Review*, No. 125, January–April 1886, pp. 207–12 and pp. 219–22.
25 See for example, the introduction to their co-published essay on *Shelley's Socialism*: 'although I am the reader, it must be understood that I am reading the work of my wife as well as, nay more than, myself.' Edward Aveling and Eleanor Marx Aveling, *Shelley's Socialism and Popular Songs*, The Journeyman Press, London & West Nyack, 1975, p. 13.
26 I'm using this surname form just for this section because it seems appropriate to the context of a major philosophical work co-written in the Marx–Engels tradition.
27 EM and EA, *The Woman Question*, p. 28.
28 Ibid., p. 16.
29 Vladimir Lenin, 'The State', lecture delivered at Sverdlov University, 11 July 1919, in *Vladimir I Lenin: Collected Works*, Vol. 29, Progress Publishers, Moscow, 1974, p. 473.
30 Eleanor Marx, 'The Gotha Congress', in *Justice*, 7 November 1896, p. 8.
31 Ibid.
32 EM & EA, *The Woman Question*, p. 16.
33 Ibid., p. 11.
34 Ibid., p. 14.
35 Ibid., pp. 15–16.
36 Ibid., p. 14.
37 Ibid., pp. 13–14.
38 Ibid., p. 14.
39 Ibid.
40 Ibid., p. 15.
41 Ibid.
42 Ibid., p. 17.
43 Ibid.
44 Ibid., p. 21.
45 Ibid., p. 13.
46 Ibid., p. 21.
47 Ibid., p. 20.
48 Ibid., p. 27.
49 Ibid., p. 28.
50 Ibid., p. 22.
51 Ibid., p. 17.
52 EM letter to Socialist League, 10 May 1886, IISH.

Chapter 16 – Lady Liberty

1 EM to Liebknecht, November 1880, cited in Tsuzuki, *The Life of Eleanor Marx*, p. 133.
2 EM to Wilhelm Liebknecht, 17 July 1886, IISH.
3 EM to LL, 14 September 1886, IISH.
4 Ibid.
5 Eleanor Marx quoted in *New Yorker Volkszeitung*, 11 September 1886.

6 Edward Aveling, *An American Journey*, Lovell, Gestefeld & Co., New York, 1892, p. 14.
7 EM to LL, 14 September 1886, IISH.
8 Ibid.
9 *New Yorker Volkszeitung*, 11 September 1886.
10 EM to LL, 14 September 1886, IISH.
11 *New Haven Workman's Advocate*, 19 September 1886.
12 Eleanor Marx, speech published in *Knights of Labor*, 4 December 1886.
13 *New Yorker Volkszeitung*, 15 September 1886, and Eleanor Marx-Aveling and Edward Aveling, *The Working Class Movement in America*, Swan Sonnenschein, London, 1888, pp. 139–40.
14 *John Swinton's Paper*, 26 September 1886.
15 *New York Herald*, 21 and 23 September 1886.
16 EM and EA, *The Working Class Movement in America*, p. 172.
17 Ibid.
18 Ibid., p. 154.
19 Ibid.
20 Ibid., p. 155.
21 Ibid., p. 156.
22 Ibid.
23 Ibid.
24 Ibid., p. 157.
25 Ibid., p. 158.
26 Bridget Bennet, 'Eleanor Marx and Victoria Woodhull', in Stokes (ed.), *Eleanor Marx*, p. 161.
27 EM and EA, *The Working Class Movement in America*, p. 177.
28 EM and EA, *The Woman Question*, p. 22.
29 Ibid., p. 177.
30 Ibid., p. 178.
31 Ibid.
32 Ibid.
33 Eleanor Marx, speech published in *Knights of Labor*, 4 December 1886.
34 EM and EA, *The Working Class Movement in America*, p. 116.
35 Ibid.
36 Ibid., p. 117.
37 Ibid., p. 121.
38 Ibid., p. 125.
39 Ibid., p. 132.
40 EA, *An American Journey*, p. 109.
41 EM and EA, *The Working Class Movement in America*, p. 138.
42 Ibid., p. 181.
43 *New York Times*, 25 April 1886.
44 Justice Ingham, *The Accused – The Accusers: The Famous Speeches of the Eight Chicago Anarchists in Court*, Socialist Publishing Society, 1886, http://www.chicagohs.org/hadc/books/b01/B01.htm
45 EM and EA, *The Working Class Movement in America*, p. 161.
46 Ibid.
47 Eleanor Marx, in *John Swinton's Paper*, 19 September 1886.
48 EM and EA, *The Working Class Movement in America*, pp. 159–60.
49 EM and EA, *The Working Class Movement in America*, p. 160.
50 These were: that the original trial of 21 June took place too near the events of 4 May in point of time and in point of place. A change of venue was necessary for justice to be done. The arrests were made without legal warrant, four months of detention without trial for some of those arrested. The offices and homes of the suspects had been broken into without proper search warrants. The post-facto

discovery of bomb-making equipment and incendiary devices in Chicago were uncorroborated by evidence. Finally, the jury was made up of men proven to be prejudiced against the accused.

51 EM and EA, *The Working Class Movement in America*, p. 160.
52 *New Yorker Volkszeitung*, 24 December 1886.
53 Ibid.
54 Edward Aveling, circular to sections of the SLP, 26 February 1887, MML.
55 Ibid.

Chapter 17 – Essentially English

1 *Commonweal*, 4 December 1886.
2 *Justice*, 30 April 1887.
3 *New York Herald*, 30 December 1886.
4 *Evening Standard*, 13 January 1887.
5 FE to LL, 24 February 1887, *MECW*, Vol. 48, 2001, p. 12.
6 FE to Florence Kelly Wischnewetzky, 9 February 1887, IML.
7 FE to Friedrich Adolph Sorge, 8 August 1887, IML.
8 *Daily Telegraph*, 12 April 1887.
9 FE to Friedrich Adolph Sorge, 4 May 1887, IML.
10 For a summary of this letter, see Tsuzuki, *The Life of Eleanor Marx*, p. 149.
11 Zinaida Vengerova, cited in Kapp, *Eleanor Marx*, Vol. 2, p. 205.
12 Eleanor and Edward both refer to this brief, but never specify which newspaper commissioned them. Their upfront expenses were paid, but the article series never published, so it's not possible to identify the publication.
13 EM to LL, 30 August 1887, IISH, and see Evans and Meier, *The Daughters of Karl Marx*, p. 197.
14 EM to LL, 24 June 1888, IISH.
15 Today Dodwell Park is a popular holiday camp and family leisure resort.
16 EM to LL, 30 August 1887, IISH.
17 Cited in E. P. Thompson, *William Morris*, p. 568.
18 Ibid.
19 Ibid.
20 Ibid.
21 EM to Havelock Ellis, December 1885, quoted by Ellis in *Adelphi*, October 1935.
22 EM to LL, 30 August 1887, IISH.
23 Havelock Ellis, in *Adelphi*, October 1935.
24 EM to LL, 25 September 1887, IISH.
25 Ibid.
26 Ibid.
27 16 November 1887, http://www.marx-memorial-library.org
28 *Pall Mall Gazette*, 8 November 1887.
29 *Today*, November 1887, in David Roediger and Franklin Rosemont (eds), *Haymarket Scrapbook*, C. H. Kerr, Chicago, 1986, p. 152.
30 *Illustrated London News*, 29 October 1887.
31 EM to LL, 16 November 1887, IISH.
32 FE to Paul Lafargue, 16 November 1887, IML.
33 Dan Laurence (ed.), *Bernard Shaw Collected Letters*, Max Reinhardt, London, 1965, p. 177.
34 EM to LL, 16 November 1887, IISH.
35 *Pall Mall Gazette*, 14 November 1887.
36 *Ibid*.
37 EM to LL, 31 December 1887, IISH.
38 EM to LL, 16 November 1887, IISH.

39 Ibid.

40 Annual report of the Bloomsbury branch of the Socialist League, May 1888, and 'Parliamentarianism in the Socialist League', unpublished letter to the editor of *Commonweal*, 16 May 1888.

41 EM to LL, 16 November 1887, IISH. 'Tomorrow I am going to some people in Lisson Grove (the <u>west</u> end). A father, most "respectable" man, with "excellent character", willing to do any work, and who is overjoyed at the prospect of earning 2/6 a week cleaning the streets for the vestry; eight children, who for days have tasted nothing but bread, and who have not even that now; the mother lying on some straw, naked, covered with a few rags, her clothes pawned days ago to buy bread. The children are little skeletons. They are all in a tiny cellar. It is pitiable but all round them people are in the same state, and in the East it is just the same.'

42 *Dramatic Review*, 3 December 1887.

43 EM to Dollie Radford, 28 December 1887, Radford Archive, British Library.

44 EM to George Bernard Shaw, 16 December 1887, IISH.

45 EM to LL, 31 December 1887, IISH.

46 Ibid.

47 Havelock Ellis, in *Adelphi*, October 1935.

48 EM to Dollie Radford, 23 February 1888.

49 'For the title of this play, En Folkfiende literally "a folk enemy" or "an enemy of the people" no exact idiomatic equivalent can be found in English. "An Enemy of Society" has served the most satisfactory rendering available.' EM in Henrik Ibsen, *The Pillars of Society and Other Plays*, ed. Havelock Ellis, Camelot Series: Walter Scott, London, 1888, p. 199.

50 EM to LL, 24 June 1888, IISH.

51 Havelock Ellis, in *Adelphi*, October 1935.

52 EM, cited in *Adelphi*, December 1888.

53 EM to Havelock Ellis, in *Adelphi* (2), December 1888.

54 EM to LL, 24 June 1888, IISH.

55 Ibid.

56 Ibid.

57 Ibid.

58 Ibid.

59 Ibid.

60 Friedrich Engels, Paul Lafargue, Laura Lafargue, *Correspondence, Vol. 2: 1886–1890*, translated by Yvonne Kapp, Foreign Languages Publishing House, Moscow, 1960, p. 121.

61 EM to LL, 9 July 1888, IISH.

62 See Hunt, *The Frock-Coated Communist*, p. 316.

63 Engels, cited in Hunt, *The Frock-Coated Communist*, p. 317.

64 FE to LL, 6 July 1888, *MECW*, Vol. 48, 2001, p. 194.

65 Ibid.

66 EM to LL, 9 August 1888, IISH.

67 Cited in Hunt, *The Frock-Coated Communist*, p. 318.

68 EM to LL, 30 October 1888, IISH.

69 EM to LL, 21 August 1888, IISH.

70 FE cited in Hunt, *The Frock-Coated Communist*, p. 319.

71 EM to LL, 11 September 1888, IISH.

72 Ibid.

73 Ibid.

74 Ibid.

75 FE to LL, 6 July 1888, *MECW*, Vol. 48, 2001, p. 194.

76 *Dramatic Review*, 15 January 1888.

77 EM to LL, 11 April 1889, IISH, and see Evans and Meier, *The Daughters of Karl Marx*, p. 210.

78 EM to LL, 19 December 1890, IISH.
79 Stephen Winster, *Salt and His Circle*, Hutchinson, London, 1951, pp. 84–5.
80 Edward Aveling and Eleanor Marx Aveling, *Shelley's Socialism*, p. 14.
81 Ibid., pp. 33–8.
82 Ibid., pp. 23–4.
83 Ibid., p. 24.
84 Ibid., p. 13.
85 Ibid.
86 Ibid.

Chapter 18 – Our Old Stoker!

1 EM, introduction, *History of the Paris Commune*, http://www.marxists.org/history/france/archive/lissagaray/introduction.htm
2 Will Thorne, *My Life's Battles*, George Newnes, London, 1925, p. 77.
3 EM to LL, 30 May 1892, IISH.
4 EM to LL, 11 April 1889, IISH, and see Evans and Meier, *The Daughters of Karl Marx*, p. 209.
5 Ibid.
6 FE to LL, 28 June 1889, *MECW*, Vol. 48, 2001, p. 343.
7 Ibid.
8 EM to LL, 11 April 1889, IISH, and see Evans and Meier, *The Daughters of Karl Marx*, p. 210.
9 EM to LL, 1 June 1889, IISH, and see Evans and Meier, *The Daughters of Karl Marx*, p. 217.
10 EM to LL, 1 June 1889, IISH.
11 EM to LL, 11 April 1889, IISH, and see Evans and Meier, *The Daughters of Karl Marx*, p. 210.
12 Eduard Bernstein, in *Die Neue Zeit*, No. 30, 1897–8, pp. 120–1.
13 Edgar Longuet, unpublished private letter cited in Kapp, *Eleanor Marx*, Vol. 2, p. 317.
14 EM to LL, 10 April 1889, IISH.
15 Eleanor Marx, 'Sweating in Type-Writing Offices', *People's Press*, 5 June 1890.
16 Ibid.
17 Ibid.
18 S.B. Boulton, 'Labour Disputes', *The Nineteenth Century*, Vol. 27, June 1890, p. 988.
19 Cunninghame Graham, in *Labour Elector*, 7 September 1889.
20 Thompson, *William Morris*, p. 527.
21 Ben Tillett, *Memoirs and Reflections*, John Long, London, 1931, p. 119.
22 Ibid., p. 135.
23 Tom Mann, *Memoirs*, Spokesman Books, Nottingham, 2008, pp. 68–9 and p. 86.
24 Thorne, *My Life's Battles*, p. 117.
25 EM to LL, 25 December 1889, IISH.
26 Ibid.
27 FE to Friedrich Adolph Sorge, 19 April 1890, *MECW*, Vol. 48, 2001, p. 485.
28 EM to LL, 12 December 1889, IISH.
29 Strike committee manifesto, 10 December 1890.
30 EM to LL, 12 December 1889, IISH.
31 Ibid.
32 Eleanor Marx, 'Northampton', in *People's Press*, 19 April 1890.
33 Eleanor Marx, *People's Press*, 13 December 1890.
34 Eleanor's nimble use of language in the political sphere was part of her great genius – and one that the suffragettes both admired and envied. Suffragette rhetoric, by defining its starting position as the rights of women, immediately

sounded like it was something different to the rights and needs of men, who consequently stopped listening, or heard the assertion of singularity as complaint – another reason not to listen.

35 FE to August Bebel, 9 May 1890, *MECW*, Vol. 48, 2001, p. 492.
36 Report of Eleanor Marx's speech on the first May Day, Hyde Park, 4 May 1890, MML.
37 Ibid.

Chapter 19 – Ibsenist Interlude

1 FE to Friedrich Adolph Sorge, 9 August 1890, *MECW*, Vol. 49, 2001, p. 439.
2 Henrik Ibsen, *The Lady from the Sea*, trans. Eleanor Marx Aveling, Digireads. com Publishing, 2008, p. 74.
3 Ibid., p. 93.
4 Edith Lees Ellis, *Stories and Essays*, Free Spirit Press, New Jersey, 1924, quoted in Sally Ledger, 'Eleanor Marx and Henrik Ibsen', in Stokes (ed.), *Eleanor Marx*, p. 54.
5 Cited in Ledger, 'Eleanor Marx and Henrik Ibsen', in Stokes (ed.), *Eleanor Marx*, pp. 54–5.
6 Harley Granville-Barker, ed. Walter de la Mare, *The Eighteen Eighties*, Cambridge University Press, Cambridge, 1913, p. 159.
7 Quoted by William Archer, 'The Mausoleum of Ibsen', *Fortnightly Review*, July 1893.
8 George Bernard Shaw, 'What about the middle class?', *Daily Citizen*, 19 October 1912.
9 GBS, quoted in Holroyd, *Bernard Shaw*, p. 214.
10 GBS in *Saturday Review*, quoted in Holroyd, *Bernard Shaw*, p. 214.
11 Cited in Errol Durbach, 'A Century of Ibsen Criticism', in (ed.) James McFarlane, *The Cambridge Companion to Ibsen*, CUP, 1994, p. 233.
12 Eleanor Marx and Israel Zangwill, 'A Doll's House Repaired', *Time*, March 1891.
13 Ibid.
14 Ibid. Eleanor and Israel rearrange Ibsen's plot by giving Krogstad his job back at the bank by sacking his new wife, Christina, who is to be sent home to her proper domestic sphere. In a manly aside, Helmer warns Krogstad that she'll need retraining: 'a woman who has once tasted the forbidden fruit of independence is like a pet tiger who has once tasted blood.'
15 EM open letter to *People's Press*, 31 August 1890.
16 Ibid.
17 Clementina Black, in *People's Press*, 13 September 1890.
18 EM to *People's Press*, 31 August 1890.
19 Der Sozialdemokrat, *Neue Zeit*, *Time* and *Volksblatt*!
20 EM to *People's Press*, 13 September 1890.
21 EM to FE, 14 September 1890, IISH.
22 Ibid.

Chapter 20 – I Am a Jewess

1 Edward Aveling, 'Frederick Engels at Home', *Labour Prophet*, September 1895.
2 EM to LL, 19 December 1890, IISH.
3 Ibid.
4 August Bebel to Victor Adler, 20 December 1890, in Friedrich Adler (ed.), *Victor Briefwechsel mit August Bebel und Kautsky*, Wiener Volksbuchhandlung, Vienna, 1954, p. 66 (letter trans. Bettina Meyer).
5 EM to LL, 11 November 1893, IISH.

6 EM to LL, 12 August 1891, IISH.
7 EM to LL, 25 September 1891, IISH.
8 EM to LL, 19 December 1890, IISH.
9 EM to LL, 15 April 1892, IISH.
10 Eleanor Marx, National Union of Gas Workers and General Labourers' *Report to the Delegates of the Brussels International Congress*, 1891, p. 16, IISH.
11 EM to LL, 7 January 1893, IISH.
12 EM to LL 30 May 1892, IISH.
13 EM to LL, 11 November 1893, IISH.
14 EM to LL, 6 July 1891, IISH.
15 Eleanor Marx & Edward Aveling, 'Die Wahlen in Grossbritanien', *Neue Zeit* (1891-1892), pp. 596-603.
16 Ibid.
17 EM to LL, 26 July 1892, IISH.
18 *Workman's Times*, 21 March 1893.
19 EM to Anna Kuliscioff, 15 September 1892, IISH.
20 EM to LL, 30 May 1892, IISH.
21 EM to Dollie Radford, 25 January 1893, IISH.
22 William Diack, *History of the Trades Council and the Trade Union Movement in Aberdeen*, Aberdeen Trades Council, Aberdeen, 1939, p. 62.
23 Beer, *Fifty Years of International Socialism*, p. 72.
24 For an excellent critical account of Vengerova's stature as an important modern intellectual, literary critic and pioneer Symbolist, see Rosina Neginsky, *Zinaida Vengerova: In Search of Beauty – A Literary Ambassador Between East and West*, Peter Lang, Canterbury, 2004.
25 Zinaida Vengerova, 'On the Daughter of Karl Marx', undated manuscript memoir, MML.
26 Ibid.
27 Founded in 1888 as the Federation of Minor Synagogues, it scrapped the diminutive shortly after in order to assert equivalence to the United Synagogue.
28 Vengerova, 'On the Daughter of Karl Marx', MML.
29 Ibid.
30 Ibid.
31 EM to Karl Kautsky, 28 December 1896, IISH.
32 TUC Library Collections, London Metropolitan University.
33 As recorded by *Commonweal*, 4 January 1890, when it reported on the mass meeting of Jewish workers at the Great Assembly Hall.
34 EM to (unnamed) 'Comrade', 21 October 1890, IISH.
35 Jack Jacobs, *On Socialists and the Jewish Question after Marx*, New York University Press, New York, 1992, p. 184.
36 Ibid.
37 Report on the International Socialist Workers Congress, 1891, IISH.
38 EM, in *Justice*, November 1897.
39 The paper was originally launched as *Der Poilisher Yidel* (The Little Polish Jew), changing its name to *Die Tsukunft* shortly after. Vinchevsky emigrated to New York in 1894, where the journal was published as *Tsukunft* (*Zukunft, Future*).
40 Morris Vinchevsky (Benzion Novochovits), *Collected Works*, ed. Kalman Marmor, 10 Vols, Farlag Frayhayt, New York, 1927-8.
41 Ibid.
42 Ibid.
43 Ibid.
44 See Beer, *Fifty Years of International Socialism*, p. 73.
45 Ibid.
46 EM to Nathalie Liebknecht, 14 January 1898, IISH.
47 EM, in *Justice*, 22 January 1898.

48 Beer, *Fifty Years of International Socialism*, p. 74.
49 See Wheen, *Karl Marx*, pp. 55–6.

Chapter 21 – 'Oh! for a Balzac to paint it!'

 1 EM to LL, 26 July 1892, IISH.
 2 EM to LL, 22 February 1894, IISH.
 3 FE to Friedrich Adolph Sorge, 21 March 1894, *MECW*, Vol. 50, 2004, p. 282.
 4 Hunt, *The Frock-Coated Communist*, p. 352.
 5 EM to LL, 7 September 1894, IISH. Tussy was amused that whilst the first and second 'Louises' got along very smoothly, 'Karl seemed to be feeling he cd be happy with either were t'other dear charmer away.'
 6 Proceedings of the International Socialist Workers' Congress in Zurich Town Hall, 1894, IISH.
 7 Ibid.
 8 Ibid.
 9 EM to Ernest Radford, 16 September 1893, Radford Archive, British Museum.
10 Beer, *Fifty Years of International Socialism*, p. 74.
11 Ibid.
12 EM to LL, 11 November 1893, IISH.
13 Ibid.
14 EM to LL, 22 February 1894, IISH.
15 Ibid.
16 Louise Kautsky to EM, 22 February 1894, IISH.
17 EM to LL, 22 February 1894, IISH.
18 Ibid.
19 EM to LL, 2 March 1894, IISH.
20 EM to LL, 22 February 1894, IISH.
21 EM to LL, 2 March 1894, IISH.
22 EM to LL, 22 March 1894, IISH.
23 Ibid.
24 Ibid.
25 Louise Kautsky to EM, 22 February 1894, IISH.
26 EM to LL, 5 November 1894, IISH.
27 FE to LL, 12 November 1894, IISH.
28 EM to LL, 5 November 1894, IISH.
29 Ibid.
30 Edward Aveling, in *Clarion*, 3 November 1894 and 10 November 1894.
31 EM to Karl Kautsky, 10 November 1894, IISH.
32 Interview between Eleanor's biographer, Yvonne Kapp, and Henry Demuth, cited from transcript in Kapp, *Eleanor Marx*, Vol. 2, p. 437.
33 Ibid.
34 Ibid.
35 Ibid.
36 EM to LL, 26 July 1892, IISH.
37 EA postscript to EM to LL, 22 November 1894, IISH.
38 Friedrich Engels to August Bebel and Paul Singer, 14 November 1894, *MECW*, Vol. 50, 2004, p. 362.
39 EM to LL, 22 November 1894, IISH.
40 Ibid.
41 EM to LL, 15 December 1894, IISH.
42 EM to LL, 25 December 1894, IISH.
43 Ibid.
44 EA to LL, 25 December 1894, IISH.
45 EM to LL, 25 December 1894, IISH.

46 Ibid.
47 EM to LL, 2 January 1895, IISH.
48 EM to LL, 25 December 1894, IISH.
49 Ibid.
50 FE to LL, 19 January 1895, *MECW*, Vol. 50, 2004, p. 424.
51 EM to Wilhelm Liebknecht, 7 March 1895, IISH.
52 EM to Wilhelm Liebknecht, 14 March 1895, IISH.
53 Friedrich Engels, last will and testament, 29 July 1893, codicil 26 July 1895, IISH.
54 FE to EM, 5 July 1895, IISH.
55 Eleanor Marx, Introduction to George Plekhanov, *Anarchism & Socialism* (1895), trans. Eleanor Marx Aveling, Dodo Press, Milton Keynes.
56 Sam Moore to EM, 21 July 1895, IISH (facsimile) and MML.
57 Louise Freyberger to EM, 5 July 1895, IISH.
58 EM to John Burns, 8 August 1895, IISH.

Chapter 22 – The Den

1   EM and LL, October 1895, MML.
2   Hobsbawm, *The Age of Capital*, p. 303.
3   EA letter to William Diack, cited in Diack, *History of the Trades Council and the Trade Union Movement in Aberdeen*, p. 63.
4   Diack, *History of the Trades Council and the Trade Union Movement in Aberdeen*, pp. 62–3.
5   Ibid.
6   EM to LL, 19 October 1895, IISH.
7   EM to Louise Freyberger, 15 September 1895, IISH.
8   Ludwig Freyberger to EM, 4 October 1895, IISH.
9   EM to LL, 24 October 1895, IISH.
10 EM to Karl Kautsky, 17 August 1895, IISH.
11 Ibid.
12 EM to LL, 24 October 1895, IISH.
13 Ibid.
14 EM to LL, 17 November 1895, IISH.
15 EM to LL, 24 November 1895, IISH.
16 One pound in 1895 corresponds to the buying power of about £55–60 today, so the absolute value of their legacy in today's terms was about £275,000–300,000; however, in terms of purchasing power this fails to account for relative historical values in prices and the cost of living.
17 EM to LL, 24 October 1895, IISH.
18 EM to LL, 19 October 1895, IISH.
19 EM, 17 November 1895, IISH.
20 Ibid.
21 EM to LL, 10 December 1895, IISH.
22 LL to EM, 1 September 1896, IISH.
23 Eleanor Marx, 'The Proletarian in the Home', *Justice*, 21 November 1896, p. 6, http://www.marxists.org/archive/eleanor-marx/1896/11/proletarian-home.htm
24 *Justice*, 16 November 1895, p. 5.
25 *Justice*, 23 November 1895, p. 8.
26 Ibid.
27 Ibid.
28 Ibid.
29 EM to LL, 10 December 1895, IISH.
30 EM to LL, 14 January 1896, IISH.

31 EM to LL, 17 January 1896, IISH.
32 Ibid.
33 Ibid.
34 Ibid.
35 EM to to Karl Kautsky, 18 September 1895, IISH.
36 EM to LL, 19 October 1895, IISH.
37 KM to FE, 23 November 1850, *MECW*.
38 EM to LL, 2 January 1897, IISH.
39 EM to Karl Kautsky, 19 April 1896, IISH.
40 EM to LL, 5 March 1896, IISH. Tussy was relaxed about Edward's amiable traction with the SDF and soft-soaping of the Fabians because it cleared their path to tackle head-on the anarchist tendencies threating to hijack the London congress. Social democrat to her DNA, Tussy scorned anarchism above all other muddle-headed, anti-democratic irrationalism. She was not fundamentally opposed to armed military resistance in a just cause. She opposed the anarchist use of violence because it was unrepresentative and ungrounded in a broad-based consensus. Individualistic action cut loose from a broadly debated and, however uncomfortably, shared democratic consensus was not only politically irresponsible, it was, in Tussy's view, immoral and dictatorial.
41 *Justice*, 23 May 1896, MML.
42 Ibid.
43 Sylvia Pankhurst, *The Suffragette Movement* (1931), Virago, London, 1977, p. 128.
44 Ibid.
45 Wilhelm Liebknecht, in *Reminiscences*, p. 133.
46 Ibid.
47 EM to LL, 24 December 1896, IISH.
48 Wilhelm Liebknecht, in *Reminiscences*, p. 133.
49 EM, in *Justice*, 13 March 1897.
50 EM, in *Justice*, 22 January 1898.
51 EM to Karl Kautsky, 10 November 1896, IISH.
52 EM to LL, 23 December 1896, IISH.
53 EM to Karl Kautsky, 16 November 1896, IISH.
54 EM to Karl Kautsky, 28 December 1896, IISH.
55 EM to LL, 26 December 1896, and EM to Karl Kautsky, 28 December 1896, IISH.
56 EM to Karl Kautsky, 28 December 1896, IISH.

Chapter 23 – The Boldest Pause

1 *Labour Leader*, 10 April 1897.
2 EM, in *Justice*, 9 January 1897.
3 EM, in *Justice*, 23 January 1897.
4 Ibid.
5 EM to LL, 3 March 1896, IISH.
6 EM to Karl Kautsky, 15 March 1897, IISH.
7 EM to Karl Kautsky, 27 April 1897, IISH.
8 Ibid.
9 EM, in *Justice*, 6 February 1897 and 8 May 1897.
10 EM, in *Justice*, 6 February 1897.
11 Jeff Guy, *The View Across the River: Harriette Colenso and the Zulu struggle against Imperialism*, David Phillip, Cape Town, 2001, p. 416.
12 Ibid.
13 EM to Karl Kautsky, 8 February 1896, IISH.

14 *Justice*, 30 July 1898, IISH.
15 EM, in *Justice*, 26 June 1897.
16 For an excellent account of Edith Lanchester, see Karen Hunt: *Equivocal Feminists: The Social Democratic Federation and the Woman Question, 1884–1911*, Cambridge University Press, Cambridge, 1996.
17 EM to Karl Kautsky, 19 June 1897, IISH.
18 Thorne, *My Life's Battle*, p. 148.
19 *Vorwärts*, 5 April 1898.
20 EM to Karl Kautsky, 19 June 1897.
21 EM to Wilhelm Liebknecht, 2 June 1897, IISH.
22 Ibid.
23 At twenty-two, Eva Frye was coincidentally exactly the same age as Aveling's first wife, Isabel Campbell Frank, had been when she and Edward married twenty-five years previously in 1872.
24 EM to Karl Kautsky, 19 June 1897, IISH.
25 EM to Freddy Demuth, 30 August 1897, in article by Keir Hardie, *Labour Leader*, 30 July 1898; and article by Bernstein, *Justice*, 30 July 1898 and IISH.
26 Ibid.
27 Ibid.
28 Ibid.
29 Ibid.
30 Ibid.
31 Ibid.
32 EM to Karl Kautsky, 21 September 1897, IISH.
33 Eleanor Marx, 'Remarks on a letter by the young Marx', in *Reminiscences*, pp. 256–7.
34 EM to Karl Kautsky, 21 September 1897, IISH.
35 EM to Karl Kautsky, 19 July 1897, IISH.
36 Ibid.
37 Cited from correspondence between Yvonne Kapp and the Aveling family in Kapp, *Eleanor Marx*, Vol. 1, p. 258.
38 EM to Karl Kautsky, 28 September 1897, IISH.
39 Ibid.
40 EM to Benno Karpeles, 1. January 1898, IISH.
41 EM to Freddy Demuth, 5 February 1898, in article by Keir Hardie, *Labour Leader*, 30 July 1898; and in article by Bernstein, *Justice*, 30 July 1898 and IISH.
42 EM to Karl Kautsky, 1 January 1898, IISH.
43 Ibid.
44 EM to Wilhelm Liebknecht, 24 December 1897, IISH.
45 Ibid.
46 EM to Nathalie Liebknecht, 1 January 1898, IISH.
47 EM to LL, 8 January 1898, IISH.
48 EM to Wilhelm Liebknecht, 24 December 1897, IISH.

Chapter 24 – White Dress in Winter

1 George Bernard Shaw to Ellen Terry, 5 January 1898, in Chistopher St John (ed.), *Ellen Terry and Bernard Shaw, A Correspondence*, Theatre Art Books, New York, 1949, pp. 262–3. Shaw exaggerated Eleanor's legacy from Engels, but the point stood.
2 EM to LL, 8 January 1898, IISH.
3 EM to Nathalie Liebknecht, 1 January 1898, IISH.
4 Ibid.
5 EM to Karl Kautsky, 1 January 1898, IISH.

6 EM to LL, 8 January 1898, IISH.
7 EM to Nathalie Liebknecht, 14 January 1898, IISH.
8 EM to Freddy Demuth, 3 February 1898, in *Labour Leader*, 30 July 1898.
9 Ibid.
10 Ibid.
11 EM to Freddy Demuth, 5 March 1898, in *Labour Leader*, 30 July 1898.
12 Ibid.
13 Ibid.
14 EM to Freddy Demuth, 7 March 1898, in *Labour Leader*, 30 July 1898.
15 EM to Karl Kautsky, 10 February 1898, IISH.
16 EM to Wilhelm Liebknecht, 9 February 1898, IISH.
17 EM to Karl Kautsky, 20 February 1898, IISH.
18 Hyndman, *Further Reminiscences*, p. 144.
19 EM to Freddy Demuth, 20 February 1898, in *Labour Leader*, 30 July 1898.
20 EM to Wilhelm Liebknecht, 1 March 1898, IISH.
21 EM to Freddy Demuth, 1 March 1898, in *Labour Leader*, 30 July 1898.
22 EM to Karl Kautsky, 15 March 1898, IISH.
23 EM to Freddy Demuth, 1 March 1898, in *Labour Leader*, 30 July 1898.
24 Inquest report published in *North Eastern Daily Gazette*, 4 April 1898, p. 2; *Forest Hill & Sydenham Examiner and Crystal Palace Intelligencer*, 8 April 1898, p. 2; and *The Manchester Weekly Times*, Friday 8 April, 1898, p. 3. Eleanor's death, inquest and funeral were also reported in the *The Times of London*, 4 April 1898, p. 14; *Northampton Mercury*, 8 April 1898, p. 2; *The Lincoln, Rutland and Stanford Mercury*, 8 April 1898, p. 3; *Labour Leader*, 9 April 1898; *Justice*, 9 April 1898; *Daily Chronicle*, 4 April 1898, p. 3; *Reynolds Newspaper*, 10 April 1898, p. 2; *Daily News*, 4 April 1898, p. 9; and the *Evening Telegraph* reprinted the story from the *Daily Chronicle*, 4 April 1898, p. 3.
25 Ibid.
26 EM, will, 16 October 1895, PRO; *Reynolds Newspaper*, 28 April 1898.
27 EM, codicil, 28 November 1896, PRO; *Reynolds Newspaper*, 28 April 1898.
28 Cited in Eduard Bernstein, *Neue Zeit*, April 1898.
29 Eduard Bernstein to Victor Adler, 5 April 1898, Victor Adler Papers, IISH.
30 Bernstein, in *Justice*, 30 July 1898.
31 The *Communist*, 21 May 1921.
32 Leah Roth to Eleanor and Edward Marx-Aveling, 19 January 1898, IISH.
33 Gertrude Gentry to Edith Lanchester, 1 May 1898, IISH.
34 Karl Kautsky to Victor Adler, 9 April 1898, IISH.
35 Eduard Bernstein to Victor Adler, 5 April 1898, Victor Adler Papers, IISH.
36 Olive Schreiner to Dollie Radford, Radford Collection, British Library Manuscripts, June 1898.
37 Ibid.

Afterword

1 Eduard Bernstein, 'What Drove Eleanor Marx to Suicide?', in *Justice*, 30 July 1898, pp. 2–3, http://www.marxists.org/reference/archive/bernstein/works/1898/07/death-eleanor.htm – the translation of Bernstein's title from the German 'Was Eleanor Marx in den Tod trieb' (from *Neue Zeit*, Vol. 16, No. 42) is debatable; it might equally be rendered 'What Drove Eleanor Marx to Her Death?'
2 Ibid.
3 Ibid.
4 Ibid.
5 Ibid.
6 Ibid.
7 Ibid.

8 Ibid.
9 Ibid.
10 Ibid.
11 For the most thorough analysis refuting that Karl Marx was Frederick Demuth's father, see Terrell Carver, 'Gresham's Law in the World of Scholarship', written for *Marx Myths and Legends*, University of Bristol, February 2005, http://www.marxmyths.org/terrell-carver/article.htm; Creative Commons Attribution-NonCommercial-NoDerivatives Licence 2.0.
12 See, for example, Freddy Demuth to LL, 7 October 1910, IISH, and Freddy Demuth to Eduard Bernstein, 29 August 1912, IISH.
13 Karl Marx, 'Peuchet: On Suicide' (1846), *MECW*, Vol. 4, p. 597, http://www.marxists.org/archive/marx/works/1845/09/suicide.htm
14 Ibid.
15 Ibid. See also Hal Draper, 'Marx and Engels on Women's Liberation', July 1970, http://www.marxists.org/archive/draper/1970/07/women.htm
16 Eduard Bernstein, 'What Drove Eleanor Marx to Suicide?', *Justice*, 30 July 1898, pp. 2–3.
17 Eleanor Marx Aveling and Edward Aveling, *The Woman Question*, p. 21.
18 Gertrude Gentry to Edith Lanchester, 1 May 1898, IISH.

BIBLIOGRAPHY OF ELEANOR MARX'S KEY WORKS

'Marx's Theory of Value', *Progress*, June 1883
'Underground Russia', *Progress*, London, August–September 1883
'Karl Marx', *Progress*, May and June 1883
'Record of the International Popular Movement', *Today*, London, January–July 1884
'The Irish Dynamiters', *Progress*, May 1884
'The Working Class Movement in England', *Today*, London, 1884
'The Trades Union Congress at Liverpool', *Time: A Monthly Miscellany*, London, October 1890
'Literature Notes', *Time*, London, August 1890 – February 1891
Report from Great Britain and Ireland to the Delegates of the Brussels International Congress, 1891, presented by the Gas Workers and General Labourers' Union; the Legal Eight Hours and International Labour League; the Bloomsbury Socialist Society; and the Battersea Labour League, London, 1891
Eleanor Marx & Israel Zangwill, 'A Doll's House Repaired', *Time: A Monthly Miscellany*, London, March 1891
'French and German Classes for the SDF', *Justice*, September 1896
'The Gotha Congress', including 'Comments on Clara Zetkin's Speech', *Justice*, October 1896
'The Proletarian in the Home', *Justice*, November 1896
'Socialist Municipalities and Communes in France', *Justice*, January 1897
'Suggestions for Propaganda Work', *Justice*, January 1897
Eleanor Marx & Laura Lafargue, *Karl Marx's Capital*, March 1897
Biographical notes on Karl Marx, *Neue Zeit*, Vol. 1, Stuttgart, 1897–8

With Edward Aveling

The Factory Hell, Socialist League, London, 1885
'The Woman Question: From a Socialist Point of View', *Westminster Review*, No. 125, London, January–April 1886; first printed as separate stand-alone edition by Swan Sonnenschein & Co., London, 1886
Campaign Against Child Labour, Social-Democratic Federation, 1887
'The Chicago Anarchists: a statement of facts', *Today*, London, 1887; first printed as separate stand-alone edition by W. Reeves, London, 1888
Shelley's Socialism: Two Lectures, privately printed, London, 1888
The Working Class Movement in America, Swan Sonnenschein & Co., London, 1888
'The Difference Between Byron and Shelley', *Die Neue Zeit*, Vol. 6, Stuttgart, January 1888
'Dramatic Notes', *Time*, February 1890–February 1891

Selected Works Translated by Eleanor Marx

'An Account of Abbé Vogler', in *Browning Society Papers*, published 1881, and published in Frederick Furnivall (ed.), *Fifty Earliest English Wills*, Early English Text Society, London, 1882

Gustave Flaubert, *Madame Bovary: Provincial Manners*, Vizetelly & Co., London, 1886

Hippolyte Prosper Olivier Lissagaray, *History of the Commune of 1871*, Reeves & Turner, London, 1886

Henrik Ibsen, *An Enemy of Society and Other Plays*, Walter Scott Publishing Co., Newcastle-upon-Tyne, 1888, revised edition published as *An Enemy of the People*, London, 1890

Henrik Ibsen, *The Pillars of Society and Other Plays*, Walter Scott Publishing Co., Newcastle-upon-Tyne, 1888

Henrik Ibsen, *The Lady from the Sea*, T. Fisher Unwin, London, 1890

Henrik Ibsen, *The Wild Duck*, W. H. Baker, Boston, 1890

Alexander Kielland, 'A Ball-Mood', *Time*, London, May 1890

Eduard Bernstein, *Ferdinand Lassalle as a Social Reformer*, Swan Sonnenschein & Co., London, 1893

George Plekhanov, *Anarchism and Socialism*, Twentieth Century Press, London, 1895

Wilhelm Liebknecht, 'A Bad Quarter of An Hour', *Social-Democrat*, London, February 1897

Selected Works Edited by Eleanor Marx

Friedrich Engels, *Revolution and Counter-Revolution, or, Germany in 1848*, Swan Sonnenschein & Co., London, 1896 (Engels's work is incorrectly attributed to Marx)

Karl Marx, *The Eastern Question: A Reprint of Letters written 1853–56 dealing with the events of the Crimean War*, Swan Sonnenschein & Co., London, 1897 – includes letters by Engels

Karl Marx, *Value, Price, and Profit, addressed to Working Men*, Swan Sonnenschein & Co., London, 1898

Karl Marx, *Secret Diplomatic History of the Eighteenth Century*, Swan Sonnenschein & Co., London, 1899

Karl Marx, *The Story of the Life of Lord Palmerston*, London, 1899

BIBLIOGRAPHY

A guide to sources

The primary archival sources used for this book are from the Marx-Engels papers and related holdings at the International Institute of Social History (IISH) in Amsterdam, Netherlands and the Marx Memorial Library in Clerkenwell Green, London. In addition to the core Marx-Engels papers at the IISH, sources include the facsimile reproductions from the Russian State Archive of Social and Political History (RGASPI) and archival items on the First International (International Working Men's Association) and the Second International in personal papers from the period, including those of Johann Philipp Becker, Hermann Jung, Victor Adler, Karl Kautsky, Henri van Kol and Pieter Troelstra. The Local History and Archives Centre of the London Borough of Lewisham, the London Metropolitan Archives, the National Archives at Kew and the TUC Library Collections, London Metropolitan University provide other key sources. The British Newspaper Archive and Colindale Newspaper Library (www.britishnewspaperarchive.co.uk) and the London Library provided a wide range of contemporary newspapers and journals. The Marxists Internet Archive https://www.marxists.org, compiled by scholars and experts, is the most comprehensive and reliable online free open source of Marxist archives.

All primary sources are referenced directly in the endnotes, including correspondence, manuscripts, newspaper and journal publications, memoirs and autobiographies. Readers wishing to follow the complete articles, speeches and correspondence discussed can access them on the open source of www.marxists.org – Marxists Internet Archive. The following select bibliography provides a guide to key secondary sources used.

Select bibliography

Adams, William Edwin, *Memoirs of a Social Atom*, Vol. 2, Hutchinson, London, 1903

Alvarez, Al, *The Savage God: A Study of Suicide*, Bloomsbury, London, 2002

Atkinson, Dorothy, *Alexander Dalin and Gail Warshofsky Lapidus: Women in Russia*, Stanford University Press, 1977

Auerbach, Nina, *Ellen Terry: Player in Her Time*, W. W. Norton & Co, New York and London, 1987

Baxendall, Lee, and Stefan Morawski (eds), *Marx and Engels on Literature and Art*, Progress Publishers, Moscow, 1976

Berlin, Isaiah, *Karl Marx: His Life and Environment*, Oxford University Press, Oxford, 1948

Blumenberg, Werner, *Karl Marx*, Verso, London, 1998

Booth, Michael, *Theatre in the Victorian Age*, Cambridge University Press, Cambridge, 1991

Brandon, Ruth, *The New Women and the Old Men: Love, Sex and the Woman Question*, HarperCollins, London, 1991

Brome, Vincent, *Havelock Ellis: Philosopher of Sex: A Biography*, Routledge & Kegan Paul, London, 1979

Browning, Robert, *The Pied Piper of Hamelin*, George Harrap & Co., London, 1934

Calder-Marshall, Arthur, *Havelock Ellis: A Biography*, Rupert Hart-Davis, London, 1959

Chernaik, Judith, *The Daughter: A Novel Based on the Life of Eleanor Marx*, HarperCollins, London, 1970

Derfler, Leslie, *Paul Lafargue and the Founding of French Marxism, 1842–1882*, Harvard University Press, Cambridge MA, 1991

Durkheim, Emile, *On Suicide (1897)*, Penguin Classics, London, 2006

Eagleton, Terry, *Why Marx Was Right*, Yale University Press, New Haven CT and London, 2011

Eichenbaum, Louise, and Susie Orbach, *Understanding Women: Feminist Psychoanalytic Approach*, Basic Books, New Haven, 1984

Engels, Friedrich, *The Origin of the Family, Private Property and the State (1884)*, in Friedrich Engels and Karl Marx, *Selected Correspondence*, Progress Publishers, Moscow, 1965, reprinted by Penguin Classics, London, 2010 (with a new introduction by Tristram Hunt)

Evans, Faith, and Olga Meier (eds), *The Daughters of Karl Marx: Family Correspondence 1866–1898*, Andre Deutsch, London, 1982

First, Ruth, and Ann Scott, *Olive Schreiner*, The Women's Press, London, 1989

Florence, Ronald, *Marx's Daughters: Eleanor Marx, Rosa Luxemburg, Angelica Balabanoff*, Dial Press, New York, 1975

Glennie, John Stuart, *Europe and Asia: Discussions of the Eastern Question in Travels Through Independent, Turkish & Austrian Illyria*, Chapman & Hall, London, 1879

Grosskurth, Phyllis, *Havelock Ellis: A Biography*, Random House, New York, 1980

Guy, Jeff, *The View Across the River: Harriette Colenso and the Zulu Struggle Against Imperialism*, David Phillip, Cape Town, 2001

Hastings, Michael, *Tussy Is Me*, Weidenfeld & Nicolson, London, 1970

Healey, Edna, *Wives of Fame*, Sidgwick & Jackson, London, 1986

Henderson, William Otto, *The Life of Friedrich Engels*, Vols 1 & 2, Routledge, Oxford, 1976

Hetherington, Naomi, and Nadia Valman (eds), *Amy Levy: Critical Essays*, Ohio University Press, Athens OH, 2010

Hobsbawm, Eric, *The Age of Capital 1848–1875*, Weidenfeld & Nicolson, London, 1996

Holroyd, Michael, *A Strange Eventful History: The Dramatic Lives of Ellen Terry, Henry Irving and Their Remarkable Families*, Random House, London, 2009

Horne, Alistair, *The Fall of Paris: The Siege and the Commune 1870-71*, Penguin, London, 2007

Hunt, Karen, *Equivocal Feminists: The Social Democratic Federation and the Woman Question, 1884–1911*, Cambridge University Press, Cambridge, 1996

Hunt, Tristram, *The Frock-Coated Communist: The Revolutionary Life of Friedrich Engels*, Penguin, London, 2009

Ibsen, Henrik, *A Doll's House*, J. M. Dent & Sons, London, 1943

—, *Ghosts & Two Other Plays: The Warriors at Helgeland & An Enemy of the People*, J. M. Dent & Sons, London, 1930

Juszkiewicz, Jennifer, *The Iron Library: Victorian England and the British Museum Library* (MA thesis), University of Notre Dame, Indiana, 2009

Kapp, Yvonne, *Eleanor Marx: Vol. 1, Family Life*, Lawrence & Wishart, London, 1972

—, *Eleanor Marx: Vol. 2, The Crowded Years*, Lawrence & Wishart, London, 1976

Kautsky, John Hans, *Karl Kautsky: Marxism, Revolution and Democracy*, Transaction Publishers, New Brunswick, 1994

Lawrence, D. H., *Studies in Classic American Literature (1923)*, ed. Ezra Greenspan, Lindeth Vasey and John Worthen, Cambridge University Press, Cambridge, 2002

Lissagaray, Prosper-Olivier, *History of the Paris Commune of 1871*, Charles River Editors, Cambridge MA, 2011 (translated by Eleanor Marx)

McDonald, Deborah, *Clara Collet, 1860–1948: An Educated Working Woman*, Routledge, London, 2004

McFarlane, James (ed.), *The Cambridge Companion to Ibsen*, Cambridge University Press, Cambridge, 1994

McLellan, David, *Karl Marx: His Life and Thought*, Harper & Row, New York, 1973

—, *Marx before Marxism*, Macmillan, London, 1980

Mehring, Franz, *Karl Marx: The Story of His Life*, Routledge, London, 2003

Meintjes, Johannes, *Olive Schreiner*, Hugh Keartland, Johannesburg, 1965

Moi, Toril, *Henrik Ibsen and the Birth of Modernism: Art, Theatre, Philosophy*, Oxford University Press, Oxford, 2006

Neginsky, Rosina, *Zinaida Vengerova: In Search of Beauty – A Literary Ambassador Between East and West*, Peter Lang, New York, 2006

Nicolaevsky, Boris, *Karl Marx: Man and Fighter*, Methuen, London, 1936 (translated by Otto Maenchen-Helfen)

Pankhurst, Sylvia, *The Suffragette Movement*, Virago, London, 1977

Peters, Heinz Frederick, *Red Jenny: A Life with Karl Marx*, Allen & Unwin, London, 1986

Peters, Sally, *Bernard Shaw: The Ascent of the Superman*, Yale University Press, New Haven CT, 1998

Reid, Piers Paul, *Game in Heaven with Tussy Marx*, Weidenfeld & Nicolson, London, 1966

St John, Christopher (ed.), *Ellen Terry and Bernard Shaw: A Correspondence*, Theatre Art Books, New York, 1949

Schreiner, Olive, *The Story of an African Farm*, T. Fisher Unwin, London, 1924

Service, Robert, *Comrades: A World History of Communism*, Macmillan, London, 2007

Slovo, Gillian, *An Honourable Man*, Virago, London, 2012

Stokes, John (ed.), *Eleanor Marx: Life, Work, Contacts*, Ashgate, Farnham, 2000

Thompson, E. P. , *William Morris: Romantic to Revolutionary*, Merlin Press, London, 1977

Townsend-Warner, Sylvia, *Summer Will Show*, Virago, London, 1987

Tsuzuki, Chushichi, *The Life of Eleanor Marx, 1855–1898: A Socialist Tragedy*, Oxford University Press, Oxford, 1967

Wheen, Francis, *Karl Marx*, Fourth Estate, London, 1999

Whitfield, Roy, *Engels in Manchester: The Search for a Shadow*, Working Class Movement Library, Salford, 1988

Winsten, Stephen, and George Bernard Shaw, *Salt and His Circle*, Hutchinson, London, 1951

Wollstonecraft, Mary, *A Vindication of the Rights of Woman: With Strictures on Political and Moral Subjects (1792)*, Penguin Classics, London, 2004

Zola, Emile, *The Debacle*, Penguin Classics, London, 1972

ACKNOWLEDGEMENTS

The librarians, archivists and staff of the International Institute of Social History in Amsterdam, the Marx Memorial Library in London, the Local History and Archives Team of the London Borough of Lewisham, the London Metropolitan Archives, the London Library and the British Library. All the specialists, who gave generously of time, expertise and criticism, reading various iterations, sharing advice and material, prodding me to further research, thought and exploration of the Marx and Engels *Nachlass*. You know who you are, and that I am greatly in your intellectual debt.

Thank you: Lisa Appignanesi, Ann Baskerville, Jane Beese, Victoria Brittain, Omar Burjaq, Polly Clayden, Alistair Constance (best ex), Morgan Cooper, Nicole Crisp, Najwan Darwish, Nathan Geffen, Ann Grant, Omar Robert Hamilton, Suheir Hammad, Nathalie Handal, Sarah Hickson, Kiyo Inoue, John Jolly, Remi Kanazi, Jude Kelly, Helena Kennedy, Laura Miller, Bill & Jeanine Mitchell, Gillian Moore, Tania, Bassem and Hanna Nasir, Susie Nicklin, Margie Orford, Maha Khan Phillips, Yoko Reijn, Margaret Reynolds, Philippe Riviére, my godson Rufus Shaljean, Muneeza Shamsie, Raja and Penny Shehadeh, Faisal Slamang, Ahdaf Soueif, Jana Stefanovska, Saleh Totah, Dalli Weyers. Andrew Davies, especially for the print of your BBC TV series *Eleanor Marx* (1977). Jacqueline and Alison Rose for the script of Alison Rose's *Tussy*, produced by the RSC at the Almeida Theatre in London in August 1985. Helmut Pibernik for German Geschick and for being my second father.

Socrates & Rosa; Latifa & Hakim; Poppy & Monti; all the denizens of Café La Vie, and Silver & Spike for your generosity in sharing your homes and giving me space to write. My champion godmother Ann Baskerville and my second mother Sarah Holmes, who built *A Doll's House* re-visioned.

My editor Bill Swainson: consistently supporting and encouraging me when I 'gone fishin', and for securing me tight lines. The thanks I owe you demand superlatives you would never allow in print. Natasha Fairweather, my superb and redoubtable agent. Alexandra Pringle, inspired in all things. The terrific Bloomsbury team who made this book: managing editor Anna Simpson, copy-editor Emily Sweet, genius designer David Mann, publicist Eleanor Weil, and editorial assistants Oliver Holden-Rea and Imogen Corke.

Tahmima Anam and Bee Rowlatt, sowster supernovas. Soul sister Josie Rourke got Tussy back on the boards. Carmen Callil, for feminism's flotilla and Tussy insights. Gillian Slovo for the primacy of material facts and unconditional humanity. Greg Mosse generously shared his brain, sound advice and Amsterdam. Susie Orbach for an infinity of new perspectives. Kate Mosse, stalwart sorority sister, always answering with exactly what's needed. Barometer and pioneer Louise Shaljean. My sister Karen Holmes, especially for her expertise when I needed it most.

Zackie Achmat and Jack Lewis – our General – from inspiration to the last word. Your encyclopaedic Marxian knowledge, sharing of Karoo dawn hours and ability to make me laugh was essential. Kamila Shamsie, camerado, Ur-friend of the open seas. Jeanette Winterson, the midwife without whom. So many thanks.

Jonathan Evans, for all the reasons he knows. He has been love and generosity itself, sharing his life with Tussy and her family and investing in this book with unstinting encouragement, patience, infinite care and ingenious support. He is a great reader and champion of all writers.

This work is dedicated, with thanks and love always, to my mother, Karin Anne Pibernik, née Silén, and to the memory of her mother, my purple, white and green grandmother, 'Speedy' Haste.

INDEX

A NOTE ON THE AUTHOR

Rachel Holmes is the author of *The Secret Life of Dr James Barry* and *The Hottentot Venus: The Life and Death of Saartjie Baartman*. She is co-editor, with Lisa Appignanesi and Susie Orbach, of *Fifty Shades of Feminism* and co-commissioning editor, with Josie Rourke and Chris Haydon, of *Sixty-Six Books: Twenty-First Century Writers Speak to the King James Bible*. She lives in Gloucestershire.

A NOTE ON THE TYPE

The text of this book is set in Linotype Stempel Garamond, a version of Garamond adapted and first used by the Stempel foundry in 1924. It's one of several versions of Garamond based on the designs of Claude Garamond. It is thought that Garamond based his font on Bembo, cut in 1495 by Francesco Griffo in collaboration with the Italian printer Aldus Manutius. Garamond types were first used in books printed in Paris around 1532. Many of the present-day versions of this type are based on the *Typi Academiae* of Jean Jannon cut in Sedan in 1615.

Claude Garamond was born in Paris in 1480. He learned how to cut type from his father and by the age of fifteen he was able to fashion steel punches the size of a pica with great precision. At the age of sixty he was commissioned by King Francis I to design a Greek alphabet, for this he was given the honourable title of royal type founder. He died in 1561.